PROLEGOMENA ON METRE AND TEXTUAL HISTORY OF THE ṚGVEDA

HERMANN OLDENBERG

Prolegomena on Metre and Textual History of the Ṛgveda

Metrische und textgeschichtliche Prolegomena, Berlin, 1888

Translated into English by

V.G. Paranjape
M.A. Mehendale

MOTILAL BANARSIDASS PUBLISHERS
PRIVATE LIMITED • DELHI

First Edition: Delhi, 2005

ISBN: 81-208-0986-6

MOTILAL BANARSIDASS
41 U.A. Bungalow Road, Jawahar Nagar, Delhi 110 007
8 Mahalaxmi Chamber, 22 Bhulabhai Desai Road, Mumbai 400 026
120 Royapettah High Road, Mylapore, Chennai 600 004
236, 9th Main III Block, Jayanagar, Bangalore 560 011
Sanas Plaza, 1302 Baji Rao Road, Pune 411 002
8 Camac Street, Kolkata 700 017
Ashok Rajpath, Patna 800 004
Chowk, Varanasi 221 001

Printed in India
BY JAINENDRA PRAKASH JAIN AT SHRI JAINENDRA PRESS,
A-45 NARAINA, PHASE-I, NEW DELHI 110 028
AND PUBLISHED BY NARENDRA PRAKASH JAIN FOR
MOTILAL BANARSIDASS PUBLISHERS PRIVATE LIMITED,
BUNGALOW ROAD, DELHI 110 007

Dedicated

To the Sacred Memory of the

LATE ACHARYA SHRI VISHNU PRABHAKAR LIMAYE

A Great Sanskritist and Freedom-fighter at

whose suggestion I undertook to complete

PROF. PARANJAPE'S

unfinished translation of this text

Translator's Note

The late Prof. V.G. Paranjape had started to translate into English H. Oldenberg's 'Metrische und text-geschichtliche Prolegomena'. Instead of first completing the translation and then going to the press, Prof. Paranjape chose, perhaps due to old age, to send to the press as and when his translation progressed. Unfortunately, he died when his work had progressed up to p. 199, i.e. when he had completed the translation of the first chapter and the first nine pages of chapter II.

Some time in 1983 the late Shri Acharya V.P. Limaye sent a word to me asking me if I would be willing to complete Prof. Paranjape's unfinished task. I consented, no doubt with some hesitation. I first started the work where Prof. Paranjape had left, but subsequently started from the very beginning of chapter II. My work went on unusually slowly as I could not devote my full time to this job. I am happy that at long last, after nearly seven years, I have been able to complete the translation.

During my work, I found that it was not easy to translate Oldenberg's text and I often came across difficulties for which I sought help from my friend Prof. H.P. Schmidt. This he readily gave. But not only this. He also very kindly offered to go through the entire translation. His inspection has saved me from many an error and awkward expression.. I am greatly indebted to Prof. Schmidt for spending his valuable time for improving this work.

Instead of simply reprinting the text of Prof. Paranjape's translation of chapter I, it was felt that it would be advisable to revise it in order to bring some kind of uniformity in the entire translation. This was, therefore, also done by me. Prof. H.P. Schmidt kindly consented to go through this revised version and I am again obliged to him for his corrections and suggestions.

I am also indebted to Prof. Schmidt's two pupils Mrs. Mona Reddick and Ms. Cheryl Steets who went through the text and corrected it from the point of view of English expression. Due to their assistance the translation now reads better than what it otherwise would have been. But in spite of these attempts at improvement some awkward expressions persist on account of the involved style of Oldenberg.

Prof. Radhe Shyam Shastri, Hon. Professor at the Bhogilal Leherchand Institute of Indology, Delhi, took great interest in seeing that the work of unfinished translation got started again. He has since shown the same interest in the progress of the translation work and its publication. My sincere thanks are due to him. I am also thankful to M/s Motilal Banarsidass for undertaking to publish the translation.

Bhandarkar Oriental Research Institute, M.A. MEHENDALE
Pune (INDIA)
411004
April, 1990.

Contents

* Page numbers given here are in accordance with the page numbers of the translation; for internal references see f.n. 1 to preface p. xi.

Preface

[III][1] When the generation of scholars to whom we younger men look upon as our teachers felt called upon to make the text of the Vedic Saṁhitās available to the learned public, this work could be and had to be undertaken only in the sense that it would reproduce that form of the text which has remained fixed in India for two thousand years or more. Works of pre-eminent merit were produced in response to that call of duty and thus was laid the foundation of all future Vedic research. Lexicographical, grammatical and exegetical researches were based on that foundation and by dint of hard-fought, but victorious battles these researches managed to make themselves free from the authority of the quasi-scientific Indian authorities like Yāska, Pāṇini and Sāyaṇa, and learnt to apply the rules of the philological science to the Veda with ever-increasing acuteness and energy. At the same time one cannot ignore the fact that Vedic *textual criticism* has not kept equal pace with grammar and exegesis. The two latter disciplines have of course made ample contributions also towards the restoration of the original text of the Veda with the traditional text as the starting point. But the problem was approached always merely in a casual manner and never figured in the foreground as an object of independent research. The present work is an attempt to remedy this deficiency so far as the Ṛgveda is concerned [IV] and the present volume is intended to be the preliminary part of it. The ultimate objective is to give the Ṛgveda text in a form approaching its original

---

1. The figures in square brackets throughout this translation refer to the page numbers of Oldenberg's original German book and not to the page numbers of this translation.

composition in so far as the available traditional text and the ability of research, of the author as well as that of others, will allow.

The way whereby to reach this objective need not be described to the expert; that way has not to be discovered now, we have simply to follow it. We might, however, be permitted to hint at a few points. First of all, it appeared to us indispensable to make as complete a collection as possible of citations of the Ṛgveda stanzas in the later Vedic texts and to list the variants appearing in them. It was necessary to pursue the question in a more planned way than what has happened so far of determining the text-historical nature and the value of the variants through their ramifications : a portion of the prolegomena that follows seeks just to fulfil this task. Although in opposition to the widely prevailing views it turns out that the yield from the text-critical point of view derived from the other Vedas is relatively very small—and this in fact is the opinion of the present author—the line of investigation indicated above is nevertheless not without its value; we are not justified in dispensing with anything, however small, which can contribute to the knowledge of the original text; and moreover, while the inferiority of the other sources as against the textual tradition of the Ṛgveda is revealed, positive results regarding the latter (Ṛgvedic textual tradition) are obtained the characteristics of which provide an important basis for our treatment of the text. Also for the splitting up of composite hymns, handed down as single hymns, [V] into their composite parts and for the treatment of the hymns made up of strophes, the listings of the citations in the other Vedas and, together with them, the complete collection of the citations of whole hymns, parts of hymns and stanzas in the Aitareya and the Kauṣītaka Brāhmaṇas, in the Āśvalāyana and the Śāṅkhāyana Śrautasūtras, to be provided in our edition, will offer an indispensable basis. It appeared necessary to devote special attention to those splittings of composite hymns into single hymns and of groups of strophes into single strophes. Nothing can induce us, out of regard for the traditional form of the text, to hold back from the splittings up where we are in a position to proceed almost with mathematical precision—the splittings up which affect so decisively the general look of the hymns. It is, however, an essential part of the tasks of these preliminary investigations to bring that precision in this process of splitting up of hymns to the highest attainable level and to make it proof against all suspicion of a play of subjective thinking into it.

Another main task of Vedic textual criticism concerns the phonetic aspect of the text which has undergone far-reaching changes in the tradition. It was necessary to study systematically the procedure of the old diaskeuasis which was directed to the phonetic form. We have to attempt, one might say, to compose a Prātiśākhya of the Ṛgveda from our own point of view, or, what comes to the same thing, to interpret the rules of the old Prātiśākhya in such a way that there would be a detailed discussion of how far these rules are valid for the Ṛk-text because they were, in fact, in force in the language of the Vedic poets, and how far because they were introduced by the transmitters of the text. It was not possible to apply the approach outlined here to all the phonetic phenomena [VI] concerned within the scope of this volume; the treatment here offered to the majority of the most complicated among the relevant problems will in the meanwhile give the necessary clue for those that have not been specifically discussed.

If the views, stated so far, are characterized collectively as a textual history of the Ṛgveda, or at least as the main chapter of it, then it also appeared indispensable—and no specific arguments need be advanced in its support—to give a systematic exposition of the Vedic *metre* in this connection. As regards some other subjects of investigation, which in principle should have formed part of these introductory investigations, the author begs the reader to refer to his detailed expositions set forth at other place: thus to the two essays in ZDMG, XXXVIII, 439 ff. and XXXIX, 52 ff. dealing with the characterization of some of the most prominent varieties of the Vedic poetical technique, for instance the hymn of the Hotṛ and that of the Udgātṛ, the prose-poetical narrative (Ākhyāna) and the Dānastuti; as regards the discussion of the Vedic peoples and races the reader is referred to an excursus in "Buddha" (pp. 399 ff.), and to another essay in ZDMG, XLII, 198 ff. dealing with relationships, and especially the relative chronology of the Vedic authors. The author has not felt it necessary to investigate anew the problem of the interference of the system of writing on the transmission of the Ṛgveda text; he regards it as already settled; such an interference in times which alone we are now considering, times in which one could speak of a history of the text, is excluded.

The orthography followed in this Prolegomena could [VII] not be consistent throughout, since it had mainly to reproduce either the traditional or the original phonetic form of the text. From the point of view of the investigations undertaken here accent-marks, barring a few individual exceptions, appeared to be superfluous. However, the author regarded it as expedient to mark the caesura in the case of the Triṣṭubh and the Jagatī lines.

The critically restored text of the Ṛgveda itself accompanied by the critical apparatus consisting of the material contained in the other Saṁhitās, the Brāhmaṇas and the Sūtras, will follow the present volume as early as the nature of such a large task beset with such considerable difficulties would allow[1].

The editor expresses his respectful thanks to His Excellency the Royal Prussian Minister for Instruction whose liberality has rendered it possible for him to undertake this new revised edition of the Ṛgveda.

HERMANN OLDENBERG

---

1. Translator's note: Oldenberg later dropped the idea of publishing this restored text of the Ṛgveda.

CHAPTER 1

The Prosody of the Ṛgveda

[1] Vedic stanzas are formed of lines of eight, eleven or twelve syllables along with which on rare occasions we have lines of five syllables. These lines (pādas) are the units with which Vedic prosody is concerned; beyond these, if we scan and classify the metrical material which builds up the lines, viz. the long and the short syllables, we do not arrive, or in any case we do not invariably arrive, at any clear and definite indications which would make it possible for us to postulate smaller units like feet, as for instance in the Greek prosody. Only at the end of the pāda we can see a fixed or a relatively fixed rule of the alternation of long and short quantities. It is the last four or five syllables in a line which are in this way governed by a rule, viz. the one which relates to the alternation of long and short quantities. This contrast between an irregular opening and an ordered cadence is absent only in the case of lines of five syllables, which is natural on account of the small length of the line, and in this case there is a relatively fixed scansion observable throughout the length of the line. This distinction between the regular and the irregular sections, and next, in the case of the eleven-syllabled and the twelve-syllabled lines the caesura, are the only [2] components within the line with which our investigations have to deal, since, as we have pointed out and shall have to substantiate further on, the conception of a foot in the sense in which it is used in the ancient classical prosody is not applicable in the present case.

So far, we have spoken of the nature of the individual syllables, of the regular and the irregular construction of the line and its sections only in so far as the *quantitative* definiteness of the syllables is concerned. If we turn, however, from a consideration of the long and short quantities to that of the *rising and falling accents*[1], we thereby move away significantly from what is given as data. If the tradition gives abundant materials enabling us to say, at least on the whole, where in the Veda is to be found a long or a short quantity, it fails us fully in our search to find where a rising accent occurs in the Vedic stanza. Of course, in so far as we deal with only the *close* of the line, we can very easily make up this deficiency. It cannot be easily doubted that at the close of the line, where there is a regular alternation of long and short quantities, there is at the same time an alternation of the rhythm of rising and falling accents. The case is more difficult to judge at the opening and in the middle portion of the line in the case of lines of eleven and twelve syllables. Are we to suppose that here also there occurs the equally invariable rhythm—for instance the same iambic and trochaic rhythm—as at the close, only with this difference that this rhythm here is more indifferent towards the linguistic matter, that is the rising and the falling accents may occur without distinction, or at least with less distinction than at the end, on *any* syllable? [3] Or, does the greater latitude and variety in the occurrence of the long and short quantities, which prevails in the opening part of the line, reveal a correspondingly greater latitude and variety in the distribution of the rhythmic beats ? For deciding this matter we have no other way than to try to discover, in the inclinations or disinclinations of the Vedic poets in respect of the various possible combinations of the short and long syllables, some indications of a rhythm, which, as we may expect, acts as a determining factor in the choice of those

1. R. Kühnau (die Triṣṭubh-Jagatī Familie, Göttingen, 1886) has earned the merit to have brought prominently into relief all the relevant problems with particular energy, although we can hardly regard his endeavour to resolve them as successful.

combinations. By doing this we think—and the following expositions will have to accomplish it—that we shall obtain intelligible results—intelligible at least if the intelligibility is not measured by the unsuitable standards as those used for the Greek rhythmics—if we suppose that the stress accent occurs on those long quantities in the place of which short quantities are not tolerated and, on the other hand, the falling accent occurs on short quantities and on those long quantities which can change places with short quantities. We have no reason to suppose that artificialities, as for instance dactylic anapaests with the scansion ⏑͡⏑́ –, exist in Vedic prosody; in Vedic prosody all phenomena are absent which might have formed a homogeneous surrounding for such artificialities and we find no traces which, to an unprejudiced mind, might disclose their existence. The fact that before a pause even a short quantity has to be regarded as capable of carrying the stress accent requires hardly any special mention; but we shall have to investigate more thoroughly the phenomenon that the Vedic poets are occasionally satisfied with a short quantity to carry the stress accent where, as a rule, there should have been a long quantity—and this either due to negligence or because the poets did not have a completely exact feeling for the difference in quantity (for instance, they use *dadhiṣe* or *vasavaḥ* [4] at the end of a Jagatī line): exceptions which, we have to admit, do not cancel the apparently prevailing rule that the rising accent requires a long quantity.

If we now try on the strength of the statements, to be substantiated by the observation of the different metres in detail, to take a decision between the two alternatives set forth above, it will be found that in the first alternative there is indeed a certain element of truth: the strictness with which a certain rhythm also requires a certain definitely fixed form of metrical material is to a certain extent less operative in the opening part of the line than in the cadence. But along with it and in a much more prominent manner the second alternative claims to have its own sphere of validity; a series of important phenomena in the prosodial build-up of the Vedic verse clearly shows a wide range of *flexibility* in the character of the rhythm which is to be attributed to the opening part and the middle of the line as against its cadence[1].

What has been said so far relates only to the construction of a *single* pāda. The pādas, however, always combine—as a rule in groups of three or four mostly similar pādas—to form stanzas (*ṛcas*); sometimes stanzas are combined to form longer units. In the earlier period, the stanza was invariably so constructed that [5] a pāda, if it recurred inside a stanza, had the same form, or, to put it more precisely, showed without any distinction any of its forms which were regarded as of equal value; it was only at the end of the Ṛgvedic period that a differentiation was made in the forms, which according to their distinction were considered to be appropriate to the same pāda at different places in the stanza.

What kind of *pre-history* it was which led to this state of the Vedic metre which in general was marked by its peculiar mixture of a well-determined and an indeterminate sequence of quantities is a problem which is not quite without the prospect of solution. In this case, before everything else, we have to follow certain indications afforded by the study of the Avestan literature. No one can compare the Avestan poetry with the Indian poetry in its content, in its style of

---

1. If this view, to be substantiated further on, of the *fluidity* which is characteristic for the rhythm of the opening and the middle of the pāda is correct then it is clear to what doubts and limitations the utilization of the *post-Vedic* form of the metre is subject for the rhythmical explanation of the Vedic form. If we see amongst the numerous possibilities standing side by side in the Vedic period one attaining predominance in later times—perhaps one still of secondary importance in the Veda—we cannot on that account deem ourselves justified in projecting the rhythmical nature of this type into the other parallel types of the Veda.

expression, and in its entire colouring, without coming to the conclusion, on account of their agreement in small details which force themselves on us at every step, that both the literatures point not only to a common origin of these two *peoples* and their *religions,* but also to a community of Indo-Iranian *religious poetry,* developed in well-established forms. We may declare the attempts[1] to discover a common possession of metrical forms in the distant nebulous world of the *Indo-Germanic* pre-history as an exercise of either a well-justified scholastic venture, or of hopeless audacity: the question regarding the nature of the *Indo-Iranian* poetry lies definitely within the limits to which our researches may and must go. For, it was since long, especially from the side of the Avestan studies[2], **[6]** that the inter-connection of the metres in the Avesta with the most fundamental forms of the Vedic prosody were recognized and were given due prominence: repetition of the octo-syllabic line, three-, four-, or five-times to form stanzas in the Avesta are exactly like the Gāyatrī, the Anuṣṭubh and the Paṅkti of the Veda; and the four-lined stanza of eleven-syllabled lines with the caesura after the fourth syllable corresponds to the Triṣṭubh. Thus, the fixed number of syllables of the lines, the caesura, and the strophical combination of the lines into stanzas are points in respect of which the Veda and the Avesta agree. In regard to the metrical and rhythmical construction of the individual lines we have no basis for a more detailed comparison; in the Avesta, as is well-known, the syllables in a line are simply counted without there being any rule to regulate the alternation of the long and short quantities and consequently we fail to obtain any direct foothold enabling us to recognize the rhythm which certainly could not have been absent even

1. We might recall especially the very ingenious attempts of Usener.
2. See, for instance, Geldner's "Metrik des jüngeren Avesta," pp. VII, XIV.

in the Avestan versification. If, however, to begin with we take into account only the number of syllables in the line and their quantities, the facts already pointed out would inevitably lead to the supposition—and this has not escaped the acute eye of Westphal—that the prosodial art of the Indo-Iranian period had taken just that stand-point which has been preserved in the Avesta, viz. a simple juxtaposition of a certain fixed number of syllables, irrespective of their quantities. As a matter of fact, it appears to me, that even without its Iranian counterpart the Vedic metre would point to just this proto-type of an earlier period which had been superseded. For example, if we follow the Triṣṭubh and the Jagatī metres in their historical development, we can see how as if before the eyes of the investigator who starting from the earliest examines ever more recent periods the prosodial definiteness, [7] restricted first to a limited portion of the line, makes constant encroachments on larger fields and continuously acquires greater rigidity: so that if we suppose the same tendency to be at work in the pre-Vedic times, we have to assume as the starting point of the development just that condition which we actually find preserved in the Avesta. If we further probe into the nature of the Gāyatrī, we find in the Veda itself two different directions in which the stanza, having apparently an identical base of construction, develops its forms: two different forms which coincide only at the point of prosodial indifference as characterized by the Avesta. We cannot, however, ascribe, if what we have said so far is correct, a very clearly defined validity and an unchangeable character to the *rhythm* in the Indo-Iranian poetic art. If it had possessed these characteristics, the rhythmical variability in the opening part of the Vedic line, which we observe there, would hardly have developed; also the cadence of the Gāyatrī, as we believe to have discovered it, would hardly have been capable of a double rhythmical development working in two opposite directions. The number of syllables and the caesura were, it seems, the only two characteristics which had reached a complete definiteness in the structure of these lines which were only imperfectly permeated by any rhythmical liveliness. But in spite of the gaps and uncertainty in our information, which we shall hardly be able ever to overcome at this point, there cannot be any doubt as to the fundamental fact of the intimate connection between the Indian and the Iranian art of versification. And, thus, the Vedic prosody, which has offered the basis for all later Indian prosody, points to distant periods of the past which escapes our direct knowledge, periods during which the forgotten generations of the Indian, and then still further back, [8] of the Indo-Iranian ṛṣis sang in those same most ancient metres of eight-syllabled and eleven-syllabled lines of the divine majesty of the Asuras and of the pressings of Soma growing on the mountains.

I

The Eight-syllabled Pāda and the Metres Gāyatrī Anuṣṭubh and Paṅkti Formed from it

The simplest among the most frequently used pādas is the octo-syllabled; in its case, which is different from the case of the eleven-syllabled and the twelve-syllabled pādas, there is no caesura which gives rise to a manifold internal arrangement and a multiplicity of equivalent forms standing side by side. For the purposes of our investigation the octo-syllabic pāda naturally gets divided into two four-syllabled halves, the first being slightly, the second to a higher degree, metrically defined.

We shall begin with the second half. For this an iambic scansion is the rule; both the short quantities may justifiably be regarded by us as having the falling accent and the long quantities as having the rising accent (◡ ˊ– ◡ ◡́; the last syllable of the pāda is here, and everywhere in Vedic prosody, anceps); e.g.

◡   – –   ◡ – ◡◡
āgnim   *īḷē*   *purohitam*

– – ◡   – ◡   – ◡◡
yājñāsya   *devam*   *ṛtvijam*

– – –   – ◡ – ◡ ◡
hotāraṁ   *ratnadhātamam.*

How great is the frequency by which we can assure ourselves of the above-mentioned rule of iambic scansion can be best established by us in the context of the description and the statistics of exceptions. We shall note for some **[9]** long series of Gāyatrī hymns the number of the different metrical forms which the four last syllables assume in the place of the iambic rhythm; in doing that it will be appropriate to note the particular pāda of the Gāyatrī stanza in which the relevant deviation from the rule takes place. Those stanzas in the construction of which there is a serious deviation from the normal type have been excluded, since for the present, we wish to have an idea of the variations which may be regarded as lying within the limits of the regular Gāyatrī. The sections on the basis of which we have given our statistical figures are as follows :

Mand. I. 1-9 (270 pādas), 12-23 (leaving 22.11; 23.19-24) (408 pādas), 37; 38 (leaving st. 2, 7-9); 41 (leaving st. 7-9); 42; 43.1-6 (147 pādas).

Maṇḍ. VI. 16.1-24, 28-45; 45; 53 (leaving st. 8); 54-57 (338 pādas).

Maṇḍ. VII. 15; 31.1-9; 66.1-9; 89.1-4; 94.1-11 (144 pādas).

Maṇḍ. VIII. 5.1-35; 6; 7 (leaving st. 30 and 32-35); 11.1-9; 14; 17.1-13; 32; 38; 43-45; 64-65; 67; 72-73; 75-76; 82-85; 93-94 (leaving 94.2); 102 (1521 pādas).

Maṇḍ. IX. 1-67 (leaving 5; 62.4-6; 66.16-18; 67.30-32) (1767 pādas).

So now we have the following results:[1]

Scansion	First Pāda							Second Pāda							Third Pāda						
	I, 1fg.	12 fg.	37 fg.	VI.	VII.	VIII.	IX.	I, 1fg.	12 fg.	37 fg.	VI.	VII.	VIII.	IX.	I, 1fg.	12 fg.	37 fg.	VI.	VII.	VIII.	IX.
⏑ ⏑ ⏑ ⏓	4	9	6	2	6	15	9[1])	2	—	1	2	2	8[1])	4	—	1	1	4	2	7	3[1])
– ⏑ – ⏓	6	1	—	—	1	3	—	—	1	—	—	1	1	—	—	—	—	—	—	2	—
⏑ ⏑ – ⏓	—	—	—	—	—	4	3	1	—	1	—	1	1	—	1	—	—	—	—	1	2
– – – ⏓	—	—	1	—	—	1	1	—	—	—	—	—	—	—	2	—	—	—	—	—	—
– ⏑ ⏑ ⏓	2	—	2	—	—	6	2	1	—	—	—	1	1	—	2	—	—	1	—	2	1
⏑ – – ⏓	—	—	—	—	—	3	1	—	—	—	—	—	1	—	1	1	—	—	—	—	—
– – ⏑ ⏓	—	—	3	1	—	2	4	—	—	2	2	—	3	1	—	1	1	—	—	2	3[2])

1. A case is repeated twice.
2. A case is repeated five times.

---

1. I have left out here and there a pāda of doubtful or deficient scansion; long vowels with a scansion of two syllables (see below) like the *ā* of the gen. pl. have been counted as two short quantities.

Some cases, in which another form of the word than that given in the traditional text has to be accepted and the regular metrical form has to be restored on its basis (as *mṝḷ*, [**10**] in the place of *mṛḷ*), have been from the very outset left out of consideration. In some other cases the form of a word to be accepted may be doubtful; we shall investigate these problems further below. On the whole, any research showing discretion will be very cautious in the matter of eliminating the irregular quantities in the stanzas and providing the Vedic language with the corresponding modified word-forms. If we were to force upon the language for every word which happens to violate the metrical rule a secondary form then there will be no end to it. However, it will not be superfluous here to make a distinction between the Vedic *language* and the Vedic *recitation*. [**11**] For, just as it is today a different matter whether we pronounce *bewilligetest, entsetzlichere* in the way of natural speech or whether we pronounce these words at the end of Platen's less successful pentameters, so and even to a greater extent we are justified in allowing the Vedic poets to contract and stretch the words. The table given above shows that about a half of the entire number of deviations from the rule shows the type ◡ ◡ ◡ ⏓, that is the third syllable from the end portion of the line has a short quantity instead of a long one, e.g.

babhrave nu svatavase
kratvā dakṣasya rathiam
martasya devi avasaḥ
asuryāya pramahasā
yad adya sūra' udite.

It is not difficult to imagine a manner of recitation in which the stress in such lines occurred at its usual place; either by lengthening the vowel or the consonant following it, the third syllable from the end of these pādas can so easily be approximated to the long quantity that the end-part of the pāda could very well be accepted by the ear as an iambic one[1]. [12] That this kind of procedure was perceived only as a last resort, which in no way stood entirely on the same level as a rigid observance of the norm, appears to me to be revealed by the fact that according to the proof afforded by the statistical table given above, the metrical

---

1. As has been already pointed out it is not in every case possible to draw with any degree of certainty the line between those words allowed sporadically or more frequently to fill the metre and those which only apparently violate it but—in a form different from that transmitted—actually fill it. We refer to the discussion of the second case—to be given later in the context of the textual history—which naturally is in many respects contiguous to the first case we are concerned with here. In the first category a particularly frequent case, perhaps the most frequent one, concerns *avase* (or *avasaḥ* and similar forms); I have counted not less than 28 instances in which *avase* occurs at the end of a Gāyatrī- or Jagatī-pāda and its first syllable thus substitutes for a long quantity (for the rest *avase* occurs 70 times immediately after the caesura of the Jagatī- or Triṣṭubh-pāda, 10 times in other prosodially indifferent position): here we have a striking example of how a form not *fully* satisfying the metre was tolerated to an extent that it became the decisively preferred form. That eventual attempts to vindicate somehow or other the scansion — ∪ — of the form *avase* would be misplaced can be clearly seen from the use of the related nom. and acc. form *avas* which, apart from prosodially indifferent places, appears six times at the end of the Gāyatrī, three times at the end of the Jagatī, four times as the penultimate word of the Gāyatrī and the Jagatī before a two-syllabled end-word, once the same way in a Triṣṭubh line before a monosyllabic end-word: so then in all these fourteen places with the first syllable of the word counting as a short quantity. The fact that consequently the use of *avase* at the end of the Gāyatrī in no way is matched by a similar use of *avas* at the end of the Triṣṭubh leaves no doubt whatsoever as regards the nature of that anomaly.—It is certainly not saying too much when we say that in more frequently used words there is no short quantity—naturally in so far as the surrounding situation suits the scheme of the metre—which would not be occasionally used in the third last place of an octo-syllabic pāda in the place of a long quantity. This is, of course, especially the case in regard to the first syllable of those three-syllablled words, the middle syllable of which is short; the consonant which occurs after the vowel seems to be of no consequence. Besides *avase,* just now mentioned, we mention also the following words as of a frequent

(Continued on next page)

scansion ∪ ∪ ∪ ⊻ — exactly the same way as on an average the remaining scansions deviating from the norm, appears to have about the same frequency in the first pāda of the Gāyatrī as in the second and the third pādas taken together. This can only mean that a deviation from the pure iambic metre which was not entirely concealed by the recitation was felt as such and it was tolerated more in the opening of the stanza than in its continuation and close. As a matter of fact several other metrical scansions appearing in the place of the iambus— **[13]** it will be noticed that in fact in our statistical table all possible combinations are represented— are indeed so palpably different from the iambus that they manifestly will have to be regarded simply as *deviations* from the metrical norm which cannot be explained away. One may examine, for instance, lines like the following :

ukṣānnāya vaśānnāya
agne rathīr adhvarāṇām
nū no rayim mahām indo
tuaṁ soma pavamānah.

If we consider how the use of such lines in the later stages of the Ṛgveda and in the following period in certain *fixed places* in the stanzas obtained an ever-increasing extension and ultimately the status of a fixed rule—in places where nobody would accept iambic scansion with syllables the quantities of which are somewhat free—, then we shall not describe the present anomaly by saying that the poet composed lines in an iambic metre which turned out to be

---

(Continued from previous page)

occurrence: *śavasaḥ, varuṇaḥ, marutām, manasā, atithim, adite, ajaram, apām* (*ā* counting as two syllables); further *cikituḥ, akṛtam, atasam, atirat, udaram, udabhiḥ, sṛjataḥ, tapuṣim, sakhiam, amithitaḥ, pathibhiḥ, vidhataḥ, sanitā, namuceḥ, harivaḥ, tarutā, aruṣī, kṛṇavate, gaviṣe, iṣām* (the end-vowel counting as two), *svayaśasaḥ, guhiā, bṛhataḥ, pramahasā, vimahasaḥ, vahata.* Of less frequent occurrence, in the position described above, we find short syllables as the final or the penultimate of a word: *sparase nu, madhu piba, ratham ava, suaśvayur upa, na' uṣaḥ,* etc.

only approximately correct but that he has in a place, where the iambic scansion is required, used scansions which are no iambic.

We shall now turn to the consideration of the first four syllables of the octo-syllabic line. Its prosodial nature may be clearly illustrated by the following table compiled from an analysis of about 1300 pādas..

No.	*Metrical analysis*	I.1-11	VIII.5-7	IX.1-24	*Total*
1	∪ – ∪ –	50	65	101	216
2	– – ∪ –	57	51	85	193
3	∪ – – –	55	57	101	213
4	– – – –	71	58	106	235
5	∪ – – ∪	10	25	24	59
6	– – – ∪	15	16	21	52
7	∪ – ∪ ∪	7	14	10	31
8	– – ∪ ∪	10	6	8	24
9	∪ ∪ – –	14	28	51	93
10	– ∪ – –	37	29	32	98
11	∪ ∪ – ∪	5	7	27	39
12	– ∪ – ∪	10	10	16	36
13	∪ ∪ ∪ –	4	1	1	6
14	– ∪ ∪ –	5	4	16	25
15	∪ ∪ ∪ ∪	—	—	—	—
16	– ∪ ∪ ∪	—	1	—	1

The study of the statistics forcibly draws our attention, first of all, to the prominence of the first *four* cases. They stand close to one another, but between these cases and those that follow there is a wide gulf; the first four together form a total which is almost the double of the remaining twelve. These four cases relate just to the four combinations **[14]** in which the second and the fourth syllables are both long (⏑̲ – ⏑̲ –). We can with very great probability conclude that these syllables are to be regarded as having the stress accent. In the same way, and this can evidently be regarded as a natural corollary, both the stress accents on the four syllables constituting the cadence stand as a counterpart to the two stresses on the first four syllables constituting the opening part of the line (⏑̲ –́ ⏑̲ –́ ⏑̲ –́ ⏑ ⏑̲́), and here, as in the case of the cadence, there is an iambic rhythm: the only difference being that this rhythm in the cadence as such is a very rigidly dominant factor of the linguistic *ruthmizómenon,** so that in the cadence not only the stress accent requires a long syllable, but the falling accent also must fall on a short syllable, while here in the opening part the quantity of the syllable carrying the falling accent is treated indifferently.

[15] The combinations ⏑̲ – ⏑̲ – give us thus the possibility to distinguish the *essentially* long quantities which have the stress accents from the *unessential* ones, which have the falling accent and therefore can very well be short quantities. If for a long quantity of this latter type we substitute a short one then, since the character of the metre does not change from what it was by this substitution, it is possible to expect for this prosodial combination the same preference of the poets and therefore the same frequency number in our statistics as for the parallel form with the long quantity.[1] If, however, we substitute a short quantity for an *essentially* long one, we can expect that such an alteration will be characterized by a difference in the inclination of the poets towards these combinations which is reflected in the statistics. That thus, for instance, in the metrical scansion — — — — the second and the fourth,

* [Translator's note: The Greek word means rhythmic pattern or type]

1. We can easily convince ourselves that the way *how language material is constituted* does not allow any essential preference for the short or the long quantity.

but not the first and the fourth, are the essential long quantities can be seen from our table where for 235 cases of — — — — nearly the same number, i.e. 216, is of ∪ — ∪ —, while for the scansion — ∪ ∪ — there are only twenty five occurrences.

We believe that in these statistical methods of investigation we also have a ready means of discovering from the smaller frequency of the syllabic combinations what the essential long quantities, that is those carrying the stress-accents, are. The twelve combinations (numbers 5-16 in the table) in their sequence given above form six pairs so that in each one of them the first syllable can be optionally short or long; the frequency of occurrences pair-wise is approximately constant[1], **[16]** and this will show that the two cases forming a pair are co-ordinated with each other and consequently, as we believe we are entitled to conclude from this co-ordination, that a long initial syllable can never be regarded as carrying the stress-accent since a short quantity can very well be a substitute for it.

Since, as we have seen, the prevailing circumstance here is that in the second as well as in the fourth place there is a long quantity, we have to change now one after another the conditions of this normal type and to examine the resulting combinations in the manner described just now. We shall first take up those cases in which the second syllable is a short quantity instead of a long one (i.e. cases 9-16 in

1. Only in the case of *one* of the pairs, the two cases giving ⏓ ∪ ∪ — (Nos. 13-14), there is an exception to this equality of frequency; just with these small numbers the correct appearance of the average figure in the statistics is of course least reliable. Later on, when we give statistics for the first four syllables of the Triṣṭubh line, we shall find that the statistical position is just reversed. Besides, a relatively large total for the cases of the type — ∪ ∪ — rests on only *one* of the three item-sums (in the columns of our table), the occurrences from Maṇḍala IX, where the statistics have been influenced especially by the constant repetition of the initial word *eṣa* in the third and the fifteenth sūkta.

the table). At the first glance these fall into two groups. The quantity of the third syllable here is no longer, as in the first four main types, a matter of indifference, but it is now decisive: the cases of a long third syllable (Nos. 9-12) preponderate in frequency of occurrence over all those with a short third syllable (Nos. 13-16), partly very considerably; on the one side there is a total of 266 occurrences, while on the other there are 32.[1] We, therefore, state the result as follows: the second syllable, which most often is long, may also appear as a short one, but *in that case* the long quantity is decidedly preferred in the third place. From among the four resulting cases. ⏓ ⏑ — ⏓ we find, as nothing else is to be expected, that the two combinations ⏓ ⏑ — — claim a decided **[17]** preponderance; the long quantity in the fourth place, which is the normal case under all circumstances, gets also here preponderance over the short quantity. On the other hand, whether the scansion is ⏑ ⏑ — — or — ⏑ — —, or whether it is ⏑ ⏑ — ⏑ or — ⏑ — ⏑, is proved to be irrelevant by the frequency figures of our table. Now, what is it that we learn from the results so far arrived at in relation to the distribution of the rising and falling stress-accents? In all probability it is this that *the* rising accent, of which the normal place is the second long syllable, will be on the third syllable[2] if the second

1. Moreover, the main item of the latter total appears to have been relatively higher only *by chance*; cf. the preceding note.
2. Whosoever collects for himself the figures of the quantities for each syllable will notice that even in the case of the third place the long quantity predominates, although not so decisively as in the case of the second and the fourth place. This fact should not dissuade us from our supposition that we have a regular iambic rhythm in the case of the first four syllables, recognizing that an *implicit* explanation is contained in what has been said here for the relevant circumstance: in the normal case (⏓ – ⏓ –) there is about equal frequency of the long and the short quantity in the third place; in the most important of the alternative cases, however, the third is regularly long if the second syllable is short.

syallable is short, so that by the side of the regular form ⊻ ⏑́ — ⏑ ⏑́ — there results the secondary form ⊻ ⏑ —́ —́ as the most important one[1]. It would be in fact difficult to imagine by considering simply the quantities of syllables why the form with a *short* third syllable along with a second short — ⏑ ⏑ — should not have received the necessary importance as the other forms which contain even *three* short syllables (⏑ — ⏑ ⏑, ⏑ ⏑ — ⏑). It can, however, be understood as a requirement of the rhythmical feeling that, in order to maintain in a way the balance of the opening part of the line, it was felt that one of the *middle* syllables out of the four must have the stress-accent: and herein will lie the explanation of the well-known rule which is still more sharply pronounced in the case of the śloka metre, **[18]** that *both*[2] the second and the third syllables cannot easily be short syllables.[3]

Alongside the scansions ⊻ ⏑ — —, we came across the

1. After what has been observed it is not necessary for us to give any special proof for saying that we have to regard — ⏑ — — as — ⏑ —́ —́, but not, for instance as —́ ⏑ —́ —; the frequency figures for both the parallel forms, ⏑ ⏑ — — and — ⏑ — ⏑, indicate it.
2. That this combination was avoided already in the Veda is indicated with particualar clearness also by the choice of certain forms with a long end-vowel instead of the usual short one which was determined by metrical considerations; cf. our section below on these "lengthenings".
3. Compare for the disinclination against the metrical scansion ⊻ ⏑ ⏑ ⊻ my observations in ZDMG XXXV. 187, n. 2; XXXVII, 63, n. 1; Jacobi, Ind. St. XVII, 447 ff., assigns as a reason for this disinclination the fact that an octo-syllabic pāda in this way "would acquire the rhythm of the Jagatī [⊻ – ⏑ –] – ⏑́ ⏑ – ⏑ – ⏑ –". I do not think this to be a convincing reason. In the first place this does not explain the prevalence of the same disinclination also in the beginning of the eleven-syllabled and the twelve-syllabled pādas. Then again, when Jacobi makes the comparison with the Jagatī line, this can obviously be done only in its form which has cadence of eight syllables, that is to say, with the caesura after the fourth syllable;

(Continued on next page)

cases of the second syllable being short in the scansions ⏓ ⏑ — ⏑ (Nos. 11 and 12 of the table) as a secondary possibility; they lead us to consider those cases where the *fourth* syllable is short (Nos. 5-8; 11; 12; 15; 16). Here, as is to be expected, those cases in which the second syllable has its normal form stand in the forefront; a decisive preference for a third long syllable is no less evident: we may as a consequence assume that the tendency arose to have the stress, displaced from the fourth syllable, transferred to the third.[1] Alongside the resulting most frequent form ⏓ —́ —́ ⏑ there occur those in which there is a short quantity in either the second or the third place in addition to the one in the fourth place: ⏓ ⏑ — ⏑ and ⏓ — ⏑ ⏑; that is to say, surely, ⏓ ⏑ —́ ⏑ and ⏓ —́ ⏑ ⏑. **[19]** One cannot close one's eyes to the possibility that here forms with a *single* stress-accent instead of the normal two occur. That in individual cases the manner of recitation occasionally might have made even a short quantity approach the validity of the rhythm, which as a rule went only to a long quantity, must, as already remarked, be regarded as possible (cf. above p. 11).[2] This is why we have to pre-suppose that, generally speaking, types such as ⏓ — ⏑ ⏑ and ⏓ ⏑ — ⏑, which were evidently felt and recognized as such, signify what they

---

(Continued from previous page)

the last eight syllables of the Jagatī line, when the caesura falls after the fifth syllable, lie far outside the comparability with the Gāyatrī pāda. Why then in this pāda just the rhythm ⏓ ⏑ ⏑ —, and why not rather the rhythm ⏓ ⏑ — — which has a far greater frequency in the scansions of the syllables 5-8 in that form of the Vedic Jagatī (ZDMG XXXVII, 61), should have caused aversion?

1. Our statistics moreover show that the disinclination for two consecutive short quantities in the third and the fourth places was smaller than for short quantities in the second and the third places. Compare also the section on metrical lengthenings.
2. We cannot easily believe that this possibility was realized in the beginning of the line to a substantially larger measure than what we have conjectured above for the closing part of the line; otherwise forms like ⏑ ⏑ ⏑ ⏑ or — ⏑ ⏑ ⏑ in our table would have played an altogether different role.

seem to signify, and we cannot be prevented from seeing that in them by mere *a priori* considerations. What could justify us in setting up at our discretion limits to the changeability of the rhythm which cannot be denied in the present place, limits which cannot at all be demonstrated on the basis of the extant material? Why should a metrical scansion with only a single stress-accent in the first half of the line like ∪ ∪ —́ ∪ ∪ —́ ∪ —́ (e.g. *pavamāna rucā-rucā*) not have been bearable to the Indian ear, as it undoubtedly is for ours?

It must further be pointed out that while, generally speaking, a long quantity in the second place has been more firmly established than in the third place, still in the case of a short quantity in the fourth place the forms ∪̲ ∪ — ∪ are not only regarded as equally justifiable, but are even preferred to ∪̲ — ∪ ∪: obviously it appeared that the third syllable, on account of the middle place it occupied, was more suitable than the second to carry the stress alone by itself which otherwise fell on the second and the fourth syllables.[1]

[20] From the above observations on the combinations with short second and third syllable it follows that the remaining possibility in the case of a short fourth syllable, ∪̲ ∪ ∪ ∪, is almost entirely excluded.

If the observations regarding the statistical table are taken into account in their entirety, it becomes obvious that here the concept of *foot* is altogether inapplicable. To begin with, only the number of syllables remains constant; there may be four long syllables, but there may also be one long

1. We can formulate the following rule: to carry the weight of the entire opening of the line as a sole long syllable, the third syllable is best qualified, next the second, *viz.* the two middle syllables. For this purpose the fourth syllable is little suitable, the first unsuitable. There may be openings without a length altogether, but they certainly are of negligible rarity.

and three short syllables. Also the distribution of the stress-accent's is of extensive variety. For, I hope, in our exposition sufficient proof will be found for the view that in the opening of the line a fixed rhythm does not impose itself on any substrate of long and short syllables, but that the changing prosodic forms are the outward appearances of changing rhythms.[1] Is it at all imaginable that, while at the end of the line a strong feeling concerning the metrical material determined by rhythm manifested itself, in the opening it seemed tolerable to press any content into one and the same form? And what is the purport of the facts brought to light by us regarding the validity of the different syllable combinations [21] if here the rhythm was indifferent to the quantities of the text? Especially, what is the purport of the requirement of a long third syllable after a short second one, if a short second accomplished for the stress the same purpose as a long one? In addition, we here refer to the later discussion of the opening of those Triṣṭubh- and Jagagī-lines which have the caesura after the fifth syllable: the constantly occurring length in fifth position after a short fourth syllable (while characteristically the fifth syllable is prosodically quite indifferent) will provide another proof for our view that in place of a regularly occurring long syllable in certain cases a short one is substituted in such a way that the function of that long syllable is shifted to the neighbouring syllable which must now be long,—and what could this function be if not the carrying of the stress-accent?

To put it in a nutshell, the actual position of the Vedic Gāyatrī regarding the iambic rhythm seems to be the

1. Compare the various types of the short line in the Edda (Sievers, Proben einer metrischen Herstellung der Edda-lieder, p. 8): –́ ⏑̲ –́ ⏑̲, ⏑̲ –́ ⏑̲ –́, ⏑̲ –́ –́ ⏑̲, etc. One is reminded of the Vedic aversion to the type — ⏑ ⏑ — when one notices that in the Edda and in Anglo-Saxon poetry (Sievers, *loc. cit.*, p. 2) the four-syllabled verse allows the form –́ ⏑̲ ⏑̲ — only under the condition that one of the two unaccented syllables takes a secondary stress.

following. This rhythm is clearly discernible in the second half of the line. In the first half it may also be present openly, but it may, so-to-say, also be present latently; latent in the sense that, in freer manipulation the iambic distribution of the stresses is represented by other distributions which, by receiving light from the end of the line, prove to be representations of the iambic rhythm or to work towards it. Equal distance of the stresses from one another is not required; in this respect a freedom makes itself felt which in later Vedic and post-Vedic times develops into a conscious exclusion of the all too regular recurrence of the stresses. But, within the permissible variations **[22]** of the movement, in the opening the unchangeably fixed number of four syllables, the number of two stresses, which is at least mostly retained, and finally the marked prevalence of the forms ⏓ — ⏓ — remind the hearer constantly of the fact that the verse is following the iambic rhythm to which the end of the line leads back again and again.

Even though in general it goes beyond our present task to follow the development of the metrical forms of the Ṛgveda in the later literature, it may be permitted to give a brief indication of the changes the opening of the eight-syllabled line undergoes, e.g., in Fausböll's statistics of the Dhammapada.[1] Here the co-ordination of the four forms with long second and fourth syllable and their prevalence as the proper normal metres is completely overturned. Other combinations come into the foreground: in frequency the scansion — ⏑ — — takes the lead, partly considerably, over three of those four forms, the scansion — ⏑ — ⏑ over two of them, — — — ⏑ and ⏑ ⏑ — — at least over one of them. We do not go into the question which

1. p. 439 of his edition. We have, of course, to choose for comparison the numbers of the first, not the third of the quadrisyllabic units of the Anuṣṭubh line because of the special restrictions to which the latter was subject in Buddhist times, so that the end of the hemistich did not get more than two iambi (ZDMG XXXVII. 64).

positive tendencies have caused this far-reaching change of the facts given in our table: in our context we are satisfied with having stated the retreat of the originally prevalent iambic scansions (⏑̲ — ⏑̲ —) as against other forms. Can we conjecturally project the process we see working between the times of the Ṛgveda and the Dhammapada [23] back into the time of the prehistory preceding that of the Ṛgveda? Then the prevalence of the iambic rhythm in the Ṛgveda would appear only as the remnant of an older, more far-reaching absolute power of the iambus—this, however, must be understood in the light of what was said above [p. 7] about the nondescript character of the old rhythms.[1] But here we have already reached or perhaps transgressed the limits within which we do well to confine our guesses.

The prevalent form of the Gāyatrī stanzas consists of three[2] eight-syllabled pādas of the pattern established by us above.[3] There is a Gāyatrī of entirely different structure; it is relatively of rare occurrence, but guaranteed as a fixed metrical form in the Vedic poetry by its occurrence in a number of hymns

1. In the opening part of the Vedic Gāyatrī we find along with the pattern ⏑ —́ ⏑ —́ the pattern — —́ — —́ and, on the other hand, the pattern ⏑ ⏑ —́ —́. We can surmise from this that the deviations of the latter two patterns from the first have different historical significance in so far as the pattern — —́ — —́ with its long first and third syllables does not arrive at the iambic standpoint, but the pattern ⏑ ⏑ —́ —́ with its displacement of the first stress-accent has already left the iambic standpoint—in so far as this had been arrived at in the opening at all.
2. Stanzas consisting of only *two* Gāyatrī-pādas occur only in a single tṛca IX.67.16-18. We will speak later about Gāyatrī-pentads and Gāyatrī-hexads.
3. I would regard the traditional splitting up of the Gāyatrī by a main section after the second pāda as foreign to the original character of the stanza and I would regard the sectional cut between the first two pādas to be neither greater nor smaller than the one between the last two. The traditional *avasāna* of the Gāyatrī has been evidently formed in imitation of that of the Anuṣṭubh, the Triṣṭubh, etc.

and stanzas. We find it, for instance, in the following stanza (VIII. 71.1):

∪ – ∪ – – ∪ – ∪
tuaṁ no' agne mahobhiḥ

– ∪ – – – ∪ – –
pāhi viśvasyā' arāteḥ

∪ – ∪ – – ∪ – ∪
uta dviṣo martiasya.

[24] The striking characteristic of these pādas is the long penultimate syllable; usually, with lesser regularity, a short syllable precedes it, so that the closing of the line approximates the trochaic rhythm. In the following table I give statistics for VIII.2.1-39 (leaving out of consideration those cases where a single vowel counts for two syllables; 117 pādas) and for VIII.16 (leaving aside the very irregular stanza 9; 33 pādas).

	First Pāda		Second Pāda		Third Pāda		Total
	VIII.2	VIII.16	VIII.2	VIII.16	VIII.2	VIII.16	
Penultimate short	2	7	2	6	1	6	24
Penultimate long	9	30	9	30	10	32	120
Third syllable from the last short	9	18	9	24	7	29	96
Third syllable from the last long	2	21	2	13	4	9	51

We see that here we do not even find even nearly the same regularity as in the Gāyatrī stanzas with iambic cadence. The fourth syllable from the end can no longer be counted at all as part of the line somewhat fixed metrically; the first four syllables seem to have the same form as in the lines having an iambic cadence described above. Then again, pādas or whole stanzas of that more common form often intrude into hymns which as a rule show trochaic cadence, and on the whole anomalies of all sorts lend the metre of these hymns a peculiarly motley appearance.

I doubt if this form of the Gāyatrī developed as a variety from the so much more rigorously defined iambic form which in its rhythm is directly opposed to it. [25] If we regard the metrical lines of the Ṛgveda as having evolved in the last analysis from lines which were fixed only as to the number of syllables, but not as to the quantity of the syllables, and whose rhythm was not strong enough to exclude developments in *different* directions, then we shall be inclined to recognize the trochaic eight-syllabled line—if this term is permitted for the sake of brevity—as a form standing *parallel* to the iambic form, as an independent development of the original eight-syllabled line which was prosodially indifferent. The small extent of the part of the line which had gained metrical regularity and the very weakly developed character of this regularity seem to me to be indications of antiquity by which this not very popular metre, which, in my opinion, had remained at an early stage of development, is markedly distinguished from the other metres of the Veda: still, this type has so much common ground with the others that its indefiniteness will caution the Vedic researcher not to measure even the rather greater definiteness of other metres by standards whose applicability to Vedic poetry we must deny.

The following are the places in which the trochaic Gāyatrī appears in the Ṛgveda: I.3.4; 22.11; 27.1-6; 10-12; 30.13-15; 38.7-9; 41.7-9; 43.7-9; 90.1-5; II.6 (in several stanzas of this hymn); III.40.3; 41.3, 8; IV.55.8(?); V.19.1-2; 68.2-5; 70; 82.7-9; VI.16.25-27; 61.10-12; VIII.2.1-39 (the only long section of this type); 3.21[1]; 7.30(?), 32-35 (metrically a motley); 16; 71.1-9; 79; 81; 94.2; 95.7[1]; IX.62.4-6; 66.16-18; X.20.2-8; 185.

[26] The *Anuṣṭubh*[2] is a strophe consisting of two lines of

1. An anuṣṭubh which, however, due to its metre seems to belong here.
2. The name certainly denotes a stanza which is accompanied (*anu*) in the course of its recitation by *stubhas,* or *stobhās,* i.e by such joyful exclamations or interjections (*auho, hāu* etc.) as the musical form of the Sāman often indicates. We may compare, for instance, the Anuṣṭubh stanza of which the musical form has been given in the Sāmaveda edition of the Bibl. Ind. I, p. 239. Each pāda of it is followed by interjections like *iyaïyāhāi* etc. We find similar interjections very often. —Yāska VII.12 has a different view.

two eight-syllabled pādas. In the earlier period of Vedic poetry it was much less popular than the Gāyatrī. Later the relation was reversed and, while the Gāyatrī more and more disappeared, the Anuṣṭubh, developing step by step, set about to become the most prominent form of Indian versification.[1]

The pāda of the earlier Vedic Anuṣṭubh is the same eight-syllabled pāda with iambic cadence as described above:

ā yas te sarpirāsute
agne śam asti dhāyase
aiṣu dyumnam uta śravaḥ
ā cittam martieṣu dhāḥ. (ṚV.V. 7.9)

In the course of time an opposition began to develop in a more and more marked way, as we have observed it also with the Gāyatrī in hardly noticeable incipient form: the first and third pādas of the Anuṣṭubh or, more briefly, the first pāda of each Anuṣṭubh-hemistich—for, now the closer cohesion, given by the nature of things, between two pādas in each hemistich exercised its influence also on the metrical structure of the individual pādas—began **[27]** to move away from the strict observance of the iambic cadence, now in isolated cases, then more frequently, while in the final pāda of each hemistich the old rule was not only maintained, but applied with even greater strictness. Thus, a greater variety of prosodic modulation is created: beside hemistichs with iambic cadence in both halves now appeared hemistichs which introduced a contrast between non-iambic or at least not purely iambic cadence of the first half and iambic cadence of the whole, apparently not without intention.[2] We may consider IX.112 and X.60.7-12[3] as hymns

---

1. With what follows compare my observations in ZDMG. XXXVII.62 ff.; Jacobi Ind. Studien XVII.447 ff.
2. Compare the characteristic ending of the fifth and the opening of the sixth stanza in X.135: *anudeyī yathābhavat, yathābhavad anudeyī.*
3. The metre of IX.112 has been given as Paṅkti, but if we disregard the refrain *indrāyendo pari srava,* then we have an Anuṣṭubh. The same is the case with X.60.8, 9.

which allow us to observe this development in one of its earliest stages. Of the 16 pādas of the former, the 24 of the latter, 14 and 20 respectively have an iambic cadence; the exceptions are:

IX.112. 2	*jaratībhir oṣadhībhiḥ*
4	*śepo romaṇvantau bhedau*
X.60. 7	*subandhav ehi nir ihi*
10	*yamād ahaṃ vaivasvatāt*
11	*niag vāto' ava vāti*
12	*ayam me hasto bhagavān.*

All these pādas, with the only exception of X.60.7 (which can very well be brought near the iambic scheme in recitation), form *first* halves of hemistichs; they thus show the nascent tendency of the Vedic poets to assign its own role to the first pāda, yet much outweighed **[28]** by adherence to the old usage which makes the first pāda similar to the second.[1]

In the subsequent stage of this development the end of the first pāda appears in a form in which the preponderance of the iambi has disappeared and all the other schemes without exception are allowed side by side with them (iambi). In hymns of this type we need not, as a rule, read much to find represented all imaginable forms of the syllables 5-8 of every hemistich. The following statistics will give an idea of the nature of these syllables:

1. We might still mention VIII.8, a hymn consisting of ninetytwo pādas in which there is only six times a deviation from the iambic cadence. Among these six cases two are of the first and four are of the second pāda. There appears to be an analogy to this in the case of the Gāyatrī in IX.5. In this hymn, which occupies a place which really does not belong to it according to the number of stanzas and which even according to its contents (it is a purely playful transfer of the Āprī invocations to Soma) stands isolated, there is a strikingly full measure of deviations from the iambic scheme. These deviations occur five times in the first pāda and twice in the third pāda. Besides this, the first and the third pāda of the Anuṣṭubh stanza 10 do not have the iambic cadence.

Scansions	X.85 1-13,15	X.90 1-15	X. 97	X.135	X.136	X.137	X.145	X.146	*Total*
⏑ — — ⏓	4	11	8	4	3	4	2	3	39
— — — ⏓	7	6	3	—	5	2	—	3	26
— ⏑ ⏑ ⏓	3	4	3	—	—	—	1	2	13
— — ⏑ ⏓	3	—	6	2	2	2	2	1	18
⏑ ⏑ — ⏓	3	2	—	2	—	—	2	—	9
⏑ — ⏑ ⏓	4	2	18	5	1	5	5	2	42
— ⏑ — ⏓	1	1•	4	—	—	—	—	—	6
⏑ ⏑ ⏑ ⏓	3	4	2	1	3	1	—	1	15

After a closer observation we cannot fail to see that in this irregularity itself there prevail certain tendencies in which rules of a later time are anticipated. **[29]** If we compare the preceding table with the statistics of the table given on p. 9 as regards the irregular combinations of syllables 5-8 in the Gāyatrī pādas composed in the ancient style—irregularities which we find continued in quite a similar way, only with less frequency, also now in the *closing* pāda of the half-line—we shall find that the frequency of the various scansions show characteristic differences between the two tables. In the other table, among all the deviations from the iambic norm, the form ⏑ ⏑ ⏑ ⏓ appeared most frequently, the frequency being practically equal to the combined frequency of the remaining forms. In the present table that same scansion has rather a subordinate place; at the top of the deviations from the iambic norm stands rather the antispast ⏑ — — ⏓ and which has almost reached right now the most frequent form [viz. the iambic one] in frequency: the antispast starts with an iambus, but almost violently by the clash of two long quantities turns into a trochaic rhythm, and this antispast, as is well-known, has been raised in later prosody to an almost exclusive validity at this place of the stanza. The next place after the antispast is occupied by the foot — — — ⏑̲ which in the same way stands in most distinct contrast to the iambic of the end of the line with its colliding long syllables. The scansions of the lowest frequency in our table, ⏑̲ ⏑ — ⏑̲, are also in the later prosody entirely or almost unusual. Thus, the apparent irregularity prevailing in our statistics in fact turns out to be in its deviations from the irregularity of the material of our earlier table—though it is undoubtedly connected with it—the prior stage of a new regularity. The later total disappearance of the feet ⏑̲ — ⏑ ⏑̲, which already here occupy a much more limited field than they claimed originally, and then the later further prominence of the feet ⏑ — — ⏑̲, already preferred at this stage, **[30]** have given to the main metre of the post-Vedic poetry which derives from the Anuṣṭubh, viz. the epic śloka, its distinct character.

This description of the late-Vedic Anuṣṭubh has to be supplemented by stating further that we find the same disinclination against the altogether monotonous prevalence of the iambic scansions, which we found for the close of the first pāda, also for another place, viz. in the opening syllables of the second pāda. We find now an endeavour both to limit the use of the iambic cadence, which was required for this pāda at all times, as also to bring it into prominence as there arose a tendency to use non-iambic measures immediately before those final iambi. So now in the third syllable of the pāda we find the old preponderance of the long quantity being intensified; still, if there is a short syllable in this place, then the fourth syllable also is short, so that the iambic series at the close of the line does not immoderately increase. In both the passages selected for the statistics mentioned above, IX.112 and X.60.7-12, which appeared to show the type described here in its formative stage, we cannot yet observe this rule; here we find the second pādas like

hiraṇyavantam icchati
subandhav ehi nir ihi
jīvātave na mṛtyave
ayaṁ śivābhimarśaṇaḥ.

It cannot be however a mere accident that in the hymns collected for the last table—with the exclusion of the somewhat negligently handled hymn X.137—amongst the 156 half-stanzas we find iambi only in two places which immediately precede an iambic cadence.

X.85.12 *viāno'*[1] *akṣa' āhataḥ*
97.3 *puṣpavatīḥ prasūvarīḥ.*

[31] In conclusion we must add that although we can be sure that the Anuṣṭubh stanzas of the type just described, which set aside the exclusive occurrence of the iambic measure at the end of the first and the third pāda, may be assigned to the latest period of the Ṛgvedic poetry, still in no way can we affirm with the same certainty the opposite, i.e. we cannot assign to the older period of composition the Anuṣṭubh hymns which do not show that modern characteristic. Rather, along with the tendency to construct stanzas of the newly invented type, knowledge and occasional use of the old Anuṣṭubh type continued. For instance, we may compare X.134; 141; 143; 152; 176; 179.1 which nobody will ever be tempted to regard as older than the numerous Anuṣṭubh hymns of the later type which occur in the same portions of the Saṁhitā.

The hymns, respectively the stanzas, in which I would see the younger Anuṣṭubh type to be present are the following: I.50.10-13; 126.6; 158.6; 164.51; 187(?); 191; III.24.1(??); 29.10, 12; 33.13(?); 53.22; IV.57.4, 7; V.40.5, 9; 61.5(?); 78.6 ff.; VI.47.23; 75.13, 15-17, 19; VII.55.5-8; VIII.8 (see above p. 28 f.n.1); 47 (end of the hymn); 69 (an initial form of this type); 91.7; 100.8, 9; IX.67.31-32; 112 (see above); 113;

1. The end-syllable of this word is a short quantity; see the presentation of Sandhi.

114; X.14.13, 16; 19; 24.4-6; 26; 58; 60.7-12 (see above); 62.5; 72; 85; 90; 97; 109.6, 7; 126(?); 135-137; 142.7, 8; 145; 146; 151; 154; 155; 159; 161.5; 162-164; 166; 173; 174; 184; 190; 191. We can easily see also how, in the distribution of these passages within the ten Maṇḍalas, the modern character of the metrical form is reflected.

---

[32] Stanzas Composed of More than Four Gāyatrī Lines

The frequent form of the stanza consisting of *five Gāyatrī lines* (Paṅkti) appears in most cases in such a way that the fifth pāda is characterized as an extension of a stanza consisting by itself of four pādas.[1] In some places in a hymn, consisting wholly of stanzas of five pādas, the fifth pāda recurs in every stanza as a refrain; in some cases at the end of an Anuṣṭubh hymn there is a Paṅkti which repeats the fourth pāda, with an unimportant variation, at the fifth place.[2] An entire Paṅkti hymn without the refrain-pāda occurs only once in I.81; somewhat oftener we come across end-stanzas as Paṅkti in which the fifth pāda does not stand in the relation described above to the fourth pāda.[3] Apart from those typical cases of Paṅkti hymns and concluding stanzas in the Paṅkti metre, Paṅkti stanzas occur seldom. Sometimes they occur sporadically inside Anuṣṭubh hymns

1. Hence, the regular place for the Avasāna in the traditional text, with which the conceptual and constructional segmentation is in complete agreement, is after the second, and not after the third pāda. With this also corresponds the fact that when sometimes the Paṅkti stanzas follow one another they have the *three* last pādas in common: I.29; VIII.31.15-18; 35.22-24; X.60.8-9.
2. Instances of the first type: I.80; 82; 105; V.6; 75; 79 etc.; those of the second type: V.7.10; 18.5; 20.4 etc.; a similar case after a preceding Gāyatrī: VIII.56.5.—It will be useful to observe that all kinds of pentad constructions are especially popular in Maṇḍala V; cf. also the section on the Triṣṭubh pentads.
3. V.9.7 etc.—X.134.7 contains such a Paṅkti at the end of a hymn of which each stanza consists of 6 Gāyatrī pādas.

in which a single stanza is extended beyond the four pādas to one of five pādas.[1] Elsewhere the Paṅktis can be pointed out only in metrically chequered texts like VIII.69 (st. 11, 16) and **[33]** especially the Dānastutis (V.52.16[2], 17; VIII.5.37; 19.37[3], 46.21, 24, 32; 56.5).

Combinations of *six* (occasionally *seven*) Gāyatrī lines occur naturally almost only then when a shorter stanza appears extended by a refrain; thus the hymns VIII.47 and X.134.1-6 consist of Anuṣṭubh stanzas of which each one has a refrain, consisting of two more eight-syllabled pādas (the second being a variation of the first), to follow. In X.133 we have such a refrain (here, however, without the variation), following a basic composition, once of four (st. 4-6) and then of five (st. 1-3) eight eight-syllabled lines so that they constitute partly hexads and partly heptads. In VIII.39-41 the pentads have been extended to hexads by the addition of the refrain *nabhantām anyake same.*[4] X.59.8-10 are hexads of which the last three pādas (the second being a variation of the first) form the refrain[5].—Hexads without repetition of the nature of a refrain are to be found only in the concluding stanzas of two Anuṣṭubh hymns, V.86.6 and X.166.5; in both the cases the sixth pāda is a variation of the fifth.—The basic component of the Mahānāmnī litany is formed by a longer series of eight-syllabled pādas

1. Cf. V.9.5; 10.4; 52.6. We are not entitled to remove the unevenness with the help of textual criticism: note that all these three passages occur in a Maṇḍala which is most prone to the pentad constructions. —A somewhat different case is to be seen in VIII.91.1, 2.
2. Here, quite like as in the Triṣṭubh pentads in V.41.16, 17 it is the second, and not the fourth pāda, to which the repetition with the variation is attached. In this case, therefore, the Avasāna rightly falls, not after the second pāda, but after the third.
3. This Paṅkti, as it seems, forms the second half of a peculiar Pragātha. Cf. Prātiśākhya 1009, 1010.
4. In VIII.40.2 there is even a heptad.
5. Stanza 8 has one pāda less.

(apparently 7, 7 and 5 pādas) (Ait. Ār. IV; SV. II. pp. 366 ff., Bibl. Ind. edn.); these are interspersed with additions of different metrical measures[1] which, as additions, are known to the Indian tradition[2].

---

[34] Forms of Eight-syllabled Lines with a Surplus or Deficient Number of Syllables

It cannot be easily affirmed, much less can it be proved, that the Vedic poets are above any suspicion of occasionally having composed pādas with too many or too few syllables. We may just compare with their poetry the methods adopted by the Buddhist religious poets or by the lesser poets of classical antiquity whose poetry we know abundantly from inscriptions, and we may ask ourselves whether the large number of Vedic poets and poetasters, man for man, had remained free from human frailties which came their way at every step. It is definite that in individual cases, the basic conditions of the Vedic textual criticism being what they are, the problem must often remain undecided whether we have before us a metrical error or a textual corruption: whosoever thinks of being able to arrive at a definite decision in each such case surely seeks what is impossible in the very nature of things. Even in those several places where in the Saṁhitā we can observe a repetition of identical type of supernumerary and deficient lines, the possibility in itself that all these cases are results of corruption cannot be considered eliminated. Once the words had been actually interpolated into the text or had been dropped they could hardly fail, considering the mass of these hymns, to be repeatedly inserted or dropped at the same places in the metre. But certain cases will be found where there are

---

1. I can discover no metre in the opening part of the litany: *vidā maghavan vidā gātum anu śaṁsiṣo diśaḥ.*
2. See Lāṭyāyana VII.5.9; Comm. on Pañc. Br. XIII.4.2 and cf. Ind. St. VIII.68.

supernumerary or deficient lines about which it can be understood more easily than in other cases how a more free or negligent practice of the Vedic poets might have led them to deviate from the normal forms and which are then instanced in the traditional text **[35]** in long series of examples which can perhaps be eliminated in some of their parts, but surely not as a whole, without excessive text-critical violence. In this case, due to the very nature of things, cases of surplus syllables are capable of being subjected to a surer treatment than the cases of deficient syllables. For, there are verses enough, also such as are too long, in the case of which it is not easy even to remove a single syllable from the traditional text, but there is not a single verse in the Ṛgveda in the case of which if a metrical deficiency has to be remedied, some expletive cannot be found which is good enough at least to be possible.

The form of the Gāyatrī line, called catelectic by the ancient Greek writers on metre, having seven syllables instead of the normal eight, and having on the whole in the cadence the scansion ◡ — $\underline{◡}$ instead of ◡ — ◡ $\underline{◡}$ is, in my opinion, amply attested to be recognized as a standard type of metrical deviation. Numerous cases of this type of line are apparently to be found where a genitive plural in *-ām* or some other form of the same category, which we would define exactly later, appears at the end of an apparently seven-syllabled line (e.g. *asya pītvā madānām*). We shall, however, later endeavour to prove with proper evidence that the views, doubted currently by many researchers, according to which at such places we have to read *madānaam* etc. so that the length of the line becomes normal, is in fact quite correct, and cases of this type have purely an external resemblance with the seven-syllabled lines which we are discussing just now: whereby, of course, is not ignored the fact that in individual cases the determination whether a vowel in a line has to be regarded as equivalent to two syllables or whether **[36]** there is a case of metrical deficiency will and must often remain uncertain.

It seems to me that in the following passages[1] we have seven-syllabled lines of the type described above:

I. 132.6 *dūre cattāya chantsat*
gahanaṁ yad inakṣat
134.3. *pra bodhayā purandhim*[2]
175.1 *vṛṣā te vṛṣṇa' induḥ*
175.4 *vaha Śuṣṇāya vadham*
kutsaṁ vātasya aśvaiḥ
176.5 *ājāv indrasya indo*
191.12 *viṣasya puṣyam akṣan*[3]
III. 8.3 *sumitī mīyamānaḥ*
V. 52.16 *pra ye me bandhueṣe*[4]
VIII. 4.7 *mā bhema mā śramiṣma*
5.35 *dravatpāṇibhir aśvaiḥ*
10.4 *yayor adhi pra yajñāḥ*[5]
11.3 *yuyodhi jātavedaḥ*
11.4 *anti cit santam aha*
yajñam martasya ripoḥ
17.11 *ayaṁ ta' indra somaḥ*
68.16 *suabhīśū̄r Ārkṣe*[6]
[37] 68.16 *surathā̄ Ātithigve*[7]
68.17 *ṣaḷ aśvā̄ Ātithigve*[7]
72.2 *ni tigmam abhi aṁśum*
74.13 *ahaṁ huvāna' Ārkṣe*[1]
103.12 *purupraśasta' eṣaḥ*

1. For some further examples see below the section "Hymns of Stanzas of Irregular Construction".
2. Grassmann's reading *purandhiam* has even a more uncertain foothold in another passage cited by him in support of it, viz. X.64.7, than in the present case. Cf. Lanman 371.
3. Grassmann's reading *puṣiam* is improbable, because it disturbs the iambic cadence.
4. Grassmann adds at the end of the line an *ā*.
5. Uncertain; the last *ā* can be counted as two syllables or the sonant [Stimmton] *ñ* can be counted as a syllable.
6. A doubtful case.
7. Or *Ātithigue* ?

IX.	12.3	*sindhor ūrmā vipaścit*
	53.1	*ut te śuṣmāso' asthuḥ*[2]
X.	24.2	*tuāṁ yajñebhir ukthaiḥ*[3]
	119.11	*divi me' anyaḥ pakṣaḥ*
	191.4	*samānī va' ākūtiḥ*[4].

I add further the following cases in which, however, I regard the presence of this type as very doubtful:

V.	7.7	*hiriśmaśruḥ śucidan.*

The sonant [Stimmton] *m* can supply the deficient syllable, or it is possible, as is made evident by X.96.8, to read *hiriśmaśāruḥ* (or *hariśm.*).

X.	152.5	*vi manyoḥ śarma yaccha.*

A comparison with I.102.3 *maghavañ charma yaccha naḥ* will show us the way how the deficient syllable is to be supplied. Compare also I.114.10; II.27.6; III.54.20; V.83.5; VII.5.9; 16.8 etc. The following two pādas finally belong to a text which shows a trochaic rhythm of the type described above (p. 24):

VI.	16.27	*te te' agne tuotāḥ*
	61.10	*saptasvasā sujuṣṭā.*

[38] If we regard the scansion of *agne* in the first pāda as three-syllabled (with the extension of the sonant nature of *n* [Erweiterung des Stimmtons des *n*] to form a syllable) and if we read *saptasuasā* in the second pāda we can restore the expected rhythm in both the places.

To the cases so far discussed in which it is the cadence of a pāda which shows a real or an apparent deficiency,

---

1. A doubtful case.
2. The scansion of *ā* in *śuṣmāsaḥ* as two syllables is rendered improbable on account of the metre and comparison with IX.50.1.
3. Or *ucathaiḥ*? *ukthiaiḥ*?
4. Or can the requisite number of syllables be made up by counting one vowel as having the scansion of two syllables?

the following offer a contrast and apparently it is the opening part of the line that contains the deficiency :

I.	133.4	*tat su te manāyati*[1]
	187.11	*taṁ tuā vayaṁ pito*
	191.1	*kaṅkato na kaṅkataḥ*[2]
V.	50.2	*te te deva netaḥ*[3]
VIII.	74.8	*sā te' agne śaṁtamā*[4]
	84.1	*preṣṭhaṁ vo' atithim*[5]
IX.	113.5	*saṃ sravanti saṁsravāḥ.*

Just as we had to list above, in the terminology of the ancient Greek prosody, a number of catalectic lines, so also the formation of hypercatalectic nine-syllabled lines, if not frequent, seems to have been not quite unheard of. Here are the instances :

[39] IX.	67.30	*tam ā pavasva deva soma*
		ākhuṁ cid eva deva soma
X.	20.2	*agnim īḷe bhujāṁ yaviṣṭham*
	140.2	*pāvakavarcāḥ śukravarcāḥ*[6]
	158.2	*pāhi no didyutaḥ patantyāḥ*
	164.5	*jāgratsvapnaḥ saṁkalpaḥ pāpaḥ.*[7]

---

1. There is a good reason to account for the deficient number of syllables in this pāda : it is manifestly intended to correspond to the pāda that follows : *takat su te manāyati.*
2. The words that follow are : *atho satīnakaṅkataḥ.* Have we perhaps to suppose that in *na kaṅkataḥ* there lurks another compound, which we naturally cannot determine, of *kaṅkata.* with the first member *having two syllables*?
3. We must count *netaḥ* as consisting of three syllables.
4. Or is *agne* to be regarded as making three syllables?
5. In the *e* of *preṣṭham* we see, as often, two syllables lurking; in spite of that there is still one syllable less. It is remarkable that also in a second stanza I.186.3, which begins with the same words as in the passage before us: *preṣṭhaṁ vo' atithiṁ gṛṇīṣe* there is one syllable less, even counting *e* as two syllables. Are we to restore the defective syllable by assuming *svarabhakti* in the consonant group *pr*?
6. That this line is to be regarded as a Gāyatrī line is rendered probable when we compare it with st. 1.
7. Perhaps also I.88.1 *vayo na paptatā sumāyāḥ.* It is possible, however, that we have to restore here a Triṣṭubh line (cf. st. 5).

A whole additional iambus is to be found in the following lines :

VIII. 29.5 *śucir ugro jalāṣabheṣajaḥ*[1]
40.6 *vayaṁ tad asya sambhṛtaṁ vasu*
46.31 *adha śvitneṣu viṁśatiṁ śatā.*

I. 129.11 *rakṣohaṇaṁ tvā jījanad vaso* is probably to be ascribed to a corruption. There is a tendency in the last pāda of this hymn and of the neighbouring hymns to repeat the concluding words of the preceding pāda (in this case: *adhā hi tvā* ‖ *janitā jījanad vaso*); sometimes, however, this repetition is not quite exact (cf. 129.6; 130.6). It is therefore probable that the pāda had its normal number of syllables as *rakṣohaṇaṁ tvā jījanat,* and that subsequently *vaso* intruded from the preceding pāda.

We close this discussion with some of those cases in which we consider the metrical defect—be it that it is complicated by misgivings of a different kind, be it that its appearance by itself alone favours more the supposition of a corruption than that of the negligence of the poet—to be only apparent which we try to remedy, or at least would try to remedy, by conjecture if the transmitted **[40]** data were sufficient to give a definite direction to our surmises.

I. 187.1 *pituṁ nu stoṣam* — ∪ ⏑̲
VI. 75.19 *yo naḥ suo' araṇo*
yaś ca niṣṭyo jighāṁsati.

The metre is Anuṣṭubh of the type described on pp. 28 f. Perhaps before *araṇo, yo* is to be added.

VIII. 39.6 *agnir jātā devānām*
agnir veda martānām apīciam.

---

1. If we drop one of the two words, the line can easily be brought to the required length. But how has the word intruded in the text ?

Agni is Jātavedas not because he knows *martānām apīciam*, but because he knows *devānāṁ ca martānāṁ ca janimāni;* cf.

VI.15.13 *viśvā veda* ‖ *janimā jātavedāḥ*
devānām ‖ *uta yo martiānām.*

Hence here, in the second pāda, by the removal of *apīciam* we bring the line to the correct number of syllables; the addition is to be ascribed to a diaskeuast who in the sentence *agnir veda martānām* thought that a word in the accusative case on which *martānām* depended was missing.

VIII. 50.9 *etāvatas te vaso*
vidyāma śūra navyasaḥ.

The parallel passage (49.9) which, in the style of the Vālakhilya hymns, corresponds to these words shows that *etāvatas te* is not to be corrected. Then there is a deficiency of one syllable before *vaso,* most likely a vowel or a vowel-initial, so that the *te* here, as in 49.9, might be treated as a short syllable. We must then accept the reading *avasaḥ* for *vaso,* and the diaskeuasts felt themselves compelled, in accordance with the Prātiśākhya rule 139, to read it as *'vaso.* The genitive *avasaḥ* is as suitable for *navyasaḥ* as it is especially also for *vidyāma* (cf.II.27.5 *vidyām ādityā'* ‖ *avaso vo' asya.* VIII.75.16; IX.58.2).[1]

[41]VIII. 69.8 *arcata prārcata*
Priyamedhāso' arcata.

At the end of the first pāda we have probably to add *naraḥ* following the Sāmaveda I.362. There is no doubt whatsoever that the text had *prārcatā* before the line was mutilated.

VIII.102.7 *agniṁ vo vṛdhantam.*

It will not do to fill in the deficiency by adding a verb meaning 'to invite' and VIII.71.12 shows also that such a

1. Grassmann in his Wörterbuch (under *navyas*) has correctly seen the correction as recommended here, but has unaccountably given it up in his translation.

verb is not necessary[1]. Thus for the emendation of this passage there is not enough support and changes like that of *vṛdhantam* to *vṛdham antamam* can certainly be proposed, but cannot be proved.

X. 93.2 *yajñe-yajñe sa martiaḥ*
⏑̲ — *devān saparyati*[2]
X. 184.3 *hiraṇyayī araṇī*
yaṁ nirmathanto' áśvinā
taṁ te garbhaṁ havāmahe
daśame māsi sūtave.

The metrical deficiency in the first pāda is connected with a fault in the construction. The Aśvinā are the subject and one expects the churning sticks *from which* they produce the *garbha* by friction to be in the ablative case.[3] Thus we can conjecturally restore:

hiraṇyayā(ḥ) araṇiā(ḥ)[4]

[42] That in the text where the word *araṇī* occurred the dual form has intruded need not cause any surprise.

II

The Eleven-syllabled and the Twelve-syllabled Pāda. The Triṣṭubh and the Jagatī Metres[5].

The twelve-syllabled line is different from the eleven-syllabled only in one respect, namely that it has one syllable more at

---

1. Ludwig in VIII.102.7 admits the continuation of the construction of st. 6, but these two stanzas belong to different tṛca strophes.
2. Or should it be *devān* ⏑̲ — *saparyati*? It could have been something like *devān devān* corresponding to *yajñe-yajñe.*
3. Cf. for instance Śat. Br. XII.4.3.3 *taṁ haika ulmukād eva nirmanthanti.* Whosoever made the change in this passage had surely a feeling for the correct construction: *hiraṇyayī araṇī yābhyāṁ nirmanthatām aśvinau devau* (Śat. Br. XIV.9.4.21).
4. For the singular number cf. ṚV.5.9.3. The instrumental *hiraṇyayā* occurs many times in the ṚV which induces me to form an ablative *hiraṇyayāḥ* and not *hiraṇyayyāḥ.*
5. Compare the detailed study of Kühnau which has been cited above on p. 2, f.n. 1 and my review of it in DLZ for 1887, col. 196, as well as Kühnau's rejoinder: Rhythmus und indische Metrik (Göttingen 1887).

the end; instead of the *anceps syllable,* which forms the ending of the latter, the former has the syllable ∪ ⊻. In other respects the relatively complicated metrical scansions of both these metres agree so much with each other that they allow and even require a common description. In each case there are two principal forms according as the caesura appears after the fourth or the fifth syllable.[1] The versification of the line in respect of the choice of long or short syllables is not independent of the placing of the caesura, as is the case with Homeric hexametre, where in all cases of essentially similar sequence of syllables the line is divided into sections either through the penthēmimerês* or the tomê katà tríton trochaîon*. In the Vedic versification with which we are concerned here the characteristic metrical constructions which tend to occur after the caesura when it comes after the fourth syllable are not distinguished from those which occur after the caesura coming after the fifth syllable, **[43]** but they occur, in case where the latter caesura appears, again after it, and are thus, in their relation whether at the beginning or at the end of the whole line, merely displaced by one syllable. That, from the very beginning, these two forms, distinguished only by this peculiar displacement, should have been there independently of each other is something which no one can regard as probable, and that therefore one will be inclined, when one considers the relationship between the eleven-syllabled and the twelve-syllabled lines, to derive the one from the other. From what we have observed above about the relations of the Vedic with the Avestic metre we shall be justified if we attach a decisive weight to the testimony of the latter in determining

1. Bartholomae's views on the position of the caesura after the *seventh* syllable (Arische Forchungen, II.16 f.) are unacceptable to me for the Veda.

* Translator's note: The first Greek word means 'consisting of five halves', a technical term meaning 'caesura after the first two feet and a half of the line'. The second expression means: 'caesura after every third trochee'.

which of these two metres and which place of the caesura inside the line is to be regarded as the older one. The type in which a line gets divided into segments by the caesura at a definite place belongs to the Indo-Iranian period; it is a well-known fact that in the Avesta it dominates the versification of the Gāthās, while the remaining Avestan texts are marked by the eight-syllabled line which has no definite location for the caesura, exactly as is the case with the eight-syllabled line in the Ṛgveda. Then again, as we have already observed above, among the prosodies of the Gāthā-stanzas the one which has four eleven-syllabled lines with a caesura after the fourth syllable[1] is in striking agreement with the Triṣṭubh of the Ṛgveda, a fact which has not escaped the observation of the Avestan scholars. As a consequence we may with great probability declare an older date for *this* caesura[2] and so also for the *eleven-syllabled* line as compared with the [44] twelve-syllabled one;[3] we can assume that the twelve-syllabled line was created by an extension of the eleven-syllabled line by a syllable[4]. We have observed the

1. That for the Gāthā-metre *this* must be regarded as the basic form of the line, from which one proceeds, will have to be adhered to even if we follow Bartholomae regarding his statements about the other forms of the Gāthā line (Arische Forschungen, II.15 ff.).
2. Can we attribute the rise of the type of the line with the caesura after the fifth syllable to the influence of the five-syllabled Virāj line?
3. That the twelve-syllabled line of the Gāthās belongs to this category is extremely doubtful; it has the basic form of 7 plus 5 syllables.
4. Whoever chooses to say in this connection that the twelve-syllabled line is the result of the resolution of the last syllable, treated as having a long quantity (and appearing as anceps only because it comes at the end of the line), of the eleven-syllabled line into two short quantities would be in my opinion unjustifiably importing into the Vedic prosody ideas which belong to more sharply developed metrical systems. Just as the Triṣṭubh line was lengthened to the Jagatī line, so was from the Jagatī line, by the addition of one more syllable, formed the Atijagatī line (e.g. VIII.97.13); and in this way the alternation each time of a long and a short syllable will be maintained so that the syllable which in the Jagatī, as a final one, is anceps would here become a long one as occurring in the penultimate position.

fact that the eight-syllabled line does not form a unit of the stanza of the eleven-syllabled line, but does so of the twelve-syllabled one with which it has the iambic cadence in common, in several forms of poetry of rigidly developed type, often related to each other; and this leads us to assume that just the influence of the eight-syllabled line on the eleven-syllabled one, viz. the endeavour to bring the cadence of the latter into conformity with the iambic rhythm of the former, may have led to the development of the twelve-syllabled line.

A number of observations proves that the caesura, as compared with the end of the metrical line, is to be regarded as a considerably weaker break. In numerous stanzas the caesura does not fall at the proper end of a word, but between the two components of a compound, or it separates from the body of a word a suffix like *-tama* enjoying an independent status. Sometimes the caesura occurs before an enclitic; in some places the saṁdhi goes beyond it: contractions or blendings of final *e* or *o* with following *a* [45] are to be found, although only in isolated instances, taking place beyond the caesura. And finally, cases are not wanting in which the caesura is completely neglected.[1] These are anomalies which would not have been possible if also in

1. The following are examples from the seventh Maṇḍala for the caesura coming in between the two members of a compound: 2.7b; 3.10b(?); 4.5d; 8.6d; 14.1c; 23.5b; 38.2d, 5d; 58.2b; 60.8d; 81.4c. Besides these, very frequently, which is only self-evident, we observe the same thing in compounds formed of names of gods such as *mitrāvaruṇā, indrāsomā, dyāvāpṛthivī,* which as a matter of fact have to be interpreted as two distinct words. —Examples of caesura before the suffix of the superlative degree *-tama* : I.62.6 (twice); IV.1.4, 6; 22.3; 23.6; X.115.5. —caesura before *īm* I.71.5; before *iva* V.53.16; X.4.2; 68.5; 94.13 (twice); before *vām* III.58.8; before *cit* X.93.7. —Examples of contraction IX.87.5: *mahe vājāyāmṛtāya śravāṁsi.*—Crasis of *e* + *a*, *o* + *a:* I.118.7; 186.8; VII.1.19(?); X.103.1 and in several more cases. —Instances of a complete neglect of caesura from the seventh Maṇḍala: 2.7c; 4.9d; 7.1b; 20.6a, 7d; 36.5c; 57.6b; 60.1a; 61.1d; 67.5b; 68.3c; 88.3d, 6c; 97.3b, 9a. Generally the pādas without caesura can be

(Continued on next page)

the regularly constructed stanzas the caesura had not formed just a break which was insignificant and therefore likely to disappear easily. Moreover, several phenomena, related to the regular use of the caesura, lead to the same result. The quantity of the fourth syllable of the metrical line, when this occurs before the caesura, is less strictly observed than when the caesura does not come after it[1]; but the way this syllable is treated even in the former case is still far remote from the **[46]** kind of complete freedom which is allowed to it at the end of the line as a consequence of the pause that comes after it. We shall discuss this subject in detail when we deal with the prosodial character of the opening part of the line and then we shall try to establish in relation with it another thesis of ours, which is equally important for understanding the nature of caesura, viz. that the position, although not without exception still in any case regularly, exercises its influence beyond the caesura. And finally we have to point out another phenomenon which lies in the same direction as what has been mentioned so far: the prejudice of the Vedic poets against the hiatus is evident also in the case of words separated by caesura, although in this case it may not be as strong as in the remaining portions

---

(Continued from previous page)

easily accommodated with the regular types; they show the construction of one or the other regular type, only that the caesura is neglected. For instance, X.103.2 *saṁkrandanenānimiṣeṇa jiṣṇunā* obviously corresponds with the form ⏓ — ⏓ — ⏓ | ⏑ ⏑ — ⏑ — ⏑ ⏓. Yet it is noticeable how often (especially among the cases just cited from the seventh Maṇḍala) the type ⏓ — ⏓ — ⏑ — ⏑ — ⏑ — ⏓ occurs. The long quantity in the sixth place does not suit the more frequent type *having* the caesura. It would appear that in the case of these lines which lack the normal scansion a certain tendency had developed for a simple alternation of the long and short quantities; however, it might be a little bold to see in this development the traces of a prehistoric 'catalectic trimeter'.

1. We find this confirmed if we confront the fourth syllable, with the caesura to follow, with the fourth syllable of a five-syllabled opening of a metrical line, as well as with the fourth syllable of the Gāyatrī pāda.

of a line[1]. When we discuss the saṁdhi we shall have to return to this subject.

For the division of the eleven-syllabled and the twelve-syllabled lines on which we have to base our review of their metrical characteristics, we have to suppose caesura as the first point in segmentation and, as the second, the place where the metrically well-regulated cadence starts, i.e. the point between the seventh and the eighth syllables. Thus, we avoid the error due to which, for instance, Benfey was prevented from obtaining a clear picture of the Triṣṭubh metre: while Benfey invariably counts the syllables 5-8 as constituting the middle "foot" and seeks to establish metrical schemes for them, he overlooks the fact that, for instance, the sixth or the seventh syllable **[47]** on the whole does not always play the same role, but that each time, according as the changing position of the caesura, corresponds to just those rules or tendencies which are valid in one group of stanzas for the sixth syllable and in the other for the seventh, and that to what in the latter stanzas is the sixth corresponds to that which in the former is the fifth[2].

So far as I am in a position to judge, within each of the two main cases which we have to distinguish from each other (the caesura being after the fourth or the fifth syllable), the different forms of metrical structure in the opening of the line are in no way related to the varieties which are

1. It is also to be observed that of the double forms of the nom. and acc. dual (in *-ā* and *-āv*) before the caesura, when a vowel follows, as also in every other place in the interior of the line before a following vowel, the form in *-āv* is found but not the one in *-ā* which comes at the end of the line.
2. I regard the term used by Kaegi (Ṛgveda 34) with reference to the Jagatī and the Triṣṭubh as equally inadmissible as Benfey's division into the feet: it is to the effect that the two lines contain respectively twelve and eleven syllables and therefore form a trimeter or catalectic trimeter. Such terms, if one wants, may be used in conjectural statements offered on the *pre-history* of the Indian metres; in a description of the Indian metres *as they are* this use of the terms of the Greek prosody can only be misleading.

possible for the middle of the line. The end-part of the line, then, has its own fixed form, except for certain anomalies, which obviously have likewise nothing whatever to do with the variety of the forms of the preceding portion. It is therefore desirable and even necessary to consider these three segments of the line independently of one another.

If we investigate the individual cases of these segments it will become apparent that the rising and the falling accents, predominantly in the opening and regularly in the cadence, alternate with each other. In the middle segment this alternation is interrupted, but perhaps it is not a mere accident that beyond this interruption the movements in the opening and the cadence point to each other, that is **[48]** the rising accents in the cadence are found exactly on those syllables which should have received the rising accents if the movement in the opening had uniformly continued. Hence, it appears that the entire line is to be regarded as an iambic line in the sense that, first, a similar freedom prevails in the opening segment as in the case of the Gāyatrī line, then in the middle segment the iambic rhythm is interrupted with the deliberate intention of providing a contrast, but the cadence, interlocking itself with the opening beyond the middle segment, reveals the dominance of the iambic rhythm on the entire line.

Regarding the *opening* of the line, that is depending on the position of the caesura the first four or five syllables, I give below in a tabular form, as was done by me in the case of the Gāyatrī lines, the results of my statistics. These are based on VII.1-13, 18 and then IX.68-86.[1] As regards the cases which do *not* correspond to the predominant norm

---

1. I have left out in counting the entirely irregular pāda IX.86.43a; some of the pādas without caesura have been taken into consideration in accordance with the place where the caesura, following the metrical look of the pāda, appeared to have been intended (see above p. 45, end of f. n. 1).

which is thus brought out (i.e. all cases other than the first four in table A and the first eight in table B) it appeared desirable to undertake a more extensive compilation of the statistics; therefore I have done the same for all the Triṣṭubh and Jagatī pādas of Maṇḍala IV, but here I have left out of consideration the normal cases (A 1-4 and B 1-8).

[49] Table A: *Caesura after the fourth syllable*

No.	*Scansion*	VII.1-13,18	IX.68-86	IV	*Total*
1	∪ — ∪ —	53	62	?	—
2	— — ∪ —	48	38	?	—
3	∪ — — —	38	28	?	—
4	— — — —	42	33	?	—
5	∪ — — ∪	9	10	42	61
6	— — — ∪	10	12	34	56
7	∪ — ∪∪	14	9	42	65
8	— — ∪∪	12	3	30	45
9	∪∪ — —	9	9	34	52
10	— ∪ — —	22	7	32	61
11	∪ ∪ — ∪	2	6	8	16
12	— ∪ — ∪	4	6	10	20
13	∪ ∪ ∪ —	4	1	21	26
14	— ∪∪ —	2[1]	1[1]	12	15
15	∪ ∪ ∪ ∪	-	-	5	5
16	— ∪ ∪ ∪	1	2	2	5

1. The scansion of two of these passages (VII.2.6 and IX.68.1) would rather be — — ∪ —, if we read for *barhiṣadā* and *barhiṣadaḥ* the forms with a doubled *ṣ* (i.e. as *barhiṣṣadā* and *barihiṣṣadaḥ*).

Table B: *Caesura after the fifth syllable*

No.	*Scansion*	VII.1-13, 18	IX.68-86	IV	*Total*
1	⏑ — ⏑ — ⏑	27	77	?	—
2	⏑ — ⏑ — —	28	77	?	—
3	— — ⏑ — ⏑	31	67	?	—
4	— — ⏑ — —	25	69	?	—
[50] 5	⏑ — — — ⏑	28	29	?	—
6	⏑ — — — —	17	35	?	—
7	— — — — ⏑	21	33	?	—
8	— — — — —	18	33	?	—
9	⏑ — — ⏑ ⏑	2	—	2	4
10	⏑ — — ⏑ —	1	4	4	9
11	— — — ⏑ ⏑	—	—	3	3
12	— — — ⏑ —	1	8	6	15
13	⏑ — ⏑ ⏑ ⏑	1	1	2	4
14	⏑ — ⏑ ⏑ —	3	8	11	22
15	— — ⏑ ⏑ ⏑	1	—	1	2
16	— — ⏑ ⏑ —	1	4	15	20
17	⏑ ⏑ — — ⏑	1	3	10	14
18	⏑ ⏑ — — —	2	2	10	14
19	— ⏑ — — ⏑	6	6	9	21
20	— ⏑ — — —	1	3	11	15
21	⏑ ⏑ — ⏑ ⏑	—	—	—	—
22	⏑ ⏑ — ⏑ —	1	3	8	12
23	— ⏑ — ⏑ ⏑	1[1]	—	2	3
24	— ⏑ — ⏑ —	1	5	4	10
25	⏑ ⏑ ⏑ — ⏑	3	2[2]	3	8

1. This (VII.4.9d) is a case with a pāda without caesura, a completely doubtful case.
2. This includes the doubtful metrical line, IX.79.1c.

No.	*Scansion*	VII.1-13, 18	IX.68-86	IV	*Total*
26	∪ ∪ ∪̣ — —	1	2	7	10
27	— ∪ ∪ — ∪	1	2	4	7
28	— ∪ ∪ — —	2	1	6	9
29	∪ ∪ ∪ ∪ ∪	1[1]	—	—	1
30	∪ ∪ ∪ ∪ —	—	—	2	2
31	— ∪ ∪ ∪ ∪	—	—	—	—
32	— ∪ ∪ ∪ —	—	1	—	1

[51] We shall now investigate these figures in the same way as we did in the case of the opening segment of the Gāyatrī. If the method followed there was the correct one it must be so here also, although, for understandable reasons, the small figures here, into which the 48 cases (instead of the 16 there) break up, cannot always reveal quite as clear agreements and deviations as was the case there.

We shall begin with the opening of the line consisting of four syllables. In the same way as in the Gāyatrī lines here also the normal scansion turns out to be the one which, with the notation of the stress accents, would appear as ∪̲ –́ ∪̲ –́ [2]. The secondary forms, however, which are attached to these primary forms show, when compared with the secondary forms of the opening types of the Gāyatrī, a

1. This is an absolutely doubtful case (VII.8.2a); we have to assume that it is probably the four-syllabled opening ∪ ∪ — ∪ (*ayam u ṣya*, not *ṣia*); then we would have before us, unless a syllable has dropped out, a defective pāda form which is not rare.
2. We have to observe that here the forms with a short third syllable appear to get preference — and this was not the case with Gāyatrī; in the same way, when the opening part of the line is of five syllables, the scansion ∪̲ — ∪ — ∪̲ is preferred to ∪̲ — — — ∪̲. This is perhaps not a mere accident. Since the middle part of a Triṣṭubh or a Jagatī line is metrically free from the iambic rhythm, the stamp of the iambic rhythm might have been felt all the more essential in the beginning of the line.

just as much characteristic as understandable shifting; there appear in particular those kinds of forms which correspond in other respects to the main form, except that they have in the fourth place a short quantity: ⏓ — ⏓ ⏑. Of course it is the caesura coming after the fourth syllable which produces this effect, viz. that the quantity here, although not absolutely indifferent — because the long quantity has still such predominance that it cannot be an accident — is employed with a noticeably weaker rigidity. Thus here, as in other matters, we see very clearly the intermediate nature of the caesura showing half as much affinity with the end of the pāda as half as much difference from it. Evidently however [52], the short quantity, which on account of the caesura is here capable of being equivalent to a long quantity, bears the accent equally as the long quantity which it replaces; thus we get the scansion ⏓ —́ ⏓ ⏑́[1].

We have so far quietly passed over a preliminary question which has a decisive influence on this point of our statistics, and, along with it, on the other views that have been just expressed: are we to regard position (the effect of a following conjunct consonant on the preceding short vowel) effective beyond the caesura? Perhaps, in this respect also a certain wavering is something which may most easily be expected on the part of the authors of the hymns, and this will be in accordance with the nature of the caesura as seen elsewhere. For the purposes of our statistics we must naturally accept one or the other of these two interpretations to serve as

1. If the short fourth syllable did not itself carry the accent, then obviously we must expect that this fact would be revealed, as is the case with the opening portion of an eight-syllabled pāda, in the preference given to a long third syllable (see above p. 18). This, however, is clearly not the case with the numbers 5-8 of A of our Table; in the case of Nos. 11, 12, 15 and 16 of Table A the predominance of a long third is due to the second syllable being short.

basis, and the interpretation that appeared to me as naturally presenting itself was that the position was effective beyond the caesura. The nature of the resulting statistics, I believe, offers enough testimony to show that with it we reach, if not what is correct, then at least what most closely approaches it. As a check on this I have compiled another set of statistics in which the fourth syllables having a naturally long quantity, those long by position, and the short ones, get separated from one another. Thus, first of all, it followed that *the* even *a priori* hardly thinkable assumption, viz. that only the naturally long quantity without taking into account the position was alone regarded as the regular one, was excluded. Now there remained two possibilities. Either the long quantity was the rule, but then also the long one by position. Or, the short had equal right as the long one. **[53]** After further examination of these two possibilities the latter appeared to be out of the question: if the short quantities were permitted to occur otherwise than in secondary validity (i.e. long only by position), then if we look at the distribution of the quantities at the word-finals of the Vedic words elsewhere we should find in larger measure clear short quantities (which are not set aside by position) at the fourth place.[1] Thus, the only interpretation that remained was that generally speaking the long quantity was the rule and that in this the position was to be taken into account. However, in the case of the fourth syllable, when the caesura falls after it, the occurrence of the long quantities is by far not so predominant as that observable in the case where the caesura falls after the fifth syllable :[2] and it appears to me that it is in the very nature of things that, when thus the

1. One may compare the interrelation of the long and short quantities at the fifth syllable in Table B, Nos. 1-8 (counted likewise under the presupposition that the position has its effect beyond the caesura). Obviously, in these cases we find the natural relation not disturbed by any metrical considerations.
2. Cf. ZDMG XXXVII.55.

caesura was *occasionally* treated like the pause at the end of the line with reference to the occurrence of the *anceps syllable*, then also the effect of the position beyond the caesura will not have been found as absolutely necessary.

It remains now only this much to be mentioned in connection with the scansion of the four-syllabled opening of the line that even here a short quantity in the second place requires a long quantity in the third place with a predominating regularity: a rule which, however, does not find so rigid an expression here as it does in the opening of the Gāyatrī line[1]. Thus, we have the scansion of the type ⏑ ⏑ –́ –́ and, along with it, [54] another with the short quantity justified by the caesura, i.e. of the type ⏓ ⏑ –́ ⏑́, and finally we have the rare scansion in which a short quantity appears both in the second and the third place.

Now if we turn to the consideration of the *five syllabled* pāda-opening, obviously here also the scansions ⏓ –́ ⏓ –́ ⏓ predominate as the normal ones[2]. In their case as well as in the case of rarer scansions, statistics shows that the quantity of the first syllable in all cases is immaterial. The same thing must be said also of the fifth syllable for the normal cases, but in regard to it we cannot say the same in connection with all the remaining cases. Our table shows the following result:[3]

---

1. There the rule holds good in the eight-ninths of the counted cases, while here it holds good only in three-fourths of the cases.
2. To the fifth syllable no accent of its own is to be attributed since, as will be shown later, this syllable can take over the accent of the fourth syllable while substituting for it and then, as to the quantity, it behaves in a way that is not observed in the normal case.
3. For the purpose that we have in view, in this grouping of the sum-totals it is not of importance that for the first of the horizontal series given here only Maṇḍalas VII and IX are drawn upon and for the following ones Maṇḍala IV comes in addition.

⏓ — ⏓ — —	302	⏓ — ⏓ — ⏑	313
⏓ ⏑ ⏓ — —	48	⏓ ⏑ ⏓ — ⏑	50
⏓ ⏓ ⏑ — —	350	⏓ ⏓ ⏓ — ⏓	363

We have on the other hand

⏓ ⏓ ⏓ ⏑ —	91	⏓ ⏓ ⏓ ⏑ ⏑	17

We thus see that the quantity of the fifth is indifferent only where the fourth syllable is short; *in more than five-sixths* of the cases[1] the fifth is long and obviously it is the representative-bearer of the accent, which has been **[55]** now displaced from its normal place on the fourth syllable.[2] The seventeen exceptional cases[3] cannot surprise us; in fact, if they had not been there, it would have been a striking riddle: if the caesura after the fourth syllable has the effect that a short syllable will be tolerated as an accent-bearer, the same obviously cannot be excluded when the caesura comes after the fifth syllable.[4] So in this case if the fourth syllable is short, we may present as the first eventuality the scansion x x x ⏑ —́, and as the next one x x x ⏑ ⏑. We

1. From similar statistics of all the Triṣṭubh and Jagatī lines of X.61-74 it turned out that after a short fourth syllable, when the caesura was after the fifth, a long quantity occurred 32 times in the fifth place, and a short one 6 times: thus then the statistics given above is seen to repeat itself with almost complete exactness.
2. This, as also the other facts discussed here, finds confirmation also in the metrical "lengthenings" of short end-syllables; one may compare their description below.
3. Besides, as we have mentioned in connection with our tables, several of these 17 exceptional cases are of a doubtful nature. Two of them come from the single stanza IV.40.5 and the peculiar manner of expression in this stanza has occasioned them.
4. It may be observed by the way that in the regularity of the results mentioned here we have a new confirmation of the assumption underlying our statistics, viz. that the position operates beyond the caesura. It cannot be a mere accident that after a short fourth syllable the originally short fifth syllable becomes so often long by position that the general rule formulated by us follows when we take this into consideration.

cannot expect that the short fourth syllable has an effect on the third syllable in such a way that in that place the long quantity would be preferred since rather the fifth syllable has turned out to be the place for the compensation needed; the statistics actually shows that such an effect of the fourth syllable on the third does not take place.[1]

It is to be expected, and it is also confirmed by our statistics, that even in this case if there is a short syllable in the second place there is a regular practice, although we cannot by any means say that there are no exceptions, to compensate it with a long third syllable (thus ∪ ∪ –́ –́ ⏓, and along with it ⏓ ∪ –́ ∪ –́ etc.)

[56] Now we turn to the discussion of the syllables following the caesura and upto the cadence which is characterized by its metrical definiteness. The syllables with which we have to deal here, if the caesura comes after the fourth syllable, are the fifth and upto the seventh; if the caesura comes after the fifth syllable, then the sixth and the seventh. In the former case the three indicated syllables have by far in most cases the form ∪ ∪ —, and in the latter case the form ∪ ∪: since, however, the eighth is regularly a long quantity we can say off-hand that in both these alternatives there is an anapaest coming habitually after the caesura, the only difference being that, when the caesura is after the fourth syllable this anapaest *comes before* the metrically fixed scansion of the cadence,[2] while when the caesura comes after the fifth, the anapaest *intrudes* with one syllable *into* the cadence.

---

1. The cases with a long third ⏓ –́ — ∪ ⏓́ are 31, ⏓ ∪ –́ ∪ ⏓́ are 25; with a short third ⏓ –́ ∪ ∪ ⏓́ are 48, ⏓ ∪ ∪ ∪ ⏓́ are 4. The rarity of this last case is explained naturally by the disinclination against the combination of a short *second* and a short third syllable.
2. Thus in this case two long syllables, viz. the last syllable of the anapaest and the first of the cadence, come consecutively. If the caesura comes after the fifth syllable, then in this position there remains only one long syllable.

The regular alternation of long and short quantities as it appears in the iambic rhythm in the opening of the line and correspondingly in the iambic, respectively in the trochaic, rhythm of the cadence is thus *interrupted* in the middle of the line, manifestly not without conscious intention.

Among the three syllables which form the anapaest in the case of the first alternative, the second is most securely constant as regards its quantity; less unchangeable is the quantity of the first and the third syllable, so that along with the foot ∪ ∪ —, we have also other arrangements of the three syllables which, arranged according to their approximate frequency, are as follows:
— ∪ —, ∪ ∪ ∪, — ∪ ∪, and finally the rarest ∪̲ ∪ ∪̲

If the caesura comes after the fifth syllable, then evidently on account of the less distance in this case between the caesura and the fixed form of the cadence, we find essentially more constant **[57]** conditions than in the case when the caesura came after the fourth syllable. The first of the two short syllables which regularly come after the caesura gives place to a long quantity considerably more seldom than in the other case; the case of the second of these two syllables being replaced by a long one is altogether rare.[1]

The description of the state of things given here remains on the whole valid without change upto the latest period of the Ṛgvedic poetry. If we find here and there certain variations in statistics regarding quantities of individual syllables these remain within the limits which can and must be attributed to chance or to the individuality of the

1. The same idea can be expressed inversely: pādas with a long second syllable after the caesura have the caesura oftener after the fourth than after the fifth syllable.

different poets.[1] They hardly reveal a change in the metrical tendencies in the course of time which took place in an appreciable way in the Triṣṭubh and Jagatī metres, only after the period of the Ṛgvedic poetry. The only perceptible difference between the later Ṛgvedic metre and the older one appears to be that the sixth syllable, if the caesura precedes it, has even more rarely a long quantity in the later as against the earlier period: a prelude to the complete banishment of the long syllable in the sixth place to be observed in the Brāhmaṇa period.

To illustrate what we have said above with the help of statistics I give below statistical findings embodying my investigations of a few hymns and I refer the reader for supplementary information to the statistics, published earlier by me, in ZDMG, XXXVII.61, as also to the statistics of Kühnau.

[58] *Form of Syllables* 5-7 *respectively* 6-7		VI. 1	VI. 17[2]	X. 27	X. 65	X. 108	X. 111	X. 129[3]	X. 168	*Total*
Caesura after the 4th Syll.	◡ ◡ —	26	12	33	16	8	21	5	5	126
	— ◡ —	5	7	4	12	5	10	3	—	46
	◡ ◡ ◡	2	13	5	—	5	1	2	2	30
	— ◡ ◡	1	2	1	1	3	—	1	—	9
	⏑̲ — ⏑̲	—	2	2	2	1	1	—	1	9
Caesura after the 5th Syll.	◡ ◡	16	18	49	28	22	5	15	7	160
	— ◡	2	3	2	—	—	2	—	1	10
	◡ —	—	—	—	1	—	—	—	—	1

1. Especially considerable fluctuations in allowing the long quantity in the second syllable after the caesura are seen even among the hymns which can hardly be assigned to different periods of the Vedic poetry.
2. The third pāda of stanza 10, which has no caesura, has not been taken into account.
3. The pādas 6b and 7b have not been taken into account.

The preponderance of the long seventh syllable in the first of these two groups[1] renders it probable that this syllable is to be regarded as carrying the stress accent (thus ◡ ◡ —́), the more so as in the parallel group with the caesura coming after the fifth syllable, where also the combination ◡ ◡ — results, the long syllable, as belonging to the cadence, is obviously also the carrier of the stress accent. The ground for the stress accent is prepared and emphasized by one short syllable (— ◡ —́), very often even by two (◡ ◡ —́) which precede it. It appears to me that in the scansion ◡ ◡ ◡, where the stress on the third syllable is abandoned, three, instead of two, short syllables continually lead to the stress on the eighth syllable. Since along with ◡ ◡ ◡, the scansion — ◡ ◡ appears in a similarly secondary position, as — ◡ — along with ◡ ◡ —, I have my doubts whether we should ascribe the stress to the long syllable of — ◡ ◡; I would rather prefer to regard — ◡ ◡ as a less sharply pronounced equivalent of ◡ ◡ ◡.

[59] That in the scansion ⏓ — ⏓ there is only a negligent rendering, mainly of the regular type ◡ ◡ —, and then also of the other types contiguous to it, is improbable in my view: if that had been the case, we would expect in the different forms of the scheme ⏓ — ⏓ most often the type ◡ — — (as standing for ◡ ◡ —). This, however, is not the case; ◡ — ◡, as compared with ◡ — —, has rather greater, and not less frequency. It appears that, by renouncing to consider them as imprecise equivalents of the other types, we have to group the forms with a long sixth syllable in such a way that we place ◡ — ⏓ (esp. ◡ — ◡) at the top as most frequent one; — — ⏓ comes next. I do not venture a conjecture regarding the question whether the sixth syllable is to be regarded as carrying the stress accent.

---

1. The same is also recognizable in metrical lengthenings.

It remains now for us to discuss the cadence, i.e. the four last syllables of the Triṣṭubh pāda and the five last syllables of the Jagatī pāda. The form of these syllables accepted by the Vedic poets as the norm is –́ ⏑ –́ ⏓, respectively –́ ⏑ –́ ⏑ ⏓́. The great regularity due to which the place of the long syllables in the scheme produce forms like *janayā, kṛṇuhī* etc. testifies to the definiteness with which that metrical form was considered to be the required one.

Deviations from this fixed scheme, which due to their high frequency can be characterized so to say as regular of the second grade, are found just in *one respect* : instead of the first long syllable of the cadence[1] a short may appear, if it is the *end-syllable* of a word. Occasionally these end-syllables are to be found in *those* words ending in vowels which in the Vedic tradition also appear as long finals (such as the imperative ending *-hi* etc.); **[60]** and as a consequence of the extraordinary preponderance of the long vowel in this place in the stanza as transmitted by the tradition one might be inclined to resort to changing the text of the passage.[2] But in general these two occurrences—the short end-syllable appearing in the place indicated in the line instead of a long syllable and the appearance of certain end-syllables with long vowels instead of the normal short ones—are obviously to be separated from each other. In the fourth place from the end of the Triṣṭubh line appear

1. This means the fourth syllable from the end of the Triṣṭubh, and the fifth from the end of the Jagatī.
2. Compare the section on Metrical lengthenings; we have in particular to draw attention to those texts where after an end-vowel of that kind there is immediately a word with an initial vowel and where consequently in the traditional text there is a resulting semi-vowel or a saṁdhi-vowel. How shall we resolve *cātayasvāmīvām* and *śnathihy amitrān,* as *catayasvā a.* or *cātayasva a., śnathihī a-* or *śnathihi a-* ? It is clear that the Prātiśākhya rule forbidding lengthening before a following vowel cannot be held as operative against *śnathihī amitrān.*

numerous short syllables—vowels at the word-end and vowels coming before all sorts of final consonants without any distinction—which lie outside the sphere of the vowels, recognized as lengthenable by the tradition; and just in this regard the tradition has remained particularly faithful.[1] On the other hand, we have to recognize the possibility of lengthening syllables like the affix *-hi* in all kinds of different places of all metres: the appearance of a short final syllable, however, as is to be seen in the fourth syllable from the last in the Triṣṭubh line, is a phenomenon which in no other places of the Vedic metres recurs with even approximating similar frequency. Accordingly, in my opinion, quite independently of the possibility of lengthening certain end-vowels, we have to ascribe, secondarily, to *all* the short syllables the capability to represent the length at the fourth-last place in the Triṣṭubh (respectively the fifth-last place in the Jagatī) which preponderantly occurs there. The word-final made it possible to have a pause **[61]** in the recitation and the duration of the preceding short vowel was so much lengthened that it appeared to be adequate to the Vedic poets for this particular place in the line.

In order to illustrate with the utmost concreteness the treatment of the fourth syllable from the end of the Triṣṭubh line I give below a list, and I hope that it is not very far from being complete, of all the passages in the seventh Maṇḍala, which is particularly rich in Triṣṭubh hymns, showing a short syllable in this place. First a list of cases where the short syllable is the word-final syllable:

1.1 *dīdhitiibhir araṇyoḥ*
gṛhapatim atharyum
3 *dīdihi puro naḥ*

1. Cf. the subject dealt with in Metrical Lengthenings.

7 *apa daha arātīḥ*[1]
cātayasva amīvām
15 *aṁhasa' uruṣyāt*
18 *surabhīṇi viantu*
19 *mā rakṣasa' ṛtāvaḥ*
3.1 *nidhruvir ṛtāvā*
5 *tam uṣasi yaviṣṭham*
6 *rocasa' upāke*
4.3 *saṁsadi anīke*
6.4 *tamasi madantīḥ*
17.7 *vi dadha' iyānaḥ*
19.5 *namucim utāhan*
7 *sūriṣu siāma*
11 *mimīhi upa stīn*
20.1 *nṛṣadanam avobhiḥ*
21.9 *viśvaha siāma*
25.2 *śnathihi amitrān*
2 *kṛṇuhi ninitsoḥ*
5 *devajūtam iyānāḥ*
27.5 *vavṛtyāma maghāya*
28.3 *tūtujir aśiśnat*
4 *anṛtam anenāḥ*
5 *brahmakṛtim aviṣṭhaḥ*
29.2 *śṛṇava' imā naḥ*
35.6 *iha śṛṇotu*
39.2 *bīriṭa' iyāte*
40.1 *dadhīmahi turāṇām*
4 *varuṇa' ṛtasya*
aditir anarvā
6 *āghṛṇa' irasyaḥ*
41.7 *gomatīr na' uṣāsaḥ*
42.3 *ririca' upāke*
4 *vāriam iyatyai*

1. I would include this and other analogous texts of the category referred to in the second note before this (p.60) with the reservation that necessarily follows from what is said there.

45.3 *amatim urūcīm*
52.3 *savitur iyānāḥ*
56.15 *ādabhad arāvā*
21 *maruto nir arāma*
[62] 59.8 *prati sa mucīṣṭa*
61.2 *dīrghaśrud iyarti*
65.4 *ukṣatam iḷābhiḥ*
68.8 *apinvatam apo na*
70.3 *mūrdhani sadantā*
73.3 *pathām urāṇāḥ*[1]
[75.1 *tama āvar ajuṣṭam*]
84.2 *kṛṇavad ulokam*
86.3 *varuṇa didṛkṣu(ḥ)*
4 *jighāṁsasi sakhāyam*
6 *kanīyasa' upāre*
92.1 *madiam ayāmi*
4 *yudhā nṛbhir amitrān*
93.6 *somasutim upa naḥ*
95.5 *sarasvati juṣasva*
6 *sarasvati Vasiṣṭhaḥ*
98.3 *mahimānam uvāca*
99.4 *cakrathur ulokam*
100.5 *tavasam atavyān*
104.12 *yatarad ṛjīyaḥ*
17 *rakṣasa' upabdaiḥ.*

Here belong the following passages in the rare Jagatī metre:

32.5 *saharāṇi śatā dadat*
18 *didhiṣeya radāvaso*
59.2 *tirate vi mahīr iṣaḥ.*

This list would be much longer if one were to include

1. This text would belong here if the *ā* in *pathām* is held as the equivalent of two short vowels.

those cases from the traditional text where there is a final *nn* which in fact are to be written with a single *n*, and also those with a final *e* and *o* followed by *a*, the final syllable of which is in reality short. As against these, there remain only the following cases in which the fourth or respy. the fifth syllable from the end of the line is *not* a short one forming the end of a word:

12.1 *viśvataḥ pratiañcam*
19.10 *narām nṛtama tubhyam*
38.2 *savitaḥ śrudhi asya*
42.6 *viśvapsniasia staut*
[63] 49.1 *ȧniviśamānāḥ*
50.1 *varuṇā iha rakṣatam.*

Thus, from the entire Maṇḍala fewer cases of short syllables, which are *not* end-syllables, than those from the first hymn alone of this Maṇḍala for short end-syllables can be adduced, so that this peculiar treatment of the final syllable in the particular place noted above of the eleven- or twelve-syllabled line has been confirmed beyond any doubt.

As in the case of the fourth syllable from the end of the Triṣṭubh line which is not the final syllable of a word, so also in the remaining positions of the cadence there occur sporadic cases of inattention to the quantity, and relatively rare anomalies. We shall not suppose, as we did in certain formations of the eight-syllabled line, that in these cases we have another rhythm which can be the substitute of the regular one, but that that rhythm is just occasionally clothed in a language which only imperfectly suits it. In certain cases the constant recurrence of the same apparent irregularities in an identical word, sometimes even the direct absence of instances where a particular word occurs *without* causing disturbance to the metrical norm disclose a form which is different from the traditional form of the word (e.g. *pavāka* for *pāvaka, mṝḷ* for *mṛḷ* etc.); we shall have to return to cases of this type in another part of this work. Generally speaking, however, the absolutely sporadical character of these anomalies and the form of the words concerned which defy all orthoepic conjectures, shows that here we have only licenses of the Vedic poets which neither demand any further explanation nor admit of it.

As regards the ninth place of both these kinds of lines a few citations of the cadences where long syllables occur in the place of [**64**] short ones will be sufficient. For instance, at the end of the Triṣṭubh lines we find words like *nakṣanta, maṁsīṣṭa, vītaṁ naḥ, hotādhruk, sūryasya, Kutsāya, indo vāyūn, adrer aurṇoḥ, tāṁ śikṣa,* and at the end of the Jagatī lines (apparently these cases are less frequent there than in the Triṣṭubh lines) we have *mṛlatām* (read *mṝlatām*), *aśvinā, āyur jīvase, somasudbhiḥ, somapāḥ, yābhis tūrvatha* etc.

In the tenth place of the line, i.e. the penultimate syllable of the Triṣṭubh and the last but two syllables of the Jagatī, the anomalies are somewhat more frequent. It appears that the Triṣṭubh does not allow all kinds of short syllables in this place with equal ease. Although it is hardly feasible to formulate hard and fast rules in this case we can nevertheless say this much that the short penultimate belonging to the root of a disyllabic word in the cadence of the Triṣṭubh is more readily tolerated in the place of a long syllable than the penultimate forming part of a suffix in a word consisting of more than two syllables. We cite the following as used at the end of the Triṣṭubh line: *viśaḥ, uṣāḥ, naraḥ, patim, rasam, rajaḥ, vidat, udan, ahan, ratham, sakhā, iṣe* etc. In the case of polysyllabic words the superlatives in *-tama,* so also the declined forms of *iṣira,* are specially frequent; there are also isolated cases like *girvaṇasam* VI.50.6, *rathavate* I.122.11, *yunajan* VI.67.11 and more such others. The third syllable before the last of the Jagatī line, which stands precisely under the same prosodial circumstances as the third syllable before the last of the Gāyatrī, appears as a short syllable somewhat in the same group of words which have been mentioned in connection with the Gāyatrī; at the end of the Jagatī we have words like *taviṣīḥ haviaḥ* (frequent), *dadhiṣe, vasavaḥ, avasā* (frequent), *vipravacasaḥ, duritā,* but also *āmurim uta* etc.

A long syllable in the penultimate position of the Jagatī is extremely rare (examples being *dadhidhve* I.168.1, *Pākasthāmānam* VIII.3.24, *dīrghaśrut* VIII.25.17).

---

[65] Triṣṭubh- and Jagatī-stanzas of More or Less Than Four Pādas

Almost nowhere do we find stanzas of other than four lines in the *Jagatī* metre. Only in IX.110.4-9 do we find Jagatī stanzas of *three* pādas each: probably an imitation of Gāyatrī stanzas. *Pentads* appear in II.43.2, VI.15.6 (end of a tṛca): in both cases the fifth pāda is a slightly varied repetition of the fourth pāda.

This kind of stanza-formation is more frequent in the case of the *Triṣṭubh* metre. Especially stanzas of *three* lines, called *Virāj* by the Indian authors, appear very frequently as regular formations running through entire hymns. The hymn X.157[1] consists of *dyads* and in addition to this hymn we have to mention as a dyad an isolated stanza VI.47.25 belonging to a Dānastuti. Possibly VI.10.7 and 17.15 (both coming at the end of a hymn[2]) also are to be regarded as dyads, provided that these lines are not to be attached to the preceding stanzas forming, together with them, hexads. *Pentads* are to be found rather frequently, but they are also isolated and do not form hymns. As a rule they stand at the end of a hymn, preferably at the end of a Triṣṭubh hymn, of course mostly in such a way that the fifth pāda is a repe-

1. The treatment given to this hymn in the Sāmaveda confirms the fact that the combination of two pādas has to be regarded as a stanza.
2. Both these texts protect each other to counter all text-critical objections. That already the Saṁhitākāras assumed here separate stanzas of two pādas is in the second case proved by the sequence of the hymns.

tition of the fourth with slight variation[1] (e.g. IV.27.5, V.2.12 etc.). At a place other than the end of the hymn stands such a pentad only once in VI.31.4; further V.41.16, 17 where, however, not the final pādas of the entire stanza but of the first hemistich are picked up for the repetitions. [**66**] Pentads *without* such repetition and not coming at the end of a hymn are to be found in IV.17.14, 15; V.42.16. 17 = 43.15, 16.[2]

THE TRIṢṬUBH AND JAGATĪ LINES HAVING SUPERFLUOUS OR DEFICIENT NUMBER OF SYLLABLES[3]

The most frequent anomaly in the case of the Triṣṭubh and the Jagatī lines which are due to either too great or too small a number of syllables can *a priori* be foreseen on the basis of the metrical theory of these lines and, quite as in the Ṛgveda, it recurs in the metres of the late Vedic texts and also in the Buddhistic texts:[4] the two types, distinguished by the placing of the caesura, are contaminated in such a way that either the caesura occurs after five syllables and the line continues as if the caesura had occurred after four syllables, or it occurs after four syllables and the line continues as if it had a five-syllabled opening. In the first case there is a syllable too many; in the other there is a syllable too few: in which latter case naturally there are manifold difficulties which beset the task of separating such formations from those in which a syllable has been lost by textual corruption as also from those in which a long vowel is to be

---

1. Where this is not the case, the tradition (cf. Prātiśākhya 994) counts the fifth pāda as a separate stanza, e.g. V.41.19, 20; VI.63, 10, 11.
2. Each single stanza counted as two by the tradition. One may note among the last-cited cases, the prominence of the fifth Maṇḍala which specially tends to pentad-formations.
3. I would refer in general to my observations made on p. 34 above in connection with the Gāyatrī lines having superfluous and deficient number of syllables.
4. See my observations in ZDMG XXXVII.75 and Deutsche Litteraturzeitung (DLZ) for 1884, p. 1459.

regarded as having a scansion of two syllables. I give the examples of both these anomalies as complete as possible.

[**67**] 1. Instances of a line having a superfluous syllable on account of the mixture of the two types[1].

I. 35.9 *abhi kṛṣṇena* || *rajasā dyām ṛṇoti*
110.9 *ṛbhumā̃ indra* || *citram ā darṣi rādhaḥ*
120.3 *tā no vidvāṁsā* || *manma vocetam adya*
164.17 (cf.18) *avaḥ pareṇa* || *para' enāvareṇa*[2]
167.1 *sahasram iṣo* || *harivo gūrtatamāḥ*
169.6 *adha yad eṣām* || *pṛthubudhnāsa' etāḥ*
II. 4.8 *kṣumantaṁ vājam* || *suapatyaṁ rayiṁ dāḥ*
43.2 *vṛṣeva vājī* || *śiśumatīr apītiā*
V. 4.6 *so' agne pāhi* || *nṛtama vāje' asmān*
44.15[3] *agnir jāgāra* || *tam ṛcaḥ kāmayante*
agnir jāgāra || *tam u sāmāni yanti*
agnir jāgāra || *tam ayaṁ soma' āha*
VI. 17.7 *upa dyām ṛṣvo* || *bṛhad indra stabhāyaḥ*
23.5 *asmai vayaṁ yad* || *vāvāna tad viviṣma*
51.2 *devānāṁ*[4] *janma* || *sanutar ā ca vipraḥ*
52.14 *ubhe rodasī* || *apāṁ napāc ca manma*
mā vo vacāṁsi || *paricakṣyāṇi vocam*
75.18 *somas tvā rājā* || *amṛtenānu vastām*[5]
uror varīyo || *varuṇas te kṛṇotu*
VIII. 21.4 *yā te dhāmāni*[6] || *vṛṣabha tebhir ā gahi*
22.14 *mā no martāya* || *ripave vājinīvasū*
[68] 46.19 *rayim asmabhyaṁ* || *yujiam codayanmate*

---

1. In many of these cases we can easily suggest alterations which remove the anomalies.
2. Are *para' enā* to be contracted ?
3. There is a parallelism between this stanza and stanza 14 which is composed in the regular Triṣṭubh [there we have (*yo* instead of *agniḥ*)], and this must have caused the anomaly.
4. Grassmann and Lanman (Noun-inflection, p. 354) propose, and that is quite probable, the reading *devām* for *devānām*; the change is not, as one can see, metrically necessary, but is recommended by parallel passages.
5. Or is there a saṁdhi beyond the caesura ?
6. Or should we read *dhāma* ?

46.22 *ṣaṣṭiṁ sahasrā* || *Aśviasyāyutāsanam*[1]
59.6 *indrāvaruṇā* || *yad ṛṣibhyo manīṣām*
7 *indrāvaruṇā* || *saumanasam adṛptam*
dīrghāyutvāya || *pra tiratam na āyuḥ*
101.12 *mahnā devānām* || *asuriaḥ*[2] *purohitaḥ*
IX. 87.5 *mahe vājāya* || *amṛtāya śravāṁsi*[1]
X. 28.1 *jakṣīyād*[3] *dhānā'* || *uta somaṁ papīyāt*
50.2 *viśvāsu dhūrṣu* || *vājakṛtyeṣu satpate*
51.9 *tava prayājā'* || *anuyājāś ca kevale*
61.1 *krāṇā yad asya* || *pitarā maṁhaneṣṭhāḥ*
13 *tad in nu asya* || *pariṣadvāno' agman*
82.4 *ṛṣayaḥ pūrve* || *jaritāro na bhūnā*
87.14 *parā śṛṇīhi* || *tapasā yātudhānān*
93.14 *pra Rāme vocam* || *asure maghavatsu*
98.10 *tebhir vardhasva* || *tanuaḥ śūra pūrvīḥ*
103.7 *abhi gotrāṇi* || *sahasā gāhamānaḥ*
11 *asmākam indraḥ*[4] || *samṛteṣu dhvajeṣu*
122.3 *dāśad dāśuṣe*[5] || *sukṛte māmahasva*
128.8 *uruvyacā no* || *mahiṣaḥ śarma yaṁsat.*

Instances of a line containing one syllable less on account of a mixture of the two types:

I. 64.9 *rodasī ā* || *vadatā gaṇaśriyaḥ*
77.3 *mitro*[6] *na bhūd* || *adbhutasya rathīḥ*
120.4 *vi pṛcchāmi*[7] || *pākiā na devān*
[69] 127.3 *didīāno* || *bhavati druhaṁtaraḥ*
9 *tuam agne* || *sahasā sahantamaḥ*

---

1. Or is there a saṁdhi going beyond the caesura?
2. Or *asuryaḥ*?
3. I would, however, propose *jakṣyād*; the corruption has arisen due to *papīyāt*.
4. Lanman (p. 321) wants here the pronunciation *asmākendraḥ*, but if we accept a typical metrical anomaly, it becomes superfluous.
5. Should we read for *dāśad dāśuṣe* (with the fourth syllable short) *dadāśuṣe*?
6. Or does it have three syllables?
7. Is *ṛ* two-syllabled?

I.	127.10	*pra vo mahe* ॥ *sahasā sahasvate*
		uṣarbudhe ॥ *paśuṣe na agnaye*
	130.10	*vāvṛdhīthā'* ॥ *ahobhir iva dyauḥ*
	135.5	*imam indum* ॥ *marmṛjanta*[1] *vājinam*
	145.5	*sa īm mṛgo'*[1] ॥ *apio vanarguḥ*
	173.10	*viṣpardhaso* ॥ *narāṁ*[2] *na śaṁsaiḥ*
	174.2	*ṛṇor apo'* ॥ *anavadya arṇāḥ*
	180.6	*preṣad*[3]*veṣad* ॥ *vāto*[2] *na sūriḥ*
	186.3	*preṣṭhaṁ*[3] *vo'* ॥ *atithiṁ gṛṇīṣe*
	7	*tam īm giro* ॥ *janayo na patnīḥ*
II.	18.1	*prātā ratho* ॥ *navo yoji*[4] *sasniḥ*
	19.5	*sa sunvata'* ॥ *indraḥ sūryam*[5] *(?)*
	20.3	*sa no yuvā* ॥ *indro johūtraḥ*[6]
	31.7	*śravasyavo* ॥ *vājam*[2] *cakānāḥ*
IV.	1.19	*śuci ūdho'* ॥ *atṛṇan na gavām*
	3.14	*rārakṣāṇaḥ* ॥ *sumakha prīṇānaḥ*[7]
	40.2	*satyo*[8] *dravo* ॥ *dravaraḥ pataṁgaraḥ*
V.	19.5	*tā' asya san* ॥ *dhṛṣajo*[1] *na tigmāḥ*
	41.10	*śociṣkeśo* ॥ *ni riṇāti vanā*
	57.8	*satyaśrutaḥ*[9] ॥ *kavayo yuvānaḥ*
VI.	3.7	*vṛṣā*[10] *rukṣa'* ॥ *oṣadhīṣu nūnot*
[70]	20.2	*hann*[11] *ṛjīṣin* ॥ *viṣṇunā sacānaḥ*
	7	*puro vajriñ* ॥ *chavasā na dardaḥ*

1. Is *ṛ* two-syllabled ?
2. This *ā* two-syllabled.
3. The anomaly disappears if in the two words *preṣat* and *preṣṭham* (that is of course *prayiṣṭham*) one assumes Svarabhakti.
4. Read *ayoji* here?
5. Both the last two words are three-syllabled.
6. Grassmann reads *johavitraḥ*, a new creation of his. The *ū* of *johūtraḥ* could be looked upon as having two syllables.
7. Read *priṇānaḥ*.
8. Hardly *satio*.
9. Hardly *satiaśrutaḥ*.
10. Should it be read as *vṛṣabho* ? Or *ṛ* to be counted as two syllables?
11. It is obvious to assume *ahann*.

VI.	30.5	*tuam apo* || *vi duro*[1] *viṣūcīḥ*
	65.5	*idā hi ta'* || *uṣo' adrisāno*
	66.10	*arcatrayo*[2] || *dhunayo na vīrāḥ*
VII.	5.1	*pra*[3] *agnaye* || *tavase bharadhvam*
	9.2	*hotā mandro*[4] || *viśāṁ damūnāḥ*
VIII.	19.18	*ta' id vediṁ* || *subhaga*[5] *ta' āhutim*
	33	*iasya te'* || *agne'*[6] *anye' agnayaḥ*
	24.17	*ud ānaṁśa* || *śavasā*[7] *na bhandanā*
	27.12	*ni dvipādaś* || *catuṣpādo' arthinaḥ*
	96.21	*sa vṛtrahā* || *indra'*[8] *ṛbhukṣāh*
X.	3.1	*ino rājann* || *aratiḥ samiddhaḥ*
	13.3[9]	*akṣareṇa* || *prati mima' etām*
	14.5	*vivasvantaṁ* || *huve yaḥ pitā te*
	8	*saṁ gachasva* || *tanuā suvarcāḥ*
	23.4	*ava veti* || *sukṣayaṁ sute madhu*
	27.6	*ghṛṣuṁ*[10] *vā ye* || *ninidhuḥ sakhāyam*
	39.14	*atakṣāma* || *bhṛgavo*[11] *na ratham*
[71]	45.8	*yad enaṁ dyaur* || *janayat*[12] *suretāḥ*
	49.3	*ahaṁ Kutsam* || *āvam ābhir ūtibhiḥ*[13]

---

1. Can we read perhaps *vi dudravo* ?
2. Is there a corruption lurking behind this hápax legómenon?
3. Is *pra* to be counted as two syllables ?
4. Is *mandro* to be counted as three syllables ?
5. To be read *subhagāsas* ?
6. To be counted perhaps as three syllables with the development of vocalic quality between *g* and *n*.
7. To be read perhaps as *na śavasā na bhandanā*. Cf. st. 15.
8. To be read as three syllables.
9. Is here an imitation of I.164.24, in such a way that the necessary substitution of *mimīte* by *mime* explains the anomaly ?
10. Does the *ṛ* count as two syllables ?
11. According to the convincing conjecture of Geldner-Kaegi we have to read *ṛbhavo* for *bhṛgavo*. This text is an imitation of IV.16.20 where the caesura comes after five syllables and the pāda has the correct number of syllables.—We can also count *ṛ* in *ṛbhavo* as two syllables.
12. We presume, however, that we have to read *ajanayat* here; compare the parallels from the other Vedas.
13. Or should we count *ā* in *āvam* as two syllables ?

X. 53.4 *ūrjaada' ǀǀ uta yajñiyāsaḥ*[1]
61.3 *aśrīṇīta ǀǀ ādiśaṁ*[2] *gabhastau*
63.15 *suasti naḥ ǀǀ pathiāsu dhanvasu*
80.2 *agnir ekaṁ ǀǀ codayat samatsu*[3]
84.4 *akṛttaruk ǀǀ tuayā yujā vayam*
95.9 *saṁ kṣoṇībhiḥ ǀǀ kratubhir na pṛṅkte*
10 *vidyun na yā ǀǀ patantī davidyot*
108.5 *imā gāvaḥ ǀǀ sarame yā' aichaḥ*[4]
112.2 *yas*[5] *te ratho ǀǀ manaso javīyān*
157.1 *indraś*[6] *ca ǀǀ viśue ca devāḥ*
164.3 *yad*[7] *āśasā ǀǀ niḥśasā abhiśasā*

Similar to these cases is:

X.17.13 *yas te drapsa ǀǀ skanno yas te' aṁśuḥ.*

The missing syllable shall not induce us to adopt the reading *ias* for the first *yas;* here is a simple repetition **[72]** of st. 12 (*yas te drapsa ǀǀ skandati yas te' aṁśuḥ*) in which the expression has been so varied that here, as also in other cases, the metre is disturbed.

Apparently to this category belongs also the first of the

1. Shall we read this as *uta ye yajñiyāsaḥ* ? Cf. st. 5.
2. Does the *ā* count as two syllables ?
3. Perhaps this should be read as *codayati* (or *codayate* ?). The pāda then, as follows, may appear obvious:

   agnir ekaṁ ca ǀǀ dayate samatsu

   agnir vṛtrāṇi ǀǀ dayate purūṇi

   But passages like VI.75.13 would render any change involving the dropping of the verb *codaya* improbable.
4. But *aichaḥ* can very well be three-syllabled.
5. To read *ias* would be difficult.
6. To be counted as three-syllabled.
7. We cannot possibly read *yad* as *iad,* since thereby the metrically regular form of the opening of the line of the traditional text would be distorted. Perhaps, however, an emendation, as made obvious by the hiatus, is possible in the second half of the line which should read *niḥśasā yad abhiśasā,* even though the reading of the Tait. Br. III.7.12.4 and the Atharvaveda VI.45.2 can have no proving force, since that reading is obviously intended to suit the metre.

following two pādas:

IX. 79.1 *vi ca naśan* ǀǀ *na' iṣo' arātayaḥ*
aryo naśanta ǀǀ *saniṣanta no dhiyaḥ.*

The dictionaries of Böhtlingk-Roth and Grassmann take *vinaśan* under *naś* "to vanish". A comparison, however, with the two passages II.35.6 and X.133.3,[1] which are not to be separated from our passage, leaves no doubt that the root *naś* "to attain" is rather to be thought of. From this, however, it follows that in IX.79:1 there is a corruption lurking behind the missing syllable and the enclitic pronoun following the caesura, for the poet can impossibly say: "May the *arātis* reach our food." That the reading of the Sāmaveda (I.555 *vi cid aśnānā' iṣayo arātayo' ryo naḥ santu saniṣantu no dhiyaḥ*) cannot serve as a basis for the emendation, but that it is itself to be regarded as an unsuccessful attempt at an emendation is beyond doubt.[2] Obviously the meaning of the passage must be "may the *arātis not* reach our food,[3] or "may the *aratis* who reach our food reach (instead of it) the enemies". The easiest suggestion appears to me to be:

vi ca naśan ǀǀ *na*[4] *na' iṣo' arātayaḥ*
aryo naśanta ǀǀ *saniṣanta no dhiyaḥ.*

[73] "And may the *arātis* not reach our food; they may reach the enemies; may our prayers be successful."

A further anomaly of the Triṣṭubh, which is not rare, appears to have been influenced by the similarity of the eleven-syllabled line with the combination of two five-

1. For this passage as well as for IX.79.1, a comparison also with X.142.2 is essential.
2. Cf. Böhtlingk-Roth S.V. *iṣi.*
3. This is also Grassmann's rendering in his translation where he departs from his WB; he does not specify his idea about the reading.
4. Cf. for this *na* Delbrück Synt. Forsch. I.121.

syllabled Virāj lines :

⏓ — ⏓ — ⏓ || ⏓ ⏑ — ⏑ — ⏓
⏓ — ⏓ — ⏓ || ⏓ — ⏑ — ⏓.

We shall have to point out when we discuss the Virāj metre that the hymns in that metre contain several lines in the Triṣṭubh metre: a co-related phenomenon is the appearance of the Virāj lines in the Triṣṭubh hymns. Although naturally not each one of the examples can be regarded as absolutely certain, generally speaking, this phenomenon cannot be explained away with conjecture without doing some violence to the text :

I.	153.1	*yajāmahe vām* ‖ *mahaḥ*(?) *sajoṣāḥ*
	174.8	*bhinat puro na* ‖ *bhido'*(?) *adevīḥ*
II.	11.17	*yāhi haribhyāṁ* ‖ *sutasya*[1] *pītiṁ*
IV.	3.11	*sam aṅgiraso* ‖ *navanta*[2] *gobhiḥ*
	50.2	*pṛṣantaṁ sṛpram* ‖ *adabdham ūrvam*
V.	15.5	*padaṁ na tāyur* ‖ *guhā dadhānaḥ*[3]
	41.12	*śṛṇvantu āpaḥ* ‖ *puro na śubhrāḥ*
	15	*siṣaktu mātā* ‖ *mahī*[4] *rasā naḥ*
VI.	66.3	*vide hi mātā* ‖ *maho mahī ṣā*
	6	*ā amavatsu* ‖ *tasthau na rokaḥ*
	68.5	*iṣā sa dviṣas* ‖ *tared dāsvān*[5]

1. Possibly one could think of *suṣutasya.*
2. The conjecture *anavanta,* proposed by Grassmann, is obvious.
3. Compare the similar stanza I.65.1, which actually is Virāj.
4. Grassmann proposes the reading *mahiā.* Cf. Lanman 356.
5. *dāsvān* to be read as three-syllabled.

[74] VII. 87.6 *drapso na śveto* || *mṛgas*[1] *tuviṣmān*
IX. 91.6 *evā punāno'* || *apaḥ suar gāḥ*
X. 1.6 aruṣo jātaḥ || *pada'*[2] *iḷāyāḥ*
6.6 *saṁ yasmin viśvā* || *vasūni jagmuḥ*
83.3 *tapasā yujā* || *vi jahi śatrūn*
89.8 *yujaṁ na janā* || *minanti*[3] *mitram*
99.8 *kṣayāya gātuṁ* || *vidan no' asme*
upa yat sīdad || *induṁ śarīraiḥ*
101.7 *prīṇīta aśvān* || *hitaṁ jayātha*
120.1 *anu yaṁ viśve* || *madanti ūmāḥ*
124.6 *hanāva vṛtraṁ* || *nirehi soma.*

Perhaps to this list also belongs, with the neglect of caesura,[4] the following:

1.148.2 *juṣanta viśvāni asya karma.*

There is little probability of the first of the following two pādas belonging to the type described here:

IV. 26.7 *ādāya śyeno'* || *abharat somam*
sahasraṁ savā̃ || *ayutaṁ ca sākam.*

The facts that there is one syllable missing and that there is complete deviation from the regular metrical pattern combine to recommend a change of the text; *abharat* shows the regular form of the syllables as they should be after the caesura; we may read *somasya* in the place of *somam.*[5]

We really find *Jagatī* lines similar to the type which we are describing here, i.e. different from it only in [75] having an additional syllable at the end. Since the Virāj line is a step further away from such a Jagatī line, it explains why there is a rare appearance of such pādas. I can quote only the following pāda, of which the first part is very doubtful:

II. 36.1 *tubhyam hinvāno* || *vasiṣṭa gā' apaḥ.*

It is obvious to read with Grassmann *avasiṣṭa* (cf. IX.89.2);

---

1. Is *ṛ* to count as two syllables ?
2. Grassmann proposes to read *padā ā.*
3. Should we read *praminanti* or, with Grassmann, *āminanti*?
4. Also in the case of the Virāj proper (see below) the caesura is not always paid attention to.
5. In that case, however, the third syllable from the end of the pāda is a long quantity, but the same anomaly is to be seen in not less than three pādas of the preceding stanza.

if this was the reading of the text, then according to the Prātiśākhya rule 139 the *a* had to be elided in the diskeuasis so that the reading *vasiṣṭa* could easily come into existence. The next case which we are quoting appears to be more certain and the passage appears in several Yajus texts and essentially also in the Atharvaveda:

VI. 47.31 *sam aśvaparṇāś* || *caranti no naraḥ.*

Next also :

X. 64.10 *ṛbhukṣā vājo* || *rathaspatir bhagaḥ*
93.7 *viśve devāso* || *rathaspatir bhagaḥ.*

We find greater deviations from the regular form when after the caesura both the first two syllables are missing. Instances are found for both the placings of the caesura, and for the Triṣṭubh as well as the Jagatī lines. In each case it is of course easy to supply the missing syllables, but it is more difficult to prove that here the limits upto which deviations from the metrical norm are thinkable have been overstepped. Instances of lines with the caesura after the fourth syllable are as follows:

X. 61.27 *ta' ū ṣu ṇo* || *maho yajatrāḥ*
79.5 *ājyair*[1] *ghṛtair* || *juhoti puṣyati*
112.6 *pibā somam* || *enā śatakrato.*

[76] The following lines have three instead of two missing syllables:

I. 132.2 *uṣarbudhaḥ* || *svasminn*[2] *añjasi*
X. 144.5 *yaṁ te śyenaś* || *cārum avṛkam*[3]

The caesura comes after the fifth syllable in the following:

I.33.9 *pari yad indra* || *rodasī ubhe*
141.8 *ratho na yātaḥ* || *śikvabhiḥ kṛtaḥ*[4]
149.5 *ayaṁ sa hotā* || *yo dvijanmā*

---

1. It is possible to read *ājyair* as *ājiair* or *ṛ* in *ghṛtair* might count as two syllables. In that case the pāda would belong to the type described immediately before.
2. To be read as *svasmin.*
3. The pāda can easily be completed by inserting *pītaye, pātave* or something like that before *cārum* (cf. IV.49.2; IX.17.8).
4. To be read as *śikvabhiḥ pariṣkṛtaḥ* or something like that?

IX. 107.9 *anūpe gomān* || *gobhir akṣāḥ*[1]
X. 32.5 *eko rudrebhir* || *yāti turvaṇiḥ*
95.4 *astaṁ nanakṣe* || *yasmiñ cākan.*

We can be bold to judge with greater confidence than is the case with these stanzas, those stanzas having a trochaic cadence which due to negligence, which again does not cause the least surprise, has a superfluous trochaic foot. Thus arise lines of thirteen syllables instead of the Triṣṭubh pādas and of fourteen syllables instead of the Jagatī pādas. Sometimes the superfluous foot can be removed very easily (especially where it is formed with the name of one of the gods); other cases of the same anomaly, however, will caution us against changing the text.

Instances of the thirteen-syllabled type are as follows:[2]

I. 88.1 *rathebhir yāta* || *ṛṣṭimadbhir aśvaparṇaiḥ*
133.6 *avar maha'* || *indra*[3] *dādṛhi śrudhī naḥ*
[77] VI. 10.1 *prayati yajñe'* || *agnim adhvare dadhidhvam*
15.14 *agne yad adya* || *viśo' adhvarasya hotaḥ*
26.2 *tuāṁ vṛtreṣu* || *indra satpatiṁ tarutram*
VII. 104.15 *adyā murīya* || *yadi yātudhāno' asmi*
X. 114.4 *ekaḥ suparṇaḥ* || *sa samudram ā viveśa*
121.7 *tato devānāṁ* || *sam avartatāsur ekaḥ*
139.4 *tad anvavaid* || *indro*[4] *rārahāṇa āsām*[5].

The following line is undoubtedly to be emended:

VI. 46.12 *adha smā yacha* || *tanve* (rather *tanue*) *tane ca chardiḥ.*

---

1. Perhaps *gobhir akto akṣāḥ* (cf. IX.96.22)? Both *akto* and *akṣāḥ* have similar beginnings and one of the two words could easily be lost.
2. From the Yajurveda compare e.g. Taitt. Saṁh. I.2.3.3.=Vāj. Saṁh. IV.1: *edam aganma* || *devayajanaṁ pṛthivyāḥ*. Taitt. Saṁh. III.1.4.4: *namaḥ paśubhyaḥ* || *paśupataye karomi.*
3. To count as three syllables. Benfey (Quantitätversch. II.30) reads *mahendra.*
4. To count as three syllables.
5. X.87.12: *śaphārujaṁ yena* || *paśyasi yātudhānam* is a thirteen-syllabled pāda, but the surplus syllables in it seem to form part of the section preceding the caesura.

Since the pāda stands in a Pragātha storphe it must be in the Jagatī metre. According to the transmitted reading the *ca* which has a long quantity on account of position happens to be in a place where regularly there should be a short syllable; as against this first syllable of *chardiḥ* would have the value of a long quantity, whereas it is well-known that in the Ṛgveda the metre everywhere else invariably requires the reading *chadiḥ*. Consequently these syllables have been displaced by one step from the place which really belonged to them. This displacement can be removed and the pāda could be made to conform to the correct Jagatī line if we remove that *ca,* as also in VIII.68.12 *tanue tane* occurs without *ca*:

adha smā[1] *yacha* || *tanue tane chadiḥ.*

The thirteen-syllabled type has been used at a certain place with such frequency that it allows us to recognize it as a form which has been handled with deliberate intention. In the case of the three stanzas VIII.97.13-15, which manifestly **[78]** belong to a tṛca,[2] in the first stanza all the four pādas are thirteen-syllabled, in the second and in the third stanza they are thirteen-syllabled intermixed with regular eleven-syllabled Triṣṭubh lines (1 plus 2 of one type as against 3 plus 2 of the other). Both the superfluous syllables in one case (i.e. in the first pāda) come before the caesura;[3] otherwise they always come in such a way that they constitute the lengthening of the trochaic cadence by one trochaic foot. The pādas run thus:

VIII. 97.13 *tam indraṁ johavīmi* || *maghavānam ugram*
satrā dadhānam || *apratiṣkutam śavāṁsi*

1. Rather *sma*; see the section on Metrical Lengthenings.
2. From the hymn VIII. 97 the Sāmaveda has taken stanzas 1, 4, 7, 10 and 13 as Yonis and stanzas 10-12 as a tṛca.
3. This may apply also to the fifth of the pādas concerned.

maṁhiṣṭho gīrbhir || ā ca yajñiyo vavartat
rāye no viśvā || supathā kṛṇotu vajrī
14 *vi ojasā || śaviṣṭha śakra nāśayadhyai*
15 *apo na vajrin || duritāti parṣi bhūri*
viśvapsniasya || spṛhayāyiasya rājan.

The fourteen-syllabled type of the variety described above based on a lengthening of the cadence of the Jagatī line appears in the following cases:[1]

I.	133.6	*apūruṣaghno' || apratīta śūra satvabhiḥ*
IV.	1.2	*sa bhrātaraṁ || varuṇam agna' ā vavṛtsua*
VIII.	90.5	*tuaṁ vṛtrāṇi || haṁsi apratīni eka' it*
	97.10[2]	*sajūs tatakṣur indraṁ || jajanuś ca rājase*
	103.5	*sa dṛḻhe cid || abhi tṛṇatti vājam arvatā*
X.	142.1	*sahasaḥ sūno || nahi anyad asti āpiam.*

We have further to adduce as one of the more frequent anomalies the incompleteness of the opening of the line. Those **[79]** cases in which the opening has four syllables instead of five have been already explained above as instances of the contamination of the two regular types and listed; now we have to cite cases of the openings with three syllables instead of four:

I.	64.9	*rodasī || ā vadatā gaṇaśriyaḥ*[3]
	104.4	*añjasī || kuliśī vīrapatnī*
	169.5	*te ṣu ṇo || maruto mṛḻayantu*
	173.4	*jujoṣad || indro dasmavarcāḥ*[4]
II.	4.3	*priyaṁ dhuḥ*[5] *|| kṣeṣianto na mitram*
	4.8	*tṛtīye*[6] *|| vidathe manma śaṁsi*
	31.7	*atakṣann*[7] *|| āyavo navyase sam*

1. In most of these cases the removal of the surplus syllable is easy.
2. I have included this pāda here although the lengthening in this case belongs to the section *preceding* the caesura.
3. Or does the caesura come after *ā* ? [See above p. 68.]
4. The deficiency can easily be made up.
5. To be corrected as *dadhuḥ*? Cf. X.49.2.
6. Is the *ṛ* to count as two syllables ?
7. To be read as *atakṣan yā* ?

V.	45.1	*vi duro* || *mānuṣīr deva āvaḥ*
VI.	4.8	(and often) *madema* || *śatahimāḥ suvīrāḥ*[1]
	15.15	*avā no* || *maghavan vājasātau*
	24.3	*akṣo na* || *cakrioḥ śūra bṛhan*
	7	*stomebhir* || *ukthaiś ca śasyamānā*
	30.1	*bhuya' id*[2] || *vāvṛdhe vīriāya*
	47.31	*ketumad* || *dundubhir vāvadīti*
VII.	100.3	*trir*[3] *devaḥ* || *pṛthivīm eṣá etām*
VIII.	46.17[4]	*mīḻhuṣe'* || *araṁgamāya jagmaye*
IX.	86.43	*añjate* || *vi añjate sam añjate*
[80] X.	31.6	*abhavat*[5] || *pūrviā bhūmanā gauḥ*
	93.9	*kṛdhī*[6] *no'* || *ahrayo deva savitaḥ*
	95.13	*pra*[7] *tat te* || *hinavā yat te' asme*
	99.6	*ṣaḻakṣaṁ* || *triśīrṣāṇaṁ damanyat*
	105.6	*ṛbhur*[6] *na* || *kratubhir mātariśvā.*[8]

Lastly we mention the stanzas where the appearance of superfluous syllables is to be explained as due to a longer list of, for example, the names of gods which exceeds the framework of the line or due to the fact that the line refers back to a preceding normal line—as, for instance, an answer to a question—in a way which causes a disturbance of the metrical form. Here belongs the stanza already referred to above on p. 67 (V.44.15) as well as the following pādas in

---

1. There is a way, not impossible, but artificial, to convert this pāda into a normal one and that is to assume the caesura after *śata-* and to count the *ā* of *himāḥ* as two syllables.
2. Should we read *bhūyasa' id* instead ?
3. Is *trir* to count as two syllables with a svarabhakti ?
4. Unless the pādas of this stanza are to be split in a different way.
5. Presumably, however, this pāda, like the preceding and the following, began with an *asya* so that it was *asyābhavat.*
6. Does the *ṛ* count as two syllables ?
7. Is *pra* to count as two syllables with svarabhakti ?
8. Is I.88.1d to be taken as a deficient Triṣṭubh line ? Instead of the transmitted three syllables, five syllables would be required, not four as in the above cases. Presumably something has been omitted: e.g. *vayo na* [*achā*] || *paptatā sumāyāḥ.*

which, however easy an emendation, I would hardly dare recommend it:

VIII. 35.13 *mitrāvaruṇavantā* ॥ *uta dharmavantā*
X. 128.9 *vasavo rudrā' ādityā*[1] ॥ *uparispṛśam mā*
10.12 *na vā' u te* ॥ *tanuā tanuaṁ sam papṛcyām*
(cf. st. 11 *tanuā me* ॥ *tanuaṁ sam pipṛgdhi*).

The different types of cases so far cited will give a picture of the abnormalities which *can* be traced to negligence or laxity in the [81] metrical composition. Other irregularities, of which we give examples in the following portion, distort the correct form of the stanzas in such a way that they can hardly be attributed to the poet, but must be attributed only to decays in the tradition, all the more so, since with this metrical defect are associated many other kinds of objections from which we have to conclude that there has been corruption of the text.[2] The exact knowledge of the

1. The Atharvaveda (V.3.10), as is obvious, drops one of the god's names and regularizes the pāda. The Taitt. Saṁh. and the Vāj. Saṁh. agree with the Ṛgveda.
2. For judging the corruptions which are revealed by the metre the comparison of the numerous cases in which the later Vedic Saṁhitās give a metrically abnormal stanza is instructive. In these cases the Ṛgveda-text with its higher authority enables us to restore the original and at the same time metrically correct form. It would be enough to cite a few passages of this kind from the Taitt. Saṁ. I.4.10.1 *ye devā* ॥ *divi ekādaśa stha*: the ṚV reading is *ye devāso*; III.1.11.4 *ād it pṛthivī* ॥ *ghṛtair vi udyate*; the ṚV reading is *ād id ghṛtena* ॥ *pṛthivī vi udyate*; III.2.5.4 *kim asmān* ॥ *kṛṇavad arātiḥ*; the ṚV reading is *kiṁ nūnam asmān* ॥ *kṛṇavad arātiḥ*; IV.6.1.4 *ye devā devānāṁ* ॥ *yajñīyā yajñiyānām*; the ṚV version drops *devā*; IV.7.14.3 *devaṁ savitāram* ॥ *abhimātiṣāham*; the ṚV version is *devaṁ trātāram* etc.; VII.4.18.2 *pṛchāmi tvā* ॥ *bhuvanasya nābhim*; the ṚV version is *pṛchāmi yatra* ॥ *bhuvanasya nābhiḥ*; VII.5.24.1 *ye te panthānaḥ* ॥ *savitaḥ pūrviāsaḥ*; the ṚV version has *ye te panthāḥ*. We cannot overlook the fact that in the case of several of these passages it would hardly be possible, without the testimony of the Ṛgveda, to find the correct form amongst the several possible ones, an observation which it will not be superfluous to bear in mind when we deal with the similarly circumstanced corruptions of the Ṛgveda where parallel testimonies of other Vedas are mostly wanting.

regular metrical pattern, which we hope to have gained from our discussions so far, will place us, generally speaking, in a position to locate the mistake. It need hardly be said that suggestions for filling up the gaps make no further claim than to give an idea of what the authentic form of the stanza *could* have been; for the rest, in certain places it appears advisable even to desist from making any such suggestions.

We shall start with those cases in which the opening of the verse is the place where the mistake is located:

[82] I. 148.5 *na yam* ⏑ — || *ripavo na riṣaṇyavaḥ*
garbhe santaṁ || *reṣaṇā reṣayanti*
X. 61.27 *ye sthā* ⏑ — || *nicetāro' amūrāḥ.*

In the following example the deficiency goes beyond the caesura :

I. 122.6 *sukṣetrā sindhur adbhiḥ.*

The poet invokes a number of gods to listen to him; in the other three pādas of the stanza we find the use of expressions like *śrutam me, uta śrutam, śrotu naḥ*. We have to supply some such expression also here. Since in IV.54.6 the words *sindhur adbhiḥ* appear at the end of the line, we shall be doing proper thing in allowing them to remain also here in the place where they belong. Hence something like

sukṣetrā [*naḥ* || *śṛṇavat*] *sindhur adbhiḥ.*

Perhaps the following passages also belong here:

X. 132.4 *mūrdhā rathasya cākan*
5 *avor vā yad dhāt tanūṣu*
avaḥ priyāsu || *yajñiyāsu arvā.*

In both these cases probably we have before us mutilated Triṣṭubh pādas. In stanza 5 we have to read *avor vām,*[1] if we compare it with VI.67.11 and VII.67.4; for the rest I refrain

1. So far as I know this suggestion is not new; but I do not find now my predecessor in this respect.

from any attempt at emendation which can have only a subjective value.

We find lacuna quite close to the caesura, as for instance in the following place :

X. 132.1 *ījānam id dyaur* ǀǀ ∪ ∪ — *gūrtāvasuḥ*
VI. 12.6 *sa tvaṁ no' arvan* ǀǀ [*vi muco*] *nidāyāḥ.*[1]

[83] In the same place, i.e. close to the caesura, the lacuna could be located in the first of the two following pādas:

I. 88.2 *rukmo na citraḥ* ǀǀ *svadhitīvān*
pavyā rathasya ǀǀ *jaṁghananta bhūma.*

What could be the golden ornament furnished with an axe? Perhaps we have to conjecture an addition in the following way:

rukmo na citro ǀǀ [*gaṇaḥ*] *svadhitīvān.*

A double lacuna may be found in the following passage:

VII. 50.4 *yāḥ pravato* ǀǀ *nivata' udvataḥ*
udanvatīr ǀǀ *anudakāś ca yāḥ.*

The metre of the hymn is a mélange of Triṣṭubh and Jagatī. In my opinion, the way of filling in the lacuna in the first pāda is shown by the following lines:

III. 2.10 *sa udvato* ǀǀ *nivato yāti veviṣat*
X. 142.4 *yad udvato* ǀǀ *nivato yāsi bapsat*
75.2 *bhūmyā' adhi* ǀǀ *pravatā yāsi sānunā.*

So the emendation could be something like

yāḥ pravato ǀǀ *nivato yānti udvataḥ.*

In the second pāda, a comparison with passages like the Atharvaveda XI.8.21 *rātayo 'rātayaś ca yāḥ;* st. 26 *akṣitiś ca kṣitiś ca yā* and similar others makes it probable that *anudakās' ca yāḥ* has to be left as it is as the end of the line. The substantive itself, which is qualified by the adjective, presents for the filling in of the lacuna:

1. This is Grassmann's restoration and it deserves preference to the one made in the Pet. Wörterbuch which is *pāhi no arvan.* We can think also of other possibilities *pra muco, spṛṇuhī* etc.

udanvatīr | | *āpo' anudakās' ca yāḥ.*[1]

In the following passage the mistake may also be located rather towards the end of the line:

[84] X. 85.34 *tṛṣṭam etat kaṭukam etad apāṣṭhavad viṣavan naitad attave.*

Atharvaveda XIV.1.29 in exactly like this, only the second *etad* is missing. Both the pādas quoted form the first half of the stanza; after them come two eight-syllabled pādas. In the former we must either supply words to form the two twelve-syllabled lines or we have to regard these as a twelve-syllabled line followed by an eight-syllabled one. In favour of the second alternative is the fact that then we can do with an extraordinarily easy emendation:

tṛṣṭam etat | | *kaṭukam tad apāṣṭhavat*
viṣavan naitad attave.

The lacuna occurs at the end of the line:

IX. 88.4 *paidvo na hi tvam* | | *ahināmnām*
hantā viśvasya | | *asi soma dasyoḥ.*

The horse of Pedu is *ahihan* (Atharvaveda X.4.5 ff; Bergaigne II.452); so obviously we have to supply *hantā* at the end of the first pāda, and this word could easily have been omitted on account of the following *hantā:*

IX. 110.10 *somaḥ punāno'* | | *avyaye vāre*
śiśur na krīḷan | | *pavamāno' akṣāḥ.*

Here in the first pāda the falling accent between the two rising accents at the end is missing; perhaps:

somaḥ punāno' | | *avyaye 'dhi vāre*[2].

X. 74.3 *dhiyaṁ ca yajñaṁ ca sādhantaḥ.*

---

1. Cf. the Ath. Veda XIX.9.1 *śāntā' udanvatīr āpaḥ.* Was *āpaḥ* in the RV dropped because someone took objection to waters being described as rich in waters and as waterless ? —Further changes that could be thought of are: *udanvatīr* | | *audakās' ca yahvīḥ*—or *udanvatīr anudakās' ca yayiyaḥ* (cf. X.78.7).

2. Cf. the frequent phrase *adhi sāno' avye (avyaye);* IX.86.3; 91.1 etc.

The hymn metrically is quite uneven; in this pāda perhaps the caesura has been neglected just as in the case of st. 1:

dhiyā vā yajñair vā rodasīoḥ.

If we accept the sonant in the nasal* of *yajñaiḥ* as having the validity of a syllable we have then the correct number of syllables. In the same way, in exact parallel to st. 1, **[85]** we may have to interpret st. 3 which then lacks only the falling accent of the last but two syllables; so perhaps:

dhiyaṁ ca yaj^{a}naṁ ca sādhayanta[1].

X. 93.14 *ye yuktvāya* || *pañca śatāsmayu.*

The meaning not being certain, it is not permissible to propose the change, that suggests itself most readily, of *śatāsmayu* to *śatāni asmayu* (cf. the similar cases in Lanman 348), except with due reservations.

X. 129.7 *iyaṁ visṛṣṭir* || *yata' ābabhūva*
yadi vā dadhe || *yadi vā na.*

I regard it as quite probable that the missing falling and the rising accents at the end of the second pāda are to be restored conjecturally. The conjectural restoration by Grassmann *yadi vā dadhe na* gives us a word order which is not otherwise to be found in the Ṛgveda; it would be better to think of *yadi vā na dadhe* against which there cannot be any decisive objection on account of the short quantity of the penultimate syllable (cf. I.103.4 *yad dha sūnuḥ* || *śravase nāma dadhe;* IX.107.10).

The lacuna appears to extend beyond the border between the two pādas in the reply of Yamī to Yama

X. 10.13 *bato batāsi* || *yama naiva*
te mano || *hṛdayaṁ cāvidāma.*[2]

It is not probable that the first line ended as *naiva te manaḥ*. It is true that the Jagatī ending is not unthinkable,

---

* Oldenberg's words : Stimmton des Nasals.

1. Cf. I.94.3, 4; II.3.8.
2. Cf. Bollensen, ZDMG, XLI.500 f.

but it is certainly Triṣṭubh which is to be expected here; in only *one* case out of the 56 pādas of the hymn there is a Jagatī line (viz. 14C). Besides, we shall then have to assume a gap here, separating *manaḥ* from *hṛdayam ca* which is certainly not to be recommended. Therefore let us allow *te mano* to remain in the second **[86]** pāda, then *naiva* apparently belongs to the first; these words, if placed in the second pāda, would give one syllable too many and will give a short quantity in the fourth syllable (with caesura after the fifth syllable); on the other hand, just after *yama* in the first line, *naiva* gives the required scansion. Thus between *naiva* and *te* there remains a gap of two syllables (— ⏑̲) in the first pāda and a gap of one syllable (⏑̲) in the second pāda. For the second pāda we get very naturally the word *na* as a completion of the gap; in the first pāda the sense appears to be: "Thou art a poor wretch, and thou art not this and that." What particular word stood there can naturally not be made out.

The deletion of a word which may have to be applied also in the case of many of the pādas with superfluous syllables quoted above will be the correct expedient for the restoration of the metre in passages such as the two following ones, and about this there can hardly be any difference of opinion:

III. 59.2 *na hanyate* ⏐⏐ *na jīyate tuotaḥ*
nainam aṁho' aśnoti ⏐⏐ *antito na dūrāt,*

where evidently, as in X.39.11, we have to read

nāṁho' aśnoti.[1]

So also, as was thought long ago

X. 78.8 *subhagān* [*no*] *devāḥ* ⏐⏐ *kṛṇutā suratnān*
asmān stotṝn ⏐⏐ *maruto vāvṛdhānāḥ.*

---

1. Do we have *enam* here from I.94.2 ?

Varieties of Triṣṭubh-and Jagatī-lines

We now turn from the sporadic irregularities of the Triṣṭubh- and the Jagatī-lines to those few cases in which the individual invention of particular poets remodelled the normal type and thus created types were more or less consistently applied in a poem.

[87] The clearest example among these is to be found in the hymn II.11[1]. In its 84 pādas the following rule emerges with sufficient certainty from which only in relatively few instances there are deviations. After the caesura, which by far oftner comes before than after the fifth syllable, there follow three trochaic feet _ ∪ _ ∪ _ ∪̲. In the case of an opening with four syllables the line falls short of the normal Triṣṭubh line by one syllable; with an opening of five syllables it exactly represents a Triṣṭubh line with only this difference that the first syllable after the caesura has a long quantity which, though otherwise allowable, is much less common.

The following are examples of pādas with a four-syllabled opening:

śrudhī havam || *indra mā riṣaṇyaḥ*
ni parvataḥ || *sādi aprayuchan*
asme rayiṁ || *rāsi vīravantam*
ukthebhir vā || *sumnam āvivāsān*
ni arbudaṁ || *vāvṛdhāno' astaḥ*
avartayat || *sūrio na cakram*
bhinad valam || *indro' aṅgirasvān*
sajoṣaso || *ye ca mandasānāḥ.*

The following are examples of a five-syllabled opening:

uktheṣu in nu || *śūra yeṣu cākan*
śubhras tvam indra || *vāvṛdhāno' asme*
uta stavāma || *nūtanā kṛtāni.*

1. This hymn by its metre and also its vocabulary is characterized as taking a special place among the surrounding hymns.

Many of the pādas of the first group would get explained as normal Triṣṭubh lines if they would have occurred in another hymn and the missing syllable could be supplied by counting svarabhakti as a full syllable (thus in the case of the first and [88] the seventh example above), or through the scansion of a single vowel as equivalent to two syllables (thus in the case of the second, the third, and the sixth example above); in *this sūkta,* however, we clearly see[1] the inapplicability of those expedients based on the metrical form prevailing elsewhere. Nevertheless, it is not improbable that the poet of this hymn may have been inspired to invent his new type by cases of svarabhakti and by counting one syllable as two; if he had before him a regular Triṣṭubh line with three-syllabled *indra* or *pāti* after the caesura, and if he took these words as two-syllabled ones, as they are actually found in an overwhelming number of cases, then he had found his new type which is short by one syllable and has the long quantity after the caesura. If he then extended this type to the line with a five-syllabled opening, pādas of normal Triṣṭubh length like those quoted above resulted, e.g.

uta stavāma || *nūtanā kṛtāni,* etc.,

in which the preference for a long quantity after the caesura, which ran counter to the general practice, can hardly be explained otherwise than by regarding it as an endeavour to give the same form to the second half of the pāda which

1. We shall not think of attempting in the manner indicated above to explain away completely all the departures from the norm of the type prevailing in the hymn II.11. In the first place there would remain enough cases where no svarabhakti or counting a syllable as two can supply the missing syllable. Then again, if the deficiency of a syllable is only an apparent one, how are we to account for the unheard-of heaping up of words in all of which there occurs just this *apparent* deficiency of a single syllable? And how to get a long syllable after the caesura in the case of a five-syllabled opening of the pāda?

we have tried to establish for the four-syllabled opening of the pāda. We can see easily that in this metrical line the relationship between the two main forms of the pāda, according as the opening is of four syllables or of five turns out to be entirely different from the one observed in the **[89]** regular Triṣṭubh. There the same number of syllables is found in the entire line; if the first half is longer or smaller by one syllable, the second half would have correspondingly one syllable less or more. Here, on the other hand, the form of the second section makes the length of the whole pāda vary, sometimes being of ten syllables, sometimes of eleven. Characteristic of this fixed nature of the second part and the variable nature of the first part are cases like the following in which each time now a four-syllabled, then a five-syllabled opening is combined with a nearly identical second part:

9. *kanikradato* || *vṛṣṇo' asya vajrāt*
10. *aroravīd* || *vṛṣṇo' asya vajraḥ.* —
3. *tubhyed etā* || *yāsu mandasānaḥ*
14. *sajoṣaso* || *ye ca mandasānāḥ*
15. *viantu in nu* || *yeṣu mandasānaḥ.*

The deviations from the form of the ten-syllabled or eleven-syllabled lines of the hymn II.11, described above, are not important enough for the recognition of the prevailing type as such to be called into question. Occasionally there occurs in the place of the first trochee after the caesura a spondee (thus the stanza 1c, 2c, 4a etc.), or more rarely a pyrrhic (10d, 12b, 21d[1]). Once the caesura fails to appear in the expected place (17d). Sometimes, and

1. In both the last-named cases, where the caesura comes after the fifth syllable, there occurs the scansion ⏑̲ _ ⏑̲ _ ⏑̲ || ⏑ ⏑ _ ⏑ _ ⏑̲ : well, the oftenest occurring form of the regular Triṣṭubh which appears here as a rare departure from the norm. Moreover, we need not include verse 21d here inasmuch as it is the standing refrain of the Gṛtsamada hymns.

this will not surprise any one, in between the shortened Triṣṭubh pādas a regular Triṣṭubh pāda is inserted (1d, 2b, 5a etc.). Finally there remain a few scattered aberrations which confront us with the usual [90] alternative, a textual corruption or a metrical anomaly, but we have nothing new to learn from them about the character of the prevailing metrical type in the sūkta.[1]

It is most suitable now to turn to the hymn I.61 which shows similarity with II.11. Most of its pādas are regular Triṣṭubh lines (thus, e.g., all the four pādas in stanza 2, 7, 9, 16); in between there are numerous lines in which after an opening of four syllables the portion following the caesura has the scansion — ⏑̲ — ⏑̲ — ⏑̲, thus for the two short syllables regularly following the caesura we have a substitution of long quantity, just as in the case of II.11: a peculiarity with which very often is associated neglect of the caesura. As example I quote:

indrāya brah- || *māṇi rātatamā*
bharāmi āṅ- || *gūṣam āsiena*
asmā' id u || *stomaṁ saṁ hinomi*
asmā' id u || *tvaṣṭā takṣad vajram*
giraś ca gir- || *vāhase suvṛkti*
Turvītaye || *gādham turvaṇiḥ kaḥ*[1].

1. At the end of the pāda in stanza 3 one syllable is short:
ukthеṣu in nu || *śūra yeṣu cākan*
stomеṣu indra || *rudriyeṣu ca.*
perhaps the *ca* is to be changed to *cākan.*—In stanza 6a either the word *indra* is to be dropped or we have to accept here four trochaic feet instead of three.—In stanza 7d a syllable before the caesura appears to have been dropped. This appears to be the case also in st. 15c, but this supposition is unnecessary if the *ā* in *asmān* is counted as two syllables.

[91] We have two cases of a short fourth after the caesura:

vṛtrasya cid || *vidad yena marma*
gor na parva || *vi radā tiraścā.*[2]

The metrical peculiarity of two passages X.46 and VI.44. 7-9 is somewhat further removed from those peculiarities just discussed. VI.44.7-9 is a tṛca which can be recognized as an independent text by the metrical form under consideration here and by also the further analysis of the texts of VI.44 which form only an apparent unity.

We have already made a reference above [p.73] to the circumstance that a Virāj line consisting of two groups of five syllables and a Triṣṭubh line of two sections of five and six syllables occasionally pass into each other: the consequent mixing up of these two types is what gives to the metre of both the mentioned sections its character. Some stanzas of X.46 show a pure Triṣṭubh metre (3, 4, 8-10); in the remaining, undoubted Triṣṭubh pādas—in most cases with the caesura after the fifth syllable which, under the circumstances, is quite explicable—, undoubted Virāj lines,[3] and finally pādas which can belong to one or the other type according as the vowel of the seventh syllable is to be scanned

1. In a few cases it is possible to resolve a long vowel coming after the caesura into two syllables so that the deficiency of a syllable can be made good; but, on the one hand, through this means not all the cases under consideration are explained, and, on the other, the large number and the regularity of the occurrence of these cases requiring a two-syllabled scansion would remain an odd fact that cannot be easily set aside.
2. The first of these passages could be eliminated if we read *avidad* for *vidad* and the second if *gor* is counted as two syllables, which is not improbable (see below).
3. It is to be observed that some of the five-syllabled complexes of this hymn—whether they are the opening sections of Triṣṭubh pādas or Virāj pādas—recur in other ṚV passages word for word as valid Virāj pādas; thus *padair anu gman* in st. 2 is identical with I.65.2, *guhā catantam* occurs in I.65.1, and *apām upasthe* in st. 1 occurs in X.109.13.

as one syllable or two get mixed up. **[92]** The following are examples of these three categories:

I. *yantā vasūni* | | *vidhate tanūpāḥ*
guhā catantam | | *uśijo namobhiḥ.*
II. *dadhir yo dhāyi* | | *sa te vayāṁsi*
paśum na naṣṭam | | *padair anu gman*
ni pastiāsu | | *trita stabhūyan.*
III. *nṛṣadvā sīdad* | | *apām upasthe*
mūrā' amūram | | *purāṁ darmāṇam.*

Something similar holds good for the section from the sixth Maṇḍala[1], mentioned above, in which further the often neglected caesura between the two Virāj halves [see below p.97] is noteworthy.

If the metrical varieties so far described are offshoots of the Triṣṭubh, we have finally to point out one such variety which derives from Jagatī. It appears in the two hymns X.77,78[2] mixed in many ways with the normal Jagatī pādas and apparently understood as equivalent of Jagatī pādas. Obviously we are not dealing here with a perfectly fixed representation of a thoroughly executed metrical concept of a single poet;[3] it has gone through several intermediate stages from the starting point of its development and the pādas which represent these stages have been mixed up together. In individual cases the difficulty in arriving at an understanding increases on account of the several liberties taken in the treatment of the metrical form, so that any attempt to offer an explanation can claim to have only a hypothetical value.

1. Cf. Kühnau 231 f.
2. Cf. M. Müller, Translation, Preface p. CIV; Benfey, Quantitätsverschiedenheiten, II, 38; Kühnau pp. 225 ff.
3. It is to be noted that according to the rules followed for the arrangement of Maṇḍala X, hymns 77 and 78 form together a dyad separated from what precedes as well as from what follows.

[93] The frequent appearance of pure Jagatī lines along with those of the particular variety we are dealing with amply indicates that the Jagatī is the basic element of the generally available metrical material from which the newly invented form is derived. This new form agrees with the Jagatī not only in the opening part of the line—where all Vedic metres are indeed more or less identical—, but also in the cadence of the pāda. In the middle of the pāda, however, changes have been introduced in the Jagatī type, of which the first stage appears to me to be in the following pādas:

X.	77.1	*sumārutaṁ na* ∣∣ *brahmāṇam arhase*
X.	77.4	*prayasvanto na* ∣∣ *satrāca' ā gata*
X.	78.5	*aśvāso na ye* ∣∣ *jyeṣṭhāsa' āśavaḥ.*

Here in the Jagatī form with the caesura after the fifth syllable, the two short syllables coming after the caesura are substituted by a long syllable: a recognition of the equivalence of one long syllable with two short ones, which in the Ṛgvedic metre finds expression only in a few isolated points. A new motif is introduced in this type by a second caesura after the seventh syllable; it occurs so often that it is improbable that it is a mere accident. Moreover it is remarkable that the fifth syllable, which in the Jagatī which forms the basis and in the three pādas just cited is *anceps,* appears in the pādas which have the new caesura almost regularly as a short one; we have thus the following scheme of scansion:

⏑̲ — ⏑̲ — ⏑ ∣∣ — — ∣∣ ⏑ — ⏑ ⏑̲.

Perhaps the short quantity of the fifth syllable is only the accidental result of the fact that in both the hymns the word *na* appears with a special frequency in that place; but perhaps we have also in that short quantity an expression of the endeavour to carry through an unbroken series of iambuses up to the second caesura. [94] One has the impression that the author of this metre could have had before his eyes a combination of two iambic series somewhat of the following type:

⏑̲ —́ ⏑̲ —́ ⏑ —́ ⏑ || ⏑ —́ ⏑ ⏑́

but, it seems, not being able to realize his intention perfectly, he, still half-dependent on the Jagatī type from which he started, took over two traits which appear odd in the new metre: the caesura after the fifth[1] and the long quantity of the seventh syllable[2].

Examples of this newly created pāda-form are:

abhrapruṣo na || *vācā* || *pṛṣā vasu*
śriye maryāso' || *añjīr* || *akṛṇvata*
divas putrāsa' || *etā* || *na yetire*
pājasvanto na || *vīrāḥ* || *panasyavaḥ*
devāvio na || *yajñaiḥ* || *suapnasaḥ*
agnīnāṁ[3] *na* || *jihvā* || *virokiṇaḥ*
abhisvartāro' || *arkaṁ* || *na suṣṭubhaḥ.*

Examples of inexactness which naturally arise in substantial abundance in the execution itself, as well as in the oral tradition of such a newly invented type, are the following from the hymn 78.1ac:

viprāso na || *manmabhiḥ suādhiaḥ*
rājāno na || *citrāḥ* || *susaṁdṛśaḥ.*

---

1. That same has been in fact given up in 77.3a, unless we read there *pṛthiviā* and assume the metre to be usual Jagatī.
2. As regards the placing of the accents, we shall be inclined to accept here a scansion standing nearest to the Jagatī, viz. ⏑̲ —́ ⏑̲ —́ ⏑ — —́ ⏑ —́ ⏑ ⏑̲́. In that case, however, if our presupposition of a completely iambic rhythm being observed in the first seven syllables is correct, the sixth syllable, occasioned by the shortness of the fifth, should have the rising accent.
3. With *ā* counting as two syllables.

[95] For the second pāda I suggest the reading *rājāno na ye citrāḥ*[1] etc., for the first, addition either of *ye* or reading *ā* in *viprāso* as constituting two syllables, so that we have the usual Jagatī form. —In pādas of the type containing two caesuras we have the short quantity for the sixth syllable in 77.4ab, a short for the seventh in 78.6d (in the place of the reading *yāmann* which has arisen by the later saṁdhi theory we have to read *yāman*). —In the case of the pāda 77.5a the easiest way is to treat it as Jagatī by reading *dhūrṣu* as a word of three syllables.

III

The Five-syllabled Pāda and the Metre Dvipadā Virāj[2]

The prevalent form of the five-syllabled pāda is ⏑̲ — ⏑ — ⏑̲ and undoubtedly has a stress accent on the second and the fourth syllable, perhaps also—which is hardly ascertainable—on the fifth syllable. Besides the short quantity of the third syllable, which is pointedly set in relief by the two stress-bearing long syllables between which it comes, we find also a long quantity: considerably of less occurrence than the short one, yet relatively much more frequent than the long quantities taking the place of the short ones in the cadence of the metrical series described before. In the second place, however, of the five-syllabled pāda a short syllable is rather rare, and rearer still in the fourth place.

We give below the following statistics:

---

1. Cf. *agnir na ye* in 78.2, *vātāso na ye* in 78.3 etc.
2. Cf. Kühnau 237 ff.

[96] Scansion	1.65,66	VII.34.I-21	IX.109.I-21	Total
— — ∪ — ⏓	31	26	29	86
∪ — ∪ — ⏓	33	38	30	101
∪ — — — ⏓	6	8	9	23
— — — — ⏓	9	3	11	23
∪ ∪ ∪ — ⏓	1	3	—	4
— ∪ ∪ — ⏓	—	2	—	2
∪ ∪ — — ⏓	—	2	—	2
— ∪ — — ⏓	—	—	1	1
∪ ∪ — ∪ ⏓	—	—	2	2
— ∪ — ∪ ⏓	—	—	1	1
∪ — — ∪ ⏓	—	—	1	1

Apparently a combination of four, and not of twice-four pādas of the described type must be seen to form a stanza[1]. The most decisive evidence for this is the hymn IX.109: the continuation and the break in the thought-sequence, so also the quotations in the Sāmaveda[2] which are in agreement with it lead us to conclude the existence of tṛca divisions, and thereby the number of the four five-syllabled pādas is established as a stanza unit[3]. With this as a unit,

1. The Indian tradition hesitates in regard to this point. See Ṛk-Prātiśākhya 847, 855, 1001 with Max Müller's Notes; Ind. St. VIII.49 f. etc.
2. The first Ārcika of the Sāmaveda has for its Yonis IX.149.1, 4, 7, 10, 13, thus every time the first of three stanzas forms the Yoni; the second Ārcika contains the tṛcas 1-3, 4-6, 10-12 and 16-18.
3. I have to draw attention further to the following circumstance. It is well-known that two parallel hymns occur frequently with the same end-verse and the *same number of stanzas.* The hymns VII.34 and VII.56 are obviously two such hymns; that both have the same number of 25 stanzas is surely not an accident. Now these hymns contain partly Dvipadās and partly Triṣṭubhs; since, however, hymn 34 has a greater number of the Dvipadās and hymn 56 has a greater number of Triṣṭubhs, the total number of stanzas in each would be different, unless we follow the tradition in regarding 20, and not 40, syllables as constituting a Dvipadā stanza.

and not the one that has double the number of syllables, the stanzas concerned have been taken up in the collection [97] of the Sāman-yonis (Sāmaveda I) which, according to its principle, contains only single stanzas.

The line of demarkation between these pādas—or at least between pāda 1 and 2 and between pāda 3 and 4 which apparently form two units within the stanza—is not as sharp as it is in the remaining Vedic stanzas. Whereas elsewhere the rule that the end of the pāda must be the end of a word has no exceptions in the Ṛgveda, in the case of this metre, the pāda limit after pāda 1 and 3 in three instances—not an insignificant number in view of the rareness of this metre —falls within a word and thus it is rather comparable with the caesura of the Triṣṭubh and the Jagatī, which also occasionally is neglected, than with the pāda-end of those metres. The passages are as follows:[1]

I.	68.2	*bhuvad devo devānām mahitvā*[2]
	70.10	*vi tvā naraḥ purutrā saparyan*
VII.	34.17	*mā no' ahir budhnio riṣe dhāt.*

We have above on p. 73 already referred to the similarity between the eleven-syllabled Triṣṭubh line (especially of that one where the caesura comes after the fifth syllable) and a combination of two five-syllabled lines. Hence, just as we find in the Triṣṭubh hymns the former not rarely being substituted by the latter [see above; cf. also p. 91], so also we find in the Virāj hymns a Triṣṭubh pāda several times taking the place of two five-syllabled lines: I.69.8; 70.4,10. In the two long Virāj hymns of Maṇḍala VII we find, after a series of pure Virāj stanzas, a transition from Virāj to Triṣṭubh taking place inside a stanza [98]. [VII.34.21; 56.10] and

---

1. In connection with ṚV VI.44.7 f. cf. also above [p. 92.]
2. Transposition of the words *devo devānām,* as proposed by Bollensen, appears to recommend itself, but in view of the two other passages it has to be rejected as superfluous.

after this we find every time upto the end of the hymn pure Triṣṭubh stanzas.[1]

As a consequence of this tendency to combine Triṣṭubh with Virāj we find the Vedic stanza-technique to lead to the creation of a peculiar metre in *one* hymn in the Ṛgveda by combining these two types of lines: in IV.10, which consists of stanzas of three[2] five syllabled pādas and one Triṣṭubh line[3]:

agne tam adya
aśvaṁ na stomaiḥ
kratuṁ na bhadraṁ
hṛdispṛśam ǁ *ṛdhiāmā ta' ohaiḥ.*[4]

IV

Combination of Pādas of Different Types in One and the Same Stanza

1. Gāyatrī- and Jagatī-pādas

Stanzas of pādas of different types of metres result only from the combinations of Gāyatrī- pādas and of Jagatī-pādas, barring isolated exceptions or anomalies which do not have the value of a distinct type, and combinations of four-syllabled pādas which never appear as independent units. This is quite explicable. For, so far as the Jagatī and the Triṣṭubh lines are concerned the similarity, almost amounting to identity, [99] between them has on the one hand occasioned often substituting negligently one for the other: on the other hand, just for that same reason, a deliberate use

---

1. In this connection might be mentioned also IX.109.22 : after Virāj stanzas, a closing stanza formed with a Jagatī- and a Gāyatrī-pāda.
2. In st. 5 there are four such pādas.
3. Cf. Max Müller, ṚV translation, Preface p. CVI; Kühnau pp. 233 ff.
4. The *avasāna* in the traditional text is after, instead of before, *hṛdispṛśam.* A similar mistake is found in st. 7.

of these two metres inside the same stanza to form a contrast was not felt to be very effective. Very similarly unsuitable were the Triṣṭubh pādas for combination with the Gāyatrī pādas: the cadence of the former has a falling accent, while the cadence of the latter has a rising accent and this difference in their nature must stand in the way of their combination in the framework of a ṛc which required a certain rhythmical homogeneity.[1] Only between the Jagatī- and the Gāyatrī-pāda there was a perceptible contrast and, at the same time, in a way its resolution in the agreement of their rhythm in their cadences. And thus have arisen certain definite forms of combinations of great variety, of which some have been employed very frequently. Quite understandably the starting point of this new development as a whole in general was the Gāyatrī line which was preponderant also in the number of pādas belonging to it. Next came the Jagatī line, since it opens like the Gāyatrī, but in order to rise to a more lively intonation. The return to the Gāyatrī rhythm in their cadence can be looked upon as the leading back to the starting point to mark the close of the whole (Uṣṇih); this leading back can occur in a more pronounced form (especially as in the Bṛhatī) when after the Jagatī pāda a Gāyatrī pāda is added. Very often it has one or more words at the end in common with the preceding twelve-syllabled pāda: a sort of a rhyme **[100]** which doubly emphasizes the agreement between the Jagatī and the Gāyatrī cadences, and, as one can see, which would be unthinkable in the combination of one of these elements with the Triṣṭubh pādas.

The two metres, *Uṣṇih* and *Bṛhatī,* are the two principal types of stanzas having a combination of eight-syllabled and twelve-syllabled lines and which are at home not just in combination of distichs. Now if we denote a Gāyatrī pāda as

1. Compare my observations in ZDMG XXXVIII.479.

a, a Jagatī pāda as *b,* and the pādas which rhyme with the preceding ones, as just indicated, with an asterisk prefixed to them, the Uṣṇih is = *a a b,*[1] the Bṛhatī = *a a b a.* The *Atyaṣṭi,* which is rarer and is apparently confined to a single author or to a group of authors, = *b b *a, a a, b *a* (I.127 ff; IX.111[2]), to which is added the *Atiśakavrī* (*a a *a, a a, b *a*) belonging to the same group of authors (I.137).

There are other types of metres, which mostly appear in a *single* sūkta of the Ṛgveda, but are either completely or almost completely carried through in it. They are as follows:[3]

[101] *b a* VIII.29[4].
b a b IX.110.1-3.

---

1. Here we leave out of account the second form of the Uṣṇih *a b,* discussed below, consisting only of Gāyatrī pādas and an addition of four syllables.
2. That here, as everywhere else, a Triṣṭubh pāda occasionally comes in the place of a Jagatī is understandable; similarly that the response of the nature of a rhyme sometimes is inexact (I.127.1 at the end; 129.5 end etc.), or is completely absent (I.127.11 at the end). There are also other stray abnormalities in the construction of these long and complicated strophes which are of such kind that there is no ground to suppose an error in the tradition; sometimes there is not even possibility of it: this is the case with the occurrence of *b* instead of the middle portion *a a* in I.135.7 and 8; the substitution for the normal ending *b *a* by *b a *a* in I.127.6, and by *a *a* in 129.8; the opening with *b a *a* (instead of with *b b *a*) in I.129.9. There are greater doubts about the absence of the first *three* pādas in I.139.5 and the irregular cadence of I.129.11, discussed above on p. 39, obviously to be traced to a corruption.
3. Below have been added some further types which, in addition to the components *a* and *b,* have also pādas of four syllables.
4. But we should perhaps rather reduce these ten stanzas of the hymn to five stanzas of the form *b a b a;* cf. the section on the 'Arrangement of the Saṁhitā'.

b b a a X.93.5-12;[1] cf. X.18.11; 132.2, 6.[2]
b b b a VIII.35.
b b b a a V.87 (but st. 1 is rather *b b a b a*).

To the types referred to here is to be added a very large number of isolated combinations having the constituents *a* and *b*; they are the outcome of the freely changing imagination of the poet and often are not repeated at all beyond one stanza for which these combinations had accidentally presented themselves. Especially the Dānastuti section, which is least subjected to the hieratical strictness of form, is quite rich in these kinds of stanzas; in their case, as in the case of analogous stanzas—most of them being isolated hymns which offer a special place for such formations—the textual critic must be careful not to restore the regularly used forms. Sometimes again we have to note that there are cases where, strictly speaking, there was no intention of the poets to create unusual combinations, but it just happened that, while they were composing a series of Gāyatrī or Anuṣṭubh stanzas, some pāda turned up as a Jagatī pāda. Thus we find in the otherwise regular Gāyatrī hymns such stanzas like the following:

[102] VIII. 28.4 *yathā vaśanti* || *devās tathed asat*
tad eṣām nakir ā minat
arāvā cana martiaḥ
X. 60.3 *ati vārān* || *pavamāno' atiṣyadat*
kalasā̆ abhi dhāvati
indrasya hārdi āviśan.

We would hardly be justified in converting these into

1. Only stanza 9 in its traditional form appears as *b a a a a*; changes, however, by which we can probably restore the form *b b a a* seem unavoidable.—Before and after stanzas of the form *b b a a* occur in the self same hymn other formations, especially stanzas of two Triṣṭubh- and two Gāyatrī-pādas.

2. Also in X.132.1 this type may have to be restored. In st. 7 it is extended to *b b a a °a*.

regular Gāyatrīs by dropping *tathed asat* from the first stanza and *pavamāno* from the second. The anomaly found here is frequent enough[1] and is understandable enough in order to be retained as such.

As instances of these anomalies we may cite:

I.23.19; VIII.28.4; 98.9[2]; IX.60.3 *b a a.*—X.158.2 *a a b?*—I.175.1 *a b a a,* (evidently for a a a a, which is to be found in the following four stanzas)[3]. —I.187.II aba*a?—X.170.4 a a b b. X.22.3,11 baaa[4].—X.150.4.5 (b b b *a).— I.105.8 a a b a a (for a a a a a). —VIII.35.23 b a a a a (for a a a a a).—VI.15.3 b b b b*a[5].—X.140[6]: st. 1, 2 a b b a;—3-5 baba[7];—6 b b b a.—IV 1.1-3: bb *ab b *b; **[103]** b b *a b*a; b b*a b a b*a.[8]—VIII.30 a a a; b a a; a a b a; a a a a. —X.144 a a a; a a b*a; a a a; a a b?; a b b a; b a b a.

Besides these we have the following types in the Dānastutis: VIII.19.34-37 a a b; b a b a; b a a; a a a a a[9]. —VIII.46.21-24 a a a a a; *b a a a*; *a a a*; *a a a a a.* — In the same sūkta 29-33: *a a a*; *b*a; a a x;*[10] *.a a a a *a*; *a a a.* — VIII.70.13-15 *a b a; a a a a*; *b a a.* —X.93.14, 15 Triṣṭ. Triṣṭ. b(?)a; b a *a *a.

---

1. Compare the analogous cases of combinations of Triṣṭubh and Gāyatrī below on p. 117.
2. Cf. below p. 114.
3. Similarly IX 98.11 *a a b a* (Bṛhatī) instead of an Anuṣṭubh.
4. Substitute for the prevailing metre of the hymn; a Triṣṭubh pāda followed by three Gāyatrī pādas.
5. Here there is an extension of the Jagatī (*b b b b*) coming at the end of a tṛca.
6. Of this sūkta it is said in the Taitt. Saṁ. V.2.6.1 *samudraṁ vai nāmaitac chandaḥ*. Cf. Ind. Stud. VIII.108.
7. The metre is Satobṛhatī which as a rule is employed in the Pragātha strophe only as its second half (see ZDMG XXXVIII.478, n. 3). In III.23.3 there is an isolated Satobṛhatī which possibly is to be taken as forming a strophe with the preceding Triṣṭubh. V.56.3 and 7 are the Satobṛhatīs irregularly distributed between Bṛhatīs.
8. We have to point out the similarity of this stanza with the Atyaṣṭi stanza described above on p. 100.
9. Preceded (32.33) by a Kākubha Pragātha. Perhaps these stanzas also are to be regarded as constituting a strophe of two stanza, cf. Prātiś'. 1010.
10. A pāda of ten syllables is denoted here by *x*, this being a Gāyatrī pāda extended by an iambus.

The combinations of eight-syllabled and twelve-syllabled pādas which we have so far noticed only as single stanzas constitute at the same time a sphere, or, to put it in more precise words, *the* sphere in which combinations of two stanzas, differing from each other, constitute *strophes*—formations which present the same kind of conflict and the same kind of resolution of the conflict between the Gāyatrī and the Jagatī rhythms as it appears between the Bṛhatī and the Uṣṇih but in a broader framework and in a more diverse grouping of the metrical measures[1]. Besides the *Bṛhatī* (*a a b a*), which has already been mentioned, we find as constituents of regularly employed strophe-forms, the *Kakubh* (*a b a*) and *Satobṛhatī* (*b a b a*), which, as independently used metres, occur only in exceptional cases; from them are formed strophes of two stanzas so formed that the first stanza always begins with *a* and the second with *b*, but both end with *a*. Thus **[104]** arises the *Kākubha Pragātha* of the form *a b a*, *b a b a* and along with it we have the *Bārhata Pragātha* of the form *a a b a*, *b a b a*,[2] in which both the stanzas are perfectly balanced, each one of them having four pādas. The construction of the Pragāthas by itself amply shows that inside the overall unity of these strophes the individual stanzas, which we have indicated as their demarcation, were felt as having their own subordinate unity. We have already indicated this as their demarcation within the strophe; the same conclusion follows also from the fact that at the end of the first stanza the grammatical construction tends to

1. For the following portion compare my detailed discussion in ZDMG XXXVIII.476-480.
2. In my article referred to in the preceding note I have tried to prove that the Pragātha strophes were originally recited just as they appear in the traditional text and that the repetitions of single pādas by means of which they were transformed into three Bṛhatīs are secondary.

show a segmentation, and finally it will be confirmed by the verieties of the Pragātha, to be described immediately after this, that just at that place has to be assumed a provisional end point of the metrical progression.

To the two main forms of the Pragātha, mentioned above, a considerable number of other varieties are to be added. Most of them are to be found in certain hymns which have metrically a peculiarly motley character, such as V.53 and VIII.10, 46, so that we cannot and must not attribute these to an imperfect oral tradition, but to the liberties which individual authors of hymns have taken to an exceptional measure. Some other forms are found mixed up with the regular Pragāthas, but they reveal such an understandable anomaly, and they protect each other by their appearance in an identical form in different places of the text in such a way that they also elude any kind of critical objection. **[105]** In the following I first adduce those forms which appear to have arisen from the basic type of the Pragātha by easily comprehensible enlargements.

(1) The extension occurs in *one* pāda of the form *a*. The same appears at the end of the scheme and is connected with the preceding by the rhyme-like response noted above (p. 99): VI.48.6, 15[1], 21. —An extension-pāda with the response comes at the end of the Bṛhatī, one without it at the end of the Satobṛhatī : VI.48, 7, 8.

(2) The extension of the form *b a* comes after the Satobṛhatī; thus the group *b a*, which when repeated twice makes the Satobṛhatī, is repeated again a third time. VII.32. 1-3, VIII.19.25-27; IX.107.1-3, 14-16[2].

1. Here there is an additional anomaly inasmuch as the second pāda of the Satobṛhatī has the *b* form instead of *a*.
2. Compare ZDMG XXXVIII.480; Prātiś. 1017.

(3) Above (p. 101, n.3) we found along with the type *b b a a*, the type *b b a a *a* and, along with the Atyaṣṭi-ending *b *a*, the form *b a *a* (p. 100, n. 2), in the same manner the extension by *three* pādas *b a *a* develops from the one by two pādas *b a*. Pragāthas with this extension are VI.48.11-13, 16-18[1]; VII.66.14-16; VIII.4.19-21. The metrical character of VII.66.16, which we find clearly brought out beyond any doubt in this context, shows that this well-known stanza is to be read according as it is handed down by the tradition:

tac cakṣur deva- || hitaṁ śukram uccarat
paśyema śaradaḥ śatam
jīvema śaradaḥ śatam—

[106] while the attempt made in the other branches of the Vedic textual tradition. (Vāj. S., Mai. S., Tai. Ā., Hiraṇ. Gṛ., Gobhila) to carry through the Gāyatrī rhythm by the insertion of *purastāt* before *śukram*[2] is seen to be the work of an interpolator.

(4) A supplement of *four* pādas (*bba*a*) is found in the Pragātha VII.96.1-3.

(5) The extension of the Pragātha by the addition of a second Satobṛhatī is found not with the normal Pragāthas, but rather with the abnormal strophe-forms, about which we shall speak further below.—

To the extended forms of the Pragāthas are to be added also those in which there is only the component *a* in the first stanza (repeated thrice or four times so that we have either a Gāyatrī or an Anuṣṭubh): thus V.61.8, 9 (in a Dānastuti); VIII.46.8, 9; 101.3, 4; 103.10, 11; further many other forms in which not the rugular Satobṛhatī, but an anomalous combination of the components *a* and *b* occurs at the second place.

---

1. After this Pragātha comes a Bṛhatī (st. 19); whether it belongs to the preceding Pragātha must be left undecided.
2. Though by this the first pāda results in having only seven syllables (*tac cakṣur devahitam*).

And finally we have a number of isolated formations invented on the spur of the moment and limited altogether to very few places in the Saṁhitā, but in these they then usually appear in larger numbers. V.53 is a sūkta which appears to me to belong to one of the principal places where such Pragātha forms occur. Ludwig[1] regards it to belong to such passages in which stanzas composed of eight-syllabled pādas are mixed together with twelve-syllabled pādas "without symmetrical strophe-type (Pragātha-) grouping"; in the same way Grassmann finds in this hymn a stringing together of such stanzas "without **[107]** any rigid rule and without there being anything to indicate with certainty a grouping together of different hymns". Nobody will certainly like to affirm the presence of any rigid rule or of a completely observed symmetry in this sūkta; but contrary to these two scholars who have renounced to find any kind of order in the construction of the hymn, it is possible, I think, to demonstrate on the basis of a number of indications with considerable probability a grouping into strophes of mostly two stanzas—strophes in which we can recognize with an unmistakable clarity a Pragātha type which has been handled in a very free and irregular manner and yet which can be perceived by an eye which has acquired the sharpness for this type and its varieties. The scheme of the pādas is as follows:

V.53.1, 2 (Prātiś. 1020) *a b a*; *a a b a*.— 3, 4 (Prātiś. 1021) *a a a a*; *b a a*.— 5-7 *a b a*; *b a b a*; *b a b a*.— 8, 9 *a a a*; *b a b a*.— 10, 11 *a b a*; *a b a*[2].— 12-14 *a a a*; *b a b a*; *b a b a*.— 15, 16 *a b a*; *b a b a*.

I have already indicated in this scheme where in my opinion the strophe-divisions are located. The logical connection, inside the hymn here, as is the case very often,

1. Vol. III, p. 64; cf. p. 68.
2. We have perhaps to assume the end of the second pāda of st. 11 before, and not after, *suśastibhiḥ*. If this view is accepted, the form of the stanza will be *a a b*.

offers only an imperfect basis to find them out;[1] all the more indicative are the combinations of the metres. **[108]** We have divided the sūkta into seven strophes, of these *four* open with a Kakubh (a b a), and the remaining *three* with the unmixed combinations of the component *a* (Gāyatrī and Anuṣṭubh): all of these thus appear in forms which appear either in a regular Pragātha-type or at least in a repeatedly occurring variety as *first* stanza of the strophe. In any other place than the first there neither occurs in the present sūkta a Kakubh[2] nor any other stanza consisting only of eight-syllabled pādas; in the other places rather combinations beginning with *b* are predominant[3]. Six times in the hymn appear Satobṛhatīs which partly come at the second place in the strophe—which is the regular place for the Satobṛhaīi—and partly next to each other as second and third stanza in a group of two stanzas: the only kind of strophe with three stanzas in this sūkta with a double employment of the Satobṛhatī, a form which will not be regarded as improbable on account of the extended formations of Pragāthas which have been listed above. Thus, then the strophes assumed by us move within rather a very narrow space around the normal Pragātha types; the last

1. But indications of this kind are not quite without significance. We can see that stanzas 1 and 2 go together as forming a question. In st. 5-7 a picture of the rain, brought by the Maruts, is in the foreground. In st. 8-9 the Maruts are requested to come without letting any one hinder them. In st. 10 and 11 we have repetitions of the expressions *śardha* and *gaṇa.* St. 8, 10, and 12 can be clearly recognized as a new beginning detached from what precedes.
2. Except st. 11 if we adhere to the traditional version; cf. the note preceding the last.
3. Surprising is, or it would be, in a regularly constituted hymn only the Bṛhatī in the first strophe (st. 2). *Here* we can hardly venture to insert a word which changes the stanza into a Satobṛhatī (as e.g. *aitān ratheṣu* ‖ *pṛṣatīsu tasthuṣaḥ,* which is suggested by V.60.2); cf. also st. VIII.46.6, 7 and 10, 11.

variety mentioned represents directly one of these types; the deviations of the remaining types lie almost completely in directions which have been noticed by us elsewhere. In this way we may have restored order in the, what at first sight appears hopeless, metrical chaos of this hymn in so far as, in a relative sense, we can speak here of order at all.

[109] In some respects VIII.46.1-20[1] is comparable to V. 53. The scheme of the hymn might be represented as follows:

1-3 *a a a*; *a a a*; *a a a* (Gāyatrī tṛca).— 4, 5 (Prātiś. 1010) *a a a*; *b a a*.— 6, 7 (Prā. *ibid.*) *a a a*; *a a b a*.— 8, 9 *a a a a*; *b a b a*.— 10,11[2] *a a a*; *a a b a* (cf. 6, 7).— 12, 13 *a b a b*; *b b*.— 14-16 mostly uncertain; many irregular or corrupt pādas.— 17, 18 *b a a b a*? ?[3] *b a a *a x*[4]. — 19, 20 *a a b *a*; *a a* Triṣṭ. *a*.

Apart from the unmistakable tṛca 1-3 and the obscure triad 14-16, all the rest of VIII.46 is arranged in strophes of two stanzas which from 4 to 11 are well-marked in their construction: after a first stanza, which contains only the *a* element, follows another in which *a* and *b* are mixed; the two pairs of stanzas 6-7 and 10-11 correspond to each other

---

1. VIII.46 consists of four sections of which this is the first; the second consists of st. 25-28 forming two Bārhata Pragāthas addressed to Vāyu; after each of these sections there is a Dānastuti (st. 21-24; 29-33; see above p. 103). Naturally the construction cannot continue from st. 28 to st. 29 as is assumed in Ludwig's translation.
2. Here and in what follows we are making a departure from the divisions of the Prātiśākhya (st. 11-12: sūtra 1016; st. 13-14: 1019; st. 16-17: 1018—where is the place for st. 15?). That the authority of the Prātiś. in questions of that kind is not to be regarded as infallible is to be seen, for instance, from the fact that it makes Pragāthas of I.51.15—52,1; 53.11—54.1; V.56.9—57.1 (Sūtras 1015, 1030 f.)!
3. By changing the place of *mīḷhuṣe* (after *gīrbhir*) I attempt to obtain pādas which are correct to a certain extent.
4. In the above, *x* stands for a group of four syllables with an iambic rhythm (*pra adhvare*).

because of their identical construction; the Satobṛhatī occurs only in st. 9 and is in its proper place. The portions borrowed in the Sāmaveda[1] from this sūkta and **[110]** the logical connection[2] also suit the proposed division into strophes.

The two hymns VIII.10 and 22 offer further examples of anomalous Pragātha formations. The former of these consists of three Pragāthas, the last of them being regular and the other two show the forms: *a a b a*; *b a b b*.[3]— *a a a a*; *a a b b*. In VIII.22, between two normal Pragāthas we have two pairs of stanzas which are proved to be irregular Pragāthas on account of the neighbouring Pragāthas as well as of their own appearance: 7, 8 *a a b a*; *a a a a*.— 11, 12 *a b a*, *b a b b* (cf. VIII.10.2).

In VIII.103, after various other Pragātha forms, we have in stanzas 12 and 13 a Pragātha in which appear along with Jagatī lines (*b*) a Triṣṭubh line (*t*), and also along with full eight-syllabled pādas (a), short pādas of seven syllables (*á*) (one may observe the ratio *a* : *á* = *b* : *t*): the notation being *b á a*, *b á t a*.

And finally we have to mention VIII.19.34, 35. This Pragātha consists of an Uṣṇih with a following Satobṛhatī. Even though by changing the place of the transmitted Avasāna we can chage the Uṣṇih into a metrically at least

1. Four stanzas appear in the collection of Yonis (viz. 1, 4, 10, 14); all of them stand at the beginning of the strophes assumed by us.
2. Almost each one of our strophes is connected together by a clear unity of thought and is separated from the neighbouring ones. Grassmann's operations have only this advantage over the methods employed in the old days by Procrustes that this modern critic does not seek to transplant parts which he has cut off at one place to another one.
3. Grassmann seeks to establish a normal Satobṛhatī by dropping *indrāviṣṇū*—which would be possible only if the stanza stood in a context which might give us the right to presuppose a normal construction. For the rest cf. VIII.22.12.

passable Kakubh, it appears to me that just at this place in the Ṛgveda in which a special preference for the Uṣṇih metre is prominent the anomaly in the transmitted text can be considered tenable.

[111] 2. Combinations of Four-syllabled Pādas

Four-syllabled pādas, which never by themselves constitute stanzas and also never appear at the beginning of a series of pādas, are to be found sometimes affixed to Gāyatrī lines, more seldom to Jagatī lines. They show an iambic structure[1] and thus correspond to the iambic rhythm of the cadence to which they are affixed[2]. In many cases in an entire sūkta or in a tṛca such a four-syllabled pāda is repeated throughout in the respective place of each stanza; especially often prominent catch-words, for instance a vocative addressed to a god etc., form such a pāda[3].

Individually the following cases are to be mentioned:

(a) Four-syllabled pādas joined to *four eight-syllabled* lines (of an Anuṣṭubh). The four syllables are repeated after each Anuṣṭubh stanza (*a a a a x*): VII.55.2-4 and X.126. The same occurs without the repetition of the words in *x* : VIII. 97.11, 12 (cf. Sāmaveda Vol. III. p. 544 f. Bibl. Ind.); and also with the form *a a a* **a x* : VIII.46-18. Or, after each of the two last Anuṣṭubh pādas come the four syllables: thus the well-known refrains of the Vimadas *vi vo made* and *vivakṣase* X.21; 24.1-3; 25. Or, finally, they come alone after the penultimate Anuṣṭubh pāda: VIII.62.7-9. Since this penultimate pāda together with the four-syllabled supplement is similar to a twelve-syllabled (Jagatī-) pāda it appears as if the whole stanza

---

1. This sentence is subject to the same limitations as the rule for an iambic end-part of the Gāyatrī line; cf. V.24.4 *sakhibhiaḥ*; I.84. 7-9 *indro' aṅga*.
2. They do not occur after a Triṣṭubh having a trochaic cadence.
3. For instance, *śatakrato, śacīpate, vicarṣaṇe*; or also *ati dviṣaḥ ni ṣu svapa* and many similar expressions.

[112] forms a Bṛhatī (*a a b a*), and actually the Indian tradition calls the stanza by that name[1].

(b) Four-syllabled pādas after *three eight-syllabled lines.*

α The most oft-occurring case is that the four-syllabled pāda comes at the end of a stanza. The stanza thus constituted (*a a a x,* where *x* denotes the four-syllabled pāda) stands in relation to the Uṣṇih (*a a b*) exactly the same way as the stanza described above stands to the Bṛhatī; and therefore this stanza is not only called Uṣṇih in the Indian terminology, but actually in some places it is found used *promiscuously* with the Uṣṇih in the sense of this term discussed above. The distinction between these two Uṣṇih types cannot possibly be made in each individual case with complete certainty; where, however, there is a series of stanzas, it hardly remains doubtful whether what follows the first two lines belongs to the type having a word-end after the fourth or the fifth syllable, or to the other type having a word-end after the eighth syllable; whether the sixth syllable is consistently long corresponding to the Gāyatrī rhythm, or whether, according to the rules of the Jagatī lines, it is predominantly short. Thus, we have an Uṣṇih of the type *a a a x* (IX.106.3):

asyed indro madeṣu ā
grābhaṁ gṛbhṇīta sānasim
vajraṁ ca vṛṣaṇam bharat
sam apsujit—

as against an Uṣṇih of the type *a a b* (*ibid* 14):

ayā pavasva devayuḥ
madhor dhārā' asṛkṣata
rebhan pavitram // *pari eṣi viśvataḥ.*

[113] Very often the pāda *x,* and sometimes along with it also the preceding last pāda *a,* has throughout the hymn or

1. Cf. with this verse also p. 113, n. 2 below.

throughout the tṛca identical refrain-like wording[1].— As an instance of the mixture of both the Uṣṇih types we can mention III.10. Stanza 6 shows the unmistakable Jagatī cadence :

mahe vājāya | | *draviṇāya darśataḥ.*

But the remaining stanzas also equally unmistakably have the eight-syllabled pāda with the extension of four syllables:

7. *hotā mandro vi rājasi*
ati sṛdhaḥ
8. *bhavā stotṛbhyo' antamaḥ*
suastaye, etc.

We may have also to see the influence of the Jagatī type when in VIII.13.15 after clear stanzas of the form *a a a x* we have the following in which across the boundary between *a* and *x* we have an Abhinihita sandhi:

yad vā samudre' andhaso 'vited asi[2].

β. The four-syllabled pāda, combined with three eight-syllabledlines, comes in a place other than at the end. Thus, we have this in both the tṛcas in VIII.98.7-12. The second (10-12) is more regular; it shows constantly the form *a a x a.* The first tṛca has this form only in st. 7[3], while in st. 8 [114] the *x* comes at the end, and, st. 9 consists of *b a a* in which *b* is unmitakably equal to *a* plus *x*. As we have learnt a variety of the Bṛhatī of the type *a a a x a* and of the Uṣṇih of the type *a a a x, a a x a* can be recognized as a sub-variety of the Kakubh.

---

1. Thus, for instance, the pāda *x* has been repeated in VIII.12, tṛca for tṛca, and also the last eight-syllabled pāda is repeated in the ninth and the tenth tṛca.
2. From the Uṣṇih form *a a a x* some light is shed on the st. VIII.62. 7-9 *a a a x a,* already mentioned above p. 111. The remaining tṛcas from VIII.62 consist of Anuṣṭubhs of which each one has been enlarged into a Paṅkti by the addition of the refrain *bhadrā' indrasya rātayaḥ.* The same pāda also comes constantly in st. 7-9 after *x* at the end of the stanza. It is thus not perfectly correct to interpret these stanzas *a a a x a* as Anuṣṭubhs, enlarged by the addition of *x*; these are actually Uṣṇihs (*a a a x*) extended by a refrain-pāda *a.*
3. Read *kāmān* as *kāmaan.*

(c) Here we have four-syllabled pādas along with *two eight-syllabled lines.* This is the case[1] in V.24 and X.172, where the form *a a x* appears. As in the case of the tṛca described in the last paragraph, the placing of the *x* is not quite constant; we can understand X.172.3 without doing any violence only as *a x a*.

(d) Here four-syllabled pādas come along with *Jagatī lines or with mixtures of Jagatī and Gāyatrī lines.* To this type belong the two hymns VIII.36, 37. They are exactly parallel to each other; each one of them consists of seven stanzas of which the last one in both the cases—barring some minor undoubtedly intentional differences—is an identical Jagatī. The first six stanzas in each hymn show a great similarity in their construction, but not complete identity. We can see clearly how in these combinations a just approximate sameness has been felt to be equivalent. By far the largest portion of the text is repeated in the case of each of the two hymns, stanza for stanza; the pertinent sections in the scheme coming up here are given in square brackets:

36.1-6 *b* [*a x*, *a b x a*].
37.1 *b x* [b^2, *b x a*].
37.2-6 *b* [b^2, *b x a*].

[115] Exactly the same difference in connection with the appearance or non-appearance of the *x*-element as in VIII. 37 is also to be found in II.22. Here we have the following scheme:

Stanza 1 *b x b x b x* [*b* x^3].
Stanzas 2, 3 *b x b x b* [*b* x^3].

---

1. Cf. Sāmaveda Vol. I, pp. 898 f., 902 Bibl. Ind. It is to be observed that the four-syllabled supplements in some of the forms of the hymn given there have been provided with especially ample ornamentations, while in other places they have been left out.
2. In the place of this *b* we can also take it to be *x a*.
3. That the explanation of the expression *sainaṁ saścad devo devaṁ satyam indraṁ satya' induḥ* by the form *b x* is possible only in a forced manner cannot be denied. There are perhaps two Gāyatrī lines with a trochaic rhythm.

The case of stanza 4 is difficult, where the expression *pravāciam kṛtam* appears to form a six-syllabled line. If we drop the superfluous *kṛtam*[1] and restore the expected four-syllabled form, then we have the scheme *a b x, b x, b a x.*

Finally, the type *b b x* is to be found in VIII.46.15 in a surrounding especially rich in abnormal formations.

3. Other Types of Combinations of Different Kinds of Pādas in the Same Stanza

As already mentioned, in the Ṛgveda combinations of Triṣṭubh lines with lines of another type in the same stanza are never, or practically never, found to have *the character of normal combinations,* so that they are repeated constantly throughout a hymn. The number of occurrences of the most frequent combination of this type, it is true, would without doubt exceed that of many other forms of stanza, which we have to consider as regular, but it also has a character of a licence which one took the liberty to use to the largest extent, but it would have hardly made any sense to use it in regular recurrence, and indeed no attempt has been made to do so. I am here speaking of the stanzas in which there is a *mixture of Triṣṭubh and Jagatī lines* such as are found in the different **[116]** parts of the Veda with different degrees of frequency in all imaginable combinations of these two elements, and yet scarcely anywhere in such a thorough-going manner that the character of a sūkta, whether composed in Triṣṭubh or Jagatī, would become thereby doubtful. Occasionally the kind of combination with which we are concerned appears mixed with another related one, which we shall discuss later on, viz. the alternating of the whole Triṣṭubh stanzas with the whole Jagatī stanzas in one

1. In this case the construction is: *tava tyad . . . apaḥ . . . pravāciam, yad* etc.

and the same hymn. When occasionally the distinguishing point between the trochaic and the iambic cadence of a line falls inside a stanza, it can be looked upon as a continuation or a modification of the latter phenomenon, which then represents a juxtaposition of the Triṣṭubh– (*t*) and the Jagatī- (*b*) components. Thus, for example, the form of I.53.10, *b t t t* unmistakably gets related with the fact that the first nine stanzas of this hymn are composed in pure, unmixed Jagatī metre, while the end stanza (st. 11), as is often the case with Jagatī hymns, is a Triṣṭubh: st. 10 in respect of its first pāda is related to what precedes and in the case of the last three pādas to what follows. So also the scheme *b t t t* of VI.75.7 is manifestly occasioned by a Jagatī which precedes and the Triṣṭubh stanzas which follow.—In other places there is either a standing formula occurring at the close of the hymn or some other stereotyped expression by the use of which at the end of a stanza there is a resulting exchange of eleven-syllabled and twelve-syllabled lines; thus, for instance, in VII.54.1 we have the formula *śam no bhava* || *dvipade śaṁ catuṣpade* at the end of a Triṣṭubh; in II.42.3 we have the traditional hymn-ending of the Gṛtamadas *bṛhad vadema* || *vidathe suvīrāḥ* after a Jagatī. In the large majority of cases however—especially frequent are these in the tenth Maṇḍala—we have before us an alternation of Jagatī and **[117]** Triṣṭubh lines only as a licence, which neither requires nor is capable of any further explanation.

We shall now turn to the combinations of the *Gāyatrī* and the *Triṣṭubh lines* (*a* and *t*). These are partly explained as due to the licence noticed in the case of the exchange of the Jagatī and the Triṣṭubh lines: thus, forms which consist of a combination of *a* and *b* components, when *t* takes the place *b*, turn into combinations of *a* and *t*. Thus, we find Triṣṭubh lines, which take the place of Jagatī lines, combining themselves with eight-syllabled pādas in the Bṛhatī metre (e.g. VII.16.5; VIII.46.20), in the Satobṛhatī (e.g. VIII.54.8; 103.13; IX.107.9), in the Uṣṇih (I.150.1, 3; VIII.25.18; 26.22), in the Atyaṣṭi (I.127.1; IX.111.1). For the main metre in

X.93, viz. *b b a a* (see above p. 101), *t t a a* is often[1] substituted; for *b b a a* of VIII.35 is substituted *t b b a* (st. 6, 13-15) and *b t b a* (st. 10-12).

A combination of *t* and *a* components is found systematically carried out in a single sūkta X.22, in which the stanzas are of the form *t a a a*.[2] Elsewhere these kinds of combinations are to be found in only isolated cases in which the poet has lapsed from the Triṣṭubh rhythm into that of the Gāyatrī, or from the latter, which did not offer him sufficient room for the expression of his thought, into the former. This happens in X.126.5 where, instead of the predominant metre *a a a a x*, we have *a a t a x* ; the text bears decisively the impress of an authentic tradition. In I.164.42 between Triṣṭubh stanzas we have the form *t t a a*; in V.33.7 and X.81.2 we have the form *a t t t*; between admixture of the Triṣṭubh and the Jagatī we have in I.162.14 [118] *b a t t*.[3] The ritual formulae composed in the Triṣṭubh

1. This is in st. 1 and 4; as to stanza 14, which is supposedly corrupt, it could have the scheme *t t b a*.
2. This is obviously the norm; *b a a a* in st. 3 and 11, *a a a a* in st. 7 are deviations from it.
3. The scheme *t t a t* (between pure Triṣṭubhs) appears in the traditional text of I.122.5 which runs thus:

   ā vō ruvaṇyum ‖ *auśijo huvadhyai*
   ghoṣeva śaṃsam ‖ *arjunasya naṁśe*
   pra vaḥ pūṣṇe dāvana' ā (*ā̆* in the traditional text)
   achā voceya ‖ *vasutātim agneḥ*.

   Just at the place where an eight-syllabled line appears in the place of an eleven-syllabled line, the context shows a lacuna which points to the corruption of the text. We expect an imperative as in st. 4 *pra vo napātam* ‖ *apāṁ kṛṇudhvam*. The dative *pūṣṇe* must depend on a similar imperative, and hence passages, cited below, seem to be the places on the basis of which the restoration would have to be modelled: VIII.89.3 *pra va' indrāya . . . brahma arcata*; VII.31.1 *pra va' indrāya mādanam . . . gāyata*; I.37.4 *pra vaḥ śardhāya ghṛṣvaye . . . brahma gāyata*; VIII.32.27 *pra va' ugrāya niṣṭure . . . brahma gāyata* etc. Thus we can think of supplying after *pūṣṇe* a word like *arcata* or *gāyata*. For *dāvana' ā* in the end-part of Triṣṭubh cf. *dama' ā* in VII.42.4.

about the *drapsa skanna* (X.17.11-13) lapse towards the end into the Gāyatrī; thus we have in st. 13 the form *t a a a.*[1] In III.21.4, 5 we have a case of slipping over from the Triṣṭubh form to the Pragātha form *t t t a*; *b a b a.* This hymn in which we come across this anomaly is altogether a meeting place of changing metres; perhaps it might be more correct to speak of it not as a "hymn", but as a collecton of ritual formulae relating to one particular point in the ritual, namely the *stokas.* The *sītā-* formulae (IV.57) have a similar character: and among them we find a similar combination of Gāyatrī and Triṣṭubh components of the type *t a a* in st. 5.[2] Finally, to hymns consisting of mixed metres belong the stanzas I.88.5 with the form *t t a t* (perhaps st. 1 is also to be so restored); ibid. stanza 6 with the form *t t a a*; V.19.5 with the form *a t t t*; also IX.67.30 may be mentioned here with the combination of a Triṣṭubh line with two **[119]** nine-syllabled pādas described above [p. 39.]

On pp. 73 and 97 f. above we have described the combinations of *Triṣṭubh* and *Virāj.*

V

Formations of Strophes and Composite Hymns

It is rather rare that we have a stánza standing alone by itself, whether in ritual employment or whether in the middle of a narrative prose frame serving as a complement. Almost always the stanzas either get connected together directly as

---

1. Thinkable, but by no means necessary, is the restoration of the form *a a a a* by deleting *skanno* which could have been interpolated due to the *skandati* of the preceding stanza.
2. The rendering of this stanza in the Tai. Ār. as *a a a* by omitting *juṣethām* is an unsuccessful attempt at emendation.

hymns[1], or they get arranged in small units—we will call them *strophes*—of which then the hymn is formed. Hymn and strophe coincide in the very frequent appearance of hymns which have the extent of a strophe.

The strophe-formations show two different basic types. Either the stanzas composed in *different* forms are grouped together and they constitute a whole, the unity of which rests on the systematic interchange of its component parts. Or the strophe is formed by the repetition of a certain number of stanzas of *similar* composition, among which we count also grouping of *different* stanzas *in case* it does not show an organic structure but occurs as an exceptional licence in the same way as occasionally also within the hymn stanzas of different structure alternate **[120]** quite irregularly: such strophes are obviously characterized as varieties of those strophes consisting of similar stanzas if only this form is handled with a certain licence.

The first of these two types is present only[2] in the *Pragātha strophe* and its varieties discussed above pp. [104 f.] It seems that in the Vedic period the feeling for the form was not developed far enough to enable the poets to combine differently formed components into a homogeneous whole beyond the extent of these two-stanza strophes[3].

---

1. These have, in so far as they do not consist of a Pragātha, less than three stanzas in quite rare exceptional cases. Obviously the extent of a strophe was regarded as the minimum extent of a hymn.
2. Or, *almost* only, if we count several times recurring strophes consisting of one Anuṣṭubh and two Gāyatrīs as belonging to this type. The Indian terminology would justify this, cf. Pañc. Br. IX. 1.1 which does it. This can, however, be done only with a certain sophistry: it cannot certainly be doubted that such strophes actually have resulted from that kind of poetical form to which the Gāyatrī tṛca belongs, and not from that form to which the Pragātha belongs.
3. That these strophes occasionally increase to three stanzas in extended forms is of course of little importance.

The second type of strophes appears by preference in the Gāyatrī metre, and next, in the other metres which are preferred by the Udgātṛ priest (the Bṛhatī, the Uṣṇih, the Paṅkti), but seldom in the Triṣṭubh, the principal metre of the liturgy of the Hotṛ priest. Since also the Pragātha-strophe belongs to the Udgātṛ, the connection of the composition in the strophes with the liturgical technique of the singer-priests (as opposed to that of the reciting priests) becomes thus manifest. The organic connection of the stanzas forming the same strophe and the separateness from the remaining strophes will have been indicated by the melody, and next, as soon as these came to be employed, by the intertwinings of the *Stoma*, which play such a great part in the liturgy of the Udgātṛ. **[121]** As to the stanzas required for forming a strophe the *number three* proves to be of exclusive currency in so far as the more or less definite criteria for assuming strophe-formation suffice to draw conclusions. Only in exceptional cases the three stanzas forming a strophe and, in the same way, only in exceptional cases the strophes which together form a hymn differ from one another in respect of metre.[1] Finally it has to be added that at the end of hymns composed of strophes it is not seldom that an isolated end-stanza appears which stands out from the strophe-grouping and is sometimes in a metre different from that of the strophes.

With these few remarks we have said everything that has to be said in describing the form of the Vedic strophe; there are, however, some peculiar difficulties in connection with the almost insuperable uncertainty which frequently occurs in deciding individual cases, where a particular hymn must be understood as arranged in the strophe-form, so far described, where, on the other hand, it is to be regarded as being composed purely line by line, and finally where we have before us indications of triads of stanzas for which we

---

1. See on this matter the next section.

cannot assume a strophic arrangement of a hymn, but rather a juxtaposition of several independent single-strophed hymns, which in the Vedic tradition have been combined into a seemingly single unit.[1]

Although the last-named case by itself is in no way connected by its nature with the problems which we are just now discussing about the formation of the Vedic hymns consisting of strophes, still it is so indissolubly connected with the understanding of **[122]** those problems that it will not do for us to leave it aside in our present investigation. For, the indications which signal a splitting up are on the whole the same, whether it concerns the splitting up into strophes or into independent hymns, and very often the decision between these two types of splittings up will have to be withheld: since by no means everywhere where we are dealing with a hymn consisting of strophes, the encompassing unity of the whole hymn is marked by sure characteristics, and, on the other hand, for large portions of the Veda we are denied that proof which would, at least with approximate certainty,[2] allow us to deduce the division of a hymn into several independent hymns: for instance, the arrangement of the hymns according to the descending order of the number of stanzas, of which the apparent violations can be removed by the splitting up of the hymns which have been combined by the diaskeuast.

The event of this fusing of independent hymns, of the obfuscation of all knowledge of the correct boundaries of the large mass of small hymns that have been grouped together in our Saṁhitā, must have taken place somewhere between the formation of the Saṁhitā and the composition of the Brāhmaṇa texts. It is clear that when these hymns were being arranged in their present sequence, their real

---

1. What is said here and in the next section is an attempt to develop further my investigation presented in ZDMG XXXVIII.451 ff.
2. Cf. ibid. 460 for the exceptions.

beginnings and ends were known[1], since it was on this knowledge that the actual place of the small hymns was determined in those series which have been arranged according to their number of stanzas. The beginnings and the ends of the hymns were also known while—after **[123]** the Ṛk-Saṁhitā assumed its final form, as I am going to show in another place—the system of sacrifice, taught or pre-supposed in the SV and the YV Saṁhitās, as also in the Brāhmaṇas, assumed a definite form; we shall immediately go deeper into the question how exactly that sacrificial system offers us an important means for the knowledge of the demarcation of the hymns. On the other hand, however, the traditional list of the authors of the hymns, which was known to the Brāhmaṇa-theologians already[2], pre-supposes the loss of the knowledge of these lines of demarcation, the adoption of the long hymn-complexes such as we have them in the transmitted Ṛgveda.

By recording the parallels from the other Vedas and the citations in the Brāhmaṇas and the Sūtras our edition of the Ṛk-text will provide a picture as complete as possible of the use made of the Ṛk-materials in the later ritual and thereby of the knowledge exhibited in the ritual of the divisions of (composite) strophes or hymns (into smaller units). It will suffice for the present to give a review of a portion of this large field of research and thus clearly to set forth the methods pursued in the treatment of the problems which recur in a similar way in the neighbouring fields. For giving an idea of how a composite text can be split up into

1. Here we are dealing only with groups of Pragāthas, hymns of three stanzas, four stanzas, etc., which are combined into large hymns; that quite independently of the fate which overtook these hymns, in some places in the Saṁhitā (e.g. very prominently in VII.1) there are to be found sporadically older amalgamations of several sūktas already existing before the authors of the arrangement according to the decreasing number of stanzas is a matter which does not concern us here.
2. See my paper on the names of authors, ZDMG, 1888.

its components we choose the second Ārcika of the Sāmaveda: that portion of the Sāma-Saṁhitā which offers especially important evidence for the question of dividing the composite hymns. Since, while a tṛca occurring in that text must obviously have been regarded as such by the Sāmaveda theologians, it can, as easily understandable, be claimed for the Yoni-stanzas of the first Ārcika in many, but by no means in all cases, with certainty or even only with probability **[124]** that they were understood as the opening stanzas of tṛcas or of other Sāman-texts. Now, in what follows, our idea is to survey in the first instance the treatment which the hymns and the stanzas of the *ninth* Maṇḍala and also of the *eighth* Maṇḍala have received in the second collection of Sāman texts: the well-known preference given, just to these Maṇḍalas in the liturgy of the Sāmaveda, added to this, the relatively simple conditions prevailing in Maṇḍala IX and, the extraordinary richness of the strophic hymns of the eighth Maṇḍala, lend to these books a special value for the purpose of our investigation. In doing this we shall have several occasions to adduce, beside the basis, which the citations in the Sāmaveda—and naturally quite analogously in the other Vedas—provide for the division of the hymns, also the other relevant criteria and to demonstrate their application.

We shall begin with the *ninth* Maṇḍala:

(a) The following hymns from amongst the hymns of Maṇḍala IX —the word hymn is taken here for the time being to mean the traditional text without taking into consideration the division of hymns into smaller sections—occur in their *entirety* in the Sāmaveda[1] 2, 3, 4, 7, 8, 10, 12, 13, 15, 20, 24, 27, 28,[2] 37, 38, 39, 41, 48, 49, 50, 53, 55, 57, 58, 111[3].

---

1. Some of these hymns have been enlarged there by additions: thus the hymn 7, consisting of 9 stanzas, by the addition of the tṛca 65.28-30.
2. Hymns 27 and 28 exchange one stanza between themselves in the SV.
3. We can see that the borrowing of complete hymns is confined to the Gāyatrī portion of Maṇḍala IX. No. 111 alone is an Atyaṣṭi hymn, but it contains only a single tṛca.

(b) In the case of a number of hymns the Sāmaveda confirms in a certain way the divisions as transmitted in the Ṛgveda in so far as it borrows from texts having many stanzas often *one triad,* **[125]** namely the stanzas 1-3: 1, 9, 18, 19, 25, 29, 32, 40, 51, 54, 70, 75, 76, 82, 83, 87, 93, 102 and 104.

(c) Several (and in some cases very numerous) *tṛcas* from the same hymn occur especially from the long hymns which (apparently) violate the rules of arrangement of the ṚV; the beginnings and the ends of these tṛcas agree with regular and continuous divisions of the Ṛg-hymn into three (e.g. 1-3, 4-6, 7-9 etc.). These hymns are: 61-67 (everyone of them), 86, 97, 101 and 109. Out of these eleven hymns no less than 59 tṛcas have been taken into the SV. From among the remaining parts of the ninth Maṇḍala several triads agreeing with the tṛca divisions of the ṚV-hymn have been extracted, only from three more hymns which make seven triads: 11.1-3, 4-9[1].—33.1-3, 4-6.—105.1-3, 4-6.

(d) We find *triads* in the SV which do *not* correspond with the tṛca division of the ṚV-hymn: 69.6, 2, 4.—88. 1, 2, 7.—90.2-4.—96.5-7, 17-19.—98.1, 5, 3,—7, 6, 10,—10, 12, 7.—99.2-4.—100.6, 7, 9.—110. 1, 3, 2,—8, 6, 9,—7, 5, 4.

(e) Dyads of stanzas in considerable number (13) have been taken from hymns 107 and 108; these are Pragāthas. At another place the SV has taken as a group of two stanzas the last two stanzas of hymn 106 which remain after a tṛca division; but to this is added 101.13 to make a tṛca. The last two late stanzas of hymn 67—the praise of one *'yaḥ pāvamānīr adhyeti'*—occur in the SV together with several others which in the ṚV appear as a Khila-supplement to the hymn.

[126] (f) *Individual* stanzas have always been so taken over into the SV that they appear there as members of a newly-formed tṛca. Mostly, however, they appear also in some another place of the SV in their natural setting, testified by

1. Strictly speaking the SV does not extract here three groups of three stanzas (3 + 3 + 3), but one group of three stanzas and another of six stanzas (3 + 6).

the ṚV, so that the SV itself prevents the conclusions which we might draw from that use: 3.9; 11.1; 61.13; 66.19; 101.13 [see above under (e)]. Our last remark does not apply only to the following two stanzas: 19.6; 42.4.

We shall now try to formulate the results of all the facts noted above.

The most important and at the same time most striking of the results is the pronounced antithesis, on the one hand, between the long hymns [as noted in (c) above] from which a very large number of triads has been borrowed, but never a larger piece than a triad, and, on the other hand, the short hymns from which the SV takes *one* triad and specifically the first triad [see (b) above], not less frequently, however, it takes over the hymns in their entirety, up to the length of ten stanzas [as in (a) above]. In the regular divisions of those hymns, and in the especially significant absence among so numerous borrowings of such ones which go beyond the tṛca-boundaries is recognizable the clear knowledge of the break of logical connection between the end of one tṛca and the beginning of another. I have already given a detailed exposition of my view in another place[1] that our observations on the continuity and the break of logical connection, the metrical peculiarities etc. have been throughout confirmed by the cuts indicated in the SV. The SV admittedly does not say whether the divisions are divisions into strophes or into hymns. Actually, we have to assume divisions into hymns: this is shown by the absence **[127]** of all characteristics which would indicate longer units composed of several tṛcas, next, by the appearance of clearly marked concluding stanzas of hymns in the midst of the transmitted composite hymns[2], and finally by the sequence

1. ZDMG XXXVIII. 458.
2. Thus 97.3 and 6 containing the refrain *yūyaṁ pāta* || *svastibhiḥ sadā naḥ*—i.e. the hymns of the Vasiṣṭhas. Then, in the *same sūkta,* are found traces of other singer-families; in stanza 51 one finds *ārṣeyaṁ Jamadagnivat;* stanza 58 concludes with the end-words recurring in the collection 1.94 ff.

of the hymns whose order according to the descending number of stanzas, which is apparently violated, is restored when those long hymns which exceed by far[1] the extent elsewhere observed in the ninth Maṇḍala, are divided into hymns of three stanzas.

A second observation which is occasioned by our compilation is regarding the *dyads* of stanzas which appear in the SV: These appear only at places where we have before us the Pragātha strophes. If the three-stanza hymn is a constant and favourite form, the two-stanza hymn is never met with outside the Pragāthas, and since there is a clear connection between the type of a hymn consisting of three stanzas and the strophe of three stanzas, we can conclude with reasonable probability that the type of a strophe with two stanzas did not exist.

As an instance of the division into strophes of *four stanzas* we have the hymn 96 [see above (d)]; both the tṛcas which have been taken up from this hymn (5-7; 17-19) are the first three stanzas of the second and the fifth tetrad.[2] Thus from the point of view of their nature, the borrowings from hymn 96 can be placed by the side of those noted above under (b). From some other hymns also which have not been used in SV II, we get other indications[3] for the divisions into tetrads, that is independent hymns of four stanzas **[128]** have been pressed together in an apparent single hymn. The appearance of such groupings of tetrads before the grouping of triads is in exact consonance with the principle of arrangement according to the descending number of stanzas. For the rest, hymns containing tetrads are not frequent enough to permit us to assume *a priori* also the existence of a corresponding strophe-type formation.

The manner in which the tetrads of hymn 96 have been marked in the SV by the appearance in each case of the first

1. ZDMG XXXVIII. 457.
2. Grassmann has already recognized this fact.
3. ZDMG XXXVIII. 458, 459.

three stanzas of such tetrads enables us to draw a definite conclusion, or to confirm a conclusion arrived at from other premises about the division of the hymn 100 which so far as I can see has not yet been properly dealt with[1] [see above under (d)]. This hymn belongs to the Anuṣṭubh series and the hymns in this series have the following number of stanzas: 98: 12 st.; 99.8 st.; 100:9 st.; 101:16 st.; the last hymn [see (c) above] turns out to be a grouping of tṛcas[2] and thus forms the end of the series according to the descending number of stanzas. The hymn 100, however, as it stands, violates the principle of arrangement. The contents of the hymn as well as its treatment in the SV are not at all favourable for an attempt to divide it likewise into tṛcas; also in that case the diaskeuasts would have presumably combined all the tṛcas (of 100 and 101) into a *single* sūkta. The way out, suggested by Grassmann, to delete stanza 8 so that we can get a number corresponding to the principle of arrangement is as hazardous as most of his suggestions for deletions; besides it goes against the experience to be met with almost everywhere in dealing with the violations of the rule of arrangement, that it is not single interpolated stanzas which disturb the arrangement, **[129]** but it is either the lumping together of several independent hymns, or—occurring *after* the composite hymns to be resolved this way—the appearance of younger supplementary hymns. The hymn 101, a conglomerate of triads which comes after hymn 100, shows that we have here the former of the two alternatives and since, as we have seen already, the hymns combined in hymn 100 could not have been tṛcas, there remains only *one* possible resolution of this hymn of nine stanzas which can satisfy the rule of arrangement and which is *a priori* thinkable, viz. that it is a combination of two hymns of five and four

1. I believe that even Bergaigne in his observations in JA. VIII.8.217 has not finally settled the question.
2. Except an irregularity at the end.

stanzas respectively. And how does the SV deal with this hymn? It takes from it a tṛca consisting of stanzas 6, 7 and 9, i.e. it treats st. 6 as marking a new beginning and takes a tṛca from the tetrad which begins with this stanza, exactly as it does from the tetrads of hymn 96 discussed above: it is merely by chance that we have not a tṛca consisting of 6-8, but of 6, 7, 9 as frequently the order of the ṚV stanzas is changed in the SV. The style of the hymn does not go against stanza 6 being regarded as a new beginning; it even supports the supposition[1].

Just as in the case of the hymns 96 and 100 so also we can conclude, generally speaking, in the case of the other texts where the sections taken by the SV cross the boundaries of a triad-division [see (d) above] that we have no triad-groupings in those hymns. Actually in most of the hymns of this type we have other criteria showing that they are homogeneous and are not divisible[2]. Only in the case of 110.4-9 we may entertain doubt. **[130]** This hymn 110 is a complex of several pieces composed in different rare metres. According to the metres the hymn, in the first instance, is divided in the following manner: 1-3, 4-9, 10-12; the middle of these sections [see (d) above], with which we are here concerned, has been taken over in the SV as two tṛcas, arranged against the ṚV order, as 8, 6, 9, and 7, 5, 4. That the SV occasionally combines stanzas, originally unconnected, into tṛca form is beyond doubt [see above under (f)]; as a rule this will not happen by mere coincidence just in such a way that stanzas from two independent tṛcas

1. The beginning of 6 is *pavasva vājasātamaḥ*; the word *pavasva* in the beginning of a stanza is especially favoured at the beginning of the hymns, or of portions which turn out to be hymns after necessary divisions.
2. In the case of hymn 69, compare the end-stanza with that of the hymn 68 (dyāvāpṛthivī); here are two parallel hymns with similar end-stanzas. Hymn 90 is also shown to be a complete hymn by its concluding stanza (cf. 89). No. 88 is characterized as a unit clearly by its contents.

which, however, stand next to each other in the Ṛgveda are combined and thus create the appearance of a homogeneous text. But exceptionally, just in the present case, the occurrence of such a coincidence, improbable on the whole, suggests itself. For the metre in which stanzas 4-9 are composed (these are ṛcs each consisting of three Jagatī lines) is found in the whole of the ṚV only in these six stanzas so that if one had to form new tṛcas one had only these stanzas at his disposal.[1] In my opinion then this reshuffling in the SV of stanzas 4-9 is not entitled, as in most other cases, to be regarded as indicative of a homogeneous unit: an uncertain result which unfortunately can scarcely be made more definite by an examination of the contents and the context.

If the divisions, for which the evidence from the Sāmaveda has been discussed so far, always pointed to independent hymns **[131]**, then we must now ask what has the SV to say regarding the assumption of the *strophe*-divisions in those hymns of the ninth book which stay there as homogeneous hymns. It appears to me that the Sāmaveda is not quite favourable to such an assumption. However the Sāmaveda has resolved in a few cases [see the end of (c) above] nine-stanza or six-stanza hymns into triads; but the fact that here and there where triads are so conveniently obtained were picked up does not by itself prove much[2] unless other criteria intervene—one even managed to extract two tṛcas from the five-stanza hymn V.68 by making the two parts overlap each other (1-3; 3-5)—; such cases, however, are only sporadic, and in an overwhelming majority of cases other methods

1. Cf. the exchange of a stanza between the two Gāyatrī hymns 27 and 28 each containing six stanzas; these are two hymns in which each stanza begins with *eṣa*.
2. Cf. my observation in ZDMG XXXVIII. 469: "In some places we can observe that hymns which were not meant for tṛca division but easily admitted of division, e.g. VII.22 (containing 9 stanzas), VI.57 (containing 6 stanzas) have been split up into tṛcas in the SV."

[above (a) and (b)] are as a rule available which do not provide any support for divisions into strophes. If we examine the remaining evidence available for and against strophe divisions the frequency of hymns of nine and six stanzas in the Gāyatrī of the ninth Maṇḍala—by the way only in this Maṇḍala—is striking: the hymns of nine stanzas are as numerous as those of ten and eight stanzas taken together, those of six stanzas even one and a half times as frequent as those of seven and five stanza taken together.[1] In a number of hymns the text shows sub-divisions corresponding to a triad division, and these do not appear to be merely due to chance[2]. **[132]** On the other hand, we cannot possibly think of a *complete* rule of strophe-division on account of the hymns of eight, of five stanzas etc., and many hymns of nine stanzas and six stanzas can be accommodated to a tṛca-division only with difficulty. Under these circumstances we have to give up the idea of laying down any general valid rule of divisibility or non-divisibility for the group of hymns that we are considering. However unwilling we may be to do without such a rule just in the present case where, even more clearly than in any other portion of the ṚV text, we have a fixed type of the form of the hymns, we must still be on our guard against the desire to gain from the available evidence

1. 8 hymns of nine stanzas against 4 each of ten and eight stanzas; 22 hymns of six stanzas against 7 of seven stanzas and 6 of five stanzas.
2. Cf., for instance, hymn 6: st. 1-3 addresses to Soma in the imperative; st. 2 and 3, besides, are connected on account of the opening words *abhi tyam* and *abhi* in the third pāda. St. 4-6: we pass on to a new thought; Soma is no longer addressed here; stanzas 5 and 6 are held together by *yam ... tam*. St. 7-9 again a noteworthy break; in both the stanzas 7 and 8, the second pāda ends with *pavate sutaḥ*; st. 9 is the concluding stanza with the opening word *evā* which constantly recurs in these stanzas.—Hymn 11 [see (c) above as regards its division in the SV], st. 1-3: st. 3 is logically connected with the preceding stanza and clearly indicates the end. St. 4-6: there is a new beginning in st. 4 as in st. 1; and the three stanzas are held together by the recurring 2nd per. pl. imperative, an address to the priests. St. 7-9: recurring address in 2nd pers. sg. to Soma.—As to the *six*-stanza hymns, cf. e.g. 30 and 45.

more definite and more plain results than those which, all considered, the evidence can deliver in this case.

Now we shall turn to the other important Maṇḍala which appears predominantly important in the SV, viz. the *eighth,* and we shall indicate under the same headings as those for the ninth the various ways in which the material has been utilized[1].

(a) *Whole hymns* do not appear in the SV, as there are altogether no borrowings of more than three stanzas.

(b) Among the cases in which only *one tṛca* is taken from a hymn, **[133]** the borrowing of st. 1-3 predominates only moderately, and there is no reason to consider them as a special type.

(c) *Several stanza-triads,* corresponding to the triad division of the Ṛg-hymns, have been taken over from the following hymns: 2, 6, 15, 24, 33, 45, 72, 84, 92, 93, 95, 98, 102. —*One triad,* corresponding to the Ṛk-division, from the following: 11, 13, 34, 38, 64, 68, 69, 74, 75, 76, 81, 89,[2] 94, 97,[3] 103.

(d) Cases of one or more *triads* which, however, do not agree with the Ṛgveda division into threes are: I.24-26. — 14.1-3; 5, 7, 8.—17.1-3; 11-13.—44.4-6; 12-14; 16-18[4].

1. In the case of Maṇḍala VIII we have especially to note that there are numerous borrowings from it in the Ath. Veda XX.
2. St. 5-7 also correspond to the ṚV tṛca division inasmuch as st. 1-4 form two Pragāthas.
3. That VIII.97.10-12, and then naturally also the three following stanzas up to the end, form tṛcas has to be accepted simply on the testimony of the SV. There is no ground for condemning the facts as uncertain as Grassmann has done by speaking of "Fragmente anderer Lieder"; cf. ZDMG XXXVIII. 471.
4. We do not go into the question of how the division of these sūktas into tṛcas stands where there is no correspondence between the order of stanzas in the ṚV and their divisions in the SV since this has nothing to do with our present subject. I shall content myself here with indicating my opinion that the ṚV is correct in the case of hymns 14 and 44; I think that the SV has grouped together, as an

(Continued on next page)

(e) From the Pragāthas occur numerous dyads; a detailed enumeration is superfluous. *Otherwise no dyads are found.*

(f) In the SV, part II, we have the following *single stanzas* standing all by themselves: 69.2; 93.19.

[134] One can see that here where the type of the longer Sāman-hymn, corresponding to a whole sūkta of the ṚV and appearing almost exclusively in the Pavamāna-hymns, is absent, *two* types which are more simply and sharply marked occur side by side: *dyads* in the Pragātha metre; *triads*—but neither longer not shorter pieces—in other metres. The justification for the Pragātha division is self-evident; but the SV leaves naturally the question open whether the Pragāthas which have been combined together into a sūkta in the ṚV constitute hymns or strophes of a hymn (see below). The tṛca-divisions, the justification for which has to be examined, deserve a more detailed study. For that purpose we proceed with the purely external criterion of the number of stanzas in a particular hymn as they stand in the ṚV. If we, as a matter of course, leave aside the Dānastutis and similar appendages, as well as the Pragāthas which are mixed up in a hymn and then naturally must alter the division of stanza into groups of three, then for the hymns which have been cited under group (c), we get the following numbers of stanzas :

Divisible by 3: 45, 42, 33 (twice), 27, 18 (twice), 15 (thrice), 12 (five times), 9 (three times), 3 (twice).

(Continued from previous page)

exceptional case, stanzas from different strophes. About hymn 17 cf. below [p. 139, n. 1]. It is hopeless to try to bring order into the chaos of the hymn 1. And yet—with the exception naturally of the two Pragāthas at the beginning and the concluding Triṣṭubhs—it is quite likely that originally a tṛca grouping was in existence. We may note that in the SV st. 24-26 form a tṛca (as also in the Āśvalāyana VII.4.3); thus there remains up to the Dānastuti the tṛca 27-29, and then in the Dānastuti up to the concluding Triṣṭubhs the tṛca 30-32. The st. 12-14 finally have been taken out in the Pañc. Br. IX.10.1 and in the Śāṅkh. Śraut. XIII.12.16.

Not divisible by 3: 40, 34, 22, 16, 13 (twice), 10 (twice)[1].

One can easily observe that the numbers which are not divisible by three, when divided by three, always leave a remainder of 1, which recurring as it does in eight cases, can hardly be a mere coincidence. Thus the hypothesis suggests itself that in the eighth Maṇḍala we find hymns of a frequently occurring type which are *arranged in triads, but have at the end a single concluding stanza standing outside this arrangement.* **[135]** A closer scrutiny of the pertinent hymns does not leave in fact any doubt as to the existence of such a type. The 38th hymn, for instance, belongs to the cases where this type is clearly characterized. The tṛca division is indicated at the first glance inasmuch as the last pāda is always common to each group of three stanzas (e.g. 1-3 *indrāgnī tasya bodhatam*; 4-6 *indrāgnī ā gataṁ narā;* 7-9 *indrāgnī somapītaye);* then follows the tenth stanza, isolated from the rest[2]: *āham sarasvatīvator indrāgnior avo vṛṇe yābhyāṁ gāyatram ṛcyate.*—Not less striking to the eye is the same construction in hymn 93,[3] where the continuity of the content is observable within each group of 3 stanzas and a new section is observable in the beginning of the next. In a characteristic manner the tṛca division becomes even sharper in st. 19-21; their opening words are *kayā, kasya, abhī ṣu naḥ*—manifestly in imitation of the tṛca which has acquired a special significance as the text of the Vāmadevya Sāman (IV.31.1-3): *kayā naś citra' ābhuvat, kas tvā satyo madānām, abhī ṣu ṇaḥ sakhīnām.* From 25 to 33 we have three tṛcas which are marked as such by the individual refrain characterizing each of them; at st. 33 stops the last tṛca passage of the SV taken

1. These are the hymns : VIII.2, 11, 15, 38, 68, 75, 93 and 102.
2. That this stanza does not share the refrain of the last tṛca shows that it (and equally the end stanzas altogether) must not be regarded as an extension of the tṛca, as e.g. in an Anuṣṭubh hymn very often the last Anuṣṭubh is extended to a Paṅkti. The end stanza as a matter of fact rather stands *outside* the tṛca division.
3. Cf. here besides the parallels of the SV also those of the Ath. Veda.

out from this hymn. Thus st. 34 remains as the end-stanza which has been relegated to the supplement by Grassmann as he has done systematically with all these end-stanzas, but actually it is in its proper place where it stands **[136]** and to leave it there is as much beyond dispute as it is also guaranteed by the type of the hymn formation which requires it there. When we consider the hymn 102 in the light of these patterns we also arrive at quite a different interpretation than that of Grassmann. Of the 22 stanzas of this sūkta, the testimony of the Sāmaveda easily proves a tṛca division for the first 15 stanzas; st. 16-18, according to their contents, similarly form a tṛca. Now remain four stanzas. The method requires naturally that we examine if there exists any objection to taking 19-21 as a last tṛca and st. 22 as the concluding stanza. One can easily see that that is not the case, that st. 19-21 are rather connected clearly together by their thought content: Agni is requested to accept in lieu of costly offerings even insignificant ones. Everything is thus in perfect order. In addition to this, the Agni ritual as laid down in the Yajurveda offers testimony for the close connection between at least st. 20 and 21.[1] Now Grassmann has seen correctly that st. 22 belongs to the end part of the entire hymn, but since he does not recognize the type of tṛca-division with a surplus end stanza, he has to reject one stanza in order to ensure the tṛca-division and so he arbitrarily removes st. 21 from its proper place, which is guaranteed by the content as also by the Yajurveda: an operation for which there is not a shadow of authority left the moment we recognize the type of hymn-construction which is pre-supposed here.

It need not be mentioned that when once our eye has become accustomed to this type, we can recognize it even

1. These stanzas are found close to one another in all the five recensions of the YV; see the citations given by von Schroeder, Maitr. S. IV. p. 290.

in many other cases, where it is not possible for us to compare the Sāmaveda, and also such which are outside the Maṇḍala VIII; **[137]** cf. VIII.18[1]; 26.1-19[2]; 66[3]; 80[4]; —I. 27; 30.1-16[5]; 42[6]; and so on.

If then the type of hymn discussed here implies by its very nature the homogeneity of a complete hymn across its strophes, finding its most evident expression in its end stanza, then the recognition of this form and of its frequent occurrence in the eighth Maṇḍala justifies us, as a matter of course, in expecting that also those tṛca-hymns of this Maṇḍala which do not have the end stanza are to be regarded as homogeneous hymns with a strophe-division and not as a conglomerate of independent hymns, each of three stanzas, as in the case of the ninth Maṇḍala. The fact that the tṛca-strophes—and also the Pragāthas—belong to homogeneous units in numerous sūktas of the eighth Maṇḍala is confirmed in an absolutely doubtless way, and accordingly it is highly probable that also those hymns in which there is accidentally no evidence have to be judged

---

1. VIII.18 gives an instructive example of the manifold evidence which indicates a tṛca division. Stanzas 4-6 contain a prominent mention of the goddess Aditi (St. 7 being linked to it, as also st. 10 is linked to the refrain of 7-9); 7-9 have the refrain *apa sridhaḥ;* there is also a frequent recurrence of *śam, śaṁtāti*; st. 10, 11 are connected by *yuyotana, yuyota;* st. 13-15 by *martia* (st. 14-15 also by *dvayu* and *advayu);* st. 20 and 21 have Mitra, Varuṇa and the Marutaḥ in common. In the first three tṛcas there is the one type of the Uṣṇih and in the following tṛca there is the other type (their notation, according to the notation used by us above, being: *a a a x* and *a a b*).
2. A manifestly by itself to be recognized as hymn to the Aśvins; the following hymn is addressed to Vāyu.
3. A Pragātha hymn, the end stanza being Anuṣṭubh.
4. Here, as in many cases, the end stanza is in another metre than that of the tṛcas.
5. An Indra hymn; after this come two clearly unconnected tṛcas addressed to the Aśvins and Uṣas.
6. The tṛcas and the end stanza have been correctly separated by Geldner-Kaegi.

in the same way[1]. **[138]** The indications of homogeneity may be of various types: in some cases it is the contents, the context which enable us to recognize the homogeneity which extends over the strophes; or it is the parallel nature of several hymns[2]; or it is the concluding portion—for instance a Dānastuti[3]—which assures the homogeneity of the entire hymn; or it is a refrain which is repeated in the entire hymn (e.g. 34, 47, 62, 85); or a refrain[4] which changes in each succeeding strophe; or it is a metrical peculiarity, for instance the trochaic rhythm of the Gāyatrī cadence (16, 71, 79, 81); or it is some less usual form of the tṛca-grouping (an Anuṣṭubh and two Gāyatrīs : 63, 74, cf. 68); or such a peculiarity as the frequent ending of the last two pādas of a stanza with the same word (70)[5]. But the strophes **[139]** which form the section of a hymn—whether it be the Sāmaveda, which gives a clue regarding their division, or

---

1. Naturally here it cannot be denied that also in the eighth Maṇḍala there is good deal of what is heterogeneous which has been grouped together and that to tṛca hymns, strophes not belonging to them, have been occasionally added (cf. below the section on the Arrangement of Maṇḍala VIII): but in saying this we are not saying anything about the fact that the predominant type in this Maṇḍala is the one of the strophe-hymns and not the one of individual strophes occurring as hymns.
2. The most prominent kind of this being the Vālakhilya hymns.
3. Or an end like that as in 79.9: *rājan(n) apa dviṣaḥ sedha mīḍhvo' apa sridhaḥ sedha,* and the like.
4. This is the case with the stanzas of hymn 35 in which three stanzas are combined into one strophe each, this being in addition to a much deeper similarity of expression.
5. My investigations into the *arrangement* of the Saṁhitā, which will be given later on, would furnish further arguments for my opinion that in Maṇḍala VIII the strophes are to be looked upon quite predominantly as parts of hymns handed down by tradition, but not as hymns by themselves. One may further consider also cases like the following. The Agni hymn 75 and the series of three Indra hymns 76-78 consist almost exclusively of Gāyatrī tṛcas. The Soma hymn 79 consists similarly of three Gāyatrī tṛcas, but with a predominantly trochaic end. If there was here a grouping together

(Continued on next page)

whether it is the refrain, or the metre, or whatever else—are always Pragāthas or tṛcas[1].

And this same result is to be found constantly repeated in the case of the remaining Maṇḍalas: even if here and there a tetrad of stanzas occurs in a single context, which has led to their being extracted together in the Sāmaveda[2]: **[140]** traces of any regular tetrad divisions continuing through a hymn are found in the Sāmaveda just as little as

---

(Continued from previous page)

of independent tṛcas, how come that exactly all those tṛcas which are addressed to Soma have that metrical characteristic which is not found in the others ? Or, how is it that in the group of the Vatsa hymns the troop of the Maruts is always glorified in Anuṣṭubh tṛcas (hymn No. 7) and Indra always in Gāyatrī tṛras (No. 6)? Facts of this nature in the distribution of metres show that we are dealing here with long hymns, consisting of strophes, and not with series of independent hymns, each consisting of a single strophe.

1. Of exceptions—if at all they are to be regarded as such—I find only the following irrelevant cases. In hymn 17 we have 13 stanzas if we leave aside the final Pragātha. The parallels from the other Vedas and the stanzas used in the ritual of the Hotṛ (Āśv. Śr. V.10.28; VI.4.10; VII.2.3) yield the tṛcas 1-3; 4-6; 11-13, so that 7-10 remain as an apparent tetrad. In whatever way one may explain the disturbance to the *regular order of the triads*—considerations of the sequence of hymns (cf. the section on the Arrangement of the Saṁhitā) recommend to look upon st. 10 as the end stanza of a tṛca hymn and st. 11-13 as an independent hymn—one will not in any case like to use this hymn to deduce a type of Vedic strophe consisting of tetrads. 31.15-18 is clearly not a tetrad-strophe, but a hymn of 4 stanzas. 32.19, 20 form a dyad in a long tṛca-hymn (cf. ZDMG XXXVIII.470 f; st. 30 is an end stanza outside the strophe-grouping); are we to suppose that a stanza has been lost ?
2. From the fact that VI.75.18-19 united with a Khila stanza, and X.152.3-4 united with a stanza not found in the ṚV have been formed into tṛcas in the SV we cannot say that *dyads* have been borrowed in the SV; elsewhere the rule applies in full rigour that where the SV borrows a group of two stanzas from the ṚV it is always a Pragātha. As to *tetrads* I find I.13.1-4 taken over in the SV: Āprī stanzas and therefore not under any suspicion of being strophes. Then again, we find III.12.5-8: but just this hymn of 9 stanzas is at the same time

(Continued on next page)

traces of dyad-divisions (excepting of course the Pragāthas) or of pentad-divisions. And what the Sāmaveda yields, yields also the same way the other evidence such as the formation of the refrain etc., and thus so long as for postulating dyad- or pentad-hymns[1] more reliable and more objective characteristics than those which the votaries of that kind of divisions have found are not determined, we shall not feel justified in postulating in the ṚV strophes other than tṛcas and Pragāthas.

VI

Hymns in Various Metres

The use of one and the same metre for a hymn is, as is well-known, the rule for the Veda. While studying the exceptions to this rule we have to subject to many-sided and penetrating scrutiny the large number of hymns composed in various metres which seems to be indicated by a survey of the traditional text or of the Anukramaṇī. A considerable part of this material is thereby eliminated at the very outset. First of all we have to think in this connection of the division of those large hymn-complexes about which the investigations into the principles of the Arrangement of the Saṁhitā[2] as also [141] the borrowings

---

(Continued from previous page)

found in the SV with the division 1-3; 4-6; 9, 7, 8. Further, of the hymn I.7 the first four stanzas are found in the SV and also in the Yajurvedas; the hymn has 10 stanzas so that a division into tetrads is not conceivable. Finally I.22 : a hymn in which at first sight we could possibly think of a tetrad-grouping. The hymn is segmented, according to the deities to whom it is addressed, in the following divisions and the SV has taken from them (wholly) only the last segment: 1-4 ; 5-8 ; 9-12 ; 13-15 ; 16-21. In my opinion the hymn in fact is made up of independent hymns of 4, 4, 4, 3 stanzas and two tṛcas; cf. the section on the Arrangement of the Saṁhitā.

1. As regards the attempts of Geldner-Kaegi, Grassmann and Delbrück tending in this direction, see my observations ZDMG XXXVIII.453 f.
2. See below the section on this subject.

in the other Vedas[1], tell us that they are to be looked upon as groups of independent hymns combined together only supreficially. When this is done, in many cases the different metres which appear to be used in the same sūkta get separated from one another[2]. A similar result is often obtained when we separate late additions to the original Saṁhitā which are indicated by the rules of the Saṁhitā arrangement. But our scrutiny by no means need stop to scan all those cases where the rules of arrangement do not give rise to any doubt against the traditional text or where they even positively show to be existent *at the time of the arrangers of the Saṁhitā.* It goes without saying that in the first place deviations of a single or groups of stanzas from the metre of the neighbouring stanzas point to interpolations and, on the other hand, combinations of independent hymns in the period *prior* to the formation of the Saṁhitā. Thus, in the hymn IV.1: here the first three stanzas show longer structures consisting of twelve-syllabled and eight-syllabled components, resembling the Atyaṣṭi (see above p. 102); then follow Triṣṭubh stanzas (4-20). Grassmann accordingly splits the hymn at stanza 3; in my opinion he has followed the correct way, only that he has been somewhat too rash. If we look at the hymn from the point of view of the contents, there is a definite section consisting of st. 1-5, being a prayer to Agni to propitiate Varuṇa; from st. 6 onwards we have, on the other hand, a normal Agni hymn without any reference to Varuṇa. Thus then the hymn must be split up after st. 5, **[142]** by which procedure the metrical unevenness is certainly not removed, but its appearance is modified; it will thus be referred to one

1. See above [pp. 121 f.]
2. For instance, the "complicated symmetries and responsions", discovered by Ludwig (III, p. 58) in I.84 get separated from one another in this way—a fact which has been already shown by Grassmann. Other such cases occur in I.79; III.62; VI.15, 16, 44, 51, 52, 59, 60; VII.31, 66 and so on.

of the types which we will come to know as regular[1].—Similar is the case with VII.1 (1-18 Virāj; 19-25 Triṣṭubh). If we divide the sūkta as indicated by the appearance of the same concluding stanza twice, stanza 20 = stanza 25, two hymns result, the first with a changing metre, but changing in a typical manner, and the second metrically uniform.—Also in the case of VI. 71 the general tenor and the style of expression make it likely that there is a new hymn starting with st. 4, and this agrees also with its ritual use[2]; this way we have a pure Jagatī hymn and a pure Triṣṭubh hymn, and these two hymns together, as the arrangement of the hymns indicates beyond all doubt, were valid for the arranger of the Saṁhitā as one hymn.—We may also further point to II.24.12 where the appearance of a Triṣṭubh in the place of a Jagatī, combined with a striking breach of coherence points to the removal of that stanza (Grassmann actually did it), or we may point to VI.68 where, if we remove the supplementary stanzas, some composed in Jagatī and some in Triṣṭubh metres, there is a pure Triṣṭubh hymn left up to st. 8[3]. Naturally it must be left to the text-critical treatment of the individual cases to dispose of the large number of cases which are more or less analogous to those touched here; **[143]** for the purpose of our present discussion it suffices to characterize in a general way the manner in which a considerable number of cases of metrical dissimilarity, also in passages where the form of the hymns as it was in the hands of the arrangers of the Saṁhitā has been correctly preserved,

---

1. Thus the first of the two hymns combined into IV.1 consisting of eight-syllabled and twelve-syllabled constructions concluded by two Triṣṭubh stanzas, the second hymn being metrically homogeneous.
2. Ait. Br. IV.32, V.8 and other ritual texts.
3. While reading the Atharvaveda we can very often have the experience that when we separate the basic component of a hymn and the later additions with the help of the Ṛgvedic parallels, then simultaneously a metrically variegated hymn is reduced to a metrically homogeneous one. With all the difference between the Ṛk- and the Atharvan-text, one may see here a pointer, although to be used with great care, for the treatment of the former.

has nevertheless to be eliminated by our critique or at least to be reduced from an anomalous form to a typically fixed one.

But even among those cases which *textual criticism* has no business to question, not a few become irrelevant for the investigation of the hymn-types with changing metre because the apparent combination of various metres is eliminated by way of *exegesis*: viz. those cases in which utterances or formulas are strung up which do not form a continuous hymn but are meant to be recited separately from each other in different places of the same ritual or the same epic narrative context — in the latter case with interspersed prose passages. In this way, if not everywhere, but at least in many passages of the funeral- (X.14ff.) and marriage-formulas (X.85), of the Yūpa-formulas (III.8), the ploughman-formulas (IV.57), the formulas for the armour (VI.75) and other similar collections of formulas, what is metrically different gets separated from one another. This is also the case with the narrative hymns of Agastya, Indra and the Maruts (I.170 f.), of Agastya and Lopāmudrā (I.179), of Indra, Vāyu and the fight with Vṛtra (VIII.100) and with those Ākhyānas for which I may be permitted to refer to my views expressed earlier at another place.[1] Also in the case of [144] the Dānastutis and similar supplementary texts, not seldom can the cases of combination of metrically different components be eliminated by untying the loose band which connects them to the preceding hymn[2].

It is quite plain that even if we eliminate from our investigation the categories of cases mentioned just now, in so far as they can be identified, this does not at all mean that the remaining material can be considered as assured. If it is often easy to separate with absolute certainty parts which only apparently form a homogeneous whole, it is, on the other hand, difficult as a rule directly to prove the real

1. ZDMG XXXIX.52 ff.
2. As regards the nature of this connection see the article in ZDMG, mentioned before, pp. 83 ff.

and original—not just the one available to the arrangers of the present Saṁhitā—unity of any components: a demonstration which due to the frequent uncertainty to obtain results regarding the unity of a hymn from the continuity of thought, can as a rule succeed really satisfactorily at least only then when we have either strophe-formations or when, of several parallel hymns, one guarantees the substance of the other. Certain types of combinations of different metres turn out to be undoubtedly fixed by their constant recurrence as also by their intrinsic conceivability; in addition to them there is a small remnant left of more or less irregular metrical combinations which cannot be totally rejected, although naturally, in the treatment of individual cases no definite results are often obtainable.

First of all we have to recognize the occurrence of a different metre at the *end of a hymn* as regular and as typical. An end-stanza in Triṣṭubh appears oftnest of all and this [145] again quite explicably, especially in the hymns composed in the metre which is nearest to the Triṣṭubh, viz. the Jagatī, after which the Triṣṭubh, with its contrasting cadence, marks palpably the end of the hymn. In most cases it is a *single* Triṣṭubh which closes the Jagatī hymn (I. 34, 52, 54, 64, 102, 106 etc. etc.)[1]; often there are *two* Triṣṭubh end-stanzas (I.51, 53, 94 etc., at the end of parallel hymns X.35, 36; 43, 44; 63, 64); occasionally there are three (I.58, 168), or even four (I.101). In many cases it is a fixed end-stanza or an end-pāda in Triṣṭubh peculiar to a ṛṣi, or a group of ṛṣis, the use of which has occasioned a Triṣṭubh-closing for a Jagatī hymn. It goes without saying that very often an irregular appearance of the Triṣṭubh in the

1. Cf. the collections made by Ludwig in III.59. The second Maṇḍala is especially rich in such cases.

interior of a hymn (see below) is related to the occurrence of Triṣṭubh at the end.

As compared with this main type, a Triṣṭubh-ending of one or occasionally two stanzas after a metre other than Jagatī occurs considerably less often, but such cases do exist for each of the metres that are not quite uncommon. Thus we have a Triṣṭubh end-stanza for Gāyatrī tṛcas in I.27.10-12; 30.13-15[1], and after the hymns VIII.11, 80[2] consisting of Gāyatrī-tṛcas. Further we have it also after Gāyatrī in X.20 (Virāj and Triṣṭubh). After Anuṣṭubh : I.175, 176 (parallel hymns); VI.2 and 14 (in both cases the same pentads of Triṣṭubh pādas); X.90 (the end-stanza taken from I.164.50). After Bṛhatī **[146]** III.9; after Uṣṇih V.40.4; 78.4; after Paṅkti I.105(?); after Mahāpaṅkti VIII.40 and X.133; after Atyaṣṭi I.130; 136; 139; after Virāj consisting of three Triṣṭubh pādas VIII.1 (see above p. 142), 22, 68; after other rarer metres II.11; X.22, 126 (IV.12.6 being repeated as the end-stanza); about IV.1 which likewise belongs here we have spoken in more detail above [p. 141].

Anuṣṭubh end-stanzas, understandably, mostly occur after Gāyatrī hymns[3]; thus I.90(?); II.8; III.37; IV.30; VIII.33.16-19; X.9 (two end-stanzas). The supposition, even otherwise recommendable, that we have to assume the end of the hymn at VIII.31.9 is supported by the fact that st. 9 is an Anuṣṭubh after the Gāyatrīs which precede. —In the last stanza of a Gāyatrī hymn, especially of a Gāyatrī tṛca, we

1. As regards the divisions of hymns concerned, I refer the reader to the section on the Arrangement of the Saṁhitā.—The case of I. 93.12, as I have shown there, could be set aside by changing the place of the concerned stanza.
2. From this it is easy to conjecture that in VIII.63.12 we have an end-stanza which must have a place after the preceding Anuṣṭubh-Gāyatrī-triads. Can it be that an Anuṣṭubh preceding st. 10 has been lost?—We can regard X.62.11 also as forming a Triṣṭubh-close after the triad consisting of Anuṣṭubh and Gāyatrī.
3. Cf. Ludwig III.62.

find very often that the third pāda is repeated, with variations, so that we have an Anuṣṭubh end-stanza; thus I.43.9 (the hymn begins with st. 7); VI.16.27; 45.33; 56; VII.94; VIII.79; IX.66.18. Just as after a pure Gāyatrī, the Anuṣṭubh end-stanza also occurs after a Gāyatrī extended by a four-syllabled pāda (i.e. Uṣṇih of the type *a a a x*) in VI.51.16[1].

In a series of mostly doubtful cases we have an Anuṣṭubh end-stanza after Triṣṭubh hymns; partly the lack of sure cohesion raises the suspicion that we may have a late addition or discontinuity due to the ritual; partly doubts based on the rules of the arrangement of the hymns must be raised against the transmitted text. These cases are: I.158; **[147]** IV.39; X.103[2], 109 (two Anuṣṭubhs), 142[2], 161.—We have Anuṣṭubh end-stanza after a mixture of Triṣṭubh and Jagatī in VI.28 and VII.104; after Pragāthas in VI.48; VIII.66, 103; after Uṣṇih in VIII.24.

Jagatī end-stanzas are rare, even after a preceding Triṣṭubh[3]. They occur after Gāyatrī in VII.89; after Paṅkti in I.82; after longer combinations of eight-syllabled and twelve-syllabled pādas in VIII.36, 37 (these being parallel hymns).

There is a *Bṛhatī end-stanza* after Gāyatrī tṛcas in VIII.78; after Anuṣṭubh in VI.42.

We have already spoken about the *Paṅkti end-stanzas* above [p. 32].

Thus all the usual metres have been used with more or less frequency for the end-stanzas of hymns in another metre. Only the Gāyatrī has been to all appearances excluded

---

1. The hymn starts with st. 13; see below the section on the Arrangement of the Saṁhitā.
2. See my observations on the end of these sūktas below in my discussion on The Arrangement of Maṇḍala X.
3. See the references in Ludwig III.59. Hymn IV.50 is to be excluded from them on account of the divisions which have to be done for this hymn. The metre of X.128.9 is Jagatī only for the very superficial judgement of the Anukramaṇī.

from this use; this complete lack of instances[1] can hardly be accidental. Did the lack of balance in the Gāyatrī on account of its three pādas make this stanza appear unsuitable to the Vedic poets to signal the end of a hymn ?

Just like the end, so also the *opening* of a hymn, or of a tṛca, could be marked by a metre different from that of the rest. But this happens much more rarely; it is conceivable that that kind of prominence to be given to the opening was not felt to be as effective **[148]** as it was palpably the case at the end. The most positive example of this variety is an Anuṣṭubh-opening before the following Gāyatrīs. It is found in individual tṛcas and in its regular recurrence in the case of whole tṛca series—so that we have the tṛca-form, already mentioned on p. 120, n. 1, of Anuṣṭubh plus Gāyatrī plus Gāyatrī—, and occasionally even in longer passages: e.g. III.24; V.28.4-6; 82. 1-3; VIII.2.28-30; 9.19-21; 63[2]; 68; 74; 92.1-3; IX.101.1-3; X.20[3]; 62.8-10.

From the analogy of an Anuṣṭubh opening before a Gāyatrī we might infer that also in a series of cases with Jagatī openings (one, occasionally two stanzas) before Triṣṭubh we have to see perhaps something different from a purely accidental combination of the frequent mixture of Jagatī and Triṣṭubh stanzas; cf. VII.41, 44; X.69, 83, 117, 130, 177.

If we leave the subject of end-stanzas and opening-stanzas, we approach more and more the subject of the irregular mixture of metres.

We can still speak of a certain orderliness when an interchange of metres concerns the strophe-division; thus,

---

1. That the Gāyatrī also occasionally occurs at the end in motley intermixtures of metres is of course of no consequence.
2. St. 5 is Anuṣṭubh instead of Gāyatrī; it would be overbold, even if not difficult, to change it.
3. St. 1 has to be omitted, see below [p. 161].

for instance, in the combination of Uṣṇih and Gāyatrī VIII.26.1-19[1], of Upariṣṭājjyotis and Paṅkti VIII.35; of Paṅkti and Bṛhatī VIII.62; of Anuṣṭubh, Gāyatrī and mixed combinations VIII.69. In this context we may mention also combinations of Pragātha strophes with Bṛhatī tṛcas (VIII.70; VIII.1 also appears to belong here) and with other strophes in which the eighth Maṇḍala abounds; meanwhile these combinations only seldom exclude the possibility of dissecting the composite hymns.

[**149**] There are a number of other cases in which, without there being an arrangement in strophes, we have the transition from one metre to another in a hymn, so that one portion of it is composed in one and the other in another metre. This is the case with the typical transition from the five-syllabled Virāj pādas to Triṣṭubh (above p. 97), the transition from Gāyatrī to Anuṣṭubh in the Āprī hymn IX.5—a particularly reliable example[2] in virtue of its ritual nature—and the transition from Triṣṭubh to Jagatī in X. 84[3]. Accordingly, if we find such combinations occasionally extended to metres which have little in common with each other, e.g. Triṣṭubh and Gāyatrī in III.59, we cannot readily take it for granted that we have here different hymns or fragments of hymns grouped together. We shall content ourselves with stating that this particular hymn—different from numerous other similar-looking hymns—has been regarded as constituting a single unit in the arrangement of

1. The end-stanza after the strophes is st. 19; with st. 20 begins a new hymn.
2. It is less certain whether in I.28 (Ait. Br. VII.17) the Anuṣṭubh piece and the Gāyatrī piece stand in a continuous, homogeneous connection.
3. The circumstance that guarantees the reliability of this instance is that each beginning of a stanza is related to the end of the preceding stanza throughout. In X.32, on the other hand, we can hardly miss the fact that the transition from Jagatī to Triṣṭubh coincides with a break in the context.

the Saṁhitā; it will not be possible to reach a more definite result than this.

Other combinations of metres—except those of Triṣṭubh and Jagatī—are relatively rare and only stray ṛcas in one metre may be found scattered in a hymn which has been composed throughout in another metre; as a rule we have here rather sūktas with a continuous, or at least very frequent, change of metres, so that we cannot in their case regard any one particular metre as the dominant one. The affinities among such metres which show a particular predisposition [**150**] for combination with one another are frequently an active factor in both cases, although we cannot say that there are not exceptions. The most outstanding example of this type is found with *Triṣṭubh* and *Jagatī*. Just as there was a more careless practice, especially with the later Vedic poets, often to introduce promiscuously in a single stanza Triṣṭubh and Jagatī pādas, similarly in the view point of that same lax practice an interchange of a whole Triṣṭubh stanza with a whole Jagatī stanza was not felt to be an interchange of metres. Apart from those cases mentioned above concerning the end-part and the opening-part of a hymn, it appears to me that it would be a mistake to try to discover any rules or any endeavour at symmetry in these interchanges.[1] As in the case of Triṣṭubh and Jagatī so also, although not so frequently, we find an interchange of *Gāyatrī* and *Anuṣṭubh*. We find a single Gāyatrī between two Anuṣṭubhs in X.19.6[2] and I.176.2; an Anuṣṭubh between two Gāyatrīs in IV.30.8; V.61.5;[3] VI.53.8; other combinations of the two metres occur

1. Ludwig holds a different opinion III.59.
2. However, it is quite possible to supply from the opening of st. 8 the pāda which is lacking to make up an Anuṣṭubh. How easily in the traditional text an interchange between Gāyatrī and Anuṣṭubh forms could take place is seen if we compare I.23.20 with X.9.6.
3. It is possible that there is a sort of a new beginning with this stanza.

e.g. in I.187; VIII.55; X.9.6 ff. (= I.23.20 ff.).— Especially in the strophic hymns of the eighth Maṇḍala as well as in many Dānastutis we have a further range of metres whose affinity renders them suitable to be used next to each other: these are the metres formed with eight-syllabled pādas alone or in combination with twelve-syllabled pādas, i.e. Gāyatrī, Anuṣṭubh, Paṅkti, Kakubh, Bṛhatī, Uṣṇih, Purauṣṇih metres, while **[151]** Triṣṭubh, Jagatī and Virāj (3 × 11 syllables) form a distinct group, closely related among themselves. This grouping of metres is clearly recognized for instance in VIII.9. The 21 stanzas of this hymn, according to their sequence are: 1-3 Bṛhatī-Gāyatrī-Gāyatrī; 4-6 Bṛhatī-Kakubh-Bṛhatī; 7-9 Anuṣṭubh; 10-12 Triṣṭubh-Virāj-Jagatī; 13-15 Anuṣṭubh-Bṛhatī-Bṛhatī; 16-18 Anuṣṭubh; 19-21 Anuṣṭubh-Gāyatrī-Gāyatrī. As I have already indicated in this synopsis it appears clear to me that here we have tṛcas. It is true that those metres which are distinct from the eight-syllabled and the eight-plus-twelve-syllabled group are not absolutely wanting, but they form a single tṛca which is composed of them exclusively (10-12). Two tṛcas (7-9, 16-18) are composed entirely in Anuṣṭubh; one tṛca (19-21) shows the typical form, described above on p. 148, consisting of one Anuṣṭubh and two Gāyatrīs; finally, the remaining three tṛcas are composed in the metres, viz. Anuṣṭubh, Gāyatrī, Bṛhatī and Kakubh which belong to the affinity-group mentioned above.[1] Thus, if I mistake not, the apparently irregular nature of this hymn—Bergaigne has characterized this sūkta as *'metrically misshapen'* (*métriquement informe*)—in fact shows a composition, of course not quite approaching the one of fixed order, but of one in which some sort of arrangement is not entirely wanting[2].

---

1. From the point of view of the contents, the tṛca division is confirmed by the fact that the glorification of the Aśvins together with Uṣas is marked off by the tṛca 16-18.
2. Comparable is the structure of the Pragātha-formation in the following sūkta VIII.10; see above [p. 110].

Further cases in which affinities of the metres mentioned above can be recognized are frequent enough; I shall confine myself here to giving only a few references. In VIII.69 we have besides one tṛca in Gāyatrī and several in Anuṣṭubh [cf. p. 148] two tṛcas **[152]** having a mixture of metres: 10-12 Anuṣṭubh-Paṅkti-Anuṣṭubh; 16-18 Paṅkti-Bṛhatī-Bṛhatī. In VIII.26 at the end of a hymn to the Aśvins we have a separate hymn to Vāyu consisting of two tṛcas: 20-22 Anuṣṭubh-Gāyatrī-Uṣṇih; 23-25 Uṣṇih-Uṣṇih-Gāyatrī. In VIII.30 we have the metres Gāyatrī, Purauṣṇih, Bṛhatī and Anuṣṭubh. The Dānastuti VIII.70.13-15 contains Kakubh[1], Anuṣṭubh, Purauṣṇih. The Praüga hymn II.41, although composed in Gāyatrī, contains one tṛca (16-18) consisting of one Anuṣṭubh and two Bṛhatīs.

Thus then in the course of these discussions the field of absolutely irregular combinations of different metres has been more and more narrowed down. But the *elimination* of this field cannot and should not be considered as the ultimate goal of our textual criticism. There will be a remainder which owes its existence to the pure accidental caprice of the Vedic poets, even though naturally the delimitation of this remainder will always be in individual cases subject to various and partially irresoluble doubts. It is simply impossible to assert that certain combinations of different metres are to be absolutely excluded and that their mere appearance in the transmitted text suffices to postulate the elimination of the irregularity by textual criticism or exegesis[2]. What the change of metre—in so far as it is not *a priori* beyond doubt because of conforming to one of the typical forms—should invite the critic to do is only to examine whether other aberrations—as regards the sense, the ritual use, the arrangement of the hymns—**[153]** *combine* with the metrical aberration and thus make it possible to

---

1. The placing of the avasāna and correspondingly recognizing the metre of the stanza as Uṣṇih by the tradition is wrong.
2. I mean here what I have said above [p. 143].

draw further conclusions. We have come to know in the first part of this section several groups of cases in which such a combination of evidence in fact occurs and as a consequence we are justified in resolving into smaller sections a bigger unit in which in the present tradition are brought together metrically disparate components; and our investigations into the arrangement of the Saṁhitā will show later at every step that in those cases in which the segmentation of composite hymns into separate units is indicated it is most often the metre that shows the point of segmentation. In other cases, however, the examination to which we are led on account of the change in metres will not be in a position to find other grounds to doubt the homegeneity of the hymn; a prudent critic, then, will not regard the tradition as free from doubt on metrical grounds, still he will not consider it as proven to be defective. And finally, in several cases we will even discover factors that prove directly the homogeneity of the metrically disparate groups. In the hymn IV.7 after a Jagatī opening we have first Anuṣṭubh and then Triṣṭubh stanzas; but there is no other Agni hymn which shows smoother and less questionable continuity and of which several components are bound together by various relations. We can imagine no more appropriately placed stanza than the Anuṣṭubh VII:103.1 which commences the frog-hymn composed in Triṣṭubh, or the Satobṛhatī which appears between Triṣṭubhs as the third stanza in the Agni hymn III.23[1]. Also the well-known Anuṣṭubh stanza IV.20.10 **[154]** (the rest of the hymn is in Triṣṭubh) has been rejected, in my opinion, with questionable justification. As I understand the context, the

1. In IX.98.11 and so also in 99.1, according to the Anukramaṇī, there is an isolated Bṛhatī between Anuṣṭubhs and, superficially, this appears quite correct. Actually, however, we can hardly here think of there being a *stanza* in another metre; clearly the case is such that every time a single *pāda* was composed by the poet in another form, as it should have happened in a regular construction. Similar cases occur not seldom.

poet praises Indra and at the same time recommends himself as the negotiator of the divine help, so to say as the hirer of the god. But, he says, one must make sure of receiving this divine help in time; whosoever sacrifices to the god today (*adya* st. 7) becomes his friend. As soon as need arises everybody longs for Indra; when the war broke out, people began to haggle foolishly;[1] they offered too little and I—the priest, the proprietor of the god—went home quite at ease without having sold the god. And here the poet continues (st. 10): "Who will purchase this Indra of mine for ten milch-cows? When Indra has killed the enemies for him, then he must return him to me." It is not merely the superficial echo of *krīṇāti* with *avikrīto* of st. 9 by which this stanza is connected with the preceding one,[2] but hardly anywhere else[3] in the Ṛgveda the same range of ideas pervades so explicitely as in st. 10 together with the preceding one: whoever wants to buy too late and is stingy will get nothing; therefore: who is going to buy now ? Nevertheless the invitation to buy, directed to the audience, contrasts with the warning to the misers, and this nuance may have motivated the change of metre. To our taste this change may perhaps appear strange, but in this case, as in similar ones, there is **[155]** no probability, not to speak of a compelling ground, for assuming an interpretation on the basis of the metrical irregularity.

VII

Hymns with Irregularly Constructed Stanzas

In some of the hymns of the ṚV we find, with such frequency and partly at least decisively shielded from text-

1. I understand *dīnā dakṣā* (st. 9) as instrumental; cf. IV.54.3 *dīnair dakṣaiḥ*.
2. Kaegi, Ṛgveda, p. 156.
3. X.27.1 ff. form an approximately similar text and Geldner-Kaegi have correctly pointed out the analogy.

critical objection, so many pādas the extent and structure of which deviate from the norm generally accepted elsewhere, that it becomes necessary to postulate for them not merely negligence on the part of the poet but a deliberately freer treatment of the metres. Already in ancient times this fact of a free use of metres has been noted; thus in the Kauṣītaki Br. (VIII.5) the stanzas I.120.1-9 have been characterized as regards their metres as "aimless" (*akūdhrīcyaḥ*) and the expression which the Ait. Br. (I.21) has used with reference to the same stanzas, viz. *vichandas*, occurs as a designation of a special category of metres already seen in the formulae of the Yajurveda ritual.[1] The Tai. Saṁ. V.1.8.4 says of the Āprī hymn used at the altar construction that the stanzas are *aparimitachandasaḥ, ūnātiriktāḥ*; the metre is called 'hairy' (*lomaśam*)[2].

First come the two sūktas I.120 (st. 1-9) and X.105 as representing the freer metrical types to be discussed here. Side by side, it would be appropriate to include in this investigation also the Āprī hymn of the Agni ritual, peculiar to the Yajurveda, which was just mentioned **[156]** (Tai. Saṁ. IV.1.8.1-3; Mai. Saṁ. II.12.6; Vāj. Saṁ. XXVII.11-22): for, while both those ṚV hymns, just on account of their not well-defined metrical form are full of corruptions and obscurities, the YV hymn, handed down in several parallel recensions[3] and protected by typical characteristics of an Āprī hymn, offers a considerably firmer basis for investigation.

There can be no doubt whatsoever that the hymns in fact consist of stanzas and not prose. The division into individual ṛcas, not only in the Āprī hymn—where the ritual nature of the text requires it to be such—but equally in both the

1. E.g. Tai. Saṁ. V.2.11.1: *sachandā yā ca vichandā.*
2. Cf. also Mai. Saṁ. III.4.6; Ind. St. VIII.108 note.
3. Among them the Tai. Saṁ. (T) and the Vāj. Saṁ. (V) agree closely and apparently offer a preferable text; the Mai. Saṁ. (M) differs considerably.

other hymns, is quite clear. Within the stanzas the pādas are clearly delineated. Many of these pādas show the well-known regular types; and when they are combined with others which deviate from that type, then even in these departures and as well as in the groupings of such pādas with the regular ones we cannot fail to see certain norms, a tendency towards regularity, although of an imperfect nature, which makes it impossible to characterize these stanzas simply as formless.

Now in order to illustrate this in detail let us start with the Āprī hymn which, as we have observed, has been best transmitted. We can formulate the following rule for this hymn that each stanza contains three pādas: the first pāda and also the last, with a few exceptions, are always in Triṣṭubh; the second pāda is never Triṣṭubh, but has mostly a form which deviates from the usual **[157]** metrical formations[1]. In some cases it contains *five syllables*, e.g. in st. 7 *uṣāsānaktā,* in st. 10 *tvaṣṭā suvīram* (*suvīryam* ?), in st. 11 *tmanā deveṣu,* in st. 12 *indrāya havyam.*[2] We find in these

1. In st. 2-5 M has a distribution of the pādas among the ṛcas which is different from the two parallel texts and which would not agree with the rule given above. The version of M is, however, not acceptable on several grounds. In the case of the god Narāśaṁsa (st. 3) as well as Tanūnapāt (st. 2) we expect a reference to the *madhu* which is characteristic of both these gods (cf. ṚV I.13.2, 3: 142.2, 3): hence the pāda *madhvā yajñam* etc. belongs to the third (thus T V) and not to the second (as in M) stanza. The fourth stanza as in M cannot be properly construed; the sentence which is without a predicate, viz. *īḍāno vahnir namasā* undoubtedly belongs to the preceding *achāyam eti śavasā ghṛtena* and this latter sentence with its *achā ... eti* offers for the otherwise unintelligible *agnim sruco adhvareṣu prayatsu* the obviously necessary completion (cf. ṚV V.21.2; VIII.60.2); therefore also the delimitation of st. 3, 4 is correct in T V and not in M. In st. 5 the redactor of M appears not to have felt as sufficient the obvious reference in *suprayasaḥ*(?) to *barhis* (cf. BR under *suprayā*) and that is why he has made an addition here; any decision, however, in this matter is uncertain on account of the very corrupt nature of the text.
2. To this list belongs also the *third* pāda of st. 9 which, as an exception, is not Triṣṭubh: *mahī gṛṇānā.*

pādas (⏓ – ⏓ – ⏓) the form of the five-syllabled Virāj line and of those five-syllabled pādas which appear in the Śakvarī lines (e.g. *evā hi śakraḥ* etc.). The following pādas contain *seven syllables*:[1] st. 2 *devo deveṣu devaḥ*, st. 6 *vratā dadante agneḥ*.[2] The following contain *nine syllables* : st. 1 *ūrdhvā śukrā śocīmṣi agneḥ*, st. 8 *agner jihvām abhi gṛṇītam*, st. 9 *iḍā sarasvatī bhāratī*. We can see that in these pādas there is a predominantly iambic rhythm; the number of their syllables is odd so that the cadence as a rule has the falling rhythm, as is the case with the Triṣṭubh which is related to them; the *even* number of syllables (6 or 8) is to be seen in the second pādas only of [**158**] st. 3-5: *narāśaṁso agne, īḍāno vahnir namasā, sa īm mandrā suprayasaḥ*(?)

We have thus obtained an idea of this metrical type in which a stanza consists of two Triṣṭubh pādas and in between them a pāda containing seven syllables (or nine syllables etc.) and now we shall turn to an investigation of ṚV X.105. Whatever doubts may arise in individual instances due to the obscure and in many respects hopelessly corrupt state of the text, the metrical type which we have just now described turns out to be the most clearly prevalent one: between two Triṣṭubh lines there is another which in this hymn is mostly a seven-syllabled pāda, as a rule of the following form ⏓ – ⏓ – ⏑ – ⏓[3]. We recognize easily the Triṣṭubh form in the *first* pādas of stanzas 1, 2, 3[4], 4, 10 and 11 (in addition 7, where instead of the Triṣṭubh we have the Jagatī); likewise in the *third* pādas of stanzas 2, 4, 5, 7, 8, 9 and 11. The seven-syllabled *second* pāda, depending on the

1. Cf. above [p. 35 f].
2. To this may be added a *third* pāda, viz. st. 8: *kṛṇutaṁ naḥ suiṣṭim.*
3. Stanza 11 with its five pādas can easily be reduced to the form of the stanza of three pādas: the second, and then also the third pāda of the normal metrical scheme have been used twice, so that the text is repeated with insignificant variation.
4. The comparison of stanzas 3 and 4, which are parallel in expression, leads to the conjecture *apāyor* (i.e. *apa ayor*) for *apa yor*: *without* them (i.e. the two *haris*) Indra is weak; *with* them, he is praised.

condition of the text, is found, with more or less certainty, in stanzas 1, 2, 4, 5, 7, 9, 10 and 11. To give an example we quote stanza 2 where we have the normal structure of the three pādas:

harī yasya ॥ *suyujā vivratā veḥ*
arvantā anu śepā
ubhā rajī na ॥ *keśinā patir dan.*

Deviations from this type which would only partly disappear even if we had a better text **[159]** are to be found in a third of the total number of pādas. Very often (once also in the second pāda of the stanza) we find Triṣṭubh lines with three instead of four syllables before the caesura [cf. p. 79 above]; e.g. in stanza 6c: *ṛbhur*[1] *na* ॥ *kratubhir mātariśvā* (so also in st. 3b, c, also probably in st. 6a). Nine-syllabled pādas, mostly ending with the falling rhythm of the Triṣṭubh cadence occur in 1c, 5a, 8a and 10c (e.g. *adhi yas tasthau keśavantā*). Finally, we have the following eight-syllabled pādas: 6b, 8b (this pāda possibly even seven-syllabled), and 9a.

The hymn I.120 (st. 1-9), to which we shall now turn, has, with the two hymns just described, this in common viz. the extent of the stanza which is of three pādas and, further, the combination, which turns out to be regular, of two Triṣṭubh lines[2] with one anomalous line. But the arrangement of the three pādas is different; the anomalous line is placed regularly at the end of the stanza. It is sometimes a seven-syllabled line (st. 2, 5, 6, 8), sometimes a nine-syllabled line (st. 1, 3) and has in the end-portion the falling Triṣṭubh rhythm *ākṣī śubhas patī dan, stanābhujo' aśiśvīḥ, kathā vidhāti apracetāḥ etc.*). In st. 4c we find a line

---

1. In itself we can think of a two-syllabled scansion of the vowel *ṛ* as we shall show in a later section.
2. I regard verse 3b as Triṣṭubh having the anomaly mentioned above [p. 67]; also a appears to me to be a Triṣṭubh-pāda which is corrupt in the end.

consisting of 13 syllables with a similar end (*pātaṁ ca sahyaso yuvaṁ ca rabhyaso naḥ*). In st. 3 the first place is taken by a nine-syllabled pāda and apparently also in st. 1; in st. 1 and 2 seven-syllabled pādas occupy the second place. The difficult st. 7 consists of four partially obscure pādas; in the third pāda there may be the nine-syllabled type which occurs frequently in these hymns (*tā no vasū sugopā syātaṁ*)[1]. Finally, stanza 9 is made up of three lines in Triṣṭubh, **[160]** of which the third pāda is a repetition of the second with minor variation and thus marks the end of the hymn.

There still remain in two more passages freer metrical structures which do not share the peculiarities of the three sūktas examined above; in the tṛca VIII.46.14-16 and in the refrain of the magial charm I.191.10-13. It appears that each stanza of that tṛca ends in one or more exclamation-like words going beyond the metre, as they very often appear at the end of the stanza in the song-books of the SV: st. 14 *yathā*, st. 15 *nūnam atha*, st. 16 *nūnam aty atha*, or perhaps, if one may try to secure a regular Jagatī ending, *yato nūnam aty atha*, from the preceding obscure *kṛpayato*, which would mean that there remains something like *kṛpā*(?) as the end of the preceding pāda. If we disregard these small appendages to the three stanzas, then they show in their main part the following forms: st. 14: Gāyatrī-pāda, a five-syllabled part[2], Gāyatrī-pāda, Jagatī-pāda.—st. 15, 16: each with two Jagatīpādas.

The refrain which appears after stanzas 10 and 11 in I.191 and with certain alterations also after stanzas 12 and 13 shows the irregular sequence of seven-syllabled and six-syllabled pādas. Thus, stanza 10 = stanza 11:

---

1. Or, Triṣṭubh by two- syllabled scansion of *ā* in *sugopā* and by reading *siātam*?

2. *madeṣu gāya*; for similar sections see above [p. 157]. That we have to divide this way and that *abhi vo vīram andhaso madeṣu* is not to be regarded as a Triṣṭubh line is confirmed by the word-division in the Sāman form of the stanza.

(7) *so cin nu na marāti*
(6) *no vayam marāma*
(7) *āre' asya yojanam*
(6) *hariṣṭhā madhu tvā*
(6) *madhulā cakāra.*

[161] May I mention in connection with these six-syllabled lines the well-known stanzas of the Pañcālas[1] cited in the Nidānasūtra which have quite a similar rhythm?

Finally, in this same connection we may allude to the isolated fragmentary stanza X.20.1 *bhadram no' api vātaya manaḥ.*[2] We can easily see that these words are borrowed from one of the hymns (X.25.1) that follow :

bhadram no' api vātaya
mano dakṣam uta kratum[3]

It is therefore clear that in this fragment we cannot speak of a metre except in so far as the metre of the passage from which it is borrowed is meant. How is it, however, that this fragment of a stanza comes to be at the place where we find it? The passage appears at the beginning of the Vimada hymns, of a group which is characterized as a collection standing by itself on account of certain striking characteristics. It is perhaps not due to accident that this collection—after that fragment *bhadraṁ no* etc. which stands at the outset—begins with just those words with which begins the whole Ṛgveda : *agnim īḷe.* Now there was a wide-spread custom in the Brāhmaṇa period as well as in the Sūtra period to begin the recitation of certain passages of the text with a request for correct recitation and hearing and with benedictory words of a similar import; formulae of this type are found not seldom prefixed to the texts concerned as if they belonged to them. Thus we read before Ait. Āraṇyaka

1. Indische Studien VIII.90.
2. As is well known, according to Yāska this is the only *ekapadā* in the Ṛgveda (Prātiśākhya 993).
3. Bollensen (ZDMG XXXV.452) sees here a blunder of the copyist who skipped some pages at the beginning of X.20 and resumed at X.25.1: a view inadmissible due to obvious basic reasons.

I, Tai. Ār. I etc. **[162]** the stanza like *śivā naḥ śantamā bhava sumṛḍīkā sarasvati* etc.; so also the stanza *bhadraṁ karṇebhiḥ śruṇuyāma devāḥ* (ṚV I.89.8), and other similar lines. These parallel passages in my opinion do not leave any doubt whatsoever as regards the significance of this fragmentary stanza before us: it was a prayer, taken over from one of the Vimada hymns, in which the reciter who proceeded with this section invoked the deity for the correct disposition[1].

---

[163]

Supplement

Vowels treated as Equivalent to two Syllables

In our above discussion of the lines of stanzas which fall short of the normal number of syllables (see pp. 35 f.) we have not taken into consideration a case which, according to the interpretation of several scholars, would belong to that type of metrical anomaly: the deficiency of one syllable in the number required by the metre which is seen repeatedly especially where the genitive plural forms in *-ām* occur, but also in a mumber of other forms and words (e.g. *akṣār, pānti, śreṣṭha* etc.).

Are we to regard these as cases of the obfuscation by tradition of the forms of words used by the poet, or are we to seek the explanation of the phenomenon on metrical grounds? For instance, is a pāda like

rājantam adhvarānām

to be pronounced as written here following the tradition, and be explained metrically by importing some idea like catalexis, or are we to read it as

rājantam adhvarāṇaam

1. It has also to be noted that the hymn as it stands now of ten stanzas is indeed in the Varga division not according to the prevailing rule as 5 plus 5, but as 6 plus 4 stanzas: a definite proof that the arranger of the Vargas did not count the first 'stanza'. As is well known the stanza has also not been divided into padas in the Padapāṭha.

so that its metrical form will correspond exactly with the norm ?

For deciding this question we should have first of all a clear idea of the facts in all their details. We must, **[164]** on the one hand, show how far this particular phenomenon is bound to certain definite places in the metrical scheme and, on the other, in what words and forms it reveals itself.

If we in the first place confine ourselves to the case, which occurs most often and in its individual occurrences is least doubtful, of the genitive plural in *-ām*[1] we find, first, inside the eight-syllabled (Gāyatrī-) line[2] that syllable appearing as equivalent of two syllables in a number of different positions. Most often the syllable *-ām* occurs in the seventh and the eighth places. Thus, for instance, in the hymn VIII.39 alone we have :

2. *tanūṣu śamsam eṣām*
4. *urjāhutir vasūnām*
5. *sa hotā śaśvatīnām*
6. *agnir jātā devānām*
   agnir veda martānām [cf. above p. 40].

Next come numerous cases in which this syllable occupies the fifth and the sixth places in the Gāyatrī line, e.g.:

VIII. 40.2 *śaviṣṭham nṛṇām naram*
46.22 *daśa śyāvīnām śatā*
53.3 *ā no viśveṣām rasam.*

But this use of *-ām* is to be observed also in the first half of the Gāyatrī-pāda although it is considerably rarer there. Thus, in the third and the fourth syllables:

VIII. 25.23 *harīṇām nitośanā*
31.15 f. *devānām ya' in manaḥ*
41.2 *pitṝṇām ca manmabhiḥ.*

---

1. That the genitives formed with a nasal, a sibilant (in the pronominal inflection), or merely with *-ām* are to be considered in the same manner has been shown already by Kuhn in his Beitr. IV.180.
2. Obviously it makes no difference whether the combination in which the line occurs is Gāyatrī, or Anuṣṭubh, or Pragātha etc.

[165] Finally in an isolated case in the second and the third syllables :

VIII. 20.14 *teṣām hi dhunīnām.*

Thus in the second half of the pāda, which more or less as a rule requires an iambic rhythm, that *-ām* which is the equivalent of two syllables occurs in all places where an iambus falls. In the first half of the pāda which enjoys greater, although not complete, freedom from the iambic rhythm, *-ām* occurs at least in an overwhelming number of cases in an analogous position. However, besides in the first and the second syllables, where its occurrence is naturally impossible, it is excluded from those pairs of syllables where the second one is short, i.e. the fourth and fifth, and the sixth and seventh.

If we now turn to the Triṣṭubh and the Jagatī metres, we come across exactly analogous situations. We find that *-ām*, first, very often occurring in such a way that it fills in the second and the third place after the caesura, thus in a complex which in its regular form begins with a short syllable. This occurs specially frequently in two-syllabled genitives like *apām* (cf. Grassmann s.v.; Lanman p. 484), *purām, girām* which are regarded as equivalent of an anapaest: this is just the only place where the Vedic metres easily tolerate an anapaest. E.g.:

I. 61.12 *iṣyann arṇāṁsi* || *apāṁ caradhyai*
122.3 *mamattu vāto* || *apāṁ vṛṣaṇvān*
VI. 24.1 *dyukṣo rājā* || *girām akṣitotiḥ.*

In the same manner genitive forms with three syllables like *marutām* fit in in such a way in a line that *-ām* fills the third and the fourth place after the caesura: that is to say when the caesura occurs after the fourth syllable of the pāda those two syllables have in the regular metrical scheme the scansion ⏑̲ _ . E.g.

[166] V. 56.1 *viśo' adya* || *marutām ava hvaye*
VI. 48.12 *yā mṛḷīke* || *marutām turāṇām*
VIII. 20.3 *śuṣmam ugram* || *marutāṁ śimīvatām.*

Then we also find it in the cadence of the Jagatī in the place of the iambus (i.e. in the fourth and the third place from the end or the penultimate and the last syllables);[1] further before the caesura in a Jagatī or in a Triṣṭubh line especially in the third and the fourth syllables, thus again at a place where the metrical tendency favours the iambus. If I cannot give illustrations of the occurrence of that *-ām* in the third and the penultimate position from the end of a Triṣṭubh (with the scansion ∪ _), this is simply due to the fact that then the pāda must end with a monosyllabic word after the genitive plural. I cite a few illustrations of the cases mentioned:

VII.	35.13	*śaṁ no' apāṁ* ǀǀ *napāt perur astu*[2]
	56.24	*janānāṁ* ǀǀ *yo' asuro vidhartā*
VIII.	70.12	*dharmāṇāṁ na* ǀǀ *saṁ gṛbhāya asmayuḥ*
	71.13	*agnir iṣām* ǀǀ *sakhie dadātu naḥ*
	60.9	*pāhi gīrbhis* ǀǀ *tisṛbhir ūrjāṁ pate*
VII.	32.5	*śravac chrutkarṇa'* ǀǀ *īyate vasūnām*
	32.7	*bhavā varūthaṁ* ǀǀ *maghavan maghonām.*

From what has been said up to now we can expect that in the five-syllabled Virāj (⏓ _ ∪ _ ⏓ _) the use of the genitive in *-ām,* described here, can hardly be a frequent one; this syllable must, in order to form the equivalent of an iambus, occupy the third syllable from the end or the penultimate syllable and the line must close with a monosyllabic word after the genitive plural. Thus, for instance, if we go through the Virāj hymns of Parāśara **[167]** collection (I.65-70) then, while according to the circumstances existing elsewhere we would be justified in expecting a number of cases of the two-syllabled *-ām* in the numerous genitive forms, we actually find only a single

1. The occurrences of *-ām* at the end of Jagatī are doubtful inasmuch as, as is well known, for the Jagatī lines Triṣṭubh lines are very often substituted.
2. Or is it that here the *ā* in *napāt* is to be treated as constituting two syllables ?

passage, viz. I.67.10 *cittir apām*. If we do not choose, following the example of I.70.3 (*garbho yo' apām*), to read here *cittir yo' apām*— which change, however, is a doubtful way out— then *-ām* actually would occupy the place of two syllables of the form — ⏑̲ in the metrical scheme. It is evident that an isolated case of that type[1] cannot be a sufficient proof against the result so far arrived at for the metrical value of the *-ām*, the more so as the occurrence, by way of exception, of a short syllable in the penultimate place in the Virāj line is by no means rare.

Before we proceed from the genitive forms discussed so far to the examination of other cases, we summarize the result obtained as follows: the genitive forms in disyllabic *-ām* whose first syllable is short occur in most diverse positions in most diverse metres[2]. Above [p. 35] we have expressed the opinion that the occasional appearance of 'catelectic' pādas or of pādas defective in other places than the end has to be admitted in the Ṛgveda: but it seems to be clear that here we have a phenomenon which has nothing in common with that of disyllabic *-ām* but the accidental and superficial coincidence of the fact that here as well as **[168]** there the text in its transmitted form is each time deficient by one syllable. The extraordinary frequency of this phenomenon which we are discussing, its connection with certain words or components of words having a long vowel, as especially with the genitives in *-ām*, its not being connected with any

1. Both the cases of the metrical scansion ⏑ — given by Kuhn (Beitr. IV.180 end) viz. IV.1.19 and X.88.6 are absolutely doubtful.
2. In some passages (e.g. in V.24) after Gāyatrī lines we find small independent metrical feet with the scansion ⏑ — ⏑ ⏑̲ [see above p. 112]. If I mistake not, there is not a single case of the two syllabled *-ām* among them, and obviously this is an accident such as can be easily understood on account of the great rarity of these feet. We have instances of other long vowels to be treated as two syllables also in those feet, e.g. *rayiṁ dāḥ* in st. 2 and *samasmāt* in st. 3 of V.24.

particular place in the metrical line[1] make it palpably different from the phenomenon of catalexis. We must regard it rather as a definite peculiarity of just that long vowel with which we are concerned: we have to say either that in this long vowel is hidden just a two-syllabled complex obscured by the tradition, or that the Vedic poets must have attributed to *this* long vowel, as distinguished from the other long vowels, the capacity to occupy the place of two syllables of the metrical scheme: which obviously would point to an opposition between over-long and simple long vowels. We shall later have to return to the discussion of this problem and here only remark that the course which Lanman has adopted in his description of the nominal flexion—to separate a part of the pertinent cases from the evaluation of the remaining ones which are in fact absolutely analogous—appears to us the most inadmissible of all those proposed: viz. to speak of 'catalectic pāda' when this *-ām* occurs at the end of a Gāyatrī- or Jagatī-pāda, but to allow the resolution of *-ām* into *-aam* in other metrical positions. The fact that in both cases we are dealing with a phenomenon first connected with the *-ām* and then with a certain group of other syllables leaves no doubt that at the end of the Gāyatrī or Jagatī this phenomenon must be explained in the same way as in all the remaining places of the metres.

[169] We have found so far that of the two vowels into which the *ā* of the ending *-ām* is to be split or whose place in some way or the other it occupies, the first is a short vowel[2]: we shall now investigate the quantity of the second vowel. Since this *-ām* most frequently occurs at the end of the line, or is followed by a consonant which makes the preceding syllable long by position, a decision of this problem is made difficult; I believe, all the same, that

1. Should one assume that the four-syllabled line mentioned in the preceding note is also to be regarded as of the 'catalectic' form (∪ — —)?
2. Moreover, this is also to be expected by itself on the strength of the rule *vocalis ante vocalem*.

complete statistics of all the cases which come for consideration make it possible to arrive at a rather sure decision. If we find that when the metre requires long quantity in the place corresponding to the second of the two vowels in all such cases or in disproportionately overwhelming number of cases, there is a consonant following, then we may conclude that the long quantity, due to position, is a necessity, that is the vowel itself is short. These cases that we have to consider for this investigation show us that the vowel in question partly occupies the fourth place from the end of the Triṣṭubh or, what comes to the same thing, the fifth place from the end of the Jagatī, partly— rather frequently —the third place from the end of the Gāyatrī and, in quite isolated cases, the penultimate of the Triṣṭubh, respectively the third place from the end of the Jagatī. I find that *in* 86 *passages* of the ṚV of the type described a consonant follows -*ām* and that there are only the following exceptions to these passages: *eṣām* I.134.6; *narām* I.167.10; *marutām* V.56.1; *pathām* VII.73.3[1]; *somānām* VIII.93.33; to these are to be added the following which, on account of the special metrical nature of the pertinent sūktas, are doubtful: *apām* X.46.1; *damām* X.46.7; finally *martānām* I.163.5 provided we do not have to read there *martiānām.*

[170] It appears clear to me that on the strength of this evidence we may affirm that the quantity of the second vowel contained in -*ām* is short. The cases which would indicate the long quantity of this vowel are by themselves disproportionately few[2]; and further it is to be noted that

---

1. The text is presumably corrupt. Cf. Gaedick, Accusativ, p. 183. Should we read *pathiām* ?
2. The following remarks may show what is proportionate and what is disproportionate here. Let us assume that -*ām* is not, as I think it is, equivalent to -*aam*, but to -*aām*. Let us now count in any section of the Veda those cases in which a Gāyatrī line has in the third but last place (where alone a long syllable is regularly required) a word-final

(Continued on next page)

the fourth place from the end of Triṣṭubh and the corresponding place of Jagatī, which are concerned in the majority of those cases, permits comparatively frequently just at the word-end a short vowel instead of the long one which would be required by the rule [see p. 59 f].

The evidence so far adduced showing that the ending *-ām* cannot just replace two syllables but that the *ā* in it is equivalent to two short syllables and that in order to make this ending **[171]** an iambus foot, position must be added by a following consonant will contribute to strengthen our conviction that the ground for explaining the two-syllabled scansion in question is not to be sought in any metrical syncope, but in the peculiar linguistic nature of the syllables in question, or at least—but this supposition has perhaps a less probability—in a peculiar quality conferred on them by the traditional artificial practice of the Vedic recitation.

(Continued from previous page)

syllable which stands in the same conditions as that *-ām* containing *-aām*, and observe how often it is followed by a consonant, how often by a vowel. But under the same conditions as of that syllable stands only a syllable with long vowel and final consonant: if it had a short vowel, then for metrical reasons the tendency would prevail to have the following word begin with consonant: if the syllable ended in a vowel then also this would lead to preferring the next word which begins with a consonant, if we consider the predominant aversion to hiatus and the shortening effect of a following vowel on the preceding vowel. Only the word-finals in *ai, au* and *pragṛhya*-vowels, since they are not affected by the doubts mentioned, would still have to be considered in the statistics. In the investigation of the long Gāyatrī section IX.61-67, conducted according to the criteria delineated, I have found the following: syllables of the kind described are followed by words beginning with a consonant 2 times, by words beginning with a vowel 21 times, besides we have once the case, just being discussed, of the gen. pl. (64.10 : *priyaḥ kavīnām matī*). In similar statistics regarding the fourth but last syllable of Triṣṭubh-lines I found in VII.1-3, besides six occurrences of vocalic word-initial only five of consonantal word-initial (among them 3 after a *pragṛhya* vowel). Even without carrying out further similar statistics, one can easily see that the preponderance by 17 times of the consonantal word-initial after the disyllabic *-ām* arrived at above cannot be accidental.

Now we must raise the question, how far the conclusion just reached can be generalized: are also others of those disyllabic vowels as the *ā* of the ending *-ām* to be counted as two short vowels and as iambus only in the case of position?

The investigation of this problem has been rendered considerably difficult on account of the fact that Vedic prosody nowhere *requires* two short syllables one after another; in the end portions of Gāyatrī, Triṣṭubh and Jagatī, which have a relatively fixed scansion, we always find an alternation of short and long syllables and only the place immediately following the caesura in the Triṣṭubh and the Jagatī prefers the succession of two short syllables, but this cannot even remotely be regarded as a rule. Hence, it is desirable to investigate the long vowels which are equivalent of two syllables coming before a single consonant as, for instance, the first syllable of *vātaḥ, bhāsā, sūraḥ*. These words have mostly in several of their often used cases a form which in trochaic or iambic scansion of the disyllabic vowel would be very convenient for the cadence of Gāyatrī, Triṣṭubh or Jagatī; if they are not found at these places and instead show a remarkable preference for the place immediately after the Triṣṭubh caesura then we are **[172]** justified in concluding that this vowel is a pyrrhic foot.

We may now consider the following series of passages[1]: *dāsa:*[2] I.104.2; II.20.6, 7; V.33.4; VI.26.5; X.23.2; 49.6, 7; in all these eight passages[3] we have this word (in the forms

1. Of course, I am making use of the collections made by Grassmann, although they require to be corrected and supplemented considerably.
2. It is superfluous to make a distinction between the word as accented on the first and on the second syllable (*dā́sa* and *dāsá*).
3. Besides these there are still other passages, metrically incharacterisitc, such as VI.20.10; VIII.46.32; X.148.2; finally II.11.4 which is doubtful on account of the peculiar metrical practice governing the concerned hymn. —In VI.25.2 Kuhn and Grassmann have wrongly treated the vowel *ā* as having the scansion ◡ —.

dāsam, dāsīḥ dāsasya) immediately after the caesura, that is in the only place in which the Vedic metre definitely prefers a pyrrhic foot. In Daivodāsaḥ VIII.103.2, the quantity of the first vowel contained in *ā* cannot be ascertained; the second vowel is short.

Sudās, dāsvant: I.63.7; VII.32.10. The first of these passages gives evidence for the short quantity of the first, and the second for the short quantity of the second component in -*ā*. As proofs of the short quantity of the first component there are two more passages containing the form *sudāstarāya*, viz. I.184.1; 185.9, and on account of the position naturally they can give no information about the second component. The same can be said about *dāsvant* of which several forms are found with a two-syllabled scansion of *ā* in the most different metrical positions[1]: the short quanity of the first element is sure throughout.

[173] *vāta* : I.174.5; 180.6; 186.10; VII.40.6; IX.97.52; X.22.4, 5; 23.4; 158.1. In all these places except the last (*vātaḥ* is in the beginning of an eight-sylabled line) *vātaḥ* or *vātasya* stands immediately after the caesura.

vāja : I.63.9; 162.22; II.31.7; IV.37.4; VI.13.1; VII.48.1. The forms *vājaḥ, vājāḥ, vājam, vājī, vājinaḥ* stand immediately after the caesura[2].

bhās : VI.10.4; VIII.23.11; X.3.1[3]: Only *bhāḥ* at the end of the Gāyatrī, so that the second short quantity in the vowel standing as two syllables has the benefit of the prosodial freedom of the verse-end; elsewhere (in the form *bhāsā*) the *ā* always comes immediately after the caesura in the place favouring a pyrrhic. The first and the third of the cited

1. See the citations in Grassmann. According to Gr. only *once* (II.4.3) the *ā* does not count as two syllables; but even there that metrical scansion is at least possible. So also I cannot bring myself to accept the view of Joh. Schmidt (Vocalismus II.264) according to which the *ā* in IV.2.7 makes one syllable.
2. IV.3.12 (and VI.45.29?) has no significance metrically.
3. VIII.1.28 is not significant; X.77.5 is doubtful.

passages give for the *ā,* although not with certainty the scansion ∪ ∪, yet rather dependably ∪̲ ∪; the second passage gives ∪ ∪̲ ; from the combination of both the results we can deduce the scansion ∪ ∪.

sūra, sūri, sūria[1] :

I. 61.3? *suvṛktibhiḥ* ॥ *sūriṁ vāvṛdhadhyai*
71.9 *ekaḥ satrā* ॥ *sūro vasva' īśe*
122.15 *syūmagabhastiḥ* ॥ *sūro na adyaut*
II. 11.20 *avartayat* ॥ *sūrio na cakram*
19.3 *ajanayat* ॥ *sūriam vidad gāḥ*
VI. 51.2 *abhi̤ caṣṭe* ॥ *sūro' arya' evān*
VIII. 46.24 *maṁhiṣṭhaḥ* ॥ *sūrir abhūt*
X. 59.5 *rārandhi naḥ* ॥ *sūriasya saṁdṛśi*[2].

[174] *pāyu*:

VII. 37.8 *sadā no divyaḥ* ॥ *pāyuḥ siṣaktu.*

The second passage II.1.7 in which *pāyu* appears with a two-syllabled scansion of *ā* is metrically not significant. Yet I shall take this occasion to point out that in the other forms of the concerned root *pā* the cases of two-syllabled scansion of *ā* are distributed in a remarkably uneven manner : this scansion, for instance, appears practically in only those forms—and in these quite frequently—which have a conjunct consonant after[3] *ā* (*pānti, pāntu, pāntam, pāntaḥ;* besides, also in the one-syllabled *pāt* which can conceivably not be evidence against our observation); the forms *pāti, pātu, pāhi* which are rather often used do not offer any sure example of the particular phenomenon that we are investigating[4].

1. I.149.3 and IX.111.1 have no metrical significance. The inclusion of VII.82.3 here is not justified. The two-syllabled scansion of *ū* in I.180.6 also is not probable.
2. X.37.6 is exactly similar, but without the *ū* having to be scanned as two-syllabled.
3. See Grassmann s.v.
4. Only *pāhi* I.129.11. There is little probability of a two-syllabled scansion of *pātu* and *pāhi* in X.158.1 and 2; I.120.7 (*pātam*) is metrically quite unclear.

This situation need not cause any surprise if we accept the scansion of two shorts for the two-syallabled *ā*: then, and only then, is explained the fact that for the Vedic versifier the form *pānti* (*paanti*) was more handy to use, than *pāti* (*paati*) with its three short syllables, which on account of the vocalic final, offered a considerably stiffer opposition to the metre than the short vowels in *vātaḥ, apām, dāsam* (*vaataḥ* etc.).

vīra, vīria:[1]

I. 61.14[2] *sadyo bhuvad* ॥ *vīriāya Nodhāḥ*
VI. 21.6, 8 *arcāmasi* ॥ *vīra brahmavāhaḥ*
brahmaṇyato ॥ *vīra kārudhāyaḥ*

[175] *dās'*[3]:

I. 61.11[4] *īśānakṛd* ॥ *dāśuṣe daśasyan*
76.1 *kena vā te* ॥ *manasā dāśema*
II. 20.2 *tuam ino* ॥ *dāśuṣo varūtā.*[5]

The second passage would indicate a trochaic scansion of the *ā* of *dāśema.* For the rest, the two-syllabled nature of the *ā* in this passage is not quite sure. Apart from the possibility which can be considered here as in many other passages viz. that in the case of the caesura after the fourth syllable the pāda might continue as though the caesura had come after the fifth syllable—as a consequence of which the deficiency of a syllable becomes explicable without there

1. Not metrically characterized: I.61.5(?); II.4.9(?); V.29.13; X.85.44. In the last passage we cannot be sure about the two-syllabled scansion of *ī*.
2. Uncertain on account of the peculiar metrical procedure followed in this sūkta.
3. Not characterized : *dadāśus* in I.147.1.
4. Uncertain on account of the peculiar metrical procedure followed in this sūkta.
5. One should take into consideration how conveniently *dāśuṣe, dāśuṣaḥ* would have suited the end of the Gāyatrī- or Jagati-pāda if the iambic scansion of *ā* had appeared permissible to the Vedic poets.

being need for a vowel to be treated as two syllables[1]— the question may also be raised whether in this example we should not rather take the *vā* as having the scansion of two syllables, as possibly in I.83.6 : *arko vā* || *ślokam āghoṣate divi.*

In any case in all these cases that we have so far considered, which are altogether different from one another, in the case of the word-final *-ām* with its aversion to the metrical places favourable to the trochee and its preference to occur at the end of the line or before a consonant and, on the other hand, in the case of opening syllables of words like *vāta, bhāsā* etc. with their preference for a place immediately after the caesura—for all these cases we arrive at the same conclusion viz.: a long vowel to be scanned as two syllables in all these words or parts of words has the value of two *short syllables.*

[176] I refrain from making further listings which can be easily extended to not a small number of those vowels occurring less frequently with the scansion of two syllables. Instead, I would list a few cases in which the equivalence of a long vowel with short ones is not indicated with the same definiteness by the metre.

Nom. pl. in *-āsas*[2]

There are a number of cases which agree with the conditions observed elsewhere: the first component of *ā* appears in a place where preferably the short syllable occurs; the quantity of the second component remains undecided:

I. 127.7 *dvitā yad īṁ* || *kīstāso' abhidyavaḥ*
VI. 67.10 *vi yad vācaṁ* || *kīstāso bharante*[3]

1. See above p. 68 f.
2. Compare Kuhn Beitr. IV.183. The passages are not of the sort that the two-syllabled scansion of *ā* would be firmly established.
3. Or should in these illustrative passages the *ī* of *kīsta* be scanned as a two-syllabled one ?

44.8 *śriye manāṁsi* ॥ *devāso' akran*[1]
63.7 *ā vām vayo'* ॥ *aśvāso vahiṣṭhāḥ*[2].

To this a few cases are to be added in which the question arises whether the change of *marta* to *martia* should not supply the deficient syllable; *martāsaḥ* occurs twice after the caesura, and three times in a place which is metrically indifferent.[3]

I. 38.4 *martāsaḥ siātana*
VI. 15.8 *devāsaś ca* ॥ *martāsaś ca jāgṛvim*
VII. 4.3 *yaṁ martāsaḥ* ॥ *śietam jagṛbhre*
25.2 *abhi ye no* ॥ *martāso' amanti*
VIII. 81.3 *na martāso' ditsantam*

[**177**] The metrical characteristic is lacking further in

I. 191.3 *śarāsaḥ kuśarāsaḥ.*

This is the first pāda of an Anuṣṭubh of the later period in which the end-part of the first and the third pāda of this metre had already broken off from the old rule (above p. 28). Next

VII. 97.6 *taṁ śagmāso'* ॥ *aruṣāso' aśvāḥ,*

provided here the *ā* of *śagmāsaḥ*[4] in fact is to be resolved into two vowels; but if we choose the *ā* of *aruṣāsaḥ,* then for metrical reasons the scansion of that vowel would be $\underline{\cup}$ —.

No definite metrical characteristic is available also in

II. 4.9 *suvīrāso'*[5] ॥ *abhimātiṣāhaḥ*
V. 41.17 *devāso* ॥ *vanate martio vaḥ.*

---

1. The scansion of this pāda as Triṣṭubh is not absolutely sure; we might take it to be the ten-syllabled Virāj.
2. Either *ā* or *vām* can be scanned as two-syllabled; perhpas also we may read *aśuāso.*
3. But also the metre justifies in I.38.4 and VII.4.3 to prefer the reading *martiāsaḥ* to the two-syllabled scansion of *ā.*
4. Without such a resolution of the *ā* into two syllables we could use the sonantic value [Stimmton] developed between *g* and *m* of *śagmāsaḥ* to fill in the metrical gap.
5. However, cf. note 3 on p. 174.

As real exceptions there remain, or would remain, if the metrical practice was fixed and without exceptions:

VIII. 2.10 *tīvrā' asme sutāsaḥ* (*ā* = — ∪)
X. 114.10 *rathasya dhūrṣu* || *yuktāso' asthuḥ* (*ā* = ∪—).

Then again, if the pāda concerned is to be scanned rather as Triṣṭubh than as Jagatī:

VIII. 26.22 *sutāvanto* || *vāyum dyumnā janāsaḥ* (*ā*= — ∪).

For iambic scansion of *ā* can hardly be cited V.43.14:

vipanyavo || *rāspirāso' agman.*

Here probably the first *ā* in *rāspirāsaḥ* is to be scanned as two syllables; cf. *rāspinasya* I.122.4

Suffix -*āna:*

Most of the passages do not yield any results from the prosodial point of view: **[178]** I.127.3; IV.3.14;[1] 21.5; VI.15.4; 44.8; 63.2(?); VIII.1.19; IX.18.7; 97.31; X.132.1 Apart from the doubtful, but in no way contradictory, passage I.61.13, the following agree with our rule (*ā* = ∪ ∪):

VII. 95.4 *eṣā siā* || *yujānā parākāt*
X. 30.9 *madacyutam* || *auśānaṁ nabhojām*(?)

In conflict with the rule, and at the same time with one another, are three, not at all sure, passages of which the first would yield iambic, the following two trochaic scansion of the *ā*:

IV. 4.1 *tṛṣvīm anu* || *prasitiṁ drūṇānaḥ*[2]

1. It appears that the *ā* of *rārakṣāṇaḥ*, not that of *prīṇānaḥ* (rather *priṇānaḥ)* is to be treated as two-syllabled.
2. It is perhaps possible to avoid completely resorting to a two-syllabled scansion. We have to read *druṇānaḥ* for *drūṇānaḥ*; *prasitiṁ druṇānaḥ* shows such a normal metrical form that we would like to avoid touching it by adopting a two-syllabled scansion.
3. It is from a dānastuti; the additional syllable may be obtained also by reading *yat* as *iat* or *tvā* as *tuā*.

VIII. 24.30[3] *yat tvā pṛcchād ījānaḥ*
101.9[1] *antaḥ pavitra' ‖ upari śrīṇānaḥ.*

mātar[2]*:*

There is no metrical significance in I.89.4 and X.79.3; the following fits in with our rule

X. 94.10 *krīḷayo na ‖ mātaraṁ tudantaḥ.*

The following goes against it

V. 7.8 *suṣūr asūta mātā* (*ā* = — ◡).

pūṣan:

The following would comply with the predominant rule (*ū* = ◡̲ ◡):

[179] I. 89.6 *suasti naḥ ‖ pūṣā viśvavedāḥ*
X. 26.3 *indur na pūṣā vṛṣā.*

The following goes against it (with *ū* = — ◡)

X. 26.4, 8 *asmākaṁ deva pūṣan*
ā te rathasya pūṣan.

śūra:

I. 122.10 *viśvāsu pṛtsu ‖ sadam ic chūraḥ*
II. 11.5 *ahann ahiṁ ‖ śūra vīrieṇa*
X. 78.4 *jigīvāṁso na ‖ śūra' abhidyavaḥ*][3].

The first of these passages would give an iambic scansion of *ū*.

maghon:

In some passages the forms *maghonas* and *maghonos* appear (see Grassmann) in such a way that metrically we

1. Read *śriṇānaḥ*. There is no need of a two-syllabled scansion if we accept the metre to be Triṣṭubh and not Jagati, which we have to do, for instance, for the first pāda of st. 10.
2. None of the passages confirms a two-syllabled scansion of *ā* with any certainty. In I.89.4 we can easily read *tan no mātā* and in X.79.3 and 94.14 respectively a svarabhakti of *pra* and of *krīḷayaḥ* could help.
3. Both the passages in brackets prove nothing on account of the peculiar nature of the metre of the two sūktas II.11 and X.78 (cf. above pp. 87 and 92). I.173.5 *yaḥ śūro ‖ maghavā yo ratheṣṭhāḥ* also is doubtful. Rather than the scansion of *ū* as two-syllabled, it is better to read *yaḥ* as *iaḥ* which has to be done at so many places, and avoid the unpopular opening — ◡ ◡ —.

would require two syllables with the scansion — ∪ in the place of *o*. If we do not take this as an instance of metrical inexactness, which would be quite unobjectionable, then we can easily think of the stem *maghāvan* (cf. *ṛṇāvan, ṛtāvan, aśvāvant* along with *aśvavant* etc.) for these forms from which *maghāvanas, maghāvanos* can be derived.

It appeared to me appropriate to discuss separately the above words and forms; one or two more absoulutely sporadic instances where metrically the long vowels concerned are to be regarded as an iambus or as a trochee would add nothing new to the situation as detailed above. Besides, the passages which seem to exhibit that prosodial **[180]** characteristic are so few, and moreover they come partly from a metrically degenerate environment or are in other ways doubtful, that we need not hesitate, when especially we pay due regard to the clear possibility of real deviations from the metrical norm everywhere in the Veda, to recognize the equivalence of vowels, to be scanned as two syllables, with *two short quanities,* at least as the widely prevailing one.

In what manner have we to make clear to ourselves that equivalence of long vowels with a two-syllabled complex? We have already pointed out above [p. 168] that this phenomenon, bound not so much to certain metrical places but to certain words and forms, can have nothing to do with any such idea as that of catalexis. Either the antithesis between the extra-long and long vowels comes into play here and that the former are able, in whatever place of the metre they may be, to represent two short syllables or, with additional position, an iambus: or those vowels were pronounced actually as a two-syllabled complex or something like it. However unwilling we may be, if we look at the question only from the linguistic point of view, to make up our mind to accept the formations *bhaasā, devānaam* and the like, burdened with the hiatus, yet in my opinion, if we take into account all the circumstances of the case, there is an overwhelming probability in favour of the *factual existence* of such forms to be postulated in the Veda, no matter whether its linguistic *explanation* is easy or difficult for us. Above all it seems to me an almost decisive factor that, as proved by the prosody of the Avesta, a number of the most outstanding and reliable cases of the two-syllabled scansion of vowels in the Veda can be traced **[181]** back to the Indo-Iranian period and that this is preserved by both these peoples in a uniform manner: thus the Avesta shows independently of the place in the metre where the form concerned occurs the two-syllabled scansion for the genitive plural in *-ām*, in the forms from roots ending in *ā* such as *dāṯ, pāṯ, gāṯ*, in the genitive singular *gǝ̄us* (Ved. *gos*) and in the accusatives *gām, pantām, mām.*[1] Vedic lines such as *barhir na yat* ǁ *Sudāse vṛthā vark*, or *nakiḥ Sudāso ratham* are paralleled by a number of lines from the Gāthā stanzas where several case forms of the stem *hudāh* always point to a two-syllabled scansion of *ā* (*āo*) (Bartholomae, *Gāthās* 7, 96, 166): the agreement thus extends to a number of cases from which the identity of this phenomenon in India and Iran positively follows. Now it seems to be obvious that even if one would like to attribute such a subtle differentiation as that of the long *ā* and the extra long *ā* to the poetry of the Indo-Iranian period, such nuances are much too fine than that they could with any degree of probability be expected to have in India and Iran equally survived all those influences which tend to level such differences. The mere fact of the high antiquity and the corresponding spread of that phenomenon in both the literatures appears to me to prove that here there must be something more tangible, more unambiguous and therefore more permanently resistant, than the mere difference between two long *ās* of different quantities: in other words it follows in my opinion that **[182]** the *-ām* representing two syllables is actually to be read as two syllables *-aam.*

---

1. Cf. Geldner, Metrik des jüngeren Avesta, pp. 9f., 12, 16 ff; A. Mayr, Sitzungsberichte der Wiener Akademie, 68 (1871), 758 ff.; Bartholomae, Gāthās, pp. 7f. and 171.

We are led to the same conclusion, in my opinion, as a consequence of the fact demonstrated above that, if not all, at lease many of those long vowels require position for representing an iambus. If the *ā* of these genitives is really to be pronounced as a continuous length occupying two places in the metrical scheme and if, as we see, the use of such a length in the iambic cadence is by itself not at all considered as obscuring the rhythm, then in the fact that *indro munīnāṁ sakhā* is considered correct, but e.g. *indro munīnām asat* would be not admissible or admissible only by way of licence—we would have in this fact an exaggerated subtlety which one might purely theoretically defend, whose actual occurrence however, in a field so opposed to all kinds of hair-splitting as Vedic prosody, will not be acceptable to any one who can distinguish the probable from improbable. And moreover: why does this *-ām*, with or without position, not amount also to a trochee ?

If we feel impelled to substitute for the monosyllabic form a two-syllabled one, then the opposition this procedure is expected to encounter will be least vigorous in some cases in which there is an *e*-diphthong and where it is the easiest to avoid a hiatus. If the words *śreṇi* and *śreṇiśas* in the ṚV always[1] require one syllable more than what is available in the traditional text-form [183] then the reading *śrayaṇi*[2] can in fact hardly be rejected. Similarly, the occurrence of a three-syllabled *tredhā* in an overwhelming number of cases beside the two-syllabled leads clearly to *trayadhā,* and along with *netar* and *praṇetar* we shall have to set up *nayitar* and *praṇayitar* (cf. *nayitum* in the Ait. Br. along with *netum*[3]).—Just as to the root *jū* belongs the superlative *javiṣṭha,* so to *prī, śrī* we might and must assume a three-syllabled *prayiṣṭha*

1. Not, as Grassmann says, often. Only *śreṇidan* occurring in the metrically problematic passage X.20.3 is not absolutely definite, but in any case it is not a contrary example.
2. I prefer this reading to the *śrayiṇi* proposed by Grassmann.
3. See also Saussure, Mémoire, p. 246, n. 1.

and *śrayiṣṭha* in the places where the traditional *preṣṭha* and *śreṣṭha* do not satisfy the metre.—In the case of the superlatives which belong to the roots ending in *-ā*, such as *jyeṣṭha, dheṣṭha*, the three-syllabled forms *jaïṣṭha* and *dhaïṣṭha* may have to be set up from which those forms have arisen.[1]

It will appear questionable to the linguist to allow a vowel group *aa*. Even in those cases in which the origin of two *a's* would be clear, as in the nominative plural of *a-* stems ending in *-aas*, the occurrence of hiatus still in those days when the Vedic Aryans were living separately will be conceded not without hesitation[2], and altogether the forms like *devānaam* or *asthaat*, whose employment in the known (metrical) contexts appears for the time being difficult or impossible, will be opposed by those doubts even more strongly. I believe that the investigator of the Vedic texts has, contrary to this, at least an *approximate* justification to affirm that *davānaam* and *asthaat* are, for once, vouched for by a sufficiently definite tradition **[184]** and it is immaterial whether at present it can or cannot be explained: for as at present those forms lie concealed behind the forms *devānām* and *asthāt* of the transmitted text—and if they were not already obscured earlier, they *must* lie unavoidably concealed after the orthoepic principles adopted by the later diaskeuasts—, yet in fact it is not far from as if they were actually transmitted, as good as we may consider today *martiam* or *avatu ūtaye* or *candraagrās* as in effect transmitted.

For the rest, in order to allay all doubts it may be stated explicitely that a complete explanation of all the forms that we are discussing as linguistic phenomena would not perhaps at all be one what should he done here. For, we have to bear in mind that the hieratic-artificial manner of

1. Cf. Joh. Schmidt, KZ XXVI. 380.
2. See, for instance, Joh. Schmidt. KZ XXIV.304; Saussure, Mémoire p. 91, note 1.

pronunciation of the Vedic texts, which may be assumed in all probability already for the period of their composition, can have forced on the phenomena, which the language offered them, a capricious intensification and extension which it would be wrong to ascribe to the old Indian *language.*[1] If the language for once showed in certain forms variations between one-syllabled and two-syllabled words or word-elements then the judgement of the priestly versifiers can have made a much more far-reaching use of such analogies than even the language itself would have made it.

[185] And to conclude this subject we shall, while reserving the treatment of all the details of the constitution of the text-edition, give an informative survey of the most important cases of vowels to be scanned as two syllables. The actuality of that scansion in many cases and its inapplicability in others can be recognized in a very clear way: between them, however, there is a border region of doubtful cases, since obviously on the one hand the practice of the Vedic poets here, as elsewhere, has often abandoned the norms observed in other places, but, on the other there are numerous cases which for our judgement are ambiguous or, due to defects in transmission, have been rendered doubtful. Especially in the delimitation of the cases of metrical deficiencies pointed out above [pp. 34f., 66f.] as opposed to cases of two-syllabled scansion, and also in the evaluation of forms of words in the hymns for which we thought it was necessary to assume special metrical types, e.g. in the case of II.11 or X.46, differences of opinion can hardly be avoided.

1. We may recall forms like *vāïtayāï* for *vītaye, gāyirāḥ* for *giraḥ* etc. of which the Sāmaveda is full. We cannot regard as unthinkable that as in the singing technique, so also more moderately in the technique of sacrificial recitation, similar liberties with the material offered by the language have been taken in some places.

In the *declensional forms* we come across a two-syllabled *ā,* apart from the most frequent case of the genitive plural in *-ām,* also in the abl. sg. of the *a*-stems in *-āt* (or *-smāt* of pronouns)[1], e.g. *sadhasthāt* VIII.11.7, *antarikṣāt* X.158.1, *samasmāt* V.24.3.— Nom. and voc. plural ending in *-ās*[2] of masculine *a-* and *ā*-stems, e.g. *devāḥ* (occurring often), *somāḥ* VIII.2, 7, 10, 28(?), *stomāḥ* VIII.64.1,— *gopāḥ* VIII.31.13, *sugopāḥ* V.38.5 etc.—Acc. pl. in *-ān, -īn, -ūn, -ṛn.*[3]—Nom., acc. pl. of feminine *ā*-stems ending in *-ās,*[4] e.g. *puṇyagandhāḥ* VII.55.8, *manīṣāḥ* X.26.1, **[186]** *saṁvidānāḥ* X.97.14.—Nom., acc. pl. of feminine nouns in *-īs* (to be read as *-ias*[5]?), e.g. *aśastīḥ* IV.48.2, *adevīḥ* VIII.61.16.— Nom. dual fem. in *-e* (to be read as *aī*?): *abudhyamāne* I.29.3.— Quite doubtful are certain cases in which we could possibly conjecture a two-syllabled scansion for the *-ā* of the nom. acc. pl. neut. forms[6]: same is the case with the neut. pl. in *-āni* (*-āṁsi, -ūni* etc.), with the nom. acc. du. in *-ā*[7], with the nom. acc. sg. of feminine in *-ā, -ām,*[8] *-īm,* with the instr. pl. fem. in *-ābhis.* As regards the instr. pl. in *-ais,* the passages discussed by Kuhn (Beitr. IV.189) and Laman (350) permit throughout other explanations than the assumption of án ending *-aïs.*

The assumption of a two-syllabled scansion of *ā* in the nom. sg. of the *as-* stems in *-ās,*[9] so also in nom. acc. sg. of the stems in *-tar* (*-tā, - tāram*) also rests on very slender and

---

1. Cf. Lanman pp. 337f.; Geldner Metrik d. jüng. Avesta, p. 18; Bartholomae Gāthās p. 7.
2. Lanman p. 345; Geldner p. 10.—On forms in *-āsas* see above p. 176.
3. Cf. Lanman pp. 346, 429 [This addition is given in Oldenberg's Nachträge p. 545].
4. Lanman pp. 362, 363.
5. Lanman, 371.
6. Lanman, 348.
7. In *tanūpā* VII.66.3, *gopā* VIII.25.1, *kakṣiaprā* 1.10.3 the two-syllabled scansion of *ā* can be accounted for by the root-syllable, cf. below.
8. But the two-syllabled scansion of the *ā* deriving from a nasal in forms like *abjām* (VII.34.16) has to be noted.
9. Cf. Lanman 559.

uncertain materials.—It is not unlikely that the *ā* in *mahān* in VI.25.1 and VII.52.3,[1] and possibly also in *haviṣmān* in I.27.10[2] has a two-syllabled scansion. On the other hand, some nominatives in *-ā, -mā, -vā* from stems in *-an, -man, -van* are quite doubtful, and also the nominatives in *-vān* (*vidvān* etc.) in which the deficient syllable can be obtained by the vocalic pronunciation of *v*. From the nominatives of the comparatives perhaps *sahīyān* in X.176.4 belongs to this category.

[187] The two-syllabled scansion is frequent in the case of the stems of the type *gir-, pur-* and is definitely attested for the *īr* and *ūr* in the nominative and before the consonantal case-terminations. Thus in *pūḥ, pūrbhiḥ* I.58.8;[3] 189.2; VII.15.14; *gīrbhiḥ* VI.21.2; X.92.14. This can very well explain the line VI.24.6 *ājiṁ na jagmur* || *girvāho' aśvāḥ*. It would be a temerity in textual criticism to agree with Grassmann to accept the reading *girvavāho* from the Sāmaveda which is manifestly, as is often the case in the Sāmaveda, only intended to fill in the apparent metrical gap. We have rather to accept the reading *gīrvāho* with a two-syllabled scansion of *gīr-*, cf. *dhūrṣad, pūrbhid* etc.

For the noun *go* we have frequently a two-syllabled scansion for the case forms *gām, goḥ, gāḥ,*[4] for *vi* in the genitive *veḥ*; also for the acc. *dyām*, which often fills in the place of two syllables (see the passages quoted by Grassmann; cf. Lanman 432), we may consider a two-syllabled scansion of the *ā*, as an alternative to the reading *diām*. We may further mention the *ā* in *panthāḥ, panthām,*[5] *kṣām, ksāḥ,*[6] *vāḥ*.

1. Lanman 506. The additional pasage X.46.1 cited by Grassmann is to be dropped; see the observations made on the metre of the hymn on p. 91 above.
2. Lanman 517.
3. Joh. Schmidt Voc. II.235 proposes the reading *pūrubhis* or *purubhis;* I consider *purubhis* more probable.
4. Lanman 431 etc.; cf. Geldner Metrik, pp. 12, 17.
5. Lanman 441; Geldner Metrik 17.
6. L. 485, 556; G. 16.

As already mentioned a two-syllabled scansion of *e* in superlatives is very frequent where the *a* or the *ay* of the base combines with the *i* of the suffix: *śreṣṭha, preṣṭha,*[1] *deṣṭha, dheṣṭha, yeṣṭha.* Accordingly, it would be preferable to assume for *jyeṣṭha* the reading *jyaïṣṭha* rather than *jieṣṭha*: [188] against the latter goes the rarity of the comparative *jiāyas* as well as a series of cases which render the assumption of a position-making initial *jy,* if not definite, at least probable: II.18.8; IV.22.9; VII.86.4; 97.3; X.120.1. To this list we shall add *deṣṇa, deyām, dheyām,*[2] further *netar praṇetar;* from isolated words *tredhā* (see above p. 183), *śreṇi śreṇiśas* (above p.182).

Other isolated nouns having *ā, ī, ū* in them such as *dāsa, vāja, śūra, vīra* have been already discussed above (p. 172 f.); to this list we may also add *rājan* (doubtful: X.61.16, 23; cf. X.132.7), *nābhi* (IV.44.5; X.1.6), *dūra* (IV.20.1; X.108.11) and several more.

Amongst the *pronominal forms* can be mentioned alongside the nominal forms already discussed above: the genitives in *-sām,* (*-ṣām*), accusatives like *yān, tāṁś ca, asmān,* the ablative *samasmāt.* The *ai* of *asmai*[3] also can be counted as two syllables (III.13.1; V.33.1; VIII.2.41; 31.2). Often *mām*[4] and *vām* are disyllabic. For the *ā* of *asmākam,* in my opinion, there are no *decisive* instances.

In the sphere of *verbal forms* we first come across some cases in which the sandhi of the augment with the initial root vowel has to be resolved, thus in *āñjan* VI.63.3, *aurṇoḥ* VII.79.4, *āvam* X.49.3, *aicchaḥ* X.108.5, perhaps also in *āstām* X.85.11.—The *ā* of the thematic *a* in sandhi with the

---

1. When *preṣṭham* in I.186.3 and VIII.84.1 counts as four syllables the reading *prayiṣitham* proposed by Grassmann is not acceptable. The vowel development between sibilant and *th* is out of the question and it does not solve the metrical difficulty. Just as the preposition *pra* has often to be read as *p*ᵃ*ra,* so obviously *parayiṣṭham* must be assumed.
2. Hübschmann Indog. Vocalsystem 13, 16: Aufrecht Ṛgveda II. p. XLIII.
3. Geldner Metrik 9.
4. Geldner Metrik 17; Gaedicke Accusativ 14.

subjunctive characteristic *a* can be scanned as two syllables: *sphurān* VI.67.11; *vardhās* X.50.5[1]. We may also conjecture that the forms of the subjunctive **[189]** from the roots ending in *ā* —whether subject to vowel-gradation or not—have *aa*. If the subjunctive forms *paanti, daas* existed alongside *pānti, dās* then, based on this model, the forms with *aa* could also occur for the indicative forms *pānti, dās.*[2] In the case of the nominal forms[3] derived from these roots, especially the nom. pl. forms (*gopās* beside *gopaas*) may have occasioned the two-syllabled scansion. We shall refrain from the enumeration of the numerous instances—the two roots *pā* and *dā, dhā, sthā, yā*[4] etc. are to be reckoned here.

In many cases the *ū* of the root *bhū* appears to have a two-syllabled scansion: thus in *bhūt* I.77.3; 173.8; IV.43.4; V.41.16; *bhūtā* VI.50.15; *bhūtu* I.94.12 etc.: the instances, however, are not quite certain in as much as forms like *bhuvat, bhavatu* could easily have undergone change.

The long root vowel of the sigmatic aorist often has a two-syllabled scansion: thus in *akṣār, bhāk, asvārṣṭām.* About the third person forms of the aorist ending in *-i* as *vāci* (VII.58.6), *tāri* (IX.93.5) we cannot be certain.

Finally, amongst the *prepositions* and *particles* we must first mention the preposition *ā* (e.g. I.131.6; III.62.16; IV.21.6; VI.11.1; 17.12; 29.2; VII.56.18; VIII.31.10 etc.). The cases of *vā* and *mā* appear doubtful; two-syllabled *nū*, on the other hand, is frequent. The assumption of Grassmann (Wörterbuch) and Benfey (Quantitätsversch. IV.2.27f.) that **[190]** this *nū* contains the particle *u* I would regard as

---

1. Cf. Geldner Metrik 9; Bartholomae Gāthās 7, 115.
2. That in the subjunctive there is a two-syllabled *ā* (*aa*) it to be seen also from the Gāthā dialect (Bartholomae Gāthās 7, 115 note 1, 119, 123).
3. Lanman 443 ff.
4. In the case of this root the deficient syllable can be obtained by reading *iā*; but in many places a two-syllabled scansion of *ā* suits the metre better.

erroneous: that the two-syllabled *nū* is to be found also in the Gāthā dialect (Bartholomae Gāthās 8), to which the particle *u* is unknown, is one proof against it, and then, also that in *nūtanasya* II.20.4 the *ū* appears to have a two-syllabled scansion.

Chapter 2

The Arrangement of the Saṁhitā

[191] We shall examine the arrangement of the Saṁhitā which means we shall, first of all, take up for consideration the question of the sequence of the hymns within each Maṇḍala. For this we shall start with the books II-VII, which have a similar nature, and with the book IX which is essentially similar to them, and next discuss, one after the other, the special conditions of the books VIII, I, X. During these investigations, while each Maṇḍala, for the time being, is to be looked upon as an independent unit, the question then will have to be raised regarding the circumstances and the processes due to which the entire hymn-material of the Ṛgveda was drawn up into units just of this kind, and—what is closely connected with this—an explanation will have to be sought regarding the sequence and the mutual relationship of the Maṇḍalas themselves.

I

The Family Books (II-VII) and the Soma Book (IX)

As is well known the books II-VII consist of a series of hymns, grouped according to their deities, the ninth book, in a similar way, according to [192] the metres. In the books II-VII everytime an Agni-series, followed by an Indra-series, occurs first. The rest of the series in each of these books are, as Bergaigne[1] has shown, on the whole, arranged according to the descending order of the number of the hymns, and where the number of the hymns in the two series is the same it is the number of the stanzas in the first hymn (in the descending order) which is decisive[2]; the same principle governs the ordering of the metrical series of book IX. Next, within each single series the hymns follow one another according to the descending number of stanzas in them: a rule long recognized and which was further perfected by Bergaigne by stating that when the number of the stanzas in the two hymns was the same, it was the length of the metre, here also in the descending order, that was decisive (Jagatī, Triṣṭubh, Anuṣṭubh, Gāyatrī, not to mention the rare metres).

It is not necessary to add anything new to prove the regular validity of these rules in view of the discerning statements made by Bergaigne. But it will not be superfluous to subject the exceptions which oppose these rules to a thorough examination. The demarcation of the apparent from the real among these exceptions, the inferences about the splitting up of hymn-conglomerations into their constituent hymns or, vice versa about combining separately transmitted hymns into a *single* hymn, about the elimination of later additions etc.— a consideration of all these points leads us to what may be regarded as still open questions, answers to which can be brought to the maximum possible definitiveness only by an integrated examination of all similar details.

[193] We will first take up the cases of the violations of the descending order of the hymns within single series, next,

---

1. *Journ. Asiatique*, Sept.-Oct. 1886; Févr. Mars 1887. I cite according to the off-print.
2. It follows from this that the single hymns, occurring after those which belong together as groups, and hence occurring at the end of the books, appear as arranged according to their descending length. Bergaigne I.32.

those of the sequence of equally long hymns which is determined by the metre; finally, we will examine the cases in which the arrangement of the series among themselves goes against the rules set up above.

a. Exceptions to the arrangement of the hymns according to the descending number of stanzas

Even a cursory look shows that the violations of the sequence of hymns based on the number of stanzas occur almost exclusively at the *end* of the series. We shall, therefore, first discuss separately the very rare violations of the rule *within* the series.

II. 36, 37. These hymns break the order of single hymns beginning to appear from hymn 33. Bergaigne (I.33; but cf. II.14) considers it doubtful whether the two hymns have been interpolated or whether they are to be combined into a *single* hymn, in which case the order can be restored. The second course is the correct one: this is shown by the comparison with I.15 which hymn according to the Anukramaṇī, just as the hymns II. 36, 37, is addressed to the "ṛtavaḥ", i.e. the deities of the ṛtuyājas. And even without taking into account the details of the numerous agreements between that single hymn and these two, one easily realizes that here, in a way similar to the Āprī hymns or the Praüga hymns, it is a fixed ritual sequence which runs through the *two* hymns II. 36 and 37. By combining these two into a *single* hymn one does justice to the ritual content of the hymns and at the same time removes an exception to the rule of the hymn-sequence.

V. 84. After the Parjanya-hymn 83 of 10 stanzas and **[194]** before the Varuṇa-hymn of 8 stanzas there occurs a hymn of three stanzas addressed to the Earth; if one considers that the series of single hymns begins with 83, then 84 violates the order. The hymn does not offer any indications of later origin; however, it is possible that originally it did *not* occur at that place, but was later inserted there because its contents touch closely on those of 83. That the small series of single hymns addressed to *different* deities offered less resistance to such an insertion than those clearly marked-out series in which the hymns are addressed to one and the same deity, is easily understood.

VI.15.16-19. After the tṛca-hymns in Jagatī and Triṣṭubh which are combined in 15.1-15 and before the collection of the Gāyatrī-tṛcas (VI.16) there appears a piece of four stanzas in alternating metres; its contents are closely related to those of the hymn III.29 which is likewise interpolated; also the expression *gārhapatyāni* (st. 19) speaks for the late origin. This then is clearly a case of addition which, here, by way of exception, occurs *before* the end of the series[1].

IX.5. This Āprī-hymn addressed to Soma Pavamāna with its 11 stanzas, which number is required and made certain by the ritual nature of the Āprī-hymn, stands between the hymns of ten and nine stanzas. It can hardly be doubted that this hymn is later than those in its neighbourhood. This is indicated by the word *prajāpatiḥ* (st. 9); but this is indicated above all, as is shown above [on p. 28, f.n. 1], by its metre. Just as the composition of an Āprī-hymn for Soma [**195**] is obviously a trifle arising out of the desire to supply even the ninth book with its own Āprī hymn, similarly the insertion of the hymn in question at the fifth place, instead of the first as required by its length, must have been occasioned, by an extremely superficial ground: in the rest of the Maṇḍalas the Āprī-hymn never occurs at the beginning but, always, at a few places after it, e.g. in Maṇḍala V, exactly at the fifth place.

With these four cases all the violations of the principle of arrangement which arise due to the number of the stanzas and which occur *within* the series are exhausted. Of these the first can be omitted as purely an apparent exception

1. Could it be that this piece came to be at this place at a time when VI.15.1-15 and VI.16 were already looked upon as hymn-units? Then it would be to some extent understandable that it was attracted by hymn 15 which was metrically closer to it, and not by 16.

and at least for the fourth there can be a special explanation. Hence, it can hardly be an exaggeration if we, in *this* respect, say that the rule enjoys an almost exceptionless validity. Essentially different is the case of the exceptions occurring at the *end* of the series where by the side of the apparent exceptions, also the real ones show greater frequency. The basic facts which give direction to the critic while dealing with them can very well be regarded at the moment as generally accepted and therefore not being in need of a fresh argumentation. If after the shortest hymns of numerous series there constantly occur longer sūktas, then, mostly, one can and must divide the first part of them in such a way that their length falls in line with the principle of arrangement[1]: the hymns obtained this way are only in a few cases longer than of three stanzas ; usually they are tṛcas and next **[196]** the Pragāthas of two stanzas[2]. But there further remain sūktas which thoroughly oppose their being subsumed under the rule and by their invariable placement at the end of the series they can clearly be recognized as additions to the original corpus of the collection. The means that we have at our disposal to distinguish those apparent exceptions to the rule of arrangement from these real ones are sufficient to give in most cases sure results. If such splittings of hymns are demanded or, at least, made possible by the sections in their contents, by the refrains, by the ritual use, by the parallels in the other Vedas, by the metrical

1. After Delbrück had first given an indication in this direction (Jenaer Literaturzeitung 1875, p. 867) and after Grassmann had made full use of the same in his translation, I have attempted a connected treatment of the relevant details (ZDMG, XXXVIII.439 ff.), the results of which have received valuable confirmation from the researches of Bergaigne.
2. Occasionally, at such places also strophes which belong to a larger unit have been treated by the arrangers of the Saṁhitā as independent hymns. This has been demonstrated by me (op. cit. 460) and Bergaigne (I.6 f.).

peculiarities, and if these splittings yield an extent of the hymn, respectively of the strophes, which corresponds to the rule of arrangement, then, and especially if the concerned cases—the tṛca- or Pragātha-extent etc.—*recur* at a number of places, one can hardly doubt the only *apparent* nature of such exceptions: and here one has to note that, if, this way, any given point in the apparent additions proves in reality to belong to the ordered series, then at the same time all that precedes this point is already settled[1]. On the other hand, the *real* additions are characterized by the length of the text, and by the relationship between the individual stanzas which resists the number-relationships required by the rule of arrangement: so also in many cases by a frequent change in the metre and especially by the later character of the language, of the metre (Anuṣṭubh [**197**] of the transition-period), and of their contents (ākhyāna-hymns, magic formulae, and stanzas of similar nature)[2].

Now we shall attempt to give a survey made on the basis of these viewpoints and arranged according to the order of the Maṇḍalas. This will reveal the apparent and the real additions to the ordered series[3]. Hymns which fit into the sequence when they are cut into tṛcas or Pragāthas have

---

1. The exceptional case of VI.15, discussed above [p. 194], is obviously a solitary one.
2. Further factors for distinguishing the concluding portions of the series which are required to be split and the supplements proper are obtained from Bergaigne's rules regarding the metrical sequence and the sequence of the series depending on the number of hymns. I do not discuss these for the time being since we shall have occasion later while dealing with individual cases to examine how far one can rely on those rules with certainty; first, it seems appropriate to ascertain the state of affairs as would result from an analysis carried out independently of those rules.
3. We may refer here to the section "Formation of Strophes and Composite Hymns" above [pp. 119 ff.] where the problem of splitting up of the hymns is tackled from another viewpoint and is meant to be supplemented with what is said here.

been marked with *tr.* or *pr.*; an asterisk mark (*) indicates what remains as a real supplement to the original series.

II

*32.6-8.— 41 tr. Bergaigne[1] who rejects some of these tṛcas because they go against his theory of metrical sequence overlooks the fact that these—except the last—are required to be just at this place by the ritual nature of the Praüga-śastra.[2]— *42-43.

[198] III

26-27 tr. *28-29. — 51 tr. *52-53.[3] — 62 tr.

IV

15.1-3 tr. *4-10.[4]— 30-32 tr.— 37 is perhaps to be split up on the basis of the metre (1-4, 5-8); that the two parts here, as elsewhere in similar cases, meant as one hymn to the arranger is possible.— *48 ? Or, can it be that the hymn properly belongs to the series and that only stanza 5 is to be removed ?— 50: first, 1-6 can be demarcated as a unit (stanza 6 is clearly a concluding stanza; 1-6 occur together in the Atharvaveda). What remains of the hymn is to be divided into two sections 7-9, 10-11 which do not give the impression of belonging together. The descending order of the number

1. I.17.38.
2. Cf. ṚV.I,2 and 3 with the Aitareya Br. III.1 etc.— Stanzas 1—18 of the hymn in question, when divided into tṛcas, correspond exactly with the sequence of the deities of the Praüga-litany. Stanzas 19—21 which, to all appearances, are related to the two havirdhāna-carts (Ait. Br. I.29.3), have certainly nothing to do with that litany: an independent tṛca which, of course, has got mixed up with the other tṛcas.
3. One may note the congruity between the hymns 28 and 52 both of which are supplementary.
4. Unless the whole hymn 15 is to be classed among the supplements.

of the stanzas would be quite in order in these parts, and there is nothing in itself which goes against assigning 10-11 to the original collection. Yet the decision in this regard would also go against these two stanzas (10-11) if one is inclined to believe that the stanzas 7-9 are to be rejected on account of their glorification of the office of Purohita which gives them a later appearance.— 55.1-7; 8-10.— 56.1-4; 5-7.— *57.4-8. It is possible that the first three stanzas formed a hymn belonging to the original collection.— *58.

V

25-26 tr. 27, 28 tr. or a supplement ? — *40.5-9. Stanzas 1-4 appear to be a hymn which would fit into the sequence (tṛca having a refrain; then a concluding stanza in a different metre)[1].— 51.1-4; 5-7; 8-10; *11-15.— *61. As natural sections we get the following: 1-4 invocation to to the Maruts; 5-10 Dānastuti [**199**] and similar things; 11-13; 14-16 tṛcas to the Maruts; 17-19 an invocation to the Night, as a supplement. One can see that at the most stanzas 1-4 would agree with the rule of the number of stanzas; however, since the next section as a Dānastuti seems to belong to what precedes, it is better to look upon everything as a supplement, which is also supported by the monosyllabic *kva* in st. 2.— 78.1-3 or, more probably, 1-4 (tṛca having refrain, then a concluding stanza in a different metre, cf. V.40.1-4) belong to the original collection. *78.5-9[2].— 82 tr. The regular tṛca-division

1. That the cut is to be made after stanza 4, and not after stanza 3 as Bergaigne thinks (I.17), is shown clearly by the contents. The metre does not go against this division, cf. what has been said above on p. 146.
2. It is perhaps due to the exceptional position of these stanzas that in the varga-division the hymn 78 is not, as is normally done in the case of hymns having nine stanzas, divided as 5 + 4, but as 4 + 5. The composition of the hymn 78.1-4 is exactly similar to that of the hymn V. 40.1-4 just described.

and the archaic metre of the last tṛca (Gāyatrī with a trochaic cadence) does not make it specially probable that a part of the sūkta is to be looked upon as a supplement.— *87.

VI

15.1-15 tr. (on *15.16-19 see above [p., 194]); 16 tr.—44-45 tr. 46 pr. *47.— With regard to the divisions to be made in 51 and 52, the following points, according to me, have to be considered. First, 52.1-6; 7-12 fall into two sections due to metre. Should these sections of six stanzas each be allowed to remain as they are, or should they be halved so that we have a series of hymns in the tṛca form which is so common? I think the latter. For, the difference in the contents favours the separation of 52.1-3 (prayer against the atiyājasya yaṣṭar, the brahmadviṣ) and 4-6; but if we admit two tṛcas for 1-6, then, according to the rule of the number of the stanzas, we cannot expect a hymn of six stanzas 7-12 to follow, and, in fact, st. 9 does give the impression of a concluding stanza and st. 10 of a new beginning. Besides, [**200**] the consideration of 51 also recommends the division of these twelve stanzas into tṛca-hymns – first two in Triṣṭubh, then two in Gāyatrī: the stanzas 13-16[1] at the end of this sūkta, which are obviously to be separated—not just due to metre—from the preceding ones, stand as a hymn of four stanzas quite at their proper place before the tṛcas. Thus we have the following result: 51.1-12, 13-16.52.1-12 tr. *13-17.

59.1-6; 7-10; 60.1-12 tr. It is not possible to decide definitely whether 13-15 is to be looked upon as a further tṛca belonging to the series or as a supplement[2].—61.1-12 tr.; 13-14 a hymn of two stanzas.— *74-75.

---

1. The view that the stanzas 13-16 are a later addition is, as far as I can see, not supported by anything, and the fact that they are placed *before* the tṛcas of the hymns 52, which belong to the series, goes against it.
2. If we apply the rule of Bergaigne regarding the sequence of the series very strictly, then this must be considered a later addition.

VII

15 tr.[1] 16 pr. *17. —31 tr. 32 pr. *33.—*55.[2]—59.1-6 pr.[3] 7-8 belong to the series, or are they a supplement? *9-11, *12 (the latest addition; not analyzed in the Padapāṭha). —66.1-9 tr. 10-16 pr.[4] *17-19.—74 pr.—81 pr.—94 tr.—96.1-3 (extended Pragātha; cf. above [p. 106]). 4-6 [**201**] belong to the series, or are they a supplement?[5]—*103. The frog-hymn seems to have been added as a supplement to the Parjanya-series (101, 102) due to its first stanza.—*104 (it is difficult to assign even just the first part of the hymn to the original collection).

IX

61-67.18 tr. *67.19-32. I consider it probable that 67.18 formed the end of the ordered series because the metrically peculiar tṛca 16-18 (*dvipadā gāyatrī*) would be a fitting conclusion to the Gāyatrī-section. Perhaps, 19-21 also could be considered as a tṛca belonging to the series. The

1. In the traditionally handed down text the Gāyatrī tṛcas appear as combined into a sūkta; the Triṣṭubh tṛcas of hymns 12-14, however are not, obviously only because the well-known concluding words *yūyaṁ pāta* etc. made their independent position too striking to be missed.
2. Stanza 1 could in itself be a sūkta and could be looked upon as marking the close of the ordered series; the stanza, obviously, has no connection with what follows.
3. Bergaigne suggests to split 56 into several hymns. I do not see sufficient grounds for this; its obvious parallelism with the hymn 34 decides the case *against* splitting. Cf. also the section on *dvipadā virāj* in the chapter on Metrik, p. 97 f.
4. Stanza 16 belongs, as an extension, to the Pragātha 14-15. (cf. p. 105); contents as well as metre do not permit its being joined to what follows, as Bergaigne wants to do.
5. Bergaigne (I.40) has a different opinion. I do not see why 95 should be split up into two tṛcas.

character of 22 onwards as a supplement is not in doubt. —85 is to be divided into hymns of four stanzas each. 86 tr.—96 is to be split up into units of 4 stanzas each. 97 tr. (certainly upto st. 54; in 55-58 there occurs a disturbance about whose nature I do not venture an opinion).—100.1-5, 6-9.[1] 101 tr. (st. 16 stands by itself as an isolated stanza, *perhaps* as a later addition).—106.1-12 tr.; 13-14 a hymn of two stanzas[2], presumably belonging to the original series. A critique, not willing to undertake ventures in order to impose a certain number of hymns on a given series, will hardly find an occasion to divide the preceding hymns (102-105) of the same series[3].—107-108 pr.—109 tr.; the last stanza (22) [**202**] can be considered as an extension of the tṛca 19-21 which, at the time of the arrangement, was as little noticed

---

1. For the justification of this division I refer the reader to p. 128.—My judgement on Bergaigne's (I.25) splitting up of 98, 99 will be the same as on 102-105, see f.n. 3 below.
2. That after stanza 14 another stanza which would have made the tṛca complete has been lost (Bergaigne I.26) is not probable because the Sāmaveda had to draw on IX.101.13 in order to complete the tṛca.
3. The hymns as *traditionally* demarcated have, in respect of the numbers of stanzas in them, exactly the same appearance which is to be found again and again in the rest of the series: decreasing number of the stanzas; disturbance at the end of the series. Presumably therefore one has to opt here for the same treatment as has been admitted in the analogous cases: we leave the hymns as they are as far as they conform to the descending order (here: 8.6.6.6); splitting up at the end. On the basis of other similar cases, one may say that if it was a case of only tṛca-hymns, these would have been combined into one or two complexes, but they would not appear as different hymns and that too conforming to the rule of arrangement. The text itself does not offer anything at all to admit the splittings proposed by Bergaigne (I, 25 f.); in 102, the number of the stanzas (8), in 103, the word *pari* which constantly appears at the beginning, in 104 and 105, the Vālakhilya-type parallelism between the hymns (cf. Pañc. Br. XIII.11.3-4; XIV.5.4) go against the splittings.

as, let us say, IX.107.16.—110 tr.[1]—*112-114. These Paṅkti-hymns are proved to be additions due to their non-compliance with the order, by their contents which are quite different from those of the rest of the Pavamāna-hymns, and by the features of language and metre.

b. Exceptions to the metrical sequence

Within each series, the hymns having the same number of stanzas are, as a rule, arranged in the descending order of the metres (Jagatī, Triṣṭubh, Anuṣṭubh, Gāyatrī). Although, certainly, this rule discovered by Bergaigne is, on the whole, found to be valid, I am doubtful whether, on its basis, we could venture such incisive operations as would be required by an *exceptionless* application of the rule. If we feel that owing to the violations of that rule we are entitled to admit disturbances in the original text—whether we say that single stanzas or whole hymns were added to the genuine text—then how do we explain the fact that such disturbances within a series violate so often the rule of the *metrical* sequence but never, at the same time, **[203]** the one related to the sequence depending on the *number of the stanzas*? We saw that the almost fixed place where hymns have been added later is the *end* of the series; *there* one observes again and again that the disturbances to the rule of the number of stanzas coincide with linguistic and metrical indices of late origin. We cannot say something similar about the instances where the normal order of the metres has been neglected. The hymns which will have to be eliminated on account of metrical disturbance fit into their position from the point of view of the number of stanzas in them; in most of them we fail to notice any other criterion of late origin. The single stanzas which will have to be eliminated—in a number of cases the concluding stanzas of *several* hymns

1. Unless st. 4-9 are to be looked upon as a *single* piece; cf. above p. 130.— I do not find any compelling reason to deny this piece, composed in a rare metre, a place in the original collection.

one after the other—are in themselves above doubt and do not disturb the sequence of the hymns according to the number of the stanzas. Perhaps one may want to get over this objection by distinguishing the interpolations which disturb only the metrical ordering, but not the ordering based on the number of stanzas, as the *older* layer of interpolations than the others. But, in my opinion, such an expedient is opposed by the fact that in some of the concerned cases—that it should be possible to demonstrate this in *all* cases is not to be expected—directly plausible grounds can be adduced for the assumption that the hymns have been purposely arranged in that order in spite of the resulting deviation in respect of the sequence of metres which is observed elsewhere. One may consider, for instance, the case of VI.44,45. Here we have the tṛca-complexes of an Indra-series; the metres are the following :

	44.1-6	2 tṛcas in Anuṣṭubh.
{	7-9	1 tṛca in a particular variety of Triṣṭubh.
{	10-24	5 tṛcas in Triṣṭubh.
	45	11 tṛcas in Gāyatrī.

Because, here, the Triṣṭubh, against the usual practice, [204] follows Anuṣṭubh, Bergaigne wants to eliminate the six tṛcas 44.7-24. The language of these hymns contains nothing that would point to a late origin; the regular sequence of 6 (or if one wants 5) hymns of equal length in the same metre has the clear stamp of an original, ordered collection as opposed to the irregular nature, devoid of any form, of the additions; and finally—should this Indra-series at all be without any tṛca in Triṣṭubh? We thus do not feel justified in eliminating these six tṛcas. On the other hand, it seems possible to find in a different way a satisfactory explanation of the unusual arrangement. Hymn 43 has for every stanza the refrain: *ayaṁ sa soma' indra te sutaḥ piba;* each stanza begins with a relative pronoun which is related to this *ayam*. Exactly similar is one of the tṛcas of the hymn 44, viz. the first, which occurs in the immediate neighbourhood of hymn 43: every stanza ends the same way with *somaḥ sutaḥ sa' indra te asti svadhāpate madaḥ*, which is very similar to the refrain of 43, and in every stanza a relative pronoun occurring at the beginning points to this close. Should we not consider it probable that exactly due to this formal similarity the two hymns are put next to each other and it is in *this* way that the latter—and then of course also the portion 44.4-6 which is connected with it by the same number of verses and the same metre—has found a place *before* the Triṣṭubh-tṛcas ?

Let us turn to a different case. V.57-60 are four hymns of equal length; the first and the third are composed mainly in Jagatī; a Triṣṭubh-hymn (60) occurs after them, another (58) against the practice, between them. Bergaigne would like to shorten hymns 59 and 60 at the end by one, respectively two, stanzas. It is true that these stanzas [**205**] are in a metre different from that of the hymns themselves, but just in the fifth book there is nothing more common than a change in the metre of that kind to mark the close of the hymn. I think the fact that hymns 57 and 58, even though the first was composed mainly in Jagatī and the second in Triṣṭubh, belonged together as *two parallel hymns ending with an identical stanza* was decisive for the arrangement of these hymns; these two (57, 58), which to some extent formed a compact principal part of this whole group, were placed first, arranging them according to the sequence Jagatī-Triṣṭubh, and they were allowed to be followed, in the same order, by the two unrelated hymns (59, 60).

This interpretation of mine is strengthened by the fact that also at a different place, viz. IV.43-45, the violation of the metrical sequence can be similarly explained. Among these hymns of equal length two Triṣṭubh hymns precede a Jagatī hymn: but here also the former two form a pair of parallel hymns, marked by the same concluding stanza, and as such, obviously, receive priority.

Somewhat different, but still comparable, is the situation with regard to the Ṛbhu-hymns: IV.35-36 : again a Jagatī hymn after a Triṣṭubh hymn. Here, probably, a factor found in their contents, respectively, in their ritual employment, has influenced the arrangement. The expressions *ratnadheyam, ratnadhebhiḥ ratnaṁ dhāta* occur in constant repetition throughout the hymn 35, but among the remaining hymns 33, 36, 37 of the Ṛbhu-series, they do not occur even once but occur, to be sure, in 34 and here as regularly as in 35. The common reference made by these two hymns to *ratnadheyam* has led to their being placed next to each other, and in this way 35 came to stand before 36, **[206]** although the former was composed in Triṣṭubh, the latter in Jagatī.

The above discussions surely show sufficiently that the rule of the metrical sequence cannot be considered exceptionless in the sense that it can offer sufficiently sure ground for the removal of stanzas or hymns (which go against that rule). It seems that we would hardly push caution too far if we were to moderate a little the definiteness with which that rule has been formulated by its discoverer. We would prefer to express it this way : the hymns having the same number of stanzas have been grouped together in accordance with certain other factors of relationship; among these factors, to be sure, the most constant and the most obvious was undoubtedly the metrical one. Besides this, we think, there could be other factors too, occasionally perhaps not to be ascertained, which would determine the sequence; and if we do not exclude in this regard an occasional working of even pure chance, then this lack of trust on our part in the complete, I would like to say mechanical precision of the Saṁhitā-arranger, will not, perhaps, be looked upon as absolutely unnatural.

c. The sequence of the series

If the sequence of the single hymns was on occasions governed by *tendencies*, which were certainly not exceptionless *laws,* then it is understandable that the ordering of the whole series shows similar phenomena : all the more so because for an absolutely exact handling of the ordering of the series it was necessary to look forward and backward more extensively, and the factors which came in question here [**207**] possessed much less clearness and simplicity than when it was only a matter of putting hymn after hymn. If, however, Bergaigne's (I.25 ff.) survey of the series points to an *almost*—but not *quite*—exceptionless ordering of them in accordance with the decreasing number of the hymns, in the second place, in accordance with the decreasing number of the stanzas in the first hymn, then, I think, the investigations of that researcher, which are (otherwise) so valuable, cannot be considered free from an important objection. A single Vedic sūkta for him, if I am not mistaken, is very little of a concerte, individual entity which, on account of definite characteristics of its form and content calls for a distinct handling: he sees in the sūkta too much of a mathematical notion, a hymn of so and so many stanzas in such and such a metre, over which a critic has the same control as a calculator on his arithmetical sum which he may reduce by subtraction, divide by division, without being obliged to give a closer look to the substratum which he reduces or divides. If, on the other hand, one proceeds to dissect the hymns in such a way that one gives more weight to the appearance of every single case than to the tendency to pursue certain numerical relationships through their absolute consequences, then one would here, exactly as in the case of the rule of metrical arrangement, come across such a number of exceptions to Bergaigne's rule, that one would scarcely have the courage to risk violent operations for the application of that rule. For example, we drew above [p. 201, f.n. 2 and 4] attention to the fact that the Anuṣṭubh- and the Uṣṇih-series of the ninth book do not yield, as B. would like to have, 14 respectively 12-13 hymns, but a considerably smaller number, so that their placing before

[208] the 12 Bārhata Pragāthas no larger corresponds to the rule. Similarly in the seventh book not only, as B. himself correctly admitted earlier,[1] is the placing of the Marut-series (perhaps of seven hymns) before the Āditya-series (12 hymns) not in order, but a similar impediment is experienced again with regard to the Indrāgnī-series.[2] If one treats the hymn 94 without preconception, then one will divide it, as one divides all the other hymns which apparently violate the sequence of the book VII (so long as they do not consist of the Pragāthas), into the tṛcas, as here, exactly as in all the other cases, also the contents[3] agree with this operation. But in that case the Indrāgnī-series consists of five hymns, and its placement after several series of 4 and 3 hymns is anomalous. Now if one still feels justified to undertake operations which will give to the series its correct place from the point of view of the number of hymns (3 hymns) still the fact remains that then we have a triad of hymns with an opening hymn of *eight stanzas* standing after one such which has an opening hymn of *seven stanzas* : hence, further, for the sake of the proper order, two stanzas of a hymn *standing at the beginning of the series* must be struck off.[4]—Similarly, with regard to IV.42 not everyone will be easily convinced to divide the hymn into two, for the sake of the ordering of series; but if one were to overcome the scruple against it, hymn 41 would still have at least *one* stanza more than what it should have in accordance with Bergaigne's principle.

[209] The instances cited, and it is possible to add to them, will suffice to justify our procedure to refrain from

1. 1.39. Later (II.10 f.) he attempted to remove the impediment with the help of the combination of a number of operations, of which, I think, each one for itself separately has little probability.
2. Cf. Bergaigne II.15,17.
3. Similarly also the Sāmaveda parallels.
4. I cannot find any evidence to say that 93.7, 8 should be additions.

using the criterion of sequence of series for the purpose of carrying out critical operations with regard to single hymns.

II

The Eighth Book[1]

Of the three leading factors of the Anukramaṇī-texts—ṛṣi of the hymn, deity, metre—it is the deity which, for the arrangement of books II-VII, has proved to be mainly decisive, and the metre for the arrangement of book IX. That for the eighth book these two factors, if at all, can in no case come in for consideration as the most principal ones needs hardly be proved. Hence, it is obvious that we should examine whether here it is not the third of those factors, the authorship of the hymns, which proves to be the most important principle of arrangement. And in this, if one takes into account the whole character of the names of the authors which appear in the Anukramaṇī, it becomes clear at the very outset—and this will further be confirmed by the discussion of the situations in book X which are in many respects analogous—that we have to give weight, in the first instance, to the data regarding the authors *contained in the hymns themselves.*[2] **[210]** For, in the statements which

1. It is perhaps not superfluous to observe that what follows here was written before the publication of the second part of Bergaigne's Recherches and it has been only subsequently taken note of. The demarcation of certain hymn-groups in which I agree with B. will, thus, have more weight, since it has been arrived at independently from *two* sides.
2. This characterizes an important difference of my investigation from that of Bergaigne (I.46 ff., II.76 ff.). I try, first of all, to demarcate groups of hymns which are so characterized by the naming of the authors in the text itself; on the basis of the appearance, shown by these collections, I then try to discover similar groups also of those hymns where the naming of the authors is absent. B, on the other

(Continued on next page)

rest entirely on the authority of the Anukramaṇī, one might certainly expect traces of recollections regarding the groupwise relationship of the hymns, each according to its authors, but, as a rule, these traces will not be recognizable, even with approximate certainty, in the weed of the silly inventions which grows luxuriously in the Anukramaṇī, as long as one [211] has not, in some other way, got hold of the factor to which these traces point.

(Continued from previous page)

hand, follows—at least in the first part of his investigations—the Anukramaṇī which shows the correct way in so far as it follows, in many cases, just the statements in the texts about the ṛṣis, which we also consider decisive. Where, however, these statements are absent, the Anukramaṇī mostly does not have any firm ground to offer; a number of hymns have been separated from one another, which, if one were to examine them in accordance with the model of the sure collections, show obvious characteristics of relationship and arrangement; almost everywhere in such cases the Anukramaṇī forms groups the extent of which remains way behind that of the sure groups, or, in numerous cases, it assumes single hymns of every supposed author and thereby changes the picture which one must expect on the basis of the groups which are characterized by clear features. When, in the second part of his treatise, Bergaigne takes up a position which is more independent of the standpoint of the Anukramaṇī, he obviously arrives in many cases at a more accurate demarcation of the groups; reservations nevertheless occasioned by the method adopted by him are referred to later [p. 219].—A further difference between Bergaigne and me concerns the breaking up of hymns into smaller hymns. In my opinion the hymns of the eighth book *on the whole* have been demarcated correctly by the tradition, and that the stanzas which are to be separated from one another are parts of these hymns and are not independent hymns; the indications which have led me to this conclusion have been set forth by me above [p. 137 f]. Bergaigne sees in the stanzas mostly independent hymns (cf. however his later statements, II.76 ff.); in between, sporadically, with regard to a few hymns in whose case the criteria of unity are specially prominent, he recognizes this unity. I believe that further investigations would have led him to such criteria in yet many other cases: his results, which are even now not convincing due to lack of uniformity and simplicity, would then betray more clearly the resistance of the texts to the treatment applied to it.

Now in order to obtain on the basis of maximally certain facts a criterion for deciding whether a division of the eighth book into groups of hymns by the same author, or by the same circle of authors, is feasible, we collect, first, the data on some of the more prominent names of the ṛṣis or the ṛṣis-families that are named in the eighth book. While doing this, we leave the Kaṇvas out; under their name, apparently, so many individuals are subsumed, and their name appears at so many different places in the Maṇḍala, that it will be proper to start with the names which are less diffused and therefore are more characteristic.

Vatsa is mentioned ten times; all the occurrences are to be found in the hymns VIII.6, 8, 9, 11.

Vyaśva, the *Vyaśvas, Vaiyaśva:* nine occurrences in the hymns VIII.23, 24, 26. Otherwise Vyaśva appears also three times in the Ṛgveda: in I.112.15 and VIII.9.10, while enumerating many ṛṣis, so that his mention here is a matter of pure chance and not connected with the authorship of the hymn; then, in IX.65.7, in a Pavamāna-hymn, which, in accordance with the principles of arrangement followed in the Ṛgveda, *cannot* occur with the other Vyaśva-hymns on account of its Devatā. If section VIII.23-26, thus, turns out to be related due to the mentions of Vyaśva, there appears further an additional characteristic which is suited to thus demarcate just these hymns, viz. the *almost exclusive* preponderance of the metre Uṣṇih.[1]

Sobharī: in seven passages in the hymns VIII.19, 20, 22. Otherwise it appears only in an enumeration of many ṛṣi-names in **[212]** VIII.5.26, and in the last stanza of the eighth book 103.14. Also here the section VIII.19-22, which thus emerges, is characterized by a striking metrical feature, viz. the frequent occurrence of the Kākubha Pragātha. One may note that the point at which this series ends and the point where the Vyaśva-series begins are mutually made certain.

1. Also the occurrence of the name (Varo) Suṣāman in 23, 24, 25, 26 (only here) delimits this group with the greatest sharpness.

Śyāvāśva: in six passages in the hymns 35, 36, 37, 38; frequent mentions of Atri or the Atris—as is well-known Śyāvāśva was an Ātreya—are characteristic of these very hymns. Outside this section, Śyāvāśva appears also a few times in the Atri-book (V).

Nabhāka (Nābhāka): in three passages in 40,41. The name, otherwise, does not appear in the Ṛgveda. The refrain *nabhantām anyake same* occurs in 39, 40, 41, 42. The characteristic metre of this series is Mahāpaṅkti. The point where this series begins and the point where the Śyāvāśva series ends are mutually made certain.

Thus, when one observes the occurrence of some frequent ṛṣi-names, it becomes immediately clear that there exist groups of related hymns the unity of which rests on the *identity of the poet* or of the circle of the poets. Of such groups, so far, we have found the following five: 6-11, 19-22, 23-26, 35-38, 39-42; that the Vālakhilya-hymns, characterized by the parallelism of two hymns each and by names such as Praskaṇva and Dasyave vṛka, form the sixth can be easily seen.

Before proceeding further to look for other similar groups, let us first examine whether the arrangement of the hymns in these groups themselves is subject to some recognizable principles, which then eventually could yield criteria, worth consideration, for the demarcation of the remaining groups. We [**213**] mention the deities and the number of the stanzas in the hymns of those groups.

Vatsa: Indra 48. Marutaḥ 36. Aśvinau 23, 21, 6. Agni 10.

Vyaśva: Agni 30. Indra 30. Mitrāvaruṇau 24. Aśvinau 19. Vāyu 6.[1]

Sobharī: Agni 37. Marutaḥ 26. Indra 18. Aśvinau 18.

Śyāvāśva: Aśvinau 24. Indra 7, 7. Indrāgnī 10.

---

1. In the transmitted text, the Aśvin-hymn and the Vāyu-hymn are combined into a single hymn (26).

Nābhāka: Agni 10. Indrāgnī 12. Varuṇa 10, 3. Aśvinau 3[1].
Vālakhilya: Indra 10, 10, 10, 10, 8, 8. Dānastuti 5, 5[2].

One can see from this statement, first, that the hymns addressed to the same deity within a given group always occur together. Next emerges, although not without an exception, yet so much predominant, that mere chance appears to be ruled out, the arrangement according to the decreasing number of the stanzas: without preference for Agni and Indra and without consideration for the number of the hymns belonging to a series, the series follow one another each time according to the number of the stanzas of their longest hymns, and after each longest hymn there follow the remaining hymns, addressed to the same deity, again in the decreasing order. The violations of this sequence are found only one each in the Śyāvāśva- and in the Nābhāka-group; an Indrāgnī hymn appears in the former after the shorter Indra-hymns, and, in the latter, after a shorter Agni-hymn. [**214**] The text of these hymns does not suggest any operation which would remove the anomaly, and such irregularities the like of which we shall come across more further on, do not make it expedient at all to expect here a thoroughly strict observance of the sequence.

Let us now examine the other groups not so clearly marked by the occurrence of definite ṛṣi-names.

The section 12-18 shows itself quite clearly as an arranged one. The Vatsa-series serves to demarcate it at the beginning, the Sobharī-series at the end. The absence of the authors' names, which occur so plentifully in the preceding and the following series, the common linguistic and metrical characteristics—the two metres Uṣṇih[3] and Gāyatrī

1. The Varuṇa-hymn 42.1-3 and the Aśvin-hymn 42.4-6 are, of course, to be separated.
2. The pairwise parallelism found in the Vālakhilya hymns breaks off in the last three hymns. But that does not matter: Aśvinau 4. Uncertain 3. Indrāvaruṇau 7.
3. And, to be sure, the Uṣṇih—as opposed to the Uṣṇih of the Vyaśva-

(Continued on next page)

dominate almost completely—, finally the arrangement, which will be indicated immediately, leave little doubt about the intimate connection of these hymns. We find the following deities and the number of the stanzas: Indra 33, 33, 15, 13, 12, 10, 3, 2[1]. Ādityas 22.

The remaining hymns of the first part of the Maṇḍala—those which precede the Vālakhilyas—, which we have not discussed so far, [**215**] can be arranged, in my opinion, into the following groups:

1-5. Characterized as belonging together by the Anukramaṇī (Medhātithi and/or Medhyātithi, Devātithi, Brahmātithi), by the regular appearance of the Dānastuti at the end of each hymn, and by connecting the names of the Kaṇvās and Priyamedhās. The last two characteristics are met with also in the hymn 6 (*Priyamedhastutā harī*, 6.45; cf. also 8.18), but, it seems to me, that 6.1 (*stomair Vatsasya vāvṛdhe*) is decisive for this hymn as forming part of the Vatsa-group. Due to many kinds of links this group turns

---

(Continued from previous page)

section for which it is equally characteristic—quite predominantly of that form, which may be expected *a priori* because of the combined predominance of Uṣṇih *and Gāyatrī* : three eight-syllabled pādas and one of four syllables, not two eight-syllabled pādas and one of twelve syllables.

1. In this arrangement the hymn 17—having 15 stanzas according to the tradition—has been divided into 3 parts (10 + 3 + 2 stanzas). This division, although recommended by the order of the hymns, has however not at all been made only for the sake of the order of the hymns. It has been shown above on p. 139, f.n. 1, that the parallels in the other Vedas and the selections in the Hotar-ritual lead us to assume a hymn consisting of tṛcas concluding with stanza 10: hence stanza 10 is a single closing stanza after the tṛcas 1-3, 4-6, 7-9. Stanzas 11-13 form a tṛca by themselves, as is shown by the Sāmaveda, where they occur as such; stanzas 14-15 form a Pragātha.—Bergaigne's (I.52) treatment of hymn 17 neglects many of the essentially relevant points.

out to be specially close[1] to the preceding hymns, but the clear demarcation of this section, in which the name Vatsa appears, justifies the assumption of a new section beginning with hymn 6. The deities of the hymns lead to the same result. In all the groups discussed so far the hymns addressed to the same Devatā always appear next to one another: hence the Indra-hymn 6, separated from the Indra-hymns 2-4, so also the Aśvin-hymn 8, separated from 5, indicate a new group. In the group 1-5 one finds the expected arrangement, *violated only by the first hymn:*[2] Indra 34, 42, 24, 21.—Aśvinau 39.

Hymns 27-31, 32-34. The assumption of *two* groups instead of one (27-34) is suggested by the Anukramaṇī (Manu-Medhātithi etc.) and by the frequent mention of the Kaṇvas in 32 ff., **[216]** who do not appear in 27-31. With this agree the deities and the number of the stanzas: first group, Viśve devās 22, 5, 5[3], 4. Praise of the sacrifice etc. 18.[4] The second group: only Indra, 30[5],19,18. Thus, both the groups appear in order.

43-48 ? These hymns, bounded by the Nabhāka- and the Vālakhilya-series are, perhaps, to be placed into one group. The same could, moreover, be looked upon as well ordered, only that—corresponding to the practice observed in the family books—Agni stands before Indra, although the first

1. 6.48 *Yāduaṁ janam*, cf. 1.31 *Yāduaḥ paśuḥ.*—6.47 *daduṣ Pajrāya sāmne*, cf. 4.17 *stuṣe Pajrāya sāmne.*—6.18, cf. 3.9.—8.12 cf. 5.4—8.21, cf. 5, 26.—Also the frequent mention of Turvaśa and Yadu is relevant in this connection.
2. The apparently present, but completely disarranged, division of this hymn into tṛcas suggests that some stanzas belonging to this hymn have been lost.
3. According to the tradition, 10 stanzas, each consisting of 2 pādas; the order is restored when we assume 5 stanzas of 4 pādas. The contents of the hymn neither prove nor disprove this.
4. Perhaps, hymn 31 consists of fragments. But at the time of making the collection these had possibly already developed into a single hymn.
5. Or, originally 31 stanzas, ZDMG, XXXVIII, 470 f.

Indra-hymn is longer than the first Agni-hymn: Agni 33, 30. —Indra 42, 33 (if the parts combined together in hymn 46 were already considered as a unit by the compilers)[1].—Ādityas 18.—Soma 15.

We now turn to the groups which follow the Vālakhilya-section. Their sorting out is, on the whole, more difficult and less certain because the characteristic ṛṣi-names which occur so frequently in the first part of the Maṇḍala, are absent here. However, the rule which has consistently held ground so far gives a lead for our orientation: hymns addressed to the same deity, if they do not occur together, must belong to different groups.

60-66. The Anukramaṇī ascribes these hymns to Pragātha[2] [**217**] and his several sons.—Agni 20.—Indra 18, 12, 12, 12, 12, 15. Thus, according to the order, except the last hymn whose division into different hymns (1-8, 9-15?) is not ruled out, but is not specially indicated either.

67-71. Ādityāḥ 21.—Indra 19, 18, 15.—Agni 15, or rather, perhaps, to be divided into two hymns 9, 6.—Completely in order. One can notice clearly how the two Indra-series, of this and the preceding group, are separated from each other. It is not unthinkable that also hymn 72 (18 stanzas), even if it violates the order, belongs to the Agni-series of this group; however, judging on the basis of the number of the stanzas, this hymn belongs more probably to the following group. But, in that case, and for this the contents of the hymn offer no difficulty, it will have to be looked upon as something different from the usual Agni-hymn (*haviṣāṁ stuti*,

1. They are, in fact, united by the name Vaśa Aśvia in stanzas 21, 33; of Vaśa who himself here speaks of his connection with Pṛthuśravas, so that in this hymn that, what in I.116.21 is praised among the past deeds of the Aśvins, is treated as present.
2. It may be noted that to the same Pragātha is assigned hymn 48, the last one before the Vālakhilya-group. However, it is scarcely possible that it is to be included in the group 60 ff. and consequently to assume that the Vālakhilyas are an interpolation cutting into the *interior* of a group.

as the Anukramaṇī says), since an Agni-hymn proper occurs in that group at a later place.

72-74 (or 73-74? see what has been just said): *haviṣāṁ stuti* 18.—Aśvinau 18.—Agni 15.—Hymns 73 and 74 are held together by the mention of the name Atri in the former, of Gopavana (who was an Ātreya; cf. Kāty. Śraut. X.2.21) in the latter.

75-79: Agni 16.—Indra 12, 11, 10.—Soma 9. Thus strictly according to the order. The traces of Atri-authorship cease here.

80-87: Indra 10, 9, 9.—Viśve devās 9.—Agni 9.—Aśvinau 9, 5, 6. According to the order except for the last Pragātha-hymn. One may note in this hymn the Vālakhilya-type parallelism in the first two Pragāthas; if one detaches them from the [**218**] third, then one obtains the fully ordered Aśvin-series 9, 5, 4, 2.

88-91: Indra 6, 7, 6, 7. The number of stanzas not according to the order.

92-94 : Indra 33, 34.—Marutaḥ 12. The number of stanzas not according to the order.

95-101:[1] Indra 9, 21, 15, 12, 8, 12.—Mitrāvaruṇau 6.—Aśvinau 2.—Vāyu 2.—Sūrya 2. The first and the last hymn of the Indra-series violates the order which happens to be there, perhaps, not just by chance. To assign the first hymn to the preceding group does not seem advisable; it would, in that case, stand separated from the other Indra-hymns of that group, and also the mode of expression shows special connections with the *following* hymns.[2] The end of the whole group is marked convincingly by a series of single tṛcas and

1. 101 is to be dissolved into its parts. Stanzas 13-15 seem to be a supplement.
2. Stanza 3 *tuaṁ hi śaśvatīnām* = 98.6; 4 *mahā̃ asi* = 98.2; 5 *mandrām* cf. 100. 10,11; 8 *sāmnā* cf. 98.1. Perhaps it deserves to be noted that the Anukramaṇī attributes 95 and 96 to the same author.

finally by a few probably appended stanzas[1].

102.103. Agni 22, 14.

In this way, it seems to me, the hymns of the eighth book can be arranged into groups, *within* which, *at least on the whole,* it is possible to recognize a definite arrangement. However, it is difficult to discover any regularity in the sequence of the groups among themselves. Yet Bergaigne believes (II.76 ff.) to have found one. The reasons for which I [**219**] cannot follow him are *implicit* in the above expositions. If one deals with the individual hymn-groups without prejudice, without being influenced by the desire to look for systematic number-relations, then one gets numbers of hymns in the different groups which, in my view, are far from having the appearance of such a far-reaching regularity that, the remaining irregularities could, perhaps, invite us to undertake corrections of the transmitted text. Altogether to such numerous, risky, and complicated corrections, proposed by Bergaigne who, here, if I am not mistaken, goes beyond the limits within which alone criticism remains criticism[2].

III

The First Book

Facts, recognized since long, make it certain that the principal division of the first book is the one which divides it into fifteen groups, the hymns of which, in every case,

---

1. One may note that the mode of expression of 96 and 100 shows several kinds of contacts. Cf. 96.7,8 with 100.1,2; *jaritar* 96. 12 and 100.4. The poet of this section has a special liking for the expression *viśvā jātāni* 96.6; 97.9; 100.4.
2. I must abstain here from going into the details of Bergaigne's construction of the eighth Maṇḍala. Only with regard to B.'s attempt to use the Adhyāya-division to derive support for his hypothesis, I may be permitted to refer to the comments I have made on the character of this division in ZDMG, XLI.508 ff.

belong to the same author or the same circle of authors. These groups, of which the Anukramaṇī has preserved correct awareness, are the following: 1-11, 12-23, 24-30, 31-35, 36-43, 44-50, 51-57, 58-64, 65-73, 74-93, 94-115, 116-126, 127-139, 140-164, 165-191. Mentioning of the names of the authors in the hymns themselves, regular repetition of concluding verses, metrical peculiarities confirm in many cases, and the arrangement [**220**] of the hymns in each group in all cases, the separation of the hymns into the above groups, and we may accept this as a fact which does not require renewed argumentation[1].

If we remember that the differently oriented arrangement of books II-VII on the one hand and of the eighth book on the other becomes specially clear in the use of the metres, then even a cursory survey of the metres of the first book will show that in this book occur, partly, the characteristics of book VIII, and, partly, those of books II ff. And, in fact, the hymn-groups of one type and those of the other are separated from each other rather sharply in the ordering of the groups in this Maṇḍala. The Gāyatrī, and beside, at least to some extent, the Pragātha-stanzas prevail, as in the eighth book, in the section I.1-50, except only in the hymn-group 31-35. On the other hand, in the section I.51-191, as

1. Ludwig (III.101 f.) contests the traditional division of the first two groups 1-11, 12-23; he believes to recognize, and I think without enough justification, a division at hymn 18. Against this, it is enough to refer to the Indra-hymn 16 which is separated from the Indra-series 4-11: a sure indication to show that a new group must begin between hymns 11 and 16. Now, if one includes hymn 1 (to Agni) in the former group, as one has every reason to do, then the Agni-hymn 12 shows that the point of division lies between 11 and 12, just where the tradition has it. Moreover, one may observe the following use of a single characteristic word: *upa hvaye* occurs in the ṚV I.13.3, 7, 8, 10, 12; 21.1; 22.5,12; 23.18; 164.26; X.36, 7: that is all passages, except two, in the hymns 13-23.—Of course, the question dealt with here has nothing to do with the other one, whether the Anukramaṇī is right in assigning hymns 1 ff. to a Viśvāmitrite, the hymns 12 ff. to a Kaṇvaite.

in the books II-VII, the Triṣṭubh and the Jagatī, on the whole, prevail, and beside these, as a special characteristic of the groups 65 ff. and 127 ff. the metres Dvipadā Virāj, respectively Atyaṣṭi.

We shall first take up for consideration the arrangement of the groups in the section I.51-191. *It corresponds in all essentials with the arrangement found in the books II-VII.* In the first instance, the rule that the hymns addressed to the same deity stand together prevails without an exception. Next, among the series of hymns to the deities, as in those Maṇḍalas, the Agni-hymns and the Indra-hymns, whenever they are available, receive priority: only in the Agastya-collection (165 ff.)—and it happens only here—where there is a group of hymns addressed to the Maruts, respy. to Indra and the Maruts which, from the point of view of the number of the hymns, far exceeds the Agni- and the Indra-hymns, stands at the beginning; this is then followed by the Indra-series which, from the point of view of the number of hymns, comes next to it, while an isolated Agni-hymn appears later among the hymns addressed to single deities[1].

The remaining series have been arranged among themselves according to the decreasing number of hymns addressed to the deities. If there are single hymns they have been placed at the end. This arrangement of the series holds good without exception if we consider that the hymn 121[2], addressed, according to the Anukramaṇī to Indra or to the Viśve devas, was assigned by the collectors of the hymns to the Viśve devās, and further if these collectors—what, however, may remain questionable[3]—counted hymns

1. Also in the group I.116-126 the isolated Indra-hymn would be seen following the Aśvin-series—Agni-hymns are not to be met with here—if it were not probable that the collectors attributed that hymn to the Viśve devās.
2. See the preceding footnote.
3. *In its favour* may be mentioned the decreasing order, which would thus arise in these hymns, further the occurrence of 92.13-18, as a cluster, in the Sāmaveda, finally the rearrangement of the stanzas which is possibly to be assumed for hymn 93 (see the next footnote).

91-93, just as they have been transmitted, only as three hymns, and not more[1].

[**222**] As is to be expected, here too, in each series the hymns follow one another according to the descending number of the stanzas. The exception of the hymn 70 (of 11 stanzas coming after the hymns of 10 stanzas) is probably to be eliminated, as has been long recognized[2], by the removal of stanza 11 which, in its construction, hangs in the air. Other exceptions which, exactly as in books II-VII, have to be made to conform to the rule by dividing them, or have to be explained by the assumption of additions, are the following:[3] 79 tr.—84.1-18 tr., 19-20 pr[4].—90.1-5,6-9 (or 6-8,9?)[5].—For 91, 92, 93 see p. 221, f.n. 4.—*104—120.

1. First, in the hymn 91 stanzas 1-4 get detached due to metre, 16-18 because they appear together in the Vāj. Saṁh. and due to their contents (*ā pyāyasva, ā pyāyasva, āpyāyamānaḥ*). Thus, we obtain for the remaining eleven stanzas 5-15 *a priori* the division 4+4+3 with which the text agrees very well (in 5-8 each stanza begins with *tvam*). Stanzas 19-23 could be a later supplement. —In 92, the two tṛcas 13-15, 16-18 get separated from what precedes due to their metre and their use in the Sāmaveda, and among themselves by their deities; also the division into 1-4 (metre), 5-8, 9-12 is hardly doubtful (Hillebrandt, Vedachresto. p. 2 f. holds a somewhat different opinion).—In hymn 93, the tṛcas 1-3, 9-11 get detached due to metre. Then one should expect division into Tṛcas also for 4-8, but we have only five stanzas. Would it then be too bold to suggest the placing of stanza 12, which stands alone by itself at the end and which from the point of view of the metre belongs to these stanzas, after stanza 8, in order to get two tṛcas 4-6, 7, 8, 12 which, according to their contents, are well-distinguished from each other? The clear character of stanza 12 as a concluding stanza could have, as the tṛca 9-11 grew together with the preceding ones, occasioned its being shifted to the end.
2. Grassmann Tr.; Bergaigne I.61.
3. We continue to use the method of reference adopted above p. 197 f.
4. We find here a regularly continuous tṛca-division and then the occurrence of a strophe of two stanzas after those of three. This, according to me, renders the assumption of appendages (Bergaigne I.18) improbable.
5. I mention this division of 90 together with the others, although in its case there is no apparent violation of the order.

1-9,10-12.—133.1-5,6-7[1].—135 tr.—The treatment of 139 is doubtful.—Are the hymns 162,163 (*aśvastuti*) and 164, the riddle-hymn, at the end of the Dīrghatamas-group, to be looked upon as appendages, or do they stand outside the series of the hymns to the deities because they are not ascribable to definite deities?—171 an isolated [**223**] violation of the rule due to special reasons[2].—*179.—*191.

The arrangement of the hymns of equal length in accordance with the metres (cf. above p. 202) is, also here, not without exceptions[3]. Whether we should remove these exceptions by doing some text-critical operations seems to me doubtful due to the reasons advanced above (p. 202 f.).

Let us now turn to the first six groups of the Maṇḍala which extend over hymns 1-50. Here also, within each group, the sūktas addressed to the same deity have been *without exception*[4], brought together. For the rest, however, principles of a different nature have been apparently decisive which, for each group separately, must be discussed in details.

---

1. The first part of this sūkta is clearly late, yet it seems to occur at the correct place in the arrangement since the last two stanzas form, perhaps, the last, shortest hymn of the Indra-series.
2. The hymns 170,171 contain stanzas belonging to *one* ākhyāna (ZDMG, XXXIX.60 ff.). By chance—presumably due to the wording of 171.1 which looks like a new beginning—two hymns (of five and six stanzas) were made out of these stanzas; these same stand, according to the order, after the hymn 169 of eight stanzas and before the hymn 172 of three stanzas: however, among themselves, they could not be arranged according to their length because, the natural order, determined by the sequence in the ākhyāna, was opposed to it.
3. Bergaigne I.18. Specially to be noted is the hymn 84 on which we have commented on p. 222 fn. 3.
4. If, for example, in the Medhātithi group the tṛca to the Viśve devās 23.10-12 is separated from the hymn 14 addressed to the Viśve devās, this is not to be looked upon as a real exception. The tṛca-series of the hymn 23 obviously corresponds to a series of deities fixed for ritual purposes (a variant of the Praüga-series?); hence here every tṛca had a fixed place which could not be changed and which it had to retain, even if the collectors, at the time of fixing the order, should have considered the tṛcas as independent hymns.

We begin with the *Kaṇva-group* 36-43[1] where the situation is very clear. We have the following deities and the numbers of stanzas: Agni 20.—Maruts 15, 15, 10. [224]—Brahmaṇaspati 8.—Varuṇa etc. 6, 3[2].—Pūṣan 6, 4.[2]—Rudra 6 (or 3, 3?).—Soma 3[2]. The arrangement would be in accordance with the principles governing books II-VII, except that the single hymn to Brāhmaṇaspati stands before the series consisting of two hymns. As we saw, such inaccuracies are surely to be found also in those books, but with regard to just this case, the belonging of this group to the Kaṇva family and the exclusive use of the metres Gāyatrī and Pragātha raise the question whether the arrangement of the hymns in this series is not to be interpreted as the one which is in accordance with the rule prevailing in the eighth book, so that, not the number of the hymns in a given series, but the number of the stanzas in the first hymn of each series becomes decisive. One can see that if judged on the basis of this principle the *group proves to be fully in order.*

The *Hiraṇyastūpa-group* (31-35) is in order from any point of view: in the case of these few hymns, the principles of arrangement followed in book VIII and those in books II-VII (these latter here in a section consisting of only Jagatī and Triṣṭubh, would, in fact, have more probability) lead to the same result : Agni 18.—Indra 15, 15.—Aśvinau 12.—Savitar 11.

1. On account of my differing view regarding the hymn-divisions, I differ substantially from Bergaigne (I.64 f.; II.89); cf. my remarks made while dealing with the Maṇḍala VIII, p. 210.
2. 41.4, and more decisively 42.4, do not give an impression that they begin a new hymn, but surely 41.7 (from there onwards a trochaic end) and 42.7 (from there onwards a refrain). That in 43, the tṛca addressed to Soma is to be detached goes without saying.

The *Medhātithi-group* (12-23)[1] shows itself more decisively to go along with the eighth book, for, in the first instance, the Indra-hymn (16) has received its present place simply on the basis of the number of stanzas, without any preference having been shown for the deity, and next, two Viṣṇu-hymns (22.16-18,19-21) appear after [**225**] single hymns, while, in accordance with the principles followed in books II-VII they (Viṣṇu-hymns) would have received their place before the single hymns. We find: Agni (including Āprī) 12, 12, 12.—Ṛtudevatās 12.—Indra 9.—Indrāvaruṇau 9.— Brahmaṇaspati etc. 9.[2]—Agni with the Maruts 9.—Ṛbhavas 8.—Indrāgnī 6.—Aśvinau 4.—Savitar 4.—The wives of the gods 4.—Dyāvāpṛthivyau 3.—Viṣṇu 3, 3.[3]—Finally in hymn 23 six tṛcas to different deities which form a ritual sequence (stanzas 19-24 a supplement).

It seems to me that the mode of arrangement of the eighth book is valid also for the *Śunaḥśepa group* (24-30). In individual cases, of course, there is a good deal of uncertainty. In the sūktas 25, 27, 30, apparently, there are in each case several hymns, and at the same time we note the well-known indications which favour their division into tṛcas. But it seems that sometimes a new hymn began with a new tṛca, but not always: on this point a completely certain decision cannot probably be reached. In 25, stanzas 4 and 7 probably do not signal the beginning of a new hymn[4];

1. Cf. Bergaigne I.62 with whom I am here in full agreement.
2. Even if we have to distinguish different constituents from one another in hymn 18, they must have been already unified at the time of the compilation of the hymns.
3. The divisions of the hymn 22 are on the whole clear. That the six Viṣṇu-stanzas are to be separated into two tṛcas is suggested not by the rule of arrangement alone; one may also note the occurrence of *vi cakrame* in each of the first three stanzas, but in none of the last three which, on the other hand, hold together by *paśyata . . . paśyanti, tat . . . tat, paramaṁ padam . . . paramaṁ padam.*
4. Nevertheless stanzas 7-9 form a tṛca (each stanza commences with the word *veda*). The tṛca-division in 13-15, 16-18, 19-21 is also clear.

stanza 12 appears to be a concluding stanza. In 27, the different ways of closing a line, now with an iambic, then with a trochaic end, seem to suggest separations after stanzas 6 and 9. In 30, a new beginning appears to occur after stanzas 6 and 12 (trochaic rhythm in 13 ff.!), but not after stanza 9; towards the end, a tṛca-hymn to **[226]** the Aśvins and another to Uṣas are to be detached. Accordingly, it seems to me that a series, somewhat of the following nature and agreeing fully with the mode of arrangement of the eighth book, comes to light: Varuṇa 15[1], 12, 9.—Agni 10, 6, 3, 4.[2]—Indra 9, 7, 6, 6, 4.—Aśvinau 3.—Uṣas 3.

Quite peculiar is the arrangement of the *Madhucchandas-group* (1-11): Agni 9.—Praüga-deities 9, 12 (but, probably, the two hymns were regarded as one, hence 21 stanzas?).—Indra 10, 10, 10, 10, 10, 10, 12, 8.—The arrangement in the three sections does not fit into any of the different methods. Equally striking is the violation of the arrangement according to the number of the stanzas towards the end of the Indra-series: it is related with the fact that the two last hymns to Indra have been composed in the Anuṣṭubh, while all the preceding hymns have been composed in the Gāyatrī[3].

1. I think that 24 was counted as *one* hymn (so also Bergaigne II.7) and possibly it is also one such. It could have been possible to look upon stanzas 3-5 as an independent Savitar-hymn if, in that event, stanzas 1-2 would not remain a separate Agni-hymn. As such it would have then belonged to the Agni-series; it also looks clearly incomplete: *prathamasya* in stanza 2 points to something further which has to follow, and this does, in fact, follow in the traditionally handed down text (cf. stanza 15 with 1 and 2). The way in which the hymn is made use of in the Śunaḥśepa-legend (Ait. Br. VII.16) agrees quite correctly with its nature, although this story was, without doubt, invented later.
2. At the end of the series a tṛca and a concluding stanza in a different metre: this tṛca occurs at the end so that the fourth stanza does not disturb the arrangement of the tṛcas in the middle, although in this way a hymn of four stanzas happens to come after the one with three.
3. Is it, perhaps, that just for this reason the Indra-series was placed at the end so that all the Gāyatrī-hymns could precede the Anuṣṭubh-ones ?

Finally, the *Praskaṇva-group* (44-50) is characterized by a distinct relationship of its hymns with the ritual[1]: all of them are addressed to the early-morning deities invoked in the Prātaranuvāka, to Agni—that [**227**] Agni, specially as the first illuminator of the day-break and as the bringer of *devāḥ prātaryāvāṇaḥ* is meant can be seen in many ways—, to the Aśvins, to Uṣas, and to the rising sun; connected with these invocations is the offering of Soma *tiroahnya*[2] (45.10; 47.1) which similarly belongs to the morning ritual. The hymns addressed to the individual deities are, each time, grouped together and made to follow the decreasing order (Agni 14, 10. —Aśvinau 15, 10. —Uṣas 16, 4. —Sūrya 10[3]), but the sequence of these small series among themselves is not the one which one expects. Since Agni has the first place and Sūrya the last, it is perhaps possible to think that the arrangement is influenced by the ritual sequence of the deities, in which case, however, we have to assume, that here the Aśvins, as against the sequence valid for the later ritual texts, had their place in the ceremony *before* Uṣas[4].

We shall have to return later to the question of the sequence of the individual hymn-groups among themselves in the first Maṇḍala.

---

1. Besides by its preference for Anuṣṭrubh, beside Gāyatrī and Pragātha.
2. On this see the Śatapatha Br. XI. 5.5.11 and specially the Āśvalāyana Śraut. VI.5 where, exactly as in our hymn-group, the deity-combination Agni, Uṣas, Aśvinau, Sūrya (§2) and the Soma tiroahnya (§ 24) are found together.
3. 50.11-13 (10-13 ?) are obviously a later addition.
4. As already shown by Bergaigne (Rel. Véd. II.432), the Ṛgveda allows Uṣas sometimes to precede, sometimes to follow the Aśvins. The latter, which is even attested in the passage concerned (I.46.14) is, perhaps, the original. For, are not the Aśvins to be interpreted—and this conjecture is expressed with the greatest reservation—as the horses of Uṣas from whom later, due to continuous anthropomorphisation, developed the young gods *with* the horses—Aśvins from Aśva ?

[228] **IV**

The Tenth Book

A discovery of Bergaigne[1], which has decisive importance, has shown that the tenth book is a unit which has been arranged according to a uniform principle. The Maṇḍala consists of, to adhere for the time being to the formulation adopted by Bergaigne himself, collections of hymns which have been composed by the same author; these collections have been arranged according to the decreasing number of hymns in them, and where this criterion is not decisive, according to the number of the stanzas in their first (or, eventually the only) hymn. At the beginning of the Maṇḍala occur some longer collections; immediately afterwards follow such as have three hymns each, then two hymns each; in the end appears, and this takes up nearly half of the whole book (from 85 onwards), the series of single hymns which are arranged according to the decreasing number of the stanzas.

That this understanding of the situation is essentially correct throughout is demonstrable and does not require any fresh discussion. What remains for us to do is only to suggest a change, with regard to a minor point, in the formulation of the principle of arrangement and then examine in detail the execution of the revised formulation, as also the exceptions which escape its operation.

The speculations of the Indian Vedic teachers who were responsible for determining the authors' lists are based undoubtedly in many cases on the same arrangement of the hymns which we find even today; the rule of the decreasing number of stanzas in the arrangement of the hymns must

1. I.40-45, cf. II.1 ff.

have been valid [**229**] already at the time when those authors' lists were devised. Could it be that in the case of the tenth book the things happened the other way round, i.e. the names of the authors—names such as Trita Āptya, Yama Vaivasvata, Yajña Prājāpatya which betray very little of the signs of a real, old tradition—were determined even before the hymns were brought together in this collection? A number of names like 111 Aṣṭrādaṁṣṭra Vairūpa, 112 Nabhaḥprabhedana Vairūpa, 113 Śataprabhedana Vairūpa, 114 Sadhri Vairūpa, or like 172 Saṁvarta Āṅgirasa, 173 Dhruva Āṅgirasa, 174 Abhīvarta Āṅgirasa[1]—do they not also point to the same type of inventions based on the *given* sequence, which (inventions) appear so clearly in the lists of the authors of the other Maṇḍalas? We shall show furthermore that the triads of hymns, the dyads of hymns etc. which have been grouped together in the tenth book almost always carry clear *inner* signs of relationship; there are also cases where the tradition does *not* ascribe the hymns to a common author and yet the hymns concerned have been treated as one group, and inner indications confirm the correctness of this grouping[2]. Hence, we may conclude that what decided the grouping of the hymns were not the direct statements of the Anukramaṇī about the authors, but the fact that certain hymns belonged together because they were composed by the same author or by closely related

1. From the standpoint of Bergaigne it would be difficult to answer why those Vairūpas or Āṅgirasas should have counted for the arrangement of the hymns as different authors, while apparently Yama, Śaṅkha Yāmāyana, Damana Yāmāyana etc. (14 ff.), or Ghoṣā and Suhastya Ghauṣeya (39-41) were to be looked upon as, to some extent, a single person.
2. E.g. hymns 35-38 undoubtedly form a group although Luśa is mentioned as the author only of 35,36; the ṛṣi of 37 is Abhitapas Saurya, of 38 Indra Muṣkavant. There are many cases of this type.

authors, and that this relationship was already there and was well-known [**230**]: this is quite similar to what has happened to the hymns of the fourth book: apparently they do not occur in the fourth book because they have been ascribed to the same author, but they were ascribed to the same author because they were found to occur in the same book; and they occurred and occur in the same book because since very old times they were transmitted as a closely related group. The Anukramaṇī, I think, is not directly the *basis* of the arrangement governing the tenth book: rather, the facts, which form this basis, are reflected relatively clearly in the Anukramaṇī. And it is difficult to imagine that the Anukramaṇī should prove itself to be so *ill*-informed about the names of the authors of the tenth book and, at the same time, so *well*-informed, at least on the whole, about the belonging-together of the individual hymn-groups, unless we assume that a certain awareness of this belonging-together of the hymn-groups was preserved in an old tradition that lay well behind the period when the names of the authors were invented, and that this awareness of the tradition, quite independently of the statements about the authors, which were invented relatively later, had served as the basis, which could not be lost, for the arrangement of the Maṇḍala.

We shall now proceed with the question of the demarcation of the individual hymn-groups, and while doing this, as would follow from what has been just said, the statements of the Anukramaṇī will be looked upon as important piece of evidence but they will have to be checked and supplemented by the indications which are obtained from other factors like the sequence of the hymns, the diction, the metre etc.

Demarcation of triads and dyads which follow one another in a very great number is, as a rule, sure and evident.

Difficulties arise about demarcation in the larger collections which form the first part of the Maṇḍala. [**231**] It is advisable to start with the Vimada-hymns (20-26) which is the clearest marked group. A number of indications combine to make the demarcation of this group quite certain. The name of Vimada or the Vimadas appears in X.20, 23, 24, the rare metre Āstārapaṅkti with its refrains in 21, 24, 25; the Anuṣṭubh, which is repeatedly represented, occurs also in 26 and thus speaks for the relationship of this hymn with the Vimada-group,[1] while a new series begins with 27 in the Triṣṭubh metre, almost unknown to the Vimadas, and, as we shall show later, 27 goes with the *following* hymns also due to other criteria. X.20 begins with the benediction *bhadraṁ no' api vātaya manaḥ* which is taken from 25.1 and placed *śāntyartham* at the head of the collection, and with the typical opening words *agnim īḷe.* So there can be no doubt that the Anukramaṇı has correctly determined the extent of the Viṃada-group to be 20-26: this way the arrangement of the hymns, first according to the groups Agni—Indra[2]—other gods, then according to the decreasing number of the stanzas, becomes clear. That the long Indra-hymns 27 ff. do not at all belong to the Vimada-group can be recognized already by their position which is separated from the Indra-hymns of that group.

Thus one group, beginning with hymn 20 and comprising seven hymns, is quite certain. Consequently, following the principle of arrangement, in the first 19 hymns we have to

---

1. Cf. also 26.7 *pra śmaśru haryato dūdhot* with 23.1 *pra śmaśru dodhuvat,* 23. 4 *indraḥ śmaśrūṇi haritābhi pruṣṇute* (cf. 26.3 *pruṣāyati*).—26.7 has the rare word *ina* (twice) common with 23.6; with 26.7 *vājānāṁ patiḥ* cf. 23.3 *vājasya . . . patiḥ.*
2. The end of the Indra-series, which is made up of three stanzas 24.4-6 addressed to the Aśvins, could be a short supplement (so also Berg. I.45); they appear to be very late.

look for a division of equally large or larger groups, [**232**] and of these we may most probably expect two. In order to determine their point of demarcation we note first the obvious relationship of 10-13. The hymns 11 and 12 have a common concluding stanza; they are connected with 10 due to decisive parallelisms: 11.2 *rapad gandharvīr apiā ca yoṣanā*, cf. 10.4 *gandharvo' apsu apiā ca yoṣā*, 10.11 *bahu etad rapāmi.*— 12.6 = 10.2 *salakṣmā yad viṣurūpā bhavāti.*— Also hymn 13 belongs to this group; 13.1 *vi śloka' etu* cf. 12.5 *śloko na yātām*; 13.2 *svam ulokaṁ vidāne* cf. 12.1 *svam asuṁ yan.*— Further, the hymns 14-18, addressed to the dead, belong undoubtedly together, and to these must be added hymn 19 unless it is a later interpolation.—Then the group of the seven Triṣṭubh hymns to Agni, each having seven stanzas, and ascribed to Trita becomes clear without difficulty. But the two Agni hymns 11-12, just because they stand detached from this series, are proved to belong to a different group.

If one takes all these data into consideration, one can see already now that it is not possible to carry out a thoroughly strict grouping of the hymns according to the principle of the decreasing number of hymns, or at least not unless we assume interpolations and some such remedies; groupings like 1-10, 11-19 or 1-11, 12-19, which would do justice to the principle of arrangement from the point of view of the number of hymns in a group, are out of question because the hymns 10-12 belong together. Hence, we will first proceed to look for the connections and breaks among the hymns which result from inner grounds without taking into account the number of hymns in a group.

In connection with the hymns 10-13 which we have recognized as forming a *single* group, we have to ask the question [**233**] whether they are to be combined into one and the same group with 14 ff.[1] I believe that there is much to be said for it. In the Ṛgveda, on the whole, there is little mention of god Yama; he is mostly mentioned naturally in the hymns to the dead X.14 ff.: then, it is probably not just by chance that the same Yama is mentioned not only as the hero of the narrative X.10, but is likewise mentioned in 12.6;[2] 13.4. Also the diction in both the parts shows as many contacts as can only be expected in the isolated context of the hymns to the dead.[3] The numbers of the stanzas in the hymns 10-19 are: 14, 9, 9, 5, 16, 14, 14, 14, 14, 8. Thus, it seems that first the hymns 10-13 and then the hymns to the dead 14-18, eventually with the hymn 19, form two series arranged according to the decreasing number of the stanzas.

The grounds which led to the assumption of the relationship of the hymns 10 ff. with the hymns to the dead, are absent for hymns 8,9; rather, it would appear that the hymn 8 (and then obviously also hymn 9, although in this hymn which is composed in a different metre and which is addressed to another deity, the indications of relationship are understandably absent) is to be combined with the preceding group[4]. Also the Anukramaṇī [**234**] supports this view[5]: it assigns hymns 1-7 to Trita, obviously on the basis of

---

1. That the hymn 16, addressed to Agni, stands separated from 11, 12 offers no difficulty; that hymn which is related to the ritual of the dead is no Agni-hymn in the usual sense.
2. This and the following stanzas give a fairly detailed account of Yama's realm.
3. 10.1 *ā . . . vavṛtyām,* 18.3 *āvavṛtran.*—11.3 *uśantam uśatām anu kratum,* 15.8 *uśann uśadbhiḥ,* 16.12 *uśantaḥ . . . uśantaḥ . . . uśann uśataḥ.*—11.6 *ud īraya,* 15.1 *ud īratām.*—12.1 *svam asuṁ yan,* 14.12 *asum,* 15.1 *asuṁ ya' īyuḥ.*—12.4 *asunīti* in the ṚV, besides in X.59.5-6, only here and in the hymns to the dead 15.14; 16.2.—12.8 *mitro no' atra* (i.e. in Yama's realm) *aditir anāgān savitā devo varuṇāya vocat;* 17.4 *yatrāsate sukṛto yatra te yayus tatra tvā devaḥ savitā dadhātu.*
4. 8.2 *jigāti,* cf. 6.4.—8.3 *aruṣīḥ,* cf. 5.5.—8.4 *uṣa'-uṣo hi vaso' agram eṣi,* cf. 1.1.—8.6 *niyudbhiḥ,* cf. 3.6.
5. Bergaigne (II.2) has already drawn attention to this.

the mention of this hero in *hymn* 8 (st. 7 ff.); hymns 8 and 9 are then assigned to the enemy of Trita who is mentioned at the same place, whereas from 10 onwards names from a different circle, Yama and different Yāmāyanas, prevail. The ordering of the group 1-9 offers no difficulties: hymns 1-7 addressed only to Agni are followed by hymn 8, addressed partly to Agni, partly to Indra,[1] finally the hymn 9 to the waters.

After having divided the hymns which precede the well-demarcated limit of the Vimada section into two groups 1-9, 10-19, let us now try to arrange, first, the immediately following hymns 27 ff. That hymns 27, 28, and, on the other hand, hymns 31, 32, 33 belong together can be easily seen[2]. The Aṇukramaṇī leads us to two groups, 27-29 (Vasukra) and 30-34 (Kavaṣa). The demarcation lines have certainly been correctly drawn at 27 and 34; however, I think it is probable that what the tradition looks upon as two groups, are, in fact, two series within the same group[3]. Parallelisms in tone and the mode of expression which bind the two series together are too numerous and weighty to be explained away as due to chance. [**235**] With 27. 2 *tanvā śūśujānān* cf. 34.6 *tanvā śūśujānaḥ (śūśujāna* only at these

1. Bergaigne (II.2) assumes that X.8.7-9 form an independent hymn. That is possible, but in no way certain. We would have, in that case, 10 instead of 9 hymns in the whole group. Reducing hymn 9 to three stanzas so that it is not longer than the conjectured hymn 8.7-9 seems to me bold, and not necessary; without it too, the arrangement Agni-Indra-Āpas is tenable.
2. 27, 28, and likewise 31, 32, have numerous parallel expessions; with regard to 32 and 33 it is enough to draw attention to the mentionings of Kuruśravaṇa (32.9; 33.4).
3. Decreasing number of the stanzas; hymns 27-29: 24, 12, 8 stanzas. — 30-33 : 15, 11, 9, 9 stanzas. Supplement: the dice-hymn 34 having 14 stanzas.—That the Indra-hymn 32 is not to be found among the Indra-hymns of the first group is hardly important; the latter are as little Indra-hymns as the former.

two places).—27.20 *mamandhi*, 31.2 *mamanyāt*, 32.8 *amaman*[1].—27.8 and 31.4 *svapatiḥ* (elsewhere only once in the ṚV).—29.1 and 31.9 *vane na*.—27.19 and 33.3 *śiśnā*.—27.17 *niuptā akṣāḥ* cf. 34.5,9 *niuptāḥ* and the whole thought-content of the dice-hymn 34.—27.17 *pavitravantā carataḥ punantā*; 30, 5 *oṣadhībhiḥ punītāt*.—27.18 *ayam me devaḥ savitā tad āha*; 34.13 *tan me vi caṣṭe savitāyam aryaḥ*.— 27.21 = 31.8 *enā paro' anyad asti*.—Above all, the riddle-type passages appearing in similar formulation in 27, 28 as in 31 also contribute to make the relationship of the two series 27 ff. and 30 ff. probable.

Next comes a collection obviously consisting of four hymns 35-38[2]. The relationship of not only 35 and 36, which the Anukramaṇī assigns to the same author, but also of 37 is made certain by numerous parallels; that 38 also belongs to this group is made probable by the number of stanzas in it, and the mode of expression of this small hymn, which from the point of view of its contents, stands somewhat further away from the preceding hymns, contains at least no factor which should go against the relationship[3].

Now we have reached a point where groups of three, then of two, hymns begin to appear in larger number and hence the judgement on individual cases becomes essentially easier and more certain. Following the lead **[236]** given by the Anukramaṇī we easily sort out the triads of hymns

1. That the three forms are related to the same root can be considered probable.
2. Decreasing numbers of the stanzas 14, 14, 12, 5.
3. In its *favour*, on the other hand, is of importance to note the relationship of stanza 38.5 to Luśa, the traditional author of hymns 35, 36, which is mentioned in the Pañc. Br. IX. 2, 22.

which immediately follow[1]: 39-41; 42-44; (45-47)[2]; 48-50; 51-53; 54-56. If one observes what is obvious, viz. the number of the stanzas, the deity, the metre of the hymns, parallelisms of expression, identical concluding stanzas (42-44), mention of the author (Bṛhaduktha 54.6; 56.7), finally, in one case, the string of the same narrative running through several hymns (51-53), then one sees that it gives a difinitive confirmation to the divisions stated above.

These sure hymn-triads are surprisingly followed by a section which, at least in the form in which it is handed down, represents a tetrad 57-60. Several related groups of formulae which are partly held together by the repetition of the refrains have been here arbitratrily divided into four hymns; their reduction to three hymns would easily be conceivable.

The dyads which now follow (61-84) form a clear series (Bergaigne I.42). Throughout, the Anukramaṇī assigns each time two of these hymns to the same ṛṣi[3], and the inner indications confirm this grouping. In most cases the two hymns put into the same group **[237]** are characterized by the same number of stanzas, the same metre[4], the same deity; 63 and 64 have the same concluding stanza having

---

1. Cf. Bergaigne I.44; II.5.
2. The Anukramaṇī assigns only the two hymns 45, 46 to the same author (Vatsaprī), but surely one cannot doubt that these three hymns, which appear between groups which are characterized by the Anukramaṇī as triads, form themselves a triad, especially when the Vātsapra melody to be sung on 47.1 indicates ṛṣi Vatsaprī to be the author also of this hymn. One may also note that hymns 45-47 stand as three Triṣṭubh hymns between the hymns in which Jagatī prevails.
3. Except 75, 76. Both the hymns have been composed in the same metre and exhibit the same tone, although special contacts between the two cannot be expected due to the difference of their contents (yet cf. 76.8 *suapasaḥ* and 75.7 *apasām apastamā*).
4. The fact that hymns 77, 78 have been composed in a peculiar metre is by itself of decisive importance in the issue of grouping. Similarly for 83, 84 the devatā (Manyu).

the mention of Gaya as the author, 65 and 66 likewise with the mention of "Vasiṣṭha". Further, sameness of vocabulary and of the manner of expression generally contribute to remove any doubt regarding the pairwise grouping of these hymns.

Finally there remain, as already mentioned, single hymns from 85 onwards upto the end of the Maṇḍala ; we will take up immediately the question of their arrangement.

First let us have a look at the sequence of the hymn-groups we have tried to set up: it strikes us that if we leave the traditionally handed down stock of hymns as it is without making any change then they betray only an approximate regularity. Our groups, according to their order, have the following number of hymns: 9[1], 10, 7, 8, 4; then follow triads, at the end of which, however, appears a tetrad (57-60), next diads, and finally single hymns. The inclusion of the hymn 19 into the third, instead of the second, group (Grassmann) would yield a more correct order of numbers (9, 9, 8, 8 etc.); this expedient, however, is ruled out by the fact that we have a perfectly clear arrangement as far as the Vimada group is concerned and above all by the unambiguous character of 20.1 as the starting point of a new group [see above p. 231]. It is not inconceivable that the principle of arranging the hymn-groups in accordance with decreasing number of hymns has not been applied wih the same strictness to the longer collections which on that account are more difficult to take in at a glance, as in the case of the shorter ones, and that the principle here was more easily thwarted owing to the considerations [**238**] which we cannot expect to discover. It is also possible that there have been interpolations: but the evidence is not clear enough to enable us to do anything more than express in general our doubt about the integrity of the tradition, or that it could give us the right to deny, even with only

1. Or 10; see p. 234, fn. 2.

approximate certainty, to certain definite sections their right to belong to the original collection[1].

The order in which the groups of equal number of hymns follow one another, as also the order of the hymns within the groups show likewise, on the whole, unmistakable regularity, but also show irregularities in individual cases which, in most cases, is impossible to eliminate. Attention has already been drawn to the fact that the longer groups are arranged as Agni-series, Indra-series etc., the hymns within which are arranged according to the decreasing number of the stanzas; in the shorter groups, mostly, though not always, the hymns are addressed to a *single* deity and correspondingly we have *one* sequence. That this sequence is disturbed in the group 51-53 (9, 6, 11 stanzas) is explained satisfactorily by the fact that these hymns are related to a narrative. It is more difficult to explain[2] the sequence in the group 54-56 which has two Indra-hymns of 6 and 8 stanzas followed by a hymn of seven stanzas to the Viśve devās. The suggestion to assign the second Indra-hymn to the Viśve devās, made by Bergaigne, cannot be easily accepted owing to the contents of the hymn. On the other hand, it is not impossible to believe that in the order of the hymns 54 and 55 we have an old, traditional sequence which is based, if not on chance, on criteria which escape our knowledge. However, it is to be noted that additions and omissions of the stanzas might also have caused disturbance **[239]** in the order which we find observed elsewhere. This is shown by the remarks made regarding the last large section of the tenth book (85-191). But this possibility is not of such nature that on its basis one can suggest same definite critical operation which might have at least just a shade of probability.

---

1. For example, one could *think* of hymn 19 or hymn 34 as later additions, but it is hardly necessary to point out the unreliability of that kind of suppositions.
2. Bergaigne I.43.

The pairs of hymns (61-84) reveal, as stressed by Bergaigne, greater consistency in ordering of the hymns among themselves, each time according to the decreasing length of the first hymn. In the case of the triads of hymns, this rule is violated in the series 42-44, 45-47 because hymn 42 has 11, while hymn 45 has 12 stanzas.[1] Most striking violations of the principle of ordering according to the decreasing number of stanzas occur in the series of the single hymns; they require a more detailed investigation. But before we come to it, it is necessary to offer beforehand a few remarks, just with regard to this series, on the question raised by Bergaigne in connection with the influence exerted by the metre on the ordering of the hymns of equal length.

That such an influence is to be found also here cannot be doubted: the sequence of the hymns of seven stanzas (129-137) or of three stanzas (177-191) is enough to make this clear. But if we found in the case of the other Maṇḍalas that there were cases of carelessness in the employment of the concerned principle of ordering, and their removal with the help of textual criticism appeared doubtful, the same is true here to a much greater degree. In the first instance, the distinction between Jagatī and Triṣṭubh, in determining **[240]** the order of the hymns, has been very incompletely made. However, in several series a Jagatī-hymn stands, each time, before a single or several Triṣṭubh-hymns: thus in the case of the series of hymns having nine, eight, six, or five stanzas. But in the case of the series of hymns having twelve and ten stanzas, the Jagatī-hymn occurs in the midst of the Triṣṭubh-hymns; in the case of the series of hymns having four stanzas, one Jagatī-hymn occurs before

1. The suggestion of Bergaigne (II.5) to remove stanza 45.12 does not seem to me to be sufficiently supported; that this stanza is omitted in the morning litany is explained by the fact that it is not addressed exclusively to Agni.

two Triṣṭubh-hymns and one follows them. Similarly, the distinction between Anuṣṭubh and Gāyatrī is shaky: the Gāyatrī-hymns 153 and 175 occur between Anuṣṭubh-hymns[1]. On the other hand, the distinction between Triṣṭubh-Jagatī group and the Anuṣṭubh-Gāyatrī group is apparently somewhat more strictly maintained. But, how far the disturbances of metrical arrangement are to be attributed in individual cases to the later additions to the original collection, how far to the equally thinkable change of place of the hymns in the course of transmission, how far to the carelessness of the redactor and other chance-occurrences is a question which, in my opinion, has little prospect of being solved, and I shall not quite succeed to persuade even myself to have the confidence with which Bergaigne handles it.

According to me we are considerably on more firm grounds when we take up the investigation of such cases where the arrangement depending on the *number of the stanzas* is violated in the long series of single hymns (85 ff.). Here one can definitely conclude that disturbances to the original state of affairs have taken place—disturbances, the remarkable frequency of which in this section as compared with their rarity in the books II-VII is obviously to be counted among those indications which show that the transmission of these **[241]** latest elements of the collection, which in many ways border on the sphere of the Atharvaveda, does not stand completely on the same level as those of its old, fundamental parts. If, as for example is the case in the arrangement of the groups of triads, the two hymns, whose relative length should decide their sequence, stand in many cases away from each other by several positions, negligences in adhering to the principle of arrangement cannot be

1. Is 153, perhaps, because it was thought to be addressed to Indra, attracted to the Indra-hymn 152 ?

surprising; it is, however, quite a different case here where single hymn, individually by itself, has to receive its place according to the number of stanzas: here nothing but the same regularity which, in fact, is to be found in the series of books II-VII and of book IX, is expected. But one may note, for example, the numbers of the stanzas as found in the hymns 138-176. The sequence of numbers here is as follows: 6.6.6.6.8.6.6.6.6.5.5.5.5.5.5.5.5.5.5.5.5.6.5.5. 6.6.5.5.5.4.4.4.4.4.4.6.5.4.4. No one will, I think, doubt that the hymns having eight stanzas amongst those having six, those having six stanzas among those having five, the two having six and five stanzas each among those having four stanzas have either to be reduced to the size of their neighbouring hymns by deleting some stanzas, or have to be declared as interpolations. On the whole, I think, the former expedient will have to be preferred. This is indicated by the circumstance that there is hardly a hymn among those which violate the order which has *far too many* stanzas than the expected number: one such hymn of 13 stanzas is to be found among those having twelve, one of 9 stanzas among those having eight, such of 5 stanzas among those having four and three, etc. This uniformity is more easily explained when one assumes vacillations regarding the length of the hymns so that these could be reckoned [**242**] as having one or two stanzas more or less, than when one thinks of interpolations of whole hymns in which case, obviously, once it was decided not to pay attention to the principle of arrangement even this *approximate* following of the same (principle) could not be expected.

The Vedic tradition offers also a concrete clue to confirm what has been *a priori* assumed, viz. changing the number of the stanzas of some of the hymns under consideration here: it is Bergaigne to whom our thanks are due for being the first also to refer to this point. Several of the hymns which interrupt the sequence[1] appear in the Atharvaveda in such a way that either they have there exactly the number of stanzas which would be correct according to the arrangement in the ṚV, or they have the wrong number of stanzas which disturbs the arrangement according to the number of stanzas, to be found also as the basis of the arrangement in the AV, but which, as is well-known, is very often violated: and, to be sure, they conform to the order of the AV as soon as one assigns to them the number of stanzas required for the arrangement of the hymns in the Ṛgveda. Although it is true that the Atharvaveda so often shows deviations from the Ṛgveda in respect of the number of stanzas and hence not the least importance can be attached to them for the text-criticism of the Ṛgveda,[2] yet here two alterations, which explain each other, come together with such constancy that one cannot regard it as a matter of pure coincidence[3].

[243] Let us now examine the individual cases more closely.

Hymn 163 has six stanzas in the ṚV; according to the arrangement, we expect five. In the Atharvaveda (II.33) the hymn occurs among the pentads, but has *seven* stanzas. To be sure, stanza 5 of the ṚV is missing and in its place two

1. 109.163.174.187.191. Cf. Bergaigne I.4.
2. Sometimes the AV changes the number of the stanzas of the ṚV hymn in such a way that its placing in the A. Saṁhitā fits with this changed number, but sometimes also in such a way that its placing in the A. Saṁhitā is accurate only if it had the number of stanzas it has in the ṚV. Sometimes the stanza-number of the AV agrees with that of the ṚV, but the placing of the hymn in the AV shows that the AV originally had a different number of stanzas which was later made equal to that of the ṚV.
3. As against the five cases listed in footnote 1 above there occur only two (128 and, to some extent, 173) in which the abnormal number of stanzas in the ṚV is confirmed by their placement in the AV.

stanzas are added: out of stanza 3 of ṚV. are made two stanzas (AV 3, 4), and a new stanza (AV 6), striking due to the faulty number of syllables,[1] is added. If we set aside these expansions, which as such are easily recognizable, then there remains a hymn of five stanzas, which is distinguished from the Ṛk-recension by the absence of ṚV stanza 5, and in this we might, in all probability, see that form of the sūkta which is required by the rule of arrangement of the ṚV. The character of this hymn of exorcism with its enumeration—which does not reveal any proper thought-continuity—of limbs and organs from which the disease is to be driven out rules out in itself either confirmation or refutation of the above interpretation from the point of view of meaning; nevertheless it may be noted that stanza 5 agrees, like other stanzas in the hymn, with the remaining stanzas not only in the words *yakṣmam . . . vi vṛhāmi te,* but is identical in its whole second hemistich with stanza 6. Presumably an interpolator found missing—similarly, as also obviously, the interpolator of the Atharvan recension—the mention of some body-parts which he then added in the first half of stanza 5 and then borrowed as its second half the second hemistich of stanza 6.

The conditions in 174 (= AV. I.29) are similar to those of 163; here also if we leave out [**244**] from the ṚV and the AV that which is not common to both the Vedas and therefore is to be regarded as uncertain, we get the correct number of stanzas for both of them. Then the AV loses its fourth and the fifth stanza—the latter is interpolated evidently following partly ṚV X.159.1, partly 174.5— ; from the ṚV, however, goes its fourth stanza.[2] One may note that this stanza is identical with X.159.4: since 159 also has one stanza too many, the assumption of one and the same stanza having

1. The same is also found in stanza 5 of the AV: comparison with the ṚV shows that the mistake had arisen later.
2. It may be noted that the catch-word *abhi,* which is continually repeated in the remaining stanzas, is missing in the fourth stanza.

been interpolated at both these places, which are quite similar to each other, suggests itself.

Also in the case of the hymn 191 the AV apparently leads to the correct solution. This hymn, which according to the arrangement in the ṚV should have three stanzas, has, in fact, three in the Atharvaveda (instead of four as in the ṚV), and it occurs in the book of hymns having three stanzas (VI.64). The first stanza of the ṚV is missing[1]: one may observe that the Taittirīya Brāhmaṇa (II.4.4.4) and the Maitrāyaṇī Saṁhitā (II.2.6) likewise give stanzas 2-4, *without stanza 1*, which latter, also in its contents, remains unmistakably at a distance from the rest.[2]

In hymn 109 where the text of the ṚV, judged according to the rule of arrangement, shows not too many but too few stanzas (7 instead of 11), the missing stanzas presumably have been correctly preserved in the AV. There (V.17), at one place in the collection which appears to indicate the extent of the hymns to be of eleven stanzas, occur 18 stanzas; of these the last seven are closely related;[3] in the ṚV there is no trace of these, [**245**], and there are obvious grounds to assign them to quite a late period. If we omit these stanzas then we get a hymn of eleven stanzas which has, besides the seven stanzas found in the ṚV, four additional ones: AV 4.7–9. On the analogy of the cases already discussed it must be considered as probable that we have, in this way, discovered the hymn of eleven stanzas which, in accordance with the rule of arrangement, is what is to be expected for the ṚV. It is scarcely probable that it is merely a case of deceptive coincidence if the hymn has lost four stanzas in the ṚV, or was interpolated at a place which indicates that

1. But it has been subsequently interpolated in a very peculiar way, see Bergaigne I.4, fn. 2.
2. The beginning of stanza 1, *saṁ-sam,* obviously, gave the occasion for attaching it to the saṁjñāna-hymn.
3. Every stanza begins the same way; the second hemistich, except for the last stanza, is throughout identical.

it should have four stanzas more, and then in the AV exactly four stanzas are added to it: it in not very easy to believe that these stanzas should have nothing to do with the four stanzas we are looking for. Yet, on the other hand, this has to be noted: if one examines the stanzas in question one will hardly find them to have the same level of Vedic dignity as is found in the remaining seven stanzas. The *pañca mānavāḥ* (st. 9), the rājanya and vaiśya (at the same place; but cf. ṚV X.90.12), the forms *hinasti* (7) and *vi dunoti* (4), perhaps, are not quite decisive, but they certainly come close to the limits of what is possible in the ṚV. Hence, the question has to be raised whether *even* if the place of the hymn in the Saṁhitā depends on its having eleven stanzas, the form of the hymn with seven stanzas is not the original one. It is possible that at the time when the collection of the ṚV hymns was arranged both the forms of the hymn were available and that while the hymn, by virtue of the form which is still available in the AV, received the place tradition has given it, the other form was preferred for the recension of the ṚV that is available to us.

Finally, no special remarks are called for for the hymn 187. In the ṚV it has five stanzas instead of the expected three; in the AV (VI.34) it occurs [**246**] with the same five stanzas in the section of the triads. For the removal of any two particular stanzas, there is no evidence,[1] and considering the whole character of the small text, well nothing else can be expected.

If the AV-parallels supply us with so many indications, which are also repeatedly confirmed in other ways, for obtaining the correct number of stanzas for the respective Ṛgvedic hymns which would correspond to the rule of arrangement, then we will decide to take the same course, with so much the more confidence, in many other cases

1. One might think that stanza 4 is added after the model of III.62,9. But that is only *one* stanza, while we have to deal with two.

where such parallels are not available. We had already noted that the way we have to treat the hymn 174 as suggested by the AV, also gives aids for 159: similar light is thrown by 163 [above p. 243] on 162. These two Anuṣṭubh-hymns of six stanzas, occurring next to each other, break the series of hymns having five stanzas. We pointed out that the AV points to the removal of st. 5 from 163, and noted that the identity of the second hemistich of st. 5 with that of st. 6 arouses, simultaneously, the doubt that one is an expansion spun out of the other. Stanzas 5 and 6 of 162 are found to be exactly in the same situation:[1] hence here also the required shortening is obvious and is confirmed mutually by the similar shortening in 163[2].

In the following cases also shortenings are easily suggested. Hymn 87 receives its correct length if we remove[3] either the last four stanzas which are distinguished from the rest by the metre, **[247]** or at least the last two which are missing also in the AV VIII.3.—Similarly, with regard to hymn 103, the sequence is put into order clearly by effecting a shortening at the end. The war-like invocations to Indra, and beside him mainly to Bṛhaspati, come to an end with stanza 11; as it often happens at the end of the hymns, the closing words *asmā̃ u devā' avatā haveṣu* carry over the prayer to a different circle of deities. In the Atharvaveda (XIX.13) and in the Saṁhitās of the Black Yajurveda[4] also stanza 11 marks the close of the hymn. Stanzas 12 and 13 are decidedly

1. Also the *nipadyate* seems to have been taken over by one stanza from the other.
2. One may note that the form *bhūtvā*, which later becomes extremely frequent and is otherwise unknown to the ṚV, occurs twice in 162, 5.
3. Stanza 21, due to its tone and contents, is quite suited to be the closing stanza of the hymn.
4. In the Maitr. Saṁh. II.10.4 and the Kāṭhaka XVIII.5 (Ind. Stud. XIII.279), ṚV stanzas 10, 12, 13 are absent; st. 11 marks the end. If in the Taitt. Saṁh. IV.6.4 we have a different form, the former still appears to be the one which is basic for the Taittirīyas, cf. Ind. Stud. XIII op. cit. and the scholiast cited in Ind. Stud. XII.62.

suspicious. In st. 12, no doubt, we have still the same metre as in the principal hymn, but, instead of the gods, the demon of sickness. Apuā, who does not figure elsewhere in the ṚV, is invoked; then there occurs *pratilobhayantī* from the root *lubh* which is not attested for the ṚV; the last pāda seems to be borrowed from X.89.15. Hence, it is quite possible that this stanza is a later addition, as the ṚV. Khila, the Sāmaveda, the Taitt. Saṁh., and the Vāj. Saṁh. show just in the case of this hymn many more similar additions, partly taken from ṚV VI.75, partly independent ones. Further the question whether the closing stanza 13, composed in a different metre, is to be cancelled[1] or is to be looked upon as a supplement, fully justified though having loose connection with the proper text of the hymn, has to be left unanswered; what is required for the observance of the rule of arrangement according to the number of stanzas is obtained satisfactorily [248] equally by cancelling one or two stanzas[2].—Hymn 121 receives the correct number of stanzas (9 stanzas instead of 10) as soon as we remove the concluding stanza *Prajapate na tvad etāni anyaḥ* etc. which, as is well known, has not been analysed in the Padapāṭha, and which, also from the point of view of the history of religion, is highly suspected to be of late origin.—In the hymn 142, the last two stanzas (Anuṣṭubh) get easily separated from the rest (Triṣṭubh, Jagatī); if one removes them, we have the correct number of stanzas, although the placing of the Triṣṭubh hymn among the Anuṣṭubh ones continues to be a matter of surprise. — One would be reluctant to decide to touch the hymn 95 which has the stanzas relating to the narrative of Purūravas

1. That this stanza, and not st. 12, is the one which continues to be in the text of the Vājasaneyins (so that the hymn in their recension has 12 and not 13 stanzas) does not seem to me to be so certain as it has been assumed in Ind. Stud. XIII op. cit.
2. The placing of the Indra-hymn 103 near the Indra-hymns 104, 105 with which it seems to form a group is perhaps in favour of its extent of eleven stanzas. (Whether 102 is to be considered a Indra-hymn seems doubtful.)

and Urvaśī. In spite of all sorts of obscurities of details, one certainly discovers in stanza after stanza the mark of the same uniform diction, and not the signs which would raise doubts in respect of the authorship of the individual stanzas. Yet just in the case of this hymn we possess the well-known positive evidence of the Śatapatha Brāhmaṇa (XI.5.1.10) which states the extent of the hymn to be of 15 stanzas. Hence, perhaps, it may appear possible to assume also the existence of a version which, in accordance with the rule of the number of stanzas, should have had 14 or 13 stanzas; but this assumption, as was noted above with reference to the hymn 109, need not force us to declare that the additional stanzas found in the transmitted redaction are of late origin.

There still remain five hymns which disturb the order, and all of them, to be sure, due to having *too many* stanzas: 97, 119, 124, 128, 173. Also for these hymns the foregoing discussions establish the probability, that [**249**] we have rather to alter the number of stanzas, than assume the interpolation of the whole hymn which disregards the rule of the number of the stanzas. However, in respect of individual cases, as far as I can see, we do not have the criteria which would help us to effect the required removals, and also where parallels from the other Vedas are available, they do not—except perhaps for the hymn 173—lead us any further in this direction[1].

---

1. With 97 cf. Maitr. S. II.7.13; Taitt. S. IV.2.6; Vāj. S. XII.75 ff. —With 128: AV V.3; Taitt. S. IV.7.14.—With 173: AV. VI.87 f.; Taitt. Brāhm. II.4.2.8 f.: out of the six stanzas of this hymn, for which we expect four, the AV omits the last, but has it, at another place (VII.94), all by itself, in a version which, essentially, is less suited to the general content of ṚV X.173, than the ṚV-version of the stanza. The Yajurveda texts (MS. 1.3.15; TS. III.2.8.6; Vāj. S. VII.25) also agree with the AV-form. In the Taitt. Br. stanzas 5 and 6 of the hymn are missing; the AV, as well as the TB, then make additions of a strange character. Hence, one can hardly look upon the extent of the hymn as comprising the first four stanzas only as specially well-attested.

V

The Ten Maṇḍalas and the Saṁhitā

While discussing so far the arrangement of the material contained in each individual Maṇḍala, we left out of consideration for the time being the question of determining the principles following which this material has been accommodated in those ten divisions in just the way we have it today.

In this respect it is as clear as it is well known that in each of the books II-VII we have the collections of the hymns of a single family, while in book IX we find the collection of the hymns of all the families addressed to Soma pavamāna.[1] It is less easy to answer the question why **[250]** just the Soma-hymns, but not the same way also the Agni-hymns, the Indra-hymns, etc., were brought together in collections, each according to the deity ; on the other hand, we find that out of these hymns, collections of a completely different nature have been made so that the hymns belonging to the same family go together and in them more or less all the gods are represented. A complete answer to this question in the sense that it should be possible to show that the way actually taken by the arrangers of the Saṁhitā is the only one conceivable, to the exclusion of all the others, is naturally not to be expected. Yet the procedure adopted by the arrangers will be to some extent understandable when one remembers the peculiar ritual nature of the Pavamāna-hymns. It would not be possible to prepare out of the store of the hymns of the Ṛgveda a second similarly compact mass of hymns which, from the point of view of the form and contents, are so thoroughly similar to one another. If

---

1. One should not overlook the distinction between the hymns to Soma pavamāna and simply to Soma; the former are to be found in the ninth book, the latter only in the other books.

one were to think, let us say, that all the Agni-hymns are brought together in a single collection, they would exhibit a plainly incalculable variety of ritual situations as compared with the uniform nature of the hymns to Pavamāná. He flows through the filter of sheep-hair—he shines towards the heaven—the hymns resound over him who increases the heroic strength of Indra: in these few expressions the contents of the ninth Maṇḍala are, in fact, fairly exhaustively recounted. These praise-songs, however, were not like the majority of the sacrificial-hymns, recited by the Hotars but by the Sāman-singers; among all the hymn-groups to be classified according to the deities this one (to Pavamāna) was the only one which, as it appears, at least originally, belonged *exclusively* to those (Sāman)-singers and the knowledge of which would have been a superfluous burden for the Hotṛ-priests. Although we may say that even a general separation, on principle, of the Hotar—and the Udgātar-texts was not attempted at the time of the arrangement of the Ṛk-Saṁhitā, **[251]** yet it is understandable that this sort of arrangement imposed itself just at that time as the one which was especially easy to execute and which was highly practical, for it helped to avoid the burdening of the Hotar-priests with learning the texts which they could dispense with.[1]

Besides, it is quite clear that the book IX cannot, like the books II-VII, have enjoyed an independent existence *before* these books were brought together, but that it itself is only a product of that collection. For, the composing of the Pavamāna hymns is naturally shared by just those families of Gṛtsamadas, of Vasiṣṭhas etc. who have also composed the other books: that goes without saying and is also explicitly proved in superabundance by factors like the occurrence of

1. That the knowledge of the Soma-hymns originally was not at all an acquisition common to *all* is indicated by the expressions *yaḥ pāvamānīr adhyeti ṛṣibhiḥ sambhṛtaṁ rasam* etc. ṚV IX.67.31 f.

refrains which are characteristic for these families.[1] Obviously, originally, a part of the present ninth book existed as a special possession of each family, and a larger collection of the Pavamāna-hymns, of the "*ṛṣibhiḥ sambhṛto rasaḥ*" can have been formed only later at a time when those masses of hymns coming from separate poet-families were generally collected to form a single whole. Here it is important to note that in the ninth book there appear not only the Pavamāna-materials which correspond to books II-VII, but quite similarly such as go with the first, the eighth, or even the tenth Maṇḍala. Along with the refrains of II and VII, we find in the [**252**] Pavamāna-texts signs such as the following which point to the domain of the first book: the name of Kakṣīvant (74.8), the closing line of the Nodhas hymns (93.5), and the one of the collection assigned to Kutsa (97.58), and finally the metre which is characteristic of the Parucchepa-hymns (111). With the eighth book goes the naming of Medhyātithi 43.3 and of Vyaśva 65.7. And it can hardly be doubted that even the tenth book has contributed its off-shoots to the ninth book. However, not in great number: otherwise the late features of the language and metre which characterize the tenth book would have been found more frequently in the ninth book[2], and we have also

1. However, it is noteworthy that the Jamadagnis, who appear only rarely elsewhere, enjoy prominence in the ninth book [62.24; 65.25 (cf. III.62.18); 97.51] and that we find here a mention of Kaśyapa which occurs only here (114.2): though only in a supplementary hymn; but the Vṛṣagaṇas who appear in 97.8 also belong to the family of the Kaśyapas.
2. For example, it is noteworthy that *sarva* (by itself; regarding derivatives and compounds, the matter is not exactly the same) occurs only *once* in the ninth book, and that too at a place 67.31 which proves to be an addition. The word *loka* (distinguished from *uloka*) does not occur anywhere; *tatra,* which is rare in the older hymns (it occurs, e.g., in the eighth book only in the two Vālakhilya hymns 56.4 and 58.1, in the sixth book mainly in the supplementary hymn 75), appears in the ninth book *only* in the late supplement 113.8-11. Numerous similar features can be observed.

good reason to believe that the very old art of composing the Soma-hymns, which shows contact with Avesta, became obsolete quite early with the Vedic poets, hence scarcely practised with any liveliness in the period of the tenth book: —it is significant that the two Ārcikas of the Sāmaveda which contain, as is well known, not an inconsiderable number of stanzas in addition to those which are taken from the ṚV, do not have a single Pavamāna stanza[1] which could not be found in the Ṛgveda[2]. That composition of this type [253] of Pavamāna-hymns had completely died out at the time of the formation of the tenth Maṇḍala can hardly be considered probable: but then, since in the tenth Maṇḍala there are no such hymns, those which arose later could have found their place only in the ninth Maṇḍala. A hymn of that kind to Pavamāna, which according to its composition belongs to the tenth book, seems to me to be IX.68 ascribed by the Anukramaṇī to Vatsaprī; in fact, agreement in the closing *adveṣe dyāvāpṛthivī huvema* etc. points to its belonging to X.45 (Vatsaprī).

In order to enable us to decide the circumstances in which this particular arrangement of the different divisions of the Ṛgveda was carried out, it would be of the greatest importance if there would have been preserved for us at that point, where parts taken out from all those divisions were united into a special collection, traces of the successive layers of these elements. Now, whether the success of the future researches directed towards the origin of the Pavamāna-texts and their relationships with the individual other collections be great or—as I rather think—little: traces of the nature just described will, in all probability, not be found. At many places, the arrangement of the hymns in

1. According to Whitney's table (Ind. Stud. II), SV II.109 would be an exception; this, however, is in fact ṚV IX.42.2 with a little modification made under the influence of VIII.44.12.
2. The rarity of the supplementary hymns in the ninth book surely is to be seen in the same light.

the ninth book according to the metres and the number of stanzas rules out at the very outset traces of such layers based on the origin of the hymns, and where such layers would after all be conceivable, factors which at present can be recognized seem to show that they, in fact, do not exist, that the sequence of events in which the Pavamāna-texts belonging to the different hymn-collections were collected here together at different periods, has been obliterated.

Bergaigne has shown that the arrangement of the books [254] II-VII is guided by the increasing number of the hymns; even if the dissections or removals of individual hymns suggested by us above yields a number of hymns that is somewhat different from the one assumed by Bergaigne, the underlying principle of arrangement mentioned above is not disturbed by the new numbers. That the *eighth* book, considering the number of hymns in it, does *not* continue the series of II-VII, that it has a smaller number of hymns than in VII, is not to be doubted. The arrangement of the hymns observed in the eighth book, with its principal deviations from the one which is uniformly observed in the preceding books, might not perhaps, by itself, seem sufficient to permit us to conclude an existence of an original separate collection of book VIII by the side of the collections II-VII since it can be explained as due to the special relationships of the authors of this book. Yet, the *combination* of those deviations with the break in the ascending order of the Maṇḍalas is, I think, enough to render that conclusion now sufficiently probable. What is the uniformity which binds together the hymns of the eighth Maṇḍala as distinguished from those of II-VII ? That the eighth book—"the book of the Pragāthas"—consists to a greater, perhaps even to the greatest, extent of hymns in *other* metres than just the Pragāthas, and that, on the other hand, numerous Pragāthas appear outside this book[1], is seen by anyone. The

1. They are strikingly rare in the tenth book.

bond that binds the materials collected together in the eighth book does not seem to lie in the authorship of the Kaṇvas either. In large parts of this Maṇḍala the Kaṇvas are not mentioned; at a few places are clearly to be found names of singers belonging to other families: quite apart from the role which the Kaṇvas play also outside [**255**] the eighth, in extensive parts of the first book. But perhaps, just *these* passages of book VIII in which appear poets of families, which are otherwise at home in other Maṇḍalas, give us the correct clue. The author of VIII.35-38 is one Śyāvāśva, of the family of the Atris. Could those hymns, without appearing odd in their surroundings, occur in the book of Atris (V) in which, in fact, Śyāvāśva appears many times as the name of the poet ? Scarcely: the tṛca-form of VIII.35-38, marked by the refrains which partly run through the entire hymns and partly change in each tṛca would make these tṛcas appear out of place in the fifth Maṇḍala; in the eighth book, amidst similar surroundings, they are quite in place. What, then, distinguishes the Śyāvāśva of this book from the one of the fifth is the empolyment of a poetic composition which the Kaṇvas and most of the other poets of the eighth book tend to use, viz. a hymn of strophes, no matter whether the hymn consists of the Pragātha-strophes or of tṛcas. The two hymns VIII.73, 74, belonging to the Atri-family, are similarly unmistakable tṛca-hymns. Thus, even these few hymns of the Atris in book VIII are enough to give a series of sure examples of a hymn being divided into strophes, while the Atris of book V do not, or do so at least only in sporadic exceptions, tend to use this strophic structure. Similarly, hymn 88, which is the only one in the eighth Maṇḍala to be characterized definitely as a Gotama hymn, is a Pragātha-hymn, while not a single Pragātha-hymn occurs in the whole of the Gotama-book IV, and only one in the Gotama parts of book I. This cannot be just a coincidence. Certainly, no one will think of viewing the eighth book as an extraction of the strophe-hymns from the entire Saṁhitā just as book

IX is an extraction of the Pavamāna-hymns : such an [256] interpretation would be opposed by a sufficient number of such exceptions as would not confirm the rule. But a clearly marked *preference* of the poets for strophic structure must have had some kind of relationship with the factors which governed the formation of the eighth Maṇḍala. If the Atris and the Gotamas of the eighth book have, in this regard, nothing to do with the other Atris and Gotamas, but, rather, with those like the Kaṇvas, the Vyaśvas etc. who are prominent in the eighth book, this means that, to all appearances, they were not connected with those of their family-members, but with these singers who, from the point of view of family-relationship, were strangers to them. Such a hypothesis will account for similar practices used by both of them in priestly poetry. Thus, directly neither the family of the singers, nor even the form of the hymn, was decisive for the formation of the eighth Maṇḍala; rather it was the position of a certain group, or more correctly of several related groups of ṛṣis, distinguished from the other groups of poets, whose hymns were marked predominantly, if not exclusively, by the strophic composition of the hymns. Primarily the Kaṇvas belonged to this group and, perhaps, formed its centre. But some Atris, Gotamas[1], and singers from different smaller families also practised the peculiar poetic composition which was cultivated in this group. And they all together formed a community whose solidarity was not far behind the one which prevailed within each of the singer-families of the books II-VII : this is proved by the numerous repetitions throughout the Maṇḍala of similar [257] expressions and parts of stanzas which occur here exactly as in the preceding books. The relationship that exists between that broader unity of this circle, which extended beyond the framework of the Gotra-relationship,

1. In other respects also one can observe the more close relationships of just these families with the Kaṇvas.

and. the groups which comprised that circle, but were distinguished among themselves and were demarcated by their family relationships, is throughout adequately reflected in the peculiar arrangement of the eighth Maṇḍala: to these groups correspond the hymn-groups which have retained heir peculiarity while renouncing an arrangement running hrough the whole book. And it seems that indirectly with these relationships is also related the deviations of the eighth book from the remaining ones in regard to the arrangement of the series of deities in each group: where the individual series of the deities were very little distinguished from one another in length, often consisting only of a single hymn, as was the case in these numerous, short hymn-groups, it was expedient not to let the arrangement depend on the number of the hymns in each series addressed to a deity, but to accept the number of the stanzas, which incidentally alone could count in the case of the numerous single hymns, as decisive also in the case of the series having several hymns exactly the way it has happened in the eighth book [above p. 213].—

We now turn to the problems connected with the *first* Maṇḍala. That its first part reveals a certain commonness with the eighth book has been already noted : how is it then that these hymns in the form of strophes, these Kaṇva-hymns, are separated from those of the eighth book? The second part of the Maṇḍala is more akin to the books II-VII: is it then to be looked upon, in full or partly, as the commencement of the series which we have in these books? **[258]** We shall begin with the second question. The collections from I.51 onwards have, following the dissections and the removals of interpolated hymns suggested above, the following numbers of hymns: Savya 7.—Nodhas 7.—Parāśara 9.—Gotama 30 or 41 (according as one divides or does not divide the hymns 91-93).—Kutsa 21.—Kakṣīvant 12.—Parucchepa 16 ?—Dīrghatamas 22-25.—Agastya 26.

One notices that these nine collections, with two

exceptions (Gotama, Kutsa) are in fact arranged according to the ascending length: a situation which, even if one does not take into account the following Maṇḍalas, in itself, purely from the point of view of the rule of numerical probability, does not give an impression of coincidence. Out of the two exceptions, one relates to the Kutsa-group. But just this group occupies, as is well known, a different place among the Vāṣkalas on account of the *anukramaviparyāsa* which, when compared with the Śākalas, prevails in that school: it occurs there after the Parucchepa-hymns, that is *exactly at the place which is required by the number of the hymns.* The second of those two exceptions (Gotama), however, cannot be set aside by any similar evidence, but it is a *solitary* exception that remains and it is not too daring if we consider here conceivable shifts similar to those which, by chance, left here their traces in the Kutsa-collection. Thus we find here, in all probability, a collection of nine small hymn-complexes, arranged according to the ascending order which, from the point of view of the number of hymns in each complex, fit into the series of the books II-VII, and they also manifest in their inner arrangement, as was shown above, enough agreement with the principles of ordering of those books—except such differences which are easily explained as due to the small size of these collections[1]. [259] Accordingly if we consider it possible that we have to assume *one* large series of hymn-collections from I.51 to VII then according to me, with this interpretation, the admission that some collections of the first Maṇḍala are, to all appearances, somewhat later than the bulk of the books II-VII is not at all incompatible: nothing compels us to push back the unification of the smaller books to a corpus of hymns so close to the period

1. That the smaller collections in the traditionally transmitted text have been gathered together while the larger ones are kept independent is a phenomenon similar to the one in which smaller hymns of three stanzas have been collected together after the longer ones are allowed to remain separate.

of the rise of the older books that there would not be left any time in between for the rise of markedly younger hymn-groups. The assumption of such a comprehensive unit is not excluded even by the fact that in that case the series of the Gotama-hymns would appear at three different places (I.58-64,74-93, IV) in the great series of collection. The group I.58-64, so to say, is localized by the mentions of Nodhas and the refrain *prātar makṣū dhiyāvasur jagamyāt*; this group must have been composed by a *definite* singer among the Gotamas or by a circle gathered around such a definite personality. That the hymns I.74-93 stand separated from the fourth book must also depend on detachments of similar nature. In fact the two collections (I.74-93 and IV) do show essentially different characteristics: one may note the frequency of Uṣṇih and Paṅkti as also of hymns having refrains in I.74 ff., and, on the other hand, the rarity of Triṣṭubh which predominates in IV. Chronological differences may have been equally responsible—in any case it would be premature to assert that such a detached occurrence of the Gotama-collections which are distinguished in some way [**260**] by the particular circumstances related to their origin, would be incompatible with the assumption of a Saṁhitā from I.51 to VII.

Further, on the basis of the number of hymns and, perhaps also, the arrangement of the hymns the Praskaṇva group I.44-50 could, in itself, have belonged to this Saṁhitā, but since the same cannot be said of the collections which precede it, and this group is clearly to be attached to the groups which precede it on account of the names of the authors, that eventuality loses all probability. Hence, the question that is to be asked with regard to this *first part* of the Maṇḍala is obviously not: how do these collections stand in relation to those which immediately follow them ?—but how do they stand in relation to the book VIII with which, for the most part, they are on the same niveau due to the prominence of the Kaṇvas and due to the form of the metre of the hymns ? Here also, as in the eighth book, we have a series of smaller collections each of which obviously belongs to an individual author, or to a narrow group of authors. Now, when in the first Maṇḍala, as in the eighth, the Kaṇvaites are equally prominent as authors, the conjecture suggests itself that there would be *specific* groups of authors who appear in the former Maṇḍala, *others* in the latter.[1] Just as, for example, the first book knows nothing of Vatsa, of Sobharī, respectively of the Sobharis, and of other poets of the eighth M., so on the other hand, the collection I.44-50 has the name of Praskaṇva more prominently than the eighth book[2], while **[261]** it shares with VIII.1 ff. the manifold mention of the Kaṇvas and Priyamedhas. In I.36-43 the situation is different: it shares with VIII.1 ff. the names Kaṇva, Medhyātithi, Upastuta (in addition also Turvaśa Yadu), but it lacks, perhaps not just by coincidence, the name Priyamedhas which is frequent there. That the Kaṇvas are not mentioned in some hymn-groups, and are presumably by no means the authors of all the hymns, does not, incidentally, contradict the analogy with the eighth book : we may think of the Śunaḥśepa- and the Hiraṇyastūpa-collection; it is also *possible* that the hymns I.1-11 which maintain throughout the tone of the Kaṇvas[3] have been composed, in fact, as the Anukramaṇī states, by a Viśvāmitra[4].

---

1. Ludwig (III.105) makes a similar assumption, "that at the time of the collection of the Ṛgveda there were two branches of the Kāṇvas whose sūkta-material was not brought together at the same time."
2. In VIII referred to only once (3.9) as a pious personality of the past in such a way that it would not characterize him as the author of the hymn: then, however, in a prominent manner in the Vālakhilyas, VIII.51.2; 54.8.
3. Cf. Ludwig III.101.
4. In its favour, without of course being quite decisive, can be cited I.1. 8 *gopām ṛtasya dīdivim,* cf. III.10.2 *gopā ṛtasya dīdihi;* I.5.3 = III.13.1 *gamad vājebhir ā sa naḥ;* I.10.7 = III.40.6 *indra tvādātam id yaśaḥ.* If one notes that not many parallels between the Gāyatrī-hymns of I and the very predominent Triṣṭubh-hymns of III can be expected, then the number of these parallels shown here does not seem to be quite insignificant.

However, it has to be admitted that by assuming for book I groups of authors which are different from those in VIII, it is not yet explained why one series of hymn-groups is thus separated from the other. There is the possibility that in this chronological factors play a role; it would, however, be difficult to point out such factors in individual cases. Side by side the material which is definitely late[1], as by the way such late material is also to be found at many places in the eighth book, occurs other material which can be as old as any section of the Vedic collection. The numerous parallels [**262**] and directly identical passages in I and VIII mostly do not allow to recognize which is the original; only a few cases such as those which pertain to the Praskaṇva collection, it seems to me, favour the assumption with some degree of probability that as to age *this part* of the first book rather precedes, than follows, the parallels of the eighth book. Thus, we find I.44.11 *yajñasya sādhanam* = VIII.6.3; in the eighth book this expression is used of Indra, in the first book of Agni with whom it agrees more accurately and to whom, elsewhere in the ṚV, it *always* refers[2]. In I.45.4 *rājantam adhvarāṇām* is said of Agni, in VIII.8.18 *rājantāv adhvarāṇām* of the Aśvins:[3] in favour of Agni decide I.1.8 ; 27.1; 44.9; X.46.4. In favour of book I seems to speak also I.48.15: *uṣo yad adya bhānunā vi dvārāv ṛṇavo divaḥ, pra no*

1. Thus, the occurrence of the monosyllabic *kva.* 38.2 in a group which is attributed to Kaṇva, if this had not been removed by Grassmann by a conjecture which is quite probable; among the Medhātithi-hymns *gārhapatyena* and *yajñanīḥ* 15.12; in the Hiraṇyastūpa-group *kalyāṇa* 31.9 ; in the Śunaḥśepa group particularly the two hymns 28, 29 and many more similar things.
2. III.27.2,8; VIII.23.9. Due to this frequent recurrence of the expression, it seems to me, that there exists a special relationship between just I.44.11 and VIII.6.3. This is confirmed by other numerous and significant parallels between the Praskaṇva-hymns and just *these* sections of the eighth book; see below.
3. That there is a connection between the two is shown by the pāda *Priyamedhā' ahūṣata* which is common to both.

yachatād avṛkam pṛthu chadiḥ (*chardiḥ* in the transmitted text); cf. VIII.9.1 (to the Aśvins): *prāsmai yachatam avṛkam pṛthu chadiḥ* (transmitted *chardiḥ*). It cannot be strictly proved, but can nevertheless be regarded as probable, that *yachatāt* is older than *yachatam*; such a markedly characteristic construction like *yad . . . ṛṇavaḥ . . . pra yachatāt*[1] makes the impression that it was originally thought that way, and not pieced together from fragments of a differently worded text[2]. A number of other passages which show contact of the Praskaṇva-hymns with Vatsa-hymns (VIII.6-11) [**263**] or with those initial hymns of the eighth book which are closely related to these (Vatsa-hymns) [above p. 215] are not of much consequence for deciding the question of priority[3]. I do not overlook how much the things adduced here are removed from giving us a real insight into the processes which have given these sections of the Saṁhitā their present form. We will have to be content for the present, or perhaps for ever, with making the statement that quite a large number

---

1. See Delbrück, Altindische Wortfolge, p. 4.
2. One may also note that *yachatāt* conforms more strictly with the requirements of the metre than *yachatam.*
3. I.44.2=VIII.11.2 *agne rathīr adhvarāṇām.*—I.45.1=VIII.5.33 *suadhvaraṁ janam.*—I.45.8 = VIII.6.42 (but also elsewhere) *abhi prayaḥ.*—I.45.8=VIII. 1.22 (also elsewhere) *martāya dāśuṣe.*—I.46.2 = VIII.8.12 *manotarā rayīṇām.*—I.46.3 = VIII.5.22 *yad vāṁ ratho vibhiṣ patāt.*—I.47.7 *yan nāsatyā parāvati yad vā stho' adhi Turvaśe*; VIII.8.14 likewise, but (less original?) *adhi ambare.*—I.47.8 = VIII.4.14 *arvāñcā vām* (respy. *arvāñcaṁ tvā*) *saptayo' adhvaraśriyo vahantu savaned upa.*—I.47.9 = VIII.8.2 *rathena sūriatvacā.*—I.47.10 *purūvasū,* said of Aśvin also only in VIII.5.4 = 8.12.—I.48.14 ye *cid dhi tvām ṛṣayaḥ pūrva' ūtaye juhūre' avase mahi,* cf. VIII.8.6 *yac cid dhi vām pura ṛṣayo juhūre' avase narā.*—I.49.1 = VIII.8.7 *divaś cid rocanād adhi* (similarly VIII.1.18). —I.49.1 *aruṇapsavaḥ* cf. VIII.7.7.—It could be that the same Praskaṇva who is mentioned in VIII.3.9 as a pious person of the past is in I, 44.6; 45.3 a living person; however, the late Vālakhilya passages VIII.51.2; 54.8 render this conclusion doubtful.—That the Medhyātithi who in a different section of the first book (36.10,11,17) is a personality of the past, is to be thought of as a living person in VIII.1.30 is not probable (cf. VIII.8.20).

of hymns has been placed before and another after that great collection which began with II, or perhaps with I.51, and reached upto VII, that these two sections of later additions show among themselves specially close contacts, and that out of all this mass the Pavamāna hymns were combined to make a special collection (IX).

It is this way that at a time when the tenth Maṇḍala came into being the first nine books[1] undoubtedly formed together a big corpus of hymns. [264] The poets of the tenth Maṇḍala certainly grew up with the knowledge of this corpus since they show their familiarity with it everywhere in their own hymns: it was this arrangement of the corpus which the author of the group X.20-26 had, to all appearances, before him since he placed at the beginning of his own hymn-collection the words *agnim īḷe* with which the corpus began: it was within this corpus that the sacrificial ritual as was known to the poet of X. 181 moved with the Rathantara and the Bṛhat Sāmans sung on the text of the Vasiṣṭhas (VII.32.22, 23), and on the text of the Bharadvājas (VI.46.1, 2).

Our detailed investigations of the books I-IX imply the negative result, viz. that the unevenness in the arrangement of the Saṁhitā, i.e. the emergence of a collection of hymns, governed by certain principles, preceded and followed by elements which are ordered *in a different way*, finally the independent collection of the hymns to Pavamāna, gives no information about the relative chronology of the different hymn-masses; rather, conversely, this chronology, if its knowledge could be advanced further than where it stands today, would, perhaps, be in a position to throw light on the obscure points in the genesis of those relationships. Thus, it is not with regard to the whole hymn-groups in the books I-IX, but only with regard to the single hymns which,

1. Excepting, of course, *those* elements of the ninth book which come from the poets of the tenth book [above p. 253] and the supplements which will be discussed presently.

by violating the principle of arrangement, attract our attention that it is possible to confirm the hypothesis of their late origin *on the basis of the arrangement.* As regards a *complete part* of the Saṁhitā the same can be said only in respect of the *tenth Maṇḍala,* which will now be discussed, the Maṇḍala which, according to the prevalent and unquestionably justified opinion, is a *supplement,* and which is characterized as such already by its position after the Soma-book.

[**265**] If some of the additions to the old collection have been accommodated by scattering them in the different Maṇḍalas and some others have been collected together into a separate tenth book, then it can be, on the whole, assumed that the latter additions are the older ones[1]. For once, in the additions of the first kind, in relation to the rather small number of the hymns concerned the signs of their later origin are much more frequent; then there appear in the Pavamāna book, as was shown above, hymns showing elements[2] related to the tenth book at a place where they really belong in accordance with the principle of arrangement: thus, evidently, they have been received earlier than the supplementary hymns which violate that principle.

One would, of course, go too far if one were to believe that the later age which has to be *on the whole* assigned to the tenth book can be, with the help of perceptible signs,

1. The later additions to the family books show many times—and in view of the small number of such hymns we can even say frequently —special relationships with the concerned families, respectively with their ṛṣi-ancestors (III.29.15; 53.7 ff.; VII.33): but if this fact of their thus marked relationship with these families alone was the ground for their being placed into the Maṇḍala of that ṛṣi-family and not in the general supplementary book X, the question still remains why, e.g., X.89,104 were not put into the collection of the Viśvāmitras, 105 not in that of Kutsa, 65,66,122,150 not in that of the Vasiṣṭhas.
2. As IX.68, [cf. above p. 253].

proved in the case of every single hymn. But the signs of this nature are surely distributed in such abundance throughout the whole book that one has the fullest right to presume late origin as the cause due to which any given hymn of the tenth book appears, not with the other hymns of the singer-families concerned[1], but in the tenth book. **[266]** Already the way the singer-families are named belongs to such signs: the definite receding of such notions and namings as the Kaṇvas, the Atris, the Vasiṣṭhas, and the appearance, instead, of individuals Gaya, son of Plati, Bṛhaduktha etc.: which corresponds to the individual character of small collections and isolated hymns, which make up the tenth book, in appreciable contrast to those extensive family-books which arose in the old community of the large families. Perhaps here also nothing proves the rule better than the exceptional cases, like the one of X.65, 66: the two hymns to the Viśve devās in which, quite in keeping with the tone of the seventh Maṇḍala, it is said *Vasiṣṭhāsaḥ pitṛvad vācam akrata* (66.14), *devān Vasiṣṭho' amṛtān vavande* (65.15 = 66.15). Why do such hymns not occur in the seventh book? Evidently because they are the work of a single late Vasiṣṭhaite. The identical concluding stanza of the two equally long, parallel hymns and a number of other special characteristics—we may here draw attention only to the naming of *daivyā hotārā* in 65.10 and 66.13: *the only two places* in the whole of the Ṛgveda where these spirits are invoked outside the Āprī hymns—make it certain that they are to be assigned to the same author. And that this author is younger than the seventh book is shown sufficiently by the fact that in the small space of these two hymns there occur *two* absolutive forms in *-tvī (janitvī, skabhitvī* (65.7), while in the whole of the seventh book only one form of

1. For, quite clearly, in a far overwhelming majority of cases the hymns which come into question are of the singers to whose very families the other Maṇḍalas belong.

that kind is found[1]. Among other [**267**] indications of the late origin may further be noted the dual fom *agnīṣomā* (66.7), which is so common in the later ritual but which is almost unkown to the ṚV[2], and the expression *jñātayaḥ* (66.14) which occurs *only* in the tenth book (thrice), as also in one place in the seventh (55. 6), which passage, however, due to certain clear features[3], proves to be one of the latest interpolations.

Similarly to this Vasiṣṭha of X.65,66, the Viśvāmitra of X.89, and similarly most of the apparent representatives of the old family-poetry in the tenth book and altogether most of the poets of this book prove themselves to be modern descendants. The criteria to be found in their contents and those to be found in their form, so diverse in their nature as agreeing in the result to which they lead, impose themselves at every step on the reader of the tenth book. As for the *contents* one notices that their narrowing and widening, as compared with the old parts of the Veda, has occurred side by side. The circle of the gods, to which the poetry of the family books was dedicated, does not fully retain its interest for the new period. Only a few of the so prominent hymn-types such as the Agni-hymns (inclusive of the Āprī-hymn) and the Indra-hymns continue to survive in the old way; the hymns to the Viśve devās even gain ground. But Varuṇa and Mitrāvaruṇau almost disappear, likewise Uṣas and, presumably, also the Pavamāna [see above p. 252], while the Maruts and the Aśvins continue, rather only as a speciality of the poets of 39-41, respectively 77-78. Instead, entities like Viśvakarman, Manyu, Śraddhā appear in the

---

1. *gūḍhvī* VII.80.2; beside it also *bhūtvi* VII.104.18, but this is undoubtedly a supplementary hymn. Absolutives in *-tvā* and *-tvāya* do not occur at all in book VII (all this on the basis of Delbrück's count, Altind. Verbum 228 f.).
2. Except I.93 and a passage in the hymn to the dead of the tenth book (19.1).
3. E.g. by *v* for *u* in *sastv ayam.*

forefront; numerous cosmogonic and philosophising [268] hymns, Ākhyāna-hymns, hymns for the rites of the Gṛhya-ritual (funeral, marriage, dedication of herds etc.), magic hymns, charms and many others of similar nature give the tenth Maṇḍala its special stamp.

In whichever way one examines the *formal* peculiarities of the tenth Maṇḍala they lead all the time to similar results. Only a few among many such things may be stressed here. In regard to the *metre* one may note the receding into the background of the archaic Pragātha-form, the increase, on the other hand, of the liberties in the first and the third pāda of Anuṣṭubh; in the field of *sandhi*, the rise in the number of contractions, the becoming rare of hiatus, the occurrence of *y* and *v* in place of *i* and *u*, occasionally in place of even accented *i* and *u*; in *morphology*, as observed by Lanman, the phenomena like the altered frequency-relationship of nominatives in *-āsas* and *-ās* and many similar things, the exclusive occurrence of the absolutives in *-tvāya* in the tenth book, the relatively considerable frequency of the remaining types of absolutive formations[1] in the same book as compared to the other books. As for the *vocabulary*, on the one hand, numerous archaic words go out of use in the tenth book, and on the other, the appearance of many later ones[2] is confined, most significantly, either wholly to this book or, not less significantly, to this book and to such hymns of the other books which prove there to be interpolations. Of the old words and forms which recede in the tenth book may be mentioned, as example, [269] *acchā* (in the whole of the Ṛgveda 177 times, of which, in the tenth book, only 15 times)[3]. Further, most of the forms and

1. See the classifications given in Delbrück, Altind, Verbum op. cit.
2. For the purpose of this examination we count among the 'later' words, naturally, also such which are old in themselves but have acquired more frequency only in later times.
3. The proportion of the extent of the tenth book to the whole of the Saṁhitā is about 2 : 11.

derivatives of the root *av*; I stress *avasā*, 7 times in X of 49 times in the whole of the ṚV, *avase* 10 of 108, *avasyu* not at all in X, *avitā* 4 of 36, *ūtayaḥ* not at all in X, *ūtibhiḥ* 3 of 69, *ūtaye* 10 of 87[1]. The locative *pṛtsu*[2], adjectives like *girvaṇas* and *vicarṣaṇi*, the substantive *vīti* (moreover *vītihotra, vītirādhas*[3]) are missing in the tenth book, while elsewhere they belong to the more common words; the disappearance of the particle *sīm* in the Atharvaveda is foreshadowed in the Ṛgveda by the fact that this word occurs only *once* (total occurrences 51 times) in book X.—On the other hand, among examples of late words which appear in the tenth book *alone* may be listed the verb *labh* (also *sulābhika*), *lakṣmī, loman, lohita, vijaya, yajñapati, yajñakāma, yatkāma, yathākāmam, yathāpūrvam, puṇḍarīka, puṣkarasraj*[4], *tīkṣṇa, grāmaṇī, grāmya, ājya, kāla, śvāpada, saṁjñāna, sarīsṛpa, evam.* Only in the tenth book, and besides in the interpolations of the other books (to which may be added the Vālakhilyas and such hymns as I.164 due to their late origin), are to be found e.g. *loka*[5] (as distinguished from *uloka*), *mṛtyu* (however *mṛtyubandhu* also in VIII.18.22), *mogha, visarga, brāhmaṇá* (oxytone), *dīrghāyutva, nāthita*[6], [270] *gup, gopāya, chandas*[7] (*chandasia*), *puruṣa* (*pūruṣa*[8]). As to words among whose places of use the tenth book and the additions to the other

1. One may also note the small role which the nouns *avas* and *ūti*, so common in the old language, play in the diction of the Atharvaveda.
2. Quite different is the case of the stem *pṛtanā* which is common also in the AV while *pṛtsu* is missing there. The latter is true also of *girvaṇas, vicarṣaṇi* and *vīti.*
3. Only the compound *devavīti* is found also in the tenth book.
4. *puṣkariṇī* once in X and once in an interpolation of book V.
5. Six times in X, next in the interpolated hymn VI.47.8. Otherwise only in the Ākhyāna-hymn VIII.100.12.
6. *nātha* is missing in the ṚV: *anātha* occurs only once in X.
7. But *chandaḥstubh* V.52.11.
8. 15 times in X; elsewhere only in the supplementary hymn VII.104.15. As regards *puruṣatrā* and some other derivatives and compositions, however, the case is different.

books *predominate* at least significantly may be cited *sarva, virāj, bhagavant, bhū* (noun), *prāṇa, tapas, sapatna* (*sapatnī, sapatnahan, asapatna*), *hṛdaya, strī* (*straiṇa*), the particle *kila,* the verbs *hiṁs, grah* (as distinguished from *grabh*), *har, nah* (*naddha, nahana, akṣānah* etc.), *kalp.* Also the statistics of the pronouns *kim* and *kad,* to which Grassmann has already drawn attention, may be noted: *kad* appears in X 8 times in a total of 62 passages, *kim* 28 times[1] in a total of 92 passages: thus the former, which is older, appears in the tenth book only in about one-eighth of the total number of occurrences, the latter, which is later, in almost one-third of the same.

It is hardly necessary to stress explicitly that the statements made here are meant to be, and can be, only a *beginning* of the investigations of this kind. But they are enough to give to the thesis in question a more firm and a more clear basis than it has had till now: the thesis that in the tenth book—as distinguished from all the other books—the uniformity, which binds together the materials collected there, is of a chronological nature: the tenth book is the book of the later hymn-groups and the later single hymns.

---

1. The only passage in which *kim* appears in III, and one of the two passages of IX, belong to the later additions.

CHAPTER 3

The Ṛk-text and the Text of the Later Saṁhitās and the Brāhmanas

[271] The oldest, and for a long period of time the only witnesses for the form and the fate of the Ṛgveda-text are, beside the transmitted form of this text itself, the hymns, stanzas, or parts of stanzas, taken over from it into the other Vedas. Whatever purpose for the criticism is served in the case of most of the literary monuments by the manifold, better or inferior, manuscripts, affiliated with one another in different ways, the same is—mutatis mutandis—served by the comparison of the other Vedas for the criticism of the Ṛgveda-text, the manuscripts of which come from the modern and most modern period, and which give essentially the same recension of the text which has been fixed since long ago. Sometimes it concerns such hymns of the Ṛgveda which were composed for special ritual use, for which, then, already in the early period arose separate secondary text-books : so that, on the one hand, we come across those hymns in the Ṛgveda, the ur-corpus of Indian poetry, and, on the other, also in the corresponding special collection. Sometimes, however, we meet with such Ṛgveda-stanzas which were seized by the later ritual practice for uses which were remote from their original purpose: such stanzas [272] without losing their original place in the Ṛgveda, have also been, at the same time, put into the surroundings of the most diverse heterogeneous productions of later periods. These Ṛgvedic stanzas in their new surroundings, affected by the peculiarities of their environment, provide us with

evidence to be used only with the utmost caution for determining the old form of the text. The parts of the Ṛk-text which have thus been preserved in the other Vedas take us back to a distant antiquity which lies far beyond not just our Ṛgveda-manuscripts, but also far beyond the testimony of works such as the Nirukta and the Prātiśākhyas. A comparison of such Ṛk-texts in the other Vedas, at first glance, seems to show a random vacillation in the form of the text during that period which means a scarcely restrained freedom which, during that period, every transmitter of the text claimed for himself vis-à-vis the exact details of the text. Very soon, however, limitations to this freedom are revealed in our investigations. Already in the large ritual texts of the Brāhmaṇa-period we find the form of the text, which earlier seemed to have a fluid character, almost coagulated into a fixed form. But not just this; on further penetration our investigation also reveals the clearest indications of the fact that already in that age which preceded the Brāhmaṇa-period, in which the greatest freedom in the handling of the text appeared characteristic, there existed, in fact, at the same time the opposite trend. Amidst that activity of arbitrary transmission, a central mass of the transmitted text, which formed the nucleus of the Veda tradition, was preserved, which stood incomparably much higher in fixity and greater faithfulness in respecting the available text. The authority of this nucleus emerges all the more sharply when one makes a comparative study of the branches of the tradition that deviate from it. A detailed [273] examination of the relationships referred to here, whether it brings to light much or little in point of positive results for the improvement of the Veda-text, cannot in any case be dispensed with; only with the help of such examination shall we be able to express firmly our evaluation of the text-tradition, which is founded on the knowledge of the history of the Vedic text-transmission.

We begin with the examination of the readings preserved in both the text-collections of the Sāmaveda. Here the deviations from the Ṛgveda-text are extremely numerous, and, on the whole, they run through evenly[1] all parts of the Ṛgveda and the Ārcikas. One has only to compare a few stanzas of the two texts in order to find out that, for example, the one characterizes Agni as *sudhito garbhiṇīṣu,* the other as *subhṛto garbhiṇībhiḥ,* or that the one sends Soma to the *devānāṁ yoni,* the other to the *ṛtasya yoni.* Sometimes we find, as in the cases cited, expressions which are different but close to each other in the same or related sense,[2] but sometimes also words of different meaning but similar sound have been interchanged with each other: thus *ma iha nāsti* and *mehanāsti, ditsu* and *dikṣu,* **[274]** *tvayā bhūṣanti* and *tve' ā bhūṣanti, paniṣṭaye* and *caniṣṭhayā.*

Now and then the deviations between the two texts extend over a larger extent: for example

Ṛ V V.18.1 *viśvāni yo' amartio havyā marteṣu raṇyati* runs in the Sāmaveda:

viśve yasminn amartye havyaṁ martāsa' indhate.

For Ṛ V VI.47.11 *hvayāmi śakraṁ puruhūtam indram suasti no maghavā dhātu indraḥ* we find in the Sāmaveda

huve nu śakram puruhūtam indram
idaṁ havir maghavā vetv indraḥ.

---

1. Here and there, longer parts of the Ṛgveda repeated in a bulk in the SV—and this happens only in a few cases—show unusually few variations, thus ṚV X.103,140,156.—We shall have to come back to the question of the greater frequency of the variants in the first Ārcika as compared with the second (Whitney, Proceedings Am. Or. Soc. Oct. 1883, p. XXI).
2. Very frequently it happens that in the Gāyatrī hymns to Soma Pavamāna, as it could very easily happen with the uniform contents of the Soma hymns and the loose structure of the Gāyatrī texts, whole Pādas have found their way into a different place in one Veda than they occupy in the other.

Or, one meets with a stanza in one Veda in which the name of the deity appears in the nominative and the verb in the third person, in the other in the vocative and the verb in the second person: thus IX.47.1. Or, a Gāyatrī has in the Ṛgveda trochaic, in the Sāmaveda the usual iambic rhythm (VIII.2.19). Or, a stanza which is addressed to Indra in the Ṛgveda (VI.24.6) refers to Agni in the Sāmaveda, so that beside other deviations we get the vocative Agne in place of Indra: where then in the Ṛgveda, the contents of the hymn, to which the stanza concerned belongs, determine beyond any doubt the Indra-character of the hymn, in the SV likewise its placement within the Agni-section of the Pūrvārcika establishes its reference to Agni.

We have already left here the sphere of the variations which could be attributed just to negligence and have identified text-deviations which presuppose deliberate alteration of the given text. A similar deliberateness is revealed also in the consistency with which certain variations always recur in numerous places. Thus, the genitive **[275]** *avyas*[1] (associated with *vāra*) common in the Ṛgveda, occurs in the Sāmaveda always in the form *avyās* (see the Sāman-parallels to ṚV VIII.2.2; IX.6.1; 7.6; 12.4; 20.1; 38.1; 50.3); only once we find in the Sāmaveda the adjective *avyam (vāram)* corresponding to the Ṛgveda form (IX.28.1). The difference between the two texts in relation to the archaic word *īm*, which had become[2] almost obsolete early, is not consistent: in most passages of the Sāmaveda it is preserved;

1. I do not agree with Lanman 384 in looking upon this form as gen. sg. mas., but I take it as gen. sg. fem.; in similar contexts, it is never a *meṣa*, but often a *meṣī* that is spoken of (IX.8.5; 86.47; 107.11).
2. Of the nine passages of the Athavaveda where the word appears, eight are borrowed from the Ṛgveda (see Whitney's Index).—One may compare that *sīm* does not occur at all in the AV (thus already Boehtl. Roth), and in the later parts of the ṚV it appears remarkably seldom. In ṚV 1.36.1 it has been eliminated by the diaskeuast of the SV. Cf. further above [p. 269].

but it is certainly not a matter of chance that for ṚV IX.75.3 *abhīm ṛtasya dohanā' anūṣata* and likewise for 77.1 *abhīm ṛtasya sudughā ghṛtaścutaḥ* in the SV on both occasions appears the reading *abhy ṛtasya,* that IX.86.17 *abhi dhenavaḥ payasem aśiśrayuḥ* occurs in the SV with the variant *payased,* and that in I.81.1 the SV reads *ūtim* for *utem* (= *uta īm*). With the removal of *īm* from the text, which had started but was far from being fully carried out, may be compared another phenomenon viz. that the metrically disyllabic vowels were not in general corrected and removed from the Sāmaveda-text, yet they have disappeared in a number of places which seem to be sufficient to exclude the possibility of pure chance. Thus a three-syllabled *deyām* in VIII.1.5 is replaced by *dīyase,* though it violates the construction; *akṣār* in IX.18.1 by *akṣarat; prāḥ* in VI.46.5 by *paprāḥ;* the three-syllabled nature of *śreṣṭha-* in VIII.19.4 is removed by the insertion of an *u;* of *āpat* in VIII.70.7 by the addition of *tam.* Also *drapso bhettā purāṁ* [276] *śaśvatīnām* of VIII.17.14 may be mentioned here. The Sāmaveda would hardly have destroyed the stanza by transposing the words *purām* and *bhettā* if its redactors had correctly known the form *puraam* and with it the absolutely simple and regular metrical structure of the line.[1]

---

1. Burnell (Ārṣeya Br. p. XVI f.) assumes, that the main source of the Sāmaveda variants is the modifications which the text undergoes in the *gānas.* Although this idea in itself has much to recommend, I think it does not find confirmation in the facts before us. One will scarcely be able to discover decisive differences between the variants of the SV and those of the Yajurveda texts, which had nothing to do with the art of priestly singing, and if one compares the SV-Ārcikas with the *gānas* one will have the impression that, apart from the *quite isolated* textual differences (one such, it seems to me, as is also assumed by Burnell, is to be found in the SV 1.8 where, in fact, the Ṛk-reading seems to be corrupted in the Ārcika, but is preserved in the *gāna;* Burnell's similar statements with reference to the SV 1.20 are based on an error), the *gānas* presuppose just that text which is found in the Ārcikas.

The last statements already involve the question of what *value* is to be attached to the readings of the Sāmaveda for the critique of the Ṛk-text. One feels that this question is answerable *a priori* with enough certainty. If, as it may appear, the separation of the two Vedas took place at a time when the text-form of the ritual hymns was still more or less fluid and it was considered immaterial whether one called Agni *sudhito garbhiṇīṣu* or *subhṛto garbhiṇībhiḥ* then one could indisputably draw the conclusion that it is impossible that the redaction of one Veda should have chosen—as if by a queer turn of destiny—always the good and original, and that of the other Veda always the corrupt from an unsettled stock of different text-forms passed on from mouth to mouth. Good and bad should have been **[277]** distributed on both sides, if not equally, then certainly not so unequally[1]. In fact, however, the investigation of the variants leads to a result which differs considerably from what has just been hypothetically stated. To wit, there emerges, as we shall have to show, an *exceedingly decisive* superiority of authenticity on the side of the Ṛgveda-tradition[2]. Even if one cannot say that the tradition of the Sāmaveda as compared to the other proves to be absolutely worthless, yet it certainly stands in importance so extraordinarily far below it, that we are led to call into question the premise on which the above conclusion is based: behind two masses of transmissions, of which the one is so thoroughly trustworthy, the other, except for very few points, deviates so far from the authentic, then there could not have existed, as we had assumed, one and the same fluctuating chaos of only partly-fixed texts. Even the disciplined technique of modern philological research could scarcely, and never and by no means the knowledge

1. One can say that the relationships should have somewhat corresponded to the picture which emerges from Ludwig's tables of "older readings of the Sāmaveda" and "older readings of the Ṛgveda" (Vol. III, pp. 83-94).
2. Similarly Whitney, op. cit. XXI.

and the ability of the ancient Indian liturgists, have been able to discern the old and valuable as it is found in the Ṛgveda. Hence, there must have existed in that, or by the side of that, chaos a line of tradition of greater consistency which was conspicuous also to the Indian mind. The conclusions to be drawn from this angle, however, belong to a later place.

For the present we have to demonstrate the higher value **[278]** of the text-transmission, as it is to be seen in the *Ṛgveda,* by examining a series of cases to be chosen as the most typical ones possible. First of all attention may be drawn once again to what has been already said above. When the same stanza is addressed to Indra in the ṚV, to Agni in the SV, and when the reading concerned is assured for each of the two Vedas by the place where it occurs within that Saṁhitā, then one can scarcely be in doubt as regards the original reading: no one will dispute that the old, historical arrangement of the Ṛg-hymns and stanzas give guarantees of authenticity better than the combination of the Yoni-stanzas grouped together according to secondary principles. Further, events like the above-mentioned elimination of the genitive *avyas,* the suppression of the word *īm* and the metrically disyllabic vowels, the introduction of the iambic rhythm in a Gāyatrī, which in the ṚV not only itself belongs to the trochaic type, but occurs in a hymn of Gāyatrī stanzas which have a trochaic cadence : in face of all these facts any uncertainty as regards which is the original is ruled out.

We turn to further variants which are characteristic for the relationship between the two Vedic texts.

Among the Ṛk-stanzas which are repeated in the SV, the archaic absolutive form in *-tvī* appears twice, VI.59.6 and VIII.76.10. On both occasions it has been eliminated in the SV; in the former passage, SV has *hitvā* for *hitvī,* in the latter *pītvā* for *pītvī.*

In the pāda *vi aśema devahitaṁ yad āyuḥ* ṚV I.89.8, the SV

reads *vy aśemahi*[1]. Apart from the fact that in the ṚV the optative form *aśema* occurs at several other places, but nowhere *aśemahi,* [279] the treatment of the *i* of *vi* proves the unoriginal nature of the Sāman-reading.

The word *prāṇa* is extremely rare in the ṚV and is limited to the later sections; it occurs[2], besides the three passages of the tenth book, only once in the Virāj-section of book I, and once in the late hymn III.53, which is appended to the original hymn-series. The Sāman-text shows the word several times in the stanzas originating from the ṚV. In *krāṇā sindhūnām kalaśā̃ avīvaśat* IX.86.19, the SV gives, corresponding to *krāṇā* and *avīvaśat, prāṇā* and *acīkradat;* likewise *krāṇā śiśur mahīnām* IX.102.1 with the same variant *prāṇā* in the SV. The arbitrariness of the Sāmaveda diaskeuasts who have here replaced the old and difficult *krāṇā,* which, incidentally, is assured by a considerable number of Ṛk-passages[3] but which had become unintelligible to them, by the modern *prāṇā* does not require any further characterization.

I add some more examples of occurrences of similar kind. In place of the old words of the Ṛk-style there appear in the Sāmaveda expressions of a completely different meaning which were current in the range of ideas of the later Vedic poetry. In the stanza V.39.3 *yat te ditsu prarādhiam mano' asti* etc., the SV reads *yat te dikṣu* etc.[4]; in I.37.10 it replaces the old and, undoubtedly, correct *ajmeṣu* (cf I.37.8; 87.3; V.87.7) by *yajñeṣu,* in VIII.23.14 *tapuṣā* by *tapasā.*—That the

1. The Taitt. Āraṇyaka agrees with the reading of the ṚV, the Vāj. Saṁh. with that of the SV.
2. Also the verb forms of the root *an* occur only in the tenth book and, besides, in I.101.5; 164.30. The nouns *apāna, udāna, vyāna* do not yet appear in the ṚV at all.
3. Cf., besides the Pet. WB (Nachtrag), Lanman, Noun-inflection 329, 334 and V. Bradke, Dyāus Asura, 35-37.
4. By this reading one will be reminded of the tone of the Gṛhya-hymns like Pāraskara I.4.15 : *yadaiṣi manasā dūram diśo 'nu pavamāno vā,* etc.

combinations of plural and singular (respy. **[280]** apparent singular) as *dhīyate dhanā* I.81.3, *triṣu ā rocane divaḥ* I.105.6 (cf. VIII.69.3) have been corrected in the text of the SV is a matter of course. Also the infinitives *śobhase* (for which appears the unintelligible *śobhathā*) and *cakṣase* (for which *cakṣuṣā*) I.84.10, VII.81.1 could not survive in the SV.

Very often the SV employs for the correct Ṛgvedic case ending of a substantive a wrong ending which occurs in neighbouring words and which has arisen due to their influence. Thus, *ghnantaṁ vṛtrāṇi saṁjitaṁ dhanānām* III.30.22; SV: *dhanāni*[1].—*vidyāma tasya te vayam akūpārasya dāvane* V.39.2; SV: *dāvanaḥ*.—*pra asya dhārā' akṣaran vṛṣṇaḥ sutasya ojasā* IX.29.1; SV: *ojasaḥ*[2].—*ād īm aśvaṁ na hetāraḥ* IX.62.6; SV: *hetāram*.—*induḥ paviṣṭa cetanaḥ priyaḥ kavīnām matī* IX.64.10; SV: *matiḥ*.—*vanā vasāno varuṇo na sindhūn* IX.90.2; SV: *sindhuḥ*.—As an example of a similar interchange of two cases we cite further I.127.1 *agniṁ hotāram manye dāsvantaṁ vasuṁ sūnuṁ sahaso jātavedasam* where the SV[3] reads *vasoḥ* for *vasuṁ*: there can be no doubt about the correctness of the Ṛk reading, since Agni is often enough called *vasu* and *sūnu sahasaḥ*, but not as *vasoḥ sūnu*.—Perhaps, the SV *eṣi* (for *eti*) in VII.3.3 which does not fit into the construction is occasioned by the neighbouring *īyase*.

Confusions of similar sounding words, due to which **[281]** the passages concerned become meaningless, are shown often by the SV; one may draw attention to *avasvarat* for the undoubtedly correct *avasparat* VI.42.4 (cf. VIII.66.14; X.39.6), and due to the confusion of the two sounds *v* and *p* in the reverse direction, *pṛṣṭim* for *vṛṣṭim* IX.39.2. Mix-ups like those of *goṣātiḥ* and *goṣāḥ* IX.61.20 and hybrid forms like

1. The genitive is supported by V.42.5 where, besides, *saṁjitaḥ* is nom. pl. (Ludwig), not gen. sing. (Grassmann, Lanman).—Taitt. Br. agrees with the reading of the ṚV III.30.22.
2. For *ojasā* cf. IX.39.3; 65.14 etc.
3. Similarly also the Taitt. Saṁhitā, while the Vāj. Saṁh. here, as in most cases, agrees with the ṚV.

those of *suśipra* and *śiprin* VIII.66.2; 99.2 may be likewise cited here as characteristic of the nature of the Sv.-text. Not seldom does the Sv.-text produce plain word-monsters such as *kṣāmīḥ* for *kṣāmaḥ* VIII.70.4, *adadiṣṭa* for *adediṣṭa* VIII.45.26, *diśasyati* for *daśasyati* IX.3.5 (similarly I.139.5), *dyukṣoḥ* for *kṣoḥ* IX.97.22, *sasrate* for *sisrate*[1] V.1.1, *śundhyāvatā* for *śubhrāvatā* IX.15.3, *pupuri* for *papuri* VI.46.5. Not much better is the form *saniṣan* IX.90.1 which would have to be interpreted as an aorist participle[2], instead of the clear form *saniṣyan* which is assured by a number of parallel passages, or *mahonām,* apparently the gen. pl. of *maghavan,* behind which is hidden partly the gen. *mahānām* of the stem *maha,* antiquated very early (VIII.63.1; 92.3), and partly *mahāmaha* (VIII.46.10) which likewise went out of use later.

As an example of how quite a number of small textual changes not rarely combine in the SV to distort the appearance of a Ṛk-stanza may be cited VIII.19.30. Here ṚV reads :

pra so' agne tavotibhiḥ
suvīrābhis tirate vājabharmabhiḥ
yasya tvaṁ sakhyam āvaraḥ.

[282] In contrast to this the Sāmaveda, with which here the Taittirīya Saṁhitā agrees, reads :

pra so' agne tavotibhiḥ
suvīrābhis tarati vājakarmabhiḥ
yasya tvaṁ sakhyam āvitha.

A look into Grassmmann's WB shows sufficiently that, first of all, *pra tirate,* which also suits the metre better, is to be preferred to *pra tirati.* Next, to be sure, the stem *vājabharman,* as also *vājakarman,* occurs so little outside our passage in

1. The correct form occurs also in the Taitt. Saṁh., Vāj. Saṁh. and the Atharvaveda.
2. Cf., however Whitney, Gramm. § 909.

the Ṛgveda and, as far as I know, anywhere else[1], but the word *vājaṁbhara* (ṚV) and the name Bharadvāja[2] certainly show that *vājabharmabhiḥ* is the correct reading. In this connection, one may further refer to passages in the ṚV like I.63.9; 64 13[3]; II.24.9; IV.16.16; 17.9; VIII.60.18; IX.52.1.

Finally, regarding the verb of the stanza, *āvaraḥ* respy. *āvitha,* which governs the accusative *sakhyam,* the decision in favour of the Ṛv-reading *āvaraḥ* is given by two passages belonging to the same Maṇḍala, VIII.13.21; 44.20, with which one may also compare IV.31.11; 41.7; VII.18.12; IX.66.18.

One may yet mention here III.45.1 (to Indra) as a further example of the text of a stanza or a pāda which has been changed by a series of alterations in the SV: here also, but perhaps still more clearly than in the previous case, [282] the value of the Ṛgveda-tradition is assured by each one of the differences. The transmitted text is:

(ṚV) *mā tvā ke cin* *ni yaman viṁ na pāśinaḥ*
(SV) *mā tvā ke cin* *ni yemur in na pāśinaḥ*

The reading of the Vāj. Saṁh. and of the Atharvaveda (except that AV has *vi* for *ni)* agrees with the ṚV; the Taitt. Ār. follows essentially the SV. It is clear that not *ni yemuḥ,* but *ni yaman* is to be written; that is demonstrated as much by the syntax (preceding *mā*) as by the metre (second syllable after the caseura) and the parallel passages IV.44.5; VII.69.6 (cf. also VIII.33.8). No less clear is the fact that one has to write *viṁ*; the position of *na* and the clear meaning of the whole comparison render any further comment on this point unnecessary.

---

1. Surely, *vājabhṛt* or *vājabharmīya,* the technical name of the related Sāman, offers a noteworthy indication that even in the tradition of the Sāmaveda-schools the correct reading was not totally forgotten.
2. Certainly it is due to this name that Bharadvāja was looked upon as the composer of the Sāman concerned.
3. Very similar are II.26.3; X.147.1.

If in the passages discussed so far we believe that as against the corrupt form of the SV text, the correct reading is preserved by the ṚV-tradition, then in a great majority of cases also those passages in which the ṚV has a corrupt text do not support, but even speak against the independent value of the SV tradition. In many cases the SV simply shares the corruption with the ṚV: thus, e.g., IX.61.12 where the parallel passages scarcely leave any doubt that the strange *indrāya yajyave*[1] is to be corrected to *indrāya vāyave* (cf. IX.27.2; 33.3; 34.2; 65.20; 84.1; 85.6; 86.20; 97, 25,49; 108.16). Sometimes, however, the SV deviates from the corruption of the ṚV in such a way that, far from giving the correct text, it enables one to recognize that just this same (ṚV) corruption had served, directly or indirectly, as the basis for its redactors, which then due to further [284] continuous corruption, or also due to mistaken attempts at improvement, was further distorted. Of this kind is the stanza IX.79.1, which has been discussed in detail above [p. 72]. I cite further IX.98.12 as an at least probable example of this situation. The RV reads :

taṁ sakhāyaḥ purorucam
yūyaṁ vayaṁ ca sūrayaḥ
aśyāma vājagandhiam
sanema vājapastiam.

The SV has, in the first pāda, *purūrucam.* Quite impossible are both the transmitted reading of the ṚV ("the shining in front") and that of the SV ("the one shining much"; cf. X.104.5 *pururucaḥ*; for the quantity of *u*, cf. Benefey Quantitäsverschiedenheiten V.1, p.3,34). But when one considers the constant connection of the verb *ruj* with the acc. *puras*, one will find it probable that Soma, the destroyer

1. The Vāj. Saṁh. also has this reading.

of the firm (*dṛḷhā* etc., cf. IX.34.1; 91.4; 108.6), has here received the epithet *purorujam.*

Moreover, the Sāmaveda tradition shows weaknesses similar to those concerning the reading of single words or of word-groups also in regard to the arrangement of the stanzas and their grouping into tṛcas[1]. I have already above [p. 131] referred to the not infrequent cases where the Sāmaveda produces tṛcas from the Ṛgvedic materials where originally there existed none, or it employs one and the same Ṛk-stanza now in its original, then in a new, arbitrarily constructed context. In the case of **[285]** the transpositions of single stanzas—mostly these are cases where the second and the third stanzas exchange places[2]—the continuity of thought, as is only natural, seldom helps to decide the issue. However, a more careful consideration of what in such cases is usually said and the sequence in which it is said, of the tone in which the general prayer for the blessings tends to be placed at the end of the enumeration of the special characteristics, deeds and the fortune of the deity, will at least in a number of cases, help to decide the issue; I think that an unprejudiced examination will almost without exception[3] result in a decision in favour of the Ṛk-tradition.

Besides the criteria with the help of which we have so far attempted to demonstrate the overwhelming excellence of the Ṛk-text as opposed to the one of the Sāmaveda there occur, as has been already indicated, numerous cases in which the two Vedas show two readings which by themselves

1. Here we naturally do not take into account the merit which falls to the lot of the SV for preserving the groupings that remain concealed in the Ṛk-Saṁhitā : but one may note that even in the Ṛk-tradition, whenever an *opportunity* presents itself for marking these groupings, i.e., in the ritual injunction, they prove to be perfectly known.
2. This is frequent specially in the Pavamāna texts.
3. As an exception may be cited the facts in relation to the ṚV VIII.32 discussed by me in ZDMG XXXVIII.470 f.

could equally be considered possible : how could it happen that the redactors of the SV, no matter how arbitrary and awkward a procedure they allowed themselves, should have hit in each individual case without fail upon only such readings which turn out to be impossible? When in III.9.1 *apāṁ napātaṁ subhagaṁ sudīditim* and *apāṁ napātaṁ subhagaṁ sudaṁsasam* stand face to face, or in V.38.1 *uroṣ ṭa' indra rādhasaḥ* and *vibhoṣ ṭa indra rādhasaḥ,* then a decision on the basis of inner grounds is unthinkable. Only the greater weight of attestation can decide the case here, and thus, if **[286]** the characterization of the Sāman-readings attempted above is correct, this decision in doubtful cases must always turn out to be in favour of the Ṛk-tradition—unless it were possible to confront the record of the faults of the Sāman-text, from which we have given a number of specimens, with an approximately similar counter-account unfavourable to the ṚV. That there can be no question of this has been revealed to me by a comparative examination of the two texts, the longer the more decisive. It has convinced me that in a few cases the SV, in fact, offers useful improvements for the Ṛk-text: but these cases are not remotely sufficient to render the well- justified presumption arising from the above discussions the least doubtful, and which compels us to decide doubtful cases always in favour of the ṚV. Nobody will, or at least no one should, be uncertain that in I.9.4 the prayers, which rise upto Indra, are called not 'without joy' *(ajoṣāḥ)*, but, as the SV shows, 'harmonious' (*sajoṣāḥ*)[1]. Similarly, no one will doubt that in X.156.3 Agni is invoked to smear the wheel-hole and to turn the rim around (*pavim,* thus SV), and not to make the miser (*paṇim,* ṚV) take turns

1. Ludwig also prefers *sajoṣāḥ*. In fact *juṣ* and its derivatives express in the ṚV the satisfaction, the joy which exists between gods and men; its negation would mean the opposite of this satisfaction, and hence the interpretation of *ajoṣāḥ* as 'insatiable' is not permissible.

around himself[1]. As the Sāmaveda diaskeuasts reveal to us, one would not find it very probable that in these passages they had the wrong readings of the ṚV transmitted to them and that they on their part discovered the correct ones by conjecture. **[287]** In other cases one would be in doubt. The assumption that conjectures were made, which in these cases would not at all go beyond the horizon or those text-arrangers, cannot be ruled out for the following cases: in respect of the restoration of the metre of IX.70.1 by substituting *duduhrire* for *duduhre;* in the improvement, which incidentally is not quite certain, of X.23.1 by reading *śmaśrubhiḥ* (for *śmaśru*)[2]; in filling up the metrical lacuna in VIII.69.8 by the insertion of *naraḥ* (after *prārcata*); in the possible but by no means evident reading *parame* (for *pūrvie*) *viomani* in IX.70.1.

To bring to light all the cases in which the SV offers the correct reading—either because the correct reading was so transmitted, or because it is possible to suspect its rise to be due to conjecture—must be reserved for a detailed treatment of the text. The total number of such cases—this much may already be asserted here with the greatest certainty—is exceedingly small. Vis-à-vis the position taken by most Vedic scholars it is therefore also more often necessary to dispute such cases assumed by them than one would find an occasion to polemize in the opposite direction. Even the critique of Grassmann, which on the whole can be considered reasonable, cannot, in my opinion, be absolved from the

1. Thus, also Grassmann and Ludwig L. compares with *vartayā pavim* Taitt. Saṁh. II.6.3.3; it would have been more appropriate to recall ṚV V.62.2 *anu vām ekaḥ pavir ā vavarta.*
2. X.26.7 speaks in favour of retaining the accusative, which is the only regular case employed with *dhū*. II.11.17 has locative. The instrumental would in itself, no doubt, be permissible; as to the parallel passages from the ṚV, I do not know anything more fitting to cite than IV.45.6 (Gaedicke, Accusativ 56). If one retains *śmaśru,* the metre is to be put in order by counting *pra* as two syllables, which is often required (or, following Gr., by accepting the form *śmaśāru* which is found in *hariśmaśāru* ?).

blame of over-estimating the Sāman-tradition. Thus, Grassmann would like to accept from the SV the reading *rādhāṁsi* for VIII.24.13 *pra rādhasā codayāte mahitvanā.* Certainly *rādhāṁsi* would be unobjectionable **[288]** (cf. VI.48.9), but why not the instrumental ["he may further (us) through a gift"]? Cf. I.94.15: V.43.9. If the attestation of *rādhasā* and *rādhāṁsi* were of equal value, one might hesitate; but considering a transmission so excellent as that of the ṚV a critique, which is quite clear about the guiding principles of its procedure can never, on the precarious authority of the SV, decide in favour of the reading *rādhāṁsi.*

But what has just been said of Grassmann's procedure applies in a much higher degree to that of Ludwig. His long tables of readings of the Sāmaveda, which are supposed to be older than those of the Ṛgveda, are based, almost without exception on decisions of a purely subjective judgement. As a sample (I give) only the first numbers of his list (Vol. III. p. 83):

VIII. 84.1 *preṣṭhaṁ vo' atithiṁ*
stuṣe mitram iva priyam
agniṁ rathaṁ na vediam.

Here the SV gives *ágne* (voc.), from which L. gets the gen. *agné(ḥ)* which in his opinion should be "decidedly older" than the reading *agnim.* Decidedly older? And older at all? Can the tradition be really wrong if, after the words *preṣṭhaṁ vo' atithiṁ stuṣe,* it allows the poet to continue—exactly as any one who is not prejudiced must expect, and exactly as in I.186.3, after the opening words *presṭhaṁ vo' atithiṁ gṛṇīṣe,* it is indeed continued—with *agnim*? Or does L. find any difficulty in the comparison in the third pāda: Agni who is notable like a chariot? I shall not attach any value to III.2.15 where it is said of Agni: *rathaṁ na citram.* But II.2.3, VIII.19.8 agree exactly with our stanza, passages which are all the more decisive for ours since their agreement in expressions **[289]** goes beyond simple comparison of Agni with the chariot : *mitram iva priyam, mitraṁ na . . . praśaṁsiam, praśaṁsamāno' atithir na mitriyaḥ.* Ludwig does not make a change in any of these passages; why then in ours ? And what is the sense that he seeks to obtain by his change? "The chariot of Agni is of course Agni himself" (Vol. IV, p. 389). Hence: I praise the dearest guest, who is to be looked upon as the chariot of Agni (i.e. as Agni himself)—in other words: I praise Agni, who is to be looked upon as Agni. Have these remains of the most venerable age, which we have before us in the form of Ṛgveda, no claim on something different and better than such careless arbitrariness which passes as critique ?

It is enough just to have a look at the following passages in that list of Ludwig. In VI.16.28, why not *agnir no vanate*[1] *rayim* as is handed down in the ṚV? Why is *vaṁsate* "better"? —In IV.9.1 why not *ya' īm ā devayuṁ janam iyetha barhir āsadam*? And one can go on further in a similar vein. These passages, not selected, but just taken in the order in which they are found in the list of Ludwig, show what the condition of his long list of alleged older SV-readings is; we will not be diverted by these lists, not even a hair's breadth, from the principle which should be the norm of our critique: viz. *that we have to recognize in individual cases the existence of a more genuine transmission in the SV text as against the corruption in the ṚV, but in each case where there do not exist the strongest grounds to favour the SV reading this must be considered improbable, and that in doubtful cases the presumption* **[290]** *would unconditionally be in favour of the form of the text transmitted in the RV, or in favour of the form to be obtained by conjecture from the one that already exists in the ṚV.*

On the basis of the results obtained so far it now remains for us to examine the assertion, made by several researchers,

1. About the form *vanate* as indicative and subjunctive, cf. W. Neisser, Zur ved. Verballehre I, p. 17 f. (Bezzenb. Beitr. VII. 223 f.).

that the readings of the SV have their origin in a śākhā of the ṚV different from the one that is transmitted to us. But it would serve the purpose better to return later to the questions noted here, and first discuss, as we have just done with regard to the SV, the nature of the variants of the Ṛk-text available in the different branches of the Yajurveda.

It is necessary here to preface a few remarks on the most important branches of the Yajurveda and the relationship among the transmitted redactions of this Veda.

The view regarding the fundamental difference between the black and the white Yajurveda which, as far as I can see, has been generally accepted has been expressed in the following words of Weber[1]: "While in the Saṁhitā of the black Yajus the sacrificial formulae are mostly immediately followed by their dogmatic explanations etc. and by the description of the ritual related with them, and the part called brāhmaṇam is distinguished from this Saṁhitā only from the point of view of chronology, that is, it is to be looked upon as a supplement to it, the sacrificial formulae and their ritual explanation are completely separated from each other in the white Yajus".

[291] Let us begin the remarks to be directed against these formulations, (remarks) which, I think, are of fundamental importance also for the questions of text-transmission occupying us, with the discussion of a passage which apparently is far removed, viz. a sūtra of the Śāṅkhāyana Gṛhya II.11.13, where, in connection with the order of the texts to be transmitted to a Vedic pupil, it is said: "When the Veda, ending with the Śaṁyu-Bārhaspatya hymn (i.e. the concluding hymn of the Saṁhitā adopted by Śāṅkhāyana) has been recited and (the teacher) wants to communicate (to the pupil further) the secret lesson" etc. What that "secret lesson" (*rahasya*) is, we learn from other

1. Ind. Literaturgeschichte, 2nd edn., p. 94.— Similarly Eggeling, Sacred Books, Vol. XII, XXVI-f.; Kaegi, Der Rgveda, p. 127, etc.

passages of the same Sūtra[1]: they are various parts of Āraṇyaka, i.e. not, as is often explained, of the texts meant for the hulobioi (*vānaprastha*), but of the texts which, on account of their higher mystic sanctity, are to be communicated by the teacher to the pupil in the forest instead of in the village. Thus, whereas, as a rule, one is accustomed to think that among the Vedic texts the Brāhmaṇa follows the Saṁhitā, the Āraṇyaka follows the Brāhmaṇa, here, as one can see, is given a description of the teaching of a lesson in which the Āraṇyaka follows directly the Saṁhitā. Where does the Brāhmaṇa go? If one reads the special injunctions of the Sāṅkhāyana about the Vedic teaching, then one finds detailed directives about the study of the Saṁhitā and, not less detailed directives about the study of the Āraṇyaka, but there is no word about the study of the Brāhmaṇa—in this case, the Kauṣītaki Brāhmaṇa.

What appears strange at the first sight, viz. that among the Ṛgvedins there was a teaching course in which one proceeded [**292**] from the Saṁhitā to the Āraṇyaka, thus passing over the Brāhmaṇa, becomes apparently further complicated by the fact that a great part of the Āraṇyaka, the description of the Mahāvrata, is obviously nothing more than a piece of a Brāhmaṇa, or a supplement to the Brāhmaṇa. If we read the Aitareya Brāhmaṇa we find that its author very well knew the ceremonies of Mahāvrata; he, however, does not describe them at a place where they would belong in the context of the rest of the ritual, but the Brāhmaṇa-type explanation of the Mahāvrata is given—just because of the special mystic dignity which is ascribed to this ceremony—in the Āraṇyaka. We ask again: how can, following the hymns of the Saṁhitā, the Mahāvrata—apparently a supplement of the Brāhmaṇa—be learnt but not the Brāhmaṇa itself ?

---

1. II.11.11,12; 12.13,14; VI.4.

It seems to me that on this perplexing question some light is thrown by a passage in the fifth book of the Aitareya Āraṇyaka, the text of the Aitareya school, which contains the sūtra-type section related to the Mahāvrata exactly as the first book of the Ait. Ār. is the Brāhmaṇa section pertaining to it.[1] There it is said (V.3.10): *nedam* (to wit, *mahāvratam*) *ekasminn ahani samāpayed iti ha smāha Jātukarṇyaḥ, samāpayed iti Gālavo, yad anyat prāk tṛcāśītibhyaḥ samāpayed evety Āgniveśyāyanaḥ*. Thus in the recitation of the Mahāvrata-lesson there are found the so-called *tṛcāśītayaḥ*. The Brāhmaṇa (Ait. Ār. I.4.3) only says: he (i.e. the officiating priest) recites this and that *tṛcāśīti* etc. and this means this and this. But we see now that one who studied the Mahāvrata recited, as it follows from the sūtra, the *aśītayaḥ* themselves, not the reflections on their significance **[293]** but their text. With that we come nearer to the problem why, directly after the study of the Saṁhitā, that of the Āraṇyaka could follow, setting aside the study of the Brāhmaṇa. The study of the Āraṇyaka-section of the Mahāvrata did not at all mean the study of the Brāhmaṇa-book which deals with that ceremony, but it meant the Saṁhitā-type recitation of the Mantras belonging to the Mahāvrata-litany. Hence, we must suppose that the regular teaching course of the Ṛgveda, as Śāṅkhāyana had it in mind, was confined to the Saṁhitā, and in addition the *rahasya* for the chosen ones. *Besides* there must have been separate schools where, if we may say so, the specialists studied the Brāhmaṇas. Hence, I think, it is not correct to say, as many do, that the Bahvṛcas were divided according to their Brāhmaṇas into the Aitareyins, Kauṣītakins, etc. But among the great number of Bahvṛcas who learnt the Saṁhitā of the Ṛgveda there was a section of Aitareyins, one of Kauṣītakins etc; many however—presumably by far most of them—were simply Bahvṛcas who did not busy themselves

1. Cf. my remarks in the Sacred Books, Vol. XXIX, p. 154 f.

with one of the two Brāhmaṇas and therefore had no claim to be called Aitareyins or Kauṣītakins.

If we thus have learnt that the Saṁhitā was the only fixed and essential thing in the teaching course of the Bahvṛcas, then it is quite natural that we should try to make use of these observations with reference to the Adhvaryu-schools. If one branch of the Veda-knowers felt that it was not essential that everyone of them should know the mystic-speculative explanations of the Hotar-functions offered in the Brāhmaṇas, we cannot easily assume that another branch of the Brāhmaṇas **[294]** conceded an essentially different honour to the mystic explanation of the Adhvaryu-functions. And we are strongly supported in this interpretation by passages like the Taitt. Ār. II.10: *yad ṛco 'dhīte. . .yad yajūṁṣi. . .yat sāmani. . .yad atharvāṅgirasaḥ . . .yad brāhmaṇānī–tihāsān purāṇāni* etc. Here, it may be specially noted that in a text of the *black* Yajurveda, there is mentioned first, the svādhyāya of the Vedic Saṁhitās themselves, viz. of the ṛcas, of the *Yajus,* etc., and then afterwards as a kind of second class literature alongside the Itihāsas etc. also of the Brāhmaṇas: thus even in the view of the black YV there were two kinds of activities: to recite the Yajus by themselves, and to recite the ritualistic and the mystic discussions on the Yajus given in the Brāhmaṇa style. In a word: in the black Yajurveda as well there must have been a separation of the Yajus proper and the Brāhmaṇa-type additions to them.

If with these presuppositions we undertake an examination of the black Yajus-texts as they in fact exist, then, I think, their nature with regard to the distinction of the Saṁhitā- and the Brāhmaṇa-elements will certainly appear to be essentially different from the one which we get from the point of view of the current opinion cited above (p. 290) in the words of Weber. Let us first of all consider the way in which the two largest and the most important principal chapters of the matter, which comes up for discussion in the YV, are presented in the black YV: the

New- and the Full-moon sacrifice, together with the Soma-sacrifice[1], and secondly, the instruction regarding the setting up of the Fire-altar. In the Vājasaneyi-Saṁhitā, as is well known, the Mantra-portion for the former ritual is given in **[295]** the books I-X, for the latter in XI-XVIII; the related ritual explanations are to be found in the books I-V, respy. VI-X of the Śatapatha Brāhmaṇa. Is, for example, the Taittirīya Saṁhitā really so far removed from this distinct grouping of the material and in the direction one would have to assume according to those definitions of the opposition between the black and the white YV? Exactly as the Vāj. Saṁh., also the Taitt. Saṁh. begins with the formulae *iṣe tvorje tvā;* then follow, again thoroughly as in the Vāj. Saṁh., all the formulae for the Full- and the New-moon sacrifice, followed by the formulae for the Soma sacrifice upto the Avabhṛtha bath which concludes this sacrifice: *and this entire treatment of the two principal sacrifices occurs* (TS I.1-4) *as a pure collection of formulae, not mixed up with Brāhmaṇa-type additions,* treating the subject exactly in the manner of the Vāj. Saṁh. and representing a parallel recension of the relevant sections of the Vāj Saṁh. Exactly in the same way at a different place in the Taittirīya Saṁhitā (book IV) the complete Saṁhitā for the Fire-altar ritual occurs, unaffected by the Brāhmaṇa-sections. And just as these two old extensive Saṃhitās, also the corresponding Brāhmaṇas occur within the TS. which, for their part, present themselves exactly as Brāhmaṇas without Saṁhitā-admixture:[2] the Brāhmaṇa of the Soma-sacrifice[3] (TS VI) and the Brāhmaṇa of the Agni-ritual (TS V). Similarly, the Maitrāyaṇī Saṁhitā contains the formulae for the half-

1. For the sake of brevity, I omit the remaining less important sacrifices whose description is usually connected with that of those mentioned above.
2. I say this about the situation as a *whole* : in isolated cases secondary displacements have occurred which do not alter the situation as such.
3. The Brāhmaṇa of the Full-moon and the New-moon sacrifice occurs at a different place, Taitt. Brāhmaṇa III.

monthly sacrifices and for the Soma in I.1-3, those for the Agni-cayana in II.7-13, **[296]** while the corresponding Brāhmaṇas are to be found in III.6 f. and III.1 f. The separation of the Saṁhitā- and the Brāhmaṇa-sections which is asserted here does *not*, of course, hold good in many cases in respect of the supplements which have been added to those fundamental constituents of the Yajurveda mentioned above; it goes without saying that pursuing in detail the special questions, which arise in this context regarding the structure of the Yajus-Saṁhitās, lies outside the scope of the present investigation. It should be sufficient for us to have established that as far as the great principal and basic mass of the Mantras is concerned, in the black Yajurveda, exactly as in the white, we have the Saṁhitā text which is not mixed up with Brāhmaṇa material. That these Saṁhitā elements which, for example, are found in the corpus of the Taitt. Saṁh., do not form a perfect whole with the Brāhmaṇa-elements of the same corpus can be easily seen from the comparison of the two types of texts. It can hardly be proved that, on the whole, the elements of one type are chronologically and internally in any way closer to those of the other type than the corresponding sections of the Vāj. Saṁh. to those of the Śatapatha Brāhmaṇa. Hence, when one uses the materials of the "Taittirīya Saṁhitā", whether from the point of view of the language or text-history, or from the point of view of the contents, one should be clear about the fact that under this general title are put together into an only apparent whole products of separated, probably widely separated, literary periods—elements which for the most part are available individually in such a compact form that they can be easily separated from each other and assigned to their chronologically proper place.

But perhaps we have gone too far in alluding to questions whose final solution **[297]** must await its own proper treatment. What has been said here, however, will be enough at least for the provisional justification of our standpoint, viz. that while discussing the Vedic textual history, instead of, for example, speaking of the Taitt. Saṁhitā, or the Vāj. Saṁhitā, as a whole, we prefer a different way of understanding and a different way of expression. We shall have to speak, if we wish to name here only the two principal groups of the text-elements concerned, of the Yajus-Saṁhitā of the sacrifice (Full- and New-moon sacrifice etc., Soma) and the Yajus-Saṁhitā of the building up of the fire-altar. And we shall have to treat the sections concerned of the *transmitted* Yajus-collections as recensions, standing side by side, of those two-Saṁhitās: for it can be asserted with certainty that neither the Maitrāyaṇīyas, nor the Taittirīyas, nor the Vājasaneyins are directly in possession of the mother-text of the Yajus-theology which lies at the basis of all these redactions.

Let us begin with the sūkta Vātsapra (ṚV X.45) which has been taken over in full in the Saṁhitā of the *agnicayana* in order to obtain a clear picture of the condition of the readings of the Ṛk-stanzas contained in those sources. I give the transmitted ṚV-text (R) with the variants in the Taittirīya Saṁhitā (T), the Maitrāyaṇī Saṁh. (M) and the Vājasaneyi Saṁhitā (V)[1]. As regards marking the accent, with which we are not concerned here, I follow the usual practice :

1. *divás pári prathamáṁ jajñe agnír*
asmád dvitī́yam pári jātávedāḥ |
[298] *tṛtī́yam apsú nṛmáṇā ájasram*
índhāna enaṁ jarate svādhī́ḥ ||

janate M (also Kāṭhaka), but *jarate* in the Padapāṭha of the Maitr. Saṁh. which has accepted in general many readings of the other redactions.

1. TS. IV.2.2; MS. II.7.9; VS XII.18 ff. In the case of the stanzas cited only by their Pratīkas the variant readings have been supplied from their full form occurring elsewhere in the Saṁhitā concerned; similarly in the case of st. 8, which is omitted here in the Mait. S., but appears in II.7.8. What is purely orthographic is not noted (as *ḍ* for *ḷ* and similar things).

2. *vidmā́ te agne tredhā́ trayā́ṇi*
vidmā́ te dhā́ma víbhṛtā purutrā́ |
vidmā́ te nā́ma paramáṁ gúhā yád
vidmā́ tám útsam yáta ājagántha ||

sádma víbhṛtam (for *dh.v.*) TM.—*ābabhū́tha* M.

3. *samudré tvā nṛmáṇā apsv̀ antár*
nṛcákṣā īdhe divó agna ū́dhan |
tṛtī́ye tvā rájasi tasthivā́ṁsam
apā́m upásthe mahiṣā́ avardhan ||

dívo M.— *ṛtásya yónau* (for *ap. up.*) TM.—*ahinvan* T, *agṛbhṇan* M.

4. *ákrandat agníḥ stanáyann iva dyaúḥ*
kṣā́mā rérihad vīrúdhaḥ samañján |
sadyó jajñānó ví hī́m iddhó ákhyad
ā́ ródasī bhānúnā bhāty antáḥ ||

him M (*hi* | *im* Padap.; *hīm* Kāṭhaka).

5. *śrīṇā́m udāró dharúṇo rayīṇā́ṁ*
manīṣā́ṇām prā́rpaṇaḥ sómagopāḥ |
vásuḥ sūnúḥ sáhaso apsú rā́jā
ví bhāty ágra uṣásām idhānáḥ ||

vásoḥ T.

6. *víśvasya ketúr bhúvanasya gárbha*
ā́ ródasī apṛṇāj jā́yamānaḥ |
vīḷúm cid ádrim abhinat parāyáñ
jánā yád agním áyajanta páñca ||

jajñe (for *ketúr*) M.—*rājā́* (for *gárbha ā́*) M.

[299] 7. *uśík pāvakó aratíḥ sumedhā́*
márteṣv agnír amṛ́to ní dhāyi |
iyarti dhūmám aruṣám bháribhrad
úc chukréṇa śocíṣā dyā́m ínakṣan ||

mártyeṣv VM (one MS. *mánteṣv*) Kāṭhaka.—*aruṣó* M.—*inakṣat* T.

8. *dṛśānó rukmá urviyā́ vỳ adyaud*
durmárṣam ā́yuḥ śriyé rucānáḥ ।
agnír amṛ́to abhavad váyobhir
yád enaṁ dyaúr janáyat surétāḥ ॥

uruyā́ víbhāti M.—*ajáro 'bhavat sáhobhir* M.—*ájanayat* VTM.

9. *yás te adyá kṛṇávad bhadraśoce*
'pūpáṁ deva ghṛtávantam agne ।
prá táṁ naya pratarā́ṁ vásyo ácchā
[a]bhī sumnáṁ devábhaktaṁ yaviṣṭha ॥

pratarā́ṁ T.—*dyumnám* TM.—*deváhitaṁ yaviṣṭhya* (°*ṣṭha* Padap.) M.

10. *ā́ táṁ bhaja sauśravaséṣv agna*
ukthá-uktha ā́ bhaja śasyámāne ।
priyáḥ sū́rye priyó agnā́ bhavāty
új jāténa bhinádad új jánitvaiḥ ॥

11. *tvā́m agne yájamānā ánu dyū́n*
víśvā vásu dadhire vā́ryāṇi ।
tváyā sahá dráviṇam icchámānā
vrajáṁ gómantam uśíjo ví vavruḥ ॥

vásūni T. In M the second Pāda of 11 reads as: *dūtáṁ kṛṇvānā́ ayajanta havyaíḥ.*

12. *ástāvy agnír narā́ṁ suśévo*
vaiśvānará ṛ́ṣibhiḥ sómagopāḥ ।
adveṣé dyā́vāpṛthivī́ huvema
dévā dhattá rayím asmé suvī́ram ॥

[300] Not found in T; can be omitted by the Vājasaneyins (Kāty. XVI.5.21 f., cf. Sát. Br. VI.7.4.6).—*nṛṇā́m* M.—*adveṣyé* M.—*huve* M.

The order of the stanzas in V agrees with that of the ṚV;

in T it is as follows: 1-4, 7, 6, 5, 9-11, 8 (12 is missing); in M: 1-3, 5.7.4.6 [I.96.5],[1] 9-12 (8 is missing[1]).

In spite of the small extent of the materials presented here, we shall attempt to formulate conclusions about the relationship of the different texts. It will, of course, be remembered that these conclusions stand in need of confirmation or correction with the help of further extensive examination.

At first glance the four texts compared fall into two groups. On the one hand, we have the thoroughly well-marked text which is found almost without variants in the ṚV and the VS, on the other the one, much less definitely fixed, occurring in the two black Yajurveda texts which, due to a series of readings, prove to be related[2], but separated from each other in numerous other cases. The deviations in the sequence of the stanzas lead to the same grouping; these also clearly bring into prominence the unchangeability of the character on the one hand, and the considerably less fixed nature on the other. **[301]** In cases where *only* M but not T, or *only* T but not M differs from the ṚV, it will be expedient to assume the reading in the ṚV to be in the source text of TM, and at the same time to see in the deviation of T, respectively of M, from the ṚV, a deviation from the basic text—I call it X—from which the two black Yajus-texts originate. In whatever way one may judge the value of X vis-á-vis the ṚV: no value can be attached to a reading which occurs only in T or in M, while the other one

1. Stanza ṚV I.96.5, which in the Mait. S. is inserted after st. 6, is, from the standpoint of this Saṁhitā, to be looked upon as a part of the Vātsapra hymn, for only in this way the sūkta has twelve stanzas, which number is specified in the related Brāhmaṇa-section (Mait. S. III.2.2) for that sūkta. It deserves to be noted that stanza 8 of the Vātsapra, which is missing at this place of the Mait. S., and the inserted stanza I.96.5 both occur next to each other in the Mait. S. II.7.8; hence we will be justified in considering the appearance of I.96.5 in the Vātsapra as a mistaken substitution for X.45.8.
2. Thus, stanza 2 *sadma vibhṛtam;* stanza 3 *ṛtasya yonau;* stanza 9 *dyumnam.*

of these two texts agrees with the ṚV, because it must be presumed that the former does not at all originate from X, but is of secondary origin. However, also a different construction is not quite ruled out in a case of the type described above: the reading which differs from the ṚV could have existed in X, but was later suppressed by the ṚV reading in one of the two descendants of X. One would not like to attach great value to this possibility as against the simpler interpretation stated above, especially when one considers the great freedom with which apparently both T and M treat the readings of their source. This state of affairs facilitates and recommends the assumption that each of the two texts has individually deviated from its basic source[1].

Of greater significance is the question of the relationship of the white Yajurveda text (V) with that of X than the question just touched upon above. **[302]** No one who compares the texts of the formulae for the Agnicayana in V, in T, and in M will doubt that they are, as we have said above, nothing but the three redactions of one and the same basic Saṁhitā. This also means that there existed for the Ṛk-stanzas taken over in that Saṁhitā, so to say, a basic Yajus-form; we shall call it W. Now there arises a new task for us—to discover the circumstances in which, starting from W, there arose so different a form of V on the one hand, and of X (=TM) on the other. If one first considers, what tentatively seems obvious, that V and X are simply two parallel descendants of W, whose relative value is still to be determined, then, clearly the agreement almost without exception, of V with R, a text which is outside this tradition and which has claims to great authority, would lead us to the conclusion that W, the source of VX, had nearly the same text as R, and that where X deviated from this text

1. I do not think it risky to assume a deviation also in M from its source-text X in such cases where—and this is often the case—the Kāṭhaka agrees with M; the two texts clearly represent a close family and when they are opposed to T they cannot be considered as two independent witnesses against T.

which is preserved with great fidelity in V, these deviations are just secondary: otherwise, if the text of V, as of X, were simply the more conscientiously or the more arbitrarily transmitted text of W, it would be impossible to understand such a thorough agreement with R of one of the two recensions. The consequence of this interpretation would be of the greatest fundamental importance: all the readings of the black Yajurveda, in so far as they, as is the rule, stand against the agreement of the white YV with the ṚV, would *a priori* have to be dismissed as secondary deviations from W; W itself, however, as the basic text to be reconstructed for the Yajurveda would have to be posited as almost identical throughout with our Ṛk-text. A confirmation of the age **[303]** of the latter, reaching further than that, can hardly be imagined.

Now all that could only be too good to be true. Just the striking regularity of the agreement of V with R arouses the suspicion that we are faced not with a purely natural affiliation of the Yajus-texts but with artificial changes. In other words: V could have had for its basis a Yajus-text which was much more independent of the Ṛgveda that is handed down to us, and instead could have had an appearance which is much more similar to TM, than what V actually has. The present similarity, bordering almost on identity, of V with R must, then, be attributed not to the basic text, from which V originates, but to the *later* correction that was undertaken for this text and for which R must have supplied the model.

It is easy to see in which way the decision between the two possibilities described above has to be reached. If the agreement of V with R goes back to the agreement of W with R and if the difference in the positions of V, and of TM, to R rests on the different accuracy with which the texts VTM reproduce their common basic text, then the greater fidelity of V, as against TM, in reproducing the W-text, assumed in the above supposition, must be seen not only in the stanzas originating from the Ṛgveda but, in a similar way, also in the remaining Yajus-stanzas and -formulae. It is easy for anyone to convince himself that this is not at all the case. No one who carries out the comparisons somewhat extensively would dispute the fact that on numerous occasions the white Yajurveda offers a text less original than that of the black recensions [304] of the Veda. Thus in the midst of the text of the white Yajus, which is not especially distinguished for its conservative fidelity, the Ṛk-stanzas which occur there strike one as something special. They show, when compared with the text of the black YV, a relationship which is quite different from the one which prevails in their environment. They, and they alone, in the text-form as it appears in the white YV show that in their complete agreement with R, they follow a fixed norm. The conclusion from all this is quite clear: it is not at all necessary that that agreement was found in the basic copy of the Yajus-texts; that agreement in the white YV has been brought about by manifold corrections of the stanzas originating from the ṚV for which the Ṛk-text served as the model. Hence the text of the Ṛk-stanzas in the white YV can be considered as a conclusive proof only for determining the time of the origin of the white Yajus-Samhitā itself; but it is not one which antedates the black Yajurvedas and, pushing them aside, represents the basic form of the Yajurveda[1].

Before we proceed to examine these statements more extensively which, for the present, have been made only tentatively on the strength of a single sūkta, we add a few more remarks on the different textual variants which were listed above for that sūkta (X.45). A great number of them show in themselves an unobjectionable form which could

1. It may further be pointed out here that if there is no reason to suppose that V, *against* the agreement of T and M, in many ways represents the common source W, then it is also possible to say that T, as also M, originates directly from W without there being any intermediate source; in other words what we have called X coincides with W. But the further follow-up of this question must be left for the special studies of the Yajurveda.

be considered as much justified as the one in the transmitted Ṛgveda **[305]** as long as the authority of the attestation does not decide the issue one way or the other. For example, among the readings given by TM, *ṛtasya yonau* (stanza 3, cf. IX.86.25) is in itself as much possible as *apām upasthe* (cf. VI.8.4), *dyumnam* (st. 9) as *sumnam*[1]. Of the readings represented only by T or only by M *ābabhūtha* in stanza 2 would be unobjectionable (presumably made according to ṚV X.84.5; cf. further ṚV X.129.6,7); likewise in stanza 3 *ahinvan* (cf. ṚV IX.73.2; 86.25; 97.57) and *agṛbhṇan* (perhaps originating from VI.8.4), st. 6 *viśvasya jajñe bhuvanasya rājā*;[2] st. 8 *ajaro' [a]bhavat sahobhiḥ*; st. 11 *dūtam kṛṇvānā' ayajanta havyaiḥ* (based on V.3.8; cf. X.122.7). In the last passage, however, an unfavourable factor for the black Yajus-texts comes to light in that they have removed the (apparent) combination of plural and singular in *viśvā vasu*, as also the similar connection between *dhāma vibhṛtā* in stanza 2 (cf. X.80.4). Still more characteristic is the reading *martyeṣu* in stanza 7 which probably, though not in all certainty, is to be attributed to the basic Yajurveda; it bears the clear stamp of the period in which it has originated: the period when the old form *marta* became obsolete, and by the side of the trisyllabic stem *martia*, which (besides *marta*) alone occurred in the ṚV, its disyllabic form *martya* gained ground.[3] The readings *vasoḥ* in st. 5, *pratarām* in **[306]** st. 9, which occur in T alone, do not look better[4]. The reading *vasoḥ sūnuḥ* which the Taitt. Saṁh. offers here is, of course, on a par with the Taittirīya- and the Sāman- reading *vasoḥ sūnum* of

1. But why should *dyumnam* be considered "better than the reading of the ṚV" (Ludwig)?
2. *viśvasya bhuvanasya rājā* is a very frequent phrase, and elsewhere without any other word occurring within it. With *bhuvanasya garbhaḥ* cf. X.168.4.
3. With *martyeṣu* for *marteṣu*, one may compare further *yaviṣṭhya* for *yaviṣṭha* (M in stanza 9), *advesye* for *adveṣe* (M in st. 12).
4. Ludwig, however, gives preference to the readings of T on both the occasions.

I.127.1 which was discussed above (p.280). To judge *pratarām*, Whitney offers Gramm. 1111c, 1119 the necessary materials. There remains just one passage where the Yajus-texts appear to improve on the transmitted Ṛgveda text: *ajanayat* in st. 8 for *janayat*. And even here it is doubtful, whether it is really a better reading (since the metre can be explained by the assumption of the frequent imperfection based on the mixing up the two forms of the Triṣṭubh; it is also possible to think of disyllabic *diauḥ*) and whether the improvement, if it is one, rests on the tradition or, in fact, is an obvious conjecture. Incidentally this *ajanayat*, as also the *martyeṣu* of st. 7, deserves to be stressed as an example of an occasional following of V of a text-transmission which *deviates* from R.

We will now leave this sūkta in order to test the results arrived at so far on some further examples taken likewise from the Saṁhitā of the Agnicayana. We will, first, select the hymn X.140 which is of special interest because it appears also in the Sāmaveda (S). The deviations from the available Ṛk-text to be found in the Yajurveda texts and in the S are the following:

1. *bhrājanty* TM.—2. *putráḥ pitárā* T.—*óbhé pṛṇāsi ródasī* M, *ubhé pṛṇakṣi ródasī* T.—3. *tvá éṣaḥ* M (but *tvé íti tvé, íṣaḥ* Padap.; *te viśve* Kapiṣṭhala Saṁh., *tve viśve* Kāṭh).—*bhū́riretasaś* T.—4. *darśatáṁ* (for **[307]** *sānasíṁ*) S.—*rayím* (for *krátum*) TM.—5. *niṣkartā́ram* T.—*rā́dhase mahé* T.—*rātíṁ bhṛ́gūṇām uśíjaṁ kavíkratuṁ pṛṇákṣi sānasíṁ rayím* T; M like R, only *krátum* (for *rayím*).—6. *viśvácarṣaṇim* T.—*daívaṁ mā́nuṣā yujā́* M.—stanzas 3 and 4, as also 5 and 6 are transposed in TM; besides in T stanza 2 follows stanza 3.

One sees *that here also V agrees with R without any deviation*, and further, that the text-recension represented by VR is supported, except for a single deviation in stanza 4, *also by the text of the* S. On the other hand, TM prove to belong together by some textual variants as also by the common sequence of the stanzas; however, we also find here that these texts reproduce in individual cases their common original text with many liberties and deviations. If we examine the value of the individual deviations, then scarcely any result is to be had from the deviations in the order of the stanzas[1]. The most important variant which requires consideration is the one in stanza 2, where for *pṛṇakṣi rodasī ubhe* (RVS), the black Yajus-texts have *obhe pṛṇāsi rodasī* (M), resp. *ubhe pṛṇakṣi rodasī* (T). Of the two formulations, obviously, as is made probable by ṚV VIII.64.4, we have to start from the one which appears in M, and which will have occurred in the basic text of TM, while in T this reading has been affected under the influence of the one appearing in RVS. Should the authority of the Yajus-redaction, as opposed to the Ṛgveda—in this case, in addition, supported by the Sāmaveda—prove for the rest to be adequate then naturally **[308]** there would be nothing objectionable with *obhe pṛṇāsi rodasī.* Our exposition, however, will show more and more how risky it is to rely on the authority of the Yajus as such. Moreover, it is difficult to understand and is also improbable that in a relatively later period in the good transmission of R there could arise out of *obhe pṛṇāsi rodasī,* due not only to a simple corruption but to a complete change of the whole wording *pṛṇakṣi rodasī ubhe.* The opposite course is more simple to understand: nothing is more frequent than the connection of *ā apṛṇat, ā apṛṇāt, ā pṛṇa, ā pṛṇāsi, ā paprātha* etc. with the object *rodasī*[2]. Therefore, it was quite simple for the diaskeuasts to introduce into the text this common *pṛṇāsi* in place of *pṛṇakṣi.* Next, the most convenient way to make room for the preposition *ā* was shown by the formulation *obhe pṛṇāsi rodasī* occurring in VIII.64.4. If we must make a conjecture—

---

1. The place of stanza 5 in R is irreproachable; the accusatives relating to Agni in the first half of the stanza are to be explained by the ellipsis of the verb. Perhaps, just because of these accusatives the stanza has been placed after stanza 6 in TM.
2. I.73.8; II.15.2; 22.2; III.2.7; 3.10; 6.2 (= IV.18.5; VII.13.2); 34.1; VI.46.5; 48.6; VII.20.4; VIII.64.4 etc.

which is, however, not even called for by the unobjectionable *pṛṇakṣi*[1], although it happens not to occur elsewhere with the same object as here—,then we have to proceed from the word-order found in the tradition of R and within this word-order place *pṛṇāsi* in the place of *pṛṇakṣi*; but then the preposition *ā* which cannot be accommodated would form a serious stumbling-block.[2] In a word: the reading of M would deserve consideration provided the value of the line of transmission of that Saṁhitā were otherwise established; the present passage, however, is not suitable as a proof to establish that value.

[309] *bhrājanti* in stanza 1 (against *bhrājante*) has very little to recommend for the recension available in TM; the ṚV always has *bhrājase, bhrājate, bhrājante,* not *bhrājasi* etc. Also among the readings found only in T or in M, one finds—apart from a few variants, unobjectionable in themselves—nothing which would appear more correct than the reading of the R, and much which proves immediately to be useless. Thus, the distortion of the derivative from *iṣ-kar* which appears here (st. 5) and also constantly elsewhere; the dative *rādhase mahe* (5) in place of the genitive; the interpolation of the second half of stanza 5 on the basis of ṚV III.2.4; the later, unknown to the ṚV, and besides metrically impossible, *daivam* (6), for the archaic *daiviam;* finally *mānuṣā yujā* (6) for *m° yugā,* a variant which by the way, occurs also in the Sāmaveda corresponding to ṚV IX.12.7.

Some readings from the other hymns and stanzas belonging to the Agnicayana-ritual may serve to give a still more definite picture of the condition of the text found in the Yajus-tradition. We confine ourselves, on the whole, to such variants whose relatively older age may be presumed

1. The author of this hymn liked this word, see stanza 4.
2. In *none* of the passages concerned, which are quite numerous, is *ā* missing, not even in VI.46.5 as one might assume following Grassmann. Only the compound *rodasiprā* can be cited as an example of the lack of *ā*.

on the ground of the agreement between T and M. The unfavourable results we get with regard to these variants naturally apply still more strongly to those readings which occur *only* in T or *only* in M[1].

[310] If in I.96.5 R reads *naktoṣāsā varṇam āmemyāne* and the Yajus-texts have in its place *naktoṣāsā samanasā virūpe,* one must look upon the *former* as the traditional text and assume in the latter an effort to get rid of the obscure and the inconvenient participle *āmemyāna* (cf. I.113.2) with the help of the obvious parallel found in I.113.3. ṚV III.22.5 may be mentioned further as an analogous recasting modeled on some other passage in the Ṛgveda where the variant *juṣantām havyam āhutam* for *juṣ° yajñam adruṇaḥ* is obviously explained as a result of the influence of *juṣasva havyam āhutam* in II.32.6. IV.58.6 is recast by substituting the latter half of the stanza by that of stanza 5. We add to this list VIII.102.20-21. In the first of these two stanzas the words *sarvaṁ tad astu te ghṛtam* are taken over from the second, and in the second the words *taj juṣasva yaviṣṭhya* are taken over from the first, and thus the two Gāyatrīs, which are assured as such by their environment in the Ṛgveda, have been transformed into Anuṣṭubhs. Similarly, the Uṣṇih of VIII.23.5 in the Ṛgveda has been turned into a Bṛhatī by adding the first pāda of stanza 6. The correctness of the Ṛk-recension is shown as much by the metrical nature of VIII.23, which runs through the hymn and the neighbouring sūktas (above p.211) as by the construction of stanza 6 which leaves no doubt that the pāda concerned belongs to *this* stanza. Also in II.6.4 the metre recommends the text as handed

1. As a case—and there are many similar ones—in which it is possible to follow especially clearly the successive layers of older and younger variants, may be cited VIII.93.8-9. The variants are in M: *bale* (for *made*); *ugro* (for *ṛṣvo*). In T (Taitt. Brāhm. I.5.8.3): *bale, saumyaḥ* (later word!), *vavakṣur* (sic!) *ugro.* One sees how a core of variants is increased by other inferior ones. Confirmation is given by the Sāmaveda: it knows only the older variants, not the new ones of the Taitt. Br.

down in the Ṛgveda: the pāda *vasupate vasudāvan*, with its long syllable in the penultimate position, corresponds to the metrical character of that sūkta, but the Yajurveda removes the long syllable by making the change *vasudāvā vasupatiḥ*, and the Mait. Saṁh, in addition, transforms the Gāyatrī-stanza occurring in a Gāyatrī-hymn into an Anuṣṭubh by the addition of the words *yāni* **[311]** *kāni ca cakṛma*.—Of other cases in which the Yajus-recension distorts the metre only a few more may be cited I.114.1 *yathā naḥ śam asad dvipade catuṣpade* (ṚV without *naḥ*); X.97.14 *tāḥ sarvā' oṣadhayaḥ saṁvidānāḥ* (*saṁv° oṣ°* M; ṚV without *oṣadhayaḥ*); X.14.9 *adād idaṁ yamo 'vasānaṁ pṛthivyāḥ (yamo dadāty avasānam asmai* ṚV[1]).

Archaic forms and word-combinations are not seldom eliminated in the Yajurveda; thus in the following passages:

ṚV II.33.14 *pari ṇo hetī rudrasya vṛjyāḥ*. Obviously the diaskeuast found fault with the archaic third person *vṛjyāḥ*, chiefly proper to the Ṛgveda, and perhaps also with the apparently missing syllable (*rudarasya*), and hence gave, without thought for the caesura, as is often the case, the form in which it occurs not only in TM, but also in V: *pari no [ṇo* T*] rudrasya hetir vṛṇaktu*[2].

The Ṛk-tradition gives VIII.102.20 :

yad agne kāni kāni cid ā te dārūṇi dadhmasi.

The archaic and rare *kāni kani cit*—the correct āmreḍita formation of *kāni cit*[3]—was found objectionable by the Yajus-diaskeuasts : we read in T M:

yad agne yāni kāni ca etc[4].

---

1. Similarly, the Atharvaveda and among the Taittirīya texts the Āraṇyaka (I.27.5, and in the ritual of the dead to which the stanza originally belongs VI.6.1; only T. Ār. has *dadātv* for *dadāty*).
2. One may compare for the Ṛk-formulation of this pāda further VI.28.7; VIII.84.2.
3. Cf. VIII.73.5 *karhi karhi cit;* see also Benfey, Vollst. Sansk. Gramm. § 124.
4. *yad agne yāni kāni cit,* Atharvaveda.

There is nothing different when in TM *iṣkṛtiḥ* X.97.9, *jarbhurāṇaḥ* II.10.5, *abhikhyā* VIII.23.5 have been substituted by the more current expressions; in the hymn to the *oṣadhis* X.97 occurs, instead of the old **[312]** nominative *oṣadhīḥ*, repeatedly *oṣadhayaḥ* ; in stanza 3 occurs, instead of the correct fem. *pārayiṣṇvaḥ* (Lanman 415), the more common form in *-avaḥ*, and there is more of that nature.

Occasionally, considerations for the favourable portents of the words spoken may have influenced the changes—considerations of the kind that are discussed in the Śatap. Br. I.4.1.35: one did not want to say: *hotāram viśvavedasam "ned aram ity ātmānaṁ bravāṇīti"*, and hence reworded it into *hotā yo viśvavedasaḥ*. Associations of this type would, as a rule, naturally escape the notice of even the most discerning philologue; but it may be assumed that considerations of the type that have been directly attested in the above passage were decisive in such cases when one did not say, as in the ṚV X.173.1 *mā tvad rāṣṭram adhi bhraśat*, but *asmin rāṣṭram adhi śraya* (T), or *asme rāṣṭrāṇi dhāraya* (M)[1]: it seems one wanted to avoid the ominous *bhraśat.* Similarly, when in VII.8.4 not only MT but also V reads *dīdāya daivyo' atithiḥ śivo naḥ* (cf. ṚV V.1.8; VII.9.3) for *dyutāno daivyo' atithiḥ śuśoca*, this may be due to the intention to further intensify the contents of the text that are indicative of luck.

We need not bring together more materials to prove the unreliability of the TM redaction of the ṚV-stanzas. However, as we observed in the case of the Sāmaveda, we do not rule out altogether in the present instance the possibility that in a very few cases something correct was preserved in TM and that it was at a relatively later period ousted from the Ṛk-tradition by a corrupt reading. **[313]** To such cases belongs possibly *ajanayat* X.45.8 which was discussed above (p. 306).

1. Of the Taittirīya-texts, the Brāhmaṇa (II.4.2.8) has preserved the Ṛk-reading; the same occurs also in the Vāj. Saṁh. and in the Atharvaveda.

It seems to me that for X.82.4 the Yajus-readings deserve consideration. In the ṚV we read:

ta' āyajanta draviṇam sam asmā'
ṛṣayaḥ pūrve jaritāro na bhūnā I
asūrte sūrte rajasi niṣatte
ye bhūtāni samakṛṇvann imāni II

In the third pāda, which alone we discuss here, M gives: *asūrtā* (Kap. Saṁh. *asūrtāḥ) sūrte rajasi niṣattā;* T has: *asūrtā sūrtā rajaso vimāne.* It cannot be directly proved that *niṣattā(ḥ)* is the reading originating from the common source of TM, for the absolutely flat reading *vimāne,* which has been interpolated in T from ṚV X.123.1, could have driven out a *niṣattāḥ* as well as a *niṣatte.* But *niṣattāḥ* definitely gives the impression of good transmission. One may compare X.15.2: *ye pārthive rajasi ā niṣattāḥ*: clearly it is the ṛṣis who have sat down in the *rajas*; it is not the *rajas* itself that is *niṣattam.* The preceding locatives could have easily changed *niṣattāḥ* into a similar locative[1].

Also for X.97.7 the Yajus-tradition *could* be deemed to represent a more authentic state of affairs :

[314] *aśvāvatīm somavatīm,*

where R (cf. Prātiśākhya 560) reads *somāvatīm* (similarly V). The words cited form the first pāda of an Anuṣṭubh which belongs to that stage of development when the length in the sixth place is no more the rule and the first and the

---

1. One may further ask, are the locatives *asūrte sūrte* in order? Is the *rajas* supposed to be described without light and lighted at the same time? Or, are rather beings without light in the lighted *rajas* spoken of? The Yajus texts point to the fact that only *sūrte* belongs to *rajasi,* and that *asūrtā* is to be related with *bhūtāni* (or *asūrtāḥ* with *ṛṣayaḥ*?). It deserves to be noted that Yāska (Nir. VI.15; cf. also Nighaṇṭ. IV.3), according to the text that has been handed down, appears in fact to give the Ṛk-reading, but his paraphrase shows that he really read differently: *asusamīritāḥ* (sic.!) *susamīrite vātasamīritā mādhyamikā devagaṇāḥ.* That *asūrte sūrte* as it stands in the text is correct cannot accordingly be beyond every doubt.

third pādas are frequently permitted to end as — ∪ ∪ —. Hence, the *ā* in *somāvatīm* in *this sūkta* loses the justification which it would have in most of the other hymns, and it is possible that it owes its existence at this place in the Ṛk–transmission to the mechanical application of the rule of lengthening the short vowels in the sixth position in an eight-syllabled pāda, perhaps also to its closeness to *aśvāvatīm.*

Sporadic cases of this type, however, where the readings in TM, as against the Ṛk-tradition, seem, in fact, to merit recommendation, can as little change the judgement on the value of the transmission concerned as a *whole,* as the sporadic cases of correct Sāman-readings. It is incomparably inferior to the transmission of the Ṛgveda, and unless there are the most important grounds to compel us to take a different course, it is *always* the latter from where the treatment of the text has to take its start.

After these discussions on the stage of the transmission represented by the agreement between TM, we may, at the end, mention some of the characteristic changes which M alone, going far beyond the common basic text of TM, has brought about in the text of X.121. In stanza 4 *himavanto* has been substituted by the colourless *viśve girayo.* The third pāda (R: *yasyemāḥ pradiśo yasya bāhū*) runs: *diśo yasya pradiśo pañca devīḥ*—obviously the clumsy work of a compiler who found fault with **[315]** the repetition of *yasya*[1] in the original text and who betrays sufficiently his late date by *pradiśo pañca devīḥ.* In stanza 5 the attempt has been made to substitute the words *yo' antarikṣe rajaso vimānaḥ* (cf. X.95.17) by something more easily intelligible (*yo' antarikṣam vimame varīyaḥ*); II.12.2 must have offered the material required for it. In the first half of st. 6, the archaic *krandasī,* attested

1. Cf. stanza 2: *yasya viśvā' upāsate praśiṣam yasya devāḥ.*—The Atharvaveda (IV.2.5) has a number of characterstic variants, but confirms the Ṛk-reading which is here under discussion.

only in the ṚV, was found objectionable by the diaskeuast; out of

> *yaṁ krandasī avasā tastabhāne*
> *abhyaikṣetām manasā rejamāne*

he makes:

> *ya' ime dyāvā -pṛthivī tastabhāne*
> *adhārayad rodasī rejamāne* —

One sees how parts of the stanza, handed down by old tradition, have been interspersed with familiar expressions found elsewhere (*ya' ime dy.* X.110.9; *adhārayad rodasī* I.62.7; cf. VI.17.7). If confirmation for the genuineness of *krandasī* is necessary, it is offered to us by the parallel passage of *that* hymn which is imitated[1] by the poet of X.121, viz. the hymn II.12 where in stanza 8 we read: *yaṁ krandasī saṁyatī vihvayete.* In fact the relationship which exists between the hymns II.12 and X.121 is unmistakable. On the one hand, we have the glorification of the most powerful of the gods in the old Vedic belief, the poetic elevation of Indra above all gods **[316]** and all worlds in the stanzas which always repeat anew: he who has done that and has subdued that enemy—"*sa janāsa' indraḥ.*" On the other hand, there is the praise of the unnamed god, whom the poets of a later period saw enthroned above the universe as a god higher than Indra and all the other gods of their forefathers, and about whose mysterious nature each stanza of the hymn asks: the one who does this and to whom that glory belongs—"*kasmai devāya haviṣā vidhema.*" A number of expressions of the later hymn (X.121) shows how the other hymn (II.12), which stands in such a remarkable contrast to it from the point of view of the history of the religion, floated before the eyes

1. Hence, also making full use of that very hymn by the interpolator who was responsible for the M-text was natural: the difference being that the poet of X.121 had used his model in a different and freer way than the interpolator has done.

of its poet[1]: hence the old hymn may certainly be summoned by the text-critic as a witness against the interpolator who has sought to remove from the younger hymn a word which had become obsolete quite early.

We have so far discussed the relationship of the Vāj. Saṁh. with the TM-text on the one hand and the R-text on the other on the basis of only a few sūktas. It is necessary for us now to subject it to a closer examination. But we prefer to link this topic with a few remarks on the condition of the text of the *second* of those original Yajus-Saṁhitās which for short we have called above "the Saṁhitā" of the ritual. In this Saṁhitā, which stood at the head of the great Saṁhitā-corpus both for the Vājasaneyins and also the Taittirīyas and the Maitrāyaṇīyas, are to be found almost only isolated stanzas from the Ṛgveda. Such stanzas in the Taitt. Saṁh. are 64 in number but, **[317]** in order to operate on a basis as sure as possible, we wish to consider of these only those which also occur in the corresponding sections of the Maitr. Saṁhitā. Their number is 49; among them 23 in TM agree without variants[2] with the Ṛgveda. Further, in 17 stanzas, variants occur only in T, or only in M, or independently of each other in both the texts, so that they do not jointly stand against R; in almost all these cases at least M alone, or T alone, agrees with R. Against these 40 stanzas, in whose case we have no reason to assign to the original Yajus-Saṁhitā a reading different from the one occurring in the Ṛgveda, stand only 9 where TM together deviate from the Ṛgveda. We list fully the variants concerned: I.23.23 *apo.—sam asṛkṣmahi.—āgamam.*—I.139.11 (at the beginning) *devā* for

1. Besides the parallel passages having the word *krandasī,* we cite (II.12 = a; X.121 = b); a7 *yasyāśvāsaḥ pradiśi yasya gāvaḥ,* b4 *yasyemāḥ pradiśo yasya bāhu;* a14 *yasya brahma vardhanaṁ yasya somaḥ,* b2 *yasya chāyāmṛtam yasya mṛtyuḥ;* a2 *yaḥ pṛthivīṁ vyathamānām adṛṁhat,* b5 *yena . . . pṛthivī ca dṛḷhā.*

2. Here again we do not take into account the technical peculiarities of orthography in the different Vedic schools.

devāso.—I.154.6 *tā* (or *te*) *te dhāmāny.*—*gāvo yatra.*—*viṣṇoḥ* (for *vṛṣṇaḥ*).—III.29.16 *asminn agne hotāram av°.*—*ṛdhag ayāḍ ṛdhag.*—At the end, apart from the changes in which both the texts differ, *yajñam* for *somam.*—V.42.4 *svastyā.*—*devakṛtam.*—V.85.2 *payo aghnyāsu* (*aghniyāsu*).—*vikṣu* or *dikṣu* (for *apsu*).—VII.99.3 *manave yaśasye.*—*vy ask°.*—VIII.42.1 *ṛṣabho antarikṣam* (for *asuro viśv°*).—VIII.52.7 *savanaṁ* (for *havanaṁ*).

Of the 49 stanzas in question, the Vāj. Saṁhitā has, in its corresponding part[1], 42; among these, 32 agree without variants with the Ṛk-text, while **[318]** in 10 stanzas there occur deviations which, in their number and extent, on the whole are much less than the deviations from the Ṛk-text in the T and M recensions. So here also it turns out that of all the Yajus-texts V shows the greatest agreement with R, but this agreement is notably less thorough than in the individual sūktas from the ritual of the Agnicayana discussed above. One will find it understandable that in the correction of the Yajus-texts on the basis of the ṚV, discussed above [p.304], the coherent sūktas were treated more exactly than the single, isolated stanzas in the ritual-Saṁhitā which are scattered in the Yajus-prose and therefore easily escaping the attention of the comparative text-improver. The variants of V in those 10 stanzas are the following:

I.154.6 *yā te dhāmāny.*—*uśmási* (thus accented).—*viṣṇoḥ.*—*avabhāri.*—III.29.16 *vayaṁ hi tvā.*—*asminn agne hotāram av°.*—twice *ṛdhag.*—*praj° yajñam upa y° vidvān.*—III.47.1 *pratipat* (for *pradivaḥ*).—V.42.4 *maghavant saṁ svastyā.*—*devakṛtam.*—*sumatau.*—V.44.1 *dhuniṁ* for *girā.*—V.85.2 *vikṣu.*—VI.51.16 *prati panthām apadmahi.*—VII.99.3 *manave.*—*vy ask°.*—VIII.42.1 *vṛṣabho antarikṣam.*—VIII.52.7 *savanam.*

If one compares the above list of variants with the

1. It seemed appropriate to consider only these here; stanzas in other parts of the Vāj. Saṁh. occur, as we shall show later, partly in conditions which are different from the text-critical point of view.

preceding one then even at first glance one notices that the most important source of variants, where V deviates from R, turns out to be just that what one, *a priori*, is justified to assume: the old Yajus-form of the Ṛk-stanzas for which we may consider the agreement between T and M in all probability as sufficient evidence. Only a few of the readings of TM **[319]** have been removed in V again on the basis of the R-text[1]; on the other hand, there are only a few passages in which V goes its own way or agrees with only one of the Black Yajus-texts; mostly its deviations from R are just those in which T agrees with M. If then, on account of this generally great agreement of V with R, one could be tempted to concede a special value to the deviations of V and try to see in it the traces of an old Ṛk-recension, differing from our R, which could have served as the model while reducing the white YV to the Ṛk-text form, the remarks made here should serve as a warning: it is not another Ṛk-recension, but in a majority of cases at least, it is the relics of the old Yajus-Saṁhitā which we assume to have existed in those cases where V differs from R.–

It is unnecessary to examine all the remaining sections of the Taittirīya- and the Maitrāyaṇīya-texts as it has been done for the two most important collections of the sacrificial formulae; the solution of the problems which arise and which, in their nature, are essentially the same, may be reserved for the detailed treatment of the text. It is necessary only to stress here that certain later parts of those Saṁhitās reveal an appreciably closer conformity to the Ṛk-form of the stanzas contained in them. The discussion of the text-

---

1. In some cases not by the reading of the directly parallel passages in the Ṛgveda but, as it appears, by the influence of Ṛgveda passages other than the ones directly in question. That in ṚV I.154.6, V does not read *tā te dhāmāni* but *yā te dhāmāni* seems to have been occasioned by ṚV I.91.4 *yā te dhāmāni*. In VIII.42.1 for *ṛṣabho antarikṣam* of TM, in V the exact reading of the passage III.30.9 *vṛṣabho antarikṣam* has been restored, which apparently has produced the TM variant.

form which appears here leads us to a second **[320]** period in the handling of the Ṛk-text, which is clearly distinguished from the one of the Sāmaveda and the older Yajus-texts discussed so far, and in which the arbitrariness and the desire to change the text of the earlier period begins to give way to greater respect for the text handed down by tradition. However, before we undertake a description of this change of direction in the history of the Vedic texts it is necessary for us to examine yet another document of the *older* stage of the text-treatment, which has not been considered so far, viz. the Saṁhitā of the *Atharvaveda.*

The observations made by us with reference to the Sāmaveda and the Black Yajurveda perhaps find a still stronger application for the text-form of the Ṛk-stanzas which are to be found in the Atharvaveda (with the exception of book XX). The loose connection, the much less fixed canonical character of the Atharvaveda, as compared to the other Vedas, gave occasion obviously to a more extensive effect of acts of negligence on the one hand, of the modernizing tendencies on the other, which we have established in the handling of the text by the redactors of the other Vedas. It may be sufficient for us to cite a few examples of these clearly obvious tendencies. Just as we find in the Atharvaveda a percentage higher than in the Ṛgveda[1] of certain forms, declensional endings etc. which alone prevailed in the later period as against the old forms, later suppressed, so also we notice in it a tendency to remove from the stanzas originating from the ṚV the forms current in the older period. Thus, for example, one observes in the Atharvaveda very frequently the use of the absolutive in *-tvā* **[321]** where in the Ṛgveda other forms have been transmitted which became obsolete later: thus, *hitvā* (with hiatus) for *hitvāya* of ṚV X.14.8, *kṛtvā* for *kṛtvī* X.15.12, *bhūtvā* for *bhūtvī* X.85.29, *dattvā* for *dattvāya*

1. Cf. the interesting statements of Lanman pp. 576 f.

X.85.33. Instr. pl. forms in *-ebhis* have in may cases been removed in the AV: thus *yajñiyebhis* of X.14.5, *pūrvyebhis* X.14.7; *sugebhis* X.85.32. Of the root *grabh* (*grah*) before the following *ṇ*, the AV knows almost without exception only the forms with *h*; hence, even in the Ṛk-stanzas which contain the forms with *bhṇ*, they have been substituted by the later ones: thus *gṛbhṇate* of IX.86.43; *gṛbhṇāmi* of X.85.36.—In X.85.20 the ṚV text reads: *syonaṁ patye vahatuṁ kṛṇuṣva;* the AV reads *patibhyo* and *kṛṇu tvam.* It is clear that the change of *patye* to *patibhyas* (cf. stanza 38) is due to the by far more frequent disyllabic value of *syona* in the Atharvaveda, while in the Ṛgveda it is without exception trisyllabic (*siona*)[1].—For the old nom. pl. *panthās* in X.85.23 the AV gives the modern form *panthānas,* although it then produces metrical unevenness. The old dative *yudhaye* X.84.4 has to give way to the modern *yuddhāya,* the nominative *adurmaṅgalīs* X.85.43 to the form *adurmaṅgalī*[2].—Just as we have noted even for the Sāmaveda the spread of the noun *diś* which is so prominent in the later Vedic thought and speech, the AV similarly replaces *vikṣu*[3] by *dikṣu* in X.15.2. This is similar to the case of X.85.43 where the compound *ahorātra,* which is so frequent in the later Veda [322] but which appears in the ṚV only once in the last but one sūkta of the whole collection, has ousted *ājarasāya*[4] which is definitely the correct reading. It goes without saying that in X.85.13 the old nakṣatra-names *aghāsu arjunyoḥ* of which the former had

1. Similarly also in ṚV I.22.15 *syonā pṛthivi bhava* is changed in the AV in such a way that *y* is treated as a consonant: *syonāsmai bhava pṛthivi.*
2. For the later treatment of the nom. of ī-stems, which has gained ground in the AV, cf. Lanman 376. If in X.85.33 (Lanman 377) *sumaṅgalīs* has been retained also in the AV, this is probably due to the consideration of hiatus.
3. But the Taitt. Saṁh. and the Vāj. Saṁh. read *vikṣu.*
4. The same appears also in the passage concerned in the Mantrabrāhmaṇa (I.2.12) of the collection of the Gṛhya-formulae of the Sāmaveda.

become completely and the latter almost[1] obsolete are eliminated and replaced by the later *maghāsu, phalgunīṣu* in the text.

But we cease now to list further examples and only call attention to the fact that in the Atharvaveda also, as in the case of the Sāmaveda and the Yajurvedas, we cannot deny that there are *exceptions* to the regular value of its readings in relation to the ṚV. The existence of these exceptions makes it impossible for the critic to ignore the Atharvan-readings, but the cases concerned are, notwithstanding the differences in judging doubtful cases, so few that the rule of text-criticism as such is not affected by them. Among such exceptions I would like to reckon X.85.6 where, while enumerating the objects and the persons who figure in the marriage procession of Sūryā, it is said:

sūryāyā bhadram id vāso
gāthayaiti pariṣkṛtam.

The AV reads *pariṣkṛtā*. Obviously correct: neither does the garment of Sūryā go, nor is it clothed in something, but, of course, "*she* goes[2] clothed in the gāthā". But **[323]** one should not assume with complete confidence the reading of the AV to be due to good tradition; the change is so obvious that it could have as well arisen due to the conjecture of a text-arranger. The same hesitation one feels regarding the following passage (ṚV X.85.31) where likewise the AV decisively offers the correct reading :

ye vadhvaś candraṁ vahatuṁ
yakṣmā yanti janād anu.

1. Cf. Śatap. Br. II.1.2.11; Weber, die ved. Nachrichten von den Naxatra, II.364, 365.
2. That in this context only Sūryā can be expected as 'one who goes' is shown by st. 7 *yad ayāt sūryā patim,* 10 *yad ayāt sūryā gṛham,* 12 *śucī te cakre yātyāḥ; prayatī patim.* Also Ludwig recognizes *pariṣkṛtā* as correct.

Clearly one must read, as the AV does, *janā̃ anu* (thus also Ludwig); cf. ṚV I.50.3,6; 120,11; X.14.12 (see also IX.92.3).

In the above case what occurs in the AV can as well be due to a happy conjecture as due to tradition, but it seems to me that the Atharvan-reading of ṚV I.164.10 definitely goes beyond what we may attribute to the skill in emendation of the Atharvan-diaskeuasts. In the ṚV the transmitted text runs as:

tisro mātṝs trīn pitṝn bibhrad eka'
ūrdhvas tasthau nem ava glāpayanti I
mantrayante divo' amuṣya pṛṣṭhe
viśvavidaṁ vācam aviśvaminvām II

The AV has at the end of the stanza *aviśvavinnām*[1]. In order to evaluate the high probability of the AV-reading, it is not necessary to pretend that one has understood the wisdom which has been mystifyingly introduced into the riddle-hymn I. 164. No one can miss how that sūkta loves to play with oppositions: one may call to mind stanza 4 *asthanvantam yad anasthā bibharti*; 16 *striyaḥ satīs tā̃ u me puṁsa' āhuḥ;* 19 *ye' arvāñcas tā̃ u parāca' āhuḥ* etc. So one can suppose that it is likewise necessary to recognize an antithesis in *viśvavidam* and *aviśvaminvām* **[324]** and if it were a coincidence, it will have to be considered surely an exceptionally rare coincidence that we have in *aviśvaminvām*, almost letter for letter, just the materials out of which with slight transposition it was possible to get the word *aviśvavinnām*, which was most suited to obtain such an antithesis[2]. And when we find just this word in the AV, then one who has not decided to be basically sceptical will feel

1. Besides, *ava glāpayanta, viśvavido,* the variants which we do not discuss here.
2. Ludwig also had correctly understood this situation.

himself justified to conclude that there is a good deal of probability of the old tradition being continued in that text[1].

Of course, if one keeps in view the content of the hymns on the whole—the number of stanzas in them etc.—then the conclusion regarding the value of the Atharvan-tradition turns out to be the same as in the examination of the different readings. Also here, on the one hand, the authority of this Veda proves to be by far inferior to that of the Ṛk-tradition. It is unnecessary to cite here the proofs for this, for a reader of the Atharvaveda comes across them in abundance at every step. However, our discussions above [p.242 f.] on the arrangement of the tenth Maṇḍala, following those of Bergaigne, will have sufficiently shown that we do come across cases in which the AV, as against the ṚV, has preserved, with regard to the number of stanzas in a hymn what is correct, or, at least has a trace of what is correct.

---

[325] Except for the cases where the same Ṛk-stanza appears in the different Yajus-recensions, we had till now occasion only in a few cases to examine *side by side* the text of a Ṛk-stanza as it appears in *more than one Veda.* It is not very frequent that a stanza from the ṚV has found a place *simultaneously* in the Yajurveda and the Sāmaveda, or in the Yajurveda and the Atharvaveda; the nature of those Vedas gave, on the whole, a different direction to the choice of

1. Another very striking AV-reading, the genuineness of which is advocated by Ludwig but which I cannot accept without hesitation, occurs in the marriage-formula ṚV X.85.44: *vīrasūr devakāmā syonā.* The Atharvaveda XIV.2.17-18 first gives the Ṛk-stanza concerned itself and then another one, partly in imitation of it, and has in both of them the reading *devṛkāmā.* Between the two, however, stands the prayer that the wife may be *"adevṛghny apatighnī"* and from that the reading *devṛkāmā* could easily get into the adjacent place. I, therefore, do not venture to consider the reading *devakāmā,* which in itself is thoroughly unobjectionable and which, moreover, appears in the stanza as it occurs in the Sāmaveda recension (Mantra Br. I.2.11), as a corruption.

the Ṛk-stanzas to be used by them. If the same Ṛgvedic stanza did, however, find a place in the younger Vedas, then it is understandable that in the intercourse between the Brahmanical circles which studied these different Vedas and with them officiated together at the sacrifices, the different forms of the Ṛk-text in their own individual traditions have influenced each other variously in alternating directions and this we cannot delineate in a generally valid form. For example, the Atharvaveda gives Ṛk-stanzas, which are also found in the Black YV, in the Yajus-form, while it also has such stanzas in the Ṛk-form untouched by the Yajus-redactions. However, in an overwhelming majority of cases the different Vedas go their own way in the treatment of the Ṛk-text, so that, as a rule, for every single word of the Ṛk-text, if among the Vedas in which the Ṛk-stanza secondarily appears someone shows a deviation, there is another available to give confirmation to the Ṛk-form. Thus, for example, we have already pointed out above (p.307) that in the hymn ṚV X.140 the Sāmaveda agrees with the ṚV in all cases where the Black Yajus-texts show variants, while on the other hand, **[326]** in the only case where the SV deviates from the ṚV, the Yajurveda-texts agree with the latter. As a further example of the existence side by side of several recensions may be mentioned ṚV X.128 which occurs in the Agni-section of the Taittirīya Saṁhitā (IV.7.14) as also in the Atharvaveda (V.3). The differences of the Taittirīya-readings (T) from those of the Atharvan (A) far exceed their agreement. One may just look at stanza 6 which reads in the Ṛgveda:

ange manyuṁ pratinudan pareṣām
adabdho gopāḥ pari pāhi nas tvam |
pratyañco yantu nigutaḥ punas te
'maiṣāṁ cittam prabudhāṁ vi neśat ||

The Taittirīya Saṁhitā has:

agnir manyum pratinudan purastāt
adabdho gopāḥ pari pāhi nas tvam |
pratyañco yantu nigutaḥ punas te
'maiṣāṁ cittam prabudhā vi neśat ||

The Atharvaveda reads:

agne manyum pratinudan paresāṁ
tvaṁ no gopāḥ pari pāhi viśvataḥ |
apāñco yantu nivatā durasyavo
'maiṣām cittam prabudhāṁ vi neśat ||

One easily perceives how the relationship between the three recensions becomes quite intelligible when one looks upon the text transmitted in the Ṛgveda as the common basis of the other two versions: of T, which follows more closely the original and of A, which is much freer but which, just in those points where T reproduces inaccurately the common source, has preserved accurately the text form of the latter. Similarly, in the whole sūkta, the readings of the A-text stand opposed to the deviations in T, and those of the T-text to the deviations in A; **[327]** the sequence of the stanzas in A, which is quite different from the ṚV, is opposed to the agreement of the sequence in T and R. Only in relatively few points the text of A agrees with that of T in its deviations from R: thus in the mention of god Savitar in place of Trātar in stanza 7, in the form *purukṣu* in place of *purukṣuḥ* in st. 8, above all in the addition at the end of a stanza *arvāñcam indram* etc. not found in the RV[1]: of a stanza which betrays its purpose due to the word *vihave* viz. that the point of contact of this hymn with the ritual of the *vihavyākhyā' iṣṭakāḥ,* certainly unknown at the time of the Ṛgveda, which is already to be seen at the beginning of the sūkta is marked once again by this word at the end of the sūkta[2]. As has been already noted, in such cases of

1. However, see the related Khila.
2. We may also refer to *kurmas* (*kulmas* ṚV Khila) which, however, is to be found only in the T-version of the stanza.

agreement among the different texts *against* the Ṛgveda, which are relatively less numerous,—especially when among them we come across readings of such kind as I.89.8 *vyaśemahi* SV, VS (against *vyaśema* ṚV and Taitt. Ār.), or I.127.1 *vasoḥ* TS, SV (against *vasum* ṚV and Maitṛ Saṁh.), or the distortion of VII.66.16 discussed above on pp. 105 f., to be found in *all* the texts except the ṚV—we can hardly think of recognizing in them numerous traces of a tradition having the same value as that of the ṚV. These agreements are obviously to be considered as results of the unavoidable equalizations and transfers which must necessarily have come about in the texts of different schools which were in constant touch with one another[1].

[328] Let us look back at the course which our examination has taken so far and formulate the result which the same examination leads to for the question of the age of the Ṛgveda text-tradition. *This tradition was already fixed in the form available to us today*[2] *at a time when the Sāman-, the older Yajus- and the Atharvan-texts were being fixed except for relatively*

---

1. One such transfer seems to be quite clear in the Taittirīya version of the text of the *chando'bhidhā' iṣṭakāḥ* (TS IV.4.4, cf. Maitr. S. II.13.7 f.). Since here we have groups of three stanzas each in the same metre, it was easy to look for an association with the tṛcas of the Sāmaveda, and the Taitt. Saṁh. shows such an association not only in a number of readings, which are not to be found in the Maitr. Saṁh., but also in the choice of the stanzas which in many ways are different from those in the Maitr. Saṁh.: while the latter gives ṚV V.6.4,1-2, the Taitt. Saṁh. has the stanzas V.6.4, 5, 9, which exactly in this order of combination form a sūkta in the Sāmaveda (II.372-374). Also the combination V.24.1, 2, 4 (so also in the Vāj. Saṁh., hence originating from the basic-Yajurveda ?) is to be traced back to the Sāmaveda (II.457-459). This shows that the arrangers of the Yajus-texts found and used the peculiarities of the Sāman text revision, still available today, that shows deviations from the Ṛk-tradition.
2. Hence, also in cases where the Ṛk-text is corrupt and where the parallel text in the other Vedas is available, these, in a large majority of cases (of the rare opposite cases, some have been discussed above)

(Continued on next page)

few exceptions[1], : this may be viewed in a nutshell as a result to which our investigation of the variant readings preserved in those Saṁhitās [329] has led us. Only at first glance would the state of the text of the ṛcas give the impression that it was quite unstable at the time of the formation of those Saṁhitās, and it may appear as if the arrangers of the different Vedas, and among them those of the Ṛgveda, had drawn their text-forms from a number of equally well or equally badly attested possibilities which were not definite and which were passing from mouth to mouth. A closer examination completely removes this impression. In numerous cases, found again and again, it reveals the symptoms of negligence, of arbitrariness, of modernizing tendencies which can be recognized always in the *other* Vedas as opposed to the Ṛgveda. Thereby it also establishes the presumption that in the matter of textual deviations, which by themselves would have no advantage or disadvantage over each other, we have to believe the Ṛk-tradition. There remains only a negligibly small number of passages[2] in which

---

(Continued from previous page)

share the corruption. Some such cases pertaining to the Sāmaveda have been mentioned on p. 283; the following passages may further be pointed out here. I.165.7 *marutaḥ* wrongly without the accent; similarly the parallel passage in the Maitr. Saṁhitā.—Same hymn, 9: *kariṣyā* instead of *kariṣyāḥ;* same in the Maitr. S., Vāj. S.—V.87.1 what is handed down is *girijā* [= *girijāḥ*] instead of *girija* [= *girije*]; likewise Sāma V.—VI.71.6 *kṣayasya* in place of *kṣayasi;* same in the Maitr. S., Taitt. S., Vāj. S.—VII.56.13 *vṛṣṭibhiḥ* in place of *ṛṣṭibhiḥ;* same in the Maitr. S., Taitt. S., Taitt. Br.—VIII.99.6 *śnathayanta* in place of *śrathayanta;* same in the Sāma V., Vāj. S., AV XX.—X.129.7 [above p. 85]: the text is mutilated; similarly, in the Maitr. S., Taitt. Brāhmaṇa.

1. While saying this we naturally do not take into account the details of the sandhi-treatment, orthographic trifles and similar matters; these things which, in all probability, were not finalized before the end of the Brāhmaṇa-period will be discussed below.
2. A much smaller number than would correspond to the numerical proportion of passages discussed in our investigation: it was, of course, necessary to find much more plentiful attestation for the rarer cases than would have corresponded to the numerical proportion.

a corruption has crept into our Ṛk-text while the remaining sources of these passages have remained free from corruption. Hence there is no question that except for those few cases there remain as a basis for the Ṛk-stanzas quoted in the other Vedas with all their differences in text-form no other equally or more authoritative Ṛk-texts apart from the very one that has been transmitted to us. And those deviations in the text-form betray themselves as the product of corrupting tendencies which have affected not the Ṛk-tradition but only that of the other Saṁhitās. **[330]** Thus, in this context we find that there is a contrast between the Ṛk-text and the other Vedas which is similar to the contrast that exists between the historical arrangement of the Ṛk-hymns (based on the history of their origins) and the preservation of the sūktas in their integrity as a well-preserved legacy from the distant past in the Ṛgveda and the liturgical arrangement of the sūktas and their dissection into often arbitrarily formed groups of stanzas and single stanzas in the other Vedas. And should all this surprise us ? The Saṁhitā which the Ṛgveda-schools possessed was available to them as a finished collection even before the principal parts of the other Vedas were composed at all and before the details of the later liturgical practices were fixed[1]; in that collection there existed a corpus on which the liturgical technique certainly drew, but one did not attempt, nor had one an occasion to attempt to change its form to suit the later tendencies of this technique. For, the instruction in the liturgical technique produced for its own purposes its own texts[2] as a vehicle; but the old corpus of the hymns was transmitted from generation to generation as something fixed, notwithstanding the way in which the liturgy chose to

1. See my essay on the authors of the hymns, ZDMG. 1888.
2. The relationship of the text as it appears in the Brāhmaṇas and the Sūtras to the one in the Saṁhitā will be discussed below.

develop. It is quite understandable that the Ṛk-texts have suffered less in the course of this transmission which was carefully guarded, than in the side-lines, which went on simultaneously with that principal one, when the texts were transferred to the other branches of the school which were newly springing up. Those who established this tradition had to, in the absence of such a comprehensive and traditionally handed down formation as the Ṛgveda, produce at every step something new. **[331]** They appropriated the old text, took it out of its context, and mixed it up with what had newly arisen. Obviously, quite differently than those who were responsible only for the further transmission of the old tradition, they felt justified to give to a Ṛk-stanza, which they set down as a Sāman-text or a Yajus-formula, the form which seemed appropriate to them. The controlling authority for the knower which existed within the school among those from whom he obtained his knowledge and among the throng of his colleagues who surrounded him and who were equally knowers was lost when new schools arose—schools which did not feel the necessity to have the knowledge of the Ṛk-texts in its full context and whose founders enjoyed an authority which was not limited by others who were equally authoritative. Thus, factors are not wanting which make the difference in value between the Ṛk-tradition and the text of the other Vedas quite understandable.

Before we leave this period of Vedic textual history, which we have discussed so far, in order to turn to its younger phases, it would not be superfluous to make a reference to the fact that the period of older Sāman-, of older Yajus-texts etc. forms, so-to-say, only a *second* stage in the fortunes of the Ṛgvedic hymns. Going back over it, we reach the *first* one: the period of the rise, the formation into collections of the Ṛk-literature which lived its own existence before the formation of the other Saṁhitās. Our investigations have made us familiar with the real stability attained by the text in this period which in the second period apparently seemed to have scarcely any limits as to its variability: they have shown us that where we meet with corruptions, they reach back *as a rule* **[332]** beyond this period and have been taken over in the second period from the past. There lies the scene of events in the textual history, to determine which will be the principal task of our detailed critical examination of the hymns—or we might perhaps say, *one* of its two tasks. For the other one must be seen in exposing those kinds of modifications which the phonetic revision of a later period had forced upon the text directed by grammatical considerations.

It goes without saying that when the Ṛk-text was received in the second period from the first, the text at a hundred places was not, and could not be, the same as that of the authors themselves. Today it is not necessary to fight against the belief in the infallibility of our tradition. But it ought to be expressly stated that, even though we admit certain undeniable corruptions in individual cases, *on the whole* the text, at the time when it was taken over by the second period, had reached a remarkably high level of authenticity. It is not difficult to collect quite a number of different phenomena regarding the details of the text form of which it can be said that they *had to have* become confused and effaced at a very early period, long before the conclusion of that first period, if extreme care had not been successfully devoted to the text already at that time to protect even its *letter*. On the basis of such phenomena it is easy to decide the degree of carefulness devoted in the old and the oldest times. Let us consider, e.g., the nom. acc. voc. dual in *-ā* and in *-au*. Lanman's investigations (340 f., 574 f.) have made clear the demarcation of both forms of this case on the one hand, **[333]** and the onset and increase of effacing the norm on the other. They also bring quite clearly to light what did not escape the notice of that excellent researcher, that the advance of the *-au* forms beyond their proper sphere is a characteristically predominant peculiarity of the younger parts of the Saṁhitā, of the tenth book and of the supplementary hymns of the remaining books[1]. Certainly I do not mean that in each individual case the *-ā* or the *-au* occurs exactly as the poet himself had used it. But so much definitely emerges from those facts that the theologists, among whom the tenth book arose, have devoted so much care to the transmission of the older Maṇḍalas that those two forms, which have absolutely the same meaning, which are metrically essentially equivalent, which are distinguished from each other only by a single letter, and which had begun to be mixed up in the linguistic consciousness of the singers of the tenth Maṇḍala, have been kept apart correctly, *at least on the whole,* in the text of the older hymns. One finds occasions leading to similar considerations at every step. One may recall, for example, the occurrence side by side of *gṛbhṇāti* and *gṛhṇātu,* of *jagrabha jagṛbhma* etc. and *jagrāha jagṛhe,* or the preservation of the old accentuation *pratīcī́ pratīcás* by the side of *pratī́cīm* of the late stanza X.18.14 and the frequent paroxytone forms of the Atharvaveda (Lanman 455), or the non-occurrence of forms like *karoti akarot kurute,* except the imperative *kuru* in two passages of the *tenth* book, etc. Future investigations e.g. those about the **[334]** occurrence side by side of pairs like *yatra* and *yatrā* etc., or about the sandhi *-āñ c-* and *-āṁś c-* will again and again show us the excellent preservation of all sorts of insignificant minute details, most exposed to corruption: however, in our present context we attach no importance to the kind of occurrences mentioned last

1. According to the statements of Lanman (341, 576), of the 76 places where *-au* appears before a consonant, 33 belong to the tenth book alone. In the ninth book we have only two occurrences of that type: both belong to the later supplementary hymn IX.112; and so forth.

because it is not provable, and partly even improbable, that the living consciousness of their nature had already disappeared, or also started to disappear in the old period of transmission with which we are concerned here, so that their preservation could be credited as a special merit to the care taken by this period. This much is nevertheless certain: none of the links required in the chain of proof is missing to show that the text-transmitters continuously directed their attention to the smallest detail (of the text) in the later period as well as in the older one—we will not and we cannot say right up to the old authors of the hymns themselves, but clearly recognizable up and into the period of the Ṛk-Saṁhitā itself, back up to the last, most distant *of those* guarantors whom we can recognize as using a mode of expression which is in some way *distinguishable* from the speech of the older ṛṣis. Naturally in our research we first notice here the preservation of the old transmitted text as such in a form which they as transmitters were conscious of as something *given* to them. Undoubtedly the faithfulness of the transmitters, about whom we are speaking, did not remain equally alive at every point in the transmission of the text. In the older period, predominantly single cases of inattentiveness, in the later periods mainly abandoning of some transmitted features in favour of artificial **[335]** ones based on grammatical theories which arose mostly due to the conditions prevailing in the later speech: these are the two factors which have impaired the success of that carefulness. What, however, we intend to stress here is that the text we arrive at lying behind the mistakes of one type or the other as the ultimate reachable basis, has preserved with admirable faithfulness the peculiarities of the oldest period up to the smallest detail.

In the above investigations we have on several occasions already alluded to indications that the freedom and the negligence with which the Ṛk-stanzas have been treated in the other Vedas have a tendency to diminish in the later strata of those Saṁhitās. To these belongs the conscious return to the text form as found in the Ṛgveda which is the characteristic of the Saṁhitā of the white Yajurveda as opposed to the texts which form the basis of the Yajus literature. To these belongs further the fact that the deviations from the Ṛgveda become rare in the second Ārcika of the Sāmaveda as against the first. This was first brought to notice by Whitney and was alluded to by us above on p. 273, fn. 1. It was a welcome confirmation of the result arrived at by me from considerations of a different nature, viz. that the two Ārcikas "represent two revisions of two sides of the Udgātar-science which were undertaken with different viewpoints and, without doubt, at different times and which do not merge in each other" (ZDMG XXXVIII.467). The closer agreement of the second Ārcika with the Ṛk-text combines with some other factors to reveal this Ārcika to be a secondary production by the side of the first one. And when, as Whitney has concluded, those stanzas of the first Ārcika, which recur in the second, stand out **[336]** among the neighbouring stanzas by closer agreement with the Ṛgveda, which is a characteristic of the second Ārcika, then this permits us to conclude with complete certainty that originally these stanzas occurred in the first Ārcika in a different form, deviating much more from the Ṛgveda, but then there occurred an equalization by which the later method of treating the text in which the Ṛgveda-text was more closely followed was carried over from the second Ārcika to these stanzas also in the first.

We have now to deal with some other strata within the Vedic Saṁhitās in which the same tendency to follow more closely the basic codex of the Vedic literature becomes apparent, in parts even more markedly than in the passages just alluded to. While, as I believe, we have to seek the explanation of this phenomenon in its being related to the later age, there clearly appears another additional factor, at least for part of the texts concerned, whose influence must have contributed towards the same result. It concerns the texts which, although appearing in the Yajurvedas, did not form part of the possessions of the Yajus-theologians in the same sense as, let us say, a stanza to be recited by the Adhvaryu at the Soma sacrifice. Occasionally, just the Ṛk-stanzas, whose recitation was the business of the Hotar priest, found a place in the Yajurveda due to some reason or by coincidence: i.e. where this Veda acting out of its proper character as it were refers to things which, considering their nature, belong to another Veda. Thus, the collection of the Hotar Mantras in the section of *iṣṭihautra,* Taitt. Brāhm. III.5 (cf. Taitt. Saṁh. II.5.7 ff.): in the quite considerable number of Ṛk-stanzas which are cited here occurs—apart **[337]** of course, from the deviations, more or less only orthographic, such as are unavoidable in the Saṁhitās that are fixed on the basis of diverging phonetic theories—only *one* real variant: *agniḥ pratnena janmanā* TB. III.5.6.1 for *agniḥ pratnena manmanā* ṚV VIII.44.12[1]. Much more important, however, than the section of the Taitt. Br. just referred to are the large Yājyānuvākyā-sections occurring in several Yajurvedas: the collections of the *ṛcas* which are employed as yājyā- respectively anuvākyā-Mantras in certain offerings. Here we find ourselves, in fact, on the ground of the Ṛk—rather than that of the Yajus-tradition although the texts which contain these sections are the Yajus-texts. According to their ritual character yājyās and anuvākyās are, as is known, *ṛcas,* not *yajūṁṣi,* and hence the sections in question comprise almost throughout stanzas from the Ṛgveda. It is understandable that if such compact collections of stanzas which, although they are cited in the Yajurveda, are employed in the ritual concerned in accordance with their character as stanzas of the Ṛgveda, they remain faithful to the Ṛk-form in quite a different way from the single *ṛcas*

1. The Sāmāv. has *janmanā,* the Maitr. Saṁh. *manmanā.*

in the Yajus-collections proper which are scattered among the Yajus formulae and which are employed along with them by the Adhvaryu priest. Simultaneously, of course, comes into play here the tendency of the new period, alluded to above, viz. to respect the Ṛk-form to a greater extent than had been done before: for, that the yājyānuvākyā sections form the later elements of the Yajurvedas is shown sufficiently by their placement in the Taittirīya Saṁitā[1] and in the Maitrāyaṇī Saṁhitā[2].

[338] If one examines the text of those yājyās and anuvākyās, one finds, in fact, in the Taittirīya- and in the Maitrāyaṇīya-collections an extraordinarily closer agreement with the Ṛk-text than in the case of the Ṛk-stanzas of the ritual-Saṁhitā or the fire-Saṁhitā. Only a small number of stanzas shows any variants at all. And again relatively speaking not a few of these are of such type that there does not even arise the question whether they preserve a useful tradition, rather that, for some reason, they must be rejected right from the beginning. This is chiefly the case with such stanzas which, besides being in the yājyānuvākyā-sections, appear also at another, more original place in the Saṁhitā concerned. It is understandable that Taittirīya-Brahmins when once they possessed a stanza in a form deviating from that of the Ṛgveda employed it in just that form also when it had to function as a yājyā or an anuvākyā[3].

A second chief source of variants in the yājyā- and anuvākyā-stanzas is to be found in the ritual sphere. Among the deities of the sacrifice, to whom such stanzas were to be

1. See Weber's remarks to the Taitt. Saṁh. I.1.14; 5.5; 5.11 etc.
2. At the end of the Khilakāṇḍa.
3. Examples: ṚV VII.8.4 = TS II.5.12.4; cf. TS IV.2.3.2.—ṚV IX.66.21 =TS I.3.14.8; cf. TS I.5.5.2.—Presently to be brought to notice and explained is a development of the text form apparently running in the opposite direction, i.e. the preservation of the Ṛk-reading in an old section of the TS and its change in the yājyānuvākyā-section—so that the same stanza appears in the TS twice in two different versions; see p. 339, fn. 2.

assigned, there were many rare or later deities which did not yet appear in the Ṛgveda. Since in such cases it was difficult[1] to find Ṛk-stanzas which could be used as yājyās and anuvākyās, [**339**] partly one helped oneself with the newly composed stanzas[2], partly one made changes in the stanzas of the Ṛgveda and thus adapted them to the intended liturgical use. Thus, one finds the words *sadmeva prāco vi mimāya mānaiḥ* of ṚV II.15.3 as *budhnād agreṇa vi mimāya mānaiḥ* in Taitt. Saṁḥ II.3.14.5; quite similarly for *bhinad valam aṅgirobhir gṛṇānaḥ* of the eighth stanza of the same Ṛk-hymn, the Taitt. Saṁh. (loc. cit.) has *budhnād agram aṅgirobhir gṛṇānaḥ.* This identical way of equipping both the stanzas with the words *budhna* and *agra* reveals the interpolation clearly enough, and in order to understand the intention of the interpolation we need only to look at the explanations in the related Brāhmaṇa-passage (Taitt. Saṁh. II.3.4.2 f.) of the offering for which the two stanzas were prescribed: it is a puroḍāśa: *aindra ānuṣūka* to be offered by a rājanya ānujāvara: *budhnavatī agravatī yājyānuvākye bhavato, budhnād evainam agram pari ṇayati.*—The stanzas 1 and 6 of the Mitra-hymn ṚV III.59 have been similarly treated in the Taitt. Saṁh. III.4.11.5: in stanza 1 *mitrāya havyaṁ ghṛtavaj juhota* is substituted by *satyāya havyaṁ ghṛtavad vidhema,* in stanza 6 for *dyumnaṁ citraśravastamam* appears *satyaṁ citraśravastamam.* One easily recognizes what is also confirmed by the related Brāhmaṇa-passage (TS I.8.10.1), that here it is a matter of an offering to Mitra *satya*: just this fact would be enough to show that the readings concerned are of no consequence for the critique of the Ṛk-text, even if the Taittirīyas themselves had not preserved in their

1. One may compare Śatap. Brāhmaṇa II.5.1.14 where a difficulty of this kind with regard to the Marutas svatavasas is expressly stated. Somewhat similar is to be found in Ait. Br. I.17.
2. We shall deal with them later in detail while discussing the stanzas cited in the Brāhmaṇas of the ṚV which do not occur in the ṚV.

Agnicayana-ritual stanza 6 with the correct reading *dyumnaṁ citraśravastamam*[1].

[340] If one excludes all variants of this category, then there remains a text of the yājyā- and the anuvākyā-stanzas which, even if one wanted to look upon their deviations from the Ṛk-text as equally authoritative rival forms, would still prove that there is not a small constancy of the wording of the text; so high is the preponderance of the stanzas which occur unchanged in the Yajurvedas. And further detailed investigation of the variants does not allow any doubt that the authority of the Ṛk-tradition predominates also here in the most decisive measure, so that the circumstantial evidence which might be obtained from the deviations in the Yajus-sections concerned, pointing to the former side-by-side existence of several equal possibilities within the Ṛk-tradition, is reduced to the utmost minimum. In order to illustrate the nature of those types of variants I choose as examples a few readings from the Taitt. Saṁhitā. Among the far-reaching transformations which ṚV I.164.47 has suffered there (III.1.11.4) I stress *sadanāni kṛtvā* for *sadanād ṛtasya;* while the context corresponds very well to the frequent expression *ṛtasya sadana,* the Taittirīya-reading is opposed by the fact that *kṛtvā,* which is so frequent later, does not occur even once in the Ṛgveda, but was, just like the other absolutives in *tvā,* much more favoured by the younger interpolators of the Ṛgveda. So also a Yājyānuvākyā section of the Taitt. Saṁhitā (likewise the Atharvaveda) while citing ṚV X.15.12 gives *kṛtvā* for the more archaic *kṛtvī.* If it were necessary to give further arguments against the Taittirīya-variant, one could refer to the fact that the Maitrāyaṇī Saṁhitā (likewise in the Yājyānuvākyā section) gives the stanza in a form which agrees with the Ṛgveda on all points, the Atharvaveda gives it in a form which agrees with the Ṛgveda in all essential points (so also in the one with which we are concerned here).

1. Taitt. Saṁh. IV.1. 6.3. This is the passage hinted at above on p. 338 fn. 1.

[341] In VIII.89.7 *gharmaṁ na sāman tapatā suvṛktibhir juṣṭaṁ girvaṇase bṛhat* the word *girvaṇase* has brought about for the Taittirīyas a meaningless *giraḥ* in place of *bṛhat;* the Sāmaveda supports the reading of the Ṛgveda.—The Ṛgveda VII.92.3 reads: *ni no rayiṁ subhojasaṁ yuvasva ni vīraṁ gavyam aśvyaṁ ca rādhaḥ.* The Taittirīya Saṁhitā is misled by the two adjectives *gavyam* and *aśviam* belonging to *rādhaḥ* to produce a third such adjective *vīravat* out of *vīram,* so that on account of the addition of a syllable, it becomes necessary to read *aśvyam* as having two syllables: a form[1] *bordering on* the unusual for the Ṛgveda[2].—In VII.96.5 ṚV has: *ye te sarasva' ūrmayo madhumanto ghṛtaścutaḥ, tebhir no 'vitā bhava.* The Taitt. Saṁhitā just as also the Maitr. Saṁh. (Yājyānuvākyā-section) gives the last pāda in the following form: *teṣām te sumnam īmahe.* It is clear that the ṚV has the correct reading, and that the other is an interpolation influenced by passages like III.42.6.—Finally we may cite the Taittirīya-variant *tuviṣmaṇasam* for *tuviṣvaṇasam* (V.8.3): a malformation which is occasioned, without doubt, by the influence of the frequent *tuviṣmant.*

As a result of such tests one would hesitate to ascribe greater weight to the variants found in the Yājyānuvākyā-sections than to the readings in the other parts of the Yajurveda discussed above, especially because, as a rule, at least *one* of the two black Yajurvedas agrees with the ṚV. And thus the result that the pertinent sections yield for the textual history of the ṚV may be formulated in such a way that their overwhelming agreement **[342]** with the Ṛk-text speaks for the essential fixed form of that text at a time when those sections of the Yajurveda were edited. Their deviations from the Ṛk-text, however, are based not on fluctuations in the Ṛk-tradition but on the fact that traces of

1. Of the three passages which Grassmann cites for it, only one (IV.41.10) is certain.
2. The Maitr. Saṁh. (yājyānuv.-section) agrees with the ṚV.

the liberties, which the arrangers of the Yajus-Saṁhitās proper have allowed themselves, are still to be found also with the editors of these later supplements.

We may here only briefly refer to some other sections of the Yajurvedas which, in so far as their relation to the Ṛk-text is concerned, are somewhat on the same line as the Yājyānuvākyā-chapters, namely to the hymns and formulae of the horse-sacrifice. We cannot find an example of a sharper contrast than the one to be found between the arbitrary way in which the hymns, e.g. X.45 or X.140 discussed above, are treated in the black Saṁhitās of the Agni-ritual and the almost complete identity between the Ṛk- and the Yajus-texts for the hymns I.162,163[1] employed in the horse-sacrifice or other hymns and stanzas like, let us say, VI.75[2] or X.169[3] which appear in the Aśvamedha-ritual.

To the same series of materials which characteristically give more careful attention to the fixed text-form in the **[343]** later Saṁhitā-period belong some testimonia of the Yajurveda which give evidence for the *Sāman text-form* of certain stanzas. We found that in cases where the Yajus-texts do not cite a Ṛk-stanza as a Yajus but, so to say, refer to it for its quality as a ṛc we regularly observe a remarkable

1. 163 not in Maitr. Saṁh.; there , hymn 162 shows deviations scarcely due to any other reason than the transposition or omission of the stanzas; in the TS the hymn hardly differs at all from the Ṛk-text. One may note that 163.1 which appears in the Aśvamedha ritual of the Taitt. Saṁh. (IV.6.7.1) in exactly the same form as the Ṛk-text, appears in the same Saṁhitā also in the ritual of the Agnī-cayana (IV.2.8.1): there, however, with such arbitrary handling of the text as is characteristic of the older part of the Yajurvedas. One may also note how ṚV I.162.21 is treated *outside* the section on the horse-sacrifice in the Maitr. Saṁ. I.2.15, and how I.163.1 in the Maitr. Saṁh. I.6.2: nothing can illustrate more clearly the differences in attitude which the various great layers of the Yajus-literature reveal towards the traditional Ṛk-text.
2. Especially in the Tattirīya-version; the Maitr. Saṁh. has some rather insignificant variants.
3. To be found only in TS, not in MS.

approximation to the text form as is transmitted in the Ṛgveda. Now, when a Yajus-text mentions a stanza *as meant for Sāman-recitation,* should we not expect to find a form close to the one transmitted in our Sāmaveda ? Would the Yajurvedas then not confirm the understanding which appeared to us to arise in a different way, viz. that the readings of a given stanza, which we find in the Ṛgveda and also in the Sāmaveda, were not confused even in old times in the consciousness of the Vedic liturgists but that the one had validity as a firmly recognized Ṛk-form and the other as an equally firmly recognized Sāman-form ?

For the moment I have been able to discover only a small amount of material for this question, but even what I am in a position to produce makes it possible to answer the question. First of all, I refer to an observation which is closely connected with the problem raised here. We saw (p. 327, f.n. 3) that in the text related to the *chandobhidhā' iṣṭakāḥ* in the Agni-ritual, where the use of a series of three stanzas each, in the same metre, recommended the consideration of the Sāmaveda due to its constant tṛca-form, the Taittirīya-text does, in fact, permit us to recognize in the choice of the stanza-triads as well as in a number of variants, the influence of the text-form as it appears in the Sāmaveda. Further indications of the fact that the Yajurvedins knew and paid attention to the Sāman-recension as such are the following :

[344] Taitt. Saṁh. V.4.12.1:[1] *pavasva vājasātaya' ity anuṣṭuk pratipad bhavati; tisro 'nuṣṭubhaś catasro gāyatriyaḥ.*—As the scholiast states and the context as well as the parallel passages (particularly Pañcaviṁśa Brāhmaṇa XXI.4.5) confirm, this pertains to the *stotra* of the Aśvamedha, that is to a Sāman-recitation; in this recitation the three Anuṣṭubh-stanzas, whose beginning is cited, are to be transformed

1. I discuss the passage here although it does not belong to the Saṁhitā-but to the Brāhmaṇa-section of the TS.

'*pādatrayaparigaṇanayā*'[1] into four Gāyatrīs. Now which are these stanzas? The pratīka *pavasva vājasātaye* occurs twice in the ṚV (IX.43.6; 107.23), but none of the two stanzas could have been intended, for both the stanzas are neither Anuṣṭubh nor do they occur at the beginning of a tṛca. The Sāmaveda has the pratīka *pavasva vājasātaye* II.366; the stanzas 366-368 form a tṛca in Anuṣṭubh, thus they satisfy the requirements of the Taittirīya passage. And with the help of the SV it is now possible to trace the pratīka also in the ṚV; the tṛca has been taken from ṚV IX.100.6,7,9, but in the ṚV the pratīka reads *pavasva vājasātamaḥ*. We thus see that the Taitt. Saṁh. cites a stanza, the text of which differs in the ṚV and the SV, in a context which is related to the use of the stanza in a Sāman in the form in which it occurs in the Sāmaveda.

The following is a similar case. In the Vāj. Saṁh. XXXVIII.22 the stanza *acikradad vṛṣā hariḥ* etc. is cited. In the corresponding Brāhmaṇa passage (Śatap. Br. XIV.3.1,26) it is said: *athāha vārṣāharam sāma gāyeti*. That stanza is the Yoni of just this Sāman, and thus it occurs in the Vāj. Saṁh., without any doubt, in its quality as a Sāman-text. Now in the text traditionally handed down **[345]** the Ṛgveda (IX.2.6) and the Sāmaveda (I.497) agree with each other in the first two pādas and, as is to be expected, also with the Vāj. Saṁhitā. The third pāda, however, shows a deviation:

ṚV : *saṁ sūryeṇa rocate.*
SV : *saṁ sūryeṇa didyute.*
VS : *saṁ sūryeṇa didyutat.*

The result again is the same: if the stanza which is cited in the Yajurveda as a *Sāman-stanza* differs from the ṚV it

1. Thus the schol. on the Pañc. Brāhm. loc. cit.

gives the reading of our Sāma-Saṁhitā, or one which is very close to it[1].

Finally, we turn to some sections of the 27th book of the Vāj. Saṁ. which fall within the same context. Of this book, which contains paralipomena [i.e. material omitted from the Yajus-collection] of the Agni-ritual, stanzas 23-44 come up for consideration in the critique of the Ṛgveda. In 23-34 occur the collections of the anuvākyās and the yājyās; one is justified in expecting here[2] the Ṛk-text and this, in fact, does occur throughout except the quite obvious mistake *pīvoannā* for *pīvoannān* (stanza 23 = ṚV VII.91.3). From stanzas 35 onwards, on the other hand, the Sāman-texts follow; they belong to the hymn-recitations which the Adhvaryu has to recite on the wings, the tail etc. of the fire-altar which is piled up as a bird. The stanzas are ṚV VII.32.22-23; VI.46.1-2; IV.31.1-3; VI.48.1; VIII.60.9; VI.48.2. As is natural, they all occur again in the Sāmaveda, and to be sure, with the following two **[346]** readings which differ from the Ṛk-text: VI.46.1 *sātau* for *sātā*; IV.31.3 *ūtaye* for *ūtibhiḥ*. The Vāj. Saṁh. has in the ten stanzas, when compared with the ṚV, the same two variants, no more, no less. The tendency of this Veda, found throughout the Saṁhitā, to follow the Ṛk-text, is an exceedingly significant sign showing that the special form of the text which was to be utilized for Sāman-recitations was fixed before book XXVII of the Vāj. Saṁh. was edited and that this form was noted by the redactors when it concerned Sāman-recitations[3].

---

1. However, in the Taitt. Ār. (IV.11.6) we find *rocate* as in the ṚV; but it seems the stanza occurs there without connection with the Sāman-singing. The corresponding passage in the Maitr. Saṁh. (IV.9.11) mentions the sāman, but does not give its text.
2. Only two of these twelve stanzas do not occur in the ṚV.
3. The situation is different in the corresponding Maitr. Saṁh. passage (II.13.9): the text given there is purely the Ṛk-text.

At the end of these discussions concerning the Ṛk-stanzas and hymns which are found in the other Saṁhitās we wish to mention a peculiar compilation consisting of elements almost solely from the Ṛgveda which is looked upon as the *twentieth book* of the traditional Saṁhitā of the *Atharvaveda*, although while doing so we are undoubtedly taking a step which goes far beyond the limits of the Saṁhitā period proper. It has been noticed for a long time that this book, which deviates considerably from the rest of the contents of the Atharvaveda, has been compiled for ritual purposes of the Śrauta-sacrifice. A closer definition of these purposes, which, as far as I know, have not yet been precisely stated, can engage us here only in passing, and I wish to reserve further expatiations for a special investigation to be given at some future time. When it was decided to stamp the Atharvaveda as the Veda of the Brahman-priests it was understandably found that the texts of that Veda did not suffice at all for the ritual recitations of those priests. This was most perceptible **[347]** in the case of the Brāhmaṇācchaṁsin who, from the point of view of his proper character as being related rather to the Hotar priest, had to recite many recitations having the nature of a Śastra, and who was only at a relatively later period assigned to the Brahman group for the sake of the symmetrical grouping of the priests into four times four Ṛtvij. Hence, the recitations connected with the Soma sacrifice and its variants which were to be recited by the Brahman-priests, chiefly by the Brāhmaṇācchaṁsin, were collected together in a special small Saṁhitā. This was naturally assigned to the Atharvaveda: and this is just the twentieth book in question[1].

1. It is easy to adduce proof for the above statements especially with the help of the *Vaitānasūtra* as soon as one knows how to obtain from the statements of this sūtra the clear and consistent reference to the Brahman-priests, in most cases especially to the Brāhmaṇācchaṁsin. This reference is made evident e.g. by a comparison with the Āśvalāyana.

Now as far as the importance of this book for determining the Ṛk-text is concerned the details of the wording do not come into question at all since in this respect, as is well known, the Atharvan-text is identical with our transmitted Ṛk-text, as also the Padapāṭha of the former has been simply taken over from that of the ṚV (see Whitney, Ath. Prāt. p. 99. fn.). For our investigation we need only consider the tṛca-divisions, the additions of stanzas which are not to be found in the ṚV, and so forth. First, it must be noted, as it emerges from what has been just specified, that the XXth book of the AV can be considered only as a very late testimony. Both the fictions on which the whole compilation is based are of a late date: that the Atharvaveda is the Veda and the Brāhmaṇācchaṁsin an assistant of the Brahman priest. Also, as is well known, the twentieth book has not been taken into consideration in the Atharva-Prātiśākhya. **[348]** Hence we shall not be wrong if we judge the deviations from the ṚV as if they were based on the evidence of some Sūtra-text[1]. Moreover, it must also be noted that not the transmitted sequence of the stanzas, but rather the traditional divisions into the sūktas is in many respects absolutely arbitrary and quite removed from the original intention. Thus, the hymns XX.19,20 belonging to the first Rātriparyāya rather ought to be so divided so that 19,20.1-4 (ṚV III.37) makes the first, 20.5-7 the second sūkta. The Division of ṚV VIII.14 = AV XX.27, 28, 29 (cf. Vaitāns. 31.22) is meaningless. No less absurd is the grouping together of the four stanzas of XX.13 into a unit; the fourth (Vait. 23,3; Āśv. V.19.7) must surely follow the first three (Vait. 22.21; Āśv. V.5.19), but it is something new and unconnected with what precedes,—and there are more things of this kind.

Only in a few places—here we do not take into account

1. See especially the statements made below on the modifications of the Ṛk-hymns in Śāṅkhāyana.

the Kuntāpa sūkta[1]—does the compilation contain sūktas or stanzas which are wanting in our Ṛgveda. Thus, there is a series of ritual formulae of a Yajus-nature making sūkta 2, and the two tṛcas 48.1-3; 49.1-3: the assumption that here we find traces **[349]** of a richer inventory of a lost Ṛgveda-recension is for the former of these texts quite out of the question and with regard to the other two there is nothing to warrant such an assumption. We shall further on come across similar cases of intermingling of Ṛk-stanzas with some other ṛcas, not belonging to the transmitted ṚV, for ritual use.—In sūkta 34 = ṚV II.12, the Atharvan text has three stanzas (12, 16, 17) which are missing in the ṚV. In this instance, in fact, it is not enough to assume, as in the case of those tṛcas, that some other material also, besides the one originating from the ṚV, was used in the ritual; the intention of the ritual-arranger here must have been that the sūkta II.12 as such should be recited (cf. Āśv. VIII.7.11), and those three stanzas, connected with the rest by a common refrain, must have been looked upon simply as stanzas belonging to that sūkta. It cannot be denied that here, in fact, we have before us a variant to our Ṛk-text, hardly however a variant which we would prefer to the vulgate. The authority of the text which contains the three stanzas cannot, as such, compete with the weight of the Ṛk-transmission; moreover, expansions of the original text are in themselves more likely than the loss of stanzas; finally,

1. These have been included in the AV because their recitation on the sixth day of the Pṛṣṭhya-ṣaḍaha forms the duty of the Brāhmaṇācchaṁsin (Vaitānas. 32; Āśv. VIII.3).—The many differences in the Atharvan-text of these hymns when compared with Śāṅkhāyana—while the AV *almost* completely agrees with the information found in the Āśvalāyana—are in line, I believe, with the fact that the whole of the 20th book agrees with the Śākala-text of the ṚV, while presumably differences would show up if a comparison is made with the Vāṣkala-text which seems to stand closer to the text of the Śāṅkhāyana.

even if the hopeless condition of the transmitted text does not permit us in individual cases to arrive at any sure judgement regarding the diction of those stanzas, one shall have to treat as suspect the fact that in stanza 16 *none* of the two hemistiches begins with a relative pronoun whereas elsewhere in the sūkta in every stanza this pronoun stands at the commencement of both halves or at least of one of them[1].—Finally, the stanza 107. 13 is not to be found in the ṚV—an **[350]** expansion of the Ṛk-text which vis-à-vis the Ṛgveda cannot claim any significance: comparison with AV XIII.2.34, 35 reveals the origin of the addition[2].

The Ṛk-text and The Brāhmaṇas

In a discussion on what the Brāhmaṇas—including the Rahasyas written in the style of the Brāhmaṇas—have to teach about the history of the Ṛk-text, quite clearly one has to distinguish between the Brāhmaṇas of the Ṛgveda[3] and those of the remaining Vedas.

Among the many hundreds of pratīkas and other text-portions of the Ṛgveda which are cited in the Aitareya and the Kauṣītaka one does not, as far as the *wording* of the text is concerned, meet with a single deviation[4]; we will speak later about the transpositions of the stanzas and similar things. This fact is not sufficient to prove adequately, as it might seem, the existence of an absolute fixity of the text, and to be sure of one and the same text, in the two great Brāhmaṇa-schools. For, even if the arrangers of those

---

1. Bergaigne also, Rech. sur l'historie de la Saṁhitā du ṚV, II.11 considers the three stanzas as suspicious.
2. One may also note the word *divākara* unknown to the ṚV.
3. I request (the reader) to supplement the remarks offered here on the Brāhmaṇas of the Ṛgveda and their attitude towards the Ṛk-text with the statements made in my essay "Die Ṛigveda-Citate im Aitareya", ZDMG XXXVIII, 472 ff.
4. Cases like the one mentioned below of ṚV II.33.1 (Ait. III.34) are no real exceptions.

Brāhmaṇas had found fluctuations in the Ṛk-text, the thorough agreement revealed by the ritual texts, as *they are available to us*, between the citations and the Ṛgveda is not only explicable but is just what one should expect. Even if *after* **[351]** the rise of the Brāhmaṇas the text-form of some pratīka or of some other passage, differing from the one which the author of the Brāhmaṇa had before him, received general recognition, then it is not that the concerned form *could* just find its way into the Brāhmaṇa: rather we may say that that is what must happen in the hands of theologians for whom the wording (of the transmitted Ṛk-text) was the only sanctified and authoritative one, and for whom it was quite clear that the śruti could not cite anything other than just that wording. One may recall how the Śatapatha Brāhmaṇa in its Mādhyandina-recension confirms the Mādhyandina-text of the Vāj. Saṁhitā, but how the Brāhmaṇa of the second available recension of the same Saṁhitā likewise gives another version undoubteldly[1] in accordance with the text of the Kāṇva-Saṁhitā. Thus, here where the Saṁhitā has been transmitted to us in *two* recensions, the corresponding variability of the Brāhmaṇa-texts can be observed even today. Even though we should expect, on the basis of other grounds, much less variation in the text of the Ṛgveda at the time of the Brāhmaṇas than for example those found in the Vāj. Saṁhitā, even then this much is clear that the supposition itself of such variations—which in this instance have disappeared from the text of the Ṛk-Saṁhitā transmitted to us and therefore also from the Brāhmaṇas—is not in any way contradicted by the nature of the Brāhmaṇa-texts as it is revealed to *us*.

But, perhaps, a more essential confirmation of our Ṛk-text than the one which results from the wording of the citations and which is not quite uncontestable is the one

1. I cannot maintain this on the basis of an actual examination of the Kāṇva-recension of the Śat. Br., but the matter can be considered obvious.

which—understandably in a considerably smaller number of [352] cases—is made available by the explanatory or symbolic observations attached to the Ṛk-texts in the Brāhmaṇas. And not less essential, rising above all other individual factors, is the whole character of the relationship of the Brāhmaṇa theology to the Ṛk-text which stands out so prominently. A text which is known this way and which is explored for getting material for ritual use, behind whose small details, metres, the numbers of stanzas, the numbers of syllables, single words the pious mystification searches and finds such an abundance of mysteries: such a text must have *essentially* had a fixed form. Even if this to some extent true about the prose formulae of the Yajurveda, still it is not possible to overlook that the theologians of the Brāhmaṇa period saw the hymn of the ṛṣis in a light different from the Yajus-formula. One perceives the difference when one reads the Śatapatha Brāhmaṇa. There, for example, the numerous different versions of the Agnihotra-formulae (*agnir jyotiḥ* etc.) are discussed as different possibilities among which the priestly acumen can choose (II.3.1.30 f.), while the same Brāhmaṇa, on the other hand (I.4.1.35), rejects the textual change suggested by some teachers for the stanza ṚV I.12.1 as an impurity brought about in the sacrifice by a human activity: *yathaivarcānūktam evānubruyāt.*

We have now to investigate a number of individual cases about which the question can be raised whether the Brāhmaṇas of the Ṛgveda reveal deviations from the text that has been handed down to us, or at least lead us to the traces of such deviations.

Quite often we find in the Brāhmaṇas statements about the contents, that such and such a hymn or such and such a longer [353] liturgical complex contains a certain number of stanzas; the statements that are further added to explain the symbolism tend to give the fullest guarantee to the statement about to the number concerned. *All* figures mentioned in such statements agree, as far as I can see, with the Ṛk-text that has come down to us. Sometimes, however, differences *seem* to arise, but I know of no case in which a thorough examination of the ritual data concerned does not eliminate the difficulty and reveal agreement between the textual form presupposed in the Brāhmaṇa and the one that is known to us. Thus, for example, there is one of the most stubborn cases, the understanding of which escaped me for a while and in which, in fact, I believed that we have to recognize the trace of a deviating Ṛk-text. This is Ait. Ār. I.2.2, 18 where the number of the stanzas in a certain litany is stated to be 97, while the actual number turns out to be 100 if one counts the Pragāthas contained therein as of three stanzas, and only 93 if one counts them as of two stanzas. The solution of the riddle lies in the method of calculating, which at first sight may appear as improbable, viz., some of the Pragāthas are to be considered as having three stanzas, others two: a method of calculation which is indeed assured beyond any doubt by the examination of the pertinent Brāhmaṇa- and Sūtra-prescriptions.

We have to note in a number of cases transpositions and omissions of certain Ṛk-stanzas in the Aitareya and the Kauṣītaka. In the case of transpositions, the question first arises whether the order concerned of the stanzas was in the eyes of the Brāhmaṇa authors the natural and only valid one, or whether the order as handed down in *our* Saṁhitā was also for them the normal one, and that it was only for ritual purposes that modifications, of which one was conscious, were made. At several [354] places clear statements of the Brāhmaṇas decide in favour of the latter interpretation. Thus, the Kauṣītaka (XIX.9), while employing the hymn I.165 for the Marutvatīya Śastra, prescribes the transposition of the ninth stanza to the end of the hymn, since this stanza is addressed to Indra alone without the Maruts, so that it was considered to some extent to form a transition from the Marutvatīya- to the Niṣkevalya Śastra. That this is just a ritual subtelty, and that the real concluding stanza of the hymn is 15 and not 9 is shown with certainty by the appearance of the hymn.— From the manner in which the Aitareya (III.37) prescribes the recitation of X.14.4, 3 and then of X.15.1,3, 2[1] it can likewise be gathered that the transposition as such was recognized;[2] besides, the text of the stanzas itself also speaks on both occasions rather for than against the transmitted order of the stanzas.— Regarding the Aponaptrīya recitation which begins with ṚV X.30.1-9,11, (then stanza 10 follows), the Aitareya (II.20) explicitly says that the first nine stanzas are to be recited *without omissions* (*anantarāyam*): thus it reflects the knowledge that stanza 10 has been left out in its normal place. The twelfth stanza of the hymn has no place at all in this litany: and yet the Kauṣītaka (XII.1), which also omits this stanza—instead mixes up several stanzas from another source with those of hymn X.30—and states that the whole hymn consists of 15 stanzas, which is in complete agreement with our Ṛk-Saṁhitā. One thus notices again: the Brāhmaṇas describe the form of the text found in the ritual not as the only one available, but as one **[355]** derived from the text which is at its basis—namely the one which is transmitted to us. And here, as in the cases discussed before, the critic, for his part, has no reason to judge the relationship of the two text-forms differently. Stanza 12 in fact fits into its traditional place as well as can only be expected. It concludes the recitation which is to be recited when the priests fetching the water are still away. The words *sarasvatī tad gṛṇate vayo dhāt* is a mode of expression frequently occurring at the *end* of a recitation. The following three stanzas are then to be recited singly when the water is brought near, when it has

1. The Atharvaveda also has the sequence 1, 3, 2. Other transpositions are to be found in the Maitr. Saṁh. and the Taitt. Saṁh.
2. *tasmād yāmīm eva pūrvāṁ śaṁset . . . anūcīṁ śaṁsati . . . dvitīyāṁ śaṁsati . . . antataḥ śaṁsati.*

arrived, and when it is placed on the sacrificial grass. Why then is stanza 12 omitted from its natural place in the liturgy described in the Brāhmaṇa-texts? Obviously simply because it has already been used on a different occasion (Ait. II.16, Kauṣ. XI.4). To one who is acquainted with the ritual it is not necessary to give references for such very frequent omissions of stanzas which have been already used or which are reserved for later use[1]; obviously it was thought that the text once recited had lost its strength[2]. Hence, the omission of stanza 12 in the Aponaptrīya-litany does not give grounds for the slightest doubt about this stanza, and similarly, the transposition of stanzas 10 and 11—there is nothing to be said either for or against it—**[356]** cannot have any value when contrasted with the higher authority of the Saṁhitā-text[3].

Beside the passages discussed above in which we found omissions or transpositions of stanzas, may be mentioned further Ait. III.34 where a change in the wording is prescribed: *tvaṁ no vīro' arvati kṣamethā'* (ṚV II.33.1) *iti brūyān nābhi na' ity, anabhimānuko haiṣa devaḥ prajā bhavati. pra jāyemahi rudriya prajābhir iti brūyān na rudrety etasyaiva nāmnaḥ parihṛtyai*. The direct testimony of the Brāhmaṇa here shows us for what artificial subtleties[4] the transmitted reading, specifically mentioned as the one that first came

1. We bring to notice only Kauṣ. Br. VIII.5: *tasya* (of the hymn X.123) *ekām utsṛjati nāke suparṇam upa yat patantam iti . . . tām uttarāsu karoti,* (Kauṣ. VIII.7), *teno sānantarhitā bhavati.*
2. Cf. Kaus. Br. XIII.2: *tad āhur yayā vai prātar yajaty ṛk sā tad ahar yātayāmā bhavati.*—Cf. further ibid. XXII.1 the discussions whether the last two stanzas of V.46 should or should not be left out on a particular occasion.
3. Regarding the transpositions of the stanzas in the ritual of the Brāhmaṇa period one may further compare the characteristic remark of the Kauṣ. Br. VIII.7: *viparyasya dāśatayībhyām vaṣaṭkuryād iti haika' āhur, yathāmnātam iti tv eva sthitam.*
4. One finds similar subtleties e.g. in the Pañc. Br. VIII. 6.12; Śatap. Br. I.4.1.35 [above p. 352].

up for consideration, was changed. It is not necessary to prove that *rudra* is correct. The genuineness of *abhi . . kṣameta* results from the usage which is characteristic just for the second Maṇḍala (II.28.3; 29.2; 33.7); cf. also Taitt. Br. II.8.6.9.

The above discussions give us a warning against the few Brāhmaṇa passages where the texts produce transpositions *without* however expressly testifying that the traditional order on which the transpositions are based was known to them. The treatment of the hymn I.28 in the narrative of Śunaḥśepa (Ait. Br. VII.17: cf. Śāṅkh. Śraut. XV.23) is more on the border line of such cases than actually belonging to them. Śunaḥśepa, bound to the sacrificial post, prays with the hymns I.24-30 successively to all the deities to whom these, in fact, have been addressed. Only I.28 **[357]** which is marked by its distinct ritual content is not suited to this situation: therefore Śunaḥśepa, when he is later released from the bonds, is made to speak this hymn while at the same time performing the rites concerned. Around this point there is considerable of evidence through which the traditional order of almost all the Sunaḥśepa-hymns as presupposed by the Brāhmaṇa is assured[1]; also the sequence of the stanzas of I.28 itself which the Brāhmaṇa seeks to alter, is discussed there on the basis of the traditional order of the stanzas. Hence, Bergaigne's view—at a time when the Śunaḥśepa legend was formulated the hymn I.28 did not belong to the collection of the Śunaḥśepa-hymns (Rech. sur l'hist. de la Saṁh. II.9)—seems less probable to me : the total picture of the position of the Brāhmaṇas and of the recitations described in them with reference to the transmitted Ṛk-

1. Ait. VII.16.7 *ata' uttarābhir ekatriṁśatā.* § 8 *ata' uttarābhir dvāviṁśatyā.* § 10 *etena sūktenottarasya ca pañcadaśabhiḥ.* § 12 = 13 *ata' uttareṇa tṛcena.* —One may note that in § 10 hymns 29 and 30 are not referred to simply as so and so many stanzas which come *next;* the omission of hymn 28 marked a break in the order, so that the pratīka of 29.1 had to be given.

Saṁhitā, in general as well as with special reference to the Śunaḥśepa-section, speaks against it, and the motive of transposing I.28 is too transparent so as to lose all its weight for text-critical considerations.

The description of the Yūpa-ritual in Ait. Br. II.2 shows stanza-transpositions in hymn III.8: the sequence is 1, 3, 2; then I.36.13-14 are inserted, and then follow stanzas 5, 4. This order of the stanzas has been, besides, unanimously accepted by the ritual texts: cf. Maitr. Saṁh. IV.13.1; Taitt. Br. III.6.1; similarly (except for an insignificant deviation), [358] Kauṣ. Br. X.2. The contents of the stanzas in question and the related ritural (Schwab, Thieropfer p. 68 ff.) do not yield anything decisive for one or the other order of the stanzas; in no case, however, will the mixup of the stanzas from I.36 with those of III.8 which is done by the ritual texts give us the confidence to assume that here, for once, by way of an exception, the later texts yield a correction to the old tradition.

There remains hymn III.13 which is cited in the Ait. Br. II.40, 41 (cf. Āśv. V.9.23) with the sequence of the stanzas 1, 5, 4, 6, 3, 2, 7. The way in which the Aitareya passage is worded would itself make it probable that the Brāhmaṇa presupposes the traditional text and is conscious of the transposition as such; on the analogy of the cases discussed earlier we cannot entertain any doubt in that regard. The very text of the stanzas is suited either to one or the other sequence; I cannot discover any grounds to judge the sequence of the stanzas given here by the Ait. as better than elsewhere.

Thus, the result of these discussions is that where the transpositions and omissions of the Aitrareya and the Kauṣītaka lead us to a form of the hymns which is different from the traditional one, we have to say that such variations neither reach nor go beyond the traditional form. The authors of the Brāhmaṇas and the arrangers of the ritual which precede them know the form of the Saṁhitā text and in their ideas take it as their starting point, but they modify it for some definite ritual purposes or for certain mystic plays: these are the facts as can be clearly demonstrated in a number of cases and therefore can be unhesitatingly assumed for the remainder of such instances. Later, in the course of discussing the Śāṅkhāyanaśrautasūtra **[359]** and Hillebrandt's theory based upon it about the ritual recension of the Vedic hymns, we shall have occasion to pursue further the observations presented here and shall find that the results obtained so far are confirmed by similar instances.

We now turn to the question of how we should judge those Pratīkas[1] cited in the two Brāhmaṇas for which we have nothing corresponding in the stanzas of our Ṛk-text. It is advisable, in this discussion, to go beyond the sphere of the Brāhmaṇas, which form the subject of our present investigation, and immediately look to those stanzas which are missing in our ṚV but which appear in the other old traditional texts in the midst of collections formed overwhelmingly out of Ṛk-stanzas : thus, the stanzas of the Sāma-Saṁhitā not found in the ṚV and the Yājyānuvākyā sections of the black Yajurvedas. In fact, from the point of view of literary history, these stanzas obviously are on a par with those cited in the Brāhmaṇas; in many cases they are even indentical with them.

If one comes across, as is not seldom the case particularly in the Aitareya, in a long series of Ṛk-pratīkas one or more which cannot be identified in the Ṛgveda, then naturally the most obvious supposition that forces itself on us is that the form of the Saṁhitā known to the author of the Brāhmaṇa had hymns or stanzas which are missing in our Saṁhitā. However, in opposition to this opinion, one should first take note of the character of our Saṁhitā which is marked by a well-preserved completeness, a completeness in which, perhaps, it was possible to think of additions to

1. See the list in Aufrecht p. 420 f. and Lindner p. 157.

the original store, but by no means so easily of losses from it. The inference that a stanza cited by the pratīka **[360]** must be found with its full text in the Saṁhitā which is at the basis of the ritual text in question obviously cannot apply strictly at least in regard to the Brāhmaṇa texts. The description of the liturgical recitations in the Brāhmaṇas is not even approximately as exhaustive as it is in the case of the Sūtras. Much is given there simply in a general outline or is completely missing, and only a chance reference at a later place shows that it is, nevertheless, assumed to be present. The task of the Brāhmaṇas is to explain the structure of the liturgy in accordance with its sacred meaning, and not to transmit it in its fullness to those who do not already know it. Hence, when a stanza is cited in the Brāhmaṇa with its pratīka, but fully in the Sūtra, that is in no way sufficient to lead us to the conclusion that such a stanza was available in the Saṁhitā known to the older author, but no longer in that of the later. The author of the Brāhmaṇa could very well presume that the stanza which he cited was known from some other source independently of the Saṁhitā. Quite clearly it will not often be possible for us to *prove* this situation in strict terms. The stanzas which are partly not much later than the Saṁhitā-period, which therefore of course, in many cases do not give any decisive evidence showing that they should be exclused from the Saṁhitā: in the case of such stanzas, how would a proof of that kind appear? We obviously must be satisfied if at least in a *part* of the stanzas in question their later origin, which excludes for them the full dignity of the Ṛgveda, is recognizable. In that case the supposition also for the remaining cases, that in them we have the remains of an another Saṁhitā-recension, is not, surely, directly refuted—and this cannot be expected— **[361]** but at least the supposition loses its positive support.

A large number of the stanzas in question, in fact, very clearly have the character of a late origin. One may immediately take up the first two pratīkas which the Aitareya cites but which are not found in the ṚV: *agnir mukham prathamo devatānām, agniś ca viṣṇo tapa' uttamaṁ mahaḥ* (Ait. Br. I.4; the full text is given in the Āśv. Śraut. IV.2.3). A number of small peculiarities would in their totality be enough to push the stanzas, at least, to the latest limit of the Ṛk-literature: what is decisive, however, is that in both of them the word *dīkṣā* occurs. The concept and the naming of *dīkṣā* cannot be traced back to the ṚV; the stanzas prescribed for the *dīkṣā,* whenever they belong to the ṚV, prove themselves clearly to be standing beyond all relationship with the rite concerned. Here we see very clearly how the later liturgists in order not to find themselves at the *dīkṣā* altogether without stanzas which really suit this rite helped themselves with their own clumsy compositions; the deities of the above stanzas are those which are principal for the *dīkṣā,* Agni and Viṣṇu: a grouping of deities not familiar in the ṚV (cf., however, Bergaigne Rel. véd. II.416). In this connection it may be pointed out that altogether the later stanzas which appear in the midst of a series of Ṛk-stanzas are frequently addressed to those deities with regard to which the Ṛgveda fails, so that one realizes the reason why the liturgist just in this situation left the domain of the Ṛk-texts. Thus, we have the Agni-Viṣṇu grouping, just referred to, in the Yājyānuvākyā sections of the Maitr. Saṁh. IV.10.1; 11.2; Taitt. Saṃh. I.8.22.1 (cf. also Kauṣ. Br. VII.2); Indra pradātar Taitt. S. I.7.13.4; Anumati Taitt. S. [362] III.3.11.3 f., Kuhū Maitr. S. IV.12.6, Taitt. S. III.3.11.5; Agni vratabhṛt Ait. Br. VII.8, Maitr. S. IV.11.4[1]; and many others.

In the case of the stanza *mahīm ū ṣu mātaram suvratānām* (Ait. I.9) of which the pratīka is cited in the Aitareya, the fact that it does not belong to the Ṛgveda is revealed in a

1. It may be noted that in many cases first a Gāyatrī occurs and then a Triṣṭubh; this indicates that these stanzas have been *composed* to serve as Puronuvākyā and Yājyā respy. (Āśv. Śraut. II.14.19-20).

different way. If the stanza were part of the Ṛgveda, the place where it should have occurred in the Saṁhitā could hardly be a matter of doubt. The Aitareya cites it along with the tenth stanza of the Gaya-hymn X.63; with the same stanza it occurs in the Atharvaveda VII.6.2, also in Maitr. Saṁh. IV.10.1, Taitt. Saṃh. I.5.11. 5, VII.1.18.2, Vāj. Saṁh. XXI.5; the two stanzas have in common the pāda *suśarmāṇam aditiṁ supraṇītim.* The diction of the stanza *mahīm ū ṣu* etc. also shows in other ways contacts with the mode of expression of the two Gaya-hymns X.63,64. Can one, in fact, locate the stanza in the Gaya-hymns ? Hardly: it cannot occur near the pendant-stanza X.63.10 for in its proximity every stanza concludes with the word *suastaye.* One cannot insert it into hymn 64 either, for that would yield a number of stanzas which would go against the rule of arrangement. Hence, the probability emerges that the stanza, intended for ritual use, was additionally composed as a counterpart to X.63.10.[1] It was composed under the influence of X.63.10 and altogether in the mode of expression prevailing in the Gaya-hymns. It was then accommodated in the Atharvaveda together with that **[363]** stanza (X.63.10) and two other Aditi-stanzas (ṚV I.89.10 and the stanza *vājasya nu prasave* which, as ἀδέσποτον, was likewise floating around) in hymn VII.6 in which scattered material has been combined into an apparent whole.

Incidentally, the Atharvaveda offers in some cases the possibility of tracing the home of the stanza in question in a genuine hymn and not just in one which is secondarily pieced together: in such cases the question of where those stanzas belong merges with the question of whether those hymns belong to the Ṛgveda. Occasionally, the question when formulated this way is decided immediately. If in Ait. VI.32 the pratīka *etā' aśvā' ā plavante* is cited, or if in Ait.

1. One may also note that in the commentary on the Vāj. Saṁh. the stanza *sutrāmāṇam,* but not *mahīm ū ṣu,* has been characterized as Gayaplātadṛṣṭā.

VIII.11 the stanza *iha gāvaḥ pra jāyadhvam* appears, then we have before us texts that belong to the Kuntāpa hymns and therefore belong to a sphere which falls *outside* the Ṛgveda.

More peculiar and more complicated is the question of the pratīkas *brahma jajñānam, iyaṁ vai pitre, mahān mahī astabhāyat*[1] which are cited in Aitareya I.19 (cf. Kauṣ. VIII.4) in the course of the Pravargya ritual. All three stanzas occur in *one* hymn of the Atharvaveda, IV.1.1, 2, 4. But there exists a piece of evidence in the exegetical literature attached to the Ṛgveda which would yield as the source of the stanzas in question a hymn, which, when contrasted with the hymn AV IV.1, shows essential differences. The *Bṛhaddevatā* (Meyer, Ṛgvidhāna p. XXII) mentions between X.103 and 104 a hymn which is not to be found in our Saṁhitā and not in the Khilas either. About this hymn it says:

[364]

brahma yat param
tatrāniruktā vaiśvadevy ṛg, ekā sūryam arcati,
gharmaṁ parāś catasras tu, savitāram abhīti yā,
sūktaśeṣas tu ṣaḷṛcaḥ sūryācandramasoḥ stutiḥ.

There is no doubt that the beginning of this passage is not to be translated as: "the following brahman," but as: "the following [hymn beginning with the word] brahma," and it is equally doubtless that the word *brahma* refers to the pratīka *brahma jajñānam.* For the fact that several stanzas of the hymn described in the Bṛhadd. should refer to the gharma agrees, on the one hand, with the often attested ritual employment (Ait. loc. cit. etc.) of *brahma jajñānam* in the Pravargya-litany and, on the other, with the words *gharmaṁ śrīṇantu* of the stanza which, in the AV, immediately follows. When next the Bṛhaddevatā lists a stanza addressed

1. The stanzas are also frequently met with elsewhere, and, to be sure, in several cases at such places where, as a rule, only Ṛk-stanzas appear: SV I.321; Taitt. Saṁh. II.3.14.6.

to Savitar and begins with *abhi*, these data agree with the fact that in the same Pravargya-litany beginning with *brahma jajñānam* just mentioned, there appears the stanza *abhi tyaṁ devaṁ savitāram oṇyoḥ*: again, one of those pratīkas to be met with in the Ait. and the Kauṣ. Br. but which cannot be identified in the ṚV (cf. also SV I.464; Śat. Br. XIII.5.1.11). If the proof that we have here actually discovered the stanzas cited in the Bṛhaddevatā beginning with the words *brahma* and *abhi* needs further substantiation, then we can point to the fact that Nakula who, as far as I know is not mentioned elsewhere, is stated to be the author of *brahma jajñānam* and of *abhi tyaṁ devam*[1]. Beside these two **[365]** stanzas, we may further attribute to the hymn described in the Bṛhaddevatā the stanza AV IV.1.2 noted above which mentions gharma, and perhaps still more stanzas from AV IV.1[2]. The stanza to the sun ("*ekā sūryam arcati*") *could* possibly be the stanza *vi yat pavitram*, which also occurs in the Pravargya ceremony and alludes to the gharma (Kauṣ. Br. VIII.5; Āśv. Śraut. IV.6.3), and which could be labelled as belonging to Sūrya, perhaps owing to its concluding words. I cannot venture any suggestion regarding the six stanzas addressed to the sun and the moon.

One thus sees that here we have another hymn beside AV IV.1, with which it had in common the opening stanza and obviously some more stanzas, but deviated from it in regard to others. The examination of AV IV.I will not leave the reader of this text in doubt, that the text *as*, or *almost as* it

---

1. Durga on Nirukta I.7 and VI.12; cf. Ṛk-Prātiś. 996; Roth, Einleitung zum Nir. XLV. The way in which the 'Nākula' is cited in the Prāt. does not prove at all, as Roth thinks probable, "that the Prātiśākhya has for its basis a redaction of the Ṛk-Saṁhitā which contains that hymn." Cf. *dāśatayīṣu . . . subheṣaje,* Prāti. 946 f.
2. These must be among the stanzas from this hymn which, according to the Bṛhadd., are addressed to *gharma.*

is transmitted is a perfect whole: in contrast, the stanza *abhi tyaṁ devam* added to it in the Bṛhaddevatā and of course also the stanzas addressed to the sun and the moon do not agree with the rest. Hence, it seems to me that the "Nākula", the hymn described in the Bṛhaddevatā, is *secondary* vis-à-vis AV IV.1; it has been pieced together by adding to the latter stanzas of different origin and made suitable for ritual purposes. Accordingly, the claims of this hymn to be considered as a part of a lost Ṛk-recension cannot be deemed strong[1]; the Nākula obviously stands rather in line with many other **[366]** apocryphal texts which are cited at many places in the Bṛhaddevatā between the hymns taken from the Ṛk-Saṁhita[2]. And there is no tenable proof to suggest that the hymn in the form as it occurs in the AV IV..1 belonged to a lost Ṛk-recension. However, considering its language, one can scarcely look upon it as *very far* removed from the later Ṛk-period, yet I believe that such things as "*brahma brahmaṇa' uj jabhāra madhyāt*" (stanza 3) would support the evidence which our Ṛk-Saṁhitā gives about the hymn by not having incorporated it.

Among the remaining stanzas whose Pratīkas are cited in the Ait. Br. but which are missing in the ṚV may further be noted that the Gāyatrī *ā yāhi tapasā janeṣv agne pāvako' arciṣā* etc. (cf. Maitr. Saṁh. IV.10.2, in the Yājyānuvākyā-section) has the stamp of a late origin: the sandhi *janeṣv agne* is in itself modern, here however, occurring between two pādas it exceeds the limits of what is possible in the Ṛgveda.

Only in passing may we further indicate that the stanzas of the Sāmaveda, which are missing in the ṚV, and which

1. One may also note that the hymn containing thirteen stanzas at this place violates the principle of arrangement.
2. The nature of these insertions found in the Bṛhaddevatā and the Ṛgvidhāna will be further discussed together below: it appeared correct to separate such an investigation from what has been said here although there are many points in common.

are obviously to be judged in the same way as those cited in the Aitareya, would considerably increase our collection of modern characteristics:[1] of course there are other **[367]** stanzas in which things of that nature do not occur. In conclusion we attempt to formulate the result of these discussions for judging the Ṛk-tradition.

When in the texts which almost exclusively cite stanzas from the Ṛgveda (thus the Ait. and the Kauṣ.) or contain them (thus the SV and the Yājyānuvākyā-sections of the black Yajus) there appear stanzas interspered among them which do not figure in our ṚV, then this does not establish a probability, in some cases not even a possibility, that these stanzas belong to a different recension of the ṚV. Between the conclusion of the ṚV and the finalization of the ritual described in these texts lies a period whose productions occasionally—especially in such places where the content of the Ṛk-stanzas was insufficient—could have acquired and did acquire validity in this ritual. One would also naturally conceive the chronological boundary between the Ṛgveda and the no-Ṛgvedic material as *only approximately* fixed in such a way that all the ṛcas which were older than a certain time-limit were included in the Ṛgveda, while all the later ones were not. Now among the materials under discussion there occurs much which, judged from its appearance, *can* go back to the Ṛk-period, and perhaps there is some material

---

1. Only a few things may be brought to the notice here. The name Kaśyapa appears in the ṚV only once, in the late supplementary hymn IX.114 (stanza 2); in stanzas peculiar to the SV it appears twice, I.90, 361: in stanzas which are also otherwise full of modernities.—I.435 *svargān* with two syllables.—II.1181 the Yajus-formula *agnir jyotiḥ* etc.—From the seventh Prapāṭhaka of the Pūrvārcika edited by Goldschmidt: st. 8 *aham annam annam adantam admi;* 18 *parameṣṭhī prajāpatiḥ;* 32 the six seasons; 40 thoroughly having the character of a formula from a Gṛhyasūtra.—The tradition ascribes most of these SV-stanzas to the ṛṣi Vāmadeva, but this does not support their origin in a tradition co-ordinated with the Ṛk-texts; cf. Ind. Stud. IX.265.

which in fact does go back that far. The scholars who are used to prefer the Ṛgveda to such a great extent over the other Vedas would do well **[368]** to give the benefit of their attention also to these areas which are immediately bordering on the Ṛgveda; but there is no occasion to suppose that any part of these areas just described were ever recognized as fully authoritative provinces of the Ṛgveda itself.

The Brāhmaṇas belonging to the Vedas other than the Ṛgveda do not offer, beyond their corresponding Saṁhitās, any fundamentally new phenomena with regard to the treatment of the Ṛk-hymns and stanzas cited there. An occasion to cite Ṛk-stanzas which do not appear in the corresponding Saṁhitā is offered sometimes by the discussion of the ceremonies which are not treated there, especially when they refer to the recitations of the Hotar; sometimes also while confirming some doctrine it is remarked that "with reference to this the stanza is—" or that "with reference to this the ṛṣi has said—," and then follows a stanza mostly[1] taken from the Ṛgveda. It is hardly to be doubted that in the period to which the citations concerned belong the Ṛk-text, in essentials, had been fixed in the form that is available to us. Nevertheless those citations exhibit a great deal of variation in their nature, each according to the school to which it belongs. Those, for example, which belong to the Pañcaviṁśa Brāhmaṇa are full of variants when compared with our Ṛk-text[2], **[369]** while the exceedingly numerous citations in the Śatapatha

---

1. Some of these stanzas, however, are missing in the Ṛgveda. I give, as I hope, a complete listing of such stanzas from the Śatapatha Brāhmaṇa. A perusal of these stanzas will show that there is no question of finding in them real Ṛk-meterial which would supplement the stock of our vulgate: III.4.2.7; X.4.1.9; XI.1.6.10 (however cf. ṚV X.54.2); XII.5.2.4; XIV.5.5.18; 7.2.28.
2. Here we find one remarkable exception to the greater strictness with which the Ṛk-text is generally treated in the later Vedic period [above p. 335 f.].

Brāhmaṇa deviate from the same almost only in details of orthography and accentuation: a condition in which the freedom enjoyed by the Sāma-Saṁhitā with reference to the Ṛgveda on the one hand, and, on the other, the close connection of the Vāj. Saṁh. with the same unmistakably continues.

It is not necessary to repeat here for the Brāhmaṇas a detailed investigation of the variants like the one attempted above with reference to the Saṁhitās. Of course, in such an undertaking the result arrived at above would be repeated, viz. that, on the whole, the ancient, well-preserved tradition of the Ṛgveda is too far above them to be corrected with the help of single stanzas preserved in other schools and mostly torn from their context, yet in isolated cases exceptions to this situation cannot be ruled out.[1] Concerning the statements regarding the number of stanzas in individual sūktas which deviate from the transmitted Ṛk-text, we may refer to what has been said above in the discussion on the sūktas in question[2].

---

1. Thus, I would consider the correction of ṚV VII.34.2 *āpo' adhaḥ* (for *adha*) *kṣarantīḥ* which follows from the Pañc. Br. I.2.9 and VI.6.17 as extremely probable.
2. About the Vātsapra (ṚV X.45), of which the Śat. Br. VI.7.4.6 gives the extent to be of eleven stanzas, see above [p. 300]; about the Apratiratha of 12 stanzas (ṚV X.103; Śat. Br. IX.2.3.6) see above [p. 247]; about the Purūravas-hymn of 15 stanzas (X.95; Śat. XI.5.1.10) see p. 248.

CHAPTER 4

The Orthoepic Diaskeuasis

[370] The text of the Ṛgveda was essentially fixed not only for the period of the Brāhmaṇas but also for the period of the composition of the later Saṁhitās : this we have learnt from the preceding investigations. But the above statement needs modification in one particular direction : that what we may in a word describe as *orthoepic details* of the text were then quite different from the form of the text available to us today; the final shaping of the text in this regard is an event that belongs to and occupies a later period of Vedic text-history. First of all we think of the treatment of sandhi: for example, definite rules and limitations on the elision and non-elision of an initial *a* after *e* and *o,* the change of *i* and *u* to *y* and *v* before vowels, the contraction of the vowels, the change or its absence of *s* to *ḥ* before *k* and *p.* Another important group of instances which received their final shape presumably in the same period is made up of equivalent forms, occurring side by side with short and long vowel, especially with short and long final vowel, the use [371] e.g. of *abhi* and *abhī,* of *tena* and *tenā* : the treatment of such pairs of forms in the traditional text, as we shall show, goes back *on the whole* to the ṛṣis themselves, but reveals the hand of the grammarians in respect of many details. In short: during the period whose activity in respect of the text of the Veda we are now going to investigate, the *words* of the text—except for some unimportant exceptions—were fixed. Such things as whether we have to read at a given place *sumnam* or *dyumnam, inakṣat* or *inakṣan* were, on the whole at least, not in doubt. But the regulation of the letters

[rather the *sounds*], i.e. differentiating between *divas pari* and *divaḥ pari,* between *pra sma vājeṣu* and *ā smā ratham,* between *divo' antān* and *indrovatu* and many more similar cases gave occasion to speculations in which the grammatical theologians did not feel themselves bound in the same way, as they did in the case of the proper content of the words, to what was given, what was transmitted to them, but considered themselves authorized to modify the phonetic forms concerned according to the norms invented by them.

If we want to define more precisely the period in which the redaction of the text was carried out on the lines described above, then it can be asserted with certainty that that task was not done before the end of the Brāhmaṇa period. Here we face the question what form the Vedic text had from the *phonetic point of view* in the Brāhmaṇa period: whether, for example, at that time they said *tvaṁ hy agne* or *tuaṁ hi agne,* whether *devāyāgnaye* or *devāya agnaye.* It is hardly necessary to stress here expressly that in order to find this out it is not enough to take into consideration only the transmitted written form of the Brāhmaṇas or of the Vedic stanzas occurring in them. If, as we believe to be the case, the artificial regulation of the phonetic form of the Vedic stanzas known to us **[372]** was achieved only *after* the rise of the Brāhmaṇas, then inevitably these revised phonetic forms must also have been subsequently carried over into the Vedic stanzas occurring in the Brāhmaṇas, indeed in many respects also into the prose passages of the Brāhmaṇas themselves. By chance, there have been preserved for us not a few direct statements in the Brāhmaṇas as to how many syllables a given word or a given group of words has; and these testimonies yield results which are not without significance for the history of the phonetic treatment of the Vedic text.

We shall here first of all draw attention to the remarks which are added in the Brāhmaṇa-sections of the Taittirīya

Saṁhitā to the stanza ṚV V.50.1. This stanza runs, in its Taittirīya-form, as: *viśve devasya netur marto vṛṇīta sakhyam, viśve rāya' iṣudhyasi dyumnaṁ vṛṇīta puṣyase.* On this the Brāhmaṇa remarks (TS VI.1.2.6): *saptākṣaraṁ prathamaṁ padam aṣṭākṣarāṇi trīṇi*[1]. That means that the damage caused to the metre in the first pāda due to *netur* (definitely for *nayitur*) was already there at that time. But the second pāda was supposed to have eight syllables: hence in those days one could not have said *sakhyam,* as was transmitted by the later diaskeuasts[2], but the old pronunciation *sakhiam* was still in vogue.

[373] The Ait. Brāhm. III.46 leads to exactly the same result where it is said about the Vāmadevya text: *tat tribhir akṣarair nyūnam.* Undoubtedly, two of these three wanted syllables in the stanzas ṚV IV.31.1-3 are to be found in the endings of the words *sakhīnām* and *jaritṝṇām* (stanza 3). Accordingly, I think that the third must be sought in the exactly similar genitive *madānām* (stanza 2). Consequently, none of the three deficient syllables remains to be seen in *bhavāsy ūtibhiḥ* (stanza 3); that means one pronounced this

---

1. Cf. also the remarks in TS V.1.9.1; Śatap. Br. III.1.4.23.
2. One should not permit the hazy notion to countinue, viz. that the later *sakhyam* is only a 'way of writing' or some such thing. As soon as one earnestly sets aside, as one must, from this group of problems all the notions connected with the writing-system, it will be immediately evident that a *sakhyam,* an *avostu* can occur in the transmitted text only because in the period which is decisive for the phonetic form of this text one *pronounced* it just that way, and not as *sakhiam* or *avo' astu.* There is no contradiction involved if in the Prātiśākhya (572, 973; cf. M. Müller ṚV. translation p. LXXVIII f.) the *vyūha* is permitted for the purposes of metrical calculations (which shows, by the way, that the pronunciation without vyūha was considered prakṛti; Prāti. 882): without such a stipulation the matter which comes up for discussion in the Prātiśākhya would have assumed immeasurable proportions. How decidedly one put into practice the rules such as the elision of an *i* and *u* before a vowel is shown by the well-known case of the words *īḍya, vīḍvaṅga* where, if the vowel was pronounced, not *ḍ* but *ḷ* should have been heard.

part as *bhavāsi ūtibhiḥ*[1]. Thus, also in these instances the existence of the deeper disfigurements of the text (*madānām, sakhīnām,* like *netur* above), on the one hand and, on the other, the non-existence of the more obvious ones is assured for the Brāhmaṇa period[2].

Further, we may refer to the Ait, Āraṇy. I.3.4.16. Here the stanza X.120.1 is treated as consisting of 41 syllables: obviously, therefore, *jyeṣṭham* and *ugras* **[374]** were counted as two syllables[3], while one had quite correctly understood the number of syllables in *madanty ūmāḥ.*

---

1. A different, but certainly not more correct, opinion is expressed by the scholiast on the Ait. Br. (loc. cit.) who, while agreeing with the characterization of stanza 3 in the Anukramaṇī as pādanicṛt, sees the deficiency not in *madānām*, but in *bhavāsi.* The Gāna-form of the stanza has correctly preserved *bhavāsi* (Sāmav. ed. in the Bibl. Ind. vol. III, p. 90 f.).
2. It may be permitted here to call attention briefly to some more statements on the number of syllables in connection with the other Sāman texts, Pañc. Br. IV.2.19; 8.15; VII.7.1,4; XII.13.20.24.: the contractions and the semi-vowels which disturb the metre have been ignored throughout.
3. The loss of the consciousness of the syllable-forming anaptyctic vowels (svarabhakti) so common in the ṚV, as in *ugraḥ* (*ug·raḥ*); similarly, *ind·ra, ag·ne, yaj·naḥ* etc.; also, what Grassmann has failed to recognize, *p·ra* (cf. Ind. Stud. XVII.240) seems to belong already to the period *prior* to the interference of phonetic diaskeuasis. It may be mentioned here that it is a characterisitic of these svarabhakti-vowels that they are used with marked preference in the most volatile syllable of the Vedic metres, viz. the second syllable after the Triṣṭubh- or Jagatī-caesura, and this is evidence for their most insignificant duration value; they occur very rarely at the beginning of a stanza; an end of a Vedic stanza like *ind·raḥ* (— ◡ ◡̲) — apart from the doubtful cases like *dhūr·teḥ* I.128.7, *at·raiḥ* 129.8 — does not occur at all; the vowel which so often appears also at the end of the stanza in the gen. loc. dual in *-tros* i.e. *-taros,* is just not anaptyctic. In my opinion also the disyllabic *ṛ* vowel disappeared from the Veda recitation in the older period (see Benfey, Vedica und Verwandtes 25 ff.; we have come across numerous attestations where one may hesitate between accepting a metrical anomaly and a two-syllabled *ṛ*, see above [p. 68f., 74, 79f.], and I would also judge similarly the cases where the Veda—just as later, the old Buddhistic Pāli poetry—contracts two syllables to make one in rapid pronunciation (see especially M. Müller, ṚV translation p. CXLII ff.).

As is well-known the word *svar* is pronounced by the Vājasaneyins as one syllable, by the Taittirīyas as two syllables (suvar). Does this difference go back to the period when the texts of the two recensions were composed, or is it to be sought in the difference between the treatments given to these texts by the later diaskeuasts? The analogy of the passages discussed so far speaks in favour of the latter interpretation, and the same is confirmed by the fact that the Śatapatha Brāhmaṇa which on many occasions speaks about the number of syllables of *svar* (II.1.4.14; XI.1.6.5; XIV.8.6.4,5) invariably assumes two syllables, that is, it prefers the form of the word given by the Taittirīya diaskeuasis. This is all the more remarkable since while making such statements the Brāhmaṇa is not dealing with metrical passages, in which case the consideration of the metre could influence the counting of syllables. —After all this it should not surprise us if *rājanya* is said to have four syllables, *dyaus* **[375]** two syllables (Śat. Br. V.1.5.14; XIV.8.15.1), the words *prāṇopāno vyānaḥ* (not in a metrical pāda) eight syllables (XIV.8.15.3). In fact one went so far as to count *y* and *v* as syllables even in the words whose syllabicity, according to the evidence of the metrical texts, is in fact totally ruled out or is very unusual: hence, one declares *tvak* to be disyllabic (Śat. Br. X.4.1.17) and *satyam* to be trisyllabic (Śat. Br. XIV.8.6.2, cf. Ait. Āraṇyaka. II, 1.5.5). One cannot think of more clear statements than these in order to show how little one thought in the Brāhmaṇa-period of theories which would have required a *y* and *v*, instead of the *i* and *u*, before vowels.

We will conclude this compilation by drawing attention to some remarks made in the Brāhmaṇas about the number of syllables in the words *uktham̐ vācīndrāya* and the related formulas; here also we are concerned with prose sentences, or at least with sentences which are not directly[1] subjected

1. However, an indrect influence of the metre on these formulas is possible, in fact not improbable, since at the time these formulas were

(Continued on next page)

to a metrical norm. In the words *ukthaṁ vācīndrāya,* the Taitt. Saṁh. III.2.9.2,4 counts seven syllables, and so also does the Ait. Brāhm. III.12[1]; that means, in the period of these Brāhmaṇa-texts, one pronounced *vāci indrāya.* With this agrees the Kauṣ. Brāhm. XIV.3 when it is said that the formula **[376]** *uktham avācīndrāya* together with the response *ukthaśāḥ* should make eleven syllables. Similarly, the Aitareya (loc. cit.) regards the formula *ukthaṁ vācīndrāya devebhyaḥ* as having eleven syllables: undoubtedly, one must have pronounced *vāci* and *devebhiaḥ*[2]. Of course, as in the Vedic stanzas, so also in the liturgical prose, whenever the occasion demanded, the number of syllables could be reduced with the help of contraction; and, in this regard too, the group of formulas we have just seen offers an example: according to the Kauṣītaka (loc. cit.) the words *avācīndrāyokthaṁ devebhyaḥ* with the response *ukthaśāḥ* make twelve syllables, which presupposes the contraction of all the vowels that can be contracted.

One can see that in the passages like the ones collected here the Brāhmaṇa texts themselves disprove by the *content* of their statements the phonetic form of the Vedic stanzas in which they have been handed down to us by them. Thus, we obtain a factor which convinces us that the sweeping as well as forceful remodelling carried out in the Vedic texts handed down to us in respect of contractions, the appearance of a semi-vowel in place of a vowel, etc. belongs to a period which is younger compared to the time of origin of the Brāhmaṇas.

(Continued from previous page)

fixed, at least in some of the available recensions, an attempt could have been made to obtain the number of the syllables required for the three principal metres (Gāyatrī, Triṣṭubh, Jagatī), and by doing so to relate those formulas to the general structure of the ritual symbolism connected with the number three. From this viewpoint the value of the concerned syllable-counting as impartial evidence is perhaps partly impaired.

1. But the *Gopatha Brāhmaṇa* (II.3.10), which generally follows the Aitareya Brāhmaṇa, characteristically deviates from it when it is said, following the later standpoint, that the formula is only *ṣaḍakṣara.*
2. The Gopatha (loc. cit.) assumes here naturally nine syllables.

Other kinds of considerations may be added which, surely, by themselves would not have the strength to prove the point, yet they are in a position to support considerably the results arrived at in a different way: consideration of the practice followed by the theologians of the Brāhmaṇa-period *in their own stanzas* in regard to the points which come up for consideration in the Vedic diaskeuasis. It would, however, be in principle wrong to assume that those who arranged **[377]** the old texts could impose only such phonetic laws, which were, in fact, accepted for the poetic practice of their own period. One easily notes that the phonetic speculation exercised on what was given by tradition, especially when the speculation was indulged in by men like Vedic grammarians who were easily amenable to unhealthy ideas just up in the air, need not feel necessarily bound to go the same way that was adopted for the phonetic treatment of the new compositions composed by them during that period. If we wanted to get an idea of the period in which the sandhi rules imposed on the Veda arose, and if for this purpose we begin to search for such texts in the later literature in which those rules have been exactly followed, we would not find them anywhere. In the Prātiśākhya itself, instances are not wanting where Śaunaka's own stanzas contradict the rules he formulated. But an element of truth that should not be neglected does remain. We expect to find that the grammarians who busied themselves with the Veda-text and the contemporary poets who produced their own compositions shared similar views on the questions of phonetic treatment. The best occasion for those grammarians to carry into the Veda sandhi rules which in fact, did not fit into the Vedic text would always be where the literary language of their period had more or less accepted these rules. In the *degree* of this recognition, in the unbridled application of such rules, the grammatical speculation of the living poetic practice might go ahead or lag behind. In many cases it might have slipped in obliquely, and it would not be possible for us to give any explanation of the arbitrary direction it had taken. But in general we would scarcely **[378]** be on the wrong path if we do not want to place the diaskeuasis, which forces upon the Veda certain phonetic rules that were in fact valid in the later literature, in a period which is still far removed from the one in which those rules came to be regularly observed. And the practice followed by the stanza-composers of the Brāhmaṇa period was, in fact, distant enough from the unrealistic extreme to which the later period and the Vedic diaskeuasis of that period had gone. The Brāhmaṇa authors however, were already on the way which led to this extreme, but we do not have to search long among the stanzas appearing in the Brāhmaṇas and those undoubtedly belonging to the Brāhmaṇa-period, even those partly belonging to times younger than this period, in order to find a number of examples of the old, natural forms of the word with *i* and *u*, instead of the later *y* and *v*, with hiatus instead of contractions. Just a few examples may be singled out from among the large number that is available. The metre demands *i* in place of *y*, e.g., Ait. Brāhm. VIII.23 *aśvān baddhvāya medhiān*; VII.17 (Śunaḥśepa-legend) *nāpāgāḥ śaudrān niāyāt, sauhārdiāya me śriyai*; Śatap. Brāhm. XIV.4.3.34 (Kāṭh. Up. II.4.9) *yataś codeti sūriaḥ,* and many similar examples. At the end of a word before the following vowel, *i* is required in the Śatap. Br. X.5.2.18 *anne bhāti apaśritaḥ,* etc. Instead of *v, u* is required in the Śatap. Br. XIV.4.3.1 *due devān abhājayat*; XIV.4.3.34 (Kāṭh. Up. II.4.13) *sa evādya sa u śuaḥ*. Hiatus between *a* and *a, a* and *ā, ā* and *a* is called for by the metre: Ait. Br. V.30 *akṛtvā anyad upayojanāya;* VII.17 *yathaiva Āṅgirasaḥ san;* VII.18 *jahnūnāṁ ca ādhipatye,* etc.

If one compares the practice of handling the sounds, as characterized by the above passages, with the one found in the Sūtra-period, which to some extent is reflected in the stanzas of the Ṛk-Prātiśākhya **[379]**, then the decision to which of these two periods the final phonetic ordering of the Ṛk-text should belong, or to which one it approaches, is automatically given. The discrepancies between the Brāhmaṇa stanzas and the norms of the Vedic diaskeuasis reveal the difference between the two periods: while one has just set out on the way leading to the later artificiality in phonetic treatment, the other has already covered it. On the other hand, the discrepancies between the Prātiśākhya-stanzas and the rules of the diaskeuasis can be easily explained by the difference in the nature of the two operations which, as we have already noticed above, relate to the editing of the old stanzas and the composition of the new ones; the factor common to both, however, is the authoritativeness of the same lifeless treatment of sounds based on theories—which are as much carried to extremes as they are wrong. Hence, the conclusion cannot be doubted that the fixation of *our* Vedic text with its artificial treatment relating to contractions, semi-vowels, etc. is not essentially older than the end of the Brāhmaṇa-period.

In order to confirm what has been said so far, the literature of about this period gives us noteworthy indications to show that just at that time the attention of certain circles was directed to phonetic questions, especially of sandhi, in a way that had never happened before. In the Brāhmaṇa literature proper, which is certainly not lacking in making use of the whole gamut of the then available ideas for their symbolic phantasies about the ritual, we hardly find traces of those kinds of observations[1], even though such observations should have interested those theologians who stood most directly **[380]** in close relationship with the form of the text that was to be recited[2]. The situation changes in

1. The remark that Vimada was a *viriphita ṛṣi* is an isolated instance, see Boehtlingk-Roth s.v. *riph.*
2. Grammatical reflection altogether—quite apart from the metrical one—is, in the Brāhmaṇas, yet in its initial stage. The relevant materials from the Aitareya have been collected by Aufrecht on p. 431 of his edition. The other texts do not yield much either; compare e.g., Taitt. Saṁ. I.5. 2.2; Śat. Br. II. 2.3.27; X.5.1.2, etc.

some passages of the Āraṇyaka-texts and the Upaniṣads, which are supplements to the Brāhmaṇas. Now begin to appear ideas such as ūṣmans and sparśas; in the "*saṁhitāyā upaniṣat*" (Ait. Ār. III, Kauṣ. Ār. VII, VIII; cf. Taitt. Ār. VII.3) a number of much ramified concepts and doctrines now occur, which are related to the different possible treatments of the Vedic text from the phonetic point of view, and also a number of names of those very grammatical theologians who are mentioned as authorities in the Prātiśākhyas: prominently names like those of Śākalya (Sthavira Śākalya[1]), Māṇḍūkeya (Śūravīra Māṇḍūkeya and Hrasva Māṇḍukeya), Māṇḍavya. These are the names which lead us from the sphere of names found in the Brāhmaṇa literature to a later period, as is also done by the sphere of thought associated with these names, and thus they reveal to us the transition from the world of ideas of the Aitareya Brāhmaṇa or the Kauṣītaki Brāhmaṇa to the mode of thinking of that literary period, whose characteristic highlights are the Prātiśākhyas and the Nirukta.

Here we find an important fixed point in the history of the Ṛgveda-transmission: Śākalya, the founder of the Śākala-śākhā and the author of the Padapāṭha[2]: younger, as we [381] saw, than the Brāhmaṇa-texts proper, but old enough so that a passage in the supplements to the Brāhmaṇas in which he is mentioned could be included among the texts to which one granted the dignity of a full-fledged śruti; older further than Śaunaka, whose Prātiśākhya is based on the Padapāṭha and who names quite frequently Śākalya together with his school; he is older than Yāska who also cites him (Nir. VI.28), and older, finally, than Āśvalāyana and Śāṅkhāyana.

1. It seems that we do not have to identify this Śākalya or his son with the Vidagdha Śākalya of the Śatapatha.
2. It is well-known that the "*saṁhitāyā' upaniṣat*" already knows the Saṁhitāpāṭha, the Padapāṭha, and the Kramapāṭha which combines the peculiarities of the two; cf. Max Müller Ṛk-Prātiśākhya p. VI f.—Also see there Einl. p. 7, and Roth on Nir. IV.4 for Śākalya as the author of the Padapāṭha.

However, this is not yet the proper place to discuss in detail the activity of Śākalya or the concept of the Śākala-śākhā. Śākalya, for the present, comes up for consideration only in so far as he is important for the chronology of the redaction which gave the Veda-text its present phonetic form. We found his name mentioned in the literature of the period which we must *approximately* assign to that redaction. We must now try to determine more exactly his relationship with the diaskeuasis of the Vedic text. Since Śākalya is the author of the Padapāṭha, while the diaskeuasis was concerned with the Saṁhitāpāṭha, we are here led to the question—or to a part of the question: how are the Saṁhitāpāṭha and the Padapāṭha mutually related ?

It is well-known and stated often enough that the Padapāṭha does not add anything new to the Saṁhitāpāṭha[1], but gives as good an analysis of the Saṁhitāpāṭha as the ancient Indian grammatical science was in a position to do. If we had only the Saṁhitāpāṭha, without difficulty we could have produced from it a similar or **[382]** in many respects even better Padapāṭha. The opposite would be impossible. Numerous genuine and important peculiarities of the Saṁhitā-text have been effaced in the Pada-text, and must be effaced in accordance with the whole practice followed in the Padapāṭha; these could never be stored from it, at least not with the scientific means offered by the Indian grammarians. The tradition which has preserved for us those peculiarities must be, according to the nature of the subject, a very old one reaching far behind the Padapāṭha. Here it is enough just to be reminded of these things in a word; to give the details would mean providing a complete list of these indications which are known to every student of the Veda. If we further add the numerous cases in which the

---

1. We have to exclude only the stanzas of the Ṛk-text which, quite peculiarly, *are not analyzed in the Pada-text*: here, indeed, we have an element of useful tradition which is peculiar to the Padapāṭha. On this see further below.

Padapāṭha gives a wrong text, i.e., a text that rests on an unmistakably wrong interpretation of the Saṁhitāpāṭha, then it becomes evident that the Saṁhitāpāṭha is definitely the older and the Padapāṭha definitely the younger text.

I do feel, however, that the factors touched on here are not sufficient to give a final decision on the question of the relative age of the two Pāṭhas. In a certain respect there remains a gap in what has been established. Even though the Saṁhitāpāṭha contains at numerous places readings which are old and, in point of the authority of the tradition infinitely superior to those in the Padapāṭha, it also reveals, as we saw, the thorough influence of certain late phonetic theories due to which the text has undergone far-reaching transformations. Cannot these younger and the youngest phases of grammatical activity directed towards the Saṁhitāpāṭha belong to the same age as that of the Padapāṭha, perhaps having their origin in the same workshops as those of the latter? In fact, Weber is **[383]** in favour of their contemporaneity in his investigations on the Padapāṭha of the Taittirīya Saṁhitā (Indische Studien XIII.2). "The composition of the Padapāṭha", he says, "presumably went on hand in hand with the *redaction* of the Saṁhitā itself; it was, in fact, also a work which satisfied the same necessity. They form, as it were, the *first* authentic commentary of the Saṁhitā". If we apply this general proposition of Weber to the Ṛgveda in particular, then it would mean that the redaction of the Ṛk-Saṁhitāpāṭha must have been executed by Śākalya himself, the author of the Padapāṭha, or at least by someone closely connected with the activity of Śākalya.

I believe that with this we have definitely moved a step forward, albeit not a big step. Of course, we cannot expect that we will be offered extensive materials to examine the above view. If we can prove a period earlier than that of the Pada-text not just for the *old text-form,* which is transparent at several places in our Saṁhitā, but also for the transmitted *redaction* of this saṁhitā, then naturally there should appear traces of an older science, unknown to the Padakāra, just in those points that concern not the *old* form of the text, but *the redaction which has been based on it,* and its technical procedure. The fact that traces of that type are almost completely absent is understandable. In an overwhelmingly large number of instances where the Saṁhitā has been changed due to phonetic diaskeuasis, the Saṁhitā- and the Pada-text are simply and naturally so opposed to each other, as in fact they should be in accordance with the principles on which the text of the two Pāṭhas rests. But, as far as I can tell, there exists at least one group of instances which exactly fits the direction of our enquiry. [384] Several nom. sg. fem. forms of stems of root nouns in *-ā* appear in the Saṁhitā-text always *without this final -ā vowel ever coalesceing with the vowel that follows.* These instances, according to the enumeration of Lanman[1] and the Prātiśākhya (Sūtra 163), are the following: VI.75.3 *jyā iyam*; VII.32.14 *śraddhā it*; VIII.48.14 *nidrā īśata;* X.4.1 *prapā asi*; X.129.5 *svadhā avastāt.* Why did the arrangers of the Saṁhitā-text, in accordance with the practice they followed elsewhere, not bring about contraction? We cannot say that the contraction was not carried out because the old, genuine text recognizable by the metre did not show contraction, since there are numerous cases which prove that this consideration did not weigh with the diaskeuasts[2]. Lanman is therefore no doubt right when he assumes that these nominatives were looked upon as ending in *-āḥ* by the redactors of the Saṁhitā-text and hence, quite naturally, contraction was ruled out. As is well-known, this interpretation of the forms is not only quite possible, but the great percentage of cases in which the

---

1. Noun-inflection 444; cf. Aufrecht Ṛgveda II², p. V note 1; Weber, Ind. Stud. XIII.104 note 2.
2. Only in the cases of nasalization (*pathā̃ anehasā* and other instances of a similar nature), which we shall discuss below, do we have, perhaps, to assume that the diaskeuasts showed some regard for this consideration. But the introduction of nasalizations appears to be older than that phase of the diaskeuasis in which vowel-contractions were carried out.

metre demands the (apparent) hiatus makes it appear almost certain, when compared with the much less frequent hiatus occurring in forms which really end in *-ā* [see below p. 385 f. note 1]. The author of the Padapāṭha, however—and this has also been stressed by Lanman—obviously misled by the nominative endings in *-ā* of stems which later became more and more frequent, set up the forms as *jyā, śraddhā,* etc. The result **[385]** was that the occurrence of the hiatus in the Saṁhitā text became an inexplicable peculiarity which has been specially noted as such in the Prātiśākhya (loc. cit.). Moreover, quite similar to these nominatives in *-ās* must have been, obviously, the case of the two other instances listed in the same Sutra of the Prātiśākhya: the case of *manīṣā agniḥ* I.70.1 and of *ayā īśānaḥ* I.87.4. In the first passage the arrangers of the Saṁhitā obviously did not carry out contraction because they correctly recongnized the acc. pl. *manīṣās,* and in the second the nom. sg. *ayās.* The Padapāṭha, however, wrongly assumed the forms to be *manīṣā* and *ayā* (cf. analogous situation in Lanman 363). Thus, in the above instances, we have quite a number of clear cases in which not only the Saṁhitā-text—which is quite often the case—shows itself superior to the Pada-text for the elements which it has *preserved of the old tradition,* but also, in one point, *the younger phonetic diaskeuasis* which has brought about the vowel contractions, etc. We have to attribute to the arrangers of the text contractions like *śukraitu* for *śukrā etu, madhyamendra* for *madhyamā indra.* Since they did not carry out contraction in the case of *jyā iyam, nidrā īśata, ayā īśānaḥ,* we have to say that they have demonstrated a more thorough knowledge, a more correct judgement, of the word-forms than what is to be found in Śākalya's Padapāṭha and Śaunaka's Prātiśākhya[1].

1. It would be in order to add here a few more remarks to what has already been said by Lanman regarding certain facts similar to the cases of *jyā iyam,* etc. L. (444) notes that the Saṁhitā text correctly gives in X.129.5 *svadhā avastāt,* but it is inconsistent since it reads in X.165.6 *svadhāsīt,*

(Continued on next page)

[386] Of course the possibility that isolated details of the Saṁhitāpāṭha, even after the conclusion of the comprehensive activity of the diaskeuasts, of which the introduction of the vowel-contractions forms one part, may have undergone changes before receiving their present form cannot be totally ruled out. But it may nevertheless be looked upon as sufficiently established that the principal characteristic peculiarities of Sandhi of the Saṁhitā-text were already present there *before* Śākalya[1]. On the other hand, we

(Continued from previous page)

and in V.34.1 *svadhāmitā* with unjustified contraction. But can it not be that in both these cases we have the nom. *svadhā* which is also to be found in the Ṛgveda (Lanman. 445), and which, in accordance with the principles of diaskeuasis, should have undergone contraction? In I.165.6 I think that the metre allows contraction, and hence the form in *-ā* is quite probable (Grassmann also scans the stanza this way; see under *svadhā* 1); in V.34.1 that form is at least quite admissible, and the occurrence of the hiatus in the original metrical text would [386] be motivated, as in a number of similar cases (see the immediately following remark), by the caesura. With regard to the nom. sg. of the feminine stems which do not have finally a root in *-ā*, the very instructive statistical account given by Lanman (355 ff.) clearly demonstrates the effort of the Vedic poets to avoid hiatus. Among the 1053 cases of such nominatives, there are only 27 where within a pāda hiatus is possible after *-ā;* this hiatus has been eliminated with the help of contraction in the Saṁhitā-text 23 times, which is in accordance with the principle of diaskeuasis; in four cases (cf. Prātiśākhya 163) the tradition preserves it. These numerical proportions alone show that the phonetic shape of these forms is different from that of the nominatives of the stems having finally a root in *-ā*, due to the extraordinary frequency of (there only apparent) hiatus which is observed in their case. It must be added that the hiatus of the nominatives in *-ā*, is largely motivated by the caesura (in 12 of the 27 cases), which softened the (metrical) harshness, but was not necessary for the forms in *-ā* [*s*]. The four cases of hiatus mentioned above, occurring even in the traditional Saṁhitā-text, pertain to the words *īṣā* (one case) and *manīṣā* (three cases, which are all to be attributed to caesura). The identical treatment of these outwardly similar words just fits the work-style of the diaskeuasts; the motive could have been given by the *apparent* hiatus in respect of *manīṣā* I.70.1 discused above [p. 385].

1. In this respect I agree with Roth who characterizes the Pada-scholars as "expounders of a text neither composed, nor even edited by them". (KZ XXVI.47).

can hardly think of a considerable interval between the great phonetic diaskeuasis and Śākalya. This is shown on the one hand by the features, described above, which prevent us from pushing back the date of the diaskeuasis right into the time of the Brāhmaṇas proper, and on the other **[387]** by the fact that the far-reaching orientation with regard to many special ideas, authoritative at the time of the Saṁhitā-text redaction, can still be found in the Prātiśākhya of Śaunaka, a work which is later than the Padapāṭha of Śākalya[1].

After these remarks on the chronolgy of the redaction which gave the Veda-text its definitive phonetic form, we shall now turn to a discussion of some special spheres of phonetic phenomena, chosen as far as possible as models which will illustrate the principal types of activity of the diaskeuasts and the method of investigation which is employed for their discovery. It is of course understood that in the following investigation it is not possible to distinguish at every step between the phonetic form obtained *due* to the diaskeuasis and the one which was obtained *before* it during the older phases of the tradition, although this may be possible in the final results of a given favourable case: the changes made in the text according to a certain plan in the former and the more natural corruptions in the latter would, as a rule, so overlap each other that distinguishing them separately becomes impossible. The discussions to which we must now turn will to some extent fill in the deficiencies of our earlier expositions on the older history of the text: the data with which we operated there could lead us only to the word-form in the text, but not to its phonetic details. While we busy ourselves here with the latter, we will **[388]** come across much which, when looked at from the point of view of the chronology of the text-history, may have to be assigned, with greater or lesser probability, to that earlier period.

1. Cf., e.g., the discussions on the Abhinịhita sandhi further below.

Throughout we shall have to stick to our final goal, viz., that the way must be found to restore the genuine, original phonetic form of the text. In view of this goal we will find it quite frequently necessary to examine the materials available in each case in the light of a definite, constantly recurring point of enquiry: we must be able to find out the standards which help us to determine *the relationship between the rule and its exception* at all places where the tradition follows certain phonetic rules and then violates them with exceptions. While considering the subjects which almost all pertain to the sphere of the Prātiśākhya, one will be surely led to such cases. Should we then rely on the conclusion which is often drawn that the diaskeuasts would not have violated the rule had not the old, fixed tradition, which we must respect, forced them to do so ? Or, should the correct approach of the critic be to recognize a levelling hand which removed from the the text exceptions in favour of a rule whenever it was possible to formulate one with sufficient certainty? In other words, we have to learn to judge from the rules and the exceptions occurring side by side what should be looked upon as inconsistencies of the old, genuine text, what as errors of the tradition propagating the text, and what as distortions due to the diaskeuasts who have worked through it.

The Abhinihita Sandhi

[389] To accomplish the above task, it seems to me that one group of features is extremely instructive, since with this group the metre almost everywhere shows with certainty what the true form of the text in every case must be: the treatment of the final *e* and *o* (or *as*) and the following initial *a*. As is well known, the tradition allows in some places the *abhinihita sandhi* to occur—the merging of *a* with *e* or *o*; in other places the vowels are allowed to stand next to each other without change. That in the original form of the text both possibilities[1] had their rightful place is shown by the metre. To assess the value of the tradition it is necessary to find out how far the diaskeuasis has been successful in demarcating correctly the two types of treatment. In order to demonstrate the relevant relationship I have collected the passages beginning from X.90 up to the end of the tenth Maṇḍala[2]. It became immediately clear that a far-reaching relationship, in fact, does exist between the genuine form of the passages concerned and the form in which they now appear in the traditional text. For example, in X.90 *pādosya* is found in st. 3 and st. 4, *brāhmaṇosya* in st. 12, but *vasanto asya* in st. 6, *virājo adhi* in st. 5, etc., and in every case **[390]** the metre confirms the reading, so that we cannot misjudge a certain tendency on the part of the diaskeuasis to preserve in individual cases the treatment of the text required by its original nature. In the text specified above I have counted in all :

(1) cases where the traditional text has brought about the Abhinihita sandhi correctly : 19 ;
(2) cases where the sandhi has correctly not been brought about : 211 ;
(3) the sandhi has incorrectly been brought about : 22 ; and
(4) the sandhi has incorrectly not been brought about: 1.

The diaskeuasis has thus correctly recognized, or perhaps we may better say, correctly known all cases, except

---

1. We understand these here only in their general, approximate nature, i.e., where the two syllables are allowed to stand we speak of *e* + *a*, *o* + *a*, and at this stage we do not try to determine what the exact nature of the first syllable, here simply expressed as *e* or *o*, is.
2. While doing this I have omitted the cases where the two vowels are at the end and the commencement of two Pādas. Here, in fact, the sandhi never takes place, but in the traditional text, it always takes place except at the *avasāna* (Prātiś. 138). These textual distortions, isolated in themselves and arising due to an understandable whim of the diaskeuasts, may be left out in the following discussion.

one(X.108.5) where sandhi had to be made. Besides, it brings about the sandhi in a number of places where it does not belong. These are the following—we arrange them into groups, the significance of which will be immediately clear:

I		II	
X.94.4	*krośantovidan*	X.95.6	*añjayoruṇayo*
99.4	*yahvyovanīr*	115.9	*ṛṣayovocan*
101.1	*indrāvatovase*	126.4	*supraṇītayoti*
102.1	*indrovatu*	5	*svastayeti*
	nova	95.5	*purūravonu*
107.11	*devāsovatā*	100.9	*vasavostu*
109.1	*tevadan*	185.1	*avostu*
113.7	*tamova*		
			III
120.7	*dadhiṣevaram*	X.95.5	*mevyatyai*
171.2	*śirova*	99.8	*śyenoyopāṣṭir*
177.2	*gandharvovadat*	181.3	*tevindan*
182.2	*novatu*		

When one compares these cases among themselves and with the Prātiśākhya, the source of the mistake becomes clear. **[391]** In the first group where an *a* has disappeared after *o* or *e*, there always follows *v* and a short vowel after it. In the second group *a* which has disappeared is preceded by *-ayo, -aye,* or *-avo.* In both these cases the Prātiśākhya (139, 141) expressly prescribes the Abhinihita sandhi. Thus, here, the correct demarcation of the cases with or without sandhi has been interfered with a dogma—I have not been able to determine how it arose—which has been forced on the text by the arrangers of the Saṁhitāpāṭha without any regard for the metre. The author of the Prātiśākhya knows not only the cases where the unsuitable rule has been applied but also knows the rule itself. Besides these cases, 19 in all, there remain only three which form our third group: these are isolated cases and I cannot discover any principle to which the mistakes contained in them can be ascribed

(Prātiśā. 144.4, 6; 151.7). Other examples of similar mistakes from all parts of the Ṛgveda are to be found in the passages cited in the Prātiśākhya 142 ff.

One will not find this discussion of the traditionally transmitted text and its mistakes superfluous with regard to any point, because we, on our part, can here restore the original text without difficulty. The less we have to refer to the transmitted text in this case, in order to reach the genuine text, the surer can we be of establishing a measure of dependability of this tradition and this we will find necessary in judging the other doubtful points of the text-treatment. The critique of the tradition, which we have employed here, enables us to give the following judgement: on the whole, the tradition has preserved what is correct; where it becomes necessary we should accept it as a useful guide in our search for what is correct. **[392]** Its defects lie mainly in its acceptance of some arbitrarily discovered principles on the basis of which the text has been forcibly altered. These principles, lacking in every conceivable rationale, must in themselves appear to us suspicious, even if the mistakes introduced into the text by application of these principles cannot be proved with the help of the metre. It was discovered that the Prātiśākhya correctly knew the principles followed by the diaskeuasis, which in the eye of Śaunaka, of course, are real rules valid for the Vedic text. Finally, it was discovered that by the side of those systematic distortions carried out on the traditional text there remains a small number of isolated mistakes whose existence must be accepted as a fact which cannot be explained any further, and with regard to which, as one can see, it would be quite pointless to treat their inexplicability as an indication of their justification[1] (to exist).

1. Thus, in order to use a rule obtained here through some other cases, it would be wrong to look for the grounds due to which in IX.107.1 (Prāt. 334) is written *parīto ṣiñcata,* or in X.63.5 (Prāt. 177) *maho ādityān,* or in VII.33.5 (Pr. 176) *tatāreva* (= *tatāra eva*), or in VIII.9.9 (Pr. 177)

(Continued on next page)

Quite surely we cannot rule out the possibility that the traditional text, just in the points discussed here, has been better preserved than on the average **[393]** because the metre in these cases could have materially contributed to guard against mistakes. In fact, I would like to say that at least in the older phase of the tradition, when the consciousness of the metre was more alive, this possibility is not incorrect; we may have to judge differently the case of later diaskeuasis since this is, as is well known, characterized by scant regard for the metre.

We now turn to other cases in which we examine the transmission of the Vedic sound inventory and try to learn the rules or practices observed by the representatives of this tradition.

Long Final Vowel in the Saṁhitā-text as Opposed to the Short Vowel in the Pada-text

We will occupy ourselves with the appearance of forms with long final vowel (*yenā, bharatā, abhī* etc.), which, as is well known, are on the whole *metri causa* and occur beside the more usual forms which show the short vowel, (*yena, bharata, abhi*) and which appear in place of them in the Padapāṭha. We may be permitted to restrict our discussion to the consideration of the final vowels. Benfey's detailed work on the quantitative differences between the Saṁhitā- and the Pada-texts has considerably lightened the task of reviewing the data and judging the numerous individual cases; thus we are spared the necessity of giving a description embracing

(Continued from previous page)

aśvineva (= *asvinā eva*). Such matters simply belong to the sphere of the irrational, which one who busies himself with the traditionally transmitted text has to accept, and one who wants to reach for the original text has to correct. The latter two cases cited above, incidentally, are especially characteristic. The anomalous contraction here goes beyond the Pāda-end; we thus see that by the side of the phenomena which are quite surely unoriginal, like the sandhi at the Pāda-boundary, there also occur anomalies of that type—a clear indication to show how wrong it would be to attribute to them some kind of historical significance.

all the details. But that great scholar was not granted the opportunity to answer a number of questions that arise in this particular sphere and which are most essential and decisive for the textual history of the Veda. **[394]** As far as possible we shall try to provide answers to these questions.

The conditions to which the investigation of the quantitative differences between vowels is subjected entail that here we can make only considerably less headway in achieving certainty, than in the case of the Abhinihita sandhi. We can say with certainty almost everywhere where we must read *yo' asmai* and where *yosmai;* but one is not in a position to judge with the same certainty whether the Vedic poet chose the form *bharata* or *bharatā* in syllables 5 – 7 of the Triṣṭubh.

We shall first try to present the basic facts regarding the alternation of the above type of pairs exactly as they are observed in the traditional text. Next, we follow this presentation step by step, in so far as we have clues to do so, to deal with the question how far the traditional text can be justified. In this way we may hope to discover at least part of the passages in which the tradition has failed to preserve the correct form, whether it was misled by the incorrect principles of diaskeuasis, or it made simple mistakes.

First we have to determine *which* end-vowels are *capable* of being lengthened[1]. Next, under which conditions, especially under which metrical conditions, the lengthening, in fact, occurs.

Benfey has already drawn attention (Quantitäsversch. II.80) to the fact that in the instances which have an unlenghened end-vowel in positions of the stanza which

1. For the sake of brevity, we will take the liberty of using the expression "lengthening" of short vowels also in such cases where actually a form with a short vowel, which is more commonly used, occurs side by side with a form with a long vowel, which is less common and occurs only under certain conditions.

[395] specially favour lengthening, the end-vowel *i* is of remarkable frequency. But closer examination reveals that the traditional text gives the vowel *i* as long quite often in certain endings, never in others. From this one is led to make an observation that, judging from the traditional text, in certain words or endings the end-vowel is very much exposed to lengthening; in some other words and endings the lengthening seldom occurs, in still others not at all. The end-vowel, e.g., of verbal forms in *-ta, -tha, -tana, -ma, -sva,* of imperatives in *-a, -hi, -dhi,* of instrumentals in *-ena,* of some adverbs like *atra,* etc. is amenable to lengthening to a specially high degree. The final vowel, for example, of the genitive in *-asya* (Lanman 338), the locative in *-i* (Lanman 411, 426), is rarely lengthened; the one found in the dative in *-āya,* the neuter nom. pl. in *-i,* the verbal forms ending in *-mi, -si, -ti,*[1] *-nti, -tu, -ntu* is never lengthened.

Can we take this opposition, so striking in the *transmitted* Ṛk-text, between the final vowels which can be lengthened and those which always remain short, back to the period of the ṛṣis themselves ? It is not difficult to ascertain this: if, for instance, *avată* had at the time of the composition of the hymns a metrical validity different from that of *avatŭ, tarată* from *taratĭ,* then we may expect that the appearance and non-appearance of these words at definite places in the metrical scheme would give us indications which are independent of the possible errors of the diaskeuasts. In fact, we do get unambiguous indications of such kind. Thus, according to M. Müller's word-index *avata* occurs in all at **[396]** 10 places, among them five times in such a way that the word-final happens to be in a position which requires a long vowel—and here the traditional text gives *avatā.* In contrast, among its 15 occurrences *avatu* has its final vowel only in three places requiring length (X.100.1; 103.7; 182.2), *and in all the three cases u is long by position.* Thus, quite apart from the diaskeuasis and the tradition, for the authors of

1. I find only *one* exception II.26.4; *uruṣyatīm aṁhaso rakṣatī riṣaḥ.*

the hymns themselves this *u* could not be used metrically the same way as the final *a* of *avata.—tarata* occurs only twice, and in one of these two places it occurs where the metre requires a long final vowel; *tarati* occurs in all at seven places, and among these at four places where a long *i* would suit the metrical scheme—but at three places out of these four the length is obtained by position, and at one place (IX.96.15) by the contraction of vowels *taratīd*, so that here also it is clear that *tarati* by itself was not, for metrical purposes, equal to *tarata.—paśyata* has in one of the six passages where it occurs a long final vowel as required by the metre, and at one other passage a long final which is at least in keeping with the metrical preference; *paśyati* (8 passages) never shows a long final, nor does it occur at any place where it would be required.—*dhāvata* (6 passages) occurs in three places in positions such that the lengthening of *a* becomes metrically necessary. Beside these, *dhāvatā* is found once at a place where the lenthening is not directly required. In contrast to this *dhāvati* (17 passages) and *dhāvatu* (4 passages) never occur at a place in the stanza where length of the final vowel would become necessary.

It cannot thus be doubted that in the phenomenon of "lengthenings" a certain quality of the vowel concerned has a role to play, which was considered to be present only in certaïn definite cases, not so much by the arrangers of the text, but rather **[397]** by the authors of the hymns themselves. It is not our task to clarify the contexts of linguistic history where this relationship belongs; we will only state that in distinguishing between the vowels which can and which cannot be lengthened the *tradition* of the Vedic text has preserved correctly a feature which can confidently be traced back to the period of the composition of the hymns[1]—

1. From what has been said one can see where the fundamental error in Benfey's presentation of the lengthenings in the sixth, the eighth, and the tenth places in the metrical sequence lies (Zweite Abh. über die

(Continued on next page)

preserved obviously not in the form of a rule known to it (we cannot expect that kind of knowledge for the diaskeuasts, and the Prātiśākhya does not show even a trace of it), but in faithful preservation of the correct pronunciation at those places, or at least at the great majority of them, which is governed by that rule.

We now turn to the question: *at which places in the metre* do the lengthenings occur? The most clear place, of course, is the one relating to the *end portion* of the stanza. Accordingly, the *sixth* syllable of the Gāyatrī metre, the *eighth*, and the *tenth* syllables of the Triṣṭubh and the Jagatī metres are, as has also been correctly stressed in the description of the Prātiśākhya, the principle places for lengthenings; in these positions the tradition gives, except for a few cases, all the vowels which are prone to lengthening as **[398]** long. Thus, the final syllable of the instrumentals in *-ena* appears almost always long in the above positions; Lanman (p. 332) gives 27 cases of this kind with the lone exception of VIII.66.9 : *keno nu kaṁ śromatena na śuśruve.* For the very numerous cases of lengthening in the forms of second person plur. in *-ta* and *-tha,* there is no exception at all; for the hardly less numerous cases of 2. sing. imperatives in *-hi, -a, -sva* there occur negligibly few exceptions recorded by Benfey (2. Abh.): s.v. *ūrṇuhi, kṛṇuhi, dīdihi, dhāva, rakṣa, sṛja, māsva*—the instance noted by him under *dhāraya* is only an apparent one. Of course, with regard to the word-classes which show lengthenings, only occasionally and by way of exception the case turns out to be different; thus, in

---

(Continued from previous page)

Quantitäts-verschiedenheiten). Benfey, following the Prātiśākhya, looks upon lengthening as a general rule and cites the passages in which lengthening does not occur as exceptions (p. 46 ff.). It was necessary to confine the rule to certain words and endings, whereby the exceptions would have been eliminated to a great or greater extent, besides, what is more, suggestions for improvements would have been prevented, e.g., the suggestion *surabhīṇī vyantu* made by Benfey (II.27) for ṚV VII.1.18 or *tanayāyā svarvit* for I.96.4.

the case of voc. sgs. of *-a* stems, for which there occur only a few cases of lengthening (*abhi tvā vṛṣabhā sute* etc., Lanman 339), there appear numerous examples where no lengthening takes place (Benfey II.50 s.v., *indra*); similarly, with genitives in *-asya* (Lanman 338 ; contrary examples are Benfey II s.v. *asya, mānuṣasya,* etc).

Our judgement on the treatment of the situations described here as transmitted by the tradition can on the whole only be one which fully confirms the traditional text. We have no reason to suppose that the almost exceptionless lengthenings, in cases which are most prone to it, are artificial; we have already noted that the great frequency with which the Vedic poets used just these end-vowels in places which demanded length—in the end-portion of the stanza—proves that they were accustomed, in fact, to pronounce those vowels long when required. I am not sure, however, what our judgement should be regarding the exceptions to the lengthenings. Can we really, for example, judge that *śromatenă* **[399]** (VIII.66.9) has been correctly preserved when it is opposed by the otherwise exceptionless tradition which gives 27 cases of *-enā* in analogous metrical conditions? It seems to me that we would be justified in assuming here a mistake similar to the one in the execution of the Abhinihita sandhi. We have already seen, while examining the Abhinihita sandhi, that we do come across, although in a relatively small number, clear, undeniable *mistakes* in the traditional text. Our faith in the tradition would have to be more unlimited than justifiable after carrying out the tests of the investigation, if we should hesitate to apply such a clear rule to the stray exceptions which the traditional text offers.

Of course, we cannot think of undertaking a similarly confident attempt to bring about uniformity in the text when we come to the sphere that lies midway between the vowels which can be lengthened and which cannot. As a matter of fact it is not improbable that the boundaries between the spheres of the vowels which lent themselves to lengthening and those which did not were not drawn with absolute sharpness and were not drawn the same way by all the Vedic poets. We shall not, therefore, lightly venture to remove from the text what we actually find in the case of, let us say, the vocatives in *-a* and genitives in *-asya.* We shall have, on the whole, just to trust the text that is, on the whole, preserved by the tradition[1]; all the more so, **[400]** for there is no occasion to suspect that in these cases the tradition has been guided by some arbitrary principles. At the same time it is true that in this sphere of fluctuations we cannot look upon any one particular detail as correctly attested and leaving no room for doubt. This is not a decisive result, but the nature of the facts with which we have to deal here do not permit us to go beyond it.

If we now turn our attention from the closing portion of the verse to its commencement, then it is understandable that its metrically less sharp nature, with which the latter distinguishes itself from the former, endows it with an indecisive character in regard to the phenomenon of the lengthenings. We first take up the *second* syllable in the metrical ordering: here we do not recognize, and on metrical grounds also do not expect a distinction between the eight-syllabled,

1. How are we to judge, for example, *a* of *upa* in four passages when, occurring as it does in the end-portion of the stanza, it should have been lengthened but occurs *without* lengthening? These are all Triṣṭubh sequences ending in *upa naḥ.* Benfey (II.54) finds that here we have "one of the greatest inconsistencies in the text of the Veda". I think, rather, that everything is in favour of showing the traditional text with *upă* as correct, because, obviously, the *a* of *upa* was not looked upon by the Vedic poets as capable of lengthening. We reach this conclusion on the basis of the fact that such a frequent preposition as *upa* has an extraordinarily rare occurrence (just those four cases) in the end, as also in the beginning of the verse where it could be counted as *upā.* Where the *a* of *upa* has to occupy the place of a long syllable it occurs almost always in position; the *a* as the second syllable of the Pāda, unless it is long due to position, is almost without an exception followed by a long vowel. Therefore, there is no question of inconsistency if *upa* is found written in a form in which, from all counts, it was known to the Vedic poets, i.e., with short *a.*

the eleven-syllabled, and the twelve-syllabled metres. We have spoken above of the poets' dislike to allow a sequence of two short syllables in the second and the third place in a metrical line; it is therefore natural to expect that lengthenings will be used as a means to avoid such a sequence. On the basis of this assumption let us then examine the distribution of the long and short syllables in the case of some more common words. We will examine, for example, **[401]** the 17 cases[1] in which *jahi* occurs at the beginning of a pāda. In 5 cases there follows a short syllable, in 12 a long. Among these 17 cases, we find that the traditional text thrice gives *jahī,* 14 times *jahi,* and it is to be noted that all the three cases are to be found among those five where a short syllable follows; only twice, or, if one chooses, once, in the identical passages IV.22.9=VII.25.3 (*jahi vadhar*) do we find a short *i* followed by a short syllable.

The case of *kṛdhi* (Benfey III.13 ff.) is similar to *jahi.* Of the 9 passages where *kṛdhi,* occurring at the beginning of a pāda, is followed by a short syllable, seven[2] show the long final *i* in the traditional text; among the 7 passages where a long syllable follows, only two show length.

More striking is the case of *yatra* (Benfey III.26). This word occurs at the beginning of the pāda[3] 20 times when it is followed by a short syllable; among these, 18 times it is written as *yatrā*[4]. Before a long syllable, it occurs 33 times, of which 8 times it occurs in the form of *yatrā*[5]. The few

---

1. Benfey, Quantitätsversch. III.15. Of course, we do not take into account those cases where *i* is long due to position; similarly, not VI.44.11 *jahy asuṣvīn.*
2. Perhaps, one (II.9.5) of the two passages where length does not occur is to be explained on the ground that *kṛdhi* is there immediately preceded by another *kṛdhi* with a position following it and hence, naturally without the lengthening of *i.*
3. Of course, leaving out the cases where the final *a* occurs in position.
4. Of the remaining two cases I.164.3, VI.16.17, the latter has *yatra* perhaps because the following word *kva* (read *kua*) makes at least apparent position.
5. Among these eight passages there are 3 where *yatrā* is followed by *naḥ,* 2 where it is followed by *somasya;* presumably in each of these two groups a mistake occurring at one place has influenced the others.

cases where *tatra* occurs (Benfey III.16) lead to a similar result.

tena (Bf. III.18; Lanman 332) with a lengthened final occurs in five passages of which four are followed by a short syllable. The 5 examples which Benfey **[402]** gives of *tena* with a short final *a* are always followed by a long syllable[1].—*yena*[2] with a short *a* before a long syllable occurs 36 times, before a short syllable 13 times; in contrast to this, with a long *ā* before a long syllable 5 times, before a short syllable 16 times[3]; thus we see that about three-fourths of the cases of both types follow the rule.

We may further note two cases each of *sedha* and *hata*, and four which pertain to *vardha* (Benfey III.35, 39): *sedhā janānām*, but *sedha rājan*; *hatā makham*, but *hata vṛtram; vardhā no' amavat, vardhā samudram* (twice), but *vardha śubhre.* Finally, we may draw attention to *abhi*, repeated nine times[4] at the beginning of a pāda in the tṛca IX.97.49-51. The distribution of length in this case is as follows: *abhi vāyum, abhi mitrāvaruṇā, abhi vastrā, abhi dhenūḥ, abhi candrā, abhi viśvā, abhi yena*—but, on the other hand, *abhī naram, abhī*

1. Among Benfey's examples there are two where find *tenā no*, three where we find *tena no*. In the first two cases a vowel follows *no;* the *nas* is thus a short syllable. In the other three cases—we have to add to these the remaining three cases, not mentioned by Benfey, where we find *tena no* or *tena naḥ:* V.62.9; VII.69.5; VIII.54.5—every time a consonant follows, so that we have length for *nas* due to position. The changing prosodic value of '*no*' depending on the sound that followed, the dependence of *tena* or *tenā* on the quantity of the following syllable, and above all the excellence of the tradition which has so clearly preserved this relationship cannot stand the test more strikingly than in the distribution of length and shortness in these eight cases.
2. Benfey III.31 ff.; Lanman 332, 334. Lanman emphasizes the point whether *tenā, yenā* are followed by a syllable with a short *vowel.* I cannot see how just the quantity of the vowel, without taking into consideration whether it makes position or not, can be of value here.
3. To these 16 cases I also add I.50.6 *yenā pāvaka:* an instance to show that *yenā* belongs to that early period when the old pronunciation *pavāka* was still valid. Cf. also V.22.1 *arcā pāvakaśocișe.*
4. The passages in which *i* appears as *y* or where it is contracted with the following *i* are naturally to be omitted.

no' arṣa: Thus, we have seven times *abhi*, **[403]** and just in these seven instances it is followed by a long syllable; twice *abhī* occurs, and on both these occasions a short syllable follows.

One therefore need not have any hesitation in setting up a rule which could be looked upon, on the whole, as valid, viz., that the vowels which are prone to lengthening occur as long when they stand at the second position in a pāda and are followed by a short syllable in the third position, and they occur as short if they are followed by a long syllable in the third position. Our investigations into the metre give us here a key to understand correctly such an apparent irregularity in handling the lengths, and the understanding thus obtained confirms vice versa the results of our metrical investigation. Evaluation of the exceptions which are extraordinarily more numerous here than at the end-portions of the verses is, however, quite difficult. The possibility that the author of the hymn himself was less consistent in his composition is not to be absolutely rejected. On the other hand, it is not surprising if the fixing of the quantity of the second syllable, about whose basis the diaskeuasts were obviously not clear, suffered in the course of transmission more severely here than at the sixth or the eighth syllable, whose nature was much more clear and was also known to the author of the Prātiśākhya. I do not think it is possible to speak here in terms of absolute certainty, but I cannot suppress the opinion that a critic who claims far-reaching authority for removing the exceptions would seem to me to have the probability rather in his favour than against. I believe that a group of examples which almost constantly agree with the rule speak more *in favour of* a fixed practice followed by the hymn-authors than other groups, even when more numerous, which do not agree with the norm, speak *against* it (i.e. a fixed practice). If a certain practice followed by the authors is not steady, **[404]** then the fluctuations would occur rather equally distributed everywhere. How is it then that, for example, the imperatives *sedha* and *vardha* are treated such that they agree with the rule, while *piba*[1], *bodha, śikṣa,* and *bhava* have their final vowel lengthened almost everywhere, oddly enough even before a position? Or, if in the case of *kṛdhī̆ nas* and *avā̆ nas* the authors of the hymns themselves had disregarded the rule in connection with the interchange of the short and long vowels, how is it that with *tenā̆ nas* the rule has been so strictly followed, as we have shown above [p. 402, note 1]? One would therefore be inclined to suppose that where the regularity prevails, which obviously lies well beyond the horizon of the diaskeuasts, we have to see in it the old and genuine composition-technique of the ṛṣis, and, on the other hand, where in similar conditions that regularity is absent, mistakes and, in a still longer number of cases the arbitrary attempts of the diaskeuasts to regularize the texts have to be assumed. The method that was in all probability followed by the diaskeuasts in their attempts towards normalization can be imagined, e.g., from the passages where the form *śrudhi* occurs at the beginning of a pāda (Benfey III.38). Often *śrudhī havam* has been transmitted according to the rule; further we have *śrudhī na' indra* and *śrudhī no' agne* which are likewise correct. Two cases remain where a short vowel is required: *śrudhi* (actual text *śrudhī*) *no hotar and śrudhi* (so also the text) *citrāmaghe.* On the basis of the passages cited, obviously, the diaskeuast formulated the rule, which, in fact, has been given as such in the Prātiśākhya (471), that *śrudhi* before *naḥ* **[405]** has a long end-vowel, and accordingly the text was fixed as *śrudhī no hotar.* Similarly, on the basis of I.25.8, 9 *vedā ya' upajāyate, vedā ye' adhyāsate*[2], the rule (Prātiśākhya 473), which at first sight appears childish, was

1. The use of *piba* (Benfey III.19 f.) corresponds to the rule only in so far as *pibā* occurs always before a short syllable, and in the three cases where *piba* is found it is followed by a long syllable. But quite often *pibā* occurs also before a long syllable.
2. Correct text, as compared with the equally correct text *veda nāvaḥ, veda māsaḥ, veda vātasya.*

formulated that in the "Śunaḥśepa hymns" the word *veda* lengthens its final vowel before *y:* accordingly in stanza 7 there must occur *vedā yo vīnām padam,* whereas in an exactly analogous situation, but outside the Śunaḥśepa hymns, the correct text has been preserved untouched: VI.51.2 *veda yas trīṇi vidathāny eṣām.* From observations like these, we may assume confidently that also in the cases where the traditionally transmitted text disagrees with the norm much more than here—one may compare, e.g., Benfey's collections of *avā, bhavā, bodhā, śikṣā*[1] — the original text was almost consistently governed by the rule which in many cases can be detected with unmistakable clarity.

If from the second syllable we now proceed to the third and the fourth syllables of the pāda, the difficulties and uncertainties perhaps multiply. With regard to the *third* syllable[2] it is certain that by itself it does not show any predominant inclination towards length or shortness. But, contrary to the prevailing practice, if the second place, and also the fourth place in an eight-syllabled pāda have a short syllable, **[406]** then the technique adopted by the Vedic poets gives preference to a long third syllable[3]. From this point of view, a very large number of lengthenings in the third syllable result. And since *at least on the whole* they are governed by an understandable rule, which was obviously early forgotten by the Indians, they throw a favourable light on the value of the tradition. As examples of the lengthened

---

1. In the case of *bhavā, bodhā, śikṣā,* if the end-vowel occurs in the second syllable of the pāda, the lengthening *always* takes place (Benfey, s.v.), *also before position,* which clearly reveals the artificial execution by the diaskeuasts of a rule which was not correctly formulated.
2. Benfey's statement (Quant. IV.1.32) that the lengthenings in the third syllable "could scarcely be due to metrical influence" is unproved, and it stands opposed to a closer observation of the occurrence of lengthenings and improved knowledge of the metre.
3. We have spoken above [p. 16, 18, 52 fn. 1, 53, 55] of the influence of the second and the fourth syllable on the use of the third.

third syllable by the side of the second short syllable may be cited[1]:

IX.	97.36	*vardhayā vācaṁ janayā puraṁdhim*
VIII.	47.1	*rakṣathā nem aghaṁ naśat*
VI.	46.9	*yāvayā didyum ebhyaḥ*
I.	174.9	(= VI.20.12) *pārayā Turvaśaṁ Yaduṁ svasti*
I.	166.8	*pāthanā śaṁsāt tanayasya puṣṭiṣu.*

The lengthened third syllable stands by the side of the fourth short one, e.g., in the following:

VIII.	13.25	*vardhasvā su puruṣṭuta*[2]
VIII.	18.11	*yuyotā śarum asmad ā*
VIII.	45.20	*rarabhmā śavasas pate*
I.	48.1	(= V.79.3, 9) *vy ucchā duhitar divaḥ*
VII.	102.3	*juhotā madhumattamam*
III.	40.5	*dadhiṣvā jaṭhare sutam.*

In contrast to this situation in the eight-syllabled pādas, such cases occur very rarely in the eleven- and twelve-syllabled pādas; this agrees fully with metrical conditions. The **[407]** transmitted text of the instances concerned must be considered as suspect. Thus we find

I.	169.4	*tvaṁ tū na' indra taṁ rayiṁ dāḥ*
VII.	37.5	*vavanmā nu te yujyābhir ūtī.*

The correct treatment in such passages, in harmony with the metrical system, would leave the short syllable unlengthened.

Relatively often we do meet with the short syllable in the

1. For a complete survey of the materials under consideration, Benfey's collections (4th Abh.) offer help most conveniently. However, they are arranged according to words and not according to their places in the metre.
2. In contrast to this is the quite correct text in V.44.5 *vardhasva patnīr abhi jīvo' adhvare.*

second and the fourth positions if the third one is lengthened, e.g.:

I. 29.7 *jambhayā kṛkadāśvam*
VIII. 45.35 *bibhayā hi tvāvataḥ*
VI. 16.41 *bharatā vasuvittamam*
V. 79.8 *ā vahā duhitar divaḥ*
II. 41.13 *śṛṇutā ma' imaṁ havam.*

Among the rare *exceptions* are ones that show a short second syllable near a third that is capable of being lengthened but remains unlengthened, e.g.:

V. 55.9 *mṛḷata no maruto mā vadhiṣṭana*
VII. 57.6 *jigṛta rāyaḥ sūnṛtā maghāni.*

It is not easy to explain why the Vedic poets did not consistently lengthen the third syllable, when it was possible to do so, in order to avoid contiguity of two short syllables at the second and the third position, just as they seem to have done in the case of the second syllable; therefore, the few passages like the ones just cited, where lengthening has not been carried out, seem to me to be corrupt.

More frequent are those exceptions where in an eight-syllabled pāda a short syllable at the second and the fourth position occurs; equally more frequent are such exceptions where the third syllable is lengthened, although it stands between two long syllables:

[408]
I. 26.5 *mandasva sakhyasya ca*
VIII. 20.20 *vandasva maruto' aha*
IX. 42.6 *pavasva bṛhatīr iṣaḥ*
59.2 *pavasva dhiṣaṇābhyaḥ.*

VII. 32.8 *sunotā somapāvne*
VIII. 20.1 *ā gantā mā riṣaṇyata*
IX. 104.3 *punātā dakṣasādhanam, etc.*

The cases in the latter group appear especially suspicious.

If we found it necessary to consider doubtful the unmotivated lengthenings of the second syllable, which in fact prefers lengthening, then this would be all the more true in the case of the third syllable which is metrically neutral.[1] As regards the cases collected in the former group, it is not possible to give a firm judgement on account of the paucity of materials.

As indicated by the metre the *fourth* syllable of the pāda by itself prefers length, if we partly exclude the case where the caesura of the Triṣṭubh or the Jagatī follows the fourth syllable. But the phenomenon is established and so strongly pronounced in the tradition that a careful critic can hardly afford to neglect the fact that the lengthenings at the fourth position form only a fraction of the frequency with which they occur at the second position; even the vowels, which by nature are prone to lengthening, mostly remain short in the fourth position. In order to understand this we must realize that the lengthenings of the second syllable **[409]** are not explained simply as a result of the tendency to produce length at the second syllable, but rather to avoid the sequence of two short syllables in the second and third positions. A similar tendency for the third and fourth syllables can be thought of at best in an eight-syllabled pāda, but here also our metrical counting shows that the tendency is scarcely as pronounced as in the case of the second and third syllables. However, just as we saw that in order to avoid feet of the type ⏓ _ ⏑ ⏑, there occurred frequent lengthenings of the *third* syllable [p. 406], we may expect that in a similar case if a vowel capable of being lengthened was present at the fourth position, the metrical practice would be inclined to lengthen this syllable also. Cases of

1. Also here it is easily understandable that the tradition, e.g., reads *uruṣyā ṇo mā parā dāḥ* in VII.71.7 because it was misled by the justified lengthenings in I.91.15 *uruṣyā ṇo' abhiśasteḥ*, V.24.3, X.7.1 Especially numerous are the shifts which *smā̆* has suffered, and this situation appears to me as original (Benfey IV.3.26 ff); see below [p. 412].

this kind are indeed a preferred and, perhaps from the point of view of textual criticism, also the surest place for the lengthened fourth syllable; thus e.g.

V.	35.8	*ratham avā puraṁdhyā*
I.	38.13	*achā vadā tanā girā*
I.	13.11	*ava sṛjā vanaspate*
IX.	46.4	*ā dhāvatā suhastyaḥ.*

Lengthenings at the fourth position when there is a *long* third syllable (e.g. III.9.8; 41.6; V.28.6) are, to be sure, not infrequent in the transmitted text, perhaps even more frequent than those which occur in the case of the short third syllable. But they prove to be extremely rare when one compares them with the numerous cases in which after a long third a fourth syllable, capable of being lengthened, has remained without lengthening; hence, we need have no hesitation in characterizing that group of cases as text-crititically doubtful.

In the case of the eight-syllabled and the twelve-syllabled pādas we confirmed that in the event of the third syllable being short, the *second* was regularly lengthened. We do not expect the *fourth* syllable to be lengthened under similar conditions **[410]** for obvious reasons. If one surveys the cases of the lengthened fourth syllables in the traditionally transmitted text, which can be done from Benfey's collections, then one, in fact, finds that the tradition in respect of this distinction between the Gāyatrī metre and the Triṣṭubh-Jagatī[1] is, on the whole, in remarkable accord with what the metrical theory leads us to expect. Among the lengthenings a *very great* majority of cases concerns the eight-syllabled pādas. We shall illustrate this with the help of a few single words. *Piba* occurs twelve times in such a way that its *a* is in the fourth position—twice in the shorter, ten

1. Cf. I.134.3 where we read in close proximity *pra bodhayā* and *pra cakṣaya:* the former is the beginning of a Gāyatrī- the latter of a Jagatī-sequence.

times in the longer sequences. Among those two cases the transmitted text has *one* case of lengthening *agram pibā madhūnām* (IV.46.1), while among the ten other cases there is not a single example. *Sṛja* occurs thrice in such a way that its *a* occurs in the fourth position. Once *a* is lengthened in an eight-syllabled pāda (I.13.11); in two cases it is short, both in eleven-syllabled pādas (I.31.18; X.16.5). *Yadi* occurs thirteen times with its *i* in the fourth position of the pāda. In all three cases where it occurs in the eight-syllabled pādas *i* is lengthened (V.74.5; IX.14.2; X.22.10); in contrast, in eight or ten cases of eleven- or twelve-syllabled pādas it is short (I.56.4; III.31.13; IV.21.6; 26.5; 27.3; V.48.4; IX.86.46; X.61.25), and long only in III.31.6; IX.97.22, and hence in these places we shall be inclined to assume that the easily understandable confusion of the two forms *yadi* and *yadī* is either due to the transmission or to the diaskeuasis. Hence, I think we should be suspicious about all lengthenings of the fourth syllable of Triṣṭubh and Jagatī **[411]**, at least when for its motivation there is nothing more than a short third syllable. The matter, though, seems to be different when the *fifth* syllable can be taken into account for the explanation of the lengthened fourth. We have shown above [p. 54] how forcefully the metrical practice requires a long fifth syllable to compensate for the short fourth when the caesura falls after the fifth. Hence, it should appear quite probable if, in the event of the caesura occurring as described above, one took recourse to lengthening the fourth syllable in order to avoid the combination ◡ ◡ for the fourth and the fifth syllables. The material offered by the tradition fortunately appears to point in the same direction which we might expect *a priori* on metrical considerations. Among the few cases of the lengthened fourth syllable, where the caesura falls after the fifth, we find the rather strikingly frequent combination in which the fourth and fifth syllables would without lengthening form the tabooed pyrrhic. Thus we find:

I.	139.1	*adha pra sū na'*	*upa yantu dhītayaḥ*
VI.	23.8	*sa mandasvā hy*	*anu joṣam ugra*
VII.	21.9	*vanvantu smā te*	*'vasā samīke*
VIII.	13.20	*mano yatrā vi*	*tad dadhur vicetasaḥ.*

As confirmation of our interpretation of these passages, it would be useful to note that the lengthenings at the fifth position also point to the same endeavour of avoiding the combination ◡ ◡ for the syllables four and five with a caesura following it. But before we turn to a discussion of the fifth syllable, let us point out somewhat more thoroughly the shifts, introduced by the diaskeuasts under the circumstances regarding the fourth syllable discussed by us, with the help of a specially striking case that offers unusually abundant materials—the case **[412]** of the particale *sma* (Benfey IV.3.26-29). The treatment of this particle in the fourth position is, however, so closely connected with the pratice adopted by the diaskeuasts when this particle occurs in other positions of the stanza that it is impossible to treat the question in isolation; if I am not mistaken, here we come across the principal area of the diaskeuasts' arbitrariness and it is worthwhile to examine it more thoroughly.

To begin with we find that the lengthenings of *sma* at the *second* position correspond, on the whole, with the rule developed above regarding the change of quantity of the syllables in the second and third positions. Thus twice we find *ā smā ratham,* further *taṁ ṣmā ratham, ye smā purā, sa smā kṛṇoti, pra smā mināti, na smā varante;* on the other hand, *ni ṣma māvate, pra sma vājeṣu, triḥ sma māhnaḥ, ut sma vātaḥ.* Against these eleven regular cases we have only two exceptions showing lengthening at the second position when a long third syllable follows: *yaṁ smā pṛcchanti* (II.12.5), *ā smā kāmam* (VIII.24.6). We shall later [cf. p. 415 n. 1] take up the case of the first of these two exceptions and now we turn to *sma* in the *third* syllable.

Since here the second syllable is always long because of

the position made by *sma,* we have only to look to the fourth syllable. Here the rule of the alternating quantities in the case of the Gāyatrī metre is observed at least in so far as a short fourth always has *smā* before it (4 cases), but *sma* is followed by a long syllable (15 cases; solitary exception I.12.5). In contrast, exceptions having *smā* and a following long syllable occur in more than a few cases (9). In *five* of these 9 cases, *hi* (or *nahi*) precedes *smā,* in two cases *adha*; instances to be considered later will confirm our feeling that, in fact, there does exist a connection between these words and the lengthening of *sma.* **[413]** Now is it possible to suppose that in the actual usage of the Vedic poets *sma* after *adha* and *hi* was treated differently than after any other word? It seems to me quite evident that here we have to imagine a rule which in its bringing about an arbitrary connection between the condition and the effect carries the stamp of the same workshop from which originated, for example, the inventions about the Abhinihita sandhi with *-ayo, -aye,* etc., elucidated by us above [p. 391][1].

In the Triṣṭubh and the Jagatī series the expected short vowel at the third syllable has been preserved only six times, the length having penetrated to 13 passages : however, among these there are *nine* where *adha* precedes, *one* where *hi* precedes, so that here, too, we clearly notice the signs of an arbitrary revision.

Let us now turn to *sma* in the *fourth* position. We have in all 20 passages. They can be arranged into the following groups:

1. Three passages with the expected short vowel: VII.32.15; X.33.1; 86.10 (not after *hi* or *adha*).

---

1. The passages in which the lengthening after *hi* occurs in accordance with the rule and which could have provided the starting point for treating the rest of the cases are VIII.21.10; 25.15; IX.20.2. —The short vowel of *sma* is preserved only once after *adha* (V.9.5; in addition a second instance from an eleven-syllabled pāda VII.3.2), once after *nahi* (VIII.7.21).

2. One passage with the expected length due to the fifth syllable being short [see above p. 411]: VII.21.9.
3. Eleven passages having *hi ṣmā.*
4. Five passages with *smā* after a word other than *hi:* I.102.5; IV.38.8; V.53.5; X.102.6; 136.7.

[414] *Two-thirds* of the cases which show *smā* in the fourth position (the cases under 2 and 3) are immediately explained as soon as we assume the rule regarding the occurrence of *smā* after *hi,* which we have supposed the diaskeuasts have used. From among the cases in question, III.30.4 deserves to be specially emphasized because here the diaskeuasts, for the sake of their liking for *hi ṣmā,* have violated the rule, otherwise almost inviolably observed, which excludes the accumulation of lengthening and position. Similarly, as we shall see later, they did not hesitate to place *smā* after *hi* even at the end of the pāda where the lengthening is not less unusual.

Of the five cases of lengthening listed under number 4 above (*smā* after words other than *hi*), I think at least two admit of a special explanation:

I. 102.5 *asmākaṁ smā ratham ā tiṣṭha sātaye*
V. 53.5 *yuṣmākaṁ smā rathā̃ anu.*

It appears that the diaskeuasts—persuaded presumably by I.51.12; 102.3; X.29.8—assumed that *sma* lengthens its vowel before the word *ratha.*

There remain still a few remarks to add about *sma* in the *fifth* position and at *the end of a pāda.* We shall see that in general there is no occasion to expect lengthenings at the fifth position and that in the traditional text, too, they occur there only with diminishing rarity. But, according to Benfey's collections, precisely in the case of *sma* lengthening occurs in *all* six cases where the word appears at the fifth position. How this fact should be judged becomes at once clear when one observes that except in *one* case *hi always* precedes. That case is:

I. 129.2 *sa śrudhi yaḥ smā pṛtanāsu kāsu cit.*

[415] Perhaps, here, it is the relative pronoun which gave the diaskeuasts an occasion for lengthening because in all the other cases where this pronoun precedes *sma*, lengthening has taken place (I.169.5; II.12.5[1]; III.62.1).

There remains one example of lengthening at the end of a five-syllabled pāda:

IV. 10.7 *kṛtam cid dhi ṣmā -*

Which is an indication of how far the diaskeuasts have let themselves be guided by their rule to have *smā* after *hi*, and a proof, in addition to others that we shall meet in the following, to show that even at the end of a pāda the long and short vowels have been affected by the transmitter's attempts at improvement carried out at the wrong places.

Thus, the treatment of *sma* gives a clear idea of the arbitrariness with which the diaskeuasts have dealt with the text in certain points: in *certain* points because not very many features of the Vedic texts invited them so pressingly to compare and equalize different, or apparently different, features and offered to their misplaced and only half-successful attempts to bring about artificial consistency such abundant material as the occurrence of *sma* and *smā*. Also here, as in the case of the Abhinihita sandhi, we see their activity goes overwhelmingly astray in one direction, so that in their hands what is exceptional—there the *ekībhāva* of the two vowels, here the lengthening—as opposed to what is regular almost completely asserts itself in the field which belongs to it but, in addition, largely appropriates to itself the field which does not belong to it[2]. **[416]** If we succeed

1. This, perhaps, explains the passage cited above [p. 412] as an exception.
2. That the shifts have mostly gone in one direction is only natural. The text-redactors quite understandably treated the exceptions as something that they had to explain. While they searched for the conditions

(Continued on next page)

in discovering[1] the false analogies on which this extension is based and remove text-interpolations which have crept in, then is revealed to us as the basis, on which rests the treatment meted out to the text by the diaskeuasts, a tradition which has preserved quite in an astonishing way the correct text that can stand the test of our research.

But from this digression, occasioned by the treatment of *sma,* we shall return to the main topic of our investigation. We must take up for consideration the exceedingly few cases where lengthening occurs in the fifth syllable of the Triṣṭubh- or the Jagatī-series[2]. On the whole we have to note the tendency to exclude metrical lengthening in this position; I would, however, like to make an exception only of a very special case already alluded to, which, as is well known, is to be found in exceedingly rare cases, that is, a **[417]** pāda which has caesura after the fifth syllable and a short fourth syllable. In such an event the tendency prevailed to compensate the missing heaviness in the fourth syllable by lengthening the fifth. In fact, among the few available examples of a lengthened fifth, the case, in itself so rare, of a short fourth with caesura occurring after the fifth, appears

---

(Continued from previous page)

under which the exceptions occur, they found that in many places where they thought the conditions were present, the expected results were missing: then they carried out the corrections in the text. If they had put the question to themselves thus: "under which conditions do the regular phenomena occur, and not the exceptions," then of course their shifts would have been in the opposite direction.

1. It is characteristic here and everywhere that the shifts of the regular ones have preferably occurred in the case of the *more frequent* words which gave special occasion for comparison of many passages and for drawing wrong conclusions.

2. Not of the Gāyatrī of course because the metrical scheme rules out length in the fifth position. In fact, in the Ṛgveda, as far as I can see, a case of lengthening occurs in that position only *once,* V.70.4 *yakṣam bhujemā tanūbhiḥ;* however, this is a Gāyatrī pāda with a trochaic finale. In addition, cf. Benfey Quantitätsversch. IV.1.15 s.v. *iva.* We have to record a case of lengthening also at the *seventh* position in a Gāyatrī pāda of *this* kind: *anābhayin rarimā te* VIII.2.1.

three or four times, i.e., considering the overall small number of such passages, relatively frequently:

I. 87.2 *ghṛtam ukṣatā madhuvarṇam arcate*
I. 166.8 *pūrbhī rakṣatā maruto yam āvata*
V. 55.5 *ud īrayathā marutaḥ samudrataḥ.*

Perhaps also belongs here:

IX. 103.1 *bhṛtiṁ na bharā matibhir jujoṣate*[1].

The remaining cases of lengthening in the fifth syllable are to be looked upon as suspicious. The metre, in fact, did not favour a long syllable in this position, but it also did not exclude lengthening in such a way that short vowels could be protected against corruptions. In this situation we cannot expect anything but that the confusion in respect of the lengthenings, from which the traditional text is not free, should occasionally appear at this position. More than this can hardly be said on the basis of the available passages. We have already discussed the case where such confusions occur most frequently, viz., that of the particle *sma* and have expressed the special doubts which arise against the traditional text in that case. Then follows *adyā* (Benfey, IV.1.11) with its large number of occurrences :

I. 34.1 *triś cin no' adyā bhavataṁ navedasā*
[418] II. 29.6 *arvāñco' adyā bhavatā yajatrāḥ*
VI. 18.13 *pra tat te' adyā karaṇaṁ kṛtaṁ bhūt*[2].

One will not attach any great importance to these passages, when one takes into account the overwhelming number (36) of counter examples in which *adya* before the caesura shows a *short* final vowel in the fifth position. The above deviating passages obviously are to be explained as due to

1. Collections providing examples of where lengthening has not taken place in the transmitted text are not available to me ; yet I cite two passages with *yadi*: I.173.8 ; X.115.1.
2. But without lengthening VII.100.5 : *pra tat te' adya śipiviṣṭa nāma.*

the confusion easily arising from the co-occurrence of *adya* and the rather frequent *adyā* in other positions of the metre.[1]

There remain only a few scattered cases of the lengthened fifth syllable:

I.	40.6	*tam id vocemā vidatheṣu śambhuvam*
I.	61.14	*dyāvā ca bhūmā januṣas tujete*
I.	89.9	*yatrā naś cakrā jarasaṁ tanūnām*
IV.	36.7	*dhīrāso hi ṣṭhā kavayo vipaścitaḥ*
VIII.	1.1	*indram it stotā vṛṣaṇam sacā sute*[2].

No one will be surprised to see that in the traditional text confusion has taken place[3] between *bhūmā* and *bhūma;* we do find *bhūmā* for the expected *bhūma* even at the end of a pāda (I.173.6). Also the remaining passages above are hardly enough to shake the doubt that arises against the tradition.

[419] The last position within a pāda to be considered in the investigation of the lengthenings is the *seventh* of such Triṣṭubh- and Jagatī-pādas which have their caesura after the fourth syllable. The metre establishes the predominant occurrence of length in this position; length overweighs shortness in frequency by three to four times. Accordingly, the lengthenings of the syllable occur relatively many times in the traditional text, enough in any case to remove doubt about the phenomenon for which there exists also a certain inner comprehensibility. Preference for

1. One may note that in two of the three passages *bhavataṁ* or *bhavatā* follows *adyā*, while among the 36 contrary examples nowhere do these or the related words follow. As regards the third passage—*adyā karaṇam*—the stimulation for the lengthening lies possibly in I.13.2 *adyā kṛṇuhi vītaye;* X.35.2 *bhadraṁ somaḥ suvāno' adyā kṛṇotu naḥ;* cf. however X.45.9.
2. I do not reckon here the passages which contain absolutive forms in *-yā* (Benfey, IV.3.34); in the case of these forms, as Benfey has shown, the length has been preserved in altogether too many cases, so that they cannot be treated the same way as the remaining "lengthenings".
3. Perhaps the preceding *dyāvā* also has given rise to *bhūmā*.—Cf. also Lanman 531.

length—and it is only a preference—in this position was not enough to bring about more than its *occasional* occurrence; the preponderant situation of course, is absence of lengthening. Thus, for example, we get *bharatā* with lengthening at I.136.1; II.14.6,7; without it at II.14.2; 37.1; III.52.8; V.43.3; VIII.100.3; X.100.2. I cannot discover any rule here, and doubt if there is one; a division of the two forms according to the different parts of the Ṛgveda can also hardly be thought of. Obviously we are here in the domain of individual arbitrariness. Again, we may not doubt, on the basis of our experience elsewhere, that what had been realized by individual choice remained unaffected by the influences of the tradition[1]. But we have no grounds to attempt a more pertinent order or disorder than what the tradition has given us **[420]** in these, fortunately, unimportant, minor details.

Our final task in this context is to investigate the *close* of the pāda in respect of the lengthenings. What we expect *a priori,* in accordance with the metrical nature of the pāda-end, and this is confirmed by the overwhelming majority of examples, is that the lengthenings are *not* supposed to take place in that position. The few cases in which the traditional text shows exceptions offer mostly special reasons, which allow us to infer that the diaskeuasts had made wrong assumptions.

Here belong, firstly, a number of cases in which the transmitters made a mistake as to where the pāda ended and hence changed the text in accordance with the rules which presuppose a metrical structure different from the one actually existing. Here we have to consider especially the Uṣṇih consisting of three eight-syllabled and one four-syllabled pādas

1. Thus, e.g., the strikingly large area in which lengthening appears with the form *cakṛmā* (Benfey, 4.2.7 f.) seems not to be above suspicion. The fact that precisely in the case of this form the long vowel is also found in position certainly reveals the hand of the diaskeuasts, which has especially here strongly favoured the lengthenings.

and also other similar combinations containing a four-syllabled pāda. The later authorities only superficially treated these stanzas, depending almost solely on syllable count and easily assumed a twelve-syllabled pāda where, rather, there was one eight-syllabled and one four-syllabled, so that they overlooked a pāda-end. In reality, the syllable which immediately precedes the pāda-division, as is to be expected in the case of the final syllable of the Gāyatrī-pāda, is very often short; in no way, therefore, can the assumption be justified that the lengthenings should have really occurred at this position. But *a priori* one can be quite sure that the tendency to produce length at this syllable must have prevailed with the *diaskeuasts,* for, for them, it was precisely a case of the eighth syllable of a twelve-syllabled pāda. Thus, in fact, we read :

[421] V. 24.1 *uta trātā śivo bhavā varūthyaḥ.*

Similarly, VIII.12.2 *āvithā;* 12.17 *raṇā,* 12.22 *anūṣatā,* 13.5 *ā bharā,* and many more similar cases.

Similar, too, is the case with the Vimada hymns where the eight-syllabled pādas, together with the following refrain *vi vo made* or *vivakṣase,* were understood as twelve-syllabled pādas by the transmitters (cf. Prātiśākhya 918,922). Here, however, as has been already noted by Benfey (Quant. II.51), side by side with the lengthening, the syllable occurring before the refrain (X.21.4; 25.7) has occasionally preserved the short vowel.

Of the remaining few cases of final-syllable lengthening, those which are related to the particle *sma* have been already discussed above (p. 415), and it was shown that the change seen in the text was effected by the diaskeuast. Quite similar is the following case (I.25.19) which confirms our judgement given earlier :

imaṁ me varuṇa srudhī,
havam adyā ca mṛḷaya.

It is obvious, as Benfey (op. cit. IV.3.16) has observed, that the numerous passages where we otherwise get the combination *śrudhī havam* have influenced this isolated passage where the two words are distributed in two pādas. Further, we have to mention a few cases (Prātiśākhya 535 ff.; Lanman 531, 540) where the nom. acc. neut. of *-man*-stems ends in *-mā*: these are mostly plural forms. To the "lengthenings" with which we are concerned I would like only to add the *singular* in *-mā*, viz., *bhūmā* (I.73.6) already mentioned above [p. 418]. There remain some absolutives in *-ya* (Benfey IV.3.34; cf. above p. 418, fn.3), and finally the isolated passage

I.182.1 *abhūd idaṁ vayunam o ṣu bhūṣatā :*

[422] surely, considering the nature of our traditional text, no adequate proof to exempt the lengthenings at the end of the pāda from our judgement expressed above.

In continuation of the above discussions we should not fail to mention the fact that the other Vedic Saṁhitās, when citing a Ṛk-stanza, agree, although not in all cases yet certainly in an overwhelming majority of cases, with the Ṛgveda in regard to the lengthenings discussed by us. Considering the liberty with which the Ṛk-text in other respects is often treated in those Saṁhitās, this agreement in a minor point, where to a great extent the texts should be exposed to corruptions, is all the more striking. Can, in fact, such a faithful conservation of the lengthenings in the different branches of the Vedic tradition mean that the agreement between the Ṛgveda and the Sāmaveda may be looked upon as proof to show that the lengthenings concerned had been firmly established at the time when the Sāmaveda branched off? In that case, not only those phenomena in general but also their aspects where one would, according to the above discussion, have to recognize *mistakes* of the text would be of such an early age that one would have good reason to doubt the validity of the criticism such as we have attempted above[1]. But the internal contradiction consisting in the fact that from a very ancient period two texts which differ from each other [423] at every step in essential points should have yet remained in agreement with the greatest exactness in respect of such a superficial point forces us to seek a different explanation of the problem. That agreement is the result of a *later* thorough revision undertaken by the diaskeuasts of the relevant orthoepic matters. Here again the phenomenon of the Abhinihita sandhi offers a sure criterion in favour of our judgement. As in the case of the lengthenings of the short vowels, so also in the treatment of that sandhi the different Saṁhitās agree in essential points, also in the readings which can be looked upon as nothing more than accidental textual corruptions not following any rule. The mistrust which one would perhaps like to entertain against the critique of the vowel-lengthenings which feels itself free from the tradition, has no place here : here it is clear without a doubt where the mistakes lie, and scarcely less clear that these mistakes do not reach back to the old period when the knowledge of the metre was fully alive. Hence, here it is certain that the agreement among the Saṁhitās has been brought about *later :* and thus we find here—as also variously in other spheres—the traces of the equalizing activity of the diaskeuasts, who respected the more serious differences among the different Saṁhitās as fixed and revealed, while in the case of those minute details which were looked upon as falling within the range of grammatical corrections, they brought about a thorough, if not exceptionless, agreement among the different texts.

---

1. One may compare, e.g., the collections of Benfey (Quantitätsversch. III.32 ff.) for *yenā* and *yena:* in a number of cases where in accordance with the interpretation expounded above [p. 402] the traditional Ṛk-text has made a mistake in the treatment of the final vowel, the other Saṁhitās agree with the Ṛk-text.

[424] FINAL *n* (respectively *ṅ*)

In the cases discussed so far the correct demarcation of certain phonetic phenomena was only partly obliterated by the tradition. We now turn to a new field in which this demarcation has been, in certain respects, completely destroyed but in others, almost fully preserved. Such unevenness of treatment is, in fact, to be expected in cases where the normal process of linguistic development alone does not govern the phonetic phenomena but is crossed by the chance exercise of grammatical consideration, which picks up one problem, but neglects the other, the one it treats with correct understanding, the other with misplaced violence.

We take up for consideration the final sound of words that in their pada form end in *n* (*ṅ*), which, as is well-known, represents partly the original *n*, partly *ns*, partly *nt*.

Here we first meet with the well-known rule (Prāt. 391) that *n* and *ṅ* at the end of a word, when preceded by a short vowel and followed by a vowel, are doubled. Now the metre shows that in the original text the *nn* (or perhaps at that time just *nt*?) was confined to the instances having originally *nt* (thus *śośucann, āpann, prathayann*)[1], but in [425] the instances where the original had *n* — those which have *ns* will be discussed below—simple *n* has to be restored in place of *nn* (thus in the vocatives like *puruhanman, vajrin*; in the locatives like *mūrdhan, ekasmin*; cf. Kuhn Beitr. III.125).

1. Can we, perhaps, think of recovering in other cases the trace of the consonants suppressed at the word final position by following the example of *nn* for *nt*? Just as we have *ahann,* one could also think of *akarr,* etc. In fact, the Ṛgvedic data are not unfavourable for an assumption of that kind for *r*. It is true that I find only three significant passages: *kar* IX.92.5, *āvar* VII.75.1, *abibhar* X.69.10 : in all these cases the *-ar* has been used as long, although not in the quite decisive fourth-from-the-last position of the Triṣṭubh, but the passages which would vouchsafe for a short syllable do not contradict this assumption. One may also recall *āvar tamaḥ* I.92.4 where *r* has been preserved obviously under the influence of the final suppressed consonant. On the other hand, as the metre proves, the final consonants after the stops have disappeared without a trace; cf. *pūrbhid* VIII.33.5; X.111.10 ; *govid* IX.55.3; *nirṇig* II.35.4; IX.10.7; *ānaṭ* VI.49.8 etc.

From this case in which the trace of an original *t* after *n* was preserved and then wrongly extended by the diaskeuasts, we move to a second similar case, which differs from the first only in that here the metre cannot be used as a check. According to a doctrine prevailing in the Prātiśākhyas, which in the Ṛk-Prātiśākhya (236) has been cited at least as the view of *some* teachers, a *t* is inserted after word-final *n* before *s*. J. Schmidt (KZ. XXVI.349) has shown that this *t* cannot be looked upon as a physiologically developed transition-sound, but that it has its origin in such cases where originally *nt* occurred; on the model of *agant sumatiḥ* was then formed *rājant soma*. *When* this generalization took place can be decided, I think, with a good deal of probability on the basis of the exact analogy offered by the extending of *nn* of *āpann amṛktam* to *mūrdhann asthāt*: since, of the two cases, the latter mix up is unknown to the original Ṛk-text, as is shown by the metre, the former, where the metre is of no avail, will be unknown to the original Ṛk-text. Hence, we should write *agant sumatiḥ*, but *rājan soma* (*rājaṁ soma* ?), since like the writing with *t* the writing without *t* also can find support from Indian authorities, who, however, know nothing about the correct demarcation of the two possibilities.

If the *t* before *s* after an original *n* is due to a later transference, then we cannot reject the possibility that the *t* after *n* for an original *ns* **[426]** (*asmānt samarye*) is to be similarly explained. Here, when the diaskeuast had once started to bring about conformity in cases whose differences had been forgotten, a generalization of that kind is just what is to be expected. J. Schmidt, however, explains the *t* of *asmānt samarye* as having arisen in a regular phonetic manner out of *s*, as in *vatsyāmi*, *vidvatsu*. But this very old phonetic change of *s* to *t* has, in most cases, undergone changes already quite early, and the "external sandhi" among all the areas is probably the one where that kind of sound change, which had started to disappear, had the last chance of lasting for a long time. Only an environment of sandhi phenomena like *śatruḍ bhayate, śatrū ḍadṛśe* (according to the model *viprudbhis, dūḍabha*) would suit such a *t*, if that is to be explained as a phonetically regular development.

If we believe that the validity of *-nt s-* in the Ṛk-text has to be narrowed down in a way similar to the case of *-nn* before a vowel, then we have also stated what our position is in regard to the writing *-ñ ch-* for *-n ś-*. It can hardly be doubted that *-ñ ch-* has arisen, in exactly the same way as *-nt s-*, out of *-nt ś-*[1]; for, the Indian authorities too, especially the phoneticians of the Ṛgveda[2], hold divergent views regarding the latter sandhi as they do about the former. In accordance with what has been just stated, we on our part would accept *-ñ ch-* only where a *t* is already available (e.g., I.100.7 *raṇayañ chūrasātau*): but cases such as *dasyūñ chimyūṁś ca* (ibid. 18) or *vajriñ chnathihi* (I.63.5) we will consider as the result of the generalization, which occurred in a later period, of that phonetic change, all the more so because we find the latter **[427]** executed without exception in the ṚV, also between pāda-end and pāda-beginning (e.g., VIII.54.3); that is, we have to consider it—exactly as the doubling of *n* before the following vowel—as belonging to *those* sandhis which the diaskeuast thought he was authorized to generalize upon. Following the authority of Śākalya (Prāt. 232), we should look upon the writing of *vajriñ śnathihi, dasyūñ śimyūṁś ca* as correct.

We have assummed that the transference of the phenomena, which belong to *nt*, to the sphere of *ns* is not old. This becomes still more probable when we find that in other spheres which, by chance, have remained more or less unaffected by the theorization of the diaskeuasts, and to which we shall now turn, the old treatment of the original *ns* has been best preserved. We mean the change of *ns* to

1. Whitney Gramm. § 207 end; J. Schmidt KZ XXVI.349; Brugmann Grundriss § 557.2.
2. Prātiśākhya 231, 232. Whitney § 203.

anusvāra or to *r̥*[1] before vowels[2] and the preservation of the sibilant when followed by *t* and *c*.

The Prātiśākhya (284.289, cf. 299) limits the cases in which, according to the point of view of the Indian grammarians, a word-final *n* before a vowel results in an anusvāra, respectively *r̥*, in such a way that this change occurs after long[3], and not after short vowels. One notices that this distinction almost completely coincides with what in reality exists: original *ns* **[428]** is almost always preceded by a long vowel (acc. pl.; nom. sg. in *-an*[4]; *s*-aorist like *ayān*), original *n* and *nt* almost always preceded by a short vowel (nominal stems in *-an, -in;* loc. sg. of pronouns in *-smin;* 3 pl. of verbs; nom. sg. of the pres. part.). But the criterion of vowel length is not correct, first of all, in the case of *-ān* for *-ānt* of the subjunctive 3rd pl. this form occurs before a following vowel in the same pāda at five places: I.84.18; III.33.8; VI.67.11; VIII.79.5; X.10.10; and *in all cases* the *-ān* has remained unchanged, that is, from the point of view of the Prātiśākhya, an exception was made, and this has also been so noted (292). One sees how, in preserving this peculiarity which must have been utterly inexplicable to the Indian grammarians, the original text, unsullied by the mechanical generalisations, has been excellently preserved. Beyond these subjunctives the traditional Ṛk-text exhibits *almost* no exception to the rule regarding the appearance of *–ām̐, –īm̐r, –ūm̐r,* before the following vowel of the same

1. About the writing system in the mss. with the sign of ardhacandra, cf. M. Müller on Ṛk-Pr. 299.
2. The writing side by side of *-ām̐ api, -īm̐r api, -ūm̐r api* clearly shows that we have to assume after *-ān* the existence of the same sound, not expressed in writing, which prevents coalescence of *-ā api* from *-ās api.*
3. To be more exact, after *ā, ī, ū.* With regard to *r̥̄* the traditional treatment shows variations (Prāt. 290; Lanman 429).
4. These are the cases of the nominative of *-vāṁs-* and *-yāṁs-*stems (J. Schmidt KZ XXVI, 341 f., 386) as also those of *-vant-* and *-mant-*stems, which is similar to the nom. of those stems in regard to the phenomena pointing to an (original) *s* (op. cit. 359; Collitz Bezz. Beitr. X.29); also *mahān* (Lanman 506) belongs here.

pāda ; after deducting the cases of the subjunctive there remain 11 exceptions to the Prātiāakhya rule concerned (292). Two of these (I.88.5; 120.2) disappear because *-ān* occurs at the end of the pāda, which was not so understood by the grammarians—a fresh proof to show that in *these* forms the text has been excellently preserved; in four other cases the exceptions noted are not at all from the Ṛk-stanzas, but from the Praiṣa-texts. Thus, there remain five real exceptions which may be unhesitantly attributed [429] to the confusion in the tradition. One may recall here the methodological principles formulated above (p. 389 f.) while dealing with the Abhinihita sandhi. One need not be surprised that such confusion has occurred, but at the most that it has not spread to many more cases[1].

The above-mentioned substitution of the criterion of vowel-length in the Indian theory, in place of what should historically be an original *ns*, proves to be insufficient not only in the subjunctive forms, but also in another case—the verbal forms of the second person of the type *agan*, having original *ns* after a short vowel[2]. The traditional text always

1. That on the whole the tradition gives here the text as it was fixed in previous times and that it was not changed according to the grammatical theories is shown by the fact that at the end of the pāda, even before the initial vowel of the next pāda, the pausa-form with *-ān* has been correctly preserved, while, e.g., in the case of the doubling of *n* before the following vowel the text-arrangers considered themselves authorized to apply their rule everywhere, thus also between the two pādas (unless the two were separated by an *avasāna*). That in a few cases *-ām̐* has occurred before a vowel even at the end of a pāda (Prātiśākhya 285; cf. 290. 1) is only a further symptom of the understandable confusion which was spoken of above.— this can be asserted with absolute certainty considering the nature of the pāda-separations. It is, moreover, to be noted that in most of the cases where *-ām̐* occurs at the end of a pāda – these cases have been listed in the Prāti. – they can be explained by the occurrence of a correct *ām̐* by its side.
2. The genitive *dan* (*patir dan*) would also belong here. But it is found only at the end of the pāda, once (I.149.1) before a following vowel, where then the traditional text has *dann*.

gives here *-ann* before vowels (e.g. *ajagann apaḥ* III.9.2; *ahann ahim* II.11.5; III.32.11 etc.), and the metre confirms the length. But is it at all possible that *-ans,* in fact, became *-ann,* rather than *–aṁ̊* when in a similar situation *-āns* has become *-āṁ̊* ? The authority of the tradition as such can hardly be given any credence here. We saw [**430**] how the rule about *nn* after a short vowel had been set up without the necessary delimitations and then, assuming its general validity, was used to 'correct' the text throughout. Just as one could say *mūrdhann asthāt* for *mūrdhan a°*, so could one say *ajagann apaḥ* for *ajagaṁ̊ apaḥ,* all the more so because this was influenced by the form of the third person that has the same phonetic form in most situations. We therefore need have no hesitation in restoring the forms of the second person to *-aṁ̊,* which ending of course has the validity of a long syllable, since after it we have to assume a sound arising out of *s* [p. 427, note 2], that is not shown in writing.

If we have thus seen that the treatment of the original *ns* before vowels permits us in all cases to conclude excellent preservation of the traditional text (except in one case where the occurrence of a short vowel before *ns* misled the diaskeuasts to apply a wrongly formulated rule), then we should now examine the same group of sounds before consonants. What we find is easily understandable: before consonants only the *n* prevails; the sibilant has disappeared except for certain traces; these traces are seen, according to the nature of the following sound, with varying frequency, most frequently before *c* and *t,* the consonants with which the sibilant combines itself easily. In pausa only *n* appears.

Before voiced consonants we find *-āṁ̊, –īṁ̊r, –ūṁ̊r* in a relatively small number of cases (Prāt.287,288; Lanman 395, 415, 512; cf. also Prāt. 227). Their authenticity is vouchsafed besides by the general faithfulness of the tradition, which is to be recognized here, in particular by the fact that they are never followed by a stop, but always by *y, v, r, l, h* (e.g. *ut paṇīr̃ hatam*).

Among the voiceless consonants, first it is *p* before which **[431]** the group appears as *-m̐ḥ* in some cases (Prāt. 297, 298): a characteristic sign of good preservation is the occurrence here side by side of *nr̥̄m̐ḥ pāhi śr̥ṇudhī giraḥ* VIII.84.3 and *rakṣā nr̥̄n pāhi asura tvam asmān* I.174, 1: in the former passage *pāhi* belongs to the preceding accusative, in the latter not.

The principal place, however, where *s* (*ś*) is preserved is the one where the later Sanskrit *always* has a sibilant, viz., when it occurs before *t* and *c*. The traditionally transmitted Ṛk-text demarcates the preservation and the loss of *s* in this case in such a way that, in general, the continuation of the old, genuine tradition is without doubt clear[1], and it is only in a few cases that confusion, which is certainly not surprising, seems to have crept in. We find the following state of affairs (cf. Prāt. 293 f.):

(a) Before *ca* (18 cases) and *cid* (3 cases) *s* is preserved[2] The Avestan sandhi, as is well known, enables us likewise to see the specially close connection of just these two enclitic particles with the preceding words. In the Ṛk-tradition, there are no exceptions in the case of *cid*, in the case of *ca* only two (Prāt. 294): II.1.16 *asmāñ ca;* I.72.6 *paśūñ ca.* I would have no hesitation to change the text here. It is obvious that in both the places a corruption has set in. By the side of **[432]** *paśūñ ca* we have *sthātr̥̄ñ caratam̐ ca;* the sandhi of the words in the latter group has influenced the former. On the other hand, by the side of *asmāñ ca* occurs, to be sure, *tām̐ś*

1. Collitz (Bezz. Beitr. X.29) emphsizes the paucity of the data for the treatment of the nominatives in *-vān* and *-yān* of the participles and the comparatives. But the data for the acc. pl. are rather plentiful, and it cannot be doubted that, on principle, the nominatives stand on the same plane as the accusatives. This would have been obviously more clearly prominent in the traditional text if *ca* would not have been, by chance, as rare after the nominatives as it is frequent after the accusatives.
2. *ca*: I.100.18; 140.12; II.1.16; III.6.9; IV.2.2,3; VI.21.9; 28.3; 38.3; 66.3; VIII.2.4; X.14.3; 15.13; 51.8; 85.41; 90.3; 114.6; 115.9. – *cid*: I.173.8; V.31.2; X.154.1-4.

ca, so that the first sandhi could be doubly surprising: the explanation, however, can be obtained from I.165.14 *asmāñ cakre*, VIII.3.2 *asmāñ citrābhiḥ*, from where the impression could have been formed that in the case of *asmāñ s* does not appear.

(b) Among the other cases, where *s* has been preserved, several of them show very close connection between both the words as it is found in the case of *ca* and *cid*: thus *tāṁs te' aśyāma* IX.91.5 (*te* is enclitic), *sarvāṁs tān* VIII.93.6; also *devāṁs tvam paribhūr asi* V.13.6 can perhaps be brought in here.

(c) There remain some cases of the preserved *s*, the conditions of which cannot be distinguished with confidence from those where *s* is lost. Accusatives: IV.33.6; IX.33.6; X.50.4; 90.8. Nominatives: III.44.2; 55.9; VIII.33.8; X.4.2. We have no right to remove these cases from the text; it is understandable that this phenomenon could be fluctuating in the borderline cases. On the other hand, we cannot be very sure about the cases where often the caesura occurs between the two words: thus in III.55.9 (= X.4.2) *antar mahāṁś carati rocanena*, where the tradition could easily have come under the influence of VIII.33.8 *mahāṁś carasy ojasā*.

(d) Next, *s* has disappeared before *ca* in the two cases mentioned above under (a), and also in the following places: accusatives: I.72.6 (?); 161.4; 165.14; II.34.14; VIII.3.2; 6.48; 26.4; X.27.2; 64.8; 154.4,5; 180.2.—nominatives: I.30, 14; 55.1; 61.7; 164.6; IV.21.2; 33.5; VI.20, 3; 41.4; VIII.17.6; X.1.1; 176.3.

[433] (e) *s* is not preserved— not even before *ca* and *cid*—when a short vowel precedes, i.e., when the final *n* corresponds to original *n* or *nt* (except for a single instance to be mentioned directly): thus in locatives and vocatives (*varṣman tasthau, maghavan tava, kasmiñ cid*) and in verbal forms (*akṛṇvan tredhā, ajagmiran te*). The lone example, if I am not mistaken, of a verbal form ending in *-an* = *-ans* is *ahañ ca* (VII.19.5; certainly second person): I consider *ahaṁś ca* to be correct, from which, at a time when the preceding short vowel was looked upon as determining the non-occurrence of *s*, *ahañ ca* has been obtained. The nominative sg. of the pres. part. which can be considered here only as an *s*-less form does not, in fact, as shown by Lanman (506), have *s* in the traditional text, not even before *ca* (*niveśayañ ca prasuvañ ca* VII.45.1). The only exception is *āvadaṁs tvam* II.43.3. Shall we correct it ? Lanman rightly emphasizes that this is a case in a particularly late passage. Now we should note that several of the late Saṁhitās sporadically give forms with *s* in such a way as to suggest a beginning of the general adoption of such forms, obviously on the analogy of the nominatives in *-vāṁs* etc., rather than mere influences of the diaskeuasis, which should have entailed greater consistency. So it is perhaps probable that the late Ṛgvedic example noted above is to be considered as the earliest attestation of that innovation.

The total result obtained from the discussion of even this group of occurrences for an assessment of the tradition and of the method we employed for our critique is so clear that it would be enough to formulate it in a few words. In so far as it concerns the natural, undisturbed preservation of the tradition and not the normalizations carried out by the diaskeuasts, [434] the traditional text proves to be completely faithful even including minute details. Confusion between possibilities, when it was difficult to keep them apart, is not totally absent, but it has occurred only in a remarkably small number of cases. However, in certain phenomena the traditional text was systematically transformed by the diaskeuasis following wrong principles: in such cases, then, the part of the tradition that has remained intact and, further, for some portion of the phenomena concerned, the metre gives the authority and, at the same time, the standard, according to which the effaced phenomena can and must be restored according to the nature of the things, even where the metre is of no avail.

Hiatus and Contraction

We now turn to certain investigations, although in them the line adopted by the diaskeuasts in their technical procedure takes second place to the question about which laws are authoritative for obtaining the original form of the Vedic text. It is necessary to examine the practice of the Vedic poets, or of those savants who handed down their text, in regard to the contact of word-final and word-initial vowels, the occurrence of contractions and hiatus in such cases, and in the case of hiatus, the shortening of the first long vowel. In this investigation special attention will have to be given to the treatment of final *e* and *o* (as well as *o* = *as*) before a following vowel and then to the group of the so-called pragṛhya vowels.

It may be considered as generally recognized that the Vedic poets strove, as far as possible, to avoid hiatus.[1] **[435]** In order to arrive at more exact decisions on how strong this aversion is and the limits within which it prevails, we may initially allow our investigation to be directed by certain tallies which I have made for two sūktas, VII.3 and X.45, chosen at random. The purpose of doing this is to state how the actual frequency of the contact of word-final and word-initial vowels stands in relation to the one which we should expect to occur if the aversion for the hiatus had not intervened. For this purpose I ascertained how often, within a pāda, consonants and vowels, appear at the end and at the beginning of a word, and how often, among these cases, the vowels are allowed to appear together, or how often this has been avoided by contraction. Of course,

1. Characteristic for this is the use of the word *īm*. Where it coalesces with the preceding vowel, that is it cannot be used to fill up a place in the metrical line, it is always (in about 60 cases with only *one* exception) followed by a vowel so that the purpose of avoiding the hiatus is clear. That this *īm* was introduced later by the diaskeuasts for this purpose is an absolutely unmotivated assumption of Grassmann.

in this calculation the words ending in *s* have been always counted as ending in consonants, even if the traditional writing, following the sandhi-rules, shows forms like *vo* for *vas*, *nṛmanā* for *nṛmanās*. The results of these tallies are the following:

	VII.3	X.45
Words ending in consonants	77	91
Words ending in a vowel other than *e*	65	60
Words ending in *e*[1]	18	21
Words beginning with a vowel	37	56
Conjunction of final *e* and a vowel	6	7
Conjunction of another vowel and a vowel, without coalescence	3	8
Coalescence	3	1

What do these numbers indicate? First, the frequency with which *e* occurs with the following initial vowel (*jajñe agniḥ*, *agna ūdhan* for *agne ūdhan* etc.) agrees with the expected frequency in so far as it can be expected to do in this small number of tallies. This situation is different from other cases of vowel contact in a highly perceptible way and thus, makes common cause with other indications (see below) to lead us to the conclusion that in *jajñe agniḥ* and other similar cases there is really no hiatus since the *e* (*a+i*) changes either to *ay*, or to *a* and a weaker consonantal echo developed out of *y*. Further, one is easily convinced that the sequence: vowel (other than *e*) + vowel is considerably rarer than what it should have been in accordance with the average expectancy. In VII.3, among the word-finals which are considered for the tally, such as those ending in a consonant or *e* : 95, in a vowel: 65. In contrast, *before an initial vowel,*

1. Or, ending in *a* which, according to the sandhi rules, stands for *e*; *o* is to be treated the same way as *e*; but cases of word-final *o*, which is not equal to *as*, are rare.

words ending in a consonant or *e:* 31, in a vowel (with hiatus or contraction): 6; thus we have here the approximate ratio of 5 : 1 instead of 3 : 2.

A closer examination of the cases where vowel contact occurs shows that the aversion against hiatus is directed not equally against all possible cases, but only against some definite ones which finds expression in the numbers given above. The cases where **[437]** vowels come in contact, e.g., in X.45, are the following: *apsu antaḥ, bhāti antaḥ, bhāti agre, rodasī apṛṇāt, marteṣu agniḥ, vi adyaut, sauśravaseṣu agne, astāvi agniḥ;* and in addition there is one case of contraction, *hīm* = *hi īm.* This shows an unmistakable preponderence of vowel combinations whose first member is *i* or *u*; they are hardly found in less quantity than what would conform with the natural expectancy. In contrast there seems to prevail a definite aversion against combinations such as *a* + *a*, *ā* + *a*, *a* + *i*, etc.; to a Vedic poet *stavāma agnim* would not have appeared in any way permissible as *astāvi agniḥ* would, in which latter sequence the transition from one vowel to another—of course with the development of an intermediate semi-vowel[1], however transient it may be—is obviously easier than in the case of a combination of two *a* sounds separated by hiatus.

1. In the Gāna-texts of the Sāmaveda we often find writings which directly note the sound concerned: *niy ātrāiṇā* for *ny atriṇam* of the source text, *vāhātiy āśāvāḥ* for *vahanty āśavaḥ, hiy ā . . . sāyi* for *hy asi, pāhiy uta* for *pāhy uta* (likewise in the body of a word *mau. . .rttiyāḥ* for *martyaḥ* etc.). Regarding the writing of the particle *u* as *u* or *uv* before a following vowel (in so far as simple *v* is not written), the different Vedas differ from one another; cf. Ṛk. Prāt. 160; Taitt. Prāt. IX.16.17 etc.; from *su* with *ūti* develops in the RV *suūtayaḥ* (VIII.47.1 ff.). For the purpose of our edition of the text, we may naturally abstain from writing the semi-vowel type transition sound, in the same way as we consider it unobjectionable to write *within a word* simply *martia, tuam etc.* While doing this we do not wish to dispute the correctness of the statements of Osthoff Morph. Unt. IV.398, Brugmann Grundriss § 117 on the transitional sound that appears in combinations *ia, ua.*— Cf. also Ṛk. Prāt. 974.

Now we offer a somewhat more comprehensive statistic which, on the basis of the tallies made so far, seems to emerge as deserving further consideration: this is with reference to the difference in the treatment of *i* + *a*, *u* + *a* on the one hand and *a* + *a*, *ā* + *a*, etc. on the other. The following figures, **[438]** of course, as in the case of the above tallies, pertain only to the contact of the final and the initial vowels *within a pāda.*

	III.1-5	VI.1-5	IX.1-15	Total
i + *a*	11[1]	13	10[2]	34
u + *a*	5	3	1[3]	9
a + *a* = *ā*	—	4	6	10
a + *a* remains	—	2	—	2
ā + *a* = *ā*	—	—	2	2
ā + *a* remains	—	1	—	1

If we noted that *ā*, and to a still greater extent *a*, happens to be a substantially more frequent word-final than *i* and still more than *u*, then we would consider that the considerably greater favour with which the Vedic poets allow the words beginning with *a* to be preceded by a word ending in *i* or *u*, than by a word ending in *a* or *ā*, as sufficiently substantiated by these figures[4].

[439] With regard to the hiatus in a narrow sense (*-a a-*

1. In addition thrice *i* + *ā*.
2. In addition twice *i* + *ā*.
3. In addition four times *u* + *ā*.
4. As to the change of the final *i*, *u* to *y*, *v* before a dissimilar vowel, Benfey has already noted (in his article on *na*, p. 1) that it occurs with greater frequency only in the case of a disyllabic prefix before the verb connected with it (*abhy anūṣi*, *praty agrabhīṣma* etc.). Whether the vowel concerned is accented (*abhí*) or not (*práti*, *pári*, *ánu*) makes no difference. Other cases where the disyllabic prepositions were felt to be sufficiently close to the following words, so that the change of *i*, *u* to *y*, *v* took place, may be illustrated with the following

(Continued on next page)

etc.) we have to add further that it was less determinedly avoided at the place of caesura in the Triṣṭubh and Jagatī lines than at other places in the pāda; in this respect also the intermediate nature of the caesura, which can be demonstrated in so many respects where the phenomena peculiar to the pāda-end constantly recur, only with less intensity, is once again confirmed. Further, it has to be noted that the hiatus—the one mitigated by the caesura as well as the other one—is much more decisively dreaded in the tenth book than in the older parts of the Saṁhitā. It would be easy to show that with the phenomenon of the hiatus becoming rare the growing preference for contraction goes hand in hand, which was decisively preferred to the former from the beginning. The use of the contraction in the late-Vedic and post-Vedic poetry, where it is employed far in excess of its actual use in the living language, unmistakably gets its start here.

This is the place to offer some remarks on the demarcation of the cases where the hiatus and the contraction occur. While doing this we believe we may for the time being ignore the shift, just referred to, which the demarcation line has undoubtedly undergone in the course of the Vedic

---

(Continued from previous page)

examples: *pary anyā. . . . yugā. . .rajāṁsi dīyathaḥ* V.73.3; *anv enān. . . bhānur arta* V.52.6; *anv asya ketam iṣitaṁ savitrā* II.38.5.— *praty u adarśi* VII.81.1.— *praty ud āyan* III.31.4.— Often, of course, *y* occurs in combinations like *pratyañc, adhyakṣa,* etc.— Of the monosyllabic suffixes I find only *ni* appearing as *ny* in the late passage I.191.3 *ny alipsata* [cf. also the combination *avyuṣṭāḥ* II.28.9].— As finals of words other than the prefixes noted above *y, v* occur only very exceptionally in the books I-IX ; thus, *ity abravītana* I.161.8; *sīvyatv apaḥ* II.32.4; *tv imā* VIII.51.4 (Vālakhilya); *haṁsy apratīni* VIII.90.5 (easily to be eliminated); *urv iva* IX.96.15 (of course more frequent in combinations like *ṛtvij, purvaṇīka* I.79.5 etc.). In the tenth book the development of *y, v* is considerably more, both in prefixes as well as in other words of all sorts; even *ī* becomes *y* in *janitry ajījanat* X.134.1 ff. — Cf. on the whole matter Edgren's investigations on the relationship of *i, u* to *y, v* in Journ. American Or. Soc. Vol. XI.67 ff.

period, [440] and we may pose the question with reference to the Ṛk-Saṁhitā as a whole.

Among the older Vedic scholars no one except Benfey had paid close attention to the relationship between hiatus and contraction. We are interested here mostly in his remarks on the treatment of the final of *ca*[1]. Benfey finds that contraction has taken place in 50 cases, hiatus occurs in 24 (except of course when *ca* occurs at the end of a pāda)[2]. He is of the opinion that the non-occurrence of contraction in these 24 cases is due throughout, or at least in a majority of cases, to semantic considerations; in some cases a group of related words is held together with the help of *ca;* the *ca* marks the conclusion of the group and since it is thus connected very intimately with the preceding word it is separated from what follows; in others *ca* indicates close relationship of the first of the two connected words with the other, or vice versa, and is therefore(?) not mutilated (by contraction); in still others, *ca* is followed by the names of gods and Benfey opined that one did not want to touch the phonetic form of the names of gods by making a contraction.

Obviously, the semantic nuances, which figure at least in the first two of the above considerations, are more subtle and disputable than is desirable [441] for Benfey's explanations to be persuasive. Is the function of *ca,* e.g., in

---

1. "Behandlung des auslautenden *a* in *na* "wie" und *na* "nicht" im Ṛgveda" (1881), pp. 23-28.
2. Some of these 24 cases, I think, have to be excluded. In V.77.2, I think *vi cāvaḥ* with contraction more likely than *vi ca āvaḥ*. In VII.4.1 there is caesura between *ca* and *agnaye* which rules out contraction at the very start; hence, the passage cannot be considered while looking for the line of demarcation between contraction and hiatus. In VIII.11.10 nothing prevents us from reading *suāṁ cāgne.* X.10.13 is to be read with contraction as *hṛdayaṁ cāvidāma.* If we now eliminate VII.4.1 as not belonging here, VIII.11.10 as uncertain, and the remaining two cases as belonging to the opposite group, we are left with 20 cases of hiatus against 52 of contraction.

mahe śūrāya viṣṇave ca arcata (I.155.1) really different from, let us say, the one in *niveśane prasave cāsi bhūmanaḥ* (VI.71.2)? And as to the third point: is it not arbitrary to recognize the tendency to preserve the names of the gods intact in the formulation of X.90.3 (*indraś ca agniś ca*), when the poet of V.51.14 or X.173.5 could say without hesitation *indraś cāgniś ca*[1]?

Perhaps we will find the correct answer more surely if we first pay attention to the external appearance of the form before we turn to meaning as the decisive factor for contraction and hiatus. I give the words which, for instance, follow *ca* in each of the first fourteen cases of Benfey's lists for hiatus and contraction with *ca*. In the case of hiatus: *āsāt, iṣṭau, arcata, āt, acchā, agnaye, acchā, imā̆* (a somewhat doubtful case), *āvaḥ agnaye, āt, advayum, ava, arhanti*. In the case of contraction, on the other hand: *aśanim, arvate, arvataḥ, adhi, ahabhiḥ, imāḥ, asi, asi, asmin, aviśat, abhajat, anu, asaparyan, ati*. In the words of the first list 12[2] begin with a long syllable, in the second only 3. Accordingly, we will be nearer the truth if we set up a rule such as: *ca* enters into contraction if a short syllable follows; if a long syllable follows there is hiatus. This is understandable enough, for the Vedic metres permit the sequence of two short syllables only in a few cases other than by way of exception; rather they show preference for the alternation of **[442]** short and long syllables. Combinations like *ca imāḥ* or even *ca ahabhiḥ, ca aviśat* would be metrically partly uncomfortable, partly impossible, while in *ca arcata, ca agnaye* we have the favourite iambic end of the line[3]. Thus, concerning *ca* we discover

1. Among the seven cases where in the ṚV the stanzas begin with *āgniḥ, āgnim, āgne,* only in two cases must we read *ā agnim* (respectively *ā agne*), in five cases *āg°*.
2. Or 13, if one takes into consideration the fact that the first syllable of VIII.19.23 metrically fills the place of a long syllable.
3. Hence, also obviously by the side of *ca agnaye* twice *indraś cāgniś ca*: here it could not be a case of bringing about iambics.

that quite independently of all considerations of meaning, surely not in all cases without exception, yet in quite a large number of cases, a purely external factor, decides whether contraction or hiatus is to take place[1]. Similar results are obtained when instead of from words ending in vowels, like *ca,* one proceeds from words beginning with vowels. In general, one notices that in every word the initial sound receives just that treatment which one would *a priori* expect in consideration of metrical convenience. Certain words, due to their prosodic form, are predestined to form hiatus with the preceding final *-a* and thereby give rise to an iambic pāda-end: thus, for example, *agnaye,* which has been already mentioned[2]. Other words would, owing **[443]** to the presence of one or more short syllables, prefer more or less exclusively only contraction. Such words are *aham, adhi,* and many augmented verbal forms. Finally, others offer both posibilities: thus *aśvam, aśvān*[3], *agniḥ, agnim,* etc.

1. It may be permitted here to point out the effect of the same metrical considerations on a related question that desreves to be looked into more carefully than has been done so far: the question regarding the interchange of *i, u* (*iy, uv*) with *y, v* (Siever's Law) in the Ṛgveda. Why one said *śarmaṇi syām, tava syām,* and not *śarmaṇi siām tava siām* can be sufficiently explained with the help of metre—a sequence of three short syllables can be accommodated metrically only with great difficulty, while the trochees in *śarmaṇi syām* offer a fitting Triṣṭubh ending. On the other hand, the Vedic metre makes use of not only the alternation of long and short syllables but also in many ways of a series of several long syllables; therefore, when one examines the occurrences of *syām* (*siām*), *syāma* (*siāma*) and other similar cases with the preceding long syllables, one must also expect to find, and one does find, *patiḥ syām* as well as *gopatiḥ siām, tarantaḥ syāma* as well as *nṛvantaḥ siāma.* When one takes into account this aspect of the question, then one would find in the materials collected by Osthoff Perf. 440 f. less support for Siever's Law than what would otherwise appear.
2. Examples are given by Benfey, op. cit. 23.
3. Hiatus: I.104.1; VII.34.4; IX.94.5; X.101.7 (not quite certain); 107.10. Contraction: V.83.3; X.39.10; 107.7; 149.4. One notices the rise in the cases of contractions in the tenth book.

However, we do not want to assert that metrical considerations of the kind described above are the *only* decisive ones in every case. A counter example is already provided by the extremely curious difference found in the treatment of *na* 'as' and *na* 'not', already discovered by Benfey. As regards *na* 'not', the Vedic poets obviously proceed each time according to metrical requirements; mostly we find contraction. In contrast, as Benfey has shown, in the case of *na* 'as' hiatus prevails with such thoroughness that any explanation based on chance occurrence is, in fact, rendered impossible. There can be no doubt that this is due to the pecularity of the figure of speech found here. I cannot find—and one can scarcely expect to find—a similar case of hiatus so sharply marked in the case of another word in the Vedic diction[1]. But it can be asserted that, generally speaking, the initial of a more important word, occurring frequently as an independent form, is less prone to contraction unless metre requires it than the initial of such words which count as small coins of the language. For example, with *aham* or *adhi* [444] I find contraction not only absolute but relatively more frequent than, let us say, with *ahim, ahiḥ, apaḥ,* which prosodically speaking have more or less the same value; words of the second, more important, type reveal where metre allows it, either a greater preference for hiatus as compared to the words of the other type, or rather a frequent avoidance of conjunction with the final *a.* On the other hand, the almost regular contraction, e.g., of *id* with the preceding vowel can hardly be due only to metrical considerations, but it must be related to the meaning of this non-independent particle which is closely attached to the

1. As a rule, to be sure, the paucity of cases does not permit a sure judgement. Perhaps it has something to do with the conceptual nature of the word when, e.g., *āt* which in most cases stands at the beginning of a pāda and introduces a new thought is not contracted, but in all cases coming under consideration forms hiatus (II.5.7; VII.66.11; VIII.82.3).

preceding word. Here, without doubt, we see the Vedic sandhi from that side where the usages of the living language, on which the ṛṣis drew, shine through their practice which was cramped by the metre. To lay bare this foundation of the Vedic sandhi that lies under the layer of those occurrences, covering a very large part of the surface, and which is purely a result of the metrical necessities, will be the task of a deeper study that is presently beyond the scope of possibility[1].

[445] As a supplement to the discussion so far let us examine, on the basis of the results for contraction and hiatus, the reconstruction suggested by Grassmann (Wörterbuch, p. VII), of forms like **mātār, *hotār, *vibhvān* at such places where the *ā* at the end of these words (appearing in the traditionally transmitted text as *mātā,* etc.) does not coalesce with a following *ṛ*. Linguistic consideration raises doubts against forms like **mātār;* it leads to the assumption that in Gk. *mḗtēr* the *r* has rather been restored afterwards on the basis of forms in the remaining cases. We, on our part, would examine purely empirically how the Vedic text stands vis-à-vis the forms assumed by Grassmann. Lanman, who leaves the question of the justification of the reconstructions concerned undecided, offers, however, materials in all thoroughness that prove their inadmissibility. With regard to the nominatives ending in *-tā* of the *r*-stems

1. For these investigations one would expect to derive important help from comparison with the Pāli prose which, without doubt, has preserved in essential points certain features of the sandhi of the Vedic period—unless it has been influenced by metrical considerations in Vedic *poetry*. These sandhi peculiarities have been completely obscured in classical Sanskrit. The reader of every old Pāli text is automatically struck by the opposition based on conceptual factors between the cases where sandhi takes place and where it does not. One may compare among the constant phrases of ecclesiastical Pāli prose instances like *mam' accayena, yass' atthāya, ten' upasaṁkami, yaṁ pan' aññaṁ khādaniyaṁ,* and on the other hand *tena . . . .samayena āyasmā Ānando. . ., maggā okkamma avidūre. . . .nisīdi.*

(p. 424) he shows that the *-ā*—leaving aside for the time being a following *ṛ*—almost always combines with the following vowel. He cites only 16 cases where we have hiatus. That such cases occur is, even without the assumption of forms like **mātār,* perfectly in order in accordance with the practice which prevails in the Veda about hiatus and contraction. Moreover these 16, or rather 15,[1] cases are such that they, even apart from their small number, rather oppose than support the assumption of a form in *-tār* being available to the Vedic poets. In 6 cases *tā* occurs before the caesura which softens the hiatus, and among the remaining there are 5 in whose case the metre makes the shortening of the final *-ā*, that is its position as *vocalis ante vocalem* not protected by any consonant,[2] **[446]** more or less probable. The passages in which the nominatives concerned appear before vowels other than *ṛ* are therefore so unfavourable for the assumption of forms in *tār* as can possibly be imagined. If such forms had really been there, would they not have revealed their existence equally before other vowels and not just before *ṛ*? Against this state of affairs the passages where *ṛ* follows will have to be particularly strong as proof if they are to offer adequate basis for *-tār.* Of such cases we have only four (Lanman 424): at two places (IV.33.5; V.46.1) *ā* and *ṛ* blend to make one syllable; once (V.45.6) they are separated by the caesura and, in the traditional text at least, also by an anunāsika; thus, there remains only one case (I.127.10) with unalleviated hiatus. Why should the hiatus not be considered permitted in the equally limited number of cases with *ṛ* as with other vowels cannot be understood. Thus, these cases fully agree with the relationships which

1. In I.61.4 perhaps we have contraction; one should take note of the peculiar metre of the hymn.
2. *ā* occurs at the second place after the caesura in I.60.4; 186.6; X.49.10; at the third place from the end in Triṣṭubh in VI.24.5; VII.40.3; the rule of *vocalis ante vocalem* will be dealt with below in details.

one expects for the traditionally *transmitted* form of the nominative endings.

As regards the nominatives ending in *-ā* of stems in *-an, -man, -van,* the materials collected by Lanman (528 f.) preclude the assumption of forms in *-ān* in a similar way. Grassmann bases his assumption on those three passages where the nominative *vibhvā,* or more exactly *vibhām̐,* occurs before a following *ṛ* without the blending of syllables (IV.33.3; 36.6; VII.48.3). In all three cases caesura occurs between *vibhvām̐* and *ṛ* : there can therefore **[447]** be no question at all of contraction[1]; in whichever way one looks at the nasalized writing of *vibhvām̐*—whether one traces it to the rule of the diaskeuasts with regard to the treatment of *-ā ṛ,* or whether one assumes transference from the *vāṁs*-stems[2]: this much is clear that the passages concerned do not give any occasion for the assumption that a nom. in *-ān* of *-an* (*-man, -van*)-stems existed in the speech materials of the Vedic poets prior to the transmitted form in *-ā.*

e, o (*as*) Before Vowels

It has long been recognized that the sounds which are written as *e* and *o* (including the *o* which arises out of *as*) in the traditional text have the value of a short vowel when followed by *a*[3]. But for the exceptions which rest on the peculiar nature of *e* and *o* in a few definite words—some cases of Pragṛhya vowels which will be considered in detail below—one can assert with confidence the shortness of those sounds,

1. In the other two cases, where *vibhvā* occurs before other vowels contraction takes place (I.190.2; V.46.4).
2. See our discussion of nasalizations further below, and cf. Prātiśākhya 168, Benfey, Vedica und Linguistica 10, Joh. Schmidt KZ. XXVI.358.
3. See especially Bloomfield "Final *as* before sonants" (Am. Jour. of Philology Vol. III) p. 15 ff. (I cite following the off-print). A. Kuhn had already hinted at this fact.

in the position described, as a fact valid for the entire Ṛgveda. In stanzas where a long vowel is required, this kind of *e* and *o* appears only in the surroundings in which any short vowel can occasionally be placed following the practice of the Vedic poets. **[448]** This is, in fact, just a question of poetic licence and not a real fluctuation in the quantity of the vowels *e* and *o*. Clear proof for it is provided by the fact that the exceptions occur *almost* always in the eighth syllable of the Triṣṭubh or Jagatī metre where, as regards the admissibility of the short finals, there is in evidence an especially extensive practice [above p. 60 f.].

As has been already correctly stressed by Bloomfield (op. cit. 19), it is not possible to explain the shortness of *e* and *o* on the basis of the principle *vocalis ante vocalem corripitur.* To prove this it is sufficient just to count the number of occurrences. The frequency of an *e* or *o* shortened before the following *a* stands in such an enormous disproportion to the rare cases in which *ā* occurs as shortened and hiatus-forming before a following vowel (cf. below) that it becomes quite clear that the conditions in which the two phenomena occur are different. One has also to note that in the case of *o* = *as* before a vowel, we have to assume necessarily the residue of the *s* that has disappeared. This residue must have had the effect of shutting off the influence of the following vowel due to which the preceding vowel is shortened: one can think of the shortening of a vowel before a vowel perhaps in *kā asmai* (written *kāsmai*), but not in the case of, let us say, *imā*[*s*] *apaḥ.*

Bloomfield (p. 19 f.) on his part gives the following explanation of the short vowels *o* and *e.* Original *ŏs* and *ĕs,* which appear as *-as* in the attested language, lost its *s* before the following vowel. The word-finals *ŏ* and *ĕ* which thus arose were, since the "Indian alphabet" [sic] did not have symbols for *ŏ* and *ĕ,* partly written as *ă* (before all other vowels except *a*), thereby preserving the correct quantity but giving up the vowel-colour; and they were partly written

[449] as *ō* and *ē* (when followed by *a*), thereby preserving the original vowel-colour but sacrificing the quantity. These *ŏ* and *ĕ*, which in the written form [sic] merged with *ō* and *ē*, drew the real *ō* and *ē*, which arose out of *a* + *u* and *a* + *i* (except in the pragṛhyas) to their proper nature as short vowels, first before *a*, then also before other vowels. Finally the *ĕ* out of *ĕs* was absorbed by the more common *ŏ* out of *ŏs:* thus there arose three vowels written as long but pronounced as short: *o* for *ŏs* and *ĕs,* plus the other *o* and *e.*

Here I do not propose discussing the doubts which can be raised against Bloomfield's understanding of the history of *ĕ* and *ŏ* of the original language up to the Vedic period and the peculiar shiftings of spheres which have to be assumed between these two vowels (see Osthoff Perfect 23 f.). For even without raising questions of the linguistic principle involved, it seems to me that Bloomfield's construction can be refuted from a different angle. One may just consider what role the "alphabet" and script play in it. We are required to assume that at a time when, according to Bloomfield's theory, the *o* and *e* which were not the results of *-as* were still pronounced long before vowels—i.e. *before* the composition of the oldest parts of our Ṛgveda: for in it the vowels concerned are already short, which in Bloomfield's view is the result of the secondary transference—one tried to find symbols among the sounds of the alphabet for the *ŏ* and *ĕ* developed from *ŏs* and *ĕs* before vowels and did not find any adequate ones. Does this mean that there was a fixed alphabet, older than the oldest portions of the Ṛgveda? And in the alphabet of the Indians, otherwise so rich in noting the smallest phonetic varieties, which distinguished *ḍ* from *ḷ* and *n, ṇ, ṅ, ñ,* which knew the long **[450]** *ḹ* vowel—in this alphabet should there be no possibility of noting or inventing letters for the *ĕ* and *ŏ* vowels, which the language at that time should have had, since it could distinguish *i* and *ī* or *u* and *ū* ? And hence should there have been the substitution of *different* signs, sometimes of *ă,* sometimes of *ē, ō* when the sound pronounced was always the same, *ĕ* or *ŏ* ? And finally there should have been such a power of the graphic representation over the spoken language at the time antedating the oldest Ṛg-hymns ! Not that the sounds *ĕ* and *ŏ*, for which inadequate symbols were used, now assumed the values of those symbols (*ē, ō*), but still more artificial: the sounds for which those signs were really and originally used, lost their original quantity for the Vedic poetry just because their graphic representations had begun to be also used for sounds of different quantity ! All this is unbelievable even if Vasiṣṭha and Viśvāmitra were "writers" in the literal sense of the word, even if there were the faintest possibility that the Vedic poets used a writing system or operated with some other method, independent of the alphabetic writing, to note a fixed phonetic system. To explain the discrepancy between the genuine phonetic form of the text which can be determined from the metre and the transmitted phonetic form in the treatment of *o* and *e* before *a*, an unprejudiced consideration will lead to anything else except an attempt to explain the rise of the Ṛṣi's own genuine sound system under the influence of the traditional alphabet. We had better say that the genuine and the transmitted form of the text obviously deviate from each other for the reason that the former is independent of, while the latter is dependent on, some kind of alternations **[451]** that are conditioned, perhaps, by the linguistic development of a later period or by the theoretical attitude of looking at language in this period. To bring precision into the nature of these alterations and, at the same time, of the old genuine phonetic system is exactly the task of our investigation.

Up to now we have learnt that the sounds which have been written as *o* or *e* before the following *a* were, in fact, pronounced short. In order to determine more precisely the nature of these short vowels, the nearest clue is offered by the observation of those sounds which appear, corresponding to *o* and *e,* before vowels other than *a.* There we find just the sound we require, viz. a short vowel, *a* : *ye aśvāḥ* but *ya ūtī; yo aśvaḥ* but *ya indraḥ,* and, as is well known, *e* = *a* + *i, o* = *a* + *u,* as well as *o* = *as* are represented, in the condition described, by *a.* First we shall take up *e, o* = *a* + *i* and *a* + *u,* respectively. The common view is that *a* + *i* before a vowel (other than *a*) first becomes *ay, a* + *u av,* and then the *y* and *v* appearing at the word-final disappear, leaving their trace behind only in the fact that the contraction of the remaining vowel *a* with the following vowel does not, as a rule, take place. Bloomfield (p. 17, cf. 18 note 1) rejects this view without adducing sufficient proof; to me that view is well founded. It is supported besides by the phonetically regular equivalence *within* a word of *ay, av* before a vowel and *e, o* before a consonant, by the treatment of the final *āi, āu,* especially of *āu,* where, when a vowel follows, the tradition sometimes preserves *āv,* but sometimes writes *ā* (Whitney § 134 end). The *āv* shows what that *ā* is: the initial constituent of the *āu*-diphthong relieved of its second element first by consonantization and then its eventual loss. **[452]** This leads virtually to the proportion *āu: āv: ā* = *o* (i.e. *a* + *u*): *av: a.* Moreover, the Ṛk-tradition has specifically preserved *av* for *o* before all non-labial vowels (*vāyav ā yāhi,* but *vāya ukthebhiḥ;* Prātiśākhya 132, 135), while before the following *u, ū* the *v* has been absorbed[1] by this

1. More unhappy is the assumption that *v* in the cases like *vāyav ā yāhi* stands for the particle *u* (Bloomfield p. 18, note 1). In the first instance a particle, inserted, which under certain purely phonetic conditions is as immutable as it is metrically superfluous, is in itself little in consonance with the style of the Vedic texts: not even with that of the diaskeuasts, for they, on the one hand, had no reason to wage a war to wipe out cases like *vāya ā* and others that are similar, since they wrote without hesitation *hṛda ā, dama ā,* etc. and, on the other, if the particle *u* was regularly introduced into the text by the diaskeuasts this would have been most probably known and

(Continued on next page)

vowel. We also find traces of *ay*—the earlier stage of *a*—, which before vowels corresponds to *e* before consonants[1]. Thus the Sāmans, whose text-form as required for singing (in the Gānas) is, on the one hand, indeed, affected in many possible ways by the activities of the diaskeuasts, such as has happened in the case of other texts, but on the other, has preserved the old form which is important from more than one point of view. For example, in the text of the several Sāmans sung on the stanza SV 1.97, we read for *śaraṇa ā: śaraṇay ō hāi* or *śārāṇāy ā:* in these **[453]** transformations of the words made to suit the requirements of singing, one cannot fail to recognize the basic text-form *śaraṇay ā*. Similarly in the SV.1.89 we have for *anīka idhyate: ānīkayā uvāye dhyāte:* where the form *anīkay idhyate* cannot be obscured in spite of all sorts of embellishments.—Now I wish to call attention to a number of passages in which variants or corruptions of Vedic texts point clearly to the pronunciation of *-ay* before the following vowel. Thus, we read for *ṛta ā* (i.e. *ṛtay ā*) *jātam agnim* (ṚV VI.7.1), in the Taitt. Saṁhitā I.4.13.1 *ṛtāya jātam agnim;* for *pāvakayā* ṚV VI.15.5 there occurs in the Taitt. Saṁh. IV.6.1.2 *pāvaka ā* (i.e. *pāvakay ā*); for *tve*[2] *ā bhūṣanti* ṚV.8.99,2 stands in the SV

(Continued from previous page)

understood as such by the Padapāṭha. There is still one more consideration that decisively goes against the particle *u* : *vāya u* certainly could have either remained without coalescence—in that case, however, we would have three syllables in place of the two that the text requires invariably here and in corresponding similar cases. Or it would, if one so likes, coalesce— I, on my part, would of course admit this possibility only as an exception; the normal course is that the final *a* appearing for *o* maintains hiatus—: if it *did* coalesce, then for the ṛṣis as well as for the diaskeuasts there must obviously arise, what invariably arose in the case of *atha* + *u*, *uta* + *u*, etc., viz. a pragṛhya *-o* ("*atho iti*", "*uto iti*"; cf. below [p. 456]), that is, a long syllable rather than a short syllable *av*.

1. Cf. with this Old Pers. *dastayā*, Avest. *zastaiā* = Sansk. *hasta ā* (Bartholomae Handbuch 95).
2. This *tve* is, however, pragṛhya.

2.164 *tvayā bhūṣanti;* by the side of *tá ā́ vahanti* (i.e., *tay ā vahanti*) of Taitt. Saṁ. I.1.2.1 we have in the Maitr. Saṁ. I.1.2 *táy ā́ vahante*[1].

If we then start to replace the diphthongs *e* and *o* first by *ay* and *av* before vowels other than *a,* and then eventually in its place by *a* (more precisely, *a'* i.e., *a* followed by a sound that obstructs contraction and which we may call spiritus lenis[2], then clearly we cannot disregard the reason why the *i-* and *u-* element of *e* and *o* before the following *a* should not have changed to *y* and *v* exactly as before any other vowel. Because in the *-ay* and *-av* which thus arise we would then get the desired, and by the metre constantly demanded, short vowel for the transmitted *e* and *o.* **[454]** We do not yet ask the question here, how are we to explain the traditionally tranmitted writing of *e* and *o* if *ay* and *av* (and from them eventually the later *a'*) were the correct old forms of the sound group in question[3]. We will take up this question later. Right here, however, we would like to point out that exactly the same kind of traces which we have for *ay* instead of the transmitted *a* before vowels other than *a* have also been preserved for *ay* instead of the transmitted *e* before the following *a.* For *anīke asthiran* SV. 1, 13 we find in the text of the related Sāman*: ānīkay āsthāyirān, anākāyikāy*

1. Padap. *táyā* I *vahante.*
2. The fact that this alternation of the originally diphthongs *e, o* with *ay, av* was a living phenomenon in the Vedic period leaves hardly any doubt about the fact that diphthongal pronunciation of those sounds had at that time not yet disappeared (cf. also the pluta-forms like *agnāi* for *agne,* etc.); see Whitney Gr. § 28. Introducing the forms *agnai, daivas* for *agne, devas* in the writing of the Ṛgveda text itself has to be avoided for obvious misgivings.
3. Incidentally, there exists a *single* passage in the Ṛk-text which, apparently, has by chance escaped the notice of the diaskeuasts who otherwise have carried out the transformations very systematically. The passages in question preserves the treatment of *e* before *a* that is really valid before *i, u, ā* etc. *stotava ambyam* VIII.72.5, Prātiśākhya 177.

āsthāyirā. For *agne aṅgiraḥ* SV I.29: *āgnay āṅgāirāḥ*. Out of *kāme asmin*, i.e., *kāmay asmin* of ṚV X.128.2 has become in the Atharvaveda (V.3.3) *kāmāyāsmai*.

Thus the difference in the treatment given by the tradition to final *e* (= *a* + *i*) and *o* (= *a* + *u*) before the following *a* and before other following vowels is nothing but a mistake—whose origin still requires explanation—of the one who transmitted the text. It is clear that the short vowel (*ay, av, a'*) has to be substituted at places where the transmitted text deviates from the otherwise prevalent treatment of that *e* and *o* before a certain vowel (*a*) and has instead of a short vowel (*ay, av, a'*) a long one and where the metre regularly indicates a mistake[1].

With the background of this knowledge we now approach the case of the final *o* = *as*. Just as with a following vowel other than *a, agnay uta, viṣṇav uta* has, in the traditional writing, **[455]** become *agna uta, viṣṇa uta* (i.e., *agna' uta, viṣṇa' uta*), similarly *indras uta* has become *indra uta* (*indra' uta*). Just as with the following vowel *a*, what is written *agne aṅga, viṣṇo aṅga,* but which due to the resulting metrical error turns out to be *agnay aṅga, viṣṇav aṅga*—and from this then obviously *agna' aṅga, viṣṇa' aṅga,* which is *that* stage of development to which *agna' uta* belongs— so also is written *indro aṅga* and here also the same metrical error is to be observed. The conclusion is obvious: here also we have to set up *indra aṅga* (*indra' aṅga*) analogous to the phase represented by *indra uta* (i.e. *indra' uta*)[2]. Thus also in the case of the final *o* = *as,* we come to the same

1. Bollensen, in fact, writes this way, e.g., *uloko yas tă adrivaḥ,* ZDMG XLI.500.
2. Just as *-is, -us* (*-iṣ, -uṣ*) becomes *-ir, -ur* no matter *whether* the following vowel is *a* or any other vowel. For one who lacks courage to declare the phonetic phenomena in the Vedic text as purely grammatical clumsiness, such as those in question here, working with the phonetic laws peculiar to the Maitr. Saṁhitā may be recommended (see Schroeder Einl. XXVIII f.).

understanding as for the final *o* = *a* + *u* and for the final *e*, viz., if we choose to repeat the expression used by Weber long ago (Kuhn's Beitr. III.401), that the whole difference between the treatment before *a* and before the remaining vowels is "only a so-to-say literary one"[1].

---

1. It has already been mentioned above that the pragṛhya *e* and *o* are not affected by the shortening before a following vowel. Bloomfield (p. 16, note 3) has already pointed out that this happens due to the specially long length of those vowels. Just as the *-e* (= *a*+*i*) of the loc. sg. of the *a*-stems becomes a^y before vowels, so also obviously the *-e* of the nom. dual of fem. and ntr. stems (= *ă* + *ī*) becomes $a + i^y$ $= e^y$ (*samudra*^{y} *andhasaḥ*, but *ubhe*^{y} *anu*). Incidentally, which *-e* and *-o* are to be understood as pragṛhya, has not been correctly determined in all cases by the tradition. The feminine and the neuter duals in *-e* are certain, and further the loc. *tve* (Prāt. 74). But *asme* does not seem to belong here. Of the 22 passages where a vowel follows this word, two passages are directly in favour of *e* as short (VIII.22.16; X.22.2); it is also to be noted that at all places where *e* before the following vowel happens to be the *second* syllable of the pāda, the third is always long. For *yuṣme* we have no way to check; but this form, of course, cannot be separated from *asme*. **[456]** The dual conjugational endings in *-āthe* etc. are doubtful; I.151.4, perhaps also I.32.13, VI.67.6 favour the pragṛhya quality of *e*, but I.2.9; VII.93.6; VIII.26.13 *contradict* it.—Of the alleged cases of *-o*, the vocatives in *o* like *viṣṇo* are to be separated (Prāt. 69,157; cf. Whitney, Ath. Prāt. I.81). In contrast, the *o* which arises from the contraction of words like *atha, uta, mā* with the particle *u* is certainly pragṛhya. Here the pragṛhya quality of the vowel seems to depend on the fact that *u* is a word in itself, and hence in the ṚV. there are as few chances of its becoming *v* as, for example, of *vi* becoming *vy*. Just as in the ṚV *tad v asti* is out of the question, similarly one can also not expect *atha v imām* in X.85.41, but only something like *athau*^{v} *imām* (where *au* does not mean a vṛddhi-diphthong but the original diphthonged pronunciation of the sound written by us as *o*).—If we look again at the pragṛhya *-ī* and *-ū*, we notice that also with them the pragṛhya-quality is proved by their remaining long before the following vowel. While the word-groups appearing in the traditional writing as *vājy asi, śipry andhasaḥ* are to be gauged as — ◡ ◡ ◡, — ◡ — ◡ ◡ (cf. Kuhn Beitr. III.119) and must be understood obviously as *vājī*^{y} *asi, śiprī*^{y} *andhasaḥ*, *ī* in *rodasī ubhe, śucī upa* remains long; they must be

(Continued on next page)

[456] The sound which arose from the disappearing *s* of *indra(s) uta*, etc., which is not seen in usual writing and which makes its presence felt only by obstructing vowel contraction has found, as is well known, positive expression at some places in the tradition. Among these **[457]** we can hardly count the writings in *-ar*[1], partly because in their case it can be said that they are based on analogy with words which really end in *-ar* (*ahar* etc.) or on forms like *havir* etc., and partly because other kinds of misunderstandings have a role to play: from the much cited *ugrar āvṛt, bhīmar āvṛt, śrutar āvṛt* etc. (Taitt. Saṁh. II.4.7; Kāṭhaka XI.9), the *ugra rāvaṭ* etc. of the Maitrāyaṇī Saṁhitā (II.4.7) has now luckily saved us. That *-ar*, in fact, does not appear for *-as* under the same conditions as *-ir, -ur* for *-is, -us* (*-iṣ, -uṣ*) is explained sufficiently by the difference in the nature of the

---

(Continued from previous page)

substituted by *rodasī*ʸ *ubhe, śucī*ʸ *upa*. The ī of the dual forms is a sure pragṛhya; apparently the *ī* in the locatives like *vedī, gaurī* (Prāt. 73, Lanman 389) is also pragṛhya, but the few passages available offer no confirmation for this, and VI.1.10 (Prāt. 174) is even opposed to it. For the pronoun *amī* (Prāt. 74) we do not have suitable passages to check. The duals in *ū* cannot be separated from those in *ī*, although the available materials would not allow us to come to any sure decision about them (see I.93.5; 116.20; VII.61.2; 68.3; X.143.6, but against this I.46.13; II.27.15; V.43.4).—The traditional view that the pragṛhya vowels cannot coalesce with the following vowel (cf. Prāt. 156) is wrong. It is not possible to conceive of any acceptable explanation and, in fact, in the ṚV cases of contraction are not wanting, which are reproduced in the Saṁhitāpāṭha almost always correctly and untouched by the mechanical processes of the grammarians' normalization (*viśpatīva, rodasīme* etc.; Prāt. 159,174,176). That we do not come across, as far as I can see, any case of a proper Abhinihita sandhi with the pragṛhya *-e* is obviously only a matter of chance, and it is quite easily understood because of the relative rarity of this sandhi. But the contraction of *-e i-* to *e*, which is essentially similar to the Abhinihita, is to be found, in fact with the pragṛhya (*kanīnakeva* IV.32.23; *vayyeva* II.3.6. Lanman 361).

1. Weber op. cit. 385 note 2, 390, 391; Whitney § 176ᶜ; Bloomfield op. cit. 7 note 2; Osthoff Perfect. 40.

vowels. In my opinion the writings in *-ay* deserve more attention than those in *-ar*[1]. Quite well-known are *adhi dhīray emi* in the stanza cited in Śāṅkhāyana (Śr. 1.6), the *apay iṣya hotar* of the formula used in the Aponaptrīya (Āśval. Śraut. V.1.1; Kāty. IX.3.2 v.l.), the *abhibhūyamānay iva* of the Maitr. Upaniṣad (II.6), the *nay ehi* of the Kauśikasūtra[2]. The Gānas of the Sāmaveda again offer here numerous similar writings. Thus, for *śukra āhutaḥ* SV 1.4 : *śukrāy āhutaḥ, śa auhovā kray āhutāḥ, śukray ā auhauhovā hotohāyi.* For *bharanta emasi* SV I.14 we have *bhārātay emāsāyi.* Similarly *-āy* for the original *-ās;* thus for *saprathā asi* SV 1.42 : *saprāthāy āsāi,* and many more similar instances. When the words *pāhi gāyāndhaso made* ṚV VIII.33.4 have become in the SV *pāhi gā andhaso made* (which, originally, [458] must have come close in pronunciation to *pāhi gāy*) we have presumably to think of the same situation[3].

Thus, we have not only before other vowels but occasionally also before *a,* traces of the writing of *y* for the final *s* after *a* or *ā.* Obviously, at the time when the phonetic form of the text was being fixed, the sound concerned had almost disappeared and was preserved mainly in the archaic pronunciation of sacred formulae and sacred songs: where from among the available sounds *y,* or the *y* "to be more lightly pronounced" (*laghuprayatnatara*) appeared to present itself as the most expedient approximation for this purpose.

On the basis of the above discussions the following system as suitably representing the sounds may be adopted for constituting the text:

For *e, o* (= *a* + *i, a* + *u*) before vowels, regardless of whether the tradition gives *e, o* (before the following *a*), or *a* (before other vowels): a^{y}, a^{v}; e.g. *agna*^{y} *agninā, agna*^{y} *ekayā,*

1. Cf. Vāj. Prātiś. IV.36; Athar. Pr. II.41; Taitt. Pr. IX.10,19 f.;—Pāṇini. VIII.3.17 ff.
2. Ind. Stud. IV.252 where more of this nature is cited.
3. Is ṚV V.75.7 *aryayā* for *arya' ā* uncertain ? Cf. ZDMG XL.126.

adhvarya^v *andhasaḥ* [correspondingly, of course, for the vṛddhi diphthongs: $\bar{a}^y$, $\bar{a}^v$].

For *o* (*as*) before vowels, regardless of whether the tradition gives *o* (before *a*) or *a* (before other vowels), in view of the passages just collected, one would be inclined likewise to recommend, a^y, or else express the sound arising from the vanishing *s* by writing it as a^s: *bharanta*^{s} *emasi; devāsa*^{s} *apturaḥ.*

However, for practical purposes it would be enough to adopt a simplified notation; therefore, at the time of printing the text I would do away with the differences of the types _*y*, _*v*, _*s* and would be content with the writing *a'* [resp. *ā'*] for all those cases.

[459] It is well known that already in the Ṛgveda—rarely in the older parts, with increasing frequency in the later ones— -a^y, -a^v, -a^s can coalesce with the following *a*- to form *one* syllable, as a result of which -$a^y a$- becomes *e*, -$a^v a$- and $a^s a$- become *o.*[1] We have already examined above [p. 389 ff.]

---

1. As regards the source of the *o*-colour of the vowel in the case of -a^s *a*-, if one does not share the views of Bloomfield on the continuation of the original *ŏ*, one can scarcely find it elsewhere than in the nature of the glottal closure of the larynx between the two vowels. Besides, we have no sufficient reason to doubt that the writing *o* is the correct one and is not imposed on the text by a later usage or a later theory. However, Roth (KZ. XXVI.51) has collected some passages where he explains *ā* of the Saṁhitā text as a contraction of *-as a-;* one may accordingly be tempted to assume that originally the product of the crasis of -a^s *a*- was rather *ā*, which just in these cases by chance must have eluded the transformation brought about by the diaskeuasts. But, to begin with, of the three cases cited by Roth the first is quite clearly to be excluded: I.164. 7 *śīrṣṇaḥ kṣīraṁ duhrate gāvo asya vavriṁ vasānā udakaṁ padāpuḥ.* I do not know why we cannot here stick to the traditional interpretation, so obvious, of *padāpuḥ* as *padā apuḥ;* where milk is milked out of the head, drinking water with the foot is certainly no more strange than many other things mentioned in the long riddle-hymn. Next, in I.51.11 (*indro vaṅkū vaṅkutarādhi tiṣṭhati*) we can very well take

(Continued on next page)

this procedure of the diaskeuasis in connection with the imposition of this so-called Abhinihita sandhi. Here it must be pointed out again that an examination of the Ṛk-text shows this sandhi to be only a special case of what, in fact, is a more general phenomenon. Just as in the case of *-a*^{y} (*-a*^{v}) and *-a*^{s} before the following *a-*, so also coalescence **[460]** going beyond a^y and a^s (and also beyond word-final *m* which is equally not capable of offereing much resistance), can occur before other vowels.[1] Hence, *rasina*^{s} *iyam* = *rasineyam* VIII.1.26; *ūrdhva*^{s} *ud* = *ūrdhvod* X.90.4; perhaps also *deva*^{s} *ekaḥ* = *devaikaḥ* X.121.8; *tura*^{s} *iyām* = *tureyām* VII.86.4, and many other similar cases. Examples for *a*^{y} : *ta*^{y} *indra* = *tendra* VII.21.9; VIII.40.9; *ma*^{y} *ud* = *mod* X. 166. 5; *vivida*^{y} *uttaraḥ* = *vividottaraḥ* X. 85.40 etc[2]. These coalescences in the Ṛgveda, not recognized by the tradition but which can be concluded on the basis of metre, are relatively hardly less frequent than the cases of the Abhinihita sandhi which have received firm recognition, since the Abhinihita sandhi is by its very nature conditioned by the overwhelming frequency of *a-* in the initial position as compared to the other vowels.

(Continued from previous page)

vaṅkutarā as dual; but if we have to admit nom. sg., then it is especially easy to admit here a corruption brought about quite superficially by the influence of *vaṅkū;* hence, this example is of no consequence for phonetic problems. There remains only one case V.61.12 where, in fact, if one does not opt for the too artificial interpretations, one must see in *śriyādhi* the occurrence of nom. pl. *śriyas* with *adhi.* Such an isolated passage is obviously not sufficient to support positing a general rule like *-a*^{s} *a-* = *ā*; one simply shall have to emend the passage (*śriyodhi*) which, apart from this, cannot be avoided in view of the accent.

1. Cf. Benfey, Quantitätsverschiedenheiten 1.31 ff.
2. The coalescence of this type is especially common when the following word is *iva,* because this word attaches itself very closely to the preceding word. That we have also cases where the first of the two coalesceing vowels is not *a* can be easily understood.

It now seems to me that it is in the writing of the Abhinihita sandhi that we have to look for the explanation of the question, left unanswered in our above discussions, as to why the diaskeuasts came to write *indra iti* and not *indra api* but *indro api, agne api.* Obviously it is the Abhinihita writing system *indropi, agnepi* which offers the solution. For it cannot be a matter of just chance that in the disyllabic spelling *-e a-, -o a-* (which, as the metre shows, is against the original pronunciation) *e,* and respectively *o,* occur *only before that one vowel* which, in the Abhinihita sandhi, can lead to the monosyllabic spelling *e, o.* For the diaskeuasts **[461]** the monosyllabic spelling (*indropi*), in accordance with the standpoint of the later period, was the obvious choice. But it did not escape their notice that in the Vedic poetry besides monosyllabic writing the disyllabic writing had even an overwhelming place. However, the question as to why it came to pass that they were earnest precisely in recognizing the disyllabic writing, while they consistently substituted the not less justified *-a a-* by *ā, -i a-* by *-y a-,* can hardly be decided. But the fact, although surprising, remains that the otherwise favoured practice of compressing the Vedic text to as few syllables as possible has been handled more moderately here than anywhere else. Can it surprise us then if the disyllabic writing was influenced by the monosyllabic one that was also in use by its side, and which was more in keeping with the understanding of the diaskeuasts? If they first understood the original *-a*^{y} *a-, -a*^{s} *a-,* as antiquated disyllabic by forms of the more common *e, o,* where the following *a-* was not lost, could they then not have fixed them accordingly as *-e a-, -o a-* ? In this way, I think we get a natural explanation of this writing method as a pure act of clumsiness on the part of the diaskeuasts[1]

---

1. It is difficult to determine exactly the point at which a real *-ē a-, -ō a-* (apart from the pragṛhyas) appear for the first time in Indian poetry. They are not known, as we saw, to the Ṛgveda. Also the

(Continued on next page)

[462] In continuation of the above discussion of final *-as*, we should discuss here the pronominal nominatives *sa* and *saḥ*[1], whose side by side occurrence brings up special questions. I refer the readers to Grassmann's Wörterbuch for forms in which they appear in the transmitted text[2]. If

---

(Continued from previous page)

Yajurveda texts and the Atharvaveda are full of metrical indices which indicate a short pronunciation of the sounds written *-e, -o* before *a*. It will not be easy to discover significant passages in the stanzas of the Brāhmaṇas and the Upaniṣads since here the Abhinihita sandhi has attained almost absolute validity. Yet I do find the Śatapatha Br. XI.3.1,5,6, the *last* pāda of a śloka repeated twice : *kathaṁ saṁtato agnibhiḥ*, respectively *tathā saṁtato agnibhiḥ;* here "*-o*" is presumably to be understood as a short syllable. Examples of *-ō a-* can be cited only from the Buddhist literature. In the Dhammapada we find the first pādas of the śloka as follows: *n'atthi rāgasamo aggi* (202 = 251), *seyyo ayoguḷo bhutto* (308), second pādas like *yo naro anuyuñjati* (247), *appatto āsavakkhayaṁ* (272). A thorough examination of the Pāli metre made on the basis of such passages will permit us to conclude that the vowel *o* is long. Thus here, and as far as my present knowledge goes, it is first here that the *o* which developed out of *as* before voiced consonants has been transferred to positions before vowels, just as in Pāli, of course, it was also transmitted to positions before voiceless consonants. Only further research will permit us to fix with absolute certainty the point of time at which this transference took place; however it is already now established that this transference is recent, as compared with the situation in the old Vedic period, that is, quite different from the way in which Osthoff Perfect 28 f., Brugmann Grundriss § 556, 3 describe the matter. Besides, if in the period of the Vedic diaskeuasts, as is likely to be the case, the phonetic form *-ō a-*, which is found in the Dhammapada, already existed in the living speech, then it is easy to understand that they assumed the same form to hold good for the Vedic texts.

1. The nominatives *sya* and *eṣa* occur more or less in a similar way.
2. Grassmann's presentation is misleading in so far as it gives the impression that the same *so* can occur before an unelided *-a* only if *a* is followed by a double consonant; the few cases which are opposed to this have been explained away by Grassmann by interpreting that

(Continued on next page)

one compares the relevant occurrences in the Atharvaveda, one finds that the stage of the later language, at least on the whole, has been reached there, i.e., *sa* was placed before consonants, *saḥ* or its sandhi-representative before vowels. The hymn-author of course had no aversion against the latter sandhi since here a real hiatus did not arise; hence, it was not of particular rarity either. **[463]** That in the Ṛgveda we meet with different situations is easily seen. First, the *sa* (*saḥ*) is—except in the tenth book—followed by a word beginning with a vowel *much more* rarely than what would correspond to the otherwise prevailing proportion of words beginning with a vowel and a consonant[1]. If the intention of the authors, which is obvious, permits us to conclude that the Ṛgvedic poets did in no way employ the form *saḥ* before a following vowel to the same extent as it has happened in the AV, then this conclusion is also proved by the fact that, unlike in the AV, the contraction with the following vowel (as in *sed, semam, sodañcam*) is in no way rare; it occurs far more frequently than what the assumption of an occasionally occurring contraction going beyond the visarga would permit us to expect. Thus, one sees that the sphere of *saḥ* in the ṚV at all events is smaller when compared with the AV, and one has to choose between the two alternatives: either to recognize for the *original* Ṛk-text only the form *sa*, or to suppose that by its side there existed

(Continued from previous page)

so as *sa u* (in V.44.8 perhaps correctly, but in both the instances occurring in I.103.5 quite arbitrarily). Altogether it is not clear why a double consonant should make a difference. That indeed *so a-* is almost always followed by a double consonant is obviously due to the fact that after the short pronunciation of *so* (before *a-*) the metre requires or favours a long syllable.

1. The cases in which *sa* (or *so*) occurs before a vowel, with or without contraction, as compared to those in which it occurs before consonants show the following proportion: Book VI, something like 1:6,6; in VII,1:4,7; in VIII.1:6,0; in IX.1:8,7; as against this in X.1:2,0! At the same time the cases of contraction in X are specially rare.

also *saḥ,* but that the latter was already on its way to acquire its later validity. I believe that the second assumption is decidedly to be preferred. In itself it is not likely that such a wide, unbridgeable gulf should separate the linguistic stage of the ṚV from that of the AV, which would be the case if we were to accept the first of those two suppositions. Moreover the existence of *saḥ* **[464]** in the ṚV is vouchsafed by the traditional text, and also by the frequency of the apparent hiatus in comparison with the contraction with the following vowel, which deviates considerably from the otherwise valid proportions. This frequency rises further in the tenth book, where in other respects hiatus is more seldom and contraction more frequent. One can hence hardly miss noticing the fact that this book comes closer to the situation in the AV[1], viz., the growing tendency to use *saḥ* in order to avoid hiatus.

Accordingly, it seems we are justified in ascribing to the poets of the ṚV the observance, perhaps not very strict yet approximate, of the following standards with regard to the use of *sa* and *saḥ:*

1. Before the consonants occurred *sa*[2]. This is what the tradition has, and it is confirmed by metrically decisive cases. The *saḥ* which could have suggested itself for the sake of position occurs only in a very few, but trustworthy, cases (III.53.21; VIII.33.16).

2. Before a following vowel *sa* is used if contraction has to occur; if not, *saḥ*. In the older period there prevailed aversion against both these eventualities; however, between the two, the latter was preferred. The tradition almost always correctly distinguishes between the case of contraction and that of the (apparent) hiatus. Especially before the following *a-* the tradition of course gives *saḥ* (*sa'*) as *so;* where metre requires contraction with *a-*, we find in the traditional text

1. This can be seen also in the data given in the preceding note.
2. *Once sā* I.145.1: not a sure case.

sā in a number of cases (cf. Prāti. 172,173; wrong in VI.12.4), in some others *so a-* or *so* with the Abhinihita sandhi : it seems to me that in all these cases *sā-* is to be restored.

[465] 3. At the end of the pāda, I believe, there was no reason to touch the *saḥ* which was obviously used where hiatus was to be avoided. The traditional text gives, at the end of the stanza and before avasāna, *saḥ,* at the other pāda-ends, each time depending on the sound that follows, that form which would be required if it occurred within the pāda (exception V.2.4). Taking the whole account into consideration, one scarcely expects anything other than this; this does not block the supposition that the form actually used at the end of the pāda was *sa.*

If one overlooks these cases of the pāda-end that are particularly exposed to the dangers of diaskeuastic alterations, then in the treatment of *sa* and *saḥ* the tradition again proves to have a knowledge that does not look like the product of grammatical reflection, but bears the stamp of a genuine reliable recollection of the past.

Vowel Before Vowel: Nasalized Final Vowel

In the preceding section we have examined the situations in which final *ī, ū, e, o* are shortened before a following vowel and in which they are not. We add here a few remarks on the treatment of *ā* in similar situation. As far as I know Kuhn[1] was the first to recognize that it was *permissible* to shorten *ā* before a following vowel[2] if no contraction took place; we may, I think, go a step further and assert that this **[466]** shortening was a rule[3]. While reviewing the relevant

1. Beiträge III.120 f. Cf. M. Müller, Ṛgveda translation LXXXVII f.
2. Of course the case where a *s* or *y* has disappeared between the two vowels (*imā' agne, asmā' id*) does not belong here.
3. When we seek to prove this rule for the case where the two vowels do not coalesce, we may not overlook that even when contraction takes place, the shortening is discernible since *-ā i-, -ā u-, -ā ṛ-* becomes *e, o, ar,* (*a ṛ*), and not *ai, au, ār.* Cf. Benfey, Ved. und Ling. 13.

material we of course neglect the insignificant cases (they are 37 or 38), in which *ā* occurs in the first syllable of the pāda, and then also those in which it occurs immediately before the Triṣṭubh- or the Jagatī-caesura (69 cases) or immediately after it (I.189.4). Equally little importance should be attached to those cases where *ā* occurs as the fourth-last syllable of a Triṣṭubh-, or as fifth-last syllable of a Jagatī-pāda[1], or as the seventh syllable of such a sequence where the caesura occurs after the fourth[2]: in these positions, as is well known, the use of the long syllable is overwhelmingly found, but the short syllable is also frequent enough. The short vowel is found first in those passages in which *ā* occurs as the second syllable after the Triṣṭubh- or Jagatī-caesura[3]. Decisive above all, however, are the cases which relate to the *end* of the stanza. Here we find *ā,* followed by a vowel, as the third-last syllable of Triṣṭubh:

I. 62.8 *vapurbhir ā carato' anyā-anyā*
I. 77.1 *kathā dāśema agnaye kā asmai*
I.140.13(?) *gaviaṁ yavyaṁ yanto dīrghā ahā*
I.165.6(?) *kua syā vo marutaḥ svadhā āsīt*[4]
I. 174.8 *sanā tā ta' ind^{a}ra navyā*[5] *āguḥ*
[467] IV. 3.13 *mā veṣasya praminato mā āpeḥ*
V. 41.16 *evayā maruto' acchāuktau*
praśravaso maruto' acchāuktau
VI. 21.8 *śaśvad babhūtha suhava' āiṣṭau*
24.5 *aryo vaśasya parietā asti*
63.1 *kua tyā valgū puruhūtā adya*
VII. 40.3 *na tasya rāyaḥ parietā asti*

---

1. These are eight cases; to these we have to add the case of the nasalized *ā* in VI.15.9 *ubhayā̃ anu vratā,* provided that we have here *ubhayā* neuter.
2. 4 or 5 cases: IV.19.6; VI.4.4; 11.1(?); X.61.18; 132.4.
3. I.60.4; 104.5; 116.16; 186.6; VIII.103.13; X.49.10.
4. But cf. above [p. 385, note 1].
5. The Padap. has *navyāḥ* and the Saṁhitāp. does not have contraction.

X. 22.5 *tuaṁ tyā cid vātasyāśvā āgāḥ*[1].

If we may venture a slight and probable correction, to this list belongs also :

X. 5.5 *icchan vavrim avidat pūṣā asya*[2].

Further, the *ā* occurs as the fourth-last syllable of Gāyatrī:

IV. 52.2 *aśveva citrā aruṣī*
V. 51.15 *punar dadatā aghnatā*
VIII.20.17(?) *yuvānas tathā id asat*
VIII. 46.29 *ṣaṣṭiṁ sahasrā asanam.*

[468] If we remove the nasalization, which is probably wrong, then the following would also belong here:

I. 133.6 *śuśoca hi dyauḥ kṣā na bhīṣā̃ adrivaḥ*
ghṛṇān na bhīṣā̃ adrivaḥ.

---

1. In this enumeration I am disregarding the numerous passages in which *tvotaḥ* or *tvōtāḥ* occurs at the end of a Triṣṭubh pāda (cf. Benfey, Quantitätsversch. IV.3.18). These would belong here if we resolve the word as *tvāūtāḥ*. Presumably, however, we have to read *tuotāḥ;* cf. the lengthening of the preceding vowel in I.73.9 *vanuyāmā tvōtāḥ*. However, in V.3.6 we have the text handed down as *vanuyāma tvotāḥ;* in X.148.1 *sanuyāma tvotāḥ;* but in the latter case the Sv. Ārcika gives *sahyāmā tvotāḥ,* and what is perhaps decisive is that the Gāna reads in both the related Sāmans *tūvotāḥ*. I also do not consider here the passages in which *tvāhuḥ* or something similar to it occurs at the end of the stanzas, and it seems that we have to resolve it as *tuāhuḥ,* not *tvā āhuḥ* (I.104.9; II.32.2; VI.44.10; VII.16.4; VIII.1.16; X.2.7; cf. also III.47.3 *ye tuānu*).
2. What is actually transmitted is *pūṣaṇásya*. This form of the name is hardly sufficiently supported by X.93.4, where *pūṣáṇaḥ* (with a different accent!) can be nom. plur. It is quite likely that *vavri* refers to the hiding place of Agni to whom the hymn is dedicated, and which is so often mentioned in the Veda. That it is Pūṣan who finds him is quite natural. It is, of course, Pūṣan's regular role to find out what is lost (Bergaigne, Rel. Véd. II.421); he is *anaṣṭapaśu* (ṚV 10.17.3), while with reference to Agni it is said *paśuṁ na naṣṭam padair anu gman* (X.46.2), cf also I.23.13,14). Incidentally, Ludwig already translates: "searching he found there the cover of Pūṣaṇa (Pūṣan his cover?)".

As far as I can determine, there is *not a single* passage with *ā* in the long penultimate syllable of a Triṣṭubh (third-last of a Jagatī) which would contradict the above passages that have *ā* at a place necessarily requiring a short syllable towards the end of the pāda. In the third-last position of a Gāyatrī, an *ā* of that sort, which is to be counted as long, should not be infrequent; in reality, however, I find it at only two places:

I. 30.14 *ā gha tvāvān tmanā āptaḥ*
IX. 66.18 *tvaṁ soma sūra' ā iṣaḥ:*

nothing, however, can confirm the rule more clearly than precisely these two exceptions, for both the pādas occur in places where trochaic intonation at the end of a Gāyatrī prevails, and hence a short syllable, rather than a long one, at the third-last position is to be expected.

In view of these firm results obtained by the investigation of the ends of the pādas, the beginnings of the pādas which have so many fluctuations in their metrical formulations do not really come for consideration, even if the unfavoured unification of two short syllables in the position of the second and the third syllable leads to the shortening of the *ā* in not quite few cases. I think it enough to put together here the material concerning the beginnings of the pādas: I.127.10; 129.9 (with the transmitted nasalisation of *ā*); II.19.3; 41.17; IV.57.7; V.45.2; 61.5; VI.23.4; VIII.16.3,7; 46.10; 101.13; IX.88.3; X.14.3; 26.1,9; 49.11; 50.2; 60.7; 61.8,9; 93.13; 105.4; 132.2; 145.3; 161.5[1].

[469] In the five-syllabled (Virāj-) pādas I find *ā* followed by a vowel at two places, on both occasions in the third syllable of the sequence which, as is well known, is predominantly short: I.69.9 *vibhāvā usraḥ*; VII.34.1 *pra śukrā etu*.

---

1. Here also belong, perhaps, the many instances in which *indrāgnī* (with four syllables) occurs at the beginning of a pāda: however, the first member *can* also be taken to be *indra-*, cf. *indra-vāyū*.

For the sake of completeness I mention further a few corrupt or abnormally constructed stanzas in which an *ā* of that kind appears or could appear: I.120.1; 173.4; X.93.14; 105.2,11; 164.3.

We may assert as the result of our investigation the regular shortening of *ā* before a following vowel. By the way, this phenomenon is not the same as the shortening of *ī, ū* in the same situation [p. 456, note 2]. In the case of the latter sounds, clearly a part of the vowel is changed to a semi-vowel, and what remains as a vocalic element is the short vowel; in the case of *ā,* on the other hand, it is nothing but the application of the rule *vocalis ante vocalem* (vowel before a vowel). Moreover, the difference in the two types is revealed in the statistics: the frequency with which the final vowel of *śuṣmī, vājī,* etc. is affected by shortening stands in notable contrast to the relative rarity of similar shortening in the case of the vowel *ā* which, *per se,* occurs so much more frequently as word-final. In this respect it must also be noted that in the case of *ā,* as the materials cited prove, it was considered essential to soften the encounter of the two vowels with the help of caesura.

The cases of the nasalization of *ā* when followed by a vowel considered above [p. 468] give an occasion to add here a few remarks on these *nasalisations* intended for the removal of the hiatus. A great **[470]** majority of these cases concern the vowel at the end of a pāda followed by another vowel at the beginning of a pāda, the two not separated by an avasāna: *ă* before *e* and *o; ā* before *ṛ* in many cases; the words *ā* and *sacā* before a following vowel[1]. On account of

1. Prātiśākhya 164 ff.; Benfey, *Vedica und Linguistica* 10 ff., 163 ff.; Lanman Index s.v. Nasalisation. That the rule about nasalization of *ă* before *e* and *o* (Prāt. 166) is declared to be valid *'Luṣād arvāk'* because the last case of that type occurs in X.34.5 (in X.121.3 the nasalization does not take place): Luṣa is the ṛṣi of X.35.

the nature of the separation of the pādas it is obvious, as has been already explained by Benfey, that here we do not have before us something which is original, but something which concerns the rules of the diaskeuasts which, whatever the notions on which they may have been based, are worthless for us. Nasalization of *ā* and in *one* instance (I.179.2) of *a* does, however, occur within a pāda.[1] It occurs only in such instances where the *ă*, according to the metrical evidence, is not to be contracted with the following vowel, but—and it is hardly necessary to state this—one cannot even remotely say that every *ā* or even just *ā* of certain forms which is not contracted with the following vowel would be nasalised; on the contrary, the concerned cases form an infinitely small minority. At the same time it is worthwhile to note that, even if the coming together of *-ā ṛ-* without contraction may be rare, in *those* situations nasalisation occurs almost in every case[2]: *kadā̃ ṛtacid* V.3.9; *mātā̃ ṛṇuta* V.45.6; *maghavām̐ ṛjīṣī* IV.16.1.[3] At some other places, I think, the situation is different: *vibhvā̃ ṛbhuḥ* IV.33.6 cf. IV.36.6: *vibhvā̃ ṛbhukṣāḥ* VII.48.3: *svavā̃ ṛtāvā* III.54.12; VI.68.5; **[471]** *svatavā̃ ṛṣvaḥ* IV.20.6. According to the explanations of J. Schmidt[4] it must be considered probable that the stems *suavas, svatavas, vibhvan* were affected by the analogy of the *vāṁs*-stems and hence formed nominatives *suavān, svatavān, vibhvān* (beside *vibhvā*). Here were found, by chance, in a number of passages just *before the ṛ-vowel* forms in *-ā̃,* which were partly really considered by the padapāṭha as *per se* ending in *-ā,* partly could very well have been considered this way. On the basis of this evidence, I

1. For the listing of passages see Benfey a.a.o; Prātiśākhya 167-170.
2. Benfey (p.11) counts *always* one syllable for the *-a ṛ-* within a pāda, hence, assumes always nasalization in the case of non-contraction. But I find at least one exception: I.127.10 *jūrṇir hota ṛṣūṇām.*
3. For the last passage cf. Benfey a.a.o. 20.
4. KZ. XXVI.357 f.

think, there was an occasion for the formulation of the rule that—except in the case of contraction—*ā* before *ṛ* is nasalized, and then due to this rule the spellings like *kadā̃ ṛtacid* etc., together with the analogous spellings at the end of a pāda, will have been introduced into the text.

According to what has been said, if the later origin of most of the cases of nasalization is certain or definitely probable, then we would be justified in distrusting the genuineness of nasalization in the remaining sporadic cases, even though it would be difficult to explain the rise of such nasalized spellings in individual cases[1]. The distrust is all the more justified since in the only case where the metre comes into question—I do not take into account the unreliable evidence of the fourth-last syllable of Triṣṭubh—the same decides the case *against* the nasalization: in the stanza I.133.6 cited above on p. 468, we obviously have to assume *bhīṣā adrivaḥ* [**472**] and apply the rule *vocalis ante vocalem.*

By the by, the fact that nasalizations never appear where metre requires contraction speaks, however, I think, for the fact that this way of spelling does not belong—at least as far as it concerns the cases within a pāda—to the younger and the youngest phases of the text-treatment given by the diaskeuasts, i.e., not to that period when one was accustomed to force on the text throughout, without any consideration for the metre, the principles concerning contraction once they were accepted.

Closer and Looser Word-Combination

In a number of phenomena related to the sentence-phonetics of the Veda, it is found that the same word-final before the

1. In I.79.2 *aminantā̰ evaiḥ*—the only case which concerns *ă*—it is easy to suppose connection with the rule Prāt. 166 which is valid for the end of the pāda. Is the rule based on this case or does the case arise rather due to an isolated extension of the rule to a point within the pāda? The chronological consideration which will be presented immediately [p.472] makes me feel that the former is more probable.

same initial of the next word assumes different forms depending on whether the connection between the two words is closer or looser. In some cases only the closer connection—especially in the case of the enclitics, but not exclusively with them—causes the phonetic effects between the final and the initial of the words corresponding to the phonetic rules which apply within the body of a word; in others, where these effects appear regularly, the looser connection, more than the closer one, favours the cancellation of the rule by the introduction of other forms, especially those which appear at the pause: for, naturally, the latter (pause forms) are most easily adopted at those places within a sentence where loose connection between the words produces an impression which more or less approximates the one at the end of the sentence. If we have on the one hand *abhy anūṣi,* but on the other *abhi* (in the transmitted text *abhy*) *aṁhuro gāt,* then this shows to us the influence exercised by the closeness of the words on the phonetic form, and **[473]** at the same time it shows how such phenomena were exposed to being leveled in the tradition. In other cases, the fates suffered by these phenomena in the course of tradition were more favourable. Thus, the preservation of *-as, iṣ, -uṣ* before *k* and *p* (the so-called upācāra) when there is greater closeness of words, but the occurrence of the pausa-forms *-aḥ, -iḥ, uḥ* in the case of lesser closeness of words[1]; correspondingly we have

1. Prātiśākhya 262 ff.; cf. Whitney Gramm. 171. Instead of trying to examine the demarcation of the phenomenon concerned in each case, we may only note that it has been on the whole well-preserved by the tradition. One may compare *haviṣ kṛṇudhvam ā gamat* VIII.72.1, *jyotiṣ kartā yad uśmasi* I.86.10 (Prāt. 266) with *uru jyotiḥ kṛṇuhi matsi devān* IX.94.5 Prāt. 270): in the latter case the caesura keeps the words *jyotiḥ* and *kṛṇuhi* apart. Similarly *divas pṛthivyāḥ pary oja' udbhṛtam* VI.47.27, but *pra ye divaḥ pṛthivyā na barhaṇā* X.77.3 (Prāt. 276). Or one may consider beside the numerous cases where the combination *divas pari* occurs, the stanza IX.8.8 = 39.2 *vṛṣṭiṁ divaḥ pari srava:* here *divaḥ* and *vṛṣṭim* belong together.

-iṣ, -uṣ before *t*, which is then cerebralized, but on the other hand *-is t-, -us t-* (*agniṣ ṭam brahmaṇā saha, sadhiṣ ṭava, niṣ ṭatakṣuḥ*, but *ūtibhis tireta*);[1] similarly, when an initial s changes to *ṣ* after a preceding *nāmin*-vowel[2] (*adhi ṣṇunā, pari ṣicyate*, but *sūriṣu syāma*), although the tradition is obviously not quite free from confusion, the factor, as I wish to call it, of greater or lesser word-closeness proves certainly to be decisive. The effects of word-closeness also clearly reveal themselves through the cerebralization, as found in the traditional text, of *n* after *r* and *ṣ* of the preceding word (Prāt. 372 ff.; *pra ṇonumaḥ, svar ṇa, pra ṇaḥ*[3], **[474]** but *pra nūnam, pra navyasā*) although this was also naturally equally exposed to many disturbances; in this, as well as in the preceding cases, the combination of the preposition and the verb offers a principal mass of materials to point to the case of words exerting stronger influence among themselves. Finally we may recall the preservation of combinations such as *-āṁś c-* in the case of greater, but their suppression by *-āñ ca-* in the case of lesser word-closeness which was discussed above [p. 431 f.].

Once phenomena of this type get confused in the oral tradition and if the corruptions are not revealed by the metre, there is of course little hope for a critic to establish in individual instances the original demarcation of the different cases. Yet it is surely our duty to indicate at least what the nature of the original form of the text must have been. Hence, we should express the supposition that the difference in the sandhi, depending on the relative closeness of the words, must have occurred also in other spheres not alluded to by us so far, but the tradition has wiped out the

1. Prātiśākhya 348 ff.; Whitney Gr. 188[b]; Osthoff Perfectum 38.
2. Prātiśākhya 348 ff.; Whitney 188[a].
3. But also quite often *pra naḥ* in the traditional text without showing that the demarcation is in any way related to the differences in the sentence structure.

difference without leaving a trace behind, as, for example, has happened in the case of *abhi* and *abhy* before a following vowel. If we find that the treatment of *-s p-*, of *-s k-* shows the form ending in *-ḥ* as at the pause, which in later language has attained general validity, but which in the Veda is valid within a sentence only when the words are thought to be not close, then I think we are justified in posing the question whether besides a sandhi between words supposed to be not close like *namo mahadbhyaḥ* we should not similarly assume also a sandhi between words thought to be close like *namas me*—with the sound-combination *sm* unchanged as within a word (*asmi*)—likewise *haviṣ me* etc.[1] **[475]** On the other hand, beside a combination *-s t-* which, on account of the identical dental character of both the sounds, is the only one that prevails in the traditionally handed-down text, should there not occur in the case of words with more word-distance—for example, where the words are held apart from each other by the influence of the Triṣṭubh-caesura—also the pausa form *-ḥ t-*? We may be permitted to give expression to such suppositions, but it is quite clear that here where the metre does not give any indication, all attempts to correct the text of individual cases accordingly would be a mere play of fantasy.

It suggests itself to assume that also in the sandhi-treatment of the final *r* similar differences occurring between the competing possibilities were obscured. Is it not likely that at many places where in the transmitted text, following the traditional sandhi-rules, the *ḥ*, as at the pause, or forms arising due to[2] the mixing up of the final *r* with the final *s* appear, instead of the final *r*, the *r*, when it occurred in closest combination with the following word, was preserved in the original pronunciation, as it has been preserved,

1. One may compare *manasmaya* (ṚV) as against later *manomaya*, *ayasmaya* (ṚV and also later) as against *ayomaya*.
2. And, in fact, maintaining exactly the same gradation of sandhi

(Continued on next page)

phonetically regularly, in the parallel situations within a word ? Since, for example, the enclitics *ca* and *cid* always prove to be in the closest combination with the preceding word, is it not probable that instead of the transmitted *svaś ca* (VII.66.9), *ahaś ca* (VI.9.1), *sasvaś cid* (VII.59.7; 60.10) we should rather admit *svar ca, ahar ca, sasvar cid,* corresponding to the [476] sound-group *rc* which is preserved without change within the word (*arcati, varcas;* cf. also *svarcakṣas; svarpati* ṚV as against *svaḥpati* SV)?

Wrong Stem-Forms

The following remarks are perhaps most conveniently made here, although, strictly from the point of view of the chronology of the textual-history, they should have occurred at an earlier place. They concern certain distortions of word-forms, which were obviously received by the founders of phonetic diaskeuasis as a legacy of the older periods.

Often in the transmitted text, declined or conjugated stems appear in such a shape that they are proved to be incorrect by the metre in all their forms. Instances of this type can for *the most part* be, at least in a majority of words, sufficiently distinguished from those in which the transmitted form is correct and, from the point of view of metre, rather a license. If the objection concerns a particular word and one finds, let us say, that the same in its traditional form, except in metrically indifferent passages, does not satisfy the metre *anywhere,* then the critic will not hesitate to look for a different fixing of the word-form. On the other hand, he will refuse to make such an attempt in cases where a given word shows only occasional violations of the metre,

---

(Continued from previous page)

depending on the closeness or distance between the words as happens in the case of *s*: thus, *pituḥ payaḥ* VII.101.3 but *pituṣ pari* VIII.6.10 as *divas pari.* On I.92.4 *āvar tamaḥ* (Prātiśākhya 259), where the *r*, by way of an exception, has resisted the penetration of the *s*-sound, see above [p. 424, note 1]; cf. Benfey Quantitätsverschiedenheiten VI.11 f.

such as are more or less common to all words, and where in a majority of cases the verse-structure allows, or even demands, the prosodic form of the word as it appears in the transmitted text: in this procedure, of course, the middle-group, consisting of doubtful cases standing between this and the group indicated above, cannot be completely eliminated. To the group of words long known [477] as absolutely sure cases of wrongly transmitted stem-forms belongs *pāvaka,* which is rather to be set up as *pavāka*[1], likewise *chadis* (which is correctly given in X.85.10) for the transmitted *chardis.* Next, several words in which for the long ṛ vowel always the short one is transmitted[2]: thus *mṛḍ-, dṛḷha, tṛḷha,* words in which the prosodic observation and the morphological consideration—we must have compensatory lengthening—support each other best[3]. One cannot describe the situation, as has sometimes happened, that "in the Veda ṛ stands not only for the short but also for the long vowel." Rather, the form which originally was *mṝḍ-, dṝḷha* was wrongly transmitted as *mṛḍ-, dṛḷha* because at the time of those who handed down the text they were really pronounced as *mṛḍ-, dṛḷha.* The Atharvaveda is a literary monument of that period in which by the side of the old prosody (ṝ), the new one (ṛ) had established itself; according to the evidence of the metre, the long vowel is represented there in the case of *mṛḍ-* in I.20.1; V.6.5-7; X.1.22; XI.2.28; XVIII.3.16, in the case of *dṛḍha* in XI.5.11; the short vowel, on the other hand, in the case of *mṛḍ-* in V.4.7; XII.1.46,47; XIX.44.5; 55.2; in the case of *dṛḍha* in V.30.1; IX.3.3.—Of not less linguisitc significance

1. The assumption of a form like *pavaka* would not, as one can easily see, sufficiently meet the difficulty. *Pāvaka* with the later prosody seems to occur in the Muṇḍ. Upan. II.1.1: this is the oldest attestation known to me at present. The Prātiśākhya, Manu etc. know natuarally the word only as *pāvaka.*
2. Cf. especially Benfey, Vedica und Verwandtes, 1 ff.
3. On *tisṛṇām* V.69.2 see Benfey op. cit 4, on *nṛṇām* the same 5 f., Lanman 430.

than the form *dṛḍha* are a series of varbal forms of the *ninth conjugation* where the metre leads us to the form *śriṇānaḥ* over the head of the transmitted *śrīṇānaḥ* VIII.101.9; likewise *śriṇītana* IX.11.6 (transmitted *śrīṇītana*); *priṇanti* IX.74.4; *apriṇāt* VIII.23.16; *priṇānaḥ* **[478]** I.73.1; II.11.17; IV.3.14; VII.13.1; *bhriṇanti* II.28.7; *druṇānaḥ* IV.4.1 (cf. Kuhn Beitr. III.122).

The examples mentioned here will be sufficient to demonstrate that the form of a word exclusively appearing in the original Ṛk-text has been equally exclusively ousted in the traditional text by another, younger form. We saw how in the Atharvaveda, in some of the cases considered above, there occur fluctuations of forms which are obviously characteristics of a transition period. One can accordingly consider *a priori* as only possible that similar fluctuations will appear also in the Ṛgveda, where, of course, such cases can be separated only with unsatisfactory certainty from those which arise due to free handling of metre. The statistical conditions and the linguistic explicability of forms which are to be considered for restitution are the factors on which alone the decision can rest and these themselves are understandably often enough insufficient to lead to a firm decision. For instance, a certain amount of probability has, I think, to be attributed to a stem *jāna,* beside *jana*[1]. For example, we have the following occurrences of *janān* where we would require the first syllable to be *long*: I.173.8; II.20.2; III.46.2; V.33.2; VI.10.5; 20.1; 49.15; 67.3; 68.5; as against these, the *short* syllable is required in I.50.3.6; 64.13; 120.11; II.2.10; VIII.19.14; 32.22; 60.16; X.14.12 (9 against 9 passages). In the case of the form *janāḥ:* those requiring a long first syllable are I.89.10; IV.38.9; VI.11.4; 51.11; in addition, perhaps, also II.24.10; X.53.5; **[479]** whilst those requiring short are I.102.5; III.2.5; VIII.1.3; 5.38; 40.7; 43.29;

1. Cf. the remarks of Saussure, Mémorie 80, on the vocalism of *a*-stems. See also Kuhn Beitr. III, 466.

46.32; 74.6 (4 to 6 against 8 passages)[1]. True, the observations made above [p. 11, note 1] on the use of *avase, avasaḥ* etc. warn us to be careful; nevertheless, in the case of *jana* the disagreement between the form required by the metre and the one actually transmitted is one that is too frequent to allow the assumption of mere metrical freedom to be probable; short words like *janāḥ* and *janān* could have been easily introduced everywhere in the stanzas without doing any harm to the metre. If *jănāḥ* could be really used so often at the place of a spondee at the Triṣṭubh-end, why then was *manaḥ,* for example, which is far more frequent, never so used? Why do all the characteristic passages that exist for this word—their number is 37—show without exception a short vowel in the first syllable?[2] Accordingly it seems to me that for the Ṛgveda the existence side by side of *jāna-* and *jana-* can be presumed with the same justification as that of *mṛḍ-* and *mṝḍ-* for the Atharvaveda[3].

[480] Moreover, just as the tradition knows pairs of forms such as *yenā* and *yena, abhi* and *abhī* and has executed their distribution on the whole correctly, so it has also preserved in other cases the two-fold prosodic possibility concerning vowels occurring within a word although this was forgotten

1. At first look it appears extremely strange that the numerous occurrences of *janam,* quite differently from those of *janāḥ* and *janān, consistently* point to a short vowel in the first syllable. Obviously this is accounted for by the fact that *janam,* but not *janāḥ, janān,* regularly requires, for semantic reasons, an adjective by its side, hence *-ṁ janam.* Since in this situation a syllable, long by position, precedes, the first syllable of *janam* itself can occur only at a neutral place or at a place where a metrically short syllable is required.
2. At the most one could cite as a counter example: *yuñjate mana' uta yuñjate dhiyaḥ* V.81.8; this is an example which, as long as it is the solitary one, can be disregarded.
3. A comparable case which applies not to the stem but to the ending is that of the traditional medial duals in *-āthe, -āte, -āthām, -ātām* by the side of which we have undoubtedly to assume forms with a short penultimate. Cf. Kuhn Beitr. III, 121; Roth KZ.XXVI.59 f.; Bartholomae KZ. XXIX.284 f.

in the case of *jāna* and *jana*. Thus, for example, is the case of *sādana*[1] and *sadana*. Both the forms are obviously distributed in the traditional text quite correctly, *except in two passages*. At the end of a pāda occurs, as required by the metre, *always sādanam, sādane, sādanaspṛśaḥ* etc. (11 passages); only *once*[2] we have *nṛṣădane* (V.7.2), presumably a mistake, which can be explained by the fact that *ā* never occurs elsewhere in the compound form *nṛṣadana*, nor has it an occasion to occur[3]. Within a pāda the word usually occurs immediately after the caesura and, to be sure, as is to be expected, with a short *ă* (55 cases); furthermore in a few cases where it occurs in other places in a pāda, it is found without lengthening, and without any occasion for it (VIII.13.2; 27.5; 143.4 and some passages having compounds of *sadana*). Only *once* does the form *sādanā* occur immediately after the caesura (X.18.13):[4] it seems to me almost certain that here we have a mistake, the wrong transfer of vowel length, which is justified at the end of the pāda, to a position in the stanza where the short vowel is assured by the overwhelming tendency of the metrical practice as seen in 55 examples.

[481] One may contrast the relationships of *sadana* and *sādana* described here with the corresponding facts, say, in respect of *savana*. Almost throughout, its first syllable comes up either in the Gāyatrī-pāda in its fourth position (16 cases) or it occurs in the Triṣṭubh or Jagatī metres immediately after the caesura (75 cases); once it occurs in the third place of the opening section of a Jagatī after a long second syllable. There remains VIII.38.5 *imā juṣethām savanā:* the

1. Saussure, Mémoire 172; Prātiśākhya 576.
2. The passage X.97.5 *aśvatthe vo niṣadanam* must be kept aside; this is the first pāda of an Anuṣṭubh of a period when the iambic finish in this position was no longer a rule.
3. Except perhaps VIII.26.24 *nṛṣadaneṣu hūmahe* (short vowel in the second and third syllable).
4. Also the parallel passages in the AV and the Taitt. Ār. have the *ā*.

only passage where the first syllable of the word, perhaps, could be looked upon as occupying the place of a long syllable : but in reality also this passage is to be omitted; the fourth last syllable equally violates the iambic rhythm, and hence we have no ground to suppose that here the poet intended to use *savanā* with the value — ∪ —.

In the different treatment of *săvana* on the one hand and *sădana* on the other in the transmitted text thus recur phenomena similar to those which we noted above (p. 396) in respect of *avatŭ* as against *avată:* the interpretation offered by the tradition, that in one case one has choice between the short and the long vowel, while in the other the quantity is fixed, proves to be authoritative even for the composers of the hymns themselves.

If one completes what has been said here by the statements made above [p. 11 f., p. 63 f.] on the cases where not a word-form other than the one traditionally handed down, but the deficient filling of the metrical scheme is to be assumed, then these discussions, although they could be extended only on a few details, selected as typical, would illustrate how according to our conviction, the attempts once so perspicaciously begun by A. Kuhn [482] to restore older Vedić word-forms with the help of the metre can often obtain important results by a renewed examination and by the application of all available controls.

ACCENTUATION

We will conclude this part of our investigations with some remarks on the *accentuation* of the Ṛgveda. The more recent discussions on the nature of the Vedic accent, especially the works of Whitney[1] and Masing,[2] make it possible for us to be brief.

1. Especially in his essay *On the Nature and Designation of the Accent in Sanskrit* (Transactions of the Am. Phil. Association 1869-1870).
2. Die Hauptformen des serbisch-chorwatischen Accents (1876), 37 ff.

I consider it as firmly established—I need not repeat here the arguments on which this is based—that each of the three signs used to mark the accent—the horizontal stroke below the line, the vertical stroke above the line, third the absence of a sign—expresses a definite accent of the syllable for which it is used: every syllable with a horizontal stroke below the line is anudātta, every syllable which is not marked is udātta or one which is similar to it (pracaya), each with a (vertical) stroke above is svarita[1]. The Prātiśākhya, the marking system in the manuscripts, the method of Veda recitation even today prevailing in India agree with one another in all essentials[2] and **[483]** mutually explain one another. We have no ground and no right to look upon this system of accentuation as arisen from a misunderstanding of the method of marking the accent which originally should have had a different meaning.

If we designate the accent of the syllable which precedes the high tone as A, the udātta of this syllable as B, the accent of the following syllable as C, the accents of the next following syllables—until we come to the next A preceding the high tone—as D, then, as is well known, we get according to the Prātiśākhya for these accents, in whose sequence is reflected the regular movement of the tone, the following values: A is anudātta, B udātta, C, to start with, higher than the udātta, then pronounced as udātta, D pronounced as udātta. As has been often noted, in this procedure it is strange that C—which one would imagine to be the

1. Thus, *agnim i̱ḻe purohltam* is to be written strictly—if we express the udātta by ´, the svarita by `, the anudātta by the absence of any sign — as *agním íḻé puróhìtám.*
2. Peculiar to the method of recitation currently practised, as described by Haug, is only the weakness of tone of the udātta as compared with anudātta and svarita. The question of tone-heights, which alone concerns us here, is not affected by this presumably modern oddity. In judging it I fully agree with L. v. Schröder (Maitr. Saṁ Einl. XXXII).

transition from the high tone to the low tone—is raised *higher* than the high tone itself[1]; the level to which we reach in C should be *lower* than the high tone, but in fact it has the same height as the high tone, which is reached in the second part of C and then is maintained in D so that many syllables which in fact have no right to do so appear to be raised (in D) to the height of the high tone. Essentially different is the situation as described by Pāṇini (I.2.29 ff.). According to him C starts at the height of the udātta and falls down to anudātta (31,32).[2] Accordingly D is really anudātta **[484]** to which is ascribed here the nature of ekaśruti (39). Equally, as in the system of the Prātiśākhya, D does not here coincide with A, i.e., the low tone *after* the high tone does not coincide with the low tone *before* the high tone; in both the systems the latter is rather lower than the former. In the Prātiśākhya, D was udātta, A anudātta; with Pāṇini (sūtra 40), where D is anudātta, A gets the name sannatara (sch. anudāttatara) which characterizes this tone as anudātta which is lowered below its usual height. One can thus see that the two systems are distinguished by a shift in which all the elements, except B, have the same relative position, but in relation to B are either pushed up or pushed down. This can be illustrated as follows[3]:

---

1. No less strange than the case of the enclitic svarita, which we are describing here, is the case of the independent svarita, the tone value of which is not differentiated from that of the enclitic svarita in the Ṛk. Pr. When *sruci iva* becomes *srucīva*, the commencement of ī does not have the tone-height of *i*, which is merged into it, but a tone higher than it!
2. Many Prātiśākhyas agree with the interpretation of C as udātta + anudātta, but in spite of this, they all agree in teaching D = B. See the statements on the Materials (to which we have now to add Ṛk-tantrá 53,61) and the excellent notes of Whitney on A. Pr. III.65.
3. If in our graphic representation the distance between the different tone-heights appears to be the same, no significance attaches to it.

R. Pr. 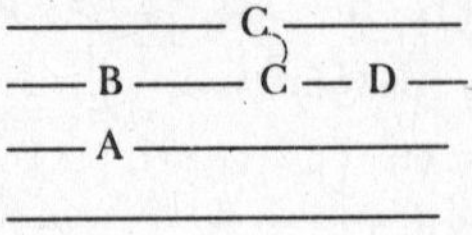 Pāṇ. 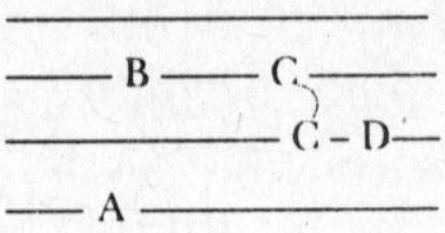

It is not to be doubted that the second scheme corresponds, more or less approximately, with that of the actual speech; the first, on the other hand, depicts a hieratic mode of recitation dependent on the shift, just described, which is purely arbitrary and artificial[1]. The nautre of the subject, in fact, decides clearly the relationship of the two systems[2]; what we pointed out as [485] strange in one case appears reasonable in the other. Moreover, if I am not mistaken, we find the intonation taught by Pāṇini in all essentials again in different Vedic Saṁhitās. Thus, to begin with, it occurs in the Saṁhitā of the Maitrāyaṇīyas. They have direct designations for our elements A, B, C; D, however, has no designation; hence, it must have been obviously understood as different from B, one having its tone-height lying between A and B. I think also the markings by numbers in the Ārcikas of the Sāmaveda becomes intelligible—without, of course, solving all its difficulties—only when we attribute to the svarita-sign 2 in its first half the value of udātta (1), in its second half an intermediate value between 1 and 3 (anudātta)[3]. The pracaya-syllables

1. Cf. Prātiśākhya 208.
2. There can be no mistake that the description of the Prātiśākhya on its part considers the way the other system looks at it as basic. It does not say that the second part of svarita is udātta, but that it is anudātta, pronounced, however, as udātta (Prāt. 191). Similarly, it does not say that the syllables following the svarita are udātta, but that they are pracaya and pronounced as udātta (205).
3. The wellknown rule that 1 is represented by 2 when 3 follows can hardly mean that the udātta before the following lowest tone is, in its first half, raised above its own proper level, but only that in its second half it is lowered below its own proper level. Thus the Ṛk-

(Continued on next page)

which follow svarita (2) have no proper marking of their own in the Sāmaveda, which means that the marking 2 continues to hold good for them: but of course this is not to be understood to mean that the two-fold tone-height 2 is repeated in every following syllable, but that the tone-height inherent in the final part of the syllable marked with 2 is to be continued for the following syllables.

The Sāman-melodies, as far as can be ascertained till now, in general are not related to the accentuation **[486]** of the text; at a few places, however, it seems to me that we cannot deny that such a relation does exist.[1] To illustrate this I give here the first stanza of the Pañcanidhanavairūpa from the Uhyagāna:[2]

```
 1 r       2            r          r
yadyāva   indra        te       śatam   | e |

 2 1          r r       2 1
śatam     bhūmīr       uta | syovā | diśam viśaṁhas |

           r  2          1   2       1r 2r      1  2     1  r       2 r
 na      tvā vajrin   sahasraṃ³   sūryā |     anu | aśvā  śiśumatī

  1          r            2          1r   2r    1
 na       jātam         aṣṭa        rodasī    | iṭ |
```

(*Continued from previous page*)

tantra (sūtra 53) also allows the first half mora of the svarita to be *at* the height of the udātta, and not *above* it; and the Nāradaśikṣā (Burnell, Ṛk-tantra, Intro. XL) says: *uccād uccataraṁ nāsti*. If the Ṛk-tantra (61) does indeed speak of the pracaya-tone as equal to udātta (cf. Nāradaśikṣā ibid. XXXIX), then it is not consonant with this interpretation of the svarita (cf. p. 483, note 2, and Whitney's note cited there), nor can it be reconciled with the method of marking the accent adopted in the manuscripts.

1. Cf. Lāṭyāyana VII.9.7: *yasya* (i.e. *sāmnaḥ*) *ārcikam udāttānudāttaṁ tad ṛgūḍham*.
2. Sāmav. ed. Bibl. Indica Vol. V p. 387.
3. *saha*^{2}*sra*^{2}*ṁ* in the Bibl. Ind. is obviously a misprint.

Accented in the usual way the text reads as: *yád dyā́va' indra te śatám bhū́mīr utá syúḥ* I *ná tvā vajrin sahásram sū́ryā' ánu ná jātám aṣṭa ródasī.*

One can see that the melody moves[1] only in the two highest tones of the scale (1 and 2)[2]. And, to be sure, every syllable having the natural udātta has the note 1; every syllable which follows it, except the one immediately before a syllable having a new high-tone, i.e. the enclitic svarita in the familiar system, has equally 1 (cf. Pāṇini I.2.37); every anudātta- and pracaya-syllable has 2[3].

A case of the independent svarita in a similar Sāman is found in *nas tanvàñ ca* SV vol. V p. 403; it is written **[487]** *ná*[2]*s tanva*[1]*ñ ca;* thus the note 1 corresponds to the natural svarita as it does to the enclitic, and, as in the case of the udātta here also the following syllable has note 1.

Other examples where the notes are assigned depending on the accents are offered by the Uhyagāna SV Vol. V p. 408 (ṚV IX.107.1,2), 433 (ṚV X.170.1-3). Even in the Geyagāna, if I am not mistaken, there occur single Sāmans where the same notation, based on accents, shines through the embellishments of the musical recital: thus SV I.193 (Bibl. Ind. Vol. I p. 420), so also I.209 (ibid. p. 443), where only the first pāda, as is often the case with prastāva, is sung wholly on note 5.

Our present knowledge of the Sāman-music is too imperfect, so that our descriptions cannot but have a purely provisional character. Nevertheless it is noteworthy that these melodies, whose age undoubtedly goes much beyond that of the Ṛk-Prātiśākhya, give evidence for the existence of a falling tone on the syllable after the udātta, for equating of

1. Every note is valid for the following syllables until a new note appears.
2. According to Burnell, Ārṣ. Brāhmaṇa p. XLII f., these are our notes F and E.
3. Only in the word *jātam* these rules are violated; I do not dare to decide if we can restore *jāta*[1]*m*.

this tone with the natural svarita—but in *this* system also at the same time with the udātta—and further for the discontinuation of the falling tone when an udātta syllable immediately follows; whereas the doctrine of the identity of the udātta and the pracaya just does not appear here, the pracaya receives rather the same treatment as the anudātta.

We will scarcely go wrong if we look upon the relationship between the accentuation of the Ṛgveda as it is handed down and the original one which, although certainly standardized under hieratic influence [488] must have at least been close to the accent system of the natural language, as somewhat similar to the relation existing between the transmitted sandhi and the original sandhi, or between the transmitted treatment of the metre and the original one. What is handed down shows at every step the hand of an artificial revision but as far as the principal features are concerned it does point to the direction in which the original lay. In the original mode of recitation there is no ground to assign a tone different from the anudātta which precedes the high tone[1] to the enclitic svarita or to the pracaya tone of the syllables following it. We may, however, justifiably assume that not only the shift of the tone-heights described above [p. 484], but also the complete equation of the enclitic svarita with the independent one belongs to the later development, all the more so because traces of the difference between the two svaritas have been in fact preserved in the Vedic tradition[2]. One may further doubt that the secondary

1. One may specially note the excellent remarks of Masing, serb. chorw. Accent 42-45.
2. Cf. Whitney Gramm. § 86.—The primary svarita is distinguished from the secondary svarita in the marking system of the Maitrāyaṇīya-mss.; that is, it was no doubt distinguished in some way also in the pronunciation of the Maitrāyáṇīyas (see Schroeder, Einl. XXX f.). —Peculiar and strange is the way in which in the Atharvan mss. a svarita after an udātta—no matter whether the svarita is independent or enclitic—is distinguished from an independent svarita after an anudātta (Whitney Ath. Pr. p. 168).—Cf. also Weber, Vāj. Saṁ. Einl. p. X.

tones surrounding the udātta had already in the original text developed, as is the case in the transmitted text, always the same way along several words, as within the same word, unhampered even by the strictest word-separations, by the Triṣṭubh-caesura etc., uninfluenced also by the tone of the verb-accent which has become latent **[489]** in the tradition, but which was not *completely* destroyed by the enclisis of the verb in the principal clause. Further, Whitney[1] has already justifiably stressed that, e.g., the mutually contradictory definitions contained in the tradition, as to when a svarita arises if there occurs a contraction of a high-tone and a low-tone vowel, have the mark of arbitrariness, not of linguistic laws, but of the rules formulated by the grammarians: it would, however, be enough for a text-critic, in these as well as in analogous points, to state this character of arbitrariness without attempting to bring order in the phenomenon concerned according to a system invented by himself.

For the purposes of our edition, it seems to me advisable to limit ourselves to the marking of the udātta and the independent svarita[2]. In any case in this way what is essential in the old system of tones is noted. We thus give the reader the basis from which he can easily supply the secondary phenomena, each to the extent which suits his views. Thus we return, although our interpretation of the accent marks used in the mss. differs from the one prevailing with most of the older scholars, in effect to the method of marking the accent employed, e.g., by Aufrecht.

1. Ath. Prāt. p. 158; Transact. Am. Phil. Assn. 1869-70, p. 28.
2. As is known, this is also how accent is marked in the Ṛg. mss. discovered by Bühler in Kashmir.

CHAPTER 5

The Śākala- and the Vāṣkala-Śākhā

[490] We have made an attempt above [p. 383 ff.] to demonstrate that the accepted principles of phonetic treatment, which can be seen in the traditional Saṁhitā text, were applied to it already *before* Śākalya. After having occupied ourselves with the closer examination of those principles, we turn to Śākalya and to the branchings of the Śākhās linked with his name.

The Caraṇavyūha (Ind. Stud. III.253) names the Śākala, Vāṣkala, Āśvalāyana, Śāṅkhāyana, and Māṇḍūkāyana as the Śākhās of the Ṛgveda. We shall see later in which marginal sense the Āśvalāyana and Śāṅkhāyana can at all be considered as schools representing the Ṛk-text itself. So we find also elsewhere in the Purāṇa tradition (see Ind. Stud. op. cit.) the mention of only three, instead of five, śākhās, viz. the Śākala, Vāṣkala, Māṇḍūka. From these again, the school of the Māṇḍūkeyas—I name them so following the Ait. Ār. III. 1. 1—is to be set aside in our investigation. Even though the name of Māṇḍūkeya or of the Māṇḍūkeyas is well known in the Āraṇyaka-, Prātiśākhya- and Sūtra-literature, we have for the present no evidence regarding the *Śākhā* of the Māṇḍūkeyas. [491] If such a Śākhā, parallel to the Śākala-Śākhā, really ever existed, its knowledge must have been lost already quite early in ancient India. So there remain for our investigation only the Śākalas and the Vāṣkalas[1].

---

1. With the 21 schools of the Bahvṛcas, which, e.g., are recorded in the Mahābhāṣya, we have to understand, as the well-known passage of Ṣaḍguruśiṣya shows, the Brāhmaṇa schools.

In Max Müller's description of the Vedic literature, of all the divisions of the Vedic schools, those of the Śākalas and the Vāṣkalas have been mentioned as the oldest (H.A.S.L. 188,376). In his view, only after they came into existence, at the second stage, did the formation of the Brāhmaṇa-schools as of the Aitareyins, the Kauṣītakins, take shape. I doubt the correctness of this view. While dealing above with the textual history of the Ṛgveda, and particularly with the role of Śākalya in it, a number of considerations were already put forth indicating that the great phonetic revision of the text of the hymns, and particularly the activity of Śākalya, which presupposes that revision has to be dated rather after the Brāhmaṇa period than in or even before it. Even though, regarding Vāṣkala, the head of the other Ṛk-school, we do not possess the same wealth of evidence as about Śākalya, yet it does give an indication of his position which, from the point of view of the literary history, is not very distant from that of Śākalya. Thus, the Vāṣkalas are mentioned as engaged in the theory of sandhi: the Upadruta-Sandhi mentioned in the Śāṅkhāyana Śrauta. XII.3 is explained as *upadruto nāma sandhir Vāṣkalānām prasiddhaḥ* (Ind. Stud. IV, 231). If we take a look at the parallel Śākhā-divisions in the sphere of the other Vedas, then this comparison offers further support for our view **[492]** regarding the period of the rise of the Śākala- and the Vāṣkala-Śākhā. It is not now necessary to establish that what we want to compare in the domain of the Yajurveda with the division of the Śākalas and the Vāṣkalas is not something like the contrast between the Taittirīyas, Vājasaneyins etc., but rather the branchings off like those of the Kāṇvas and the Mādhyandinas of the white Yajurveda, of the Āpastamba- and the Ātreya-schools among the Taittirīyas. Throughout we find that by the names of the heads of the schools, after whom these Śākhās are named, we are referred to the same period of phonetic speculations, finally laid down in the Prātiśākhyas, to which Śākalya also belongs. Just as Śākalya is the author of a Padapāṭha of the Ṛgveda, similarly, according to well-known testimonies,

Ātreya, the head of a Taittirīya school, is the author of a Padapāṭha of the Taitt. Saṁhitā. Kāṇva, the *doctor eponymous* of a Śākhā of the white Yajurveda, appears among the authorities on phonetic questions named in the Vāj. Prātiśākhya (Ind. Studien IV.70). Thus, throughout there appear as founders of the text-recensions of *this* stage—of course here I am not talking of those recensions which mean rather a different Veda (the Vājasaneyins as opposed to the Taittirīyas, etc.) but a different recension of the same Veda—not in the least the ṛṣi-type personalities of the distant past, but grammarians who belong to the same stratum in the literary history as Śākalya. The correct placement of the epoch to which the branching off of the Śākhās belongs is also shown very clearly when we, for example, try to see in the domain of the white Yajurveda which texts of the Mādhyandinas and which of the Kāṇvas have been affected by the divisions into the Śākhās and which not. It is not the Saṁhitā of the White Yajurveda alone that has branched off into the recensions of the Kāṇvas and the Mādhyandinas, but, as is well known, **[493]** quite similarly the Śatapatha Brāhmaṇa. And when the dawn of the pantheistic speculation had led to the rise of the Upaniṣad and the text-corpus of the white Yajus school was furnished with an Upaniṣad, which was assigned to the Saṁhitā (XL), and with another to the Brāhmaṇa (XIV.3 ff.), the founders of the Mādhyandina- and the Kāṇva-schools *had before them* also these texts so that the old parts of the Saṁhitā and the Brāhmaṇa, as well as these, were affected by the differences between those schools. The Taittirīyas and the Vājasaneyins had as Upaniṣads two fundamentally different texts: for, the division of the Taittirīyas and the Vājasaneyins is older than the rise of the Upaniṣads. On the other hand, the Kāṇvas and the Mādhyandinas possessed as Upaniṣads only two redactions of the same text : for, the division of the Kāṇvas and the Mādhyandinas is later than the rise of the Upaniṣads. —In the literature of the Ṛgveda the division of the Aitareyins and the Kauṣītakins was already there when the Upaniṣads were composed and hence in these schools there arose two Upaniṣads essentially different from each other. On the other hand, here did not arise, as the analogous developments in the white Yajus could lead one to expect, a Śākala- and a Vāṣkala-recension of the Brāhmaṇa or of the Upaniṣad, obviously because here—unlike the white Yajurveda—there already existed a *multiplicity* of the Brāhmaṇas, respectively of the Upaniṣads, based on one and the same Saṁhitā. Hence, it happened that when the different text recensions of that Saṁhitā came to be fixed, the same difference did not continue in a Brāhmaṇa and an Upaniṣad for that recension[1], **[494]** but the followers of one Saṁhitā-Śākhā turned to this, those of the other to that Brāhmaṇa—correspondingly to the Upaniṣads. In this process, of course, it was not ruled out that the Upaniṣads could admit additions even after the formation of the Śākhās, as has to be assumed, for example, in the case of the chapter on the "Saṁhitās" due to the frequent mention there of Śākalya [above p. 380].

Thus, we come to know that the period of the rise of these Śākhās, brought into existence by the theoreticians on phonetics, is after the dawn of the pantheistic speculations on Brahman and after the rise of the great older Upaniṣads, except for some individual parts of the latter like the Saṁhitā-chapter. We must now proceed to examine individually the differences which our sources permit us to ascertain in respect of the Śākala- and the Vāṣkala-text of the Ṛgveda.

A well-known statement of the Anuvākānukramaṇī (stanza 36) informs us that the Vāṣkala Śākhā had eight hymns more than the Śakala Śākhā: the former had 1025, the latter

---

1. The Vāṣkalopaniṣad (Ind. Stud. IX.38 ff.) and the problematic Śākalyopaniṣad (the same II.170). have nothing to do with the questions which engage us here.

1017 sūktas. Statements found in a commentary on the Caraṇavyūha[1] enable us to state exactly which these eight hymns are. That commentary tells us that the Vāṣkala Śākhā placed the first two Vālakhilya hymns (VIII.49, 50) just at the place where we have them; the following five Vālakhilya hymns (VIII.51-55) followed VIII.94[2]; the **[495]** last four Vālakhilyas were missing. At the end of the whole Saṁhitā, the Vāṣkalas had after X.191 one more Saṁjñāna hymn of 15 stanzas; the last stanza of this hymn (*tac chaṁ yor ā vṛṇīmahe,* etc.) has also been specified elsewhere as the concluding stanza of the Ṛgveda in the Vāṣkala Śākhā[3]. Thus, if we *exclude* in our counting the *Vālakhilyas* from the Śākala Śākhā, then the Vāṣkalas have eight hymns more than the Śākalas. Although I do not wish to hazard any assumption on the rise of the deviations concerned, I do wish to stress that the facts cited above do not shed a favourable light on the authority of the Vāṣkala Śākhā. The separation of the first two Vālakhilyas from the following, with which they are held together on account of the common form of pair-wise parallelism between them and other relationships, and above all the cutting off of the eighth hymn from the seventh, between which there exists exactly the same correspondence as between the preceding hymn-pairs[4]: these are the factors

1. Ms. in the possession of Prof. Weber who had received it in 1880 from Whitley Stokes of Calcutta and which he had kindly permitted me to use; fol. 22-23.
2. This statement about the different extents of Anuvāka VIII.10 in the two Śākhās disposes of the assumption of R. Meyer (Ṛgvidhāna p. XXVII note 1) that the Anuvākānukramaṇī has ascribed the hymns VIII.11,12,18-20 to the above-mentioned Anuvāka.
3. See the materials given by Weber, Nachtrag to the second edition of the Ind. Literaturgeschichte, p. 2.
4. It deserves to be noted that, just as the Ait. Br. (VI.28) mentions four pairs of the Vālakhilyas, the Kauṣītaka (XXX.4) also does so in exactly the same way. These are the eight sūktas of the Vālakhilyanāmakā maharṣayaḥ which Sāyaṇa has in mind while commenting on Ait. VI.24.5; the Vālakhilyas 9-11 of the Vulgate obviously do not have the same dignity as the rest.

in which the tradition of the Vāṣkalas in no way proves to be superior to that of the Śākalas. Also, the alleged Saṁjñāna-hymn of 15 stanzas at the end of the tenth Maṇḍala does not help to form a more favourable opinion about the Vāṣkala variations. The five stanzas which M. Müller and Aufrecht give as Pariśiṣṭa to ṚV.X.191 are doubtful enough; especially the fifth which falls out of the metre here and there and slips wholly into the character of the Yajus-prose. **[496]** The modern character of the following stanzas would be still more clearly indicated if these were really to be assigned to the hymn (see below). Moreover, the sūkta, whether it consists of 5 or fifteen stanzas, violates the principle of ordering the sūktas of the tenth Maṇḍala.

In addition to the above-mentioned differences between the two Śākhās found in the Maṇḍala VIII and X, there exists an *anukramaviparyāsa* in the first book of the Vāṣkalas as compared with the Śākalas. A well-known stanza found in the Anuvākānukramaṇī (V.21) and the Bṛhaddevatā (Ind. Stud. I.115) informs us that among the small collections of hymns in the first Maṇḍala the one of Kutsa (I.94-115) stands after that of Parucchepa (127-139) in the Vāṣkala Śākhā. Our investigations of the arrangement of the first Maṇḍala [p. 258] have shown that it is not improbable that in this point the Vāṣkala tradition is to be viewed more favourably than in respect of the points just discussed.

As far as I know these are all the available pieces of evidence about the deviations of the Vāṣkala Śākhā from the Śākala text. The good quality of our materials does not make it probable that still other differences of the same kind once existed between the two texts which then should have found mention in the Anukramaṇī; we would have then known them. The tradition is absolutely silent, as far as my knowledge goes, on the variations in *readings*[1]. That

1. It would be too bold to suggest that Sāyaṇa's statement on ṚV I.50.3 (cf. Benfey Ved. und. Ling. 123) that "śākhāntare" the reading *adṛśran*

(Continued on next page)

there could have existed radical differences [497] has been ruled out from the outset by our earlier investigations on the state of the text in the Saṁhitā and the Brāhmaṇa period. On the other hand, one would surely go too far in maintaining that the text of the two Śākhās was just identical except for the deviations in arragement noted above. We will show later that the text-variants of the Ṛgveda had not *fully* ceased to exist even with Yāska. Also the comparison with the relationships existing between the other Vedic schools does not favour the idea of *absolute* identity of the text in the two Ṛk-Śākhās. As for the Sāmaveda, however, the statements on pratīkas and some other information contained in the Anukramaṇī-texts of the Naigeya school published by Weber (Ind. Stud. XVII.315 ff.) hardly ever lead us to real variants in the received text. Most of the deviations collected by Weber (p. 319) exhibit obviously, not Śākhā-differences, but pure negligence on the part of the Anukramaṇī or of its manuscripts. Isolated cases of change of place, and additions or omissions of stanzas do exist, and one would like to assume a case of text-difference when the daivatam to II.2.1 states *pavasva pañca saumyā' uttamāyā' uttame sūryaḥ* : the text of stanza 139[1] has in the SV, as little as in the ṚV, the least connection with *sūrya*, and so it is possible that in the Naigeya-text a different third pāda—for example, *pavasva sūryo dṛśe* ṚV IX.64.30 or something like it—may have existed[2]. As for the *Vājasaneyi-Saṁhitā* not only the [498] Prātiśākhya (Ind. Stud. IV.67) leads to text-variants, but such ones occur, as is well-known,

---

(Continued from previous page)

occurs in place of *adṛśram* has reference to another śākhā of the Ṛgveda and not to the parallel Vedic texts, of which, indeed, several have *adṛśran*. Similarly, e.g., Sāyaṇa while commenting on Ait. Br. II.34.7 refers to the Taitt. Saṁ. with the expression "śākhāntare".

1. I think this stanza, and not, as Weber thinks, st. 129 is meant; to *pañca* I supply, not *ṛcaḥ*, but *tṛcāḥ*.
2. For more about the differences in the Sāmaśākhās, see Burnell, Ṛktantra p. XXVII f., XLIX.

directly in the existence side by side of the Mādhyandina- and the Kāṇva-recensions, and they are, to be sure, not quite small in number. That they are by far more numerous and more significant in the *prose* portions of the Yajurveda than in the stanzas and, specially, in the old stanzas, is quite as it should be. Therefore, also these are not lacking in variants : variants moreover in which sometimes the different Śākhās of *one* Yajus-text continue the differences which had arisen in much older times between the great main branches of the Yajus-tradition[1]. *This* source of variants naturally did not exist for the Vāṣkala- and the Śākala Śākhā, and even otherwise we may not transfer the picture which is offered to us by the Kāṇva- and the Mādhyandina-variants straightway to these Śākhās without tăking into account the much stricter consistency of the Ṛk-tradition.

In the traditional *countings* of the *stanzas,* or respectively of the *Vargas,* of the Saṁhitā there occur manifold differences, which are to be explained partly to be due to the different modes of calculation, and are partly such as I cannot explain them, at least for the present, but as far as I see, they do not allow the assumption that the Vāṣkala Śākhā has anything to do with it. In the commentary on the Caraṇavyūha fol. 16, the number of the stanzas is stated to be 10552 including, 10472 excluding, the Vālakhilyas ; in this counting the so-called *naimittikadvipadās* (which, like the dvipadā virājas, can be counted either as one or as two, **[499]** stanzas) are counted as single stanzas. A counting carried out by myself shows that the figures cited above agree with out text. Only seemingly different from these figures are those which are found in the same commentary fol. 19. There the number of stanzas (excluding the Vālakhilyas) is given as 10496 by

1. Thus, the variations between the different Yajus-Saṁhitās are also occasionally continued in the different readings found in the Maitrāyaṇīya-mss.; see v. Schröder Maitr. Saṁh. II, p. VII.

pair-wise counting of the 140 naimittikadvipadās, 10566 by counting them singly as stanzas; finally, the number is given as 10580 stanzas and a pāda (viz. X. 20. 1) with the inclusion of the Saṁjñāna hymn [above p. 495]. Among these figures, it is the figure 10566 which is to be compared with the figure 10472 in the above-mentioned countings. The difference of 94 is to be explained as due to the different way of counting stanzas which consist of three ardharcas; in the ritual use the three ardharcas are considered as one stanza, in the text-recitation as two stanzas ("*ardharcadvayena ṛg ekā, ardharcenaikā*" ms. fol. 17'); and the number of those stanzas in the Saṁhitā comes to 94[1].–The biggest of the totals just stated, 10580 stanzas and a pāda, is an old traditional figure; it has been given already by Śaunaka (Anuvākānukr. stanza 43). But I consider this seemingly so complete an agreement of this figure with the calculation of the Caraṇavyūha commentary, and respectively with our own counting done for the Vulgate text, as suspicious; I think artificial operations have been at work in order to bring about this agreement. To prove this, I shall bring together some countings of vargas of the Ṛk-Saṁhitā; the first of these countings is the one found in the Anuvākānukramaṇī (stanzas 40-42); the other occurs **[500]** in some stanzas which are several times cited and explained in the Caraṇavyūha-comm. (fol. 6.21 f.); in this the Saṁjñāna with its 4 vargas = 15 stanzas is included for calculation. The third counting is my own. The Vālakhilyas have been excluded for all the three countings; the naimittikadvipadās are counted every time two as making one stanza.

---

1. These stanzas consisting of three ardharcas and also those consisting of one ardharca help us to understand the statements of Śaunaka (M. Müller, Hist. of A.S.L. 221) to the effect that the number of half-stanzas in the ṚV is not exactly double of the number of stanzas.

Vargas	Śaunaka	Car.-comm.	My counting
of one stanza	1	1	1
of two stanzas	2	2	2
of three stanzas	97	100	99
of four stanzas	174	175	174
of five stanzas	1207	1211	1210
of six stanzas	346	345	343
of seven stanzas	119	120	121
of eight stanzas	59	55	55
of nine stanzas	1	1	1
Total number of Vargas	2006	2010[1]	2006
Total number of stanzas	10417	10419[1]	10402[2]

One will thus see that with regard to the total number of vargas, Śaunaka agrees with the data of the present text as ascertained by me. But with regard to the number of stanzas there is a difference : and this difference comes to 15, that is *exactly equal to the number of stanzas in the Saṁjñāna hymn.* Without counting this hymn—that he does not count it is shown by his 2006, not 2010 vargas—Śaunaka arrives at a total **[501]** which the traditional text yields only by the addition of the hymn. From this we further conclude that if Śaunaka specifies the total number of stanzas to be 10580 (and one pāda) and this corresponds to *our* figures *with the inclusion* of the Saṁjñānasūkta, then Śaunaka on his part must *not* have included this sūkta; the Car.-comm., however, in order to arrive at the traditional total number of 10580-

1. Thus, *without* Saṁjñāna also here the traditional figure of 2006 vargas, but 10404 stanzas: two stanzas more than what my counting leads to and also than what would be in agreement with the figures of the Car.-comm. spoken of above. I do not know how to explain this difference.
2. This figure is given also by Śaunaka in the Chandonukramaṇī, M. Müller H.A.S.L. 221 f.

1, has used the Saṁjñāna as the remedy to make up the deficiency, so that the difference between Śaunaka's estimate and the modern text is covered up. Further grounds for doubting the inclusion of the Saṁjñāna in Śaunaka's counting coincide at just this point with those set forth so far. Is it believable, what according to the Car.-commentary should have been the case, that the old counting of the Ṛg-stanzas, which yielded the figure 10580-1 included the Saṁjñāna, but at the same time did *not* count the Vālakhilyas? The Vālakhilyas, at least those which were recognized also by the Vāṣkalas, are certainly as close as the Saṁjñāna for being considered as a constituent part of the Ṛgveda. Furthermore, is not the number of the stanzas, 15, of the Saṁjñāna assumed in the counting concerned in itself doubtful ? As a Khila of our Ṛk-recension, the hymn with *five* stanzas is found in a relatively acceptable form with the traditional concluding stanza *tac caṁ yoḥ* at the end. The form of this hymn as *consisting of fifteen stanzas* (Car.-comm. ms. fol. 19'-20') has, after this concluding stanza, a good deal clumsy pieces of work which are not homogeneous and partly quite late, thus the Upaniṣad-stanza *bhūtam bhaviṣyat prastoti maham* (thus the ms.) *brahmaikam akṣaraṁ bahu brahmaikam akṣaram,* the stanza *trāyuṣaṁ Jamadagneḥ* etc., finally at the end of the whole hymn, as conclusion, *once again* the indispensable stanza *tac caṁ yoḥ* which has been there already once before ! From this it seems clear to me that the **[502]** genuine Saṁjñāna had only five stanzas and that the one with fifteen stanzas has been artificially prepared for some purpose, probably even just to obtain the total number of stanzas in the Ṛgveda which had become traditional since the time of Śaunaka[1].

---

1. This view will receive further corroboration if the supposition, expressed below [p. 507, note 1] is correct, according to which a part of the supposed longer Saṁjñāna was identical with the Nairhastya which is separated from it in the Bṛhaddevatā (VIII.19; Meyer Ṛgvidhāna p. XXVI).

If we set aside at this juncture the obvious attempts to explain away an existing difference, the fact remains that Śaunaka counted 15 stanzas more in his Ṛgveda than what we find—employing, *as far as can be seen,* the same method of counting—in ours. I would, however, scarcely believe that his text, in reality, contained more than the present-day text: in that case we should have been in all probability informed about it. It is quite possible that he counted some longer stanzas as two by separating them into ekapadās[1] or dvipadās, or he differed from our way of reckoning in some other way which we now cannot determine. That *real* deviations, if they are to be assumed at all, between his text and ours, in extent and limits of the Saṁhitā, could have been only small becomes incidentally clear in each case from the figures discussed above.

Finally, I mention one more varga-counting found in Ms. Chambers 785 which counts 2042 vargas and 10622 stanzas. We are informed about this by Weber Ind. Stud. III.255[2] and M. Müller H.A.S.L. 221. These numbers do not fit in with what we know about the Vāṣkala Śākhā; **[503]** I do not know how to explain this counting of the Ms. and only assume that some Khilas (see below) have been counted.

The assumption that a series of texts not contained in the Śākala Śākhā, but which are mentioned in the Bṛhaddevatā and the Ṛgvidhāna among the hymns of the Ṛgveda, belong to the Vāṣkala-Śākhā[3] has not—apart from the Saṁjñānasūkta—found any confirmation in the direct statements, available today, on the hymns which the Vāṣkala

1. That there were differences of opinion as to where we have to suppose ekapadās is shown by Prātiśākhya 993 f.
2. The counting according to the Anuvākānukr., which is mentioned there, agrees with the statements made above on the basis of the text itself, the only difference being that the number of the vargas having six stanzas is given, surely due to simple mistake, as 340 instead of 346.
3. Weber, Nachtrag to the second edn. of ind. Literaturgesch. p. 2 f.

Śākhā has in excess over the Śākala Śākhā [above p. 494][1]. Consequently, if these passages were *not* recognized as canonical in *any* of the two Śākhās, of which alone we have some concrete knowledge, then the chances that they were ever fully respected in some other recension of the Ṛgveda are, at the very start, not very great. However, it will not be superfluous to examine more closely the appearance of these texts, endowed with a kind of importance by those two works of the Śaunaka school by naming them[2].

R. Meyer[3] has shown that a portion of the texts in question **[504]** is identical with the *Khilas* inserted at different places, especially at the end of the Maṇḍalas, in the Ṛk-manuscripts which have been added so to speak as apocrypha to the canonical text. The places of these Khilas in the manuscripts also agrees completely with those where the Bṛhaddevatā and the Ṛgvidhāna[4] have them occur. For all that, we have to note, on the one hand, that by no means have all the Khilas been listed in the works mentioned above and, on the other, there appear many additions to the Vulgate in these very texts which cannot be detected in the Khilas available to us. Can we then conclude that such texts not known to us as Khilas must have belonged with full validity to the Saṁhitā, described just in those texts, and consequently this Saṁhitā, in respect of these sūktas, was

1. The enumeration of the concluding stanzas of the Maṇḍalas given in the Śāṅkhāyana Gṛhya IV.5 are, and I think rightly, customarily related to the Vāṣkala Śākhā.—Śāṅkh. in fact mentions *tac chaṁ yoḥ* as the concluding stanza of the tenth M.—, and in this we have a further piece of evidence which goes *against* ascribing the text-passages in question here to the Vāṣkalasaṁhitā ; as the concluding stanza of the fifth M., Śāṅkh. cites a stanza which is found also at this place in the Vulgate, while the Bṛahaddevatā (V.17) and the Ṛgvidhāna (II.21.3) have more material to follow.
2. For the materials, see R. Meyer, Ṛgvidhāna, Praefatio p XIX ff.
3. op. cit. XXI ff.
4. Some of these can definitely be shown to be absent in the Saṁhitā which has been described by the Bṛhadd. and the Ṛgv.; see Meyer op. cit. XXIII.

different from our Saṁhitā? Obviously, we have to ask: What are the means to recognize whether a passage missing in *our* Saṁhitā is a Khila or whether it represents a fully respectable part of a different Saṁhitā[1]? If we once consider ourselves authorized to treat as disputable the limits within which the content of the Saṁhitā which is to be recognized as canonical—disputable beyond the narrow limits which the tradition yields with regard to the stock of the Vāṣkalaśākhā—, then obviously we have **[505]** much more reason to reckon in regard to the Khilas with vacillations to which such products, so to say freely floating in the air, must have been exposed and having loosely been attached to the firm core of the Saṁhitā must have been exposed. Since vacillations in respect of the content of the Khilas are to be found in the manuscripts, we can expect that there were many more of them between the time of our manuscripts and the period of the Bṛhaddevatā. Hence, what does not appear in the manuscripts as Khila need not on that account be considered a fully valid hymn of another Saṁhitā. Need not be and, I mean, can*not* be *easily*. For it is not an *easy* assumption that the texts which we do not find either in the Śākala Saṁhitā, which was surely followed by the Śaunaka's school (Ind. Stud. I.107 f.), nor in the Vāṣkala Śākhā of which alone, beside the Śākala Śākhā, that school has any knowledge as a recognized part of the Veda, should be taken back to some third missing Śākhā, rather than, what is so obvious, assign that kind of texts to the floating material of the Khilas or to the Khila-like ȧdéspota.

After all that has been said, if some doubt still persists, then in order to diminish it there is no other way than to

1. With the criterion like what does not have a Padapāṭha is a Khila (thus, e.g., Weber's ms. of the Caraṇavyūha-comm. fol. 14': *yasya mantrasya padābhāvas tasya khailikatvaṁ siddham*), one can naturally not get anywhere when we are dealing with different Śākhās. Moreover, one may also note that hymn VIII.59 has been analyzed in the Padapāṭha and yet has been characterized as "*sauparṇaṁ khailikam*" in the stanza cited by Sāyaṇa on the Ait. Br. VI.25.7.

examine the look of the concerned passages themselves and at the same time investigate whether the place they occupy in the order of the hymns is in accordance with the rules of arrangement of the Saṁhitā. If the texts prove to be late and violating the proper sequence, the possibility that they were recognized as canonical in some other Śākhā of the Veda is, of course, not yet thereby excluded, but certainly very much weakened; or, the respect which that Śākhā as the guarantor of the literary-historical dignity of the texts contained in it can claim will be **[506]** lowered to a level which would be equal to the *Khilas* of our Vulgate. Incidentally, we have no reason to extend the examination of the type described above only to *those* texts which are missing in the Khilas of our Vulgate. However, great or small is the possibility that *such* a text may have had the validity of a canon in an unknown Śākhā, likewise great or small is the possibility also for the Khilas; for, that a Khila of one Śākhā can be a fully valid sūkta in another is shown by the Saṁjñāna-sūkta.

As a rule, the placing in the Bṛhaddevatā and the Ṛgvidhāna of the hymns added to the Saṁhitā already raises suspicions. Sometimes they appear at the end of a Maṇḍala: thus the Śrīsūkta, the *prajāvat-* and the *jīvaputra*-hymn, the hymn to the cows (at the end of the Maṇḍala V), the *nairhastya* (before the last hymn of the Maṇḍala X). Sometimes the placing disturbs the series of hymns addressed to a deity: this happens, for example, due to the insertion of a tṛca (No. VIII of the Khilas in Aufrecht's edition) after VI. 44 in the middle of hymns to Indra while the tṛca has nothing to do with Indra. The reason why this quite late composition has come in here is obviously its verbal similarity with VI.44.24. On many occasions in the tenth Maṇḍala, which is the principal place for additions, the principle of ordering the hymns according to the number of the stanzas is violated. Thus, the proper order is disturbed by the hymn with thirteen stanzas after X.103, which is described in the.

Bṛhadd. VIII.3 (Meyer XXII); by the Āyuṣya of eleven stanzas after X.128[1], and by the lightning-hymn **[507]** "*namas te*", placed adjacent to it (the Āyuṣya) in the Bṛhaddevatā, and which we have to imagine to be of four stanzas on the basis of AV 1.13; further by the Medhāsūkta after X.151 which, with its nine stanzas, breaks the series of the hymns of five stanzas and which has obviously been given a place after the Śraddhā-hymn simply because of the constant relationship between the notions of *śraddhā* and *medhā;* likewise by the *śivasaṁkalpa* of three stanzas (Vāj. Saṁh. XXXIV. 4-6) after X.166 inserted between the hymns of five and four stanzas. Also, the "Parākadāsa" hymn, which for the present cannot be identified, of eight stanzas (Bṛhadd. VII.24; Ṛgvidhāna III.21.4) after X.84 cannot be said to agree with the principle of ordering. Among these cases where a judgement is possible, the principle of ordering is complied with only by the Nairhastyam after X.190[2]—it seems to have had three stanzas—and further by the series of eleven stanzas after I.73, to which we shall have an occasion to return later.

The expressions and the metrical character of the texts in question—of the Khilas as also of those not transmitted among the Khilas—, as far as we know them, confirm fully the rejection of their claim to be admitted to the Ṛgveda. One may compare, for example, the Khailika portion admitted by the Bṛhaddevatā as the concluding part of hymn X.85, with the remaining genuine hymn: one needs only to read *śrīdharasya yathā śriyā* and *śaṅkarasya yathā gaurī*, or to

---

1. In the editions of M. Müller and Aufrecht, the same has twelve stanzas; however, the first stanza is to be separated and understood as a Khailika stanza concluding the hymn X. 128. This becomes evident from the Taitt. Saṁh. IV.7.14.4 etc. The real Āyuṣya begins only with the supposed second stanza.
2. Among the various kinds of elements which go to form the Saṁjñānasūkta of fifteen stanzas discussed above (p. 501) we find a piece of three stanzas which begins with the words *nairhastyaṁ senādaraṇam,* partly identical with AV VI.67. I would think of this tṛca rather than of the AV VI.65 or 66.

note that out of the twelve Anuṣṭubh half-stanzas nine have at the end of the first pāda the syllables ∪ — — ∪̲ in order **[508]** to get a sufficiently clear idea about the age of this addition. Not everything, of course, is equally late: it appears that the text of the Suparṇa-hymn listed after I.73[1], which unfortunately is for the most part even now untraceable, belongs to the most respectable ones among the concerned additions. These were eleven in number. The first ten, addressed to Aśvin, having the opening words *śaśvad dhi vām,* have not until now, as far as I know, come to light anywhere. We have the eleventh: it is hymn VIII.59 appearing in the Vulgate at the end of the Vālakhilyam, whose ṛṣi, in fact, is stated to be Suparṇa Kāṇva[2]. When those ten hymns are specified in the Kauṣ. Brāhm. as the constituent part of the Āśvinaśastra, this confers—as does the character of the eleventh hymn before us—on the Suparṇa-piece a dignity which pushes it back close to the boundary of the Ṛgveda. And yet, I mean only to the boundary; it is significant that the only hymn of our Ṛk-vulgate which belonged to that Supraṇa-text is just the last sūkta of that half-apocryphal Vālakhilyam; and hence it seems to me that the environment to which this Suparṇa, along with the Vālakhilya, belongs has been correctly characterized in the remark (in the Caraṇavyūha comm. fol. 16): *yathā praiṣādhyāyakuntāpādhyāyanividadhyāyasuparṇādhyāyas' ceti tadvat vālakhilyādhyāyaḥ.*

As the result of the preceding investigations, we might state that the pratīkas of the texts found in the Bṛhaddevatā and the Ṛgvidhāna, and which **[509]** are missing in our Vulgate, do not lead us anywhere on the track of material which could be looked upon as equal to the recognized Ṛk-

1. Bṛhadd. III, 24; Ṛgvidh. I.20.3; Meyer op. cit. XXIV f.; Weber Nachtrag to Lit.-Gesch.[2], 2 f.
2. Thus, then, the ten Aśvin-hymns also will be sauparṇāni in so far as Suparṇa is considered the ṛṣi of the hymns; a connection with the myth of the Suparṇādhyāya is scarcely probable.

texts in status and of which—except for the Saṁjñānasūkta—we could say that there is some kind of possibility that they figured as fully valid texts of the canon in some lost Śākhā of the Ṛgveda.

Only *one* text—this was not mentioned so far—which, according to the Bṛhaddevatā and the Ṛgvidhāna forms part of our Saṁhitā, has a claim on a separate, deviating judgement: a case whose special circumstance rules out any thought that what is true here could perhaps be true also of some other text, not precisely known, among those with which we are dealing. I mean the *Mahānāmnī-stanzas.* They are listed both by the Bṛhaddevatā and the Ṛgvidhāna after hymn X.191 and after the Saṁjñānasūkta that is, *after* the well-established conclusion of both the Śākala- as well as the Vāṣkala-Saṁhitā. In the Upākaraṇa ceremony of the Baudhāyana[1] we find the Mahānāmnīs mentioned after the tenth Maṇḍala in such a way as if they formed a distinct part of the Saṁhitā coordinated with the Maṇḍalas. Further light is shed on the peculiar position of the Mahānāmnīs by the statement of the Śāṅkhāyana (Gṛhya II.11,12; cf. Āśvalāyana Śraut. VIII.14, 2) that these stanzas belong to the Rahasya-texts to be studied at the end of the regular Veda-study—that is, after the study of the ten Maṇḍalas; among these they occupy the first place. Thus those stanzas also appear with the Aitareyins in the *Āraṇyaka* as its fourth book. Those stanzas which are to be studied as a Rahasya in the forest can, in accordance with its form and its place in the literary **[510]** history, belong to the Saṁhitā—and this is obviously the case with the Mahānāmnīs—as well as to the Brāhmaṇa or the Sūtra; it can be an older or a later text. Hence, we shall have to look upon, perhaps, also the Mahānāmnīs[2]

1. Known from the comm. to the Caraṇavyūha, fol. 25' of Weber's manuscript.
2. Or better, the stanzas at the basis of the Mahānāmnīs which, in their transmitted form, have been peculiarly embellished in conformity with its sanctity with the help of a number of additions.

directly as a piece of the Ṛk-Saṁhitā just as the Rahasya-chapter of the first Sāmavedārcika—as is well known the Mahānāmnī stanzas occur also here—belongs to the Sāma-Saṁhitā or the Pravargya books to the Vāj. Saṁh. But it did not find a place within the ten Maṇḍalas simply because of the technique of ritual instruction.

It is well known that the following stanzas have not been analyzed in the Padapāṭha, but are given in their Saṁhitā-form by the Pada-manuscripts : VII.59.12; X.20.1; X.121.10; X.190. The explanation of this fact, discovered long ago, viz., that these stanzas have found their way into the Saṁhitā only after the period of Śākalya or that they were at least at his time not yet recognized as belonging to those places is no doubt correct. What else could have led Śākalya to leave them without analysis? He has obviously not only not analysed them, but has not paid any attention to them at all, and the later ones who missed them in his Padapāṭha, have not dared to undertake the analysis on their own responsibility, nor at the same time to omit them altogether; they have therefore inserted the stanzas, without analysis, in the Padapāṭha although that was contrary to its character. We allude **[511]** here to this course of events, although so clear, simply because on the one hand we want to draw attention to the numerous indications of all kinds, coinciding with one another, which go to ensure the interpretation mentioned above, and on the other to stress the obvious conclusions, emerging from them, regarding the process of finalizing the Ṛk-text which had not been *quite* concluded at the time of Śākalya.

With regard to the individual stanzas not analysed in the Padapāṭha we note the following factors which confirm their late encroachment on the Ṛgveda :

VII.59.12: placement at the end of the Marut-series, *after* a supplement from which again this isolated stanza gets separated due to its character and metre (see above p. 200). *The only* place in the ṚV where Tryambaka, mentioned later so often, appears. Atharvan-type phrase *mṛtyor mukṣīya māmṛtāt*; perhaps the whole stanza is an imitation of AV XIV.1.17 or a similar model.

X.20.1: on this blessing-formula see what has been said above on p. 161. The special character just of *this* stanza makes it, however, conceivable that Śākalya knew and recognized it at this place, but, as a blessing-formula just introducing the recitation of the text proper, he did not analyse it.

X.121.10: one of the few passages of the ṚV where Prajāpati is mentioned; the only one where the later conception of him clearly comes to light. It was attracted to hymn X.121 as an answer to the constantly repeated question in the same hymn: *kasmai devāya haviṣā vidhema.* The stanza disturbs the arrangement of the hymns according to the number of stanzas (above p. 248); it occurs frequently alone by itself in the other Vedas but not at places where almost the entire hymn is reproduced, Taitt. Saṁ. IV.1.8; Mait. Saṁh. II.13.23; AV IV.2.

[512] X.190: full of late features, in a surrounding, however, in which its modern look is less offensive.

That these texts arose altogether only after the period of Śākalya is, as one can easily see, out ot the question. They prove only that *even after that period, in some isolated cases,* elements that were Vedic but not belonging to the Ṛgveda could receive a recognized place in the Ṛgveda. One may believe to have all the concerned texts together: for if there were more of them, the criterion of the Padapāṭha, which has so particularly stood the test, would certainly not have failed us here. Thus, the group of these stanzas stands in between the old additions to the hymns, already recognized as genuine parts of the text by Śākalya, many of which, for example, were discussed by us while considering the arrangement of book X, and the late ones appearing in the form of Khilas as appendices to the Saṁhitā, which could not succeed in finding their way, either as analysed or unanalysed, into the Padapāṭha.

CHAPTER 6

The Ṛk-text and the Sūtra-Literature

[513] That the Sūtras of Āśvalāyana and Śāṅkhāyana are later than the separation of the Śākala- and the Vāṣkala-Śākhā needs hardly to be proved. The well-known tradition holds Śaunaka to be older than Āśvalāyana and the work of Āśvalāyana confirms this estimation by mentioning Śaunaka a number of times as also by its conclusion *namaḥ Śaunakāya.* Now Śaunaka as the author of the Prātiśākhya, in the first stanza of which he is named as such, and furthermore as the author of the Anuvākānukramaṇī, is of course younger than Śākalya and presupposes the existence of the Śākala-text and the Vāṣkala-text. Śāṅkhāyana, on the other hand, describes the study of the Rahasya texts in such a way that it leaves no room for doubting that these texts themselves were at that time completed and settled[1]: in them, as is well known, different Śākalyas and their speculations on the phonetic questions play a prominent role. And above all, the way in which Āśvalāyana and Śāṅkhāyana, at not a few places in their Sūtras, speak in details of the phonetic technique of the Vedic recitation [514] shows that these subtleties laid down in the Prātiśākhyas were at that time long known to the Vedic authorities. Also this does not leave any doubt that the two great text-śākhās were fixed *before* the period of those Sūtrakāras.

The closer discussion of the way in which the Ṛk-text is

1. See Śāṅkh. Gṛhya II.11,12. However, the "Saṁhitās" are expressly mentioned [above p. 380] first in the sixth book of the Śāṅkh. Gṛhya, which is an expansion of the original work.

met with in the Sūtras of Aśvalāyana and Śāṅkhāyana can best be initiated by the analysis of the statements made by the oft-mentioned commentator of the Caraṇavyūha on the text of the Āśvalāyanas and the Śāṅkhāyanas. It was already pointed out [p. 490] that the Caraṇavyūha puts the Āśvalāyanas and the Śāṅkhāyanas on the same level as the Śākalas, Vāṣkalas, Māṇdūkāyanas as schools of the Ṛgveda. The commentator (fol. 13-14) makes in this context first some statements on the number of words in the Vedic text. It should be 152 585[1], in which the Vālakhilyas are not counted. Then he adds: *atha vālakhilyasahitapadasaṁkhyā* (*°saṁhitā°* cod.) *ucyaṁte* (*ucyate*?). *lakṣaikaṁ tu tripañcāśatsahasraṁ śatasaptakaṁ padāni ca dvinavatiḥ pramāṇaṁ Śākalasya ca* [1]. *ekalakṣatripaṁcāśatsahasrasaptaśata-dvinavatiś cādhikāni padāni ity arthaḥ.* 153 792[2]. *padāni vālakhilyasya arkasaṁkhyāśatāni ca adhikāni tu saptaiva vargā aṣṭādaśā smṛtāḥ* [2]. *saptādhikadvādaśaśatāni padānīty arthaḥ.* 120 (should be 1207). *ity Āśvalāyanānāṁ. Śāṁkhāyanānāṁ tu vālakhilyasahitapadasaṁkhyā ucyate. Śākalyadṛṣṭe padalakṣam ekaṁ sārddhaṁ tu vede trisahasrayuktaṁ śatāni saptaiva tathādhikāni catvāri triṁśac ca padāni carcā* [3]. *Śākalyo Māṁḍūkagaṇasthaḥ* [follows the prose enumeration of the number 153734]. *padāni vālakhilyasya* **[515]** *rudrasaṁkhyāśatāni ca ṣaṭpaṁcāśat [t]v adhikāni vargāḥ saptadaśās tathā* [4]. *ekādaśaśataṣaṭpaṁcāśadadhikavālakhilya-padānīty arthaḥ, aṣṭapaṁcāśatpadātmakaṛktrayasyābhāvāt. yam ṛtvijo vargo* (VIII.58.1-3) *nāsti. na tu*[3] *haviṣpāṁtīyasūkte dvesamīcīvarge* (X.88.16-19) *triṛcānantaraṁ eka evāgniḥ ṛk* (VIII.58.2) *yam ṛtvijo ṛk* (VIII.58.1) *khilarūpeṇa paṭhanti,*

1. For the Vāsiṣṭhas 152 514, since they omit Varga III.53.21-24 consisting of 71 words.
2. This figure comes very close to the figure 153826 given in the Anuvākānukrarmaṇī (stanza 45); I do not know how to account for the difference.
3. Read *nanu,* as it appears to have been first in the manuscript.

jyotiṣmantaṁ (VIII.58.3) *ṛcābhāvaḥ* [sic], *ṛktrayasya teṣāṁ mate padābhāvatvāt. ante vargasamāptau yāvanmātram ṛcāṁ* [sic] *paṭhanti* (X.88.19). *evaṁ dve samīcīti ṣaḍṛco vargaḥ. Āśvalāyanānāṁ caturṛcātmako vargaḥ. ity Āśvalāyana-śāṁkhāyanaśākhayor adhyayanayor bheda ity artaḥ.*

One can see that these countings are always based on the Śākala-text of 152 585 words, exclusive of Vālakhilya: on the difference in the extent which results from the addition of the Vālakhilyas to this firm principal item rests—and at the same time, according to the above description exhausts—the difference between the Ṛk-texts of the Āśvalāyanas and the Śāṅkhāyanas. If one adds the Vālakhilya as we have it in our text with its 18 Vargas and 1207 words, one gets the Āśvalāyana text.[1] If one adds the Vālakhilya of the above extent minus one Varga = 58 words,[2] we have the Śāṅkhāyana text. The latter no doubt inserts in hymn X, 88 two of the three stanzas of the varga that is left out, but it is done as khila and hence does not disturb the counting. The Vāṣkala text, however, with its **[516]** acceptance of the Vālakh. 1-7 with full validity and its rejection of the remaining Vālakhilyas remains, as one can see, completely out of consideration in these discussions. And from what has been told about the Āśvalāyana- and the Śāṅkhāyanaśākhā one cannot deduce that it is possible to maintain that corresponding to the two different namings there were two recensions of the Ṛk-text in the way we have the Śākala-recension as one such, or that they have been, in fact, maintained by our authority; rather it is merely a question of whether or not to include the Vālakhilyas in the countings, and in particular of the one point viz. that the Śāṅkhāyanasūtra should hold with reference to VIII.58 a view different from what is otherwise

1. Incidentally here again with reference to the text conceived to have this extent the expression *pramāṇam Śākalasya ca* is used.
2. There remain thus 17 vargas = 1149 words. For 1149 is given 1156 which I cannot understand; otherwise, the different items and their sums agree with one another.

valid, and which *possibly* it does, in fact, hold. The Śāṅkhāyana passage which comes into question here is obviously XVI.13: *dve srutī aśṛṇavam pitṝṇām iti brahmodgātāram pṛcchati, dvitīyayā pratyāhaikāntarayā pṛcchati, uttarayā pratyāha.* That is a ritual dialogue consisting of first X.88.15-16, then of stanza 18 and, one would think, 19. But instead of stanza 19 the commentary specifies stanza VIII.58.2 which in fact, as Sāyaṇa also notes on this stanza, answers the questions raised in stanza 18. That Śāṅkhāyana really had just this stanza in view is, if not certain, yet quite possible and agrees at any rate with the statement of the Caraṇavyūha-commentary. Accordingly, in case we have really to assume for Śāṅkhāyana at this place a different form of the text than what has been transmitted, still we should not overlook the fact that the deviation pertains to, so to say, only the periphery of the Veda text: it concerns, on the one hand one of the latest Vālakhilyas, which, moreover, is not found in several manuscripts, and on the other, an insertion in hymn X, 88 for which, **[517]** by those who made it, was claimed only the validity of a Khila[1].

The view, moreover, which seems to be the basis of the discussions of the commentary reviewed here, that the Veda-text of the Śāṅkhāyanas has closer relationship with the

1. It can hardly be supposed that the two stanzas VIII.58.2,1 should have, *in fact,* belonged to the tenth book at that place. For one thing they sound decidedly later than hymn X.88 (*anūcāna,* st. 11), and then they have to—as it is, in fact, stated—change their order in the tenth book, so that stanza 2 stands immediately after X.88.18 : in reality, however, stanza 2 is obviously to be understood as an answer to stanza 1 (*bahudhā — eka' eva*), whose author had presumably before him stanza X.88.18. The connection of the two stanzas with the Aśvin-stanza 3 is, however, not clear, but such want of clarity is not rare. One may note that Śāṅkhāyana's understanding does not, as one might have thought of doing, relate stanza three to the preceding hymn, but simply omits it : since stanzas 1 and 2 had been disposed off differently, one could not do anything more with stanza three alone.

Śākala- than with the Vāṣkalaśākhā should not go uncontested. The mention in the Śaṅkhāyana of the sandhi-term upadruta [p. 491], which is peculiar to the Vāṣkalas, as also the mention found in the Gṛhya (IV.5.9) of the stanza *tac chaṁ yor* as the concluding stanza of the Veda make it rather probable that Śāṅkhāyana was a follower of the Vāṣkalaśākhā[1]. But we can hardly conclude from this that his Sūtra could not be equally well used by the Śākalas: had it been otherwise, the manuscripts of Śāṅkhāyana today presumably would have been as few as the manuscripts of the Vāṣkalaśākhā. In the fact that Śāṅkhāyana was based on the Kauṣītaka Brāhmaṇa and Āśvalāyana, on the other hand, on the Aitareya, lay an essential, not bridgeable difference: but what concerned the Śākhās of the Ṛk-Saṁhitā itself, their deviations, **[518]** of which we know, could scarcely offer a hindrance to the use of the same Sūtra by the followers of different Śākhās[2]. Hence, it is not surprising that the commentator of the Caraṇavyūha, for whom obviously the Vāṣkalaśākhā did not have any concrete importance, used as basis the Śākala-text when he had to say something about the Śāṅkhāyana.

In sharp contrast to the tradition according to which the Veda-text of Śāṅkhāyana betrays only a vanishing, insignificant difference from the vulgate, stand the views recently advanced by A. Hillebrandt[3] on the importance of Śāṅkhāyana for the understanding of the textual history. Here we have to deal with the assertions of this researcher

---

1. However, one may note that he (XII, 11) assumes *eight* Vālakhilya hymns; cf. above [p. 495].
2. One may recall that Ṣaḍguruśiṣya says about the writing of Śaunaka: *te saṁhite* (scil. Śākala and Vāṣkala) *samāśritya*. Āśvalāyana (Gṛhya III.5.8,9) gives *both* the last stanzas of the Śākala and the Vāṣkala where the concluding stanza of the Veda is to be cited. Cf. M. Müller, H.A.L. 230.
3. "Spuren einer älteren Ṛgvedarecension" [Traces of an older Ṛgveda recension], Bezzenberger's Beiträge VIII.195 ff.

on the former existence of an authoritative "older Veda-recension preserved due to its employment in sacrifice", traces of which he seeks to establish in a number of instances from Śāṅkhāyana. Partly, he assumes that the statements of Śāṅkhāyana have no doubt been made on the basis of the traditionally handed down text, but the change of order of the stanzas in a given hymn, their omissions, etc., which have to be done in this text as prescribed by Śāṅkhāyana, point to an older form of the text. Partly, however, he also assumes (pp. 199, 202) that altogether the content of certain hymns, as known to Ś., was different from the one which we know. H., however, does not envisage an independent "recension" of the ṚV in the proper sense of that term; he conceives only of "in many respects a purer tradition which comes to light in **[519]** the ritual employment of the hymns" (ZDMG. XL.712). The importance which in principle would be attached to these views makes it necessary that we discuss them in details.

By the side of the line of transmission which has given us our Saṁhitā of the Ṛgveda, there has to be another which "owed its motivation and preservation to the ritual tradition." According to Hillebrandt, we have not to assume that this ritual form of the hymns agreed completely with our Saṁhitā "because the Saṁhitā, on account of its many parts which have very little to do with the ritual, is certainly not edited on the basis of the hymn-materials used at the time of sacrifice; on the other hand, however, the hymns used in the sacrifice did not require first their redaction in the Saṁhitā in order to find their way into the ritual." The first part of this assertion cannot be easily contested. It would not, in fact, be less absurd to look upon our Saṁhitā as one edited on the basis of purely liturgical agenda than, let us say, if one wanted to hold our New Testament as compiled out of the Sunday gospels and epistles. But what does exactly the second part of Hillebrandt's statement say ? The hymns to be employed in the sacrifice did not require first their inclusion in the Saṁhitā as is available to us? One would hardly want to say the Sunday Bible-lessons did not require first being redacted into the N. Test. in order to be valid for God's worship. It might have been perhaps *possible to think* of events which occurred in literary history which made possible the rise of the sacrificial ritual together with all the texts used in it *without* a Saṁhitā as is handed down to us having to do anything with it. That ritual would not perhaps be *in the need of* this Saṁhitā. But that is not the direction in which our **[520]** enquiry is to be directed. We have rather to ask : is the assumption certain or probable, that in the course which Vedic literature and the liturgy have *in fact* taken, our Saṁhitā—or the one *essentially* identical with it—formed the basis of the arrangement of the ritual liturgy, so that the Saṁhitā and the liturgical tradition would not, as is Hillebrandt's view, represent two parallel lines of development but that the former was *prior* and the latter *posterior*?

Here, above all, the chronological relationship between the fixation of the Saṁhitā and the fixation of the sacrificial ritual—namely *that* ritual which is essentially identical in the Vedic ritual texts, and which alone naturally comes for consideration in this investigation—assumes decisive importance[1]. Already the arrangement of the Saṁhitā proves the existence of *this* compilation of the liturgical materials in times which lie far behind those of the fixation of that sacrificial ritual. One may bring to mind the separation of the families which comes to light in the older layers of the Saṁhitā, while the later ritual is founded throughout on the combination of the different family traditions. One may further recall all those traces which enable us to follow the gradual growth of the collection, which inform us that its principal content was there already long before its conclusion

1. For what follows I refer the reader to the expositions given by me in ZDMG XLII.240-247.

giving it its present arrangement, and which make clear to us the additions of the later elements (supplements to the ordered series; book X). Then one may consider on the other hand, how the principal features of **[521]** the sacrificial system taught in the ritual texts presuppose the existence and, in consequence of what has been just said, also the arrangement of the Saṁhitā—its main content together with the additions—, and how a series of essential elements of that sacrificial system (especially the principal elements of the Yajus-liturgy) are *later* than the Saṁhitā. One may also consider how a number of ceremonies, which assume prominent significance in the later form of the sacrifice, are altogether unknown to the Saṁhitā, so that providing those rites with hymns and stanzas is partly done with the Saṁhitā-texts, which obviously are not composed for this special purpose, partly with texts which were definitely meant by their authors for those occasions but which do not have a place in the Saṁhitā and bear clear signs of later origin. Hence, one would reject at the very outset the notion of the Saṁhitā-tradition and the ritual-tradition being in existence *side by side*. One would rather find that everything shows that matters have taken a different course: *first*, —in times which possessed archaic and relatively brief sacrificial ritual— the codification of the Ṛgveda took place, and *then* the liturgists who had the knowledge of this codified Veda also brought in the later materials and fixed the form of the sacrificial ritual which is found to be essentially identical in the later Saṁhitās, in the Brāhmaṇas and the Sūtras.

However, it would of course be quite conceivable that isolated corruptions and interpolations which could have intruded in later times into the transmitted Ṛk-text should not have found their way up to the place of sacrifice or at least not up to the place of sacrifice of some definite school. But it would be advisable for us to proceed with the most wary caution while judging all the supposed cases of this sort. **[522]** If the discussion of the data found in the

Sāmaveda and the Yajurveda—that is, in the most proper "sacrificial recensions"—has already convinced us about the almost complete higher excellence of the Ṛk-tradition and its completion, well-established *in all essentials* since old times, then it will be much less probable that the ritual practice of the Ṛgveda, exposed directly and unopposedly to the influence of the Ṛk-Saṁhitā, should have preserved many variants which really come into question. On account of the artificiality and the absurd indulgence in symbolism, carried to the extreme, with which the liturgies of the later ritual are construed, the hymns employed in such rituals, of course, underwent changes often enough; stanzas were either omitted or new stanzas from other hymns were introduced, and many more such things: our investigations above [p. 352 ff.] on the Brāhmaṇas have sufficiently shown this to us. In most cases it will be possible for an attentive investigator of the ritual technique to discover the motives of the concerned changes and thereby avoid the danger of mistaking the bungling of the later liturgists for traces of very old tradition. If, however, as nothing else can be expected, here and there the hair-splittings of the Indian ritualists have taken a course, the discovery of which is beyond the strength of our divination, now or for ever, then in view of the whole condition of all these questions elsewhere, the cautious investigator will here much rather admit a residue of the unintelligible matter in the field of liturgy than dare touch the old traditional text by stanza-omissions, their transpositions and many more similar things on the basis of that kind of data.

We shall now try to demonstrate with the help of a few individual examples how the pretence of old tradition, which **[523]** perhaps could attach to the form of some Ṛk-texts used in the ritual described by Śāṅkhāyana, is only a pretence. While doing so it is desirable that we take our examples from that context where Hillebrandt believes he can prove the antiquity and value of the ritual-tradition. We begin with ṚV I.52 for which Śāṅkhāyana (IX.8) prescribes the omission of stanzas 9 and 15, as also the transposition of 13 and 14, so that stanza 13 stands at the end (Hillebrandt op. cit. 196 f.). If one first reads the hymn the way it has been handed down, one can hardly notice anything which would arouse suspicion. Stanza 9 occurs at a place which is most natural in the context, bound with the following stanza by means of some common expressions, as is altogether the case in many ways in this hymn. This does not give the slightest occasion to doubt it as a *later* addition. Likewise stanza 13 stands between 12 and 14 in as correct a place as is only possible. However, there is change of metre: whereas the hymn as a whole is çomposed in Jagatī, 13 and 15 are in Tirṣṭubh. But this cannot give any occasion for doubt. In the collection (I.51-57) to which the hymn belongs there prevails a practice which, as far as the metre is concerned, remains very much the same. The metre throughout is Jagatī, but in four hymns among the seven Triṣṭubh is found toward the end, so that always the last stanza, and along with it also one or many others, are composed in Triṣṭubh. To be sure, these Triṣṭubh stanzas do not always occur in an unbroken sequence but, as in 52, so also in 54 a Jagatī is found between them[1]. In this way **[524]** the apparent metrical unevenness in hymn 52 is in complete agreement with the type that prevails in the collection concerned.

Thus if the text of the hymn does not contain any indication which could give an occasion for making changes, then we have to ask whether the operations which Śāṅkhāyana prescribes for it can be explained on the basis of technical-liturgical grounds. Let us look at the situation in which the author of the Sūtra puts the hymn. The twelve

1. 54.10. Śāṅkhāyana, who prescribes (IX.10) the employment of hymn 54 in an analogous ceremony in a way parallel to the one of hymn 52, does not, as also Āśvalāyana (VI.4.10), prescribe any modification of the traditional text.

rātri-paryāyas belonging to the Atirātra ceremony comprise among other parts the recitation of a "jāgatam" in each paryāya. These, according to Śāṅkh. IX.7 ff. (cf. Āśvalāyana VI.4.10), are the following: I.51,—I.52 with the modifications specified. —I.53,—I.54.—X.48.—II.16.—II.17. —V.34; instead of the concluding stanza appears V.31.3.—II.21.—X.49.—I.102, instead of the concluding stanza I.103.5.—X.96.—If one surveys these texts, one finds two characteristics common to them all: they are addressed to Indra and they are composed in Jagatī, *but in such a way that the concluding stanza*—and sometimes with it also one or more other stanzas—is composed in *Triṣṭubh*. Thus the form of the Jagatī-hymn ending in a Triṣṭubh, which is so clearly discerned in the Vedic poesy itself [see above p. 145], is here picked up by the liturgical technique and executed with full consciousness[1]. On the basis of the two characteristics of this recitation noticed above, we can very well explain the selection of the texts prescribed for it. Jagatī-hymn with a Triṣṭubh-end is a favourite form of composition in the Savya- and the Kutsa-collections of Maṇḍala I, in Maṇḍala II, and in **[525]** the group of hymns attributed to Indra Vaikuṇṭha of Maṇḍala X: hence these portions of the Saṁhitā are almost exclusively represented[2] at the places concerned of the Rātriparyāyas. What was not addressed to Indra had to be eliminated. Hence, above all, the concluding stanza of V.34 which praises Śatri Āgniveśi and mentions Agni. But also the concluding stanza of I.102 with its *tan no mitro varuṇo māmahantām* etc. had to go; the later liturgists were

1. Cf. the citations in the scholium communicated by Hillebrandt p. 197, note: *aindrāṇi jāgatānīti vacanāt. . .triṣṭubbhiḥ paridadhātīti vacanāt.*
2. One may note that from the Savya-group, the first four which have Triṣṭubh as the concluding stanza have been surely chosen (and that too in the sequence of our Saṁhitā), but none of the last three. Āśvalāyana prescribes also one of these (I, 55) *but with the addition of a Triṣṭubh stanza* I.130.10.

considerably more particular in maintaining *exclusive* relationship of the recitations with the god who was invoked each time than were the old poets of the hymns who often, especially at the end of the hymn, loved to extend their invocations to a wider circle of the gods. For this reason the Jagatī hymns V.34 and I.102 lost their concluding Triṣṭubh stanzas[1] in the litany of the Rātriparyāyas and these, as we saw, had to be substituted, following the liturgical technique, in some other way. Hence on both the occasions stanzas V.31.3 and I.103.5, taken from close neighbourhood of the hymns to which they were to be supplied, were added to the litany.

After all this, the treatment of I.52 is not at all difficult to understand. First, two stanzas, for the reasons given in the cases just discussed, had to be set aside because in them Indra is not invoked alone, but with the Maruts, i.e. stanzas 9 and 15. On account of these stanzas **[526]** the hymn could—in that case of course *without* omitting them—be considered fit for use in the Marutvatīya Śastra[2]: but just what made the hymn qualified for that Śastra did not fit into the recitation of the rātri-paryāyas dedicated to Indra alone. The exclusion of stanza 15, however, removed from the hymn the necessary conclusion with the Triṣṭubh; hence as in the case of V.34 and I.102 a substitute had to be procured. This substitute was found for this hymn at a place

1. The case of V.34, which is thus settled, also figures among the traces of older Ṛk-recension in Hillebrandt's treatment p. 198. Hillebrandt's treatment of V.30 (p. 201) is to be judged in a similar way.
2. Together with I.165 and X.73 as already noted by Hillebrandt (197). But how could "the attempt to make it have there the same status as these two hymns have led to the interpolation of these two stanzas, perhaps vaguely floating around"—just the two stanzas 9 and 15 looked upon as interpolations by Hill.? Is it possible that the hymn was once without these stanzas and, although it was then purely an Indra-hymn, was chosen for the Marutvatīya Śastra and only later received its connection with the Maruts in order to have the same status as the other Marutvatīya-hymns ?

still closer than in the case of those two hymns: in stanza 13 of the hymn itself one found the desired Triṣṭubh, and what was necessary was nothing but a simple transposition in order to bring it to the place where it was required, viz. the end of the hymn.

In order to recapitulate, let us ask the question: how do we judge the two forms of the hymn I.52, the one in the Ṛk-Saṁhitā and the other of Śāṅkhāyana? The factors related to the literary history place the one as a tradition high above the other; they vindicate for the former a considerably higher age and, on the other hand, offer grounds, against the latter, to doubt it as one that has been artificially made up[1]. The sequence of the stanzas as found in the former is assured by the running relationship of the contents and of the expression; the metres, even when there is a change, agree with the practice followed by the author of the collection concerned. If we, on the other hand, examine the liturgical form of the hymn in the context of its ritual surrounding, then **[527]** at each step it becomes evident that every change made in the Saṁhitā-form is *either required* or suggests itself. Thus the older recension of this hymn which is allegedly supposed to exist in the Sāṅkhāyana disintegrates into mere illusion.

We add a few further remarks on ṚV X.81 (Hillebrandt 200 f.). Śāṅkhāyana (VI.11.9) cites this hymn but he prescribes the omission of the fourth stanza, and Hillebrandt assumes that here also the ritual-recension has preserved the older condition of the hymn. But *could* Śāṅkhāyana use at all the whole hymn without omission? At that place it is not a matter of reciting a hymn in a continuous way, but what are given are the yājyā and the puronuvākyā stanzas for a number of sacrificial animals: for every animal, respy.

1. In this connection it may also be noted that Śāṅkhāyana, on a different occasion (Hill. 197 note 2), himself pleads for the Saṁhitā form of the hymn.

for every deity to which the animal belongs, six stanzas, viz. three puronuvākyās (for the vapā, the puroḍāśa and the aṅgāni) and three corresponding yājyās. For the animal of Viśvakarman, Śāṅkhāyana took the relevant stanzas from the hymn X.81, besides X.82, the only hymn addressed to this deity. However, since the hymn had seven stanzas and the employment was only for six, one stanza obviously had to be omitted; that for this purpose just stanza 4 was singled out may be a chance or it may be due to the fact that just in this stanza Viśvakarman is less clearly conspicuous than in the rest.[1] Thus for the textual history the prescription of Śāṅkhāyana cannot yield anything since what he teaches turns out to be unavoidable on ritual grounds[2].

[528] Perhaps the cases discussed here should suffice to demonstrate the way in which, in our view, statements such as those made by Śāṅkhāyana on the changes in the consistence of the hymns before their use in the ritual must be examined, and what the constant result of such an examination is. The altered form of the hymns as used in the ritual is not explained by the assumption of an older text-recension in which the ritualists found it, but by the rules of the ritual technique which occasioned deviations from the recension available to them [the ritualists] as well as to us.

Besides the changes in the inventory of the hymns which

---

1. Āśvalāyana (Śrauta. III.8.1) chooses the six stanzas from *both* Viśvakarman-hymns X.81 and 82:81.6, 7; 82.2; 81.2; 82.3; 81.5. Should this represent traces of another older recension ?
2. It may further be pointed out that the extent of the hymn having seven stanzas is assured by the rule of arrangement. That the Vāj. Saṁ. likewise stands witness to the existence of the stanza has been already noted by Hill. himself; so also the transpositions and contamination with X. 82 found in the Taitt. Saṁh. do not at all change the fact that stanza four appears among all the remaining stanzas with full equal right. Cf. also now the Maitr. Saṁh. II.10.2; it follows from the statements in the index of Schröder that also the Kāth. and Kap. Saṁh. have stanza 4 among the others.

Śāṅkhāyana *specifies* as such, other deviations from the Vulgate text, which Śāṅkhāyana already *finds* in his Veda-text and therefore tacitly assumes, could come up for consideration. We suggested above [p. 517] the possibility that Śāṅkhāyana followed the Vāṣkalaśākhā. This, however, is not indicated by any variant in the numerous pratīkas and other textual pieces which he cites. It is possible there *were* in fact no variants with the Vāṣkalas in all these passages as compared to our text, but this cannot be concluded with certainty from Śāṅkhāyana: if the variants were there, they could and almost must have been suppressed by the readings of the Śākalaśākhā as the latter went on acquiring more and more exclusive supremacy. I also cannot discover any far-reaching deviations in the form **[529]** of the hymns[1]: apart from the case of the hymns VIII. 58 and X. 88 discussed above [516] and unimportant minor details, like the fact that the stanza VI. 63. 11 is individually recorded as ekapadā in the Vulgate, but is reckoned, together with the preceding stanza, as pañcapadā in Ś. (VI, 6). On the other hand the statements of Śāṅkhāyana expressly confirm at every step the textual form of the hymn as found in our Vulgate. Thus, to bring to the notice only a few out of the extremely numerous instances, the statements to be found in XVIII. 14 regarding a number of stanzas, which are correctly specified with their running numbers, from the most heterogeneous hymn in the whole Saṁhitā, VIII, 46, or the total numbers of stanzas as the 100 of the Śunaḥśepa-legend XV. 17ff., or the 100 Triṣṭubh XVIII. 19, or several other statements regarding the numbers of stanzas or their sums, which, from everything that I can see, prove to be correct

1. That is in the form of the hymn as Ś. had it before him in his Saṁhitā, not of that which he prescribed for the ritual after making changes expressly mentioned by him.

according to our Saṁhitā[1]. As far as it has been possible to observe [530] till now—and here I refer to my researches as well as to those of Hillebrandt who obviously has not come across *firm* traces of variants[2]—it can be said that, apart from the minor details mentioned above, the text which Śaṅkhāyana presupposes is identical with that of ours, and we have no right and no occasion to carry our assumptions further than saying that it is *merely conceivable* that differences—certainly in no case numerous and significant—*could* have once existed and were later removed in the tradition of the Śāṅkhāyanasūtra.

Much less than with Śāṅkhāyana, of course, shall we expect to find, and in fact find, variations from our text with Āśvalāyana, the pupil of Śaunaka and consequently a follower

1. The statement of Śāṅkhāyana in XII. 2 that "dāśatayīṣu" there are 47 Gāyatrīs to Mitra and Varuṇa, 44 gāyatrāṇi to Indra, and 46 Gāyatrīs to Indra and Agni does not give any room for doubt about the two last points. Even the 47 Gāyatrīs can be easily found; these are obviously the 12 single stanzas listed by Ś. in the preceding Sūtras—their sequence follows the ordering in the Saṁhitā—and 12 tṛcas (= 35 stanzas, because the stanza V.68.3 is counted in two tṛcas) to Mitra and Varuṇa, beside whom, however, in some stanzas Aryaman is also named.—As is known Lāṭyāyana X.6.3,6 makes similar statements about there occurring "*dāśatayīṣu*" 104 *aindrā bārhatāḥ pragāthāḥ* and 29 (*aindrāḥ*) *sātobārhatās tṛcāḥ*. In order to verify the first figure, one has to remember that beside the combination of bṛhatī and satobṛhatī, other combinations are also characterized as bārhata pragātha. The second statement—in which sātobārhata is understood in a sense different from the usual one, cf. Ind. Stud. VIII.97—is to be understood, according to Nidānasūtra V.3 in this way, that 87 stanzas of that type are available which can be formed into 29 tṛcas. With regard to some stanzas we may doubt whether they themselves were comprised under the metrical category in question here. There is, however, no difficulty in realizing the number 87, one way or the other.
2. One might also expect that if there were variants they would have been pointed out in the Caraṇavyūha-commentary.—In the passages mentioned in Weber's Catalogue of Berl. mss. Vol. II. p. 10 fn. 2, p. 11 fn. 3, 4 there do not exist real text-differences.

of Śākalaśākhā[1]. For when Āśvalāyana cites a number of Khilas and Khila-like texts such as the prajāvat- and the jīvaputra-hymns[2], that kind of material is obviously not enough to maintain that beyond the above there were deviations in his Saṁhitā from our Saṁhitā.

The textual variations in the Ṛk-stanzas, cited in the sūtras other than those belonging to the ṚV, give no occasion to add anything further to the parallel discussions gone into above in connection with **[531]** the Saṁhitās and the Brāhmaṇas. Moreover, such citations with notable frequency are to be found only in the Gṛhyasūtras; that the Sūtra of Pāraskara, by adopting almost exclusively[3] the readings of the Ṛgveda, distinguishes itself from the rest of the texts of this type which are rather full of variations, is a fresh noteworthy proof for the predominant tendency of the school of the white Yajurveda, observed also in the Saṁhitā and the Brāhmaṇa belonging to it, to concede special importance to the authority of the Ṛgveda in the handling of the text.

To the remarks which we had to make about the significance of the Sūtras for the textual history we will add what we have to say with reference to *Yāska's Nirukta:* in doing so we take the freedom of deviating from the strict chronological sequence, since Yāska undoubtedly belongs to the *beginning* of the Sūtra-period.

If one takes into account the traditionally transmitted form of the text of the Nirukta, then one finds that the extremely numerous stanzas from the Ṛgveda which are

1. However see p. 518, note 1.
2. See the list in Meyer, Ṛgvidhāna p. XXVII note 2.—If Āśv. II.12.5 cites the pratīka *vāyur agregā yajñaprīḥ* (cf. Vāj. Saṁh. XXVII, 31; Kauṣ. Br. XIV.4), not found in the Ṛgveda, then this is explained by the fact that the stanza concerned is a puroruc (nivid) (Āśv. V.10.4).
3. The only exception concerns the citation of ṚV X.85. 37 in Pāraskara I.4.16 in a very corrupt form.

cited in it agree *thoroughly* with the traditional ṚV-text except for some differences of the most insignificant nature. In order to explain this, assuming that there are corruptions in the Nirukta is more probable than assuming a variant Ṛk-text[1]. That in fact in Yāska's **[532]** period there existed a very firmly fixed form of the Ṛgveda, and that this form in *all essentials* is identical with the one transmitted to us, cannot be doubted if one takes into account the whole tenor of the Nirukta. In the first place Yāska's deviations from the Vulgate text of the Ṛgveda appear as differences in the pada-divisions: thus the well-known remark of Nir. VI.28 on ṚV X.29.1 where Yāska objects to the pada-division *vā yó,* which is attributed to Śākalya and which is in fact found in our Padapāṭha, instead of *vāyó* assumed by him: *udāttaṁ tv evam ākhyātam abhaviṣyad asusamāpaś cārthaḥ ;* further Nir. V.21, where Y. in ṚV I.105.18 reads *māsakṛ́d* instead of *mā sakṛ́d;* Nir. IV.15 where *kanīnakéva* of ṚV IV.32. 23 is explained—presumably correctly—as *kanīnake iva,* whereas the Padapāṭha has *kanīnakā́-iva*[2]. Sometimes, however, Yāska reveals—indeed only in very rare cases—deviations which go beyond the Padapāṭha and touch directly the Saṁhitāpāṭha. In the text of the concerned Ṛk-citations in the Nirukta available to us, however, these variations have been corrected but the paraphrase certainly proves that they were very much there. Thus here we find directly before us a phenomenon which corresponds most exactly with what we have thought of above

1. E.g. in ṚV X.53.4 Nir. III.8 reads *maṁsīya* for *masīya;* I suppose, however, as Roth also assumes, we have to restore *masīya* in Nir.—If we find in the Nir. IV.24 the Yajus-reading *ṛdhak* for *dhruvam* of ṚV III.29.16, then we should not overlook that here it is the question of explaining the very word *ṛdhak* listed in the Nighaṇṭavas and hence the passage concerned only in its Yajus-form could at all come for consideration. Citations of Yajus-type formulae are found several times in the Nirukta.
2. One would suppose with Roth that according to Nir. I.6 Yāska read in ṚV I.170.1 *abhisaṁcareṇyam* as one word.

as a conjecture [p. 350, 528] with reference to the Ṛk-citations in the Brāhmaṇas and the Sūtras—the former existence of variations which were removed later from the transmitted text. It is, however, not always easy to decide the text-form of a Ṛk-stanza accepted by Yāska on the basis of his paraphrase[1]. **[533]** Of course, every explanation does on no account really presuppose *the* form of the explained text which, according to our notions of exegesis it should presuppose, and in a doubtful case one would rather do good to attribute to Yāska a bold or impossible explanation of the traditional text than a deviation from that text. All the same one cannot altogether deny the existence of such deviations. The variant reading, which is found in the Yajurveda tradition, peeps through the paraphrase of ṚV X.82.4 (Nir. VI.15), and this has already been discussed above [p. 313]. Yāska's expalnation (Nir. IV.4)—at least as it is available to us[2]—allows us at first sight to conclude the corrupt variant *citram* in ṚV V.39.1, which, however, cannot be accepted when contrasted with the reading of the Vulgate (*citra*) which is impeccable as to meaning and is supported by the Sāmaveda and the metre[3]. On the basis of Yāska's paraphrase [VI.33] *ardanavedhinau gamanavedhinau śabdavedhinau dūravedhinau* perhaps in ṚV VIII.77.11 we have to assume a reading *ṛdūvidhā* in place of the transmitted *ṛdūvṛdhā*. Relatively frequently the Pariśiṣṭa appended to the Nirukta shows in its paraphrases—here also they occur in the paraphrases, not in the text-citations themselves in the

1. For example, it would be difficult to make out if Yāska (X.32) in ṚV X.149.1 read *antarikṣam atūrte* or *antarikṣe 'tūrte*.
2. However, it cannot be overlooked that Sāyaṇa on ṚV l.c. cites the Nirukta passage in such a way that it does not have the variant: but this may be easily due to a correction made in favour of the transmitted Ṛk-text.
3. One may note that further on at the same place Yāska expressly compares with the reading *mehanā* a different one *ma iha na;* the same occurs in the SV [see above p. 273].

form they are available to us—variants against the Ṛk-vulgate, to which, however, obviously no importance is to be attached. It would be enough to refer to the stanzas IX.97.40 (Nir. XIV.16) and I.164.15 (Nir. XIV.19). **[534].** In the former the expression *parame vyavane* corresponds, both in the adhidaivata- and the adhyātma-explanations, to *prathame vidharman* of the text which leads us to the reading *parame vyoman* for the Ṛk-text (cf. Nir. XIII.10). In the latter, the paraphrase deviates from the text in a more thoroughgoing way; we have to assume a form of the text in which the first hemistich of ṚV I.164.15 was contaminated by the second of X.82.2.

As is known, isolated deviations from the Vulgate of the Ṛk-text are to be found even in the commentary of *Sāyaṇa*; they have been listed by M. Müller in the apparatus of his great edition. This much is immediately clear: that these deviations, few and insignificant as they are, can in no case justify an *important* qualification of the view about the existence of a fixed Ṛk-text long before Sāyaṇa. But do they justify any such qualification at all? The textual variations which appear through the explanations of Sāyaṇa have—apart from some indifferent readings, also to be found here, which do not allow any judgement—the obvious character of chance mistakes of the commentator, such as could not be avoided easily in the course of such a voluminous work. One may consider such readings of Sāyaṇa as, let us say, the metrically impossible *taved idam* for *tavedam* VII.98.6 where along with the ṚV also Maitr. S., Taitt. Br., Av. (book XX) have the correct text, or in X.57.5 the meaningless *jano* for *mano* (*mano* also in Maitr. S., Taitt. S., Vāj. S.) which has been occasioned by the neighbouring pāda, or in X.160.4 the omission of *na* (AV XX has *na*) which even clashes with the metre, **[535]** or in IX.61.14 the meaningless word-separation, which entails change of accent, *saṁ śiśvarīr* (Sāmav. has *saṁśiśvarīr* which correct reading Sāy. himself admits in VIII.69.11), or the absurd *vṛjineṣu* in IX.77.5, or *ṛtasya* in X.39.3 instead of *rutasya,* whose correctness is proved by IX.112.1, or *sarvā* in IV.28.3 instead of *śarvā* (*śaruā*; cf. I.100.18), or *vahnī* in X.101.10 (caused by the neighbouring dual) instead of *vahnim* (cf. st. 11). As against the agreement of the Saṁhitā and the Padapāṭha which is fixed since old times and which is thoroughly covered by the guaranty of the Prātiśākhya—by what it says and by what it does not say—one will have to see in those kinds of Sāyaṇa's readings nothing more than lapses of memory or inattentiveness of the commentator. Of course, even the strictest fidelity of the text-transmission could at no times have excluded *such* variants.

Indices*

[The page numbers in the indices are according to Oldenberg's text. Oldenberg's number are given in the square brackets in the translation.]

I
Subject Index

* I am thankful to Dr. Madhavi Kolhalkar for copying Oldenberg's 'Register' for me.

II
Word Index

III
Index of Passages

Ṛgveda

Other Texts